# APPLIED ENGLISH
# GRAMMAR *and* COMPOSITION
## INTERNATIONAL EDITION: *for* HIGH SCHOOLS

# APPLIED ENGLISH
# GRAMMAR *and* COMPOSITION

**INTERNATIONAL EDITION** : *for* **HIGH SCHOOLS**

DEVELOPED AFTER

**Nesfield, Wren & Martin, Thomson & Martiner,**
**Raymond Murphy and Modern Oxford Authorities**


Dr P C Das

MA, BT, DELT, PhD



New Central Book Agency (P) Ltd

LONDON
HYDERABAD ERNAKULAM BHUBANESWAR
NEW DELHI KOLKATA PUNE GUWAHATI

*Exclusively Distributed by*

Bijay Pustak Bhandar (P) Ltd.

90/6A, M G ROAD, BHAWANI DUTTA LANE, KOLKATA 700009

**NCBA**

**REGD OFFICE**
8/1 Chintamoni Das Lane, Kolkata 700 009, India
email: ncbakolkata@gmail.com

**OVERSEAS**
NCBA (UK) Ltd, 149 Park Avenue North, Northampton, NN3 2HY, UK
email: ncbauk@yahoo.com

**CORPORATE OFFICE**
212 Shahpur Jat, New Delhi 110 049
email: ncbaexports@ncbapvtltd.com

**BIJAY PUSTAK BHANDAR (P) LTD**
90/6A M. G. Road, Bhawani Dutta Lane, Kolkata-700007
E-mail : bijaypustakbhandar@gmail.com

**APPLIED ENGLISH GRAMMAR AND COMPOSITION** [FOR HIGH SCHOOLS, INT EDN] ● P C Das



First Published: [English Version] July 2007
Revised Reprinted: 2010, 2011, 2012, 2013
Second Edition: April 2013
Reprinted: January 2014
Revised Reprint: 2015
Reprinted: January 2016, January 2017, January 2018, January 2019, July 2019, April 2021, June 2022, **August 2023**

**PUBLISHER • TYPESETTER**
New Central Book Agency (P) Ltd
8/1 Chintamoni Das Lane, Kolkata 700 009

**PRINTER**
New Central Book Agency (P) Ltd
Web-Offset Division, Dhulagarh, Sankrail, Howrah

**PROJECT TEAM**
Joydeep Ghosh and Subas Maitra

ISBN 978 81 7381 542 3

Price ₹ 565.00

## Some of the Multifarious Authorities Consulted

1. *English Grammar Series*—Nesfield
2. *High School English Grammar & Composition*—Wren & Martin
3. *Hints on the Study of English*—Rowe & Webb
4. *Good English—How to Write It*—Vallins
5. *A Practical English Grammar*—Thomson & Martinet
6. *Modern English Usage*—Fowler
7. *The King's English*—Fowler
8. *Current English Usage*—Wood
9. *English Colloquial Idioms*—Wood & Hill
10. *Concise Oxford Dictionary*
11. *Twentieth Century Dictionary*—Chambers
12. *The Advanced Learner's Dictionary of Current English*—Hornby, Gatenby & Wakefield
13. *English Idioms and How to Use Them*—Mc.Mordie, Revised by Goffin
14. *Collins Cobuild English Grammar*—The University of Birmingham
15. *Collins Cobuild Dictionary of Phrasal Verbs*
16. *English Conversation Practice*—Taylor
17. *English Conversation Practice*—Spencer
18. *English Pronouncing Dictionary*—Jones
19. *Oxford Dictionary of New Words*
20. *Oxford Guide to English Grammar*—Eastwood
21. *Essential English Grammar*—Murphy

**"I have milked three hundred cows into my bucket but the butter I churned is my own."**

CHESTERTON

## SOME OTHER BOOKS OF Dr. P. C. Das

*in our publication*

1. Applied English Grammar and Composition [Anglo-Bengali Edition]
2. Applied English Grammar and Composition [Anglo-Hindi Edition]
3. Applied English Grammar and Composition [International Edition]
4. H.S. Applied English Grammar and Composition [For H.S. Level]
5. Beginners' Applied English Grammar & Composition [Anglo-Bengali]
6. Spoken English and Functional Grammar
7. Essays, Reports and Letter Writing

# Preface to the Second Edition

This international edition of the book has been thoroughly revised and updated with the latest contents and methods, even with the pictorial illustrations in some more topics.

There are some linguistic features in British and American variations, and that too has been dealt with in this book.

In order to create greater cultural proximity to the learners of different countries, sufficient care has been taken in choosing the theme and names in global context—both European and non-European.

We believe, the readers are the real touchstone for evaluating the worth of a book and thus to make it a prized possession.

The author and the publisher will be glad to receive any constructive suggestions from any corner, for the betterment of the book.

Radhanagar
P.O. Nangulpara
Dist. Hooghly
West Bengal, India

P C Das

# Preface to the First Edition

I feel particularly happy to present this book which should prove itself to be a wonderful compilation of Nesfield, Wren & Martin, Thomson & Martinet, and other classical Oxford authorities along with modern applied approach in learning English.

Learners generally resort to several strategies to augment and enhance their skill in using a foreign language. But, sometimes, lack of basic knowledge of grammar lands them in a precarious situation. Little do they realise that mere misuse of grammatical points in writing English makes them a laughing stock. This book will help the learners solve the intricacies of rules and regulations of grammar—specially with the Applied Section. Due emphasis has been given on difficult points that demand detailed discussion, such as—Articles including zero article, Prepositions, Verbal Noun, Gerund and Participle, and, of course, the Tenses and Subject-Verb agreement, etc. Moreover, useful notes have been added to clarify the confusing points.

The chapters on composition comprising Letter writing, Narrating events, Paragraphs, Retelling stories, Reporting, Dialogues, Describing a Process, etc. are arranged to ensure gradual development of the learners' writing skill, original thinking and power of expression in lucid language.

Elaborate exercises have been given on both Grammar and Composition in order to acquire complete mastery over the language. Thus, this book covers a wide range of the need of the readers including those who want to score better in the competitive examinations.

I earnestly hope that this book will serve the right purpose at the right time and, the teachers and the taught will extend their supporting hands to us so that this attempt may attain an encouraging result. In fact, I believe, the readers are the real touchstone for evaluating the worth of a book with such an assiduous effort on the part of the author to make it a prized possession.

Radhanagar
P.O. Nangulpara
Dist. Hooghly

P C Das
12.01.2009

# Contents

SOME OF THE MULTIFARIOUS AUTHORITIES CONSULTED vi

PREFACE vii

## Part I: GRAMMAR

CHAPTER 1 : SENTENCE CONSTRUCTION 3-6

■ Definition—the Old View and the New Concept 3, 4 ■ Formation of Sentences 5 ■ Subject and Predicate 5, 6 ■ Exercise 6

CHAPTER 2 : KINDS OF SENTENCES AND THEIR FUNCTIONS 7-19

■ Kinds of Sentences and their Functions 7 ■ Sentence Pattern 8 ■ Question Tags 11 ■ Applied Section 13 ■ Exercise 16

CHAPTER 3 : PARTS OF SPEECH 20-26

■ Definition, Parts of Speech—NOUN, PRONOUN 20 ■ ADJECTIVE, VERB 21 ■ ADVERB, PREPOSITION 22 ■ CONJUNCTION, INTERJECTION 23 ■ Applied Section 24 ■ Exercise 25

CHAPTER 4 : KINDS OF NOUNS 27-32

■ Proper, Common 27 ■ Collective, Material 28 ■ Abstract Noun 29 ■ Gerund and Verbal Noun 30 ■ Formation of Abstract Nouns 31 ■ Exercise 31

CHAPTER 5 : COUNTABLE AND UNCOUNTABLE NOUNS 33-37

■ Illustration and Definition 33 ■ Uncountable Nouns Used as Countable 34 ■ Applied Section 35 ■ Exercise 36

CHAPTER 6 : THE NOUN : NUMBER 38-46

■ Singular and Plural Number 38 ■ How Plurals are Formed 38 ■ Foreign Plurals and Typical Plurals 41 ■ Applied Section 44 ■ Pronunciation Note 45 ■ Key to Pronunciation of Vowels and Diphthongs 46 ■ Exercise 46

CHAPTER 7 : THE NOUN : GENDER 47-50

■ Kinds of Gender 47 ■ Rules of Changing Genders 48 ■ Applied Section 49 ■ Exercise 50

CHAPTER 8 : THE NOUN : CASE 51-54

■ Different Types of Cases 51 ■ Formation of Possessive Case 51 ■ Use of Possessive Case 52 ■ Noun in Apposition 52 ■ Applied Section 53 ■ Exercise 54

CHAPTER 9 : MORE ABOUT PRONOUNS

■ Kinds of Pronoun 55 ■ Cases and Number of Pronouns 56 ■ Rules for the Use of 'It' 56 ■ Possessive Pronouns 57 ■ Reflexive and Emphatic Pronouns 58 ■ Uses of Different Types of Pronoun 58 ■ Short Forms of Pronouns and Verbs 63 ■ Applied Section 64 ■ Exercise 65

CHAPTER 10 : MORE ABOUT ADJECTIVES 68-79

■ Types of Adjectives 68 ■ Uses of Adjectives 69 ■ Formation of Adjectives 70 ■ Comparison of Adjectives 72 ■ Rules of Comparison 72 ■ Use of Degrees 75 ■ Applied Section 76 ■ Exercise 77

CHAPTER 11 : MORE ABOUT VERBS AND MODALS 80-101

■ Kinds of Verbs 80 ■ Auxiliary and Principal Verbs 81 ■ Use of Primary Auxiliaries or Tense Auxiliaries 81 ■ Uses of Modal Auxiliaries (Modals) 82 ■ Transitive and Intransitive Verbs 84 ■ Finite and Non-Finite Verbs 87 ■ Bare Infinitive 88 ■ State Verbs and Event Verbs 89 ■ Causative Verbs 91 ■ Verb Patterns 91 ■ Applied Section 95 ■ Exercise 100

CHAPTER 12 : SYNTAX : SUBJECT-VERB AGREEMENT 102-108

■ Subject-Verb Agreement Rules 102 ■ Exercise 108

CHAPTER 13 : CONJUGATION OF VERBS 109-121

■ Weak and Strong Verbs 109, 113 ■ Verbs Often Confused 116 ■ Spelling Rules of Verbs with '-ing' 117 ■ Pronunciation Note 118 ■ Exercise 119

CHAPTER 14 : TIME AND TENSE WITH MOOD 122-144

■ Illustration and Definition of Tense 122 ■ Different Forms of Tense 122 ■ Mood of Verbs 130 ■ Applied Section 132 ■ Exercise 137

CHAPTER 15 : VERBAL NOUN, GERUND AND PARTICIPLE 145-151

■ Verbal Noun, Gerund 145 ■ Gerund and Infinitive 146 ■ Participle 147 ■ Gerund and Participle 148 ■ Participle and Nominative Absolute 148 ■ Exercise 149

CHAPTER 16 : MORE ABOUT ADVERBS AND ADVERBIALS 152-168

■ Adverb and its Functions 152 ■ Uses of Adverbs 153 ■ Kinds of Adverbs 154 ■ Formation of Adverbs 156 ■ Adverbs Derived from Pronouns 159 ■ Position of Adverbs 160 ■ Adverbials/Adverbial Particles 161 ■ Degrees of Comparison of Adverbs 161 ■ Intensifiers and Downtoners 162 ■ Applied Section 163 ■ Exercise 167

CHAPTER 17 : MORE ABOUT PREPOSITIONS 169-185

■ Illustration and Definition 169 ■ Relation of Preposition 169 ■ Position of Preposition 170 ■ Kinds of Preposition 171 ■ Relations Expressed by Prepositions 172 ■ Some Important Prepositions 173 ■ Some Usages of Prepositions 175 ■ Prepositional Phrases 182 ■ Applied Section 182 ■ Exercise 185

CHAPTER 18 : APPROPRIATE PREPOSITIONS 186-209

■ Appropriate Prepositions 186 ■ Special Prepositions 208 ■ Some Common Errors in Preposition 208 ■ Exercise 208

CHAPTER 19 : MORE ABOUT CONJUNCTIONS 210-217

■ One Word Joined to Another Word 210 ■ One Word Joined to a Clause 210 ■ One Clause Joined to Another Clause 211 ■ Correlatives 212 ■ Kinds of Conjunctions for Joining Clauses 212 ■ Functions of Conjunctions 212 ■ Conjunctions as Linking Words 213 ■ Sentence Linkers or Connectors 214 ■ Applied Section 215 ■ Exercise 216

CHAPTER 20 : ARTICLES AND DETERMINERS 218-230

■ Illustration and Definition of Article/Determiner 218 ■ Definite and Indefinite Article 218 ■ Use of Articles 218 ■ Special Use 219 ■ Uses of A/An 219 ■ Uses of 'The' 221 ■ Omission of the Articles 223 ■ Repetition of the Articles 225 ■ Determiners 226 ■ Applied Section 227 ■ Exercise 228

CHAPTER 21 : MODIFIERS 231-234

■ Illustration and Definition 231 ■ Premodifier and Postmodifier 231 ■ Types and Uses of Premodifiers 231 ■ Types and Uses of Postmodifiers 232 ■ Noun Modifiers and Head Nouns 233 ■ Nominal Group/Noun Cluster 233 ■ Exercise 234

CHAPTER 22 : STRUCTURAL AND NON-STRUCTURAL WORDS 235-237

■ Illustration and Definition 235 ■ Difference between Structural Words and Non-Structural Words 235 ■ Exercise 236

CHAPTER 23 : NARRATION/REPORTING 238-259

■ Illustration and Definition of Direct Speech and Indirect Speech 238 ■ Punctuation of Direct Speech 238 ■ Rules for Changing Direct Speech into Indirect Speech 239 ■ Change of Tenses 239 ■ Narration of Assertive Sentence 240 ■ Exercise [I] 241 ■ Narration of Interrogative Sentence 242 ■ Yes-No Questions 242 ■ Wh-Questions 243 ■ Question Tags 244 ■ Exercise [II] 244

■ Narration of Imperative Sentence 245 ■ Imperative Beginning with 'Let' 246 ■ Exercise [III] 246 ■ Narration of Optative Sentence 247 ■ Exercise [IV] 247 ■ Narration of Exclamatory Sentence 247 ■ Exercise [V] 249 ■ Narration of Vocatives 249 ■ Reporting Mixed Sentences 250 ■ Applied Section 251 ■ Reporting Dialogues 251 ■ Exercise [VI] 256

CHAPTER 24 : VOICE CHANGE/DESCRIBING A PROCESS 260-273

■ Illustration and Definition of Active Voice and Passive Voice 260 ■ Rules for Changing Voice 260 ■ Verb Patterns of Passive Voice 261 ■ Objective Forms of Pronouns 262 ■ Voice Change of Assertive Sentence 262 ■ Imperative Sentences 262 ■ 'Let' in Active and Passive 263 ■ Interrogative Sentences 263 ■ Yes-No Questions 263 ■ Wh-Questions 263 ■ Negative Sentences 264 ■ Special Forms of Passive Voice 264 ■ Quasi-Passive Voice 267 ■ Passive Voice of Complex Sentences 268 ■ Some Peculiarities in Voice 269 ■ Applied Section 270 ■ Exercise 271

CHAPTER 25 : PHRASES 274-283

■ Construction of Phrases 274 ■ Difference of Phrase and Clause 274 ■ Kinds of Phrases 274 ■ Noun Phrases 275 ■ Adjective Phrases 275 ■ Adverbial Phrases 276 ■ Position of Adverbial Phrases 277 ■ Prepositional Phrases 277 ■ Participial Phrases 277 ■ Phrase in Apposition 277 ■ Absolute Phrase 278 ■ Parenthetical Phrase 278 ■ Exercise 278

CHAPTER 26 : SENTENCES AND ITS CLAUSES/JOINING/SPLITTING 284-305

■ Illustration and Definition 284 ■ Difference of Clause and Phrase 285 ■ Principal, Subordinate and Coordinate Clause 285 ■ Noun Clause 286 ■ Adjective Clause/Relative Clause 288 ■ Adverbial Clause 290 ■ Coordinating Clauses 294 ■ Some More Joining 294 ■ Contracted Sentences 295 ■ Different Clauses with the Same Linker 295 ■ Participial Phrases and Non-Finite Clauses 296 ■ Some More Joining 298 ■ Splitting of Sentences 299 ■ Sequence of Tenses 300 ■ Applied Section 300 ■ Exercise 301

CHAPTER 27 : TRANSFORMATION OF SENTENCES 306-317

■ Interchange of Interrogative and Assertive 306 ■ Exercise [I] 307 ■ Interchange of Exclamatory and Assertive 307 ■ Exercise [II] 308 ■ Interchange of Affirmative and Negative 308 ■ Exercise [III] 309 ■ Interchange of Degrees of Comparison 309 ■ Exercise [IV] 310 ■ Joining by 'Too' 310

■ Exercise [V] 311 ■ Simple to Complex Sentences 311 ■ Exercise [VI] 312 ■ Complex to Simple Sentences 312 ■ Exercise [VII] 313 ■ Simple to Compound Sentences 314 ■ Exercise [VIII] 315 ■ Compound to Simple Sentences 316 ■ Exercise [IX] 316 ■ Complex to Compound Sentences 317 ■ Compound to Complex Sentences 317 ■ Exercise [X] 317

CHAPTER 28 : WH-QUESTIONS 318-349

■ Difference of Simple Questions and Wh-Questions 318 ■ Rules of Interrogative Patterns 318 ■ Classification of Wh-words 319 ■ Framing Wh-Questions 319 ■ Structure of Wh-Questions 321 ■ Wh-Questions for Two or More Sentences 339 ■ Exercise 343

CHAPTER 29 : FORMATION OF WORDS/ANTONYMS 350-380

■ Primary Derivatives 350 ■ Secondary Derivatives : Prefixes 351 ■ Suffixes 355 ■ Antonyms 359 ■ Homonyms and Homophones 363 ■ Words Expressing the Cries of Animals 365 ■ Words Indicating Young Ones of Animals 366 ■ Single Word for a Group of Words 366 ■ Applied Section 378 ■ Exercise 379

CHAPTER 30 : WORD-FAMILY FROM ONE PART OF SPEECH TO OTHERS 381-393

■ Nouns Corresponding to Other Parts of Speech 381 ■ Verbs Corresponding to Other Parts of Speech 384 ■ Adjectives Corresponding to Other Parts of Speech 390 ■ Applied Section 391 ■ Exercise 392

CHAPTER 31 : SAME WORD USED AS DIFFERENT PARTS OF SPEECH 394-399

■ Same Words as Different Parts of Speech 394 ■ Exercise 399

CHAPTER 32 : WORDS COMMONLY CONFUSED 400-415

■ Words Commonly Confused in Spelling 400 ■ Words Commonly Confused in Meaning 404 ■ Words Commonly Confused in Usage 411 ■ American and British English 412 ■ Exercise 413

CHAPTER 33 : GROUP VERBS/PHRASAL VERBS 416-427

■ Different Group Verbs 416 ■ Applied Section 424 ■ Exercise 425

CHAPTER 34 : PHRASES AND IDIOMS 428-444

■ Idioms with Meaning and Examples 428 ■ Exercise 443

CHAPTER 35 : NOMINAL COMPOUNDS 445-454

■ Noun + Noun 445 ■ Noun + Verb/Verbal Noun 449 ■ Verb/Verbal Noun/Participial + Noun 450 ■ Adjective + Noun 450 ■ Nominal Compound of More than Two Words 451 ■ Applied Section 452 ■ Exercise 453

CHAPTER 36 : PUNCTUATION AND CAPITALIZATION 455-460

■ What is Punctuation? 455 ■ Uses of Punctuation 455 ■ Use of Capital Letter 459 ■ Exercise 459

CHAPTER 37 : COMMON ERRORS/CORRECT USAGE 461-482

■ Correct Usage of Articles 461 ■ Correct Usage of Nouns 465 ■ Correct Usage of Pronouns 466 ■ Correct Usage of Adjectives 467 ■ Correct Usage of Verbs 468 ■ Correct Usage of Adverbs 470 ■ Correct Usage of Prepositions 472 ■ Correct Usage of Tense 474 ■ Sequence of Tense 476 ■ Subject-Verb Agreement 477 ■ Miscellaneous Errors 478 ■ Exercise 482

CHAPTER 38 : FIGURES OF SPEECH 483-488

■ What is a Figure of Speech 483 ■ Metaphor 483 ■ Personification 484 ■ Transferred Epithet 484 ■ Apostrophe 484 ■ Inversion/Anastrophe 484 ■ Alliteration 484 ■ Hyperbole/Exaggeration 484 ■ Oxymoron 485 ■ Euphemism 485 ■ Climax 485 ■ Anticlimax 485 ■ Paradox 485 ■ Antithesis 485 ■ Pun 486 ■ Irony 486 ■ Epigram 486 ■ Synecdoche 486 ■ Onomatopoeia 486 ■ Some More Similes 486 ■ Exercise 487

## Part II: COMPOSITION

CHAPTER 1 : LETTER WRITING 491-527

■ Private Letters 492 ■ Letters to Pen-Friends 497 ■ Social Letters 500 ■ Business Letters 501 ■ Official and Demi-Official Letters 503 ■ Application for Employment 506 ■ Letters in Response to Advertisements 508 ■ Letters to the Editor 511 ■ Circular Letter or Notice and Draft 517 ■ Telegrams 520 ■ Do It Yourself 523 ■ Exercise 524

CHAPTER 2 : NARRATING EVENTS/REPORTS 528-539

■ Specimens 528 ■ Do It Yourself 536 ■ Exercise 538

CHAPTER 3 : PARAGRAPHS 540-565

■ Definition 540 ■ Paragraphs on Places 540 ■ Paragraphs on Persons 544 ■ Paragraphs on Objects 554 ■ Do It Yourself 558 ■ Exercise 564

CHAPTER 4 : PRESENTING PROBLEMS AND SUGGESTING SOLUTIONS 566-573

■ Pollution 566 ■ Sound Pollution 567 ■ Drug Addiction 567 ■ National Integration 568 ■ Illiteracy 568 ■ Child Labour 569 ■ Do It Yourself 569 ■ Exercise 571

CHAPTER 5 : RETELLING STORIES 574-585

■ Categories of Stories 574 ■ Stories of Eminent Persons, Folk Tales, Fables 574 ■ Real-Life Stories 579 ■ Do It Yourself 580 ■ Exercise [I] 582 ■ Exercise [II] 584

CHAPTER 6 : DIALOGUE AND REPORTING IN A SUMMARY FORM 586-592

■ Examples Worked Out—Planning a Picnic 586 ■ Booking for a Trip to Goa 587 ■ A Doctor and his Patient 587 ■ Who is More Useful—a Teacher or a Doctor? 588 ■ A Rainy Day at School 588 ■ Two Boys about a Fire 589 ■ Visiting a Patient in a Hospital 589 ■ A Father and his Son about the Son's Career 590 ■ Puja Purchase 590 ■ Two Friends on Cinema Shows 591 ■ Do It Yourself 591 ■ Exercise 592

CHAPTER 7 : SUMMARY/PRÉCIS WRITING 593-613

■ How to write a Summary/Précis 593 ■ Shortening a Sentence/Sentences 593 ■ Exercise 610

CHAPTER 8 : DESCRIBING A PROCESS 614-620

■ Ways of Describing 614 ■ Do it Yourself 619 ■ Exercise 619

CHAPTER 9 : PICTURE DESCRIPTION 621-628

■ Pollution Problem 621 ■ Three Essentials of Living 622 ■ Exercise 622

Part III: READING COMPREHENSION

READING COMPREHENSION 631-660

■ What it Means, Guidelines 631 ■ Comprehensions from Familiar Extracts 631 ■ Unseen Comprehensions from Newspapers, Journals, etc. 643 ■ Exercise 649

# PART I

# GRAMMAR

# 1 SENTENCE CONSTRUCTION

**[Special stress has been given on the STRUCTURES of sentences and their FUNCTIONS AND SITUATIONS within communicative and realistic contexts.]**

## ◆ WHAT IS A SENTENCE?

### THE OLD VIEWS

A group of words that makes a complete sense is called a sentence.

**Wren & Martin**

A combination of words that makes a complete sense is called a sentence.

**J. C. Nesfield**

**But these old views are defective in two points :**

**(i) A sentence may be single-worded or multi-worded in a given context.**
In Modern Grammar single-word sentences and verbless sentences are acceptable.

**EXAMPLES :**

Teacher : Have you done your home task?
[ Multi-word sentence ]

Student : Yes. [ Single-word sentence ]

Teacher : All right. [ Verbless sentence ]

**Some other single-word sentences :**

| | |
|---|---|
| Assertive sentences | : Yes. No. Certainly. Impossible. etc. |
| Imperative sentences | : Come. Look. Halt. Stop. Wait. etc. |
| Interrogative sentences | : Why? Where? What? etc. |
| Exclamatory sentences | : Hello! Good! Bravo! Hurrah! |
| Verbless sentences | : Not at all. Not yet. Why not? So what? etc. |

Some other sentences with verb and without verb [ side by side ]

| Sentence with verb | Sentence without verb |
|---|---|
| What's your name? | Name, please. |
| Please show me your ticket. | Ticket, please. |
| What's the time now? | Time, please. |
| It is just five past 10. | Just five past 10. |
| How much is that book? | How much for that book? |

**Note** In written form of English we usually use sentences having a group of words with verbs. But in Spoken English we often use single word or verbless group of words as sentences.

**(ii) A sentence may not sometimes convey a complete sense as a sentence may be extended from a short one to a bigger one by left branching or / and right branching.**

**EXAMPLES :**

A man is taking rest. [Key sentence]

A tired man is taking rest.
A fat and tired man is taking rest. [**Left branching**]

A fat and tired man is taking rest under a tree.
A fat and tired man is taking rest under a tree by the side of a road. [**Right branching**]

**Now the question arises :**

Can we call a sentence complete, more complete, most complete etc.?

We must say : No. (As in that case the word 'complete' itself becomes insignificant.) However, in all the examples mentioned above, there is a clear meaning. And, if we use **'clear meaning'** in place of **'complete sense'**, there is no dispute in the definition of a sentence.

**Hence, we should modify the definition of a sentence as below :**

## THE NEW CONCEPT

**A word or a group of words having a clear meaning in a given context is called a sentence.**
**P. C. Das**

For such clear meaning, a multi-word sentence must have a proper order of words.

| Not a sentence for no proper order of words | Sentence for proper order of words |
|---|---|
| Goes he to school. | He goes to school. |
| Fat man the slowly walks. | The fat man walks slowly. |
| The beggar a rupee give. | Give the beggar a rupee. |

So we see :

**A sentence must have a proper order of words and a clear meaning.**

**P. C. Das**

## FORMATION OF SENTENCES

**SENTENCE**

- **Single-worded** [ Come. Go. Stop. Wait. etc. ]
- **Multi-worded**
  - With Verbs
  - Verbless

| With Verbs | Verbless |
|---|---|
| Who is there? | Mr. Ghosh. |
| Have you got any ticket of the cricket match? | Not at all. |
| Will you take any? | Why not? |
| I am going now. | Where to? |
| Will you accompany me? | What for? |
| Where are you going now? | To see a cricket match. |

## SUBJECT AND PREDICATE

A multi-word sentence with a verb may be divided into two parts :

**SENTENCE**

- **Subject or Noun Part [NP]** — About whom or what we are speaking.
- **Predicate or Verb Part [VP]** — What is said about the subject.

1. The part which names the person or thing we are speaking about is called the subject of the sentence.
2. The part which tells something about the subject is called the predicate of the sentence.

**Wren and Martin**

**Subject or Noun Part :** The Subject part of the sentence consists of Nouns, Pronouns, or Adjectives.

**Predicate or Verb Part :** The Predicate part of the sentence consists of Finite Verbs, Objects/Complements, Adverbials and Modifiers.

| Subject | Predicate |
|---|---|
| The boy | got the prize. |
| The intelligent boy | got the prize for standing first in the exam. |

In the above-mentioned sentence, 'The boy got the prize', **'boy'** is the **'Subject Proper'** and **'the'** is the **'Adjunct to Subject'**. In the sentence 'The intelligent boy got the prize for standing first in the exam', **'the'** as well as **'intelligent'** are the **'Adjunct to Subject'**.

Usually the **Subject** comes first and then comes the **Predicate**. But **sometimes the whole Predicate or a part of the Predicate is placed before the Subject for the sake of emphasis.**

**EXAMPLES :**

| | |
|---|---|
| Those days are gone. | Gone are (*Predicate*) those days. (*Subject*) |
| The uses of adversity are sweet. | Sweet are (*Predicate*) the uses of adversity. (*Subject*) |
| I have none—silver and gold. | Silver and gold have (*Predicate*) I (*Subject*) none. (*Predicate*) |

**Note** Sometimes the Subject may be understood :

Thank you. (Here the Subject 'I' is understood.)

In almost all Imperative sentences, the Subject is understood :

Sit down. (Here the Subject 'you' is understood.)

In Exclamatory sentences, the Subject and a part of the Predicate can be understood :

Well done! (That was well done. 'That was' understood.)

No more of that! (Let us have no more of that. 'Let us have' understood.)

## EXERCISE

**1. Say something about the following Subjects :**

| | |
|---|---|
| Ratan | .................................................... |
| The boys | .................................................... |
| The girls | .................................................... |
| The cows | .................................................... |
| The birds | .................................................... |

**2. Divide each of the following sentences into Subject and Predicate :**

(i) Mary has a little lamb.
(ii) She has a good memory.
(iii) The boy stood on the burning deck.
(iv) The earth moves round the sun.
(v) Nature is the best physician.
(vi) All roads lead to Rome.
(vii) A barking dog seldom bites.
(viii) We cannot pump the ocean dry.
(ix) Edison invented the phonograph.
(x) We should profit by experience.

# 2 KINDS OF SENTENCES AND THEIR FUNCTIONS

There are five different kinds of sentences :

**SENTENCES AND THEIR FUNCTIONS**

- Assertive → Statement
- Interrogative → Question
- Imperative → Command/Request
- Optative → Desire/Prayer
- Exclamatory → Emotion

Now see the following chart :

| Kinds of Sentences | Examples | Functions |
|---|---|---|
| Assertive | Uma is a good girl. | Statement |
| Interrogative | Is she going to school? | Question |
| Imperative | Open the window. | Command |
| Optative | May you be happy. | Desire |
| Exclamatory | Hurrah! We have got a rainy day. | Emotion |

**Note** In English, each type of sentences and the first line in case of a poem, start with a **Capital Letter**. It is important to remember that the **Assertive, Imperative and Optative sentences end up with a Full Stop** [.] **whereas the Interrogative sentences with a Note of Interrogation** [?] and **the Exclamatory sentences with a Note of Exclamation** [!].

These five types of sentences are again divided into two types :

1. **Affirmative**, 2. **Negative**

| Kinds of Sentences | Affirmative | Negative |
|---|---|---|
| Assertive | He is an Indian citizen. | He is not an Indian citizen. |
| Interrogative | Does he take tea? | Does he not take tea? |
| Imperative | Sit down on the chair. | Do not sit down on the chair. |
| Optative | May he prosper in life. | May he not prosper in life. |
| Exclamatory | Hurrah! We have succeeded at last. | Alas! We have not succeeded at last. |

**Note** However, in Transformation of Sentences we can use 'not' with the opposite word or the phrase 'It is not that' to keep the meaning unchanged. e.g. Affirmative—Rohit is a good boy. Negative—Rohit is not a bad boy. Affirmative—He is an Indian. Negative—It is not that he is not an Indian.

## SENTENCE PATTERN

In English, **Assertive**, **Interrogative**, **Imperative**, **Optative** and **Exclamatory** sentences have five types of sentence pattern :

### [1] ASSERTIVE SENTENCE PATTERN

About 80 percent of sentences in English are of Assertive Pattern. The rules of arrangement of such sentences are [ **S–V–O / Comp. / Adverbials** ] :

| Subject | Verb | Object/ Complement | Adverbials/Preposition and other words |
|---|---|---|---|
| He | is | a student. | |
| Prof. Das | cancelled | our class | yesterday. |
| There | were | many students | in the classroom. |
| Sourav | plays | cricket | at the Edens. |

### [2] IMPERATIVE SENTENCE PATTERN

In Imperative sentences, the subject 'you' is omitted. Hence the verb comes first and the remaining part is the same as the Assertive sentences.

The rules of arrangement of such sentences are [ **V–O / Comp. / Adverbials** ] :

**Pattern A**

| Subject | Verb | Object (What / Whom) |
|---|---|---|
| — | Read | the book. |
| — | Write | a letter. |
| — | Shut | the door. |
| — | Give | me a glass of water. |

**Pattern B**

| Verb | Where |
|---|---|
| Come | here. |
| Go | there. |
| Walk | to the door. |
| Run | across the field. |

You smoke and your family suffers. [Assertive, not Imperative]

You must do your duty. [Assertive, not Imperative]

**Note** **Why is the Subject omitted in the Imperative?**

As the Subject is always 'You', and nothing else, it is omitted in the Imperative sentence. However, the Adverb 'Please' or 'Kindly' comes first in the Imperative in order to denote a polite request.

Please sit down. Kindly give me a glass of water.

### [3] INTERROGATIVE SENTENCE PATTERN

***Three rules of forming Interrogative sentences*** :

**(i)** The verb **Be** and its forms—is, am, are, was, were; **Have** and its forms—has, have, had; shall, should; will, would; can, could; may, might, etc. are placed before the Subject in an Interrogative sentence [**V–S–O / Comp. / Adverbials**] :

| Assertive | Interrogative |
|---|---|
| Kim is your brother. | Is Kim your brother? |
| He has got a bad tooth. | Has he got a bad tooth? |
| He will pull out the bad tooth. | Will he pull out the bad tooth? |
| The girl is dancing in the hall. | Is the girl dancing in the hall? |

**(ii)** The verb Do (do—does—did) is placed before the subject in absence of the above-listed verbs [**Do–S–V–O/Comp./Adverbials**]

Do you play football everyday?

Does Mala do her hometask every day?

Did you write a letter to your father?

**(iii)** Wh-word comes first, if necessary, in both the above-mentioned types of Interrogative sentences [**Wh–Word + Interrogative Pattern**]

Who are you?

Whose book is this?

Whom do you want?

Which is your pen?

What are you doing?

When do you eat?

Where does he live (in)?

Why do you come here?

How does he write? How many sisters have you? How much milk do you want?

**Note** The Helping verb 'do' is not required where 'who' poses itself as the subject : Who knows it? But 'do' is required to make a Negative form : Who does not know it?

## [4] OPTATIVE SENTENCE PATTERN

An Optative sentence denotes wish or prayer. The rules of forming such an Optative sentence are :

May + Assertive = **Optative**

May you live long. May God bless you. [Blessing]

May the sky break down upon you. [Cursing]

Sometimes, 'May' is omitted :

Long live the king. (= May the king live long.)

## [5] EXCLAMATORY SENTENCE PATTERN

An Exclamatory sentence is used to express sudden emotion of joy, sorrow, wonder etc. Such sentences are formed in two ways :

**(i)** By using 'Alas! Hurrah! Ah!' etc. :

Alas/Hurrah etc. + Assertive = **Exclamatory**

Alas! The man is dead.

Hurrah! We have won the match.

Hush! The man is asleep.

Fie! You are a liar. Hello! You are Amal, I see!

**(ii)** By using What, How, etc. [**What/How + S + V**] :

What a nice bird it is!

What a wonderful land it is!

How happy you are!

How cold it is today!

**Note** The Verb is placed before the Subject in Interrogative sentence with 'What' or 'How'. But the Verb is placed after the Subject in Exclamatory sentence with 'What' or 'How'.

## NEGATIVE FORMS

Now study the rules of making Negative forms. There are three ways of doing this :

**(i)** **'Not'** is placed after the **'Be'** (is, am, are, was, were), **'Have'** (has, have, had), **shall**, **should**, **will**, **would**, **may** or **might** :

| Affirmative | Negative |
|---|---|
| Amal is a good boy. | Amal is not a good boy. |
| Bimal has a book. | Bimal has not (hasn't) a book (no book). |
| I shall go to school. | I shall not go to school. |
| We can solve this problem. | We cannot (can't) solve this problem. |

**Note** However, if we like **to transform an Affirmative sentence into a Negative** one without changing its meaning, we should use the **opposite word with 'not'** or the phrase **'It is not that' with 'not'**. For example—Amal is a good boy (Affirmative). → Amal is not a bad boy (Negative). He is an Indian citizen (Affirmative). → It is not that he is not an Indian citizen. (Negative)

**(ii)** **'Not'** is placed after the helping verb **'Do'** in absence of the above-listed verbs :

| Affirmative | Negative |
|---|---|
| Go there. | Do not go there. |
| Dipak plays football. | Dipak does not play football. |
| They play football. | They do not play football. |

**Note** **'Not'** is always placed **after a Pronoun** and usually **before a Noun** in non-contracted **Negative questions**.

Amal is not going to school. → Is not (Isn't) Amal going to school?

He is not going to school. → Is he not going to school?

Dipak does not play football. → Does not Dipak play football?

He does not play football. → Does he not play football?

"Do not the police really remain?"—

**'Oxford English Grammar' by Sidney Greenbaum**

However, 'Not' may also be placed after a noun in non-contracted Negative questions.

"Can the directors not make a decision ...?"

**'Practical English Usage' by Michael Swan**

But the shortened form of Verb + not (don't, doesn't, can't, etc.) is always placed before the subject in Negative questions.

You do not play football. → Don't you play football? [Do not = Don't]

Reba does not like story-books. → Doesn't Reba like story-books? [Does not = Doesn't]

**(iii)** By using **'No'** before a Noun and **'Not'** before an Adjective :

| | |
|---|---|
| No man can do this work. | 'No' before the noun 'man'. |
| He has no enemy. | 'No' before the noun 'enemy'. |
| He is not faithful. | 'Not' before the adjective 'faithful'. |
| The girl is not beautiful. | 'Not' before the adjective 'beautiful'. |

**(iv)** By using **'never'** or **'nothing'** :

He never goes to school.

They saw nothing in the room.

**Now study Affirmative, Negative and Interrogative side by side :**

| Affirmative | Negative | Interrogative |
|---|---|---|
| I am | I am not | Am I ? |
| We are | We are not | Are we ? |
| You are | You are not | Are you ? |
| He/She is | He/She is not | Is he/she ? |
| They are | They are not | Are they ? |
| It is | It is not | Is it ? |

## QUESTION TAGS

Question tags are short Interrogative clauses added like a tail to sentences, asking for confirmation.

In Affirmative sentences, the Question Tag is made by repeating the auxiliary verb in Interrogative form in the Negative, expecting the answer **'Yes'**.

**Affirmative Statement + Negative Question Tag**

[Expecting the answer 'Yes']

You can speak French, can't you? (not 'can you?')

You have a dog, haven't you? (not 'have you?')

You will have to do this, won't you? (not 'will you?')

Suman would like to go there, wouldn't he? (not 'would he?')

Rohan is a good boy, isn't he? (not 'is he?')

Reba has gone home, hasn't she? (not 'has she?')

In Negative sentences, the Question Tag is formed by repeating the auxiliary verb in Interogative form in the Affirmative, expecting the answer **'No'**.

**Negative Statement + Affirmative Question Tag**

[Expecting the answer 'No']

Salim cannot speak Hindi, can he? (not 'can't he?')

Syed is not a good student, is he? (not 'is not he?')

They have not any house, have they ? (not 'haven't they ?')

Robert did not agree to do this, did he ? (not 'didn't he ?')

Rabeya will not come here, will she ? (not 'won't she ?')

You need not come here, need you ? (not 'needn't you ?')

**Note** (a) The main force of affirmation or negation lies in the main clause, not in the Question Tag.

(b) The Subject of a Question Tag must be a pronoun, never a noun.

(c) The non-contracted Negative Interrogative form is used in the main clause and contracted or shortened form in the Question Tag.

[The only exception is in Imperative sentence where the main clause starts with 'Don't and the Question Tag starts with 'do'—Don't go there, do you?]

(d) Guard against the common errors :

You are going to school, isn't it? (Incorrect)

You are going to school, aren't you? (Correct)

You haven't done this, is it? (Incorrect)

You haven't done this, have you? (Correct)

(e) Positive statements with the negative shortened forms :

We are ............... (positive statement) ........ , aren't we?

You are .............. (positive statement) ........ , aren't you?

He is .................. (positive statement) ........ , isn't he?

They are ............. (positive statement) ........ , aren't they?

[ But ] I am ........ (positive statement) ........ , ain't I? (not 'amn't I?')

(f) If there are two auxiliaries in the verb, only the first one is used in the formation of the Question Tag :

They should have done this, shouldn't they?

(g) The Tag for Imperative affirmative sentences usually begins with 'will'. But the Tag for Imperative negative sentences usually begins with 'Do' :

Write down your name, will you? [Imperative Affirmative]

Don't disturb me, do you? [Imperative Negative]

(h) For a positive request or command, the Tag can be either positive or negative :

Go to market, will you?

Go to market, won't you?

Please shut the door, will you?

Please shut the door, won't you?

(i) But for negative requests or commands, the Tag can only be positive.

Don't make such mistakes, will you?

Please don't make noise, will you?

## APPLIED SECTION

### (Functional Communicative Approach)

### FUNCTIONS OF SENTENCES

| FUNCTIONS | SENTENCES |
|---|---|
| **A. Assertive/Declarative** | |
| (i) Giving information/Reporting | The Second Hooghly Bridge was inaugurated on October 10 in 1992. |
| (ii) Narrating | He said that Napoleon died at St. Helena. |
| (iii) Describing | There are rows of trees on both sides of the road.  |
| (iv) Defining | Fables are short tales, usually with animal characters in them, and always with a moral. |
| (v) Hesitating/Giving opinion—not confidently | I don't know what exactly he or she is. |
| (vi) Classifying | Food substances may be classified into two broad groups—organic food and inorganic food. |
| (vii) Illustrating/Exemplifying | Some of the best Science Fiction writers are : H. G. Wells, Jules Verne and Arthur C. Clarke. |
| (viii) Stating cause | His hard labour placed him in the high position. |
| (ix) Describing a process | The preparation of butter goes through a number of steps. |
| (x) Denying a fact | No, I'm all right. |
| (xi) Asserting a fact | Yes, Sir, I am a book-binder. |
| (xii) Expressing obligation | I must go home. |
| (xiii) Supposing/Guessing | If he comes, he may receive a hearty welcome. |
| (xiv) Comparing | He is as cunning as a fox. The ruby is redder than a rose. |
| (xv) Contradicting | I don't worry but I can't keep from thinking. |
| (xvi) Apologizing/Confessing | I beg your pardon, I have hurt your feelings.  |
| (xvii) Expressing ability | I can do the sum easily. |
| (xviii) Expressing possibility | He may come here today. |
| (xix) Giving permission | You may sit in the parlour. |
| (xx) Appealing | I pray to your kind self for granting me three days' sick-leave. |

| FUNCTIONS | SENTENCES |
|---|---|
| **B. Interrogative** | |
| (i) Asking for information/Asking reason/Interrogating/Enquiring | What is the distance of Delhi from Kolkata?<br>Why did you not go to school yesterday?<br>Who does not want to be free? |
| (ii) Asserting a fact | That was really a bit of fun, wasn't it? |
| (iii) Asking for an opinion | May I have your opinion on the book?  |
| (iv) Asking for permission | May I come in, sir? |
| (v) Requesting | Could you please tell me your name? |
| (vi) Challenging | Who dares to defy me? |
| (vii) Expressing a doubt | Who knows when the country will be free from corruption? |
| (viii) Confirming a doubt | The science you have learnt is more or less the result of self-teaching, isn't it, Mr. Faraday?  |
| **C. Imperative** | |
| (i) Ordering/Commanding | Get out at once. |
| (ii) Requesting | Please give me a glass of water. |
| (iii) Advising | Don't give up hope, Mr. Faraday. |
| (iv) Suggesting/Proposing | Let's sit down here and talk the matter over. |
| (v) Instructing | To improve your English read as much as you can. |
| (vi) Warning | Be quiet, or I'll punish you. |
| (vii) Threatening | Get out, or I'll break your nose. |
| (viii) Permitting | Go wherever you like but come back before evening. |
| (ix) Prohibiting | Don't leave the place without permission. |
| (x) Reminding | Kindly remember the date and time of our meeting.  |
| **D. Optative** | |
| (i) Wishing/Desiring | Wish you good luck. |
| (ii) Praying | May God bless you. |
| **E. Exclamatory** | |
| (i) Expressing joy | Hurrah! Our club has won the trophy. |
| (ii) Expressing sorrow | Alas! The man is dead. |
| (iii) Expressing wonder | What a nice bird it is! |
| (iv) Expressing pity | Poor fellow! How changed you are. |

| FUNCTIONS | SENTENCES |
|---|---|
| (v) Expressing disgust | How shabby the statue is! |
| (vi) Encouraging | Bravo! You have saved a nice goal. |
| (vii) Greeting | Hello! How nice to meet you after years. |
| (viii) Farewell | Goodbye!/Goodnight! Hope we'll meet you again. |

**1. Giving Information [Assertive]**

Be, Have

| I am | He is |
|---|---|
| We are | She is |
| You are | They are |

| I have | He has |
|---|---|
| We have | She has |
| You have | They have |

I **am** a student. We **are** students. You **have** four brothers.

**Note** British English uses both **have** and **have got**, but prefers the second.

We **have**/**have** *got* a cottage in the village. (Possession)

Moreover, you can **have** things to eat, things to drink.

What do you usually **have** for breakfast?

We usually **have** *'muri'* for breakfast.

Do you **have** lunch at school?

No, we **have** lunch at home.

You can **have** a cup of tea/coffee, a cold drink etc.

Similarly, you can have a rest, a shower, a dream, an idea, a lesson, a lecture, a good/bad/dull/happy time, an outing, etc.

**2. (Order, Request/Instruction etc.) [Some have been done. Complete others.]**

| Verb | Where |
|---|---|
| Come | to my desk. |
| Don't sit | on the table. |
| Don't talk | in the class. |
| Don't run | ............... |

| Verb | What/Whom |
|---|---|
| Shut | your eyes. |
| Open | ........... |
| Bring | me your book. |
| Show | ........... |

| Verb | What | Where |
|---|---|---|
| Put | the book | on the table. |
| Draw | a map | ........... |
| Throw | ........ | ......... |

**3. Question and Information [Some have been done. Complete others.]**

| Question | Information |
|---|---|
| Is your school big? | Yes, it's a big one. |
| Are the elephants small? | No, they aren't. |
| Have you good friends? | .................................................. |
| Has the ant ......... legs? | Yes, the ant ................................ |
| Did you have breakfast? | Yes, I did./No, I didn't. |
| Do you like your English? | .................................................. |
| Don't you like coffee? | .................................................. |
| Does Lata sing daily? | .................................................. |
| Doesn't Pintu play regularly? | .................................................. |

[It's, aren't, don't, doesn't etc. are used in Spoken English.]

| | |
|---|---|
| Who is your English teacher? | .................................................. |
| Who lives near your house? | .................................................. |
| What's the time now? | It's ............................................ |
| Which ........... your pen? | The red one. |
| Where do you live? | .................................................. |
| When ......... your father come home? | .................................................. |

**4. Wish and Prayer :** **Express similar wishes & prayers**

| | |
|---|---|
| May you be happy. | .................................................. |
| May God bless you. | .................................................. |
| I wish I were a bird. | .................................................. |

**5. Sudden feeling or emotion :** **Express similar emotion**

| | |
|---|---|
| Alas! The king is no more. | .................................................. |
| Hurrah! It's a rainy day. | .................................................. |
| Hello! You're Nipa, I see. | .................................................. |
| What a fool you are! | .................................................. |
| How happy you are! | .................................................. |

## EXERCISE

**1. Mention the kinds of sentences in the following table. One has been done for you.**

| Sentences | Kinds of Sentences |
|---|---|
| 1. People are smoking less nowadays. | Assertive |
| 2. When will you come? | ...................................... |
| 3. Go there and wait for a while. | ...................................... |
| 4. May God bless you. | ...................................... |
| 5. Alas! The man is no more. | ...................................... |

**2. State the functions of the sentences in the following table. One has been done for you.**

| Sentences | Functions |
|---|---|
| 1. I enjoyed your letter and your notebook. | Statement. |
| 2. Don't spit here. | ................................ |
| 3. Why are you weeping then? | ................................ |
| 4. May you be happy. | ................................ |
| 5. What a beautiful flower it is! | ................................ |

**3. Write down the names of the specific functions of the following sentences :**

| Sentences | Functions |
|---|---|
| (i) "I'm all right." | |
| (ii) "No, I'm all right." | |
| (iii) What is it? | |
| (iv) Her little head is bare. | |
| (v) Her father will beat her. | |
| (vi) Her father will not beat her. | |
| (vii) She has let her matches fall in the street. | |
| (viii) "Pluck out my other eye and give it to her." | |
| (ix) I don't know what exactly he or she is. | |
| (x) Sir Humphry Davy was taken aback by the unexpected outburst. | |
| (xi) A few years in the field will cause you to change your opinion. | |
| (xii) It's a very good way to learn. | |
| (xiii) Davy nodded approvingly. | |
| (xiv) "About how long will it be before I die?" | |
| (xv) "Oh, yes, I am. I heard him say a hundred and two." | |
| (xvi) "People don't die with a fever of one hundred and two. That's a silly way to talk." | |
| (xvii) I still prefer scientific work. | |
| (xviii) Please tell me about them. | |
| (xix) "You have a trade at present, Mr. Faraday?" | |
| (xx) "What's the matter, Schatz?" | |
| (xxi) "I've got a headache." | |
| (xxii) "You better go back to bed." | |
| (xxiii) "What made him wait for it?" | |
| (xxiv) Give yourself a quarter of an hour and walk gently. | |

| Sentences | Functions |
|---|---|
| (xxv) How cool I feel! | |
| (xxvi) But I feel quite warm now, although it is so cold. | |
| (xxvii) I must be getting better. | |
| (xxviii) We shan't (shall not) see him again. | |
| (xxix) Do you know how I earn my bread? | |
| (xxx) Could you bring your camera? | |
| (xxxi) May I come in, Sir? | |
| (xxxii) You mustn't idle away your time. | |
| (xxxiii) I can walk five miles (kilometres) at a stretch. | |

**4. Write the types of sentences against the functions in the table below :**

| Functions | Sentences |
|---|---|
| (i) Expressing approval | |
| (ii) Asking for information/Enquiring | |
| (iii) Illustrating | |
| (iv) Confirming doubts | |
| (v) Expressing dislike | |
| (vi) Giving information | |
| (vii) Giving opinion | |
| (viii) Giving opinion—not confidently | |
| (ix) Assuring immediate action | |
| (x) Asking for confirmation | |
| (xi) Narrating | |
| (xii) Persuading | |
| (xiii) Expressing determination | |
| (xiv) Asserting | |
| (xv) Requesting | |
| (xvi) Expressing disbelief/doubt | |
| (xvii) Narrating an event | |
| (xviii) Expressing surprise | |
| (xix) Commanding | |
| (xx) Appreciating | |
| (xxi) Describing | |
| (xxii) Stating a fact | |
| (xxiii) Expressing disagreement | |
| (xxiv) Suggesting | |

| Functions | Sentences |
|---|---|
| (xxv) Expressing satisfaction | |
| (xxvi) Asking for opinion | |
| (xxvii) Advising | |
| (xxviii) Warning | |
| (xxix) Prohibiting | |
| (xxx) Expressing disgust | |
| (xxxi) Expressing pity | |
| (xxxii) Encouraging | |
| (xxxiii) Expressing a condition | |
| (xxxiv) Appealing | |

# 3  PARTS OF SPEECH

### What is meant by 'Parts of Speech'?

Words are divided into different classes, called **Parts of Speech**, according to their use; that is, according to the work they do in the sentence. **Wren & Martin**

Each word is actually a part of our speech. Hence, all types of words are called **Parts of Speech**. **P. C. Das**

The Parts of Speech are eight in number :

1. **Noun**, 2. **Pronoun**, 3. **Adjective**, 4. **Verb**, 5. **Adverb**, 6. **Preposition**, 7. **Conjunction**, 8. **Interjection**.

## NOUN

A Noun is a word used for naming some person or thing. **J. C. Nesfield**

A Noun is a word used as the name of a person, place or thing. **Wren & Martin**

A Noun is a naming word. **P. C. Das**

**EXAMPLES :**

**Subhas** is a brilliant boy.—**Proper Noun** (Particular name)

The **cow** gives us milk.—**Common Noun** (Common name of the same class)

Salil is the best boy in the **class.**—**Collective Noun** (Name of a group taken as a whole)

**Gold** is a valuable metal.—**Material Noun** (Name of a matter or substance)

**Honesty** is the best policy.—**Abstract Noun** (Name of quality, state or action)

## PRONOUN

A word used instead of a noun is called a Pronoun. **J. C. Nesfield**

Pronoun = Pro (in place of) + noun **P. C. Das**

The repetition of the same Noun sounds silly. Hence a Pronoun is used instead of a Noun.

| Use of the same Noun | Use of Pronoun |
|---|---|
| **Ram/Rahim** is a student. | [No Pronoun is used for the first time.] |
| **Ram/Rahim** is going to school. | **He** is going to school. (Pronoun) |
| **Ram/Rahim** is an intelligent boy. | **He** is an intelligent boy. (Pronoun) |

**Some more examples :**

**I** am a student. **You** are a doctor. **She** is a girl. **They** are players.

**Pronouns are divided into three Persons :**

**First Person :** I, we; me, us; my, mine; our, ours.

**Second Person :** you, your, yours.

**Third Person :** He, she, they; him, her, them; his, her, hers, their, theirs; it, its.

## ADJECTIVE

An Adjective is a word used for qualifying (or adding something to) the meaning of a Noun or Pronoun. **J. C. Nesfield**

Now read the following sentences :

1. Kamat is a **good** boy.
2. **He** is **blind**.
3. Our cow gives **much** milk.
4. Give me **two** pens and **three** pencils.

In sentence 1, 'good' shows the quality of a boy.

In sentence 2, 'blind' shows the infirmity of the boy.

In sentence 3, 'much' describes quantity.

In sentence 4, 'two' and 'three' show how many pens and pencils are required.

All the above words ('good', 'blind', 'much', 'two' and 'three') are Adjectives as they qualify a Noun or a Pronoun.

An Adjective qualifies a Noun or a Pronoun in two ways :

1. **Attributive Adjective**, 2. **Predicative Adjective**.

When an adjective is placed before a noun it is used attributively :

Do not laugh at the poor man. ('poor' is used as an Attributive Adjective)

But when it qualifies a noun or a pronoun and is placed after a verb, it is used predicatively :

He is an Indian. ('Indian' is used as a Predicative Adjective)

## VERB

A Verb is a word used for saying something about a person or a thing. **J. C. Nesfield**

A Verb is a word used to say something about some person, place or thing. **Wren & Martin**

A Verb is a word that denotes 'being', 'having' or 'doing' or an action or a state in any form. **P. C. Das**

**Verbs** are of **four types** :

1. **'Being' verb :** The man **is** honest.
2. **'Having' verb :** I **have** a sharp knife.
3. **'Doing' verb :** The boy **kicks** the football.
4. **An action or state in any form :** The moon **looks** bright.

**Some more examples :**

He is playing hockey. The girl is reading. The thief is running. The lady is talking.

## ADVERB

An Adverb qualifies anything except a Noun or a Pronoun. **J. C. Nesfield**

Now read the following sentences :

Salma goes **slowly**. (Adverb modifies a verb)

She is a **very** beautiful girl. (Adverb modifies an adjective)

She walks **very** slowly. (Adverb modifies another adverb)

The bird flew **exactly** over our head. (Adverb modifies a preposition)

I dislike her **simply** because she is very rude. (Adverb modifies a conjunction)

**Adverbs to denote time, place, manner etc. :**

An adverb may denote **time**, **place**, **manner**, **number**, **degree**, **reason**, **purpose**, **condition** and **contrast**.

**Time** : now, then, soon, early etc.

**Place** : here, there, far, near etc.

**Manner** : slowly, quickly, surely, probably etc.

**Number** : once, twice, thrice, again, always etc.

**Degree** : very, much, partly, wholly etc.

**Reason** : as, so, because etc.

**Purpose** : that, so that etc.

**Condition** : If, unless etc.

**Contrast** : though, although etc.

## PREPOSITION

A Preposition is a word placed before a noun or noun-equivalent to show in what relation the person or thing denoted thereby stands to something else.
**J. C. Nesfield**

A Preposition is a word used with a noun or a pronoun to show how the person or thing denoted by the noun or pronoun stands in relation to something else.
**Wren & Martin**

A Preposition is a word that is placed before a noun or a pronoun to show the relation of that noun or pronoun with any other word of the sentence.
**P. C. Das**

**Preposition = Pre + Position**

Read the following sentences :

1. The book is **on** the table.
2. The man is **under** the tree.
3. The fish is **in** the pond.
4. The bird flew **over** our head.
5. The dog is **behind** you.
6. What did you say **about** her?

In sentences 1, 2, 3 and 4, on, under, in and over are placed before the Nouns—table, tree, pond and head—and show the relation between table and book, tree and man, pond and fish, head and the bird, respectively.

In sentences 5 and 6, behind and about are placed before a Pronoun—and show the relation between you and the dog, and say and her.

Thus on, under, in, over, behind and about are Prepositions.

**Most commonly used Prepositions are :**

*at, about, above, across, along, amidst, among, around, before, behind, below, beneath, beside, between, beyond, by, for, from, in, of, off, on, out, through, up, under, with, within, without.*

## CONJUNCTION

A Conjunction is a word for joining one word to another word, or one sentence to another sentence. **J. C. Nesfield**

A Conjunction is a word used to join words or sentences. **Wren & Martin**

**Conjunction = Con (together) + junction (joining)**

Read the following sentences :

1. Reba **and** Rekha are good girls.
2. Mukesh is a boy **but** Mira is a girl.
3. Learn your lesson **or** leave the class.

In the first sentence, 'and' joins two words—'Reba' and 'Rekha'.

In the second sentence 'but' joins two sentences—'Dipu is a boy' and 'Mira is a girl'.

In the third sentence 'or' joins two sentences—'Learn your lesson' and 'Leave the class'.

Thus and, but, or are Conjunctions as they have joined either two words or two sentences.

**Most commonly used Conjunctions are :**

*and, but, or, either···or, neither···nor, otherwise, else, still, yet, nevertheless, however, only, therefore, so, also, too, if, for, because, as, as well as, after, though, although, till, until, unless, since, not only···but also, when, where, whether, whereas, while* etc.

## INTERJECTION

An Interjection is a word or sound thrown into a sentence to express some feeling of the mind. **J. C. Nesfield**

An Interjection is a word which expresses some sudden feeling. **Wren & Martin**

**Interjection = Inter (into) + jection (throwing)**

Read the following sentences :

**Hello,** Rahul! How do you do?

**Alas!** My father is no more.

**Hurrah!** Today is a holiday.

**Oh!** What a nice view.

**Fie!** You are a liar.

**Bravo!** You have done well.

**Interjections may express :**

(a) **Joy :** Hurrah! How! [How nice to meet you!]
(b) **Grief :** Alas! [Alas! The man is dead.]
(c) **Surprise :** Ah! Ha! What! How!
(d) **Encouragement :** Bravo!

Certain groups of words are also used to express some sudden feeling or emotion :

Ah me! For shame! Well done! Good gracious! Good heavens! etc.

**Note** An Interjection, grammatically speaking, is not a part of speech as it has no connection with any other word of the sentence. But, in a broader sense, an Interjection is a part of our speech. Hence it is included as a part of speech in grammar.

## APPLIED SECTION

### (Functional Communicative Approach)

**1. Read the following passage and complete the chart :**

Amar goes to Mitra Institution at Bhawanipur in Kolkata. He is in Class VIII. He goes to school by bus. He lives at Kalighat. His father, Binay Ghosh, is a shopkeeper. He sells goods at his shop.

| Who (name) | What he does | Place of work/study | Lives in | How he goes |
|---|---|---|---|---|
| 1. Amar | ..................... | ............................. | ........... | ................. |
| 2. ............... | sells goods | ............................. | ........... | ................. |

**2. Read the following passage and make a family-tree :**

My name is Gopal. Samar Sen is my grandfather. My grandmother was Shantilata. She is now no more. They have four sons and daughters. They are Tapan, Tapas, Niva and Shubha. My uncle Tapas has no son. I have a brother and a sister. They are Tablu and Tumpa.

**Samar Sen + Shantilata**

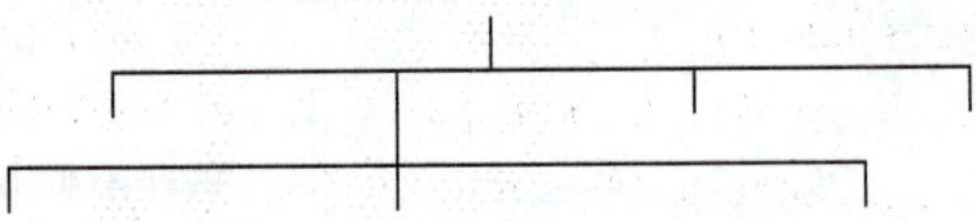

**3. Read the passage and complete the chart :**

Atghara is a small village. There is a river beside it. To the south of the river there is a cornfield. A man is ploughing in the field. There are some fishermen in the village. They catch fish in the river. Most of the villagers are farmers. They are very poor. But they live honestly and peacefully. How charming is the village life!

| Noun | Pronoun | Adjective | Verb | Adverb | Preposition | Conjunction | Interjection |
|---|---|---|---|---|---|---|---|
| ......... | ............ | ............. | ...... | .......... | .......... | ................. | ............ |

**4. Now describe your village/town/city as shown above.**

## EXERCISE

1. **What are Parts of Speech?**
2. **How many kinds of Parts of Speech are there? Give four examples of each kind.**
3. **Classify the following words according to the Parts of Speech and put them in the appropriate box :**

father, mother, brother, sister, boy, girl, you, we, his, she, they, hot, cold, beautiful, ugly, kind, cruel, red, white, break, burn, ask, keep, learn, teach, stand, sleep, swim, dance, write, weave, again, ago, daily, early, often, never, always, idly, openly, surely.

| Noun | Pronoun | Verb | Adjective | Adverb |
|---|---|---|---|---|
| | | | | |
| | | | | |

4. **Classify the following Parts of Speech and put them in the appropriate box :**

across, as, to, or, but, and, into, through, though, if, Ah, Oh, below, under, both, else, up, over, above, Alas, Hurrah, between, among, Hello, with, within, without, Bravo, towards, before, after, by, Fie, Hush, lest, behind, beyond, from, for, of, upon, till, on, Hark, goodbye.

| Preposition | Conjunction | Interjection |
|---|---|---|
| | | |

5. **Fill in the blanks with the appropriate Parts of Speech given in the brackets :**

(i) Reba was praised for her ........... (cruelty/honesty)

(ii) The boy was admired for his ........... (intelligence/intelligent)

(iii) Vidyasagar is famous for his ........... (kind/kindness)

(iv) Give ........... your pen. (I/me)

(v) ........... is a good exercise. (swim/swimming)

(vi) ........... is good for health. (walk/walking)

(vii) ........... goods are cheap. (India/Indian)

(viii) This curry is ........... (taste/tasteful)

(ix) Early to bed and early to rise makes a man ........... (health/healthy)

(x) Lipika dances very ........... (beautiful/beautifully)

6. **Point out the different Parts of Speech in the following sentences :**

(a) Abdul and Latif are brothers.

(b) Delhi is a great city in northern India.

(c) The clothes have been washed with soap.

(d) The girl has a sweet voice.

(e) Debkumar is the first boy in the class.

(f) Columbus discovered America.

(g) Solomon was famous for his wisdom.

(h) He treats his children with great kindness.

(i) The Wind and the Sun had a quarrel.
(j) The boy showed great courage.
(k) Our class consists of forty pupils.
(l) The girl's hair is long and thick and full of curls.
(m) The earth moves round the sun once in a year.
(n) Boys sometimes act like monkeys in their play.
(o) The stars shine through the branches of the tree.
(p) A boy's head has less hair than a monkey's.
(q) The days in all places are hotter than the nights.
(r) Parents must do their duty to their children.
(s) The people who live in India are called Indians.
(t) Without wealth there is no happiness.

# 4 KINDS OF NOUNS

We have already learnt—**Noun is a naming word**. Now we should learn **the kinds of Nouns**.

J. C. Nesfield shows that Nouns are of five defferent kinds : **Proper, Common, Collective, Material and Abstract**.

But Wren and Martin shows that Nouns are of four kinds : **Proper, Common, Collective and Abstract**.

However, it is convenient to classify Nouns in five categories.
1. **Proper Noun**, 2. **Common Noun**, 3. **Collective Noun**, 4. **Material Noun**, 5. **Abstract Noun**.

## PROPER NOUN AND COMMON NOUN

Read the following sentences :

**Ashoka** was a noble **king**.
**Rita** is a poor **girl**.
**Binay** is a smart **boy**.
**Kolkata** is a big **city**.

In the above sentences, 'Ashoka' is the name of a particular king, but 'king' is the common name of its class.
'Rita' is the name of a particular girl, but 'girl' is the common name of its class.
'Binay' is the name of a particular boy, but 'boy' is the common name of its class.
'Kolkata' is the name of a particular city, but 'city' is the common name of its class.
Thus, when a word denotes a particular name, it is a Proper Noun and when it denotes a common name of its class, it is a Common Noun.

**A Proper Noun is the name of some particular person or place.**
**A Common Noun is a name given in common to every person or thing of the same class or kind.** Wren & Martin

So we can say :

Ashoka is a Proper Noun while king is a Common Noun.
Rita is a Proper Noun while girl is a Common Noun.

Binay is a Proper Noun while boy is a Common Noun.

Kolkata is a Proper Noun while city is a Common Noun.

**A Proper Noun begins with a Capital Letter and does not take any article.**

**Note** Difference between a Proper Noun and a Common Noun :

A Proper Noun is always written with a Capital Letter at the beginning but a Common Noun does not require a Capital Letter. Moreover, a Proper Noun does not usually take an article before it while a Common Noun takes an article as a rule.

## COLLECTIVE NOUN

Read the following sentences :

The **crowd** has no discipline. (= a collection of people)

The **army** is formed with discipline. (= a collection of soldiers)

Niren is the first boy in the **class**. (= a collection of students)

You must watch the **fleet**. (= a collection of armed ships)

In the above sentences, crowd, army, class and fleet are Collective Nouns because they refer to a group or collection of similar individuals or things taken as a whole.

**A Collective Noun denotes a group or collection of similar individuals, considered as one complete whole.** J. C. Nesfield

**Note** Difference between a Common Noun and a Collective Noun :

There may be many sheep in a field, but there is only one flock of sheep/birds.

Here 'sheep' is a Common Noun, because it may stand for any and every sheep, but 'flock' is a Collective Noun, because it stands for a group of sheep.

**Note** **Nesfield** also shows a distinction between a **Collective noun** and a **Noun of Multitude** :

(a) A Collective Noun denotes one undivided whole and, takes, the Verb in singular :

The jury consists of twelve persons.

(b) A Noun of Multitude denotes the individuals of the group separately and, hence, the Verb is plural, although the Noun is singular :

The jury (the men on the jury) were divided in their opinions.

However, both the Collective Noun and the Noun of Multitude are followed by the definite article 'The' as a rule.

## MATERIAL NOUN

Read the following sentences :

This ring is made of **gold**.

This chair is made of **wood**.

Please give me a glass of **water**.

In the above sentences, gold, wood and water are Material Nouns because they refer to some matter or substance.

**A Material Noun denotes the matter or substance of which the things are made.** J. C. Nesfield

We should note that gold is a Material Noun but 'ring' is a Common Noun; wood is a Material Noun but 'chair' is a Common Noun; water is a Material Noun but 'glass' is a Common Noun.

But if we say :

**Glass** is transparent, then 'glass' would be a **Material Noun**, because here it does not denote the container, but denotes the matter or substance.

The **sheep** is a **Common Noun**, but **mutton** (the flesh of sheep, goat etc.) is a **Material Noun**. The **tree** is a **Common Noun** but **wood** is a **Material Noun**.

**Note** No article is usually used before a Material Noun, but when it is specified, it takes the definite article 'The'.

**Coal** is black. **The coal** of Jharia is of good quality.
He drinks **water**. **The water** of the Ganga is sacred.

## ABSTRACT NOUN

Read the following sentences :

**Honesty** is the best policy.
**Beauty** is truth.
**Kindness** is a great virtue.
He burst into **laughter**.
He is brave since his **boyhood**.

In the above sentences, honesty, beauty, kindness, laughter, boyhood are Abstract Nouns because they denote the names of some quality, action or state.

> An Abstract Noun is usually the name of a quality, action or state considered apart from the object to which it belongs. **Wren & Martin**

**Quality**—kindness, brightness, honesty, beauty, bravery, wisdom etc.
**Action**—laughter, movement, judg(e)ment etc.
**State**—boyhood, childhood, youth, slavery etc.

> **Abstract Noun relates to qualities, states or action which cannot be seen or touched.** **J. C. Nesfield**

**Note** Thus we see that four kinds of Nouns (Proper, Common, Collective and Material) previously described relate to objects of sense that can be seen or touched. But an Abstract Noun refers to qualities, states or action that cannot be seen or touched; it can only be felt.

We know that a stone is **hard**. We also know that iron is **hard**. We also know that a brick is **hard**. We can, therefore, speak of **hardness** apart from stone or iron or brick or any other object having the same quality.

The names of subjects of Arts and Sciences are also Abstract Nouns, e.g. Physics, Chemistry, Philosophy, Geography, etc.

**Abstract Nouns are formed :**

(a) **From Adjectives** :
kindness from kind; honesty from honest.

(b) **From Verbs** :
arrival from arrive; growth from grow.

(c) **From Common Nouns** :
childhood from child; slavery from slave.

## GERUND, SIMPLE INFINITIVE AND ABSTRACT NOUN

The **Gerunds** and the **Simple Infinitives** of Verbs are in fact (not in form) kinds of **Abstract Nouns**. The following sentences all mean the same thing :

**Service** is better than idleness. (Abstract Noun)

**Serving** is better than idleness. (Gerund)

**To serve** is better than idleness. (Infinitive)

**Note** No article is usually used before an Abstract Noun, but when it is specified, it takes the definite article 'The'.

**Kindness** is a great virtue. (But) **The kindness** of Vidyasagar is known to all.

## GERUND AND VERBAL NOUN

A Gerund is that form of the Verb which ends in *-ing*, and has the force of a Noun and a Verb. **Wren & Martin**

As both the Gerund and the Infinitive have the force of a Noun and a Verb, they have the same uses. Thus in many sentences either of them may be used without any special difference in meaning. **Wren & Martin**

| Infinitive | Gerund |
|---|---|
| Teach me how **to swim**. | Teach me **swimming**. |
| **To see** is to believe. | **Seeing** is believing. |
| **To walk** is a good exercise. | **Walking** is a good exercise. |
| **To give** is better than **to receive**. | **Giving** is better than **receiving**. |

### Proper, Material and Abstract Noun used as Common Noun

There are two ways in which a Proper, Material or Abstract Noun can be used as a Common Noun :

[1] by putting an article ('a', 'an', or 'the') before it.

[2] by putting it into the plural number. **J. C. Nesfield**

**Daniel** was a learned Jew. (Proper Noun)

**A Daniel** has come to judgment. (Common Noun)

**Scott** is a great novelist. (Proper Noun)

Bankim Chandra is **the Scott** of Bengal. (Common Noun)

**Mr. Bose** is not here. (Proper Noun)

**Boses** are not here. (Common Noun)

**Mango** is my favourite fruit. (Material Noun)

Give me one of your **mangoes**. (Common Noun)

**Justice** is a noble quality. (Abstract Noun)

He is **a Justice** of the Peace. (Common Noun)

**Kindness** is a great virtue. (Abstract Noun)

**The kindness** of Vidyasagar has become a proverb. (Common Noun)

**Note** Generally Proper Noun, Material Noun and Abstract Noun do not take any article before them. But they can take an article (a, an, or the) when they are used as a Common Noun.

## FORMATION OF ABSTRACT NOUNS

### Abstract Nouns formed from Adjectives :

| Adjective | Abstract Noun | Adjective | Abstract Noun |
|---|---|---|---|
| brave | bravery | honest | honesty |
| dark | darkness | kind | kindness |
| deep | depth | long | length |
| false | falsehood | short | shortage |
| great | greatness | true | truth |
| high | height | wide | width |

### Abstract Nouns formed from Common Nouns :

| Common Noun | Abstract Noun | Common Noun | Abstract Noun |
|---|---|---|---|
| agent | agency | hero | heroism |
| boy | boyhood | king | kingship |
| child | childhood | mother | motherhood |
| friend | friendship | priest | priesthood |

### Abstract Nouns formed from Verbs :

| Verb | Abstract Noun | Verb | Abstract Noun |
|---|---|---|---|
| admit | admission | enter | entrance |
| agree | agreement | fail | failure |
| behave | behaviour | grow | growth |
| believe | belief | obey | obedience |
| die | death | think | thought |

**Note** There are some Abstract Nouns which are of the same form as Verbs : desire, hope, laugh, love, taste, etc.

## EXERCISE

1. **How many kinds of Nouns are there? Give five examples of each of them.**
2. **Classify the following Nouns and put them in the table :**

Amal, Binod, Vidyasagar, father, mother, boy, girl, Solomon, postman, carpenter, hawker, Ramayana, Mahabharata, gold, silver, iron, army, class, crowd, fruit, player, club, bundle, stick, place, truth, wisdom, shoes, chair, table, ruler, strength, unity.

**Table**

| Proper Noun | Common Noun | Collective Noun | Material Noun | Abstract Noun |
|---|---|---|---|---|
| Amal<br>........ | boy<br>........ | army<br>........ | gold<br>........ | truth<br>........ |

**3. Point out the Nouns in the following sentences and say whether they are Common, Proper, Collective, Material or Abstract :**

(a) Solomon was famous for his wisdom.
(b) Our class consists of forty pupils.
(c) The elephant has great strength.
(d) The soldiers were rewarded for their bravery.
(e) Without health there is no happiness.
(f) He gave me a bunch of grapes.
(g) Cows are fond of grass as the tigers are fond of flesh.
(h) Honey is sweeter than milk.
(i) Cleanliness is next to godliness.
(j) Wisdom is better than strength.

**4. (a) Form Abstract Nouns from the following Adjectives :**

| | | | | |
|---|---|---|---|---|
| lazy | long | true | free | poor |
| cruel | strong | false | proud | wise |
| young | wide | good | novel | human |
| decent | broad | dark | modest | just |
| brave | high | deep | vacant | similar |
| bitter | short | prudent | sweet | ignorant |

**(b) Form Abstract Nouns from the following Verbs :**

| | | | | |
|---|---|---|---|---|
| live | act | choose | die | see |
| obey | hate | move | think | clean |
| laugh | serve | seize | advise | judge |
| know | starve | flatter | defend | pursue |
| steal | please | depart | protect | relieve |
| excel | believe | conceal | punish | converse |
| expect | occupy | preserve | succeed | discover |

**(c) Form Abstract Nouns from the following Common Nouns :**

| | | | | |
|---|---|---|---|---|
| boy | infant | author | bond | friend |
| man | woman | mother | priest | enemy |
| child | owner | agent | pirate | capital |
| king | rogue | hero | pilgrim | patriot |
| thief | regent | beggar | coward | bankrupt |

# 5 COUNTABLE AND UNCOUNTABLE NOUNS

**In Modern English Grammar** Nouns are broadly divided into two categories—**(a)** **Countable Noun**, **(b)** **Uncountable Noun** or **Mass Noun**.

**Countable Nouns** are those which **can be counted** and **Uncountable Nouns** are those which **cannot be counted**.

**Countable Nouns** can have **a/an** or a numerical word (**one**, **two** etc.) before them or can be used in the **plural**. But, **Uncountable Nouns** are not used with **a/an** or a numerical word or in the **plural**.

We have got three children, two cows and a dog.

Air and water are essential to human life.

In the first sentence, children, cows and dog are Countable Nouns, whereas, in the second sentence, air and water are Uncountable.

Usually **Common Nouns and some Collective Nouns are Countable Nouns**, but **Proper Nouns, Material Nouns and Abstract Nouns are Uncountable Nouns**.

However, when a Proper Noun, a Material Noun or an Abstract Noun is used as a Common Noun or used in a specific sense, it can have an article (a, an, the) before it, or it can be used in the plural.

Have you heard the name of **Daniel**?

**A Daniel** has come to judgment.

**The Boses** are highly cultured.

Africa is a country of **forests**.

**The navy** of America is powerful.

**Water** has no colour.

[But] **The water** of this tank is not pure.

**Honesty** is the best policy.

[But] **The honesty** of this boy is praiseworthy.

Moreover, Countable Nouns or Common Nouns (book, pen, boy, etc.) can have numerical words (one, two, three, etc.) before them but Uncountable Nouns cannot have such numerical words.

Besides, Countable Nouns can have **many/a few** to denote non-specific higher or lower number, while Uncountable Nouns can have **much/a little** to denote non-specific higher or lower quantity. 'A lot of' is common in both the cases.

| Countable Nouns | Uncountable Nouns |
|---|---|
| A boy, a book, a pen, etc. | Rice, water, milk, etc. |
| A few boys, a few books, etc. | A little rice, a little water, etc. |
| Many boys, many books, etc. | Much rice, much water, etc. |
| Some boys, some books, etc. | Some rice, some water, etc. |
| A lot of boys, a lot of books, etc. | A lot of rice, a lot of water, etc. |

Many men, many women, many boys, many girls, many cows, etc.

Much butter, much sugar, much salt, much tea, much honey, much money, etc.

**Note** The usage of **'much money'** needs some special attention. You may think that money can be counted. And then why 'much' instead of 'many' before 'money'? In fact, money cannot be counted as it is a Collective Noun—taken as a whole. Coins and notes can be counted, NOT MONEY. We cannot say 'one money', 'two moneys' etc., though we can say 'one rupee', 'two rupees', 'one dollar', 'two dollar' etc. Hence 'money' is an Uncountable Noun and 'much' instead of 'many' is placed before it.

**Note** '**Any**' is used in questioning and '**some**' or '**a lot of**'/'**lots of**' is used in answering before both Countable and Uncountable Nouns.

**Q.** Is there **any** water in the glass?

**Ans.** Yes, there is **some**.

**Q.** Is there **any** book in the almirah?

**Ans.** Yes, there are **lots of** books.

**Q.** Is there any sugar?

**Ans.** Yes, there is **a lot**.

**Q.** Is there any salt?

**Ans.** Yes, there is **a lot**.

**Another Point :**

If a Countable Noun is placed before an Uncountable Noun, it may have *a, an the many. a few. one two three*, etc.

A kilo of rice, a cup of tea, the cup of tea, a few cups of tea, many cups of tea, etc.

## LIST OF UNCOUNTABLE NOUNS USED AS COUNTABLE

**Article/Number + Countable + of + Uncountable**

| A | heap | of | sand | Two | tons | of | coal |
|---|---|---|---|---|---|---|---|
| A | bag | of | sugar | Three | pieces | of | bread |
| Two | bags | of | sugar | Four | kilos | of | flour |
| Many | bags | of | sugar | Five | litres | of | petrol |
| Many more | bags | of | sugar | Six | bottles | of | milk |
| A few | bags | of | sugar | Seven | bales | of | cotton |
| Many | packets | of | salt | Eight | phials | of | medicine |
| A few | boxes | of | bread | Nine | boxes | of | milkpowder |
| Several | bottles | of | honey | Ten | wagons | of | limestone |

When 'full' is added to a Countable Noun, it becomes 'ful'.

**Article/Number + Countable + of + Uncountable**

| | | | | | | | |
|---|---|---|---|---|---|---|---|
| A | bagful | of | sweets | A | spoonful | of | sugar |
| A | handful | of | rice | Three | spoonfuls | of | salt |

**Countable Nouns forming a Collective Noun**

| | | | | | | | |
|---|---|---|---|---|---|---|---|
| A | band | of | pilgrims | A | heap | of | files |
| A | batch | of | students | A | herd | of | cows/deer |
| A | bevy | of | ladies | A | hive | of | bees |
| A | board | of | directors | A | mass | of | ruins |
| A | brood | of | chickens | A | multitude | of | people |
| A | bouquet | of | flowers | A | nest | of | ants |
| A | bunch | of | keys/grapes | A | pack | of | hounds/wolves |
| A | bundle | of | pencils/sticks | A | pack | of | cards |
| A | chain | of | mountains | A | pair | of | shoes |
| A | clump | of | bamboos | A | pile | of | books |
| A | cluster | of | words | A | quiver | of | arrows |
| A | collection | of | rare books | A | range | of | hills/mountains |
| A | crew | of | sailors | A | regiment | of | soldiers |
| A | crowd | of | passengers | A | series | of | events |
| A | drove | of | cattle | A | shoal | of | fish |
| A | fleet | of | ships | A | squad | of | homeguards |
| A | flight | of | birds | A | stock | of | goods |
| A | flock | of | birds/sheep | A | swarm | of | bees |
| A | galaxy | of | talents | A | throng | of | people |
| A | gang | of | robbers | A | troop | of | soldiers |
| A | gathering | of | people | A | tuft | of | hair |
| A | grove | of | trees | A | volley | of | arrows/questions |

## APPLIED SECTION

### (Functional Communicative Approach)

**1. Uncountable (Mass) Nouns :**

Is there any sugar in the pot?

No, there is not much sugar in the pot.

Yes, there is some sugar in the pot./Yes, there is some.

Yes, there is a lot of sugar in the pot./Yes, there is a lot.

**Now write five sentences in the same way.**

Q. Is there any ...................................................................................?

Ans. Yes.

Q. ...................................................................................................?

Ans. No.

Q. .......................................................................................................?

Ans. Yes.

Q. .......................................................................................................?

Ans. No.

Q. .......................................................................................................?

Ans. Yes.

**2. Countable Nouns :**

How many rainy seasons are there in Tamil Nadu?

There are two rainy seasons in Tamil Nadu.

**Now write some other sentences in the same way :**

Q. How many ..........................................................?

Ans ......................................................................

Q. How many ..........................................................?

Ans ......................................................................................

Q. How many ..........................................................................?

Ans. ......................................................................................

**3. Uncountable Nouns used as Countables :**

I want two teaspoonful(s) of sugar in my cup of tea.

Here is a bottle of sugar. Take as much as you need.

**Now fill up the blanks :**

(i) Give me ................ slice of bread and ......................... glass of water.

(ii) There are six ...................................................................... of milk.

(iii) We want many more ........................................................ of tea.

(iv) Please give me ............................................ cupfuls of boiled water.

(v) ...................................................... squads of homeguards are on duty.

(vi) Here is a ...................................................................... of cotton.

(vii) There is a ................................................................ of passengers.

(viii) We had a ......................................... of talents in the nineteenth century.

**4. Use of 'a lot of' & 'a great deal of' :**

'A lot of' replaces 'much' and 'many'. But 'a great deal of' replaces 'much' only :

I have a lot of mangoes. I have a lot of milk.

[But] She took a great deal of (much) trouble to please us.

## EXERCISE

**1. What are Countable and Uncountable Nouns? Give some examples of each kind.**

**2. Give separate uses of 'a few', 'a little', 'many' and 'much'.**

**3. Make ten sentences with the use of 'some' and 'a lot of'.**

**4. Fill in the blanks with appropriate words :**

(a) Mother gives him ..................................................... milk. (a few/a little)

(b) Rabi takes ....................................................... oranges. (a little/a few)

(c) I have .......................................... books. (much/many)

(d) Raju has .......................................... pens. (a few/a little)

(e) Kamal eats .......................................... rice. (much/many)

(f) There is .................... money in the purse. (much/many)

(g) They have .............. wheat in the granary. (much/many)

(h) Give him .................................... sweets. (a few/a little)

**5. Make proper sentences from the following tables :**

(a)

| | | |
|---|---|---|
| I want | a few | milk. |
| He wants | a little | sugar. |
| They want | much | salt. |
| The cat wants | many | fishes. |
| Samir and Dipak want | a lot of | chairs. |
| The naughty boy wants | a | orange. |
| The greedy monkey wants | an | banana. |

(b)

| | | |
|---|---|---|
| Is there | any | milk? |
| | many | boys? |
| | much | sugar? |
| Are there | some | rice? |
| | a lot of | wheat? |

(c)

| | | |
|---|---|---|
| How much | money | is there? |
| | pens | |
| | water | |
| How many | boys | are there? |
| | milk | |
| | books | |

# 6  THE NOUN : NUMBER

**The Countable Nouns have two forms : Singular and Plural.**

| Boy | Box | Baby | Knife | Child | Ox | Man |
|---|---|---|---|---|---|---|
| Boys | Boxes | Babies | Knives | Children | Oxen | Men |

The first word of each pair denotes one and the second word of each pair denotes more than one.

Hence, *boy, box, baby, knife, child, ox* and *man* are **Singular Number**.
*Boys, boxes, babies, knives, children, oxen* and *men* are **Plural Number**.

> When one person or thing is spoken of, the noun is singular and when more than one person or thing is spoken of, the noun is plural. **Nesfield**

**Note** The Countable Noun may be either a Common Noun or a Collective Noun. A Common Noun (boy, book, etc.) or a Collective Noun (army, class, etc.) can be used either in Singular or in Plural number, but a Proper Noun (Kolkata, Delhi, etc.), a Material Noun (oil, rice, etc.) or an Abstract Noun (honesty, kindness, etc.) cannot be used in Plural number.

Moreover, a Common Noun or a Collective Noun in Singular number always takes an article or determiner (a, an, the, this, that, etc.) when it is used in a sentence.

**We cannot say :** ~~Here is boy. Navy of America.~~

**We must say :** Here is a boy/the boy. The navy of America.

The only exception is '**man**'. It can be used either as '**a man/the man**' in Singular Number, or '**man**' without any article or determiner to denote the sense of human race.

**We cannot say :** ~~The man is mortal.~~

**We must say :** Man is mortal.

## HOW PLURALS ARE FORMED

1. **The Plural of Nouns is generally formed by adding -s to the Singular :**

| Singular | Plural | Singular | Plural |
|---|---|---|---|
| Book | Books | Pen | Pens |
| Desk | Desks | Chair | Chairs |
| Cat | Cats | Table | Tables |

| Singular | Plural | Singular | Plural |
|---|---|---|---|
| Cow | Cows | House | Houses |
| Dog | Dogs | Eye | Eyes |
| Lion | Lions | Ear | Ears |
| King | Kings | Hand | Hands |
| Girl | Girls | Head | Heads |

**2. Nouns ending in -s, -sh, -ch (soft), or -x form the Plural by adding -es to the Singular :**

| Singular | Plural | Singular | Plural |
|---|---|---|---|
| Ass | Asses | Box | Boxes |
| Gas | Gases | Fox | Foxes |
| Glass | Glasses | Kiss | Kisses |
| Class | Classes | Inch | Inches |
| Lass | Lasses | Bench | Benches |
| Bush | Bushes | Branch | Branches |
| Brush | Brushes | Bunch | Bunches |
| Dish | Dishes | Church | Churches |

**Note** **If ch sounds as 'k', Plural is formed by adding -s :**

| Singular | Plural |
|---|---|
| Monarch | Monarchs |
| Stomach | Stomachs |

**3. Nouns ending in -o having a Vowel before it, take -s to form Plural :**

| Singular | Plural | Singular | Plural |
|---|---|---|---|
| Bamboo | Bamboos | Radio | Radios |
| Cuckoo | Cuckoos | Studio | Studios |
| Hindoo | Hindoos | Folio | Folios |

**4. Nouns ending in -o having a Consonant before it, take -es to form Plural :**

| Singular | Plural | Singular | Plural |
|---|---|---|---|
| Hero | Heroes | Echo | Echoes |
| Zero | Zeroes | Mosquito | Mosquitoes |
| Negro | Negroes | Mango | Mangoes |
| Buffalo | Buffaloes | Potato | Potatoes |

**Some exceptions :**

| | | | |
|---|---|---|---|
| Dynamo | Dynamos | Photo | Photos |
| Piano | Pianos | Quarto | Quartos |

**5. Nouns ending in -y having a Vowel before it, form their Plurals by adding -s :**

| Singular | Plural | Singular | Plural |
|---|---|---|---|
| Boy | Boys | Day | Days |
| Toy | Toys | Play | Plays |
| Key | Keys | Ray | Rays |
| Monkey | Monkeys | Donkey | Donkeys |

**6. Nouns ending in -y having a Consonant before it, form their Plural by changing -y into i and adding -es :**

| Singular | Plural | Singular | Plural |
|---|---|---|---|
| Army | Armies | Copy | Copies |
| Baby | Babies | Duty | Duties |
| Body | Bodies | Fly | Flies |
| City | Cities | Lady | Ladies |
| Country | Countries | Story | Stories |

**7. Nouns ending in -f or -fe form their Plural by changing f or fe into v and adding -es :**

| Singular | Plural | Singular | Plural |
|---|---|---|---|
| Calf | Calves | Self | Selves |
| Half | Halves | Shelf | Shelves |
| Knife | Knives | Sheaf | Sheaves |
| Life | Lives | Thief | Thieves |
| Leaf | Leaves | Wife | Wives |
| Loaf | Loaves | Wolf | Wolves |

**8. Several Nouns ending in -f form their Plurals by adding s :**

| Singular | Plural | Singular | Plural |
|---|---|---|---|
| Chief | Chiefs | Gulf | Gulfs |
| Cliff | Cliffs | Hoof | Hoofs |
| Brief | Briefs | Proof | Proofs |
| Belief | Beliefs | Roof | Roofs |

**9. Some Nouns form their Plural by changing the inside Vowel of the Singular :**

| Singular | Plural | Singular | Plural |
|---|---|---|---|
| Man | Men | Foot | Feet |
| Woman | Women | Tooth | Teeth |
| Gentleman | Gentlemen | Goose | Geese |
| Human | Humans [vide 'The Cage' by Bertram Chandler] | | |

**10. A few Nouns form their Plural by changing the inside Vowel and the Consonant of the singular :**

| Singular | Plural | Singular | Plural |
|---|---|---|---|
| Mouse | Mice | Louse | Lice |

**11. A few Nouns form their Plural by adding -en to the Singular :**

| Singular | Plural | Singular | Plural |
|---|---|---|---|
| Ox | Oxen | Child | Children |
| Brother | Brethren | | |

**12. Compound Nouns generally form their Plural by adding -s to the principal word or by changing the inside vowel of the principal word :**

| Singular | Plural | Singular | Plural |
|---|---|---|---|
| Son-in-law | Sons-in-law | Maid-servant | Maid-servants |
| Daughter-in-law | Daughters-in-law | Step-son | Step-sons |

| Singular | Plural | Singular | Plural |
|---|---|---|---|
| Father-in-law | Fathers-in-law | Step-daughter | Step-daughters |
| Mother-in-law | Mothers-in-law | Looker-on | Lookers-on |
| Man-of-war | Men-of-war | Passer-by | Passers-by |
| Commander-in-Chief | Commanders-in-Chief | Washerman | Washermen |
| Grant-in-aid | Grants-in aid | [But, Grown-up | Grown-ups] |

**13. Compound Nouns written without hyphen take -s to form the Plural :**

| Singular | Plural | Singular | Plural |
|---|---|---|---|
| Armchair | Armchairs | Handful | Handfuls |
| Bookcase | Bookcases | Bagful | Bagfuls |
| Pickpocket | Pickpockets | Spoonful | Spoonfuls |

**14. There are some Compound Nouns which are turned to a double Plural :**

| Singular | Plural | Singular | Plural |
|---|---|---|---|
| Man-servant | Men-servants | Lord-justice | Lords-justices |
| Woman-servant | Women-servants | Knight-templar | Knights-templars |

**15. Some Typical Examples of Plurals :**

### FOREIGN PLURALS/TYPICAL PLURALS

| Singular | Plural | Singular | Plural |
|---|---|---|---|
| Agendum | Agenda | Bacterium | Bacteria |
| Addendum | Addenda | Formula | Formulae (Formulas) |
| Alumnus | Alumni | Forum | Fora/Forums |
| Appendix | Appendices | Genus | Genera |
| Axis | Axes | Hypothesis | Hypotheses |
| Bacillus | Bacilli | Medium | Media |
| Basis | Bases | Memorandum | Memoranda |
| Bureau | Bureaux | Oasis | Oases |
| Corpus | Corpora/ Corpuses | Ovum | Ova |
| | | Phenomenon | Phenomena |
| Crisis | Crises | Radius | Radii |
| Criterion | Criteria | Serum | Sera |
| Curriculum | Curricula | Syllabus | Syllabi |
| Datum | Data | Symposium | Symposia |
| Dictum | Dicta | Terminus | Termini (Terminuses) |
| Erratum | Errata | | |
| Focus | Foci/Focuses | Vertex | Vertices |

**16. Nouns having different meanings in different numbers :**

| Singular | Plural |
|---|---|
| Advice—counsel | Advices—information |
| Air—wind | Airs—manners |

| Singular | Plural |
|---|---|
| Force—power | Forces—army |
| Good—benefit, well-being | Goods—things |
| Iron—a kind of metal | Irons—chains made of iron |
| Physic—medicine | Physics—Physical science |
| Return—coming back | Returns—accounts |
| Sand—a kind of matter | Sands—desert |
| Wood—timber | Woods—forest |

17. **Nouns with two Plural forms of different meanings :**

| Singular | Plural |
|---|---|
| Brother | Brothers—sons of same parents<br>Brethren—members of the same society |
| Cloth | Cloths—pieces of cloth<br>Clothes—garments |
| Fish | Fish—collectively fish<br>Fishes—fishes of different types |
| Genius | Geniuses—men of talent<br>Genii—spirits |

18. **Noun with one meaning in the Singular but two in the Plural :**

| Singular | Plural | Meaning |
|---|---|---|
| Arm—part of body | Arms | 1. parts of the body<br>2. weapons |
| Colour—hue | Colours | 1. hues<br>2. flag |
| Custom—habit | Customs | 1. habits<br>2. revenue duties |
| Manner—method | Manners | 1. methods<br>2. behaviour |
| Minute—1/60th part of an hour | Minutes | 1. 1/60th parts of an hour<br>2. proceedings of a meeting |
| Part—portion | Parts | 1. portions<br>2. skill |

| Singular | Plural | Meaning |
|---|---|---|
| Pain—suffering | Pains | 1. sufferings<br>2. take pains = take care |
| Premise—proposition | Premises | 1. propositions<br>2. buildings |
| Quarter—fourth part | Quarters | 1. fourth parts<br>2. lodgings |
| Spectacle—a sight | Spectacles | 1. sights<br>2. eye-glasses |

**19. Some Nouns are the same in form in Singular and the Plural : NO CHANGE IN NUMBER**

| Singular | Plural | Singular | Plural |
|---|---|---|---|
| Deer | Deer | Dozen | Dozen (Five dozen) |
| Sheep | Sheep | Score | Score (Four score) |
| Pice | Pice | Hundred | Hundred (Two hundred) |
| Public | Public | Thousand | Thousand (Three thousand) |

The public is the best judge/are the best judges—POD & COD.

['The public' may take a verb in singular or plural.]

**Note** Of course, we can say : Hundreds of students, Thousands of people

**20. Some Collective Nouns or Group Nouns are Singular in form, but are used as Plural :**

**Cattle**—These cattle are mine.

**Folk**—The old folk have gone.

**Swine**—These swine must be kept out of the garden.

**Poultry**—Whose are these poultry?

**People**—These people have returned home.

**Police**—The police are watching the house.

[But] The policeman is watching the house.

**Vermin**—The vermin destroy our property and carry disease.

**21. Some Nouns are used only in the Singular. They may be used in the Plural in some special sense :**

**Abuse**—He gave me much abuse for no fault.

**Alphabet**—He learnt the alphabet before he could read.

**Furniture**—His house is full of good furniture. (not furnitures)

**Information**—He gave me all the information. (not informations)

**Issue**—He had no issue. (child or children)

**Offspring**—These four children are his offspring.

**Poetry**—He worte very good poetry./Poetry is my favourite subject.

**Scenery**—These hills are lovely scenery./The scenery of Darjeeling is imposing.

**Note** When 'abuse' is used in the sense of 'wrong use' the plural is 'abuses'. When more than one language is spoken of, the plural of 'alphabet' is 'alphabets'. When 'issue' means result, its plural is 'issues'.

**22. Nouns Plural in form but Singular in use :**

Gallows, News, Physics, Ethics, Politics, Statistics, Economics, Athletics, Gymnastics etc.

**News**—What is the news?

**Mathematics**—Mathematics is his favourite subject.

**Statistics**—Statistics is a difficult subject. But, "These statistics are rather complicated." (= these figures).

Oxford Guide to English Grammar—**Eastwood**

**23. Some Nouns are always Plural :**

(a) Names of such instruments having two parts or **Pair Nouns** :

Bellows, Scissors, Glasses/Spectacles

Your new glasses/spectacles are very nice.

(b) Names of certain articles of dress :

Trousers, drawers, breeches, shorts

These shorts are nice. These trousers need cleaning.

(c) Names of diseases :

Measles, mumps [But Smallpox is a singular noun.]

Smallpox has broken out there.

(d) Names of games : Billiards [Plural according to **Wren & Martin**]

**Note** According to '**Oxford Guide to English Grammar**' by **John Eastwood**, 'billiards' (like the news, gymnastics etc.) is plural in form but takes a singular verb.

(e) Certain other Nouns :

Ashes, alms, assets, annals, fetters, proceeds, Aborigines, thanks, tidings, vegetables, belongings, goods, clothes, congratulations, earnings, particulars (= details), premises (= buildings), riches (= wealth), surroundings.

**Usage :** The goods were found to be defective.

My belongings have been destroyed by fire. (not my belonging).

**Note** Letters, figures and other symbols are made plural by adding an apostrophe and **s** :

Dot your i's and cut your t's. Add two 5's and three 2's.

**24. An Uncountable Noun takes a Singular Verb :**

The grass is getting long. His hair is grey. (not hairs)

**Note** When an Uncountable Noun is used countably, it will take an article/determiner before it. There is a hair in my soup.

## APPLIED SECTION

**1. Change the Subject into Singular with other necessary changes in the following sentences :**

(a) These oranges are very sweet.

(b) Those mangoes are not ripe.

(c) Three boys were present yesterday.

(d) Good children are liked by all.
(e) There are ten benches in this room.
(f) The windows facing the street are broken.
(g) The thieves were arrested last night.

**2. Change the Subject into Plural with other necessary changes :**

(a) The boy is playing in the playground.
(b) The girl is dancing gracefully.
(c) A bird is singing on the tree.
(d) The owl sleeps in the daytime.
(e) A bad boy hides his faults.
(f) The book was on the table.
(g) The shop was closed yesterday.

**3. Here is a daily routine of a boy.**

The boy gets up at six in the morning. He washes his hands and face and cleans his teeth. He takes his breakfast with his parents. He studies up to 9 a.m. Then he has his bath. After lunch he starts for school at 10 a.m. He returns home at 4 p.m. and takes some tiffin and goes to the playground. Coming back home at 6 p.m. he studies his lessons attentively. He takes his dinner at 10 p.m. and then goes to bed.

**Make the above daily routine of the boy for 'the boys'.**

## PRONUNCIATION NOTE

See the rules of correct pronunciation of the Plural Number of Nouns added with -s/-es/-en. (Vide—'**An Introduction to Descriptive Linguistics**'—by **H. A. Gleason**)

**1.** -s for Plural Number of Nouns ending with **k, p, t, f** sounds as s :

book—books (buks) cat—cats (kæts) cup—cups (kʌps) chief—chiefs (tfi:fs)

**2.** -s or -ves (**fe > ves**) for Plural Number of Nouns ending with **b, d, g, l, m, n, r, e, y, w, h** sounds as z :

cub—cubs (kʌbz) arm—arms (a:mz) baby—babies (beibiz)
hand—hands (hændz) lion—lions (laiənz) elbow—elbows (elbouz)
dog—dogs (dɔgz) brother—brothers (brʌðəz) almirah—almirahs (ælmairəz)
log—logs (lɔgz)
girl—girls (gə:lz) bee—bees (bi:z) wife—wives (waivz)

**3.** -s for Plural Number of Nouns ending with '**th**' usually sounds as s.

cloth—cloths (klɔθs)

But there are a few exceptions such as 'paths' in which -s sounds as z. e.g. paths (pa:θz).

**4.** -s or -es for Plural Number of Nouns ending with **-s, -ch, -j** or **-z** sounds as iz :

glass—glasses (gla:siz) witch—witches (wichiz)
house—houses (hausiz) badge—badges (bæjiz)

**5.** -en for Plural Number of Nouns sounds as in :

ox—oxen (ɔksin) child—children (childrin) brother—brethren (briðrin)

In brief, we can say that -s for Plural Number sounds either as s or z; -es for Plural Number sounds as iz and -en sounds as in.

## KEY TO PRONUNCIATION OF VOWELS AND DIPHTHONGS

| Symbol | Examples |
|---|---|
| ɔ [Short] | hot [hɔt], pot [pɔt], clock [kɔk] |
| ɔ: [Long] | all [ɔ:l], ball [bɔ:l], draw [drɔ:] |
| ʌ [Short] | sun [sʌn], gun [gʌn], come [kʌm] |
| a: [Long] | class [kla:s], glass [gla:s], pass [pa:s] |
| æ [Medium] | man [mæn], can [cæn], pan [pæn] |
| ə [Short] | ago [ə'gou], convert [kənvət], collect [kəlekt] |
| ə: [Long] | first [fə:st], purr [pə:], word [wə:d] |
| i [Short] | sit [sit], bid [bid], tin [tin] |
| i: [Long] | dream [dri:m], green [gri:n], free [fri:] |
| e [Medium] | bed [bed], den [den], desk [desk] |
| u [Short] | book [buk], foot [fut], put [put] |
| u: [Long] | food [fu:d], fool [fu:l], moon [mu:n] |
| ɔ: [Medium] | boy [bɔ:], toy [tɔ:], noise [nɔ:iz] |
| ei [Medium] | day [dei], main [mein], name [neim] |
| ai [Medium] | five [faiv], nine [nain], high [hai] |
| au [Medium] | how [hau], now [nau], mouth [mauθ] |
| iə [Medium] | here [hiə], hear [hiə], near [niə] |
| eə [Medium] | care [keə], dare [deə], fair [feə] |
| ou [Medium] | go [gou], toe [tou], nose [nouz] |

## SOME SPECIAL CONSONANTS

| Symbol | Examples |
|---|---|
| ŋ | bring [briŋ], cling [kliŋ], sing [siŋ] |
| θ | thin [θin], thing [θiŋ], mouth [mauθ] |
| ð | this [ðis], these [ði:z], mother [mʌðə] |
| ʃ | fish [fiʃ], dish [diʃ], shoe [ʃu:] |
| tʃ | chair [tʃe], teach [ti:tʃ], church [tʃə:tʃ] |

## EXERCISE

1. **How many kinds of numbers are there in English? What are they? Give examples.**
2. **Change the number of the following Nouns :**
   Boy, Bus, Comb, City, Country, Fool, Foot, Tooth, Eye, Ear, Baby, Thief, Knife, Life, Man, Woman, Fisherman, Gentleman, Calf, Roof, Hero, Radio, Bamboo, Body, Leaf, Chief, Child, Mouse, Son-in-law, Step-brother, Man-servant, Passerby, Sheep, Railway, Valley, Volcano.
3. **Give some examples of Nouns having different meanings in Singular and in Plural.**
4. **Give some examples of Nouns having two meanings in the Plural.**
5. **Give some examples which are same in form in Singular and in Plural.**
6. **Fill in the blanks with the appropriate word given in the brackets :**
   (a) The ..... are reading. (child, children)
   (b) That ..... is singing. (woman, women)
   (c) Ratan's ..... are white. (tooth, teeth)
   (d) These ..... are playing. (boy, boys)
   (e) The ..... are grazing. (deer, deers)
   (f) Give me ten ..... only. (pice, pices)

# 7 THE NOUN : GENDER

What in nature is called the difference of sex is in grammar called the difference of Gender.

**Nesfield**

| | | | |
|---|---|---|---|
| Boy | Lion | Hero | Boy-friend |
| Girl | Lioness | Heroine | Girl-friend |

The first word of each pair denotes the name of a male and the second word of each pair denotes the name of a female.

A noun that denotes a male is said to be of the **Masculine Gender**.

Boy, Lion, Hero, Boy-friend, etc.

A noun that denotes a female is said to be of the **Feminine Gender**.

Girl, Lioness, Heroine, Girl-friend, etc.

A noun that denotes either a male or a female is said to be of the **Common Gender**.

Parent, child, baby, infant, friend, people, servant, thief, enemy, cousin, orphan, student. doctor, teacher, police, neighbour, etc.

A noun that denotes things without life is said to be of the **Neuter Gender**.

Book, pen, chair, table, room, gold, silver, iron, knife, shirt, coat, etc.

Though 'tree' is not lifeless, yet it is Neuter Gender in English.

**Therefore, there are four kinds of Gender :**

(1) Nouns denoting male : **Masculine**

(2) Nouns denoting female : **Feminine**

(3) Nouns denoting either sex : **Common**

(4) Nouns denoting things without life : **Neuter**

## RULES OF CHANGING GENDERS

Generally there are **four rules for changing Masculine Genders** of Nouns **into Feminine Genders** :

**[1] By using different words**

| Masculine | Feminine | Masculine | Feminine |
|---|---|---|---|
| Father | mother | Son | daughter |
| Brother | sister | Sir | madam |
| Boy | girl | Bull, Ox | cow |
| Uncle | aunt | Dog | bitch |
| Nephew | niece | Fox | vixen |
| Husband | wife | Horse | mare |
| Man | woman | Boar | sow |
| Male | female | Buck | doe |
| Gentleman | lady | Drake | duck |
| Lord | lady | Drone | bee |
| King | queen | Gander | goose |
| Bachelor | maiden, spinster | Ram | ewe |
| Monk | nun | stag | hind |
| Cock | hen | Wizard | witch |

**[2] By adding -ess**

| Masculine | Feminine | Masculine | Feminine |
|---|---|---|---|
| Author | authoress | Mayor | mayoress |
| Baron | baroness | Patron | patroness |
| Count | countess | Peer | peeress |
| Giant | giantess | poet | poetess |
| Heir | heiress | Priest | priestess |
| Host | hostess | Prophet | prophetess |
| Jew | Jewess | Shepherd | shepherdess |
| Lion | lioness | Steward | stewardess |
| Manager | manageress | Viscount | viscountess |

**Note the changes in spelling in some cases : By dropping the vowel before 'ess'**

| Masculine | Feminine | Masculine | Feminine |
|---|---|---|---|
| Actor | actress | Instructor | instructress |
| Abbot | abbess | Master | mistress |
| Duke | duchess | Prince | princess |
| Emperor | empress | Seamster | seamstress |
| Governor | governess | Songster | songstress |
| God | goddess | Tiger | tigress |
| Hunter | huntress | Waiter | waitress |

**[3] By changing the Masculine word of a Compound word :**

| Masculine | Feminine | Masculine | Feminine |
|---|---|---|---|
| Boy-friend | girl-friend | Grandfather | grandmother |
| He-goat | she-goat | Great-uncle | great-aunt |
| He-bear | she-bear | Step-brother | step-sister |

| Masculine | Feminine | Masculine | Feminine |
|---|---|---|---|
| Bull-calf | cow-calf | Man-servant | maid-servant |
| Bridegroom | bride (exception) | Milk-man | milk-woman |
| Son-in-law | daughter-in-law | Peacock | peahen |
| Father-in-law | mother-in-law | Landlord | landlady |
| Brother-in-law | sister-in-law | Washerman | washer-woman |

**[4] Sometimes Feminine forms are made by adding** a, ine, ix etc.

| Masculine | Feminine | Masculine | Feminine |
|---|---|---|---|
| Hero | heroine | Administrator | administratrix |
| Sultan | Sultana | Executor | executrix |
| Czar | Czarina | Prosecutor | prosecutrix |
| Signor | signora | Testator | testatrix |

**Note** Objects without life are often personified and then they are regarded as males or females.

(a) The Masculine Gender is often applied to objects remarkable for strength or power :

The Sun, Summer, Winter, Death, Time etc.

The sun sheds his beams on the rich and the poor alike.

(b) The Feminine Gender is often applied to objects remarkable for beauty and gracefulness :

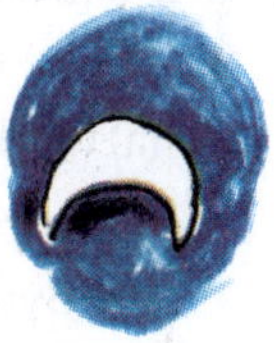

The Moon, The Earth, Nature, Autumn, Spring, Liberty etc.

The moon has hidden her face behind the cloud.

(c) A ship is always spoken of as Feminine Gender.

The ship lost all her boats in the storm.

(d) Collective Nouns, even when they denote living beings, are considered of the Neuter Gender. The army showed its strength.

(e) Lower animals are often considered as Neuter Gender.

The mouse cut the rope with its teeth.

**Some more words denoting male or female :**

| Masculine | Feminine |
|---|---|
| Mr./Mr [ with or without fullstop ] | Mrs./Mrs |
| Master | Miss |

## APPLIED SECTION

**Read the passage and change the Genders :**

Mr. Roy is a teacher. He teaches me English. He has two sons. One of them is a poet. He has a pet peacock. His uncle is a doctor. He is a widower. His grandfather was a landlord and his son-in-law is a hunter. His step-brother is a bachelor and his step-sister is an actress.

## EXERCISE

**1. Classify the following Nouns according to Gender and put them in the boxes given below :**

Baby, cock, man, chair, table, book, pen, oil, rice, tutor, hero, brother, child, teacher, doctor, son, poet, prince, tiger, master, priest, lord, aunt, wife, niece, male, host, bride.

| Masculine | Feminine | Common | Neuter |
|---|---|---|---|
| ........................ | ........................ | ........................ | ........................ |
| ........................ | ........................ | ........................ | ........................ |
| ........................ | ........................ | ........................ | ........................ |
| ........................ | ........................ | ........................ | ........................ |
| ........................ | ........................ | ........................ | ........................ |
| ........................ | ........................ | ........................ | ........................ |
| ........................ | ........................ | ........................ | ........................ |

**2. Change the Gender of the following Nouns :**

Father, boy, daughter, husband, uncle, hero, master, widow, man, nephew, sir, brother, poet, actor, son-in-law, mother-in-law, milkman, host, bride, tiger, lion, man-servant, grandfather.

**3. Fill in the blanks with the appropriate word given in the bracket :**

(a) Arthur is my ......... (sister, brother)

(b) Meera is my ......... (brother, sister)

(c) Byron is a great ......... (poet, poetess)

(d) Akbar was a great ...... (queen, king)

(e) The ............ gives us milk. (bull, cow)

# 8 THE NOUN : CASE

The relation in which a noun stands to some other word or the change of form by which this relation is indicated, is called its case. **J. C. Nesfield**

There are five cases in English—**Nominative**, **Objective**, **Possessive**, **Dative** and **Vocative**. **But in Modern Grammar** Dative is included in Objective. Hence there are four cases in English.

[**1**] When a Noun (or Pronoun) is used as the **Subject** of a Verb, it is said to be in the **NOMINATIVE CASE** :

**Tom** threw a stone. [Who threw a stone? = Tom (subject)]

[**2**] When a Noun (or Pronoun is used as the **Object** of a Verb, it is said to be in the **OBJECTIVE CASE** :

Tom threw **a ball**. Steve bowled **him** out.

[ What did Tom throw? = a ball (object) ]

The horse kicked **the boy**.

[ Whom did the horse kick? = a boy. (object) ]

**Note** To find the Nominative put **Who**? or **What**? before the Verb. To find the Objective put **Whom**? or **What**? before the Verb. The Nominative generally comes before the Verb and the Objective after it.

[**3**] The **POSSESSIVE CASE** denotes ownership or possession or relationship or authorship. The possessive answers the question—'**Whose**?'

This is **Kamat's** umbrella. (possession)

These are **Shakespeare's** plays. (authorship)

A **mother's** love is a noble thing. (relationship)

[**4**] The **VOCATIVE CASE** is practically a nominative of address :

Come here, **Ram**. Come on, **boys**.

**Note** The forms of Nouns remain the same in the Nominative Case, Objective Case and Vocative Case. But the form is changed only in the Possessive Case.

## FORMATION OF THE POSSESSIVE CASE

The rules are :

When the Noun denotes the name of a living one, apostrophe s ['s] or only apostrophe comma ['] without s is used.

(a) When such a Noun is Singular, the Possessive Case is formed by adding 's to the noun :

Ram's book. The boy's pen. Father's car. Mother's purse. Captain's bat.

**Note** The letter s is omitted and only the apostrophe comma is used in a few words where too many hissing sounds would come together : For justice' sake; for goodness' sake; for conscience' sake; Moses' laws. However, we can add either apostrophe comma (') or 's in such cases : Keats' poem (or, Keats's poem), Jones' car (or Jone's car).

(b) When the Noun is Plural and ends in s, the Possessive Case is formed by adding only an apostrophe comma :

Boys' club; Girls' school etc.

(c) When the Noun is Plural but does not end in s, the Possessive Case is formed by adding 's :

Men's club; children's books.

## USE OF POSSESSIVE CASE

(a) The Possessive 's, is chiefly used with the names of **living things**. It cannot be used with the names of inanimate things :

The boy's hand; the girl's hair.

The leg of the chair. [not, the chair's leg]

The cover of the book. [not, the book's cover]

The roof of the house. [not, the house's roof]

**Of course, of instead of 's may be used in both the cases** [**Living & non-living**] :

The leg of the boy. The leg of the chair.

(b) The Possessive 's is used with the **personified objects** :

Nature's laws; Fortune's smile; Duty's calls. India's heroes.

(c) The Possessive 's is also used with the Nouns denoting **time**, **space** or **weight** :

A day's match; a week's holiday; next year's prices; Last night's TV programme; at a stone's throw; a foot's length; a pound's weight.

(d) The noun following a Possessive Case can be left out when we talk about someone's home, some shops and services :

We are going to Mohan's (home) this evening. Are you going to the butcher's (shop)? Whose batting is this? Sourav's (batting).

(e) When the Noun is a long phrase, we use of instead of 's :

He is the brother of someone who used to give us chocolates.

## NOUN IN APPOSITION

Read the following sentence :

Kapil, our captain, made fifty runs.

Here 'Kapil' and 'our captain' mean the same person. Hence 'our captain' is in Apposition to Kapil. Such Apposition is placed just after the Noun.

[Apposition means 'placing near'.]

A Noun in Apposition is in the same case as the Noun which it explains.

**Further examples :**

1. Ramchandra, *the son of Dasharath,* went to forest.
2. Kavir, *the great reformer,* was a weaver.
3. Yesterday I met your father, *the doctor.*
4. Have you read the 'Gitanjali', *Tagore's song-offerings?*

In sentences 1 and 2 the Nouns in Apposition are in the Nominative case.

In sentences 3 and 4 the Nouns in Apposition are in the Objective case.

## APPLIED SECTION

**1. Apply the following Nouns in the Nominative Case :**
**[The Nominative answers 'Who' or 'What' questions]**

Rabindranath, Mother Teresa, Satyajit, a boy, a man, the book, girls.

***Example :***

| | |
|---|---|
| Who ? (Nominative)<br>Rabindranath  | won the Nobel Prize. |
| What? (Nominative)<br>The book | is in the desk. |

(i) ..........

(ii) ..........

(iii) ..........

(iv) ..........

(v) ..........

**2. Apply the following Nouns in the Objective Case :**
**[The Objective answers 'Whom' or 'What' questions]**

Haribabu, the boy, the man, a stone, a ball, a picture, the window.

***Example :***

| | |
|---|---|
| I know | Whom? (objective)<br>Haribabu. |
| That naughty boy broke | What? (objective)<br>the window. |

(i) ..........

(ii) ..........

(iii) ..........

(iv) ..........

(v) ..........

**3. Apply the following Nouns in the Possessive Case or in their alternative 'of' :**
**[The Possessive answers 'Whose' questions]**

Ram's, man's, girls', Shakespeare's, patient's, (of the) chair, (of the) boy.

***Examples :***

| **What is/are** | **Whose? (possessive)** |
|---|---|
| These are<br>This is the broken leg | Ram's books./books of Ram.<br>of the chair. |

(i) ..........

(ii) ..........

(iii) ..........

(iv) ..........

(v) ..........

## EXERCISE

1. **In each of the following sentences pick out the Nouns in the Nominative Case :**

   (a) Ram married Sita.
   (b) Milk is the best food.
   (c) Gopal wants to go home.
   (d) The lazy boy was punished.
   (e) Kolkata is the capital of West Bengal.
   (f) The earth moves round the sun.

2. **Pick out the Nouns in the Objective Case in the following sentences :**

   (a) Do you know the way?
   (b) Have you taken your meal?
   (c) Little Rabi read the Ramayana.
   (d) The poet met a little cottage girl.
   (e) Aladdin had a wonderful lamp.
   (f) Sir Ralph the Rover tore his hair.

3. **Pick out the Nouns in the Possessive Case in the following sentences :**

   (a) The baby's doll is lost.
   (b) The girl's voice is sweet.
   (c) He reads in a boys' school.
   (d) She reads in a girls' school.
   (e) The children's clothes are new.
   (f) The ladies' sarees are beautiful.

4. **Write the Possessive Case, Singular and Plural, of the following Nouns :**

   Man, boy, baby, lady, child, sheep, deer, ox.

5. **Combine the following pairs of Nouns by putting one of them in the Possessive Case :**

   (a) Parents, kindness
   (b) A man, labour
   (c) Books, authors
   (d) A student, books
   (e) Crown, a king
   (f) The journey, end

# 9 MORE ABOUT PRONOUNS

A Pronoun is a word used instead of a noun or noun-equivalent. **Nesfield**
Pronoun = Pro (instead of) + Noun.
Pronoun means for a noun. **Wren & Martin**

There are ten different kinds of Pronouns :

| Kinds of Pronouns | How to recognise them? | Examples |
|---|---|---|
| (1) **Personal** Pronoun | This is used instead of a person. | I, we, you, he, she, they. |
| (2) **Impersonal** Pronoun | It is used for non-living things, lower animals, etc. | It (for inanimate object and lower animals). |
| (3) **Possessive** Pronoun | It denotes possession. | Mine, ours, yours, his, hers, theirs. |
| (4) **Reflexive Pronoun** & **Emphatic** Pronoun | These are formed by adding—self/selves. | Myself, ourselves, yourself, yourselves, himself, herself, themselves. |
| (5) **Demonstrative** Pronoun | This is for a noun that has been already mentioned. | This, that, these, those, it. This is my house.  |
| (6) **Indefinite** Pronoun | This is used for a non-specific person or thing.  | Any, one, anyone, some, someone, no one, anybody, somebody, nobody, many, everyone, all. Anybody can take me home. |

| Kinds of Pronoun | How to recognise them? | Examples |
|---|---|---|
| (7) **Distributive** Pronoun | To refer to persons or things one at a time | Each, either, neither. |
| (8) **Reciprocal** Pronoun | To refer to reciprocal relation | Each other, one another. |
| (9) **Interrogative** Pronoun | At the beginning of a sentence for questioning | Who, whose, whom, which, what.  |
| (10) **Relative** Pronoun | In the middle of a sentence to join two sentences by denoting relation to the antecedent | Who, whose, whom, which, that. This is the boy who stood first.  |

**Note** When a Pronoun is used instead of a person, it is called a **Personal Pronoun**.

## NUMBER AND CASE OF PERSONAL PRONOUN

| Person | Number | Subject [Nominative] | Object [Objective] | Possessive |
|---|---|---|---|---|
| **1st person** | **Singular** | I | me | my, mine |
| | **Plural** | We | us | our, ours |
| **2nd person** | **Singular** | You | you | your, yours |
| | **Plural** | You | you | your, yours |
| **3rd person** | **Singular** | He, She | him, her | his, her, hers |
| | **Plural** | They | them | their, theirs |

**Note** Though basically Pronouns, my, our, your, his, her and their are Possessive Adjectives for their function.

## IMPERSONAL PRONOUN

There is another type of Pronoun called Impersonal Pronoun (e.g. **It**).

## RULES FOR THE USE OF 'IT'

| We use 'It' | Examples |
|---|---|
| (i) For non-living things or an idea | It is a pen.<br>Here is your book; take it.<br>It is the opinion of the public. |
| (ii) For animals, unless we clearly wish to speak of them as male or female | The horse fell and broke its leg.  |

| We use 'It' | Examples |
|---|---|
| (iii) For a young child, unless we clearly wish to refer to its sex | When I saw the child, it was crying.<br>The baby has torn its clothes. |
| (iv) To refer to some statement going before | He told a lie and he knows it.<br>He deserved his punishment as he knew it. |
| (v) To give emphasis on the Noun or Pronoun following it | It is you who are to be blamed. |
| (vi) As Subject of an Impersonal Verb (= Impersonal It) | It is raining.<br>It snows. It hails.<br>It thunders.<br>It seems to me.  |
| (vii) For denoting weather or time (= Preliminary It) | It is winter.<br>It is fine weather.<br>It is 8 o' clock<br>It is too early. |
| (viii) As a provisional Subject before the Verb 'to be' when the real Subject follows it | It is easy to find fault.<br>It is easy to say but hard to do.<br>It is doubtful whether the play will continue. |

## POSSESSIVE PRONOUNS

A Pronoun is called Possessive Pronoun when it denotes possession.

In a broad sense such **Possessive Pronouns** are : my, mine, our, ours, your, yours, his, her, hers, their, theirs, its.

But in Modern English : my, our, your, his, her, their—when used attributively before nouns—are classified as **Possessive Adjectives** or **Pronominal Adjective**.

For example : my book, our home, your name, his house, her letter etc.

The alternative forms mine, ours, yours, hers, theirs are used as **Possessive Pronouns**.

For example : This book is mine. That horse is yours.

However, 'his' may be used both as a Possessive Adjective and as a Possessive Pronoun.

For example : This is his book. This book is his.

## REFLEXIVE PRONOUNS

| Singular | Plural |
|---|---|
| I—myself<br>You—yourself<br>He—himself<br>It—itself | We—ourselves<br>You—yourselves<br>She—herself<br>They—themselves |

## REFLEXIVE PRONOUN AND EMPHATIC PRONOUN

**(i)** We use **Reflexive Pronouns** when the Subject and Object refer to the same person or thing.

(a) I cut **myself**.
(b) She blamed **herself**.
(c) Shrila is looking at **herself**.
(d) You have hurt **yourself**.
(e) You have enjoyed **yourselves**.
(f) The prisoner hanged **himself**.
(g) The refrigerator defrosts **itself**.
(h) He spoke to **himself**.
(i) She is ashamed of **herself**.
(j) They gave **themselves** much trouble.

**Note** A **Reflexive Pronoun** is used as the **Object** of a Verb or of a Preposition. Hence it **comes after a Verb** or a Preposition. Sometimes a Reflexive Pronoun is used emphatically. And such an **Emphatic Pronoun** comes **after the Subject** or after the Object. **We use a Reflexive Pronoun when an action turns back upon the Subject. We use an Emphatic Pronoun to give emphasis on the Subject or Object**.

**(ii)** **Emphatic Pronouns** are used to emphasise that the action is done by no one else. These are used just after the Subject or the Object.

I **myself** saw him (to) do it.
He **himself** said so.
She **herself** has cooked her meal.
They **themselves** admitted their guilt.
I spoke to the Chairman **himself**.

I will do it **myself**. [ = I shall do it. I won't ask anyone to do it. ]
Amar, work out the sum **yourself**. [= Amar, work out the sum. Don't ask anybody to help you.]

However, all the **Self-pronouns** are broadly called **Reflexive Pronouns**.

**(iii)** A **Reflexive Pronoun** is used with '**by**' when it means 'alone' :

She was singing **by herself**.
I was playing **by myself**.
I like to spend time **by myself**.
[= I like to spend time alone.]

**(iv)** Some Verbs must take **Reflexive Pronouns** as Object : **avail**, **exert**, etc.

You must **avail yourself** of the train. He will **exert himself** in time.

**(v)** Some Verbs do not take **Reflexive Pronouns** (dress, change, wash, bathe, shave) :

Are you **dressing**? (not 'dressing yourself').
Do you **shave** daily? (not 'shave yourself')

## DEMONSTRATIVE PRONOUNS

We use **Demonstrative Pronouns** to point out the Objects to which they refer.

**This** is a present from my elder brother. **These** are merely excuses.
Darjeeling tea is better than **that** of Assam.
**These** mangoes are not as sour as **those** mangoes.

## INDEFINITE PRONOUNS

We use **Indefinite Pronouns** in order to refer to persons or things in a general way, not to refer to any particular person or thing.

**Anybody** can do this easy task.
**One** must not praise oneself. **One** of the boys is wicked.

{ **None** of the boys **is**/**are** wicked.
{ **None** but fools **have** ever believed it.

**None** but the brave **deserves** the fair.

**None** of them **has** (**have**) come back yet. ***A.L.D.*—Hornby**

[* "None is a shortened form of not one; yet it is commonly used with plural verbs."
—**Wren & Martin**]

**Many** of them were injured but **a few** escaped unhurt.

What is **everybody's** business is **nobody's** business.

In referring to anybody, everybody, everyone, anyone, each etc. the Pronoun *he* or *she*, *his* or *her* is used according to the context.—**Wren & Martin**

I shall be glad to help **everyone** of the boys in **his** studies.

I shall be glad to help **everyone** of the girls in **her** studies.

But when the sex is not determined from the context, we use the Pronoun of the masculine gender :

**Each** must do **his** best. **Everyone** likes to have **his** way. **Anyone** can do this if **he** tries.

**Note** But we **cannot use he or she** in case of **one** :

**One** must do **one's** duty. (not, his)

### NUMBER OF REFLEXIVE, DEMONSTRATIVE & INDEFINITE PRONOUNS

| | **Singular** | **Plural** |
|---|---|---|
| **Reflexive Pronoun** | Myself<br>Yourself<br>Himself, Herself | Ourselves<br>Yourselves<br>Themselves |
| **Demonstrative Pronoun** | This<br>That | These<br>Those |
| **Indefinite Pronoun** | Any | Many, some |

### DISTRIBUTIVE PRONOUNS

We use **Distributive Pronouns** in order to refer to persons or things one at a time. For this reason they are **always singular** :

**Each** of the boys is healthy.

**Either** of the roads **leads** to the market.

**Neither** of the girls **was** late.

**Note 1** **Either** means the one or the other of the two. **Neither** is the negative of **either**.

**Note 2** The pronoun *each* may have three positions :

(i) **Each** of the boys received a prize.

(ii) These boys **each** received a prize.

(iii) These boys received ten rupees **each**.

The third order is usually placed after a numeral.

**Note 3** In the following sentences *each*, *either* and *neither* are Adjectives, not Pronouns :

**Each** boy got a prize. (each boy separately )

There are trees on **either** side of the river. (either side = on both the sides)

**Neither** accusation is true. (neither = not any one of the two)

## RECIPROCAL PRONOUNS

We use **Reciprocal Pronouns** in order to refer to reciprocal relation.

The two boys hate **each other**. They loved **one another**. The brothers quarrelled **with each other**. They stood **against one another**.

## INTERROGATIVE PRONOUNS

**[ For Wh-questions ]**

(i) **Who**, **Whom** and **Whose** are used for indicating persons :

**Who** are you?

**Whom** do you like?/**Who** do you like?

**Whose** is this book?

[But, whose book is this? = Modern usage]

(Here *Whose* is Interrogative Adjective.)

**Note** "Today **'Who' is more usual than 'Whom', especially in spoken English.**" Wren & Martin

(ii) **Which** is used for selecting a person or a thing :

**Which** is your book?

**Which** is your friend?

**Which** of the pictures is yours?

(iii) **What** is used in general sense of asking :

**What** is he?

**What** is your name?

**What** are you doing?

**Note** In the following sentences **Which** and **What** are not Interrogative Pronouns but Adjectives :

**What** book do you want?

**Which** book is he reading?

**Which** way leads to the post-office?

**Note 1** Who, Whom, Whose, Which and What are placed at the beginning of a sentence when they are used as Interrogative Pronoun or Interrogative Adjective. But Who, Whom, Whose, Which and What are usually placed in the middle of a sentence (after the antecedent) when they are used as a Relative Pronoun.

[An Antecedent is a noun or a pronoun or a noun-equivalent to which a pronoun refers.]

**Note 2** Interrogative Pronouns are sometimes used in the middle of the sentence in asking Indirect questions.

I do not know *who* is there. Tell me *what* you have done.

## RELATIVE PRONOUNS

**Relative Pronouns** are also called **'Linking Pronouns'** as they link the Dependent Relative Clause of a sentence to its Main Clause.

Read the following pairs of sentences and observe how these are joined with the help of Relative Pronouns :

I know the boy. The boy came from Kolkata.

= I know the boy **who** came from Kolkata.

This is the book. This belongs to my grandfather.

= This is the book **which** belongs to my grandfather.

This is the rat. It was caught by a cat.

= This is the rat **that** was caught by a cat.

It is you. You are to be blamed.

= It is you **who** are to be blamed.

**Note** The Nouns or Pronouns immediately before the Relative Pronouns are called the **Antecedents**. Here 'book', 'rat' and 'you' are Antecedents.

**Table to classify different uses of Relative Pronoun**

| Relative Pronoun | Used for | Example |
|---|---|---|
| Who (as Subject)  | Persons only (Both Singular and Plural) | I know the man *who* is honest. He *who* hesitates is lost. Those *who* die for others are immortal. |
| Whom (as Object)  | Persons only (Both Singular and Plural) | This is the boy *whom* all praise. These are the boys *whom* all praise. This is the girl *whom* the president offered a medal. |
| Whose (Possessive)  | Persons and things | This is the man *whose* pocket was picked. This is the man *whose* books are dropped. A triangle *whose* three sides are equal is called an equilateral triangle. |
| Which (Object & Subject)  | Things without life and animals | This is the house *which* my uncle built. This is the cow *which* is milking (= giving milk). This is the way *which* leads to the Post-office. |
| That (as Subject) | Persons, animals, things | He *that* is content is rich. A dog *that* barks seldom bites. Take anything *that* you like. |

Note that the Relative Pronouns are usually used in the middle of the sentence. But the Relative Pronouns 'What', 'Who' and 'Whom' may sometimes be used at the beginning of a sentence and sometimes in the middle when the Antecedent is understood :

What has happened is not clear.

What cannot be cured must be endured.

Who laughs last laughs best.

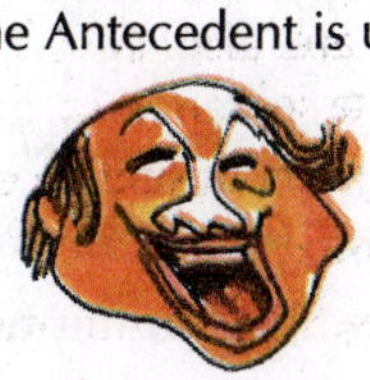

I don't know what has happened.

I say what I mean. I know who he is. This is whom I want.

## OMISSION OF THE RELATIVE PRONOUN

The Relative Pronoun is generally omitted when it is in the Objective Case :

The man (whom) I invited is my friend.

The book (which) I am reading is romantic.

I am the monarch of all (that) I survey.

> The tendency to omit the Accusative (objective) Relative is more marked in the spoken language. In the written language its omission is often felt to be undignified.
> **Wren & Martin**

## OMISSION OF THE ANTECEDENT

Sometimes the Antecedent of a Relative Pronoun is left out :

Who does not work shall not eat. = He who does not work shall not eat.

Whom the gods love, die young. = Those whom the gods love, die young.

What is done cannot be undone. = That what is done cannot be undone.

## AGREEMENT OF THE RELATIVE PRONOUN AND ITS ANTECEDENT

As the Relative Pronoun refers to a Noun or a Pronoun (*i.e.* Antecedent), it must be of the **same number and person as its Antecedent** :

The boy who was lazy was punished.

The boys who were lazy were punished.

I am the last person (that is) to admit it.

You who are mighty should be merciful.

He that is down needs no fear to fall.

Those who live in glass houses should not throw stones.

The flowers which grow in our garden are not for sale.

But the case of the Relative Pronoun depends upon its relation to the verb in the clause in which it occurs :

Ram is the boy who did it. (subject)

Ram is the boy whom I want. (object)

Ram is the boy whose pencil I want. (possessive)

## POSITION OF THE RELATIVE PRONOUN

To remove ambiguity, the Relative Pronoun should be placed as near as possible to its Antecedent :

(i) The boy **who** was walking in the field saw a dead cow.

***We cannot say***—The boy saw a dead cow **who** was walking in the field.

(ii) The boy **who** won the first prize is the son of my friend.

***We cannot say***—The boy is the son of my friend **who** won the first prize.

## COMPOUND RELATIVE PRONOUNS

Compound Relative Pronouns are formed by adding *ever* or *soever* to who, which or what :

Whoever (= any person who) comes is welcome.
Take whichever (= anything which) you like.
Whatever (anything which) may happen, I'll do this.
Whatsoever (= anything what) may happen, I'll do this.
You can call whomsoever (= anyone whom) you see.

## SHORT FORMS OF PRONOUN AND VERB

I am = I'm
I shall/will = I'll
We are = We're
We shall/will = We'll
You are = You're
You will = You'll
He will = He'll
She will = She'll
They will = They'll

He is = He's
She is = She's
They are = They're
I have = I've
We have = We've
He has = He's
You have = You've
It is = It's
That is = That's

**Note** **Its = of it. It's = It is** [These short forms of Pronouns and Verbs are often used in Spoken English.]

## SOME IMPORTANT NOTES

When Pronouns of different Persons are joined, the Verb will be Plural :

He and I have done it. You and Hari have idled away your time.

As per good manners, **2nd person first**, **3rd person next** and **1st person last** :

You and I (not I and you); You and he (not he and you);

He and I (not I and he); You, he and I (not I, you and he).

But in admitting faults the pattern will be reverse, i.e. I, he and you are guilty.

Study the following correct sentences :

These gifts are for you and me. (not I).

Nobody will help you but me. (not I. Here 'but' is a preposition)

He is taller than I (am).

He is taller than me. (This is now accepted).

**Wren & Martin**

"*Than whom* is standard English today, admitted and blessed by the Oxford Dictionary." **Good English by G. H. Vallins**

**Impersonal Pronoun :**

There is another type of Pronoun called Impersonal Pronoun (= It).

What is *it*? *It* is easy to say but hard to do.

**Possessive Pronoun and Possessive Adjective :**

A Pronoun is called Possessive Pronoun when it denotes possession.

Such **Possessive Pronouns** are : mine, ours, yours, his, hers, theirs, its.

In Modern English, my, our, your, his, her, their—when used attributively before nouns—are classified as **Possessive Adjectives**.

**For example :** *my* book, *our* home, *your* name, *his* house, *her* letter etc.

The alternative forms *mine*, *ours*, *yours*, *hers*, *theirs* are used as Possessive Pronouns.

**For example :** This book is *mine*. That book is *yours*.

However, 'his' may be used both as a Possessive Adjective and as a Possessive Pronoun.

**For example :** This is *his* pen. This pen is *his*.

## APPLIED SECTION

**1. Use appropriate Pronouns in the blank spaces of the following dialogue :**

Larry : This is ........... friend, Rahaman.

Harry : Hello, nice to meet ........... .

Rahul : Nice to meet ........... too.

Larry : Rahaman is an artist and ........... sister is also an artist.

Harry : That's interesting.

Larry : ........... work of art is very popular. Everyone in ........... town knows about ........... paintings.

Harry : Larry, aren't ........... sisters artists too?

Larry : Well, they are not artists. ........... are good musicians. ........... parents are also good musicians.

Rahul : Larry is a good cricketer. ........... plays cricket in ........... school team.

Larry : Yes, ......know that, but ........... belong to a family of footballers.

Harry : ........... family members are different from ........... family members. It does not matter. ........... are friends.

**2. Use Pronouns as Object to a Verb or a Preposition :**

[Apply correct forms given in the brackets]

(a) Can you pass ........... the salt? (I)

(b) Please send the letter to ........... (She)

(c) His mother made this shirt for ........... (He)

(d) Have you bought tickets for ...........? (They)

(e) Would you like to come with ...........? (We)

**3. Note the difference between Possessive Adjective and Possessive Pronoun :**

| Possessive Adjective | Possessive Pronoun |
|---|---|
| This is *my* book. | This book is *mine*. |

We can say the same thing in three ways :

(i) This is *my book*. (ii) This *book is mine*. (iii) This book *belongs to me*.

*Now rewrite each of the following sentences in two other ways* :

| | | |
|---|---|---|
| (i) This is his ball. | (ii) ........... | (iii) ........... |
| (i) That is your book. | (ii) ........... | (iii) ........... |
| (i) Those are our pens. | (ii) ........... | (iii) ........... |

**4. Apply Reflexive Pronouns in the following sentences :**

(i) Lila makes her bed ..........................................................................

(ii) Her mother cooks ..........................................................................

(iii) I'll do the sum ..........................................................................

(iv) Badal washes his clothes ..........................................................................

(v) The boys clean the room ..........................................................................

## EXERCISE

**1. How many kinds of Pronouns are there? What are they?**

**2. Give the various forms of Personal Pronouns in different persons and cases.**

**3. What is the difference betweeen a Relative Pronoun and an Interrogative Pronoun though they look alike?**

**4. Find out the Pronouns and classify them.**

They have lost their books. Which is your book? Which books are yours? I gave him a pen but he did not return it. Any of the boys can do it. Somebody will take it. I lost myself. He hurt himself. Who are you? What do you want? Each of the girls has gone home. Either of them can do it. Ahmed and Rahim love each other.

**5. Fill in the blanks with appropriate Pronouns in the following passage :**

A farmer had three sons. .............. always quarrelled. .............. made the farmer unhappy. One day the farmer thought of a plan. .............. called in all his sons. .............. showed a bundle of sticks and asked .............. to break the bundle. All .............. sons tried but no one could break it.

**6. Read the following passage and find out different types of Pronouns used in it :**

Once king Solomon invited the queen of Sheba to his kingdom. The queen was pleased. She said to the king's messenger, "Ours is a small kingdom and yet your great ruler wants to be our good friend. It is a great honour to me."

**7. Choose the appropriate Pronouns from the brackets and complete the sentences.**

(a) .............. went to school. (me, mine, I)

(b) .............. am talking with .............. friends. (my, me, I, mine)

(c) Can you run as fast as ..............? (he, his, him)

(d) The boys are taking .............. prizes. (our, their, your)

(e) Lila is sitting in .............. room. (his, her, their)

(f) Tell .............. about .............. school. (me, our, your)

**8. Find out the Relative Pronouns in the following sentences. Tell the Case of each and mention its antecedent :**

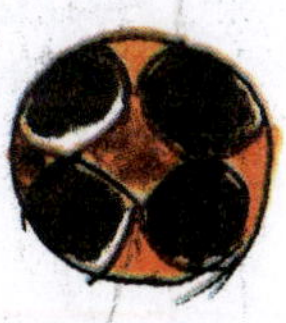

(a) The pen that you gave me is a very good one.

(b) The ball you play came from Russia.

(c) The answer which you gave is not right.

(d) I know the woman whose child was burnt.

(e) This is the boy whom I want.

(f) Bring me the letters which the postman left.

(g) This is the house that Jack built.

(h) Show me the knife that you have bought.

(i) He has not bought the knife that I asked for.

**9. Fill in the blanks with appropriate Relative Pronouns :**

(a) We always like those boys .............. speak the truth.

(b) He .............. does his best shall be praised.

(c) We saw the dog .............. worried the cat.

(d) I know .............. you mean.

(e) Most people want .............. they deserve.

(f) Where is the book .............. I gave you?

(g) God helps those .............. help themselves.

(h) No man can lose .............. he never had.

**10. Join the pairs of sentences with Relative Pronouns :**

(a) This is the boy. The boy got the first prize.

(b) This is the building. It was built in a month.

(c) The letter reached me this evening. You sent the letter.

(d) The dog barks. The dog does not bite.

(e) This is the man. I want the man.

(f) This is the girl. The book of the girl is lost.

(g) I have found the umbrella. I had lost it.

(h) A boy came to me yesterday. He is your classmate.

(i) The film is about a spy. His wife betrays him.

(j) The boys were absent. Do you know them?

**11. Join the sentences in column A to the sentences in column B using Relative Pronouns appropriately**—who, which, that, whose, whom :

| | A | | B |
|---|---|---|---|
| 1. | Here is the book | who | leads to the station? |
| 2. | I met a lame man | which | head was off. |
| 3. | The man is the Secretary | that | you lent me. |
| 4. | Is this the road | whose | you see on the chair. |
| 5. | I gave the baby a doll | whom | was walking in the field. |

**12.** **Turn the statements into questions by using Interrogative Pronouns or 'Wh'-questions.**

| Statement | Question |
|---|---|
| *Example* : I wanted his address. | What did you want? |
| A boy lived at Bhowanipur in Kolkata. | |
| His parents sent him to school. | |
| Pele is the king of football. | |
| Dipak is 14 years old. | |
| His father is a teacher. | |
| I have seen some birds in the garden. | |
| He invited some friends. | |
| He is going to buy some books. | |

# 10 MORE ABOUT ADJECTIVES

An Adjective is a word used to qualify a noun or a pronoun. **J. C. Nesfield**

Adjectives are mainly of two types : **Attributive Adjective** and **Predicative Adjective**. An Adjective is called an **Attributive Adjective** when it is placed before a noun and qualifies it. But an Adjective is called a **Predicative Adjective** when it is placed after a verb in the Predicate part and qualifies a noun or a pronoun.

The intelligent girl is reading a book. ('intelligent'—Attributive Adjective).

The girl is very intelligent. ('intelligent'—Predicative Adj. qualifies the Noun 'girl'.)

She is very lazy. ('Lazy'—Predicative Adjective qualifies the Pronoun 'she'.).

**Note** Both Attributive Adjective and Predicative Adjective qualify a noun. But only Predicative Adjective qualifies a pronoun.

However, there are eight kinds of Adjectives in terms of nature :

### TYPES OF ADJECTIVES

| Kinds of Adjectives | How to recognise them | Examples |
|---|---|---|
| (1) Proper Adjectives [*Indian* tea is better than *Chinese* tea.] | Proper Adjective is formed from a Proper name. | Asian, Chinese, French, English, African, Punjabi, etc.  |
| (2) Adjective of Quality [He is an honest man.] | It denotes the quality, weakness or state of a person or a thing. | good, bad, wise, noble, rich, poor, great, hot, cold, warm, etc.  |
| (3) Adjective of quantity [I want some salt.] | It denotes the quantity of a thing or idea. | much, huge, some, a little, all, any, half, full, whole, enough etc.  |

| Kinds of Adjectives | How to recognise them | Examples |
| --- | --- | --- |
| (4) Numeral Adjective [Some boys were in the competition but only three got the prizes.] | It denotes the number of persons or things. [ one, two, three—cardinal number. First, Second, Third—ordinal number. ] | one, two, three, four, first, second, third, fourth, all, any, many, some, several, each, every, a few etc.  |
| (5) Demonstrative Adjective [I hate such things.] | It points out which persons or things are meant. | this, that, these, those, such, etc. |
| (6) Distributive Adjective [Each boy will get a prize.] | It denotes a person or a thing separately. | each, every, either, neither. |
| (7) Interrogative Adjective [What manner of man is he?] | Before a noun for asking a question. | whose, which, what. Whose book is this? Which coat is yours? What news did he bring? |
| (8) Possessive Adjective [This is his book.] | To denote possession. | my, our, your, his, her, their. My pen is lost. |

## POSSESSIVE ADJECTIVES & POSSESSIVE PRONOUNS

**My, mine; our, ours; your, yours; her and hers**

A Possessive Adjective takes a noun after it, but a Possessive Pronoun does not require it.

This is my book. [Possessive Adjective]
This book is mine. [Possessive Pronoun]
This is our house. This is your pen. This is her doll. [Possessive Adjective]
This house is ours. This pen is yours. This doll is hers. [Possessive Pronouns]

## USES OF ADJECTIVES

**[An Adjective is a describing word]**

| | |
| --- | --- |
| This is an American boy. | (Proper Adjective) |
| He likes a Chinese dish. | ( " ) |
| Indian people do not like this. | ( " ) |
| Lipika is a clever girl. | (Adjective of Quality) |
| She is very beautiful but lazy. | ( " ) |
| The rich men are not always happy. | ( " ) |
| Bilas drinks much milk. | (Adjective of Quantity) |

The girl has a large frock. (Adjective of Quantity)
The boy wants a little sugar. ( " )
I ate some rice. ( " )
He has lost all his wealth. ( " )
I have enough sugar. ( " )
Four girls are in the common room. (Numeral Adjective)
The first boy has stood third this time. ( " )
Not a single boy is in the classroom. ( " )
Some boys are clever, not all. ( " )
Are there any mango trees in the garden? ( " )
There are enough spoons. ( " )
This boy is stronger than that boy. (Demonstrative Adjective)
These mangoes are sweet. ( " )
Those rascals must be punished. ( " )
Each boy got a prize. (Distributive Adjective)
You may take either side. ( " )
She took neither side. ( " )
Whose book is this? (Interrogative Adjective)
Which pen do you want? ( " )
What books are you reading? ( " )

**Note** Whose is this book? (Whose = Interrogative Pronoun)
Whose book is this? (Whose = Interrogative Adjective) **—Wren & Martin**

This is my book and that is your book. (Possessive Adjective)

There are two more Adjectives—**Emphasizing** and **Exclamatory** Adjectives :

**Emphasizing Adjectives :**

He was beaten at his own game. He was paid back by his own coin. Mind your own business. I saw it with my own eyes. The incident happened before my very eyes. That is the very thing I want.

Own and very are used as Emphasizing Adjectives in the above-mentioned sentences.

**Exclamatory Adjectives :**

What folly! What a fall! What an idea! What a blessing! What a piece of work is man!

## FORMATION OF ADJECTIVES

### *Adjectives from Nouns*

| Noun | Adjective | Noun | Adjective |
|---|---|---|---|
| Boy | boyish | Benefit | beneficial |
| Child | childish | Education | educational |
| Fool | foolish | Devotion | devotional |
| Beauty | beautiful | Health | healthy |
| Care | careful | Dirt | dirty |
| Hope | hopeful | Ease | easy |
| Need | needful | Storm | stormy |

| Noun | Adjective | Noun | Adjective |
|---|---|---|---|
| Peace | peaceful | Sun | sunny |
| Play | playful | Leaf | leafy |
| Success | successful | Anger | angry |
| Use | useful | Glory | glorious |
| Wonder | wonderful | Envy | envious |
| Shame | shameful/shameless | Ambition | ambitious |
| Sense | sensible/senseless | Courage | courageous |
| Cease | ceaseless | Outrage | outrageous |
| Silk | silken | Danger | dangerous |
| Gold | golden | Nerve | nervous |
| Cost | costly | Horror | horrific |
| King | kingly | Telegraph | telegraphic |
| Life | lively | Laugh | laughable |
| Man | manly | Belief | believable |
| Miser | miserly | Desire | desirable |
| Music | musical | Pardon | Pardonable |
| Crime | criminal | Office | official |
| Attraction | attractive | Voice | vocal |
| Destruction | destructive | Hand | handy/handsome |
| Distribution | distributive | Trouble | troublesome |
| Production | productive | Quarrel | quarrelsome |
| People | popular | Venture | venturesome |

## Adjectives from Verbs

| Verb | Adjective | Verb | Adjective |
|---|---|---|---|
| Act | active | Move | movable |
| Attract | attractive | Rely | reliable |
| Detect | detective | Add | additional |
| Deceive | deceptive | Edit | editorial |
| Include | inclusive | Forget | forgetful |
| Instruct | instructive | Trust | trustful |
| Talk | talkative | Invent | inventive |
| Agree | agreeable | Prevent | preventive |
| Desire | desirable | Advise | advisory |
| Enjoy | enjoyable | Love | lovely |
| Adjust | adjustable | Adore | adorable |
| Cease | ceaseless | Combat | combative |
| Convert | convertible | Cooperate | cooperative |
| Dispense | dispensable | Dispose | disposable |
| Elude | elusive | Exult | exultant |
| Extend | extensive | Solicit | solicitous |
| Produce | productive | Infer | inferential |
| Study | studious | Obligate | obligatory |

### Adjectives from other Adjectives

| Adjective | Adjective | Adjective | Adjective |
|---|---|---|---|
| Alternate | alternative | Large | largely |
| Economic | economical | Sick | sickly |
| Conic | conical | Black | blackish |
| Tragic | tragical | White | whitish |
| Three | threefold | Whole | wholesome |

**Note** A few words with 'ly'-ending look like Adverbs; but they are really Adjectives : (lovely, sickly, manly, miserly etc.) : He is a miserly man. He showed manly behaviour.

## COMPARISON OF ADJECTIVES

Read the sentences :

[1] Raju is a **tall** boy.

[2] Sibu is **taller** than Raju.

[3] Giraffe is the **tallest** of all animals.

In sentence [1], the Adjective 'tall' simply tells that Raju is tall without comparing with another. In sentence [2], the Adjective 'taller' tells that Sibu is taller in comparison with Raju. In sentence [3], the Adjective 'tallest' tells that Debu is 'tallest' of the three boys.

Thus, in the above sentences, we can see the changes in the forms of Adjective. The Adjective 'tall' is in Positive degree, 'taller' in Comparative degree and 'tallest' in Superlative degree. Hence there are three degrees of Adjective.

1. **Positive Degree** [without any comparison]
2. **Comparative Degree** [comparison between two persons or things]
3. **Superlative Degree** [comparison among three or more persons and things]

## FORMATION OF COMPARATIVE AND SUPERLATIVE DEGREES

**[1] Most Adjectives of one syllable by adding -er and -est :**

| *Positive* | *Comparative* | *Superlative* |
|---|---|---|
| Bold | bolder | boldest |
| Cold | colder | coldest |
| *Old | older | oldest |
| Old | elder | eldest |
| Clever | cleverer | cleverest |
| Few | fewer | fewest |
| Great | greater | greatest |
| Hard | harder | hardest |
| High | higher | highest |
| Kind | kinder | kindest |
| Low | lower | lowest |
| Long | longer | longest |
| Poor | poorer | poorest |
| Rich | richer | richest |
| Short | shorter | shortest |

| Positive | Comparative | Superlative |
|---|---|---|
| Bold | bolder | boldest |
| Small | smaller | smallest |
| Strong | stronger | strongest |
| Soft | softer | softest |
| Sweet | sweeter | sweetest |
| Tall | taller | tallest |
| Weak | weaker | weakest |

**Note** In case of aged person or vintage substance, generally '**old**' is used as '**older**' in Comparative form and '**oldest**' in Superlative form. In case of family relation, '**old**' is used as '**elder**' in Comparative form and '**eldest**' in Superlative form.

**[2] When the Positive ends in -e, only -r and -st are added :**

| Positive | Comparative | Superlative |
|---|---|---|
| Able | abler | ablest |
| Brave | braver | bravest |
| Fine | finer | finest |
| Late | later | latest |
| Late | latter | last |
| Large | larger | largest |
| Noble | nobler | noblest |
| Pale | paler | palest |
| True | truer | truest |
| Wise | wiser | wisest |
| White | whiter | whitest |

**Note** 'Later' and 'Latest' in relation to time : This is the later/latest edition of the book. 'Latter' and 'Last' to denote order or position. That is the latter/last issue.

Ram and Shyam are two boys; the former is strong in Bengali and the latter in English. Amar is the last boy in the class. He came last of all.

**[3] When the positive ends in a Consonant preceded by a Vowel, the Consonant is doubled before adding -er and -est :**

| Positive | Comparative | Superlative |
|---|---|---|
| Big | bigger | biggest |
| Fat | fatter | fattest |
| Hot | hotter | hottest |
| Mad | madder | maddest |
| Sad | sadder | saddest |
| Thin | thinner | thinnest |

**Note** The Consonant is not doubled in Comparative and Superlative degrees if there are two Consonants or two Vowels before a Consonant in Positive degree :

| | | |
|---|---|---|
| Thick | thicker | thickest |
| Cool | cooler | coolest |

**[4] When the Positive ends in y, preceded by a Consonant, the y is changed into i before adding -er and -est :**

| Positive | Comparative | Superlative |
|---|---|---|
| Busy | busier | busiest |
| Easy | easier | easiest |
| Dry | drier | driest |
| Happy | happier | happiest |
| Heavy | heavier | heaviest |
| Holy | holier | holiest |
| Merry | merrier | merriest |
| Mighty | mightier | mightiest |
| Ugly | uglier | ugliest |
| Wealthy | wealthier | wealthiest |

**Note** 'y' is not changed when there is a vowel before it :

| | | |
|---|---|---|
| Gay | gayer | gayest |
| Grey | greyer | greyest |

**[5] Some Comparatives and Superlatives are different from the Positive :**

[ They are formed in irregular way. ]

| Positive | Comparative | Superlative |
|---|---|---|
| Good | better | best |
| Bad | worse | worst |
| Far | farther | farthest |
| Fore | further/furthermore | furthest/furthermost |
| Little | less | least |
| Much | more | most |
| Many | more | most |

**Note** Kolkata is farther from Mumbai than Patna. (distance)
He made no further remarks. (further = additional)

**[6] Adjectives of two syllables or more than two syllables form the Comparative and Superlative by adding more and most or less and least before them :**

| Positive | Comparative | Superlative |
|---|---|---|
| Beautiful | more beautiful | most beautiful |
| Dutiful | more dutiful | most dutiful |
| Careful | more careful/less careful | most careful/least careful |
| Courageous | more courageous | most courageous |
| Difficult | more difficult | most difficult |
| Diligent | more diligent | most diligent |
| Important | more important | most important |
| Intelligent | more intelligent | most intelligent |
| Industrious | more industrious | most industrious |
| Learned | more learned | most learned |

**[7] There are some Latin Comparatives :**

*Junior, Senior, Inferior, Superior, Minor, Major, Prior, Anterior, Posterior, etc.* These Latin Adjectives take 'to' instead of 'than' after them in Comparative degree. They have no Positive and Superlative forms :

I am junior to him. He is senior to me. Amal is junior to Bimal in age but senior to him in service. This type of tea is inferior to that. This type of rice is superior to that. The Vedas are anterior to the Puranas. The Iron Age is posterior to the Copper Age.

## USE OF DEGREES

Use of positive degree : Bob is as *old* as Joe.

Use of Comparative degree : George is *older* than Mike.

Use of Superlative degree : { George is *the oldest* of all. / He is *the oldest* boy *in* his class. }

**Note** Hints for expressing degrees :

**Positive degree :** He is (as) ferocious as a wolf. (as...as)

**Comparative degree :** He is more ferocious than a wolf. (...than)

**Superlative degree :** He is the most ferocious man in the society. (the...in)
He is the best of all the boys. (the...of)

**Change of Degree without any change of meaning :**

He is ferocious as a tiger. (Positive)
= A tiger is not more ferocious than he. (Comparative)
Arthur is stronger than Kapoor. (Comparative)
= Kapoor is not as strong as Arthur. (Positive)
= Kapoor is less strong than Arthur. (Comparative)
Harry is the laziest boy *in* the class. (Superlative)
= Harry is lazier than any other boy in the class. (Comparative)
= No other boy in the class is as lazy as Hari. (Positive)
Iron is the most useful metal. (Superlative)
= Iron is more useful than any other metal. (Comparative)
= No other metal is as useful as iron. (Positive)
Gold is one of the most precious metals. (Superlative)
= Gold is more precious than many other metals. (Comparative)
= Very few metals are as precious as gold. (Positive)

**Now note the difference in meaning :**

Don is braver than Donald = (Don has more courage than that of Donald.)
Don is more brave than *prudent.* (= Don has more courage than wisdom.)

## AN IMPORTANT NOTE

The Superlative with **most** is sometimes used when there is no idea of Comparison, but merely a desire to indicate a quality in a very high degree.

This is most unfortunate.
This is a most wonderful sight.
It was a most eloquent speech.

**Note** In such cases 'the' is not used in the Superlative degree.

## APPLIED SECTION

**An Adjective gives more information about a Noun or a Pronoun. The form is the same for the Singular and the Plural.**

**Example :**

Look at the pretty bird.

Look at those pretty birds.

He and his brother are poor.

But certainly they are honest.

**1. Fill in the blanks with the opposite of the following Adjectives :**

Fat, long, big, rich, clean, easy, early, noisy, boring, sour, fierce, straight.

(a) Ruma's hair is ............ and ............ She is ............ and ..........

(b) Tinku always gets up ...........................................................

(c) Some sums are really ...........................................................

(d) Some parts of the city are .....................................................

(e) We all like to eat ...................................................... oranges.

(f) Old people like to live in ............................................ places.

(g) Most of the people in the villages are ......................................

(h) I read an ................................................... book yesterday.

**2. Put the pairs of Adjectives in the sentences in the suitable order :**

(a) Mr. Roy's room is very .......... and .......... . (clean, neat)

(b) You have a coloured TV but we have a ........ and ........ TV (white, black)

(c) Give something to that .......... man. (old, poor)

(d) Vidyasagar gave his mother a very .......... shawl. (woollen, expensive)

(e) Nila is wearing her mother's .......... sari. (lovely, Benarasi)

**3. Apply the Positives, Comparatives and the Superlatives correctly :**

**as + adjective + as**

Naren is as tall *as* Haren.

Arun is ...... old ....... Barun.

A grape is not ..... big .... orange.

**Negative Comparison**

not as ................. as

not so ................. as

not {so / as} .... as

Rabeya weighs as much as Rahima. Does she eat ............ Rahima too?

**Comparative (-er / more) + than**

Arun is older than Barun.

The net of the basket ball hangs higher than their hands.

Barun is ............ Arun. (young)

Lipika is more beautiful than Latika.

Latika is less ............ Lipika.

**Comparative only**

I think your handwriting is better.

Have you any ............ umbrella? (small)

**the + comparative ............ the + comparative**

The sooner the better. The bigger the house is the more money it will cost. The more leisure he has the .........he is. (happy)

**the + superlative only**

Asia is the biggest continent.

Which is ............ continent? (small)

Which is ............ river? (long)

**4. Comparatives and Superlatives appear much stronger in the following sentences :**

A Fiat is more costly than Maruti. An Ambassador is much more costly. A Contessa is far more costly. A Standard 2000 is by far the most costly.

**Now complete the following sentences :**

(i) Which place in West Bengal has the ......... rainfall?

(ii) The ......... picture ever sold was painted by Van Gogh.

(iii) Did Maradona play ........... he could?

(iv) Sharmila can dance ........... than many senior girls of her school.

(v) My brother reads English ......... than I can. I am rather a slow reader.

(vi) Do you feel ......... now?

**5. Compare the climate of Kolkata and that of Darjeeling. Use Comparative forms of the following words :** hot, cold, wet etc.

..........................................................................................

..........................................................................................

..........................................................................................

## EXERCISE

**1. Pick out the Adjectives in the following sentences :**

| Sentences | Adjectives |
|---|---|
| (a) Every man has his duties. | |
| (b) Do not say the same thing twice. | |
| (c) The way was long, the wind was cold. | |
| (d) He was absent last week. | |
| (e) He died a glorious death. | |
| (f) Good wine needs no push/advertisement. | |
| (g) The old man was both deaf and dumb. |  |
| (h) He is a man of few words. | |
| (i) A small leak may sink a large ship. | |
| (j) The child fell down from a tall tree. | |
| (k) Neither party is quite in the right. | |
| (l) Which pen do you prefer? | |
| (m) There should not be much talk and little work. | |

**2. Supply suitable Adjectives :**

(a) The ................ prize was won by Rahim.
(b) The ................ woman lives in a wretched hut.
(c) This is a very ................ matter.
(d) There were riots in ................ places.
(e) Every cloud has a ................ lining.
(f) Suddenly arose a ................ storm.
(g) He is a man of ................ ambition.
(h) He always walks with a ................ step.
(i) Have you any ................ reason for leaving the country?
(j) The battle of Waterloo ended in a ................ victory.

**3. Form Adjectives from the following words and place a Noun after each Adjective :**

act, doubt, ease, health, wealth, time, pity, heaven, love, hill, pain, wonder, peace, child, thought, hope, friend, quarrel, storm, star, leaf, sun.

**Examples :** [Sunny day, Stormy sea, Starry sky, leafy tree]

**4. Use each of the following Adjectives in a sentence :**

Lazy, big, small, tall, hard, sad, happy, rude, polite, rich, poor, young, old, long, short, healthy, clever, cruel, beautiful, ugly.

**5. Change the degree of the following Adjectives :**

| **Positive** | **Comparative** | **Superlative** |
|---|---|---|
| able | .............................. | .............................. |
| easy | .............................. | .............................. |
| early | .............................. | .............................. |
| busy | .............................. | .............................. |
| strong | .............................. | .............................. |
| short | .............................. | .............................. |
| hot | .............................. | .............................. |
| big | .............................. | .............................. |
| good | .............................. | .............................. |
| bad | .............................. | .............................. |
| weak | .............................. | .............................. |
| intelligent | .............................. | .............................. |

**6. Fill in the blanks with suitable forms of Adjectives :**

He is the ................................................ of all in the class. (bad)
He is........................................................... than his sister. (tall)
He is................................................ than his brother. (intelligent)
She is ..................................................... than her sister. (happy)
You are ..................................................... to me than life. (dear)
Iron is ........................................................... than gold. (cheap)
Iron is ..................................................... of all metals. (useful)
Gold is ..................................................... than iron. (valuable)

Fatema is as ........................................................ as Salma. (old)

She is her father's ........................................................ daughter. (old)

This tree is ........................................................ than that. (old)

Which do you like ........................................ rain or sunshine? (good)

**7. Fill in the blanks with suitable words from the brackets :**

I want a book of the ........................................ edition. (last/latest)

Reba is ........................................ than her sister. (older/elder)

She has lost ........................................ blood. (much/many)

Nasir has ........................................ friends. (much/many)

He came ........................................ than his brother. (later/latter)

I want the former, not the ........................................ (latter/later)

**8. Study the Table below :**

| Description | Mr. Bose | Mr. Das | Mr. Roy |
|---|---|---|---|
| Age | 35 years | 50 years | 55 years |
| Height | 1·7 metres | 1·5 metres | 1·6 metres |
| Weight | 52 kg | 48 kg | 50 kg |

**Now fill up the blanks with suitable words :**

Mr. Bose is not ............ old ............ Mr. Roy.

He has ............ weight ............ Mr. Das.

Mr. Roy is taller ............ Mr. Das, but Mr. Bose is ............

**9. Make comparison between these pairs using the words given in the brackets : [They may be equal or unequal.]**

(a) Cricket and football (interesting/exciting)

(b) English and Arithmetic (difficult/interesting)

(c) A dog and cat (pretty/faithful)

(d) The rainy season and the winter season (good/pleasant)

(e) Delhi from Kolkata and Mumbai from Kolkata (far).

# 11  MORE ABOUT VERBS AND MODALS

[ Special stress has been given on the use of **'have to + verb'**, **'must/mustn't + verb'** and **'ought to + verb'** for obligation/necessity; **'can/could/couldn't + verb'** for ability or inability and **'may/might + verb'** for expressing possibility. ]

**A Verb is a word used for saying something about some person or thing.**
J. C. Nesfield

**A Verb is a word that tells or asserts something about a person or thing.**
Wren & Martin

**A Verb is a word that denotes being, having or doing something.** P. C. Das

**A Verb may tell us—**

(1) What a person or thing is :
Mr. John is a teacher.
The dog is brown.
His shirt is white.

(2) What a person or thing has :
Shila has a pet cat.
A chair has four legs.

(3) What a person or thing does :
Latif kicks the ball.
The clock strikes ten.

## KINDS OF VERBS

Verbs are classified in four different ways :

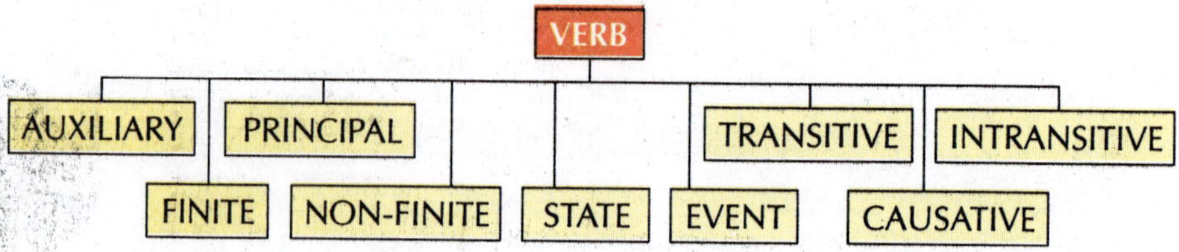

## AUXILIARY VERBS AND PRINCIPAL VERBS

Study the following table :

| Auxiliary | Principal |
|---|---|
| She is writing a letter.<br>I have come to school.<br>He does not go to school.<br>She will sing a song. | She is a teacher.<br>I have an umbrella.<br>He does his work perfectly.<br>She wills to have a prize. |

***An Auxiliary verb is one which helps a Principal verb to form a tense or mood or voice. Hence it is also called a Helping verb.***

***The Verbs which are used independently without help from other verbs are called Principal Verbs or Main Verbs.***

**Auxiliary Verbs or Helping Verbs are of two types :**

1. **Primary Auxiliaries** or **Tense Auxiliaries**. 2. **Modal Auxiliaries** :

| Primary Auxiliaries | Modal Auxiliaries |
|---|---|
| Be : be, is, am, are<br>was, were, been, being.<br>Have : Have, has, had, having.<br>Do : do, does, did. | can, could, shall, should,<br>will, would, may, might, must,<br>need, dare, used (to), ought (to). |

**Full Form of Verbs : Helping Verbs + Principal Verbs**
[ Be, have, do, Modal ] + [ Present, Present + ing, Past Participle ]

### USES OF PRIMARY AUXILIARIES OR TENSE AUXILIARIES

**To be :** For indicating continuous tense and passive voice :

I am doing the sum. (Present Progressive)
The kitten is crying. ( " )
He was sleeping at night. (Past Progressive)
The work is being done by me. (Passive Voice)
The sum has been worked out. ( " )
The work will be done by him. ( " )

**Note** **'To be'** may also be used as a Principal Verb :

I am well. He is at home. You are here. Niren is an engineer. They are brave soldiers.

**To have :** For indicating Perfect Tense forms, Passive Voice and Nominative Absolute.

I have done the work. (Present Perfect)
He had left the school before the class was over. (Past Perfect)
It has been raining for five days. (Pr. Perfect Cont.)
The work has been done. (Passive Voice)
The sun having risen, darkness disappeared. (Nom. Absolute)

**Note** **'To have'** may also be used as a Principal Verb :

He has a red shirt. She had a nice umbrella. How many children have they? What shall we have for dinner?

**Note** British English uses both '**have**' and '**have got**' but prefers the second.

We **have** / **have got** a cottage in the village.

They **have** / **have got** a small flat.

**To do :** [ As Auxiliary verb ]

(i) To make an Interrogative sentence :

**Do** you like football? **Does** he take tea? **Did** she write a letter?

(ii) To make a Negative sentence :

| Full forms | Shortened forms |
|---|---|
| I **do not** like him. | do not = **don't** |
| He **does not** go to school. | does not = **doesn't** |
| They **did not** play football. | did not = **didn't** |

(iii) To give a stress in a statement :

I **do** hereby authorise you.

He **did** help you and you should not deny that.

**Note** **'To do'** is generally used as a Principal Verb :

We **do** our homework regularly. They **did** the work sincerely.
They **do** practice 'catch' regularly.

## USES OF MODAL AUXILIARIES (MODALS)

Modal Auxiliaries are those helping verbs which help to express the mode or manner in which the action is done.

**The modals are different from other Auxiliaries 'have', 'be' and 'do' in three ways :**

(i) They do not have **-s** forms, **-ing** forms, **-ed** forms or **-en** forms :

*do—does—did* ; *have—having—had* ; *be, being, been*. But not *may—maying* or *mayed*.

(ii) Modals take only the base form of Principal Verbs after them :

I **can do** the work alone. He **may** not **come** here today.
You **must abide** by the rules.

(iii) Modals modify the meaning of the Main Verbs :

**Does** he **play** football?

('Does' not to modify the main verb 'play', but to form a mere question)

[But] He **can play** football. ['can' modifies the main verb 'play' expressing ability]

**Now see the Modals :**

| Modals | Functions | Examples |
|---|---|---|
| Will | asking | Will you go to school? |
| Would | requesting | Would you give me a table-tennis ball? |
| Shall | asking | Shall I do the work? |
| Should | suggestion | You should work hard. |
| Can | ability | He can drive a car. |

| Modals | Functions | Examples |
|---|---|---|
| Could | ability<br>requesting | He could do the sum.<br>Could you help me to do the sum? |
| May | possibility<br>permission<br>prayer | He may come here today.<br>May I come in?<br>May you live long. |
| Might | possibility<br>suggestion | His statement might be true.<br>You might go to Italy for training. |
| Must | certainty<br>obligation | It must be good. You mustn't do this.<br>You must obey your teachers. |
| Mustn't | prohibition | You must not (mustn't) run in the sun. |
| Need | necessity | He need not go there. [not 'needs not'] |
| Needn't | negation | I need not (needn't) want a book now. |
| Dare | bold assertion<br>daring courage | I dare say you are a fool.<br>He dares to stand alone.<br>[vide **A.L.D.—Hornby**] |
| Daren't | afraid to do | I dare not (daren't) follow you.<br>He dare not (daren't) do it.<br>['dares not' is incorrect] |
| Ought (to) | moral obligation<br>suggestion | We ought to love our neighbours.<br>This is really a good film; you ought to see it. |
| Used (to) | habit | He used to walk early in the morning. |

**Note** **Dare :** In the Third Person Singular (in Simple Present) the modal is 'dare' and not 'dares'—provided it is followed by a negative.

## SOME MORE EXAMPLES

**Expressing ability [Can]**

The boy can write a poem.
The girl can dance gracefully. The deer can run fast.

**Expressing request [Could]**

Could you lend me your book? Could I have a cup of tea?

**Expressing possibility [May]**

He may come home today. I may go out for a walk now.

**Asking and giving permission [May]**

May I come in, sir? May I climb the hill? Yes, you may.

**Expressing possibility (Past Tense) [Might]**

He might do the work at ease. They might join the party for the picnic. They might just as well go.

**Asking permission (Past tense) [Might]**

He asked the Headmaster if he might go home after the first period.

**Expressing certainty / obligation [Must]**

You must do your duty. He must leave the class.

**Expressing advice [Should / Ought to]**

You should have (take) a morning walk. You ought to be here at 9 a.m.

**Auxiliaries in short answers :**

To avoid repetition of the main verb, the Auxiliary Verbs 'do', 'have', 'can', 'may', 'be', etc. are used in short answers :

| | |
|---|---|
| Do you take tea in the morning? | Yes, I do. |
| Have you got your umbrella? | Yes, I have. |
| Can you drive a car? | No, I can't. |
| Is he going to school? | Yes, he is. |
| May I go out, sir? | Yes, you may. |

## TRANSITIVE AND INTRANSITIVE VERBS

**Principal Verbs are of two types :**

(1) **Transitive Verb**

We eat rice. He does his home work.

(2) **Intransitive Verb**

Rivers flow. Winds blow. Birds fly. Animals die.

> A verb is Tansitive if the action does not stop with the agent, but passes from the agent to something else.
>
> A verb is Intransitive when the action stops with the agent, and does not pass from the agent to something else.
>
> **J. C. Nesfield**

**Study the following table :**

| Transitive | Intransitive |
|---|---|
| He is eating rice. | The birds are flying. |
| She is preparing breakfast. | The boy is laughing. |
| We have caught a thief. | The lion is roaring. |
| They have bought a bicycle. | Why are you weeping? |
| The beggar wanted some money. | The old man is coughing. |

So we can say :

Transitive Verbs need an Object to complete their meaning.

Intransitive Verbs need no Object to complete their meaning.

**What is an Object?**

If we ask a Verb '*Whom*' or '*What*', the answer we get is the Object.

## Direct Object and Indirect Object :

Most Transitive Verbs take a single Object. But such Transitive Verbs as *give, ask, offer, promise, tell* etc. take two Objects after them—an *Indirect Object* which denotes the person to whom something is given or for whom something is done, and a *Direct Object* which is usually the name of something. **Wren & Martin**

**Examples : (Single Object)**

I want a book. He got a letter.

**Double Object (Indirect Object and Direct Object)**

| | | |
|---|---|---|
| His father gave | me | a book. |
| | Ind. obj. | Direct obj. |
| He told | us | a secret. |
| | Ind. obj. | Direct obj. |
| The teacher asked | him | a question. |
| | Ind. obj. | Direct obj. |

## Cognate Object :

Some Intransitive Verbs take after them an Object similar to the Verb. Such an Object is called the **Cognate Object** :

I slept a sound sleep. He has fought a good fight. She dreamt a strange dream. Dhira sang a sweet song. Shila laughed a hearty laugh. Mrs. Mukherjee cried a bitter cry. What a bitter cry Mrs. Mukherjee cried!

Most verbs can be used both as Transitive and as Intransitive verbs. **Wren & Martin**

| Used Transitively | Used Intransitively |
|---|---|
| Ring the bell. | The bell rang loudly. |
| He spoke the truth. | He spoke haughtily. |
| The driver stopped the train. | The train stopped suddenly. |
| The horse kicked the man. | This horse never kicks. |
| I feel a severe pain in my head. | How do you feel? |

Sometimes a Reflexive Pronoun used as an Object is expressed or omitted :

The man killed himself. (Reflexive Pronoun used as an Object)

The bubble burst [itself]. (Reflexive Pronoun omitted)

Please keep [yourselves] quiet. (Reflexive Pronoun omitted)

## Intransitive Verbs used as Transitives :

(i) ***When an Intransitive verb is used in a causative sense it becomes a Transitive.***

**Intransitive verb ⇛ causative sense ⇛ Transitive verb**

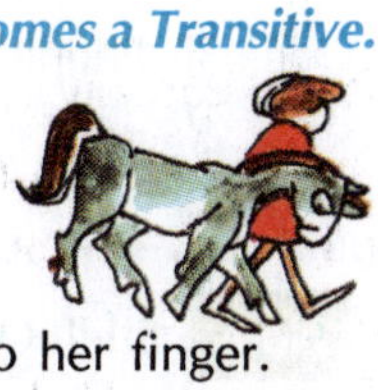

| Intransitive | Transitive |
|---|---|
| The horse walks. | He walks the horse. |
| The girl ran down the street. | The girl ran a needle into her finger. |
| Birds fly. | The boys fly their kites. |

(ii) ***A few verbs in common use are distinguished as Transitive or Intransitive by their spelling :***

| **Intransitive** | **Transitive** |
|---|---|
| Lie still on bed. | Lay the basket there. (Lay = cause to lie) |
| Rise early with the lark. | Raise your hands. (Raise = cause to rise) |
| Sit there idly. | Set the lamp on the table. (Set = cause to sit) |
| Many trees fall by the storm. | The woodcutters fell trees. (fell = cause to fall) |

(iii) ***Some Intransitive verbs may become Transitive by having a preposition added to them :***

All his friends laughed at him.

Please look into the matter.

He will soon run through his fortune.

The teacher asked for his name.

We talked about the affair several times.

I wish for nothing more.

(iv) ***Sometimes the preposition is prefixed to the verb and the verb becomes Transitive :***

Shivaji overcame the enemy. He bravely withstood the attack.

The river overflows its banks. They determined to withdraw the strike.

**Verbs of Incomplete Predication :**

(i) **Some Intransitive verbs** *e.g. come, go, fall, die, sleep, lie* can never be used transitively. Hence these Verbs do not require any word to make the sense complete. **But some Intransitive verbs** *e.g. be, become, seem, grow, taste* require a word to make the sense complete. Such a verb is called a **Verb of Incomplete Predication**.

Tom is a dog.

The earth is round.

John became a soldier.

The man seems tired.

Sharmila looks happy.

She has grown old.

She appears pleased.

Roses smell sweet.

Honey tastes sweet.

The man has fallen asleep.

**Note** Such Complements describe the Subject. Hence these are called Subjective Complement.

(ii) **Some Transitive verbs** require, besides an Object, a Complement to complete their predication. Such a Complement is called **Factitive Object** :

We considered him honest.

The players made Kapil captain.

People elected him *President.*

The jury found him guilty.

They chose him their leader.

His parents named him Bhola.

Dipen called his cousin a liar.

We consider the man trustworthy.

**Note** Such Complements describe the Objects. Hence these are called Objective Complement.

## FINITE AND NON-FINITE VERBS

**A Finite Verb** is limited by person and number of the subject and changes its forms according to tenses.

**A Non-finite Verb** is not limited by person and number as a Verb that has a Subject and is, therefore, called the Verb Infinite or simply the **Infinitive**.

**Wren & Martin**

**Note** A Finite Verb helps to complete the structure of a sentence but an Infinitive cannot do that. Moreover, a Finite Verb requires a Subject but an Infinitive cannot take a Subject.

| Finite Verb | Infinitive |
|---|---|
| Fatima goes to school. | Fatima does not like to go to school. |
| The mangoes taste sweet. | The mangoes are sweet to taste. |
| He attended three meetings. | He had three meetings to attend. |
| The boot is so heavy that he cannot walk. | The boot is too heavy for him to walk. |
| We can save India by patriotism. | Patriotism is the way to save India. |

Infinitives are mainly of three types :

**1. Simple Infinitive, 2. Qualifying Infinitive, 3. Perfect Infinitive**

### Simple Infinitive (Noun Infinitive) :

Simple Infinitives are used in the following conditions :

(i) As the Subject of a Verb :

To err is human. To steal is a sin. To forgive is divine. To see is to believe. To give is better than (to) receive.

(ii) As the Object of a Verb :

I like to play games. He likes to read stories. They tried to win the medals.

(iii) As the Complement of a Verb :

I asked him to shut the door. The window is difficult to open. Our motto is to work. His habit is to rise early. They are to start at once.

(iv) As the Object of a Preposition :

I am about to go. The runners are about to start. The patient was about to die.

(v) As an Apposition to 'It' :

It is easy to say. It is silly to talk like that. It is foolish to waste time.

(vi) After Interrogative Pronouns and Adverbs :

I do not know how to swim. I do not know where to go. Does he know when to start? I told him what to do. She could not decide which doll to play with.

### Qualifying Infinitive :

Qualifying Infinitives are used in the following conditions :

(i) To qualify the Noun :

He had no food to eat. This is not the time to weep. I have some letters to write. He is a man to be loved.

(ii) To qualify an Adjective :

The rose is sweet to smell. Fruits are good to eat. English is difficult to learn.

(iii) To modify a Verb :

We eat to live. (Purpose)

I am going to see the match. (Purpose)

She wept to see the mishap. (Cause)

He worked hard to get a prize. (Result)

(iv) After 'too'. [too...to] :

I am too tired to work. He is too proud to beg. I am too weak to walk. She is too ill to sit-up on bed.

**Perfect Infinitive (Completed Infinitive) :**

There is another kind of Infinitive that can be called 'Completed Infinitive'. When the action expressed by the Infinitive is regarded as completed, the perfect aspect of the Infinitive must be used :

He seems to have been beaten.

They seem to have forgotten to come here.

She appears to have been absent for some days.

Rivu is believed to have damaged the doll. (= It is believed that Rivu has damaged the doll.)

**'Have to' Infinitive for obligation :**

I have to go there. (obligation)

**Difference of 'Is to' and 'Has to/Have to' :**

It is wrong to suppose that 'is to' and 'has to/have to' mean the same thing. 'Is to' means 'It is settled' and 'has to/have to' means 'It is obligatory'.

He is to go there. (= It is settled that he will go.)

He has to go there. (= It is obligatory for him to go.)

**'To' after 'help' :**

'To' after 'help' may or may not be used :

I helped him to find his things.

[Or] I helped him find his things.

[The omission of 'to' after 'help' is more usual in American than in British usage.'— **'The A.L.D.'—Hornby**]

## BARE INFINITIVE [ Infinitive without 'to' ]

> The word *to* is often used with the Infinitive. But "after certain Verbs (bid, let, make, need, dare, see, hear) we use the Infinitive without *to*." **Wren & Matrin**

Such Infinitives without *to* are called Bare Infinitives.

I bade him go. Let him sit there. I will not let you go. I made him run. You need not go today. We saw him do the work. I heard him cry. You dare not do it.

## STATE VERBS AND EVENT VERBS

In Modern English Grammar, **Finite Verbs** are classified in two broad categories. They are **State Verbs** and **Event Verbs**.

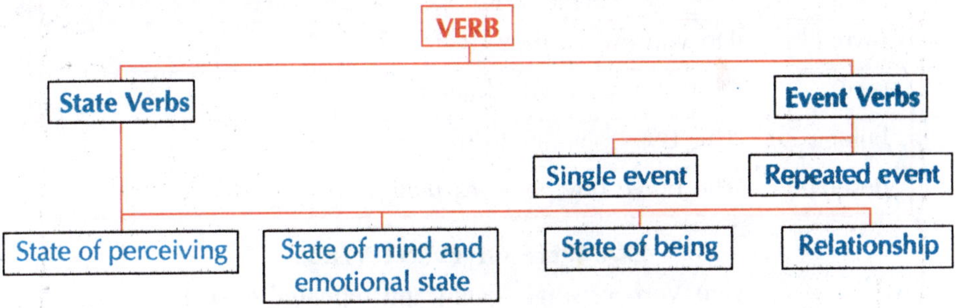


## EXAMPLES OF STATE VERBS

### State of Being

| Verb | Sentences |
|---|---|
| be | He *is* a very brave boy.<br>We *are* Indians and they *are* Chinese. |
| remain | I *remain* silent in such cases.<br>He *remains* dumb all along. |

### State of Perceiving

| Verb | Sentences |
|---|---|
| see | I see, you are a fool. |
| Hear | I hear a buzzing sound. |
| feel | I feel tired. She feels ashamed of your behaviour. |
| smell | The rose smells sweet. |
| taste | Honey tastes sweet. |

### State of mind & emotional state

| Verb | Sentences |
|---|---|
| love | Everybody loves his mother. |
| hate | You should not hate the poor. |
| like | Sharmila likes to wear white saree. |
| believe | I believe that you are telling the truth. |
| forget | I often forget his name. |
| appear | The dog appears to be mad. |

### State of Relationship

| Verb | Sentences |
|---|---|
| have | I have a brother and a sister. |
| own | Do you own a motor car? |
| owe | You owe your own house. |
| belong | This book belongs to me. |
| deserve | The brave boy deserves praise. |

## EXAMPLES OF EVENT VERBS

**Event Verb of single event and repeated events**

| Verb | Sentences |
|---|---|
| buy | I bought an orange from the market. (single event) |
| buy | I buy oranges from the market regularly. (repeated event) |

### Difference between State Verbs and Event Verbs

State Verbs are used only in Non-Progressive forms. But Event Verbs are used in both Progressive and Non-Progressive forms :

| | Progressive | Non-Progressive |
|---|---|---|
| State Verb | × I am believing you. (Incorrect) | √ I believe you. (Correct) |
| Event Verb | √ He is going to school. | √ He goes to school. |

**Note** Sometimes State Verbs may be used in Progressive forms, but then the Verbs are changed into Event Verbs and don't remain the State Verbs.

**Examples :**

He has a dog. (State Verb)

He is having his lunch. (Event Verb)

I forgot your name. (State Verb)

I am forgetting names nowadays. (Event Verb)

Honey tastes sweet. (State Verb)

He is tasting honey. (Event Verb)

**Note** There are some State Verbs which change their meaning when used in Progressive form.

**Examples :**

The boy looks (appears) like his father.

The boy is looking (becoming) more and more like his father.

You look (appear) bright today.

She is looking at (seeing) the moon.

## CAUSATIVE VERB

Some Event Verbs are sometimes used in causative sense. These are called Causative Verbs. These Verbs are formed in three ways :

(i) by using the **same verb**

| Simple Verb | Causative Verb |
|---|---|
| The bird is flying in the sky. | The boy is flying a kite. |

(ii) by using a **different verb**

| Simple Verb | Causative Verb |
|---|---|
| Mother is eating her food. | Mother is feeding her baby. |
| The girl lay (p.t. of 'lie') in bed. | The girl laid (p.t. of 'lay') her doll on bed. |

(iii) by adding **'make', 'have' or 'get'**

| Simple Verb | Causative Verb |
|---|---|
| I should go there. | I made him go there. (= compelled him to go.) |
| I cleaned the room. | I had John clean the room. |
| The barber cut my hair. | I got my hair cut. |

## VERB PATTERNS

The following tables will show the **Verb Patterns** in different constructions of sentences :

**Subject + Linking Verbs + Other aspects**

**Pattern 1**

| Subject | Linking Verb (Intr. Verb) | Noun / Noun Phrase |
|---|---|---|
| Rabin | is | my elder brother. |
| He | appears (to be) | a great leader. |
| The couple | remained | faithful to each other. |

**Pattern 2**

| Subject | Linking Verb (Intr. Verb) | Adj / Adj Phrase |
|---|---|---|
| The house | looked | deserted. |
| The soup | tasted | delicious. |
| The damage | appears | not so serious. |

**Note** Sometimes a that clause or a to-infinitive phrase may be used as a Subject when it appears to be too long to be used as a complement.

**Pattern 3**

| **Subject** [That-clause/To inf. phrase] | **Linking Verb** [Intr. Verb] | **Adj./Adj. Phrase** |
|---|---|---|
| To go further | was | impossible. |
| That he is honest | sounds | right. |

**Note** '*It*' can also be introduced at the beginning bearing the same sense.

To go further is impossible = *It* is impossible to go further.

**Pattern 4**

| Subject | Linking Verb (Intr. Verb) | Adverb/Adv. Phrase |
|---|---|---|
| Sharmila | gets up | early. |
| Arnab | was driving | very fast. |
| The milk | is | in the refrigerator. |
| Shila | was swimming | in the pool yesterday. |

**Pattern 5**

| Subject | Linking Verb (Intr. Verb) | Prepositional Phrase |
|---|---|---|
| Preetam | is coming | to dinner. |
| Students | are complaining | about ragging. |
| We | can't rely | on your cousin. |
| Oil | doesn't mix | with water. |
| Meera | can't cope | with the extra visitors. |

**Note** Sometimes prepositions are omitted in the Prepositional Phrases.

| | | |
|---|---|---|
| The meeting | lasted | (for) two hours. |
| The sea beach | extends | (for) five miles. |

**Pattern 6**

| Subject | Linking Verb (Intr. Verb) | Non-finite Clause [to infinitive] |
|---|---|---|
| I | hesitated | to phone my boss. |
| We | longed | to have a family get-together. |
| They | wanted | to go away from the crowded city. |
| We | wouldn't care | to have a fight with him. |

**Pattern 7**

| Subject | Transitive Verb | Direct Object [Noun/Noun Phrase] |
|---|---|---|
| The company | paid | a fabulous sum. |
| I | was watching | television. |
| She | is reading | a novel. |
| Dhiren | doesn't owe | his parental property. |

**Pattern 8**

| Subject | Trans. Verb | Direct Object | Adv./Adv. Phrase |
|---|---|---|---|
| I | thought (over) | the plan | deeply. |
| They | opened | the debate | again. |
| He | drives | his workers | too hard. |
| She | was driving | the car | very fast. |

**Pattern 9**

| Subject | Trans. Verb | Direct Object | Prep. Phrase |
|---|---|---|---|
| She | confused | your name | with mine. |
| The Corporation | cleared | the pavements | of rubbish. |
| The teacher | referred | the student | to a passage in the textbook. |
| The visitor | thanked | the host | for his kind treatment. |

**Pattern 10**

| Subject | Trans. Verb | Direct Object [to-infinitive] |
|---|---|---|
| I | like | to do the household work myself. |
| He | likes | to get up early in the morning. |
| She | failed | to produce her testimonials. |
| They | want | to finish the job in a week. |
| Aparna | expects | to be promoted soon. |
| Deepayan | does not like | to drive in the rush-hour. |
| The children | need | to be looked after. |

**Pattern 11**

| Subject | Trans. Verb | Direct Object [Non-finite clause with Noun/Pronoun + to-infinitive] |
|---|---|---|
| The manager | likes | the staff to work properly. |
| Arpita | hates | her husband to lose his temper. |
| Kallol | wants | his friends to get ready for the picnic. |
| Tanmay | prefers | his wife (her) to manage the household work. |

**Note** Sometimes 'bare infinitive' (Infinitive without 'to') is used in this pattern : I saw the cat (to) steal the fish. I heard him (to) slam the door. She watched the boy (to) destroy the furniture.

**Pattern 12**

| Subject | Trans. Verb | Direct Object [Non-finite clause with *-ing*] |
|---|---|---|
| The servant | started | arguing. |
| Mini | likes | watering the garden. |
| Sourav | enjoys | playing cricket. |
| Their firm | will start | operating next month. |

**Pattern 13**

| Subject | Trans. Verb | Direct Object [Non-finite clause with Noun/Pronoun + (-ing form)] |
|---|---|---|
| I | hate | him doing such nonsense. |
| Mita | dislikes | her husband's talking over the business. |
| We | don't like | him interrupting our plan. |
| Mother | doesn't like | my reading late at night. |

**Pattern 14**

| Subject | Trans. Verb | Direct Object | Object Complement (Noun/Noun Phrase) |
|---|---|---|---|
| We | made | him | captain. |
| The Housing Society | declared | him | chairman. |
| The Committee | elected | him | secretary. |
| The court | considered | her | a trustworthy witness. |

**Pattern 15**

| Subject | Trans. Verb | Object | Obejct Complement [Adj./Adj. Phrase] |
|---|---|---|---|
| Nilu | has got | a tooth | loose. |
| Nilima | prefers | her coffee | black. |
| The president | declared | the meeting | closed. |
| The lecturer | made | the lesson | interesting. |
| We | imagined | her | much taller than that. |

**Pattern 16**

| Subject | Trans. Verb | Object | Object Complement [as + Noun Phrase/ Adj. Phrase] |
|---|---|---|---|
| We | could not accept | the story | as genuine. |
| Students | recognise | him | as a leading authority. |
| The cricket-lovers | regard | him | as a world-class player. |

**Pattern 17**

| Subject | Trans. Verb | Object | Object Complement [to-infinitive] |
|---|---|---|---|
| The police | forced | him | to hand over the money. |
| The Inspector | pressed | them | to answer his questions. |
| The Corporation | declared | the place | to be free from infection. |
| We | encouraged | her | to play the piano. |

**Pattern 18**

| Subject | Trans. Verb | Indirect Object | Direct Object [that clause] |
|---|---|---|---|
| Father | told | me | that I should not be careless. |
| They | informed | us | that the show had been postponed. |
| People | warned | the driver | that the road had been blocked. |

**Pattern 19**

| Subject | Trans. Verb | Indirect Object [to + noun (phrase)] | Direct Object [that clause] |
|---|---|---|---|
| The organiser | announced | to the audience | that the singer had been absent. |
| The manager | explained | to the workers | that the job wouldn't be very easy. |
| The workers | recommended | to the employer | that the new pay-scale should be introduced. |

**Pattern 20**

| Subject | Trans. Verb | Indirect Object | Direct Object [finite clause/non-finite clause] |
|---|---|---|---|
| Experience | has taught | him | whom he can trust/whom to trust. |
| The police | showed | the thief | how he could escape/how to escape. |
| The teacher | did not tell | us | whether we should bring the books/ whether to bring the books. |
| The director | explained | to the staff | how they should handle the job/how to handle the job. |

## APPLIED SECTION

**1. Pronouns used with the Verb 'be' (full and short forms) :**

| FULL FORM | | | SHORT FORM | | |
|---|---|---|---|---|---|
| **Person** | **Number** | **Pronoun & Verb** | **Person** | **Number** | **Pronoun & Verb** |
| 1st | Singular<br>Plural | I am (not)<br>We are (not) | 1st | Singular<br>Plural | I'm (not)<br>We're (not)<br>We aren't |
| 2nd | Singular<br>Plural | Yor are (not)<br>You are (not) | 2nd | Singular<br>Plural | You're/You aren't<br>You're/You aren't |
| 3rd | Singular<br><br>Plural | He/She is (not)<br>It is (not)<br>They are (not) | 3rd | Singular<br><br>Plural | He's/He isn't<br>She's/She isn't<br>It's/It isn't<br>They aren't<br>They're (not) |

**Past form :** 'was' with singular pronouns (I, He, She, It)
'were' with plural pronouns (We, They) and with You (both singular and plural)

**2. Pronouns used with the Verb 'have' (full and short forms) :**

| FULL FORM | | SHORT FORM | |
|---|---|---|---|
| I<br>We<br>You<br>They | have (not) | I<br>We<br>You<br>They | haven't/'ve (not) |
| He<br>She<br>It | has (not) | He<br>She<br>It | hasn't/'s (not) |

**Past form** = had (not) > hadn't

**3. Pronouns used with the Verb 'do' (full and short forms) :**

| FULL FORM | | SHORT FORM | |
|---|---|---|---|
| I<br>We<br>You<br>They | do (not) | I<br>We<br>You<br>They | don't |
| He<br>She<br>It | does (not) | He<br>She<br>It | doesn't |

**4. Persons with 'shall'/'will' :**

| FULL FORM | | SHORT FORM | |
|---|---|---|---|
| I<br>We | shall/will<br>shall (not) | I<br>We | 'll<br>won't |
| You<br>He<br>She<br>They<br>It | will (not) | You<br>They<br>He<br>She<br>It | 'll/won't |

**USE OF 'BE' :**

The verb **'be'** in the present form (am, is, are) is used in the following ways :

'Be' verb (am, is, are) :

**(i) Occupation/Trade/Profession :**

Mr. Roy is a teacher.
I am a student.
These men are carpenters.

**(ii) Age / Relationship :**

He is thirteen. I am twelve. Bina is Rina's sister.

**(iii) Nationality :**

We are Indians. They are Chinese. You are British.

**(iv) Qualities / description of condition etc. :**

Sudhir is a dull boy. Sanjib is intelligent. He is ambitious. They are hard-working. The weather is fine in February.

**(v) Size and shape :**

Mr. Pal is a fat and tall man. This table is rectangular.

**(vi) Place :**

My uncle is in Delhi now. The Taj Mahal is in Agra.

**(vii) Colour :**

Her hair is black. Grass is usually green.

**(viii) Condition :**

His father is not well. He is hungry. The situation is critical.

Be it hot or humid, the dress suits all well.

**Note that 'be' is one of the most common verbs in English. It states present facts/ truths.**

Now use the proper form of be + one of the words from the list to complete the sentences. Write the short from of be where possible. One has been done for you :

(i) I'm going to have some '*muri*' (puffed rice).
I am hungry/I'm hungry.

(ii) I'm going to bed. I .........

(iii) The sums ......... not very ......... You can do them if you .........

(iv) The clown makes us laugh. He ......... very .........

(v) Don't ask a child "What are you going to be?" It .... a .... question to ask a child.
List : hungry, difficult, sleepy, silly, careful, funny.

## AMERICAN STYLE OF 'GET' INSTEAD OF 'BE'

Sometimes we use 'Get' instead of 'Be' in the passive.

**Examples :**

I slipped in the bathroom and got my left leg broken. (= my left leg was broken)

There was a fight but nobody got hurt. (= nobody was hurt)

We can use 'Get' only when things happen or change (i.e. as the Event Verb).

We cannot use 'Get' in the following sentences (as the State Verb).

**Examples :**

He is liked by everybody. (not 'gets liked'—This is not a happening.)

We also use 'Get' in the following expressions. (They are not passive in the meaning.)

**Examples :**

Get ready. (= Be ready.)

Get dressed. (= Put on your clothes.)

Get changed. (= Change your clothes.)

Get married. (Or) He is getting married.

Get divorced. (Or) She is getting divorced.

We use 'Get' mainly in informal Spoken English. But we can use 'Be' in all situations.

## HAVE & HAVE TO :

Study the use of the verb 'have' in the following sentences :

(i) **'Have' with meals, food and drink :**

What do you usually have for breakfast? Do you have lunch at home at 12 noon? What shall we have for dinner?

(ii) **'Have' with bath, shower :**

I'm going to have a shower/bath.

(iii) **'Have' with relations :**

Nita has three brothers and one sister. She hasn't many friends here. How many children have they?

(iv) **'Have' or 'have got' with possessions :**

They have /have got their own house.

We have /have got a beautiful garden.

(v) **'Have' or 'have got' with physical or mental characteristics :**

Has she (got) blue eyes? (British usage)

Does she have black eyes? (American usage)

He hasn't a good memory.

(vi) **'Have to' for obligations : [have + to + any other verb]**

I have to go to school today. We have to listen to our teachers. To do good result you have to study hard.

**Now complete the sentences. One has been done for you :**

You can have a cup of tea.

You ........................................................ a cold drink.

You ........................................................ an idea.

You ........................................................ a lesson.

You ........................................................ an outing.

You ........................................................ a break during school hours.

You ........................................................ a good/bad/dull/happy time.

**Ask and answer :**

X : Has Amal (got) brothers?

Y : Yes, he has. He's got two brothers.

X : Has he (got) any sister(s)?

Y : No, he hasn't.

[He's = He has. He hasn't = He has not]

**Now answer the questions :**

$S_1$ : Does Biman have English on Tuesdays?

$S_2$ : ........................................................

$S_1$ : Does he have Bengali everyday ?

$S_2$ : ..............................................

$S_1$ : When does he see/watch a TV ?

$S_2$ : ........................................

## OTHER VERBS :

**The 'S' form (with do, go, play, sing etc.)**

It is used when the Subject is a singular noun or a pronoun—he, she, or it in the Simple Present Tense. It is never used with I, we, you, or they :

Lata does not go to school. She studies at home.

Rinki likes chocolate, but she does not take much.

Ramen plays football every afternoon.

### Ask and answer :

x : Does she practise computer daily?

y : Yes, she practises everyday./Yes, she does.

x : Does her sister sing in the evening?

y : No, she doesn't sing in the evening?/No, she doesn't.

**Note** Answers in the dialogue may be given in full form or in the short form. In the short form 'do' verb is used instead of any verb.

### Request etc.

**Make requests or give instructions with Intransitive Verbs :**

| Verb | Where |
|---|---|
| Go | there/to the blackboard. |
| Come | here/to my desk. |
| Walk | to the windows. |
| Jump | ...................... |
| Don't sit | on the chair. |
| Don't run | ...................... |
| Don't talk | ...................... |

**Make requests or give instructions with Transitive Verbs :**

| Verb | What/Whom (+ What) |
|---|---|
| Open | the door. |
| Bring | me your book. |
| Bail | the stump. |
| Clean | ...................... |
| Shut | ...................... |
| Show | ...................... |
| .......... | her my pen. |
| .......... | your pulse. |

| Verb | What | Where |
|---|---|---|
| Draw | a map | in your exercise-book. |
| Put | the book | ...................... |
| ......... | your name | ...................... |
| ......... | your bag | down on the floor. |
| Throw | ...................... | ...................... |

| Verb | What | to/from/for + whom |
|---|---|---|
| Give | the book | to Mr. Roy, please. |
| Take | the pencil | from your friend. |
| Bring | a glass of water | for me. |
| Pick up | the piece of chalk | ........................ |
| ......... | a letter | ........................ |

## EXERCISE

**1. Choose the correct alternative from the Auxiliaries :**

(a) I don't think I (shall, should, can) be able to go.

(b) He (shall, will, dare) not pay unless he is compelled.

(c) You (should, would, ought) be punctual.

(d) I wish you (should, would, must) be punctual.

(e) You (should, would, ought) to pay your debts.

(f) (Shall, Should, Would) you please help me with this?

(g) You (needn't, mustn't, won't) light a match; the room is full of gas.

(h) She (can, will, used to) play badminton before her marriage.

**2. Name the Verbs in the following sentences and say in each case whether the Verb is Auxiliary or Principal :**

(a) The hunter killed a tiger.

(b) Do you know the fact?

(c) He did a remarkable deed.

(d) She has passed the examination.

(e) He is an intelligent boy.

(f) He is now going to the playground.

(g) Don't laugh at the poor man.

**3. Name the Verbs in the following sentences and say in each case whether the Verb is Transitive or Intransitive. If the Verb is Transitive, name the Object :**

(a) The sun shines brightly.

(b) The fire burns dimly.

(c) The policeman blew his whistle.

(d) The wind is blowing hard.

(e) An old beggar stood by the gate.

(f) Her new watch does not keep correct time.

(g) I shall bring my camera with me.

(h) She has won a reward for an act of bravery.

(i) She easily lifted the heavy-weight.

(j) Sometimes a child can speak two languages fluently.

**4. Point out in the following sentences which Verbs are Finite and which are Non-finite :**

(a) Please teach me how to swim.

(b) We made him run in the field.

(c) She wants to go to Agra to visit the Taj Mahal.

(d) Putting a cap, he went to see the cricket match.

(e) It being a rainy day, we did not go out.

**5. Combine together the following pairs of sentences by using Infinitives :**

[**Example :** He had no money. He could not buy his textbooks. = He had no money to buy his textbooks.]

(a) Every cricket team has a captain. He directs the other players.

(b) His father went to Delhi. His object was to visit Rajghat.

(c) You must part with your purse. On this condition only you can save your money.

(d) The robber took out a knife. He intended to frighten the old man.

(e) He wants to earn his livelihood. He works hard for that reason.

(f) He has four children. He must provide them.

**6. Choose the best alternative of the State Verbs and Event Verbs and rewrite the sentences :**

(a) The soldier ........... (be/is/is being) angry and he ........... (shouts/is shouting/shouted) at his enemy.

(b) You should stop before you ........... (get/will get/are getting) into trouble.

(c) By the time he ........... (receives/will receive/will have received) this letter, I ........... (am/will be) in Japan.

(d) The population of the world ........... (increased/was increased/is increasing) and we must ........... (produced/produce) more food.

(e) This book ........... (belongs/is belonging) to me and you cannot ........... (demand/are demanding) it.

**7. Use the following functions of 'have to + verb', 'must/mustn't + verb', 'ought to + verb', 'can/could/couldn't + verb' and 'may/might + verb' in six other sentences in realistic contexts :**

[**Example :** One is done for you for each pattern.]

(a) The students <u>have to submit</u> the assignments within a week.

(b) The government <u>must do</u> something about the flood-affected people.

(c) You <u>mustn't tell</u> anyone what I said.

(d) He is really needy; you <u>ought to help</u> him.

(e) Fatima <u>could hear</u> the sound of music but she couldn't understand the lyric.

(f) You <u>might come</u> here earlier as it may rain today.

**8. What would you say in the following situations? Modals are given within brackets to help you :**

(a) You think that there is a possibility of rain today. (may)

(b) You think that the Indian team is able to beat Australia. (can)

(c) You are seeking permission to go out of the class for a while. (may)

(d) You are going to advise your brother not to watch TV for long hours. (should)

(e) You think that it is not necessary for your friend to wait for you. (need)

# 12  SYNTAX : SUBJECT-VERB AGREEMENT

## WHAT IS SYNTAX?

The Syntax is the rule of placing the Verbs in agreement with the Subjects in Number and Person.

**General rules :**

**'Be' Verb :** Different forms for Subjects in Persons and Numbers :

| | | | | | | | |
|---|---|---|---|---|---|---|---|
| 1st Person—I | am | We | are | I | was | We | were |
| 2nd Peson—You | are | You | are | You | were | You | were |
| 3rd Person—He | is | They | are | He | was | They | were |

**'Have' Verb :** No change except for Subject in 3rd Person Singular in Present Tense :

| | | | | | | | |
|---|---|---|---|---|---|---|---|
| 1st Person—I | have | We | have | I | had | We | had |
| 2nd Peson—You | have | You | have | You | had | You | had |
| 3rd Person—He | has | They | have | He | had | They | had |

**Other Verbs :** No change except for Subject in 3rd Person Singular in Simple Present Tense :

| | | | | | | | |
|---|---|---|---|---|---|---|---|
| 1st Person—I | do | We | do | I | did | We | did |
| 2nd Peson—You | do | You | do | You | did | You | did |
| 3rd Person—He | does | They | do | He | did | They | did |

**Now study some important Subject-Verb Agreement rules :**

1. **A Singular Subject takes the Verb in singular and a Plural Subject takes the Verb in plural.**
   There is a cat. There are three cats. They are happy.
   But a singular subject takes a plural verb in the subjunctive mood :
   If the story were true, what would it matter?
2. **An uncountable noun, though Plural in sense, takes a Verb in Singular form :**
   Her hair is grey. The grass is getting long.
3. **We can use the + Adjective with a Plural Verb to refer to some group of people in society :**
   The old are generally respected. The poor are not always dishonest.

4. **Two or more Singular Subjects connected by 'and' usually take a Verb in the Plural. When 'and' is followed by a negative word as 'no' or 'not', the Verb agrees with the word preceding 'no' or 'not' :**

Imran and Irfan are two brothers. He and his friend have arrived here.

I, and not my brother, have done this. Only boys, and not the girl, are guilty.

5. **If two Singular Nouns refer to the same person or thing, or two Subjects together express one idea, the verb must be Singular :**

The Captain and Manager of the team is coming. (The same person)

The Captain and the Manager of the team are coming. (Different persons)

**Note** One article for the same person and two articles for different persons.

Bread and butter is his favourite food. Slow but steady wins the race.

Early to bed and early to rise—makes a man healthy, wealthy and wise.

6. **Titles and names of Plural form also take a Singular Verb when they refer to one thing :**

'Seven Dwarfs' was a very successful film.

7. **A phrase of measurement, though Plural in form, takes a Singular Verb :**

Two hours is a long time to wait. Five miles is too far to walk.

8. **We use a Singular Verb after a Subejct with every, each, any, everyone, someone, anything and nothing :**

Every pupil has a book. Each boy was wicked. *Someone* is waiting at the door. Nothing happens in this place.

**Note** When 'each' follows a Plural Subejct, the Verb is Plural :

"The pupils each have to take a test."

Oxford Guide to English Grammar by John Eastwood

9. **If two or more Singular Subjects preceded by 'each' or 'every' are connected by 'and', the Verb is usually Singular :**

Each boy and each girl was dressed with a new dress.

Every man, woman and child *was* charmed.

Every man and woman of the village was present at the festival.

Every hour and minute brings its call for duty.

10. **Two or more Singular Subjects connected by 'or', 'nor', 'either...or', 'neither...nor' take a Verb in the Singular :**

The boy or the girl is fond of sweets. Either Amal or Bimal has eaten the mango. Neither you nor I was there.

11. **When the Subjects joined by 'or', 'nor', 'either...or', 'neither...nor' are of different numbers, the Plural Subject comes latter and the Verb must be Plural :**

Nikhil or his friends have done this work. Neither Akbar nor his brothers were hurt.

12. **When the Subjects joined by 'or', 'nor', 'either...or' 'neither...nor' are of different Persons, the Verb agrees in Person with the one nearest to it :**

Either he or I have done this. Neither you nor he is to blame. Either you or he or I shall go to market.

**Note** The order of placing Subjects of different Persons are : 2nd Person, 3rd person, 1st Person (i.e. 2-3-1). But in case of confessing faults, the order is reverse—1-3-2, i.e. 1st Person, 3rd Person, 2nd Person. However, in both the cases, the Verb agrees to the Person nearest to it :

You, he and I shall watch the TV tonight. (Statement)

I, he and you have done the mischief. Either I or you are to blame.

13. **When Subjects differing in Number or Person, or both, are connected by 'and', the Verb must always be in the Plural though the placing of Persons would be according to the above note :**

You, he and I are friends. You and he are birds of the same feather. You and I (not, I and you) would enjoy the TV.

14. **A Collective Noun takes a Singular Verb when it is thought of as a whole and takes a Plural Verb when the individuals are separately thought of :**

The army was defeated. Fifty rupees is enough for me. There is a large audience.

[But] The audience are requested to take their seats (separately).

The jury has ordered to hang the man.

[But] The jury are divided in their opinion.

The committee has agreed to take unanimous decision.

[But] The committee are divided in respect of details. The committee usually raise their hands to vote 'Yes'.

15. **A lot of/A group of/A number of :**

There is a lot of boys on the ground. (Collectively)

A lot of boys are playing in the field. (Separately)

[Thus] Here is a group of boys. A group of boys are enjoying a picnic.

There is a large number of boys in his class.

A number of boys were caught copying.—**Wren & Martin**

**Special Note** from **'Oxford Guide To English Grammar'.** **John Eastwood**

"When a plural noun follows *number of, majority of,* or *a lot of,* we normally use a plural verb.

*A large number of letters were received. The majority of people have complained. A lot of people have complained.*

Here *a number of* etc. expresses quantity.

(a) But, when *number* means 'figure', it agrees with the verb. The *number of letters* we receive is increasing.

(b) The word *amount* agrees with the verb. *A large amount of money was collected. Large amounts of money were* collected."

16. **Some Nouns which are Singular in form but Plural in meaning take a Plural Verb (These include police, people, staff, dozen etc.) :**

The police are questioning a man. [But] The policeman is watching outside the house.

People have to obey the law. The staff have come to this decision. Two dozen (not dozens) make twentyfour. One dozen of eggs cost thirty rupees.

17. **Some Nouns which are Plural in form but Singular in meaning take a Verb in Singular form :**

The news is true. The wages of sin is death. Physics is a branch of science. Politics is the business of his life.

A chemical works (factory) causes a lot of pollution.

[But] Chemical works (factories) cause a lot of pollution.

18. **Some Nouns are always Plural and take** a Verb in **plural form.**

These include belongings, clothes, congratulations, goods, earnings, savings, riches (= wealth), premises, particulars, stairs, surroundings, etc. :

The goods were found to be defective. My belongings have been destroyed. Riches (= wealth) have wings.

19. **When the Subject of a sentence is a Phrase** (i.e. a group of words), **the Verb must agree with the main Noun in the Subject group :**

The quality of the oranges is not good. (not *are*)

Many leading members of the opposition party have tried to justify the decision.

The only excuse that he gave for his actions was that he was tired.

20. **When a Plural Noun is placed with a real Singular Subject (** **one**, **each** etc.) **with the help of '*of*', the Verb must be Singular, not Plural.** In such cases, a Plural Verb is often wrongly used. *One of, each of, either of, neither of* etc. take a Verb in Singular form :

One of the boys was ill. (not were)

Each of the girls is clever. (not are)

Each of the rats was given a cake. (not were)

Either of the books is stolen. (not is)

Neither of the books was interesting. (not were)

The quality of the oranges is not good. (not are)

**Note** After 'None' and 'None but' we can use either a Singular or a Plural Verb :
'None of the pupils has/have failed the test.' **Eastwood**

"None is a shortened form of not one; yet it is commonly used with Plural Verbs." **Wren & Martin**

"None of them has (have) come back yet." **A.L.D.—Hornby**

"None but the brave deserves the fair." **Shakespeare.**

"None but fools (has) have ever believed it." —COD [Also, **Wren & Martin**]

'More than one' takes a Singular Verb; but 'More than two/three or more' takes a Plural Verb :

More than one boy is guilty. [But] More than two boys are guilty.

***Some Notes from 'Modern English Usage' by Fowler and 'Current English Usage' by F. T. Wood :***

(a) *More than one* is treated as compound of one and agrees with a singular noun and a singular verb. But, *More than two* is treated as a compound of two and agrees with a plural noun and a plural verb :

*More than one man was* present there.

*More than two men were* present there.

(b) *Half, heaps, lots, two-thirds, three-fourths,* etc. take singular verbs when they are followed by singular nouns with *of* but plural verbs when followed by plural nouns with *of* :

*One-fourth* water *is* mixed with *three-fourth* milk. *Half of* the work *is* done. *Half of* the apple *is rotten*. *Half* of the apples *are* bad. There *is lots* of work to do. *Lots* of people *think* so.

(c) After *one and a half* we use plural nouns and *singular verbs* : *One and a half* lemons *was* enough.

(d) *The greater/greatest part* is *singular* when it refers to *amount or quantity, plural* when it refers to *number* :

*The greater part* of the land *is* uncultivated.

*The greater part* of the apples *are* bad. **F. T. Wood**

(e) *None*—"It is a mistake to suppose that the pronoun (*None*) is singular only and must at all costs be followed by singular verbs, etc. The Oxford Dictionary explicitly states that plural construction is commoner." **MEU by Fowler**

*None* of the letters *have* been opened yet. (Plural, because, *none* has the meaning *'not any'*.) **CEU by F. T. Wood**

**21. When words are joined by 'with', 'together with' or 'as well as' etc. the Verb agrees with the first Subject :**

The Prime Minister with all the members of his cabinet has arrived. They with their father deserve praise. Bibha as well as her friends was punished. He, and not you, (used parenthetically), has won the prize. Mr. Smith together with some of his friends is buying some books.

**22. After but or not only ... but also, the Verb agrees with the nearest Subject :**

No sound but their own voices were heard.

Not only George but also his friends *are* buying books.

Not only the boys but also the teacher is watching the TV.

**23. When the Subject of the Verb is a Relative Pronoun, care should be taken to see that the Verb agrees in number and person with the antecedent of the Relative Pronoun :**

I who am your friend should stand by you.

He who is my friend should stand by me.

You who are my friend should stand by me.

This is the boy who is my friend. These are the boys who are my friends.

I am the man who has lost his cow. Those are the men who have lost their belongings.

**24. In referring to anybody, everybody, anyone, everyone, each etc., the Pronoun of the masculine or the feminine gender is used according to the context.**

I shall help each of the girls in her studies. Each of the boys will do his duty.

**But when the sex is not determined, we use the Pronoun of the masculine gender :**

Each must do his best. Anyone can do this if he likes. Everyone likes to have his way. If anybody knows the truth, let him tell it.

**25. The Indefinite Pronoun 'one' should be used throughout.**

One should be careful of one's (not his/her) duties.

One cannot be too careful about what one (not he) says.

**26. The case of a Pronoun following *than* or *as* is determined by the sense of the context and that can be done by mentally supplying the Verb in the given context :**

Ram's house is better than Jadu's (house). Or, Ram's house is better than that of Jadu. He is taller than I (am). I like you better than he (likes you). I like you better than (I like) him. They gave him as much as I (gave him). They gave him as much as (they gave) me.

"However, 'He is taller than me' is now accepted." **Wren & Martin**

**27. Many a/Many an before a Noun is Singular in form and the Verb is usually Singular :**

Many a rose is born to blush unseen. Many an admirer praised him.

**Note** But when **'A great many'/'A good many'/'Too many'** is used instead of 'Many a'/'Many an' it is Plural in form and the Verb is also Plural :

Too many cooks spoil the broth. A great many/ A good many boys were absent from the class.

**28. Pair Nouns :**

**A Pair Noun like trousers, glasses, scissors etc. is Plural in form and takes a Plural Verb :**

These trousers need cleaning. Your new glasses are very nice. Here are the scissors.

We cannot use "a or numbers" before the Pair Nouns.

"Not a trouser and Not two trousers."

We can use "pair(s) of" such Pair Nouns with a Singular or a Plural Verb.

This pair of trousers needs cleaning. How have three pairs of scissors managed to disappear? **John Eastwood**

**29. A single Auxiliary may serve two Principal Verbs if the construction allows it :**

I have lost the pen but (have) got the book.

[Common Auxiliary for the same Subject and same Tense.]

But when the Subjects and Tenses are different, Common Auxiliary will not serve the purpose :

You have retired, but your brother has resigned.

I have resigned and a new man has been appointed.

**30. A Clause or a Phrase as a Subject takes a Singular Verb :**

To err *is* human.

That he is honest *is* known to me.

## EXERCISE

**1. In each of the following sentences supply a Verb in agreement with its Subject :**

(i) One of the helicopters .............................................. missing.
(ii) No news .............................................. absolutely good news.
(iii) Neither of the girls ...................................... quite at her ease.
(iv) The jury .............................................. divided in their opinion.
(v) Each of the robbers .............................................. arrested.
(vi) Twenty rupees ..............................................too much for this article.
(vii) Two-thirds of the book .............................................. been lost.
(viii) Shakespeare is one of the greatest dramatists that .................ever lived.
(ix) Which one of these books .............................................. yours?
(x) Two tons of coal .............................................. here.
(xi) None of the boys ..............................................done the sum.
(xii) Iron as well as copper ..............................................found in India.
(xiii) The cost of all the necessary articles ...................................... risen.
(xiv) The chief with his followers .............................................. arrived.
(xv) 'The Arabian Nights' .............................delighted many generations.
(xvi) None of the girls ..............................................present in the class.
(xvii) There ...................................... a large number of boys in the field.
(xviii) A number of boys ..............................................found copying.
(xix) Here .............................................. a group of boys.
(xx) A group of boys ..............................................going on the road.

**2. Fill in the blanks :**

(i) Time and tide .............................................. for none.
(ii) Early to bed and early to rise .............a man healthy, wealthy and wise.
(iii) Each man and each woman ......................................given a prize.
(iv) I, and not my brother, .............................................. done this.
(v) No man, no woman and no child ...................................... saved.
(vi) Only men and no child ......................... allowed to enter the room.
(vii) Two books only and no pen ..............................................required.
(viii) Each boy and each girl .............................................. present.
(ix) He as well as his friends .............................................. guilty.
(x) The boys as well as their leader ............................... running away.
(xi) The king with his guards .............................................. been killed.
(xii) Mr. Roy, together with his children, ................buying some sweets.
(xiii) If I ...................................... a king, I would ban examinations.
(xiv) Either you or he .............................................. done this.
(xv) Neither life nor property .............................................. for ever.
(xvi) Either you or your friends .............................................. guilty.
(xvii) You are the man who .............................................. done this.
(xviii) The Headmaster and Secretary of the school ...................... coming.
(xix) Not only he but also his friends ..................................... come here.
(xx) One of the boys .............................................. a liar.

# 13  CONJUGATION OF VERBS

**There are two main kinds of Conjugation of Verbs**—the **strong** and the **weak**.

(i) The forms of Past Tense and Past Participle of the Strong Verbs are done by changing the inside vowel of the Present, as bear—bore—born.

(ii) The forms of Past Tense and Past Participle of the Weak Verbs are done by adding -d, -t. or -ed to the Present, as love—loved—loved; bend—bent—bent.

**Weak Verbs** are also called **Regular Verbs** as they are changed in a regular way and **Strong Verbs** are called **Irregular Verbs** as they are changed not in a regular way.

> Verbs that form their Past Tense by adding -ed, -d or -t to the Present, with or without any inside vowel-change, are called **Weak Verbs**.
>
> Verbs that form their Past Tense by merely changing the vowel in the body of the Present, without adding an ending are called **Strong Verbs**. **Wren & Martin**

## WEAK VERBS OR REGULAR VERBS

**Rule : verb + ed**

| Present Tense = Present (Base) Form | Past Tense = Past Form | Perfect Tense = has/have/had + Past Participle |
|---|---|---|
| add | added | added |
| allow | allowed | allowed |
| appear | appeared | appeared |
| ask | asked | asked |
| boil | boiled | boiled |
| borrow | borrowed | borrowed |
| cheer | cheered | cheered |
| clean | cleaned | cleaned |
| climb | climbed | climbed |
| delay | delayed | delayed |

| Present (Base) Form | Past Form | Past Participle |
|---|---|---|
| discuss | discussed | discussed |
| dream | dreamed/dreamt | dreamed/dreamt |
| end | ended | ended |
| enjoy | enjoyed | enjoyed |
| fail | failed | failed |
| fill | filled | filled |
| fix | fixed | fixed |
| flow | flowed | flowed |
| hang | hanged | hanged |
| help | helped | helped |
| jump | jumped | jumped |
| kill | killed | killed |
| laugh | laughed | laughed |
| load | loaded | loaded |
| lock | locked | locked |
| look | looked | looked |
| mend | mended | mended |
| need | needed | needed |
| obey | obeyed | obeyed |
| own | owned | owned |
| pass | passed | passed |
| paint | painted | painted |
| play | played | played |
| pull | pulled | pulled |
| push | pushed | pushed |
| punish | punished | punished |
| rain | rained | rained |
| reach | reached | reached |
| rear | reared | reared |
| sew | sewed | sewed |
| sow | sowed | sowed |
| show | showed | showed |
| spoil | spoiled | spoiled |
| stay | stayed | stayed |
| thank | thanked | thanked |
| thrive | thrived | thrived |
| wait | waited | waited |
| wash | washed | washed |
| wish | wished | wished |
| work | worked | worked |
| walk | walked | walked |

**Rule : Verb + d**

| Present (Base) Form | Past Form | Past Participle |
|---|---|---|
| agree | agreed | agreed |
| advise | advised | advised |
| arrive | arrived | arrived |
| arrange | arranged | arranged |
| care | cared | cared |
| change | changed | changed |
| charge | charged | charged |
| close | closed | closed |
| compare | compared | compared |
| compete | competed | competed |
| complete | completed | completed |
| dare | dared | dared |
| dance | danced | danced |
| die | died | died |
| divide | divided | divided |
| gaze | gazed | gazed |
| hate | hated | hated |
| hope | hoped | hoped |
| live | lived | lived |
| lie | lied | lied |
| loose | loosed | loosed |
| loosen | loosened | loosened |
| love | loved | loved |
| move | moved | moved |
| place | placed | placed |
| stroke | stroked | stroked |
| flee | fled | fled |
| have | had | had |
| hear | heard | heard |
| sell | sold | sold |
| tell | told | told |

**Rule : Doubling Consonant + ed**

| | | |
|---|---|---|
| beg | begged | begged |
| cancel | cancelled | cancelled |
| drop | dropped | dropped |
| hop | hopped | hopped |

| Present (Base) Form | Past Form | Past Participle |
|---|---|---|
| emit | emitted | emitted |
| nod | nodded | nodded |
| pat | patted | patted |
| plan | planned | planned |
| refer | referred | referred |
| rub | rubbed | rubbed |
| stop | stopped | stopped |
| travel | travelled | travelled |
| quarrel | quarrelled | quarrelled |

**Rule : y = i + ed/d**

| | | |
|---|---|---|
| bury | buried | buried |
| carry | carried | carried |
| cry | cried | cried |
| dry | dried | dried |
| fry | fried | fried |
| try | tried | tried |
| hurry | hurried | hurried |
| marry | married | married |
| lay | laid | laid |
| pay | paid | paid |
| say | said | said |
| [ **Exception :** enjoy | enjoyed | enjoyed ] |

**Rule : Past and Past Participle ending with 't'**

| | | |
|---|---|---|
| bend | bent | bent |
| build | built | built |
| burn | burnt | burnt |
| buy | bought | bought |
| catch | caught | caught |
| creep | crept | crept |
| fight | fought | fought |
| deal | dealt | dealt |
| dream | dreamt | dreamt |
| dwell | dwelt | dwelt |
| feel | felt | felt |
| keep | kept | kept |

| Present (Base) Form | Past Form | Past Participle |
|---|---|---|
| kneel | knelt | knelt |
| learn | learnt | learnt |
| leave | left | left |
| lend | lent | lent |
| lose | lost | lost |
| mean | meant | meant |
| seek | sought | sought |
| send | sent | sent |
| sleep | slept | slept |
| smell | smelt | smelt |
| spell | spelt | spelt |
| spit | spat | spat |
| spend | spent | spent |
| spoil | spoilt | spoilt |
| sweep | swept | swept |
| teach | taught | taught |
| think | thought | thought |
| weep | wept | wept |

## STRONG VERBS OR IRREGULAR VERBS

**Rule : Changing inside vowel**

| | | |
|---|---|---|
| abide | abode | abode |
| become | became | become |
| behold | beheld | beheld |
| bid | bade | bidden/bid |
| bite | bit | bitten/bit |
| bind | bound | bound |
| bleed | bled | bled |
| breed | bred | bred |
| chide | chid | chidden/chid |
| come | came | come |
| [But] welcome | welcomed | welcomed |
| dig | dug | dug |
| feed | fed | fed |
| fight | fought | fought |
| find | found | found |
| get | got | gotten/got |
| hide | hid | hidden/hid |

**Note** **'Welcome'** is also an **Adjective**. "You are **welcome** to it." As a **Noun**—"They gave us a warm **welcome**." "As a **Verb**—I **welcome** you to our house." As an **Interjection**—"**Welcome** to England!" **A.L.D.—Hornby**

| Present (Base) Form | Past Form | Past Participle |
|---|---|---|
| hold | held | held |
| make | made | made |
| meet | met | met |
| shoot | shot | shot |
| sit | sat | sat |
| stand | stood | stood |
| withhold | withheld | withheld |

**Rule : Past Participle ending with n/en**

| | | |
|---|---|---|
| arise | arose | arisen |
| awake | awoke | awoken |
| be (am, is, are) | was, were | been |
| bear | bore | born |
| bear | bore | borne (en > ne) |
| beat | beat | beaten |
| break | broke | broken |
| choose | chose | chosen |
| do | did | done |
| drive | drove | driven |
| eat | ate | eaten |
| fall | fell | fallen |
| forbid | forbade | forbidden |
| forgive | forgave | forgiven |
| forget | forgot | forgotten |
| forsake | forsook | forsaken |
| freeze | froze | frozen |
| give | gave | given |
| go | went | gone |
| lie | lay | lain |
| mistake | mistook | mistaken |
| ride | rode | ridden |
| rise | rose | risen |
| see | saw | seen |
| shake | shook | shaken |
| speak | spoke | spoken |
| shine | shone | shone |
| smite | smote | smitten |
| steal | stole | stolen |
| strive | strove | striven |
| swear | swore | sworn |
| take | took | taken |
| tear | tore | torn |

| Present (Base) Form | Past Form | Past Participle |
|---|---|---|
| thrive | throve | thriven |
| tread | trod | trodden |
| wake | woke | waken |
| wear | wore | worn |
| win | won | won |
| write | wrote | written |
| weave | wove | woven |
| **Rule : Past > e; Past Participle > n** | | |
| blow | blew | blown |
| draw | drew | drawn |
| fly | flew | flown |
| grow | grew | grown |
| know | knew | known |
| slay | slew | slain |
| throw | threw | thrown |
| withdraw | withdrew | withdrawn |
| **Rule : Past > a; Past Participle > u** | | |
| begin | began | begun |
| drink | drank | drunk |
| fling | flang | flung |
| ring | rang | rung |
| run | ran | run |
| sing | sang | sung |
| sink | sank | sunk/sunken |
| shrink | shrank | shrunk/shrunken |
| spring | sprang | sprung |
| swim | swam | swum |
| **Rule : Past > u; Past Participle > u** | | |
| cling | clung | clung |
| dig | dug | dug |
| hang | hung | hung |
| spin | spun | spun |
| stick | stuck | stuck |
| strike | struck | struck/striken |
| **Rule : Without any change** | | |
| bet | bet | bet |
| bid | bid | bid |
| burst | burst | burst |

| Present (Base) Form | Past Form | Past Participle |
|---|---|---|
| cast | cast | cast |
| cost | cost | cost |
| cut | cut | cut |
| hit | hit | hit |
| hurt | hurt | hurt |
| let | let | let |
| put | put | put |
| quit | quit | quit |
| read | read | read |
| set | set | set |
| shut | shut | shut |
| spread | spread | spread |
| thrust | thrust | thrust |
| broadcast | broadcast | broadcast |
| telecast | telecast | telecast |

**Verbs that are often confused**

| Present (Base) Form | Past Form | Past Participle |
|---|---|---|
| beat [strike] | beat | beaten |
| bite [tear with teeth] | bit | bitten/bit |
| bear [carry] | bore | borne |
| bear [bring forth] | bore | born |
| compete [contend] | competed | competed |
| complete [finish] | completed | completed |
| fall [drop down] | fell | fallen |
| feel [perceive] | felt | felt |
| fill [make full] | filled | filled |
| fail [be unsuccessful] | failed | failed |
| leave [abandon/depart] | left | left |
| live [exist] | lived | lived |
| lie [sleep/rest lengthwise] | lay | lain |
| lie [make false statement] | lied | lied |
| lay [place or set down] | laid | laid |
| loose/loosen [untie/relax] | loosed/loosened | loosed/loosened |
| lose [forfeit/miss] | lost | lost |
| raise [lift up] | raised | raised |
| rise [ascend] | rose | risen |
| sew [fasten with stitches] | sewed | sewed |
| sow [scatter seed/plant] | sowed | sowed/sown |
| show [exhibit/display] | showed | shown |
| strike [affect/beat] | struck | struck |
| stroke [knock/rub] | stroked | stroked |

## Spelling Rules of Verbs which have *-ing* forms

| Verb + '-ing' spelling rules | Examples | |
|---|---|---|
| (a) Single 'e' is omitted before '-ing : | come | coming |
| | give | giving |
| | have | having |
| | love | loving |
| | make | making |
| | write | writing |
| (b) Double 'e' is not omitted before '-ing' : | agree | agreeing |
| | see | seeing |
| (c) Consonant (after a vowel) becomes double when it is added with any suffix—'-ed', '-er', '-ing' : | bat | batting |
| In Past Tense : | beg | begging |
| beg + ed = begged, | get | getting |
| bat + ed = batted | run | running |
| | sit | sitting |
| In Continuous Tense & Verbal Nouns : | stop | stopping |
| beg + ing = begging | hop | hopping |
| run + ing = running | pat | patting |
| | admit | admitting |
| Also in forming Nouns : | begin | beginning |
| beg + er = beggar (e > a) | forbid | forbidding |
| run + er = runner | forget | forgetting |
| | refer | referring |
| | quarrel | quarrelling |
| | travel | travelling |
| (d) Consonant is not double if there is no stress on the last syllable : | listen | listening |
| | visit | visiting |
| | prohibit | prohibiting |
| | remember | remembering |
| (e) ie > y + ing | die | dying |
| | lie | lying |
| | tie | tying |
| (f) In most cases '-ing' is added without making any change : | be | being |
| | do | doing |
| | say | saying |
|  | fry | frying |
| | try | trying |
| | buy | buying |
| | keep | keeping |
| | stand | standing |
| | carry | carrying |
| | enjoy | enjoying |

## PRONUNCIATION NOTE

See **English Pronouncing Dictionary** by **D. L. Jones** or **Advanced Learner's Dictionary** by **A. S. Hornby** for correct pronunciation of Past and Past Participle forms of Verbs, especially **'-d'/'-ed'**. The symbols of pronunciation have been used here :

### Rule 1

| **If the last sound of the Verb is 'd'/'t'/'y'/'i'/'i:'** | | **ed = id** |
|---|---|---|
| **Present** | **Past** | **Past Participle** |
| aid (eid) | aided (eidid) | aided (eidid) |
| decide (disaid) | decided (disaidid) | decided (disaidid) |
| end (end) | ended (endid) | ended (endid) |
| mend (mend) | mended (mendid) | mended (mendid) |
| hate (heit) | hated (heitid) | hated (heitid) |
| paint (peint) | painted (peintid) | painted (peintid) |
| nod (nɔd) | nodded (nɔdid) | nodded (nɔdid) |
| start (sta:t) | started (sta:tid) | started (sta:tid) |
| enjoy (enzoi) | enjoyed (enzoid) | enjoyed (enzoid) |
| die (dai) | died (daid) | died (daid) |
| carry (kæri) | carried (kærid) | carried (kærid) |

### Rule 2

| **If the last sound of the Verb is 'k'/'p'/'f'/'s'/'sh'** | | **ed = t** |
|---|---|---|
| **Present** | **Past** | **Past Participle** |
| ask (a:sk) | asked (a:skt) | asked (a:skt) |
| kick (kik) | kicked (kikt) | kicked (kikt) |
| look (luk) | looked (lukt) | looked (lukt) |
| drop (drɔp) | dropped (drɔpt) | dropped (drɔpt) |
| help (help) | helped (helpt) | helped (helpt) |
| laugh (la:f) | laughed (la:ft) | laughed (la:ft) |
| pass (pa:s) | passed (pa:st) | passed (pa:st) |
| push (puʃ) | pushed (puʃt) | pushed (puʃt) |
| fix (fiks) | fixed (fikst) | fixed (fikst) |
| wash (wɔʃ) | washed (wɔʃt) | washed (wɔʃt) |
| wish (wiʃ) | wished (wiʃt) | wished (wiʃt) |

### Rule 3

| **If the last sound of the Verb is other than the two already mentioned** | | **ed = d** |
|---|---|---|
| **Present** | **Past** | **Past Participle** |
| allow (əlau) | allowed (əlaud) | allowed (əlaud) |
| boil (bɔil) | boiled (bɔild) | boiled (bɔild) |

| Present | Past | Past Participle |
|---|---|---|
| clean (klin) | cleaned (klind) | cleaned (klind) |
| climb (klaim) | climbed (klaimd) | climbed (klaimd) |
| close (kloz) | closed (klozd) | closed (klozd) |
| delay (dilei) | delayed (dileid) | delayed (dileid) |
| dance (dæns) | danced (dænsd) | danced (dænsd) |
| fail (feil) | failed (feild) | failed (feild) |
| fill (fil) | filled (fild) | filled (fild) |
| flow (flou) | flowed (floud) | flowed (floud) |
| play (plei) | played (pleid) | played (pleid) |
| pull (pul) | pulled (puld) | pulled (puld) |
| obey (obei) | obeyed (obeid) | obeyed (obeid) |
| love (lʌv) | loved (lʌvd) | loved (lʌvd) |
| move (muv) | moved (muvd) | moved (muvd) |
| rub (rʌb) | rubbed (rʌbd) | rubbed (rʌbd) |
| sow (sou) | sowed (soud) | sow (soud) |
| show (ʃou) | showed (ʃoud) | showed (ʃoud) |

## EXERCISE

**1. Write the following Verbs in Past and Past Participle forms.**

One has been done for you.

| Verb → Present | Past | Past Participle |
|---|---|---|
| add/adds | added | added |
| ask/asks | | |
| end/ends | | |
| fail/fails | | |
| fill/fills | | |
| feel/feels | | |
| help/helps | | |
| kill/kills | | |
| loose/looses | | |
| lose/loses | | |
| play/plays | | |
| reach/reaches | | |
| leave/leaves | | |
| live/lives | | |
| lie/lies | | |
| lay/lays | | |
| sew/sews | | |

| Verb → Present | Past | Past Participle |
|---|---|---|
| see/sees | | |
| sow/sows | | |
| show/shows | | |
| think/thinks | | |
| keep/keeps | | |
| put/puts | | |
| catch/catches | | |
| bind/binds | | |
| seek/seeks | | |
| hear/hears | | |
| tell/tells | | |
| say/says | | |
| cry/cries | | |
| sell/sells | | |
| bear/bears | | |
| try/tries | | |
| send/sends | | |
| sleep/sleeps | | |
| eat/eats |  | |
| bite/bites | | |
| beat/beats | | |
| learn/learns | | |
| teach/teaches | | |
| obey/obeys | | |

**2. Give the resulting forms of the following Verbs + ing in correct spelling with their meaning.**

One has been done for you.

| Verb + ing | Resulting Forms | Meaning |
|---|---|---|
| bite + ing | biting | tearing with teeth |
| come + ing | | |
| abide + ing | | |
| arise + ing | | |
| advise + ing | | |
| loose + ing | | |
| care + ing | | |
| change + ing | | |
| charge + ing | | |

| Verb + ing | Resulting Forms | Meaning |
|---|---|---|
| close + ing | | |
| compare + ing | | |
| compete + ing | | |
| complete + ing | | |
| dare + ing | | |
| dance + ing | | |
| die + ing | | |
| lie + ing | | |
| agree + ing | | |
| see + ing | | |
| be + ing | | |
| have + ing | | |
| give + ing | | |
| make + ing | | |
| take + ing | | |
| run + ing | | |
| sit + ing | | |
| get + ing | | |
| emit + ing | | |
| drop + ing | | |
| hop + ing | | |
| plan + ing | | |
| cancel + ing | | |
| travel + ing | | |
| quarrel + ing | | |
| cry + ing | | |
| play + ing | | |
| pay + ing | | |
| fly + ing | | |
| shake + ing | | |
| strike + ing | | |
| write + ing | | |

# 14  TIME AND TENSE WITH MOOD

## WHAT IS TENSE?

**Tense denotes the time of a verb or an action or state.**

[The word tense comes from the Latin tempus or time.]

TENSE → TIME OF ACTION or STATE

| | | | |
|---|---|---|---|
| **Action** | He does his homework. | → | Action of Present time |
| | He did his homework. | → | Action of Past time |
| | He will do his homework. | → | Action of Future time |
| **State** | He is very idle. | → | State of Present time |
| | He was very idle in his boyhood. | → | State of Past time |
| | He will be idle in his old age. | → | State of Future time |

We can organise an action or state mainly in three parts of time :

(i) **Present Tense** (ii) **Past Tense** (iii) **Future Tense**

He is reading.

He was reading.

He will read.

There are four different forms of each of the three main divisions :

(i) **Indefinite**, (ii) **Continuous**, (iii) **Perfect**, (iv) **Perfect Continuous**.

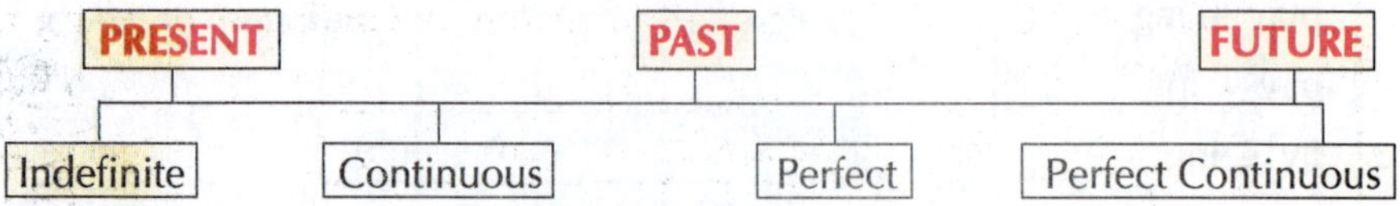


**Forms of Tenses**

| | | | | |
|---|---|---|---|---|
| **Present** | I do | I am doing | I have done | I have been doing |
| **Past** | I did | I was doing | I had done | I had been doing |
| **Future** | I shall do | I shall be doing | I shall have done | I shall have been doing |

## PRESENT INDEFINITE TENSE (SIMPLE PRESENT)

**Present Indefinite Tense** denotes an **action in the present time** or a **habitual truth**, a **historical truth** or an **eternal truth**.

**Subject + Verb (verb + s/es in case of Third Person Singular Subject)**

**General use :**

I read a book. We read books. You read a book (books). He/she reads a book. They read books.

**Habitual Truth :**

I get up early in the morning. My brother takes regular exercise every afternoon.

**Historical Truth :**

Raja Rammohun is the pioneer of modern India. Iswarchandra Vidyasagar is famous for his kindness.

**Eternal Truth :**

The sun rises in the east. Water freezes at 0° centigrade.

**Difference of 'Is to' and 'Has to/Have to' :**

It is wrong to suppose that 'is to' and 'has to/have to' mean the same thing. 'Is to' means 'It is settled' and 'has to/have to' means 'It is obligatory'.

He is to go there. (= It is settled that he will go.)

He has to go there. (= It is obligatory for him to go.)

We have to keep a record of the expenses. (Obligation)

**Different Forms of Simple Present :**

| Affirmative | Question | Negative |
|---|---|---|
| I write. | Do I write? | I do not write. |
| We write. | Do we write? | We do not write. |
| You write. | Do you write? | You do not write. |
| He/She writes. | Does he/she write? | He/She does not write. |
| They write. | Do they write? | They do not write. |

## PRESENT CONTINUOUS (PRESENT PROGRESSIVE)

**Present Continuous Tense** is used when an **action is continued** or going to be continued in near future :

**Subject + am/is/are + (verb + ing)**

I am reading a book. We are reading books. You are reading a book (books). He/She is reading a book. They are reading books.

**Near Future :**

My uncle is arriving here tomorrow. Are you coming to the meeting this afternoon?

**'going to' for near future :**

We are going to leave for Japan today. (near future)

I am going to Delhi tonight. (near future)

**These Verbs are not normally used in the Continuous form :**

(1) Verbs of perception, e.g., see, hear, smell, notice, recognize.

(2) Verbs of appearing, e.g., appear, look, red.

(3) Verbs of emotion, e.g., want, wish, desire, feel, like, love, hate, hope, refuse.

(4) Verbs of thinking, e.g., think, suppose, believe, agree, consider, trust, prefer, remember, forget, know, imagine, mean, mind, understand.

(5) Have (= possess), own, possess, belong to, contain, consist of, be (except when used in the passive).

So we must say "I see an aeroplane". (not "I am seeing an aeroplane.")

"What do you think of him?" (not "What are you thinking of him?")

"How do you feel now?" (not "How are you feeling now?")

"I feel quite well/rather tired/dizzy" etc. (not "I am feeling quite well" etc.)

"I feel her pulse." (not "I am feeling her pulse.")

**These Verbs may be used in the Continuous Tense with a change of meaning :**

I am seeing him tomorrow. (= I have an appointment with him.)

I am thinking of (= considering the idea of) going to America.

Mr. Ghosh is minding (= looking after) the baby as his wife is not at home.

Are you feeling better now? (Comparison)

**Different Forms of Present Continuous (Progressive) :**

| Affirmative | Question | Negative |
|---|---|---|
| I am writing. | Am I writing? | I am not writing. |
| We are writing. | Are we writing? | We are not writing. |
| You are writing. | Are you writing? | You are not writing. |
| He/She is writing. | Is he/she writing? | He/She is not writing. |
| They are writing. | Are they writing? | They are not writing. |

## PRESENT PERFECT TENSE

**Present Perfect Tense is used when the work has been done but its effect lasts.**

**Subject + has/have + (Past Participle of Verb)**

I have done the work. We have done the work. You have done the work. He/She has done the work. They have done the work. He has studied for hours. We have discussed this proposal in detail. I have followed their discussion with great interest.

**Just, already, since, for, yet are generally used with the Present Perfect**

They have just come here. He has already finished his homework.
I have often wished to learn music.

**Note 1** Present Perfect Tense is never used with adverbs of past time. We should not say, for example, "He has gone to Kolkata yesterday". In such cases the Simple Past Tense should be used "He went to Kolkata yesterday."

**Wren & Martin**

I received your letter yesterday. [not] I have received your letter yesterday.
He came here last Sunday. [not] He has come here last Sunday.

**Note 2** Sometimes Present Perfect Tense is used with '*after/when*' with the function of predicting a cause and effect sequence of events in the Simple Future Tense :

(a) **After he has finished** writing the letter, he **will post** it.

(b) **When she has got** the house **painted**, it **will look** nice.

**Different Forms of Present Perfect**

| Affirmative | Question | Negative |
|---|---|---|
| I have written. | Have I written? | I have not written. |
| We have written. | Have we written? | We have not written. |
| You have written. | Have you written? | You have not written. |
| He/She has written. | Has he/she written? | He/She has not written. |
| They have written. | Have they written? | They have not written. |

**Modals + Perfective**

**Could/may/might + Perfective** [to indicate a past possibility]

It may/might have rained last night. The cause of death could have been bacteria.

**Should + Perfective** [to indicate an obligation that did not occur]

John should have gone to the office. The police shouldn't have made such a bad report.

**Must + Perfective** [to indicate a logical conclusion in the past]

The grass is wet. It must have rained last night.

## PRESENT PERFECT CONTINUOUS TENSE

**The Present Perfect Continuous Tense** is used for an action which **began at some time in the past and is still continuing :**

**Subject + has been/have been + (verb + ing)**

I have been doing this work for two days. We have been living here for five years. He/She has been reading in this school for three years. Lipika has been waiting for you for a long time. Nilu has been suffering from fever since (from) Sunday last. It has been raining from (since) Monday last.]

**For, Since and From :** "Both (since and from) denote a point of time, not a space or period. But 'since' is preceded by a verb in some perfect tense, while 'from' can be used with any form of tense. Another difference is that 'since' can be used only in reference to past time, whereas 'from' can be used for present and future tense."
**Nesfield**

**Different Forms of Present Perfect Continuous :**

| Affirmative | Question | Negative |
|---|---|---|
| I have been working. | Have I been working? | I have not been working. |
| We have been working. | Have we been working? | We have not been working. |
| You have been working. | Have you been working? | You have not been working. |
| He/She has been working. | Has he/she been working. | He/She has not been working. |
| They have been working. | Have they been working? | They have not been working. |

## PAST INDEFINITE TENSE (SIMPLE PAST)

**Past Indefinite Tense** is used to denote **an action completed in the past** or **a past habit.**

**Subject + Past form of Verb**

I/We/You/He/She did the work. They did the work. He spent his boyhood in London. She began learning English since (from) the age of ten.

**Would/used to (For Habitual Past or Past Habit) :**

He would (used to) bathe in the river everyday. Apurba would (used to) play cricket every afternoon.

**Difference between 'used to' and 'would' :**

1. The servants used to tell them stories.
2. He would sit by the window and watch people at the pond.

The verbs in sentence 1 and 2 tell us about past habits.

But the first one is often used in writing and the second in speech.

Moreover these verbs express a discontinued habit :

"I used to ride a lot" means that "I rode a lot at one period of my life but that I do not ride a lot now." **A. J. Thomson and A. V. Martinet**

However, in a given context would/used to may not be repeated and simple past may also be used to denote past habits :

"He used to sit there and look out at the little pond. He watched the people come to bathe in the pond."

Simple Past may also be used with 'often', 'always', 'usually', 'regularly' etc. to denote past habits :

The servants usually looked after him. He watered the plants regularly.

**Different Forms of Simple Past :**

| Affirmative | Question | Negative |
|---|---|---|
| I played | Did I play? | I did not play. |
| We played | Did we play? | We did not play. |
| You played | Did you play? | You did not play. |
| He/She played | Did he/she play? | He/She did not play. |
| They played | Did they play? | They did not play. |

## PAST CONTINUOUS (PAST PROGRESSIVE)

**Past Continuous Tense** is used when the action was **continued for some time** in the past :

**Subject + was/were + (verb + ing)**

I was playing football. We were playing football. You were playing football. He/She was playing football. They were playing football. What was she doing last evening?

**Note** Past Progressive is often used together with a Simple Past when two clauses in the Past Tense are joined with 'when' or 'while'.

I saw you while you were playing in the field. It was raining when I reached home. When he was having his breakfast, I went to see him.

### Different Forms of Past Continuous :

| Affirmative | Question | Negative |
|---|---|---|
| I was playing | Was I playing? | I was not playing. |
| We were playing. | Were we playing? | We were not playing. |
| You were playing | Were you playing? | You were not playing. |
| He/She was playing | Was he/she playing? | He/She was not playing. |
| They were playing. | Were they playing? | They were not playing. |

## PAST PERFECT TENSE

**Past Perfect Tense** is used in **the former action between two completed actions of the past**. **Simple Past is used in the later action**.

**Subject + had + (Past Participle of Verb)**

Javed had gone before Nasir came home. She played her violin before the key-show started. The train had started before I reached the station. They had reached the school before the bell rang. I had shut the door before I got into bed. The patient had died before the doctor came. [Or] The doctor came after the patient had died. The doctor had come before the patient died. [Or] The patient died after the doctor had come.

### Past Perfect with 'When' :

I had done my exercise when Hari *came* to see me.

### Past Perfect with 'Hardly/Scarcely' :

In such case 'had' is placed just after 'Hardly/Scarcely'.

Hardly/Scarcely had we started when it began to rain.

[Or] We had hardly started when it began to rain.

### Past Perfect with 'No sooner...than' :

In such case 'had' is placed just after 'No sooner'. [Or, Simple Past—'No sooner did ...... than')

No sooner had we left the house than it began to rain.

[Or] No sooner did we leave the house than it began to rain.

### Different Forms of Past Perfect :

| Affirmative | Question | Negative |
|---|---|---|
| I had opened. | Had I opened? | I had not opened. |
| We had opened. | Had we opened? | We had not opened. |
| You had opened. | Had you opened? | You had not opened. |
| He/She had opened. | Had he/she opened? | He/She had not opened. |
| They had opened. | Had they opened? | They had not opened. |

## PAST PERFECT CONTINUOUS TENSE

**Past Perfect Continuous Tense** is used for **an action that began** before a certain point in the past **and continued up to that time**.

**Subject + had been + (verb + ing)**

We had been playing before the train started. She had been reading a novel when I went to meet her. At that time Robert had been writing a novel for two months. When I met the boy he had been crying for several hours. Your mother had been waiting for you when you went to your friend's house. Mr. Roy had been teaching there for five years. It was 10.a.m. and Jagjit was tired as he had been working since dawn.

**Differrent Forms of Past Perfect Continuous :**

| Affirmative | Question | Negative |
|---|---|---|
| I had been playing. | Had I been playing? | I had not been playing. |
| We had been playing. | Had we been playing? | We had not been playing. |
| You had been playing. | Had you been playing? | You had not been playing. |
| He/She had been playing. | Had he/she been playing? | He/She had not been playing. |
| They had been playing. | Had they been playing? | They had not been playing. |

## FUTURE INDEFINITE TENSE (SIMPLE FUTURE)

**Future Indefinite Tense** is used when an **action will be done** or will happen in future :

**Subject + shall / will + Verb**

I shall go to school. We shall go to school. You will go to school.
He/She will go to school. They will go to school.

**Note 1** Normally, 'shall' is used after 1st person and 'will' is used after 2nd and 3rd persons. But we use 'will' instead of 'shall', and 'shall' instead of 'will' when we talk about strong intention.

I will go to school. You shall not go to see the cinema show.
He shall do the work. They shall (= must) do the work.

**Note 2** When an action is planned or arranged to take place in the near future, Present Continuous Tense is used instead of Simple Future Tense :

My father is coming home tomorrow. I am going to the cinema this afternoon.

Simple Future Tense generally expresses pure or colourless future. When the future is coloured with intention, the ***going to + infinitive*** construction is preferred; e.g., He is *going to build* a new house.
But, I *shall see* him tomorrow. Tomorrow *will be* Sunday. **Wren & Martin**

**Different Forms of Future Indefinite (Simple Future) :**

| Affirmative | Question | Negative |
|---|---|---|
| I shall do. | Shall I do? | I shall not do. |
| We shall do. | Shall we do? | We shall not do. |
| You will do. | Will you do? | You will not do. |
| He/She will do. | Will he/she do? | He/She will not do. |
| They will do. | Will they do? | They will not do. |

## FUTURE CONTINUOUS TENSE

**Future Continuous Tense** is used when **an action** is thought **to be going on** in the future :

**Subject + shall be / will be + (verb + ing)**

I shall be doing the work. We shall be doing the work. You will be doing the work. He/She will be doing the work. They will be doing the work. I shall be reading the book when father comes. [Future Continuous with Simple Present]

**Different Forms of Future Continuous :**

| Affirmative | Question | Negative |
|---|---|---|
| I shall be doing.<br>We shall be doing.<br>You will be doing.<br>He/She will be doing.<br>They will be doing. | Shall I be doing?<br>Shall we be doing?<br>Will you be doing?<br>Will he/she be doing?<br>Will they be doing? | I shall not be doing.<br>We shall not be doing.<br>You will not be doing.<br>He/She will not be doing.<br>They will not be doing. |

## FUTURE PERFECT TENSE

**Future Perfect Tense** is used to indicate the completion of an action by a certain time in the future :

**Subject + shall have/will have + (Past Participle of Verb)**

I shall have written the letter by that time.
I shall have done the work before my father comes. Before you go to see him, he will have left the place. [Future Perfect with Simple Present]

**Different Forms of Future Perfect :**

| Affirmative | Question | Negative |
|---|---|---|
| I shall have done.<br>We shall have done.<br>You will have done.<br>He/She will have done.<br>They will have done. | Shall I have done?<br>Shall we have done?<br>Will you have done?<br>Will he/she have done?<br>Will they have done? | I shall have not done.<br>We shall have not done.<br>You will have not done.<br>He/She will have not done.<br>They will have not done. |

## FUTURE PERFECT CONTINUOUS TENSE

**Future Perfect Continuous Tense** is used when the doer will have been doing the work by a certain future time :

**Subject + shall have been/will have been + (verb + ing)**

By next July we shall have been living here for three years. I shall have been doing the work before my father comes. He will have been studying at Oxford before he gets his degree.

**Different Forms of Future Perfect Continuous :**

| Affirmative | Question | Negative |
|---|---|---|
| I shall've been doing.<br>We shall've been doing.<br>You will've been doing.<br>He/She will've been doing.<br>They will've been doing. | Shall I've been doing?<br>Shall we've been doing?<br>Will you've been doing?<br>Will he/she've been doing?<br>Will they've been doing? | I shall not have been doing.<br>We shall not have been doing.<br>You will not have been doing.<br>He/She will not have been doing.<br>They will not have been doing. |

# MOOD OF VERBS

## WHAT IS MOOD?

**A mood denotes the manner or way of using a Finite Verb in a sentence.**

The traditional grammar groups the Mood under three heads :

[i] **Indicative**, [ii] **Imperative**, [iii] **Subjunctive**

**Note** The traditional **Indicative Mood includes statement and interrogation.** Formerly the **Infinitive** also was called a Mood; but modern grammarians do not regard it as such, because it "merely names the action in an indefinite way, without reference to the mode or manner."

**However, Modern Grammar groups the Mood under four heads :**

**[1]** **Declarative**, **[2]** **Interrogative**, **[3]** **Imperative**, **[4]** **Subjunctive**.

### DECLARATIVE MOOD [ Making Statements ]

| Rules | | Examples |
|---|---|---|
| (i) To state a fact (affirmative or negative) (active or passive) | : | I go to school. He/She goes to school. He does not go to school. They went to school. It is done by me. It is not done by me. |
| (ii) To express an opinion | : | I think he is a scholar. It is good that you are here. |
| (iii) To make a promise | : | I must do it in time. |
| (iv) To put emphasis (by dummy 'do') | : | I do hereby authorise you. I did see her in the Coffee House. |
| (v) To express condition (or, supposition taken as a fact) | : | If it rains, I shall stay at home. If you come, I will go. |
| (vi) To ask a question to confirm something (beginning with a conjunction) | : | So you are satisfied? Then you think it is right? |

**Note** **Statements or Declarations usually end with a full stop (.).**

### INTERROGATIVE MOOD [Yes/No Questions and Wh Questions]

| Yes/No Questions | WH-questions |
|---|---|
| Are you well? | Who are you? |
| Is it true? | What is your name? |
| Have you found your book? | Which is your umbrella? |
| Do you like it? | Where are you going now? |
| Does he play cricket? | When will you come again? |

**Note 1** Wh-words are : Who, Whose, Whom, Which, What, When, Where, Why, How.

**Note 2** Verbs/Helping Verbs come before the Subject in Interrogative Mood.

**Note 3** 'Who, What, Which' do not take any Operator (Helping Verb) when they are used as the Subject. [ Who is he? What is your intention? ]

**Note 4** **Interrogative sentences always end with the question mark (?).**

## IMPERATIVE MOOD [Command, Request, etc.]

| Rules | | Examples |
|---|---|---|
| (i) To give orders/command | : | Come here. Go there. Stop talking. |
| (ii) To give force by putting 'you' in front of the verb | : | You shut up. |
| (iii) To give advice (exhortation) | : | Be steady. Be sensible. Don't be afraid of them. Try to do better. |
| (iv) To give instruction | : | Boil the egg for three minutes. Don't put your hand in boiling water. |
| (v) To give direction | : | Turn to the left first, then right, then go ahead. |
| (vi) To give warning | : | Stop talking or you will be punished. Look out. There is a snake. |
| (vii) To make request | : | Please open the door. Come in, please. |
| (viii) To make an offer/invitation | : | Have a cup of tea. |
| (ix) To put emphasis (by dummy 'do') | : | Do come on my birthday. |
| (x) To make a prayer/entreaty | : | Save me. Help! Help! Have pity on me. |
| (xi) To express supposition | : | Read and you will learn. |
| (xii) To express prohibition | : | Keep off the grass. |
| (xiii) Using 'Let' | : | Let me do this. Let him come. |

**Note** **The Imperative Mood** is used in the Present Tense, in the 2nd Person. The Subject of the verb **'You'** is usually **omitted**. The sentence **starts with the root Verb**. **'Let'** takes the Objective form of Pronouns of 1st and 3rd Persons, such as, Let me, Let us, Let him, Let them. The sentences in **Imperative Mood usually end with a full stop (.)**.

## SUBJUNCTIVE MOOD [Optative Sentences and Imaginary Condition]

The Subjunctive Mood may be divided into two groups :

[1] **Present Subjunctive**, [2] **Past Subjunctive**.

### PRESENT SUBJUNCTIVE

| Rules | | Examples |
|---|---|---|
| (i) To express wish or prayer | : | May you live long. May you be happy. |
| (ii) To express proposal or intention | : | Mind that the letter be written. It is resolved that his resignation be accepted. |
| (iii) In the subclause of condition | : | If that be the case, we are helpless. |

## PAST SUBJUNCTIVE

| Rules | | Examples |
|---|---|---|
| (i) After 'If' in imaginary condition | : | If I were you, I should not do that. |
| (ii) After 'wish' in imaginary situation | : | I wish it were Sunday. |
| | | I wish I knew her name. |
| (iii) After 'as if'/'as though' to indicate | : | She behaves as if she is a queen. |
| unreality or improbability | : | He walks as though he were drunk. |
| (iv) After 'would rather' + verb + subject | : | I would rather wish you went by air. |
| (to indicate preference) | | (vide **Wren & Martin**) |
| (v) After 'it is time' + subject | : | It is time we started. |
| (to imply that it is late) | | (vide **Wren & Martin**) |

## VERB PATTERN IN THE SUBJUNCTIVE MOOD

| Present Subjunctive | | Past Subjunctive | |
|---|---|---|---|
| **The verb 'be'** | **Other Verbs in Present Tense** | **The verb 'be'** | **Other Verbs in Past Tense** |
| I be | I write | I were | I wrote |
| We be | We write | We were | We wrote |
| You be | You write | You were | You wrote |
| He/She be | He/She write (not 'writes') | He/She were | He/She wrote |
| They be | They write | They were | They wrote |

**Note** The word 'Subjunctive' means 'subjoin', and so it is usually used in the sub-clauses. The sentences in Subjunctive Mood end with a full stop (.). However, the tendency of modern English is to discard the Subjunctive.

## APPLIED SECTION

### NOW STUDY THE USAGE OF TENSES :

**1. Simple Present is used in the following situations :**

(i) To express present actions or events or facts :

I get up at 6 a.m.
The train leaves at 7 p.m.
Leave your bed when the bugle sounds.
Lipika looks very beautiful.
Rabin goes to school.
I don't like tea, but I prefer coffee.

(ii) To express a habitual action :

I get up everyday at 6 a.m.
He takes milk every morning.
The elephant plays football in the circus.

(iii) To express a historical fact :

The Sepoy Mutiny of 1857 is a turning point in the history of freedom movement in India.

(iv) To express general truth or eternal truth :

The earth moves round the sun. Fortune favours the brave.

(v) In Imperative sentences :

Draw a straight line. Don't run in the sun.

Stop writing and hand over the answer-scripts.

(vi) In Exclamatory sentences beginning with here and there :

Here comes the bus! There goes the bell!

(vii) In quotations and reporting :

Keats says, "A thing of beauty is a joy for ever." (Quotation)

They tell me that you are a fool. (Reporting)

(viii) To indicate a future event that is a part of a present plan or arrangement :

They leave (are going to leave) for London by the next mail. His father sails for the Andamans next Sunday. When does the school reopen?

(ix) To use verbs of perception, verbs of appearing and verbs of emotion (see, hear, look, seem, feel etc.) :

I see, you are a fool. I hear the buzzing sound. You can't feel her sentiment.

(x) In clauses of time and condition :

I shall wait till you finish your lunch. If it rains we shall get wet.

**2. Present Progressive/Continuous is used in the following situations :**

(i) For an action going on at the time of speaking :

What is Lila doing now? (Interrogative)

Lila is dancing now. (Assertive)

Who are playing football? (Interrogative)

The boys are playing football. (Assertive)

The police are talking to a number of people. (Assertive)

(ii) Imagining an unseen activity :

I think Subhendu is lying in bed at home. His friends are doing Mathematics now.

(iii) For an action that is planned or arranged to take place in the near future :

Dipu and his friends are leaving Kolkata tonight.

Bela and her friends are arriving here tomorrow.

(iv) For giving information about a third person's whereabouts :

Where is Debika? She's (= she is) watering the plants in her garden.

(v) For explaining what one is doing :

What are you doing? I'm (= I am) drawing a picture.

(vi) For describing :

Which girl is Nipa? What is she wearing today?

She is slim and beautiful. She is wearing a white *sari* today.

**3. Present Perfect is used in the following situations :**

(i) To indicate a completed action in the immediate past :

He has just gone out. The clock has struck ten.

I have cut my finger and it is bleeding now.

(ii) To express past actions whose time is not definite :

Mr. Roy has been to Japan. I have never known him to be angry. Have you ever been to Delhi? Have you read 'Gulliver's Travels'? I have complained about this problem before. Sachin Tendulkar has broken the record of centuries in One-Day match.

(iii) To denote an action beginning at sometime past and continuing up to the present moment :

I have known him for a long time. We have lived here for ten years. We haven't seen Padmini for several months. He hasn't finished his work yet.

**Note** We see that these adverbs or adverbials can be used with the present perfect : just, often, so far, till now, already, since, for, never; ever (in questions only); yet (in negatives and questions).

(iv) To denote relation between what happened in the past and the present time :

I have found the letter you were looking for.

(v) To denote duration of event :

We have lived here for 5 years. Prices have fallen sharply over the past 6 months.

(vi) To denote that an action has been repeated a number of times :

He has visited Bhutan several times.

**4. Present Perfect Continuous is used :**

(i) For an action which began sometime in the past and is still continuing :

She has been sleeping for six hours. He has been playing since 4 p.m.

They have been building the bridge for several years.

**Note** This tense is sometimes used for an action already finished. In such cases the continuity of the activity is emphasized as an explanation of something.

"Why are your clothes wet?"—'I have been watering the plants.'

(ii) When we ask questions with 'How long' and get answers thereof :

How long have you been waiting for me?

I have been waiting for you for an hour.

(iii) To focus the recent activity with its present results :

Your eyes are red—have you been crying? (= recently stopped)

**5. Simple Past is used in the following situations :**

(i) To talk about a past event as a simple fact of time. It often occurs with adverbs or adverb phrases :

Haradhan left school last year. The steamer sailed a week ago.

I received his letter yesterday.

(ii) Sometimes without an adverb of time. In such cases, the time may be either implied or indicated by the context :

I didn't sleep well. (i.e. last night)

'Where did he learn Hindi?'

'He learnt Hindi in Patna.' (i.e. in sometime past)

(iii) Simple Past is also used with 'used to/would' for past habits.

He used to study many hours everyday.

My grandmother would bathe in the Ganga in her old age.

She always carried (= would carry) an umbrella.

**Note** 'Used to' is very often used in writing and 'would' in speech.

(iv) For situations that existed for a period of time in the past but not now :

The Mughals ruled here for several hundred years.

When I was younger, I played cricket for my school team.

(v) To talk about how long something went on :

How long did you live here?

I stayed here with my grandparents for 3 months.

(vi) To ask questions about a past action :

When did you arrive here? Did she reach the hostel in time?

**6. Past Continuous is used in the following situations :**

(i) To talk about any continuing process of doing something in the past :

The train was late and they were waiting at the station for three hours.

(ii) To describe a background action :

X. What were you doing in the evening yesterday?

Y. I was listening to the radio all evening.

X. You took a long time to answer the phone.

Were you sleeping?

Y. Yes, I was (sleeping).

(iii) To denote a temporary situation at or around a particular time in the past :

At the time of robbery, she was staying with her uncle.

She was shaking with fear when they turned away.

(iv) When we talk about two past actions going on at the same in past :

I was watching the TV while my sister was reading a novel.

**7. Past Perfect is used in the following situations :**

(i) To describe an action completed before a certain moment in the past :

I met him in New Delhi in 2005. I had seen him last four years ago.

(ii) If two actions happened in the past, it may be necessary to show which action happened earlier than the other. The past perfect is mainly used in such situations :

I had written the letter before she arrived. I had wanted to visit the office before I left for foreign tour.

(iii) To denote a time expression with by the time, when, etc. :

I had gone to bed when the phone rang.

The film had already begun by the time we got into the cinema.

**8. Past Perfect Continuous is used in the following ways :**

(i) To express an action that continued in the past for a given period of time :

At that time he had been reading a novel for two weeks. We had been expecting the news for some time.

(ii) To express a Past Perfect Continuous and a Simple Past with when :

He had been suffering from flu when he was interviewed.

(iii) To ask questions with 'How long' and get answers thereof :

How long had you been travelling here?

I had been travelling here for two months.

**9. Ways of talking about the Future :**

There are four different ways to talk about the near future :

(i) by using going to, (ii) by using Present Continuous, (iii) by using Simple Present, (iv) by using will, 'll, won't, shall.

Look at this table. They give the same facts :

| Mr. Roy | (i) is going to leave<br>(ii) is leaving<br>(iii) leaves<br>(iv) will leave | tomorrow morning. |
|---|---|---|

**Note** Such type of future is coloured with intention or arrangement.

But to express pure or colourless future we use only Simple Future Tense (shall/will + verb).

**10. Simple Future is used in the following situations :**

(i) To talk about simply to some future event :

I shall do this work. We shall enjoy life together. I'll have my dinner at 9 pm tonight. They will meet us in the hotel. There won't be any ceremonial party this year as we've lost a member of the club. They will not admit children under five. Will he come back this evening?

(ii) If two future actions are joined by when, the one will be in the Future Tense (any form) and the other will be in Simple Present Tense :

I shall leave the place when she comes. She will do it when you come.

**Note** Sometimes Simple Future Tense is used with a Simple Present Tense :

Don't worry, I'll get it.

**11. Future Continuous is used in the following situations :**

(i) When we talk about an activity going on at a particular time in future :

Next Thursday, we will be celebrating our Dipu's birthday.

(ii) To talk about near future :

We will be leaving for Mumbai tonight.

(iii) To refer to some future activities previously arranged :

She will be helping us to organise the party. We will be joining you at night.

(iv) To ask someone politely about the immediate future :

Will/Would you be using the computer for long?

**12. Future Perfect Tense is used in the following situations :**

(i) To denote something that will be ended in future :

We shall have finished our task before the sun sets. They will have reached school before the rain starts.

(ii) To denote the completion of some events in the past before starting an event in future :

We hope the situation will have improved before we reach there.

(iii) To describe the future events in less cartain way :

By the time you get home, I will/should have cleaned the house.

**13. Future Perfect Continuous Tense is used in the following situations :**

(i) To denote an activity by a certain future time :

He will have been studying in London when he gets his degree.

(ii) To emphasize how long something could be going on over a period of time in future :

Next year, he will have been researching at JNU for three years.

## INFINITIVE AFTER 'ABOUT'

'**About**' denotes '**about to do**'.

He was about to go to school. The rose was about to bloom but did not bloom.

## PERFECT INFINITIVE

When the action expressed by the Infinitive is regarded as completed, the Perfect Aspect of the Infinitive is used.

He seems to have acted properly. They seem to have forgotten to come here.

## SOME IMPORTANT USAGES

He came here yesterday. (not 'has come')

The president made (delivered ) a nice speech. (not 'gave')

His brother will not appear at (sit for) the examination. (not 'will not give')

He refused to come. (not 'denied')

He denied his guilt. (not 'refused')

We declined his invitation. (not 'denied')

He has come to see me. (not 'for seeing me')

He will stay in Kolkata for five days. (not 'live')

We live in Kolkata. (not 'stay')

Will you listen to his advice? (not 'hear')

They are mistaken. (not 'have mistaken')

The man was drowned in the river. (not 'sank')

The boat sank in the river. (not 'drowned')

## EXERCISE

**1. Fill in the blanks with the correct form of tense of the Verbs given in brackets :**

(i) The earth...........(move) round the sun and the sun...........(give) us light.

(ii) He always...........(buy) lottery tickets but never...........(win) any prize.

(iii) Are you...........(go) to school now?

(iv) Have you...........(do) your homework?
(v) I have...........(know) him for several years.
(vi) I...........(get) your letter yesterday.
(vii) He...........(come) here last Sunday.
(viii) She...........(not buy) anything from the shopkeeper.
(ix) I...........(wash) my hands when the telephone rang.
(x) I shall telephone you when she...........(come) back.

**2. Choose the correct Verb form from those in brackets :**

(i) He..........when my uncle entered the room.
(was studying, has studied, had studied)

(ii) I must stay here because I.................a parcel.
(have expected, expect, am expecting).

(iii) I see the price of petrol...........up again recently.
(was gone, has gone, went)

(iv) The kites...........in the sky before it started raining.
(flew, were flying, had flown, had been flying)

(v) I..........for a suitable job before I got this one.
(looked, had been looking, was looking)

**3. Complete the following passages with the correct forms of Verbs given within brackets :**

(a) While I...........(walk) back home yesterday, someone...........(snatch) the bag from my hand and...........(run) away. The police...........(not catch) him yet. I ...........(wonder) how such things...........(happen) nowadays.

(b) Every particle of matter...........(attract) or...........(pull) every other particle. That...........(be) the law of gravitation. The sun...........(attract) the earth and the earth, in turn,...........(attract) the moon.

(c) We...........(expect) him here yesterday. He...........(not come) till today. No one...........(know) what...........(happen) to him. Perhaps he...........(reach) here tomorrow. You...........(see) him then.

**4. Complete these sentences with the following Verbs. Use the Simple Present for one and the Present Continuous for the other :**

(i) Have :
We usually...........dinner at about 10 p.m.
I...........a birthday party on Friday. Are you free?

(ii) Do :
Biltu always...........his homework as soon as he goes to school. Today he ...........his homework before going to school.

(iii) See :
Dipika...........her brother off at the railway station this afternoon. Now I ...........what she means.

(iv) Get :
Tuhina has been thoroughly drenched. I think, she...........a cold. She ...........colds in the rainy season.

(v) Speak :
Bipin.........Bengali well, but no Hindi. He.........to his friend. Let's wait for him.

**5. Use the following Verb patterns in realistic communicative functions :**

(a) Present Perfect with 'after/when' with the function of predicting a cause and effect sequence of events in the future.

..................................................................................................................

..................................................................................................................

(b) Past Perfect with 'before/after/when' with the function of describing a sequence of events.

..................................................................................................................

..................................................................................................................

**6. Use the appropriate future Verb forms to complete the following conversations :**

(i) **At the ticket counter** [go, get, arrive, save, take, travel]

Passenger : Could you help me? I...........to Delhi tomorrow.

Can you tell me when the Delhi Mail...........in?

Booking Clerk : Let me see. You...........it early in the morning.

It...........about eleven hours.

Passenger : What about the Rajdhani Express?

Booking Clerk : That's a faster train. You.........at least four hours of your time.

Passenger : Then I.......not by the Delhi Mail. I.......by the Rajdhani Express.

(ii) **Offering help** [be, call, give]

Abdul : I don't feel quite well today.

Ayesha : ......................in a doctor?

Abdul : No, I think I......all right.......you......me a cup of coffee please?

Ayesha : Certainly. Do you take sugar?

Abdul : Yes, one spoon. (= one spoonful)

(iii) **A letter from the landlord** [sell, do, find, write, be]

Man : Look at this letter from the landlord. He...........this house.

Wife : But what...........we...........? We have nowhere to go. Where ...........we...........a place to live in?

Man : Don't worry. We...........a place. I...........to my friend. He ...........able to help us.

**7. Indicate the Moods of the Verbs in the following sentences :**

(i) We eat that we may live. (ii) I would help you if you needed. (iii) Stand up on the bench. (iv) Sit down, please. (v) Do not make a noise. (vi) I warn you lest you should fail. (vii) Listen to me or you will be punished. (viii) Touch it and you die. (ix) Work hard and you will succeed. (x) I wish that I were there.

**8. Now complete the following tables. One has been done for you :**

### Simple Present & Simple Past

| | | | |
|---|---|---|---|
| **1st person** | I | do the work. | did the work. |
| | We | .............................. | .............................. |
| **2nd person** | You | do the work. | did the work. |
| **3rd person** | Ram | does the work. | did the work. |
| | Lila | .............................. | .............................. |
| | He | .............................. | .............................. |
| | She | .............................. | .............................. |
| | They | .............................. | .............................. |

### Present Continuous & Past Continuous

| | | | |
|---|---|---|---|
| **1st person** | I | am doing the work. | was doing the work. |
| | We | .............................. | .............................. |
| **2nd person** | You | .............................. | .............................. |
| **3rd person** | Madhu | .............................. | .............................. |
| | Bina | .............................. | .............................. |
| | He | .............................. | .............................. |
| | She | .............................. | .............................. |
| | They | .............................. | .............................. |

### Present Perfect & Past Perfect

| | | | |
|---|---|---|---|
| **1st person** | I | have done the work. | had done the work. |
| | We | .............................. | .............................. |
| **2nd person** | You | .............................. | .............................. |
| **3rd person** | Debu | .............................. | .............................. |
| | Mini | .............................. | .............................. |
| | He | .............................. | .............................. |
| | She | .............................. | .............................. |
| | They | .............................. | .............................. |

### Simple Future

| | | |
|---|---|---|
| **1st person** | I | shall do the work. |
| | We | ................................................................ |
| **2nd person** | You | ................................................................ |
| **3rd person** | Shibu | ................................................................ |
| | Shila | ................................................................ |
| | He | ................................................................ |
| | She | ................................................................ |
| | They | ................................................................ |

Now take some other Verbs and complete such tables.

**9. Make questions for the given statements using different tenses as required :**

**Simple Present :**

He teaches Economics.

Who ........................................................................................ ?

Wha ........................................................................................ ?

The sun shines by day.

When ........................................................................................ ?

I leave office at 5 p.m.

When.......................... you ........................................................ ?

The US forces now lead their men to Iraq.

Where ........................................................................................ ?

**Present Continuous :**

I am attending my class.

What.........................you ........................................................ ?

They are reading books in the class.

What ........................................................................................ ?

Sourav is taking part in the game.

Who ........................................................................................ ?

The police are talking to a number of people here.

Who ........................................................................................ ?

What ........................................................................................ ?

**Present Perfect :**

I have complained about this problem before.

Who ........................................................................................ ?

Soumen has slipped in the bathroom and got his leg broken.

Who ........................................................................................ ?

Tendulkar has broken the record of centuries in One-Day match.

Who ........................................................................................ ?

I have found the letter in your drawer.

Where.............................you ........................................................ ?

**Present Perfect Continuous :**

The Japanese concern have been building the flyover for a few years.

Who ........................................................................................ ?

She has been learning French for one year.

How long ........................................................................................ ?

We have been working in this company for two years.

How long......................... you ................................................ ?

It has been raining all night.

How long ........................................................................................ ?

**Simple Past :**

I received this letter yesterday.

When..........................you ........................................................?

My cousin decided to continue the course.

Who ................................................................................?

He learnt Kannad at Bangalore.

Where ..............................................................................?

We stayed with our grandparents for a few days.

How long..........................you ..............................................?

**Past Continuous :**

Rahul was shaking with anger when he was punished.

Who ................................................................................?

People were working round the clock.

Were ...............................................................................?

I was reading a newspaper while my brother was watching TV.

Who ................................................................................?

He was working in a hotel when I was living in Mumbai.

Where ..............................................................................?

**Past Perfect :**

He found out that Sunita had lied to him.

Who ..................................................................... to you?

I had gone to bed when the phone rang.

Who ................................................................................?

**Past Perfect Continuous :**

I had been finishing some work in the garden.

What ...............................................................................?

We had been expecting the news for some time.

Who ................................................................................?

**Simple Future :**

I shall meet you in the hotel.

Where..........................you ........................................... me?

He will come back this evening.

When ...............................................................................?

**Future Continuous :**

Prof. Bose will be delivering his lecture at the conference.

Who ................................................................................?

An international delegation will be meeting us shortly.

Who ................................................................................?

Next Friday, we will be celebrating our sister's birthday.

When ...............................................................................?

**Future Perfect :**

I shall have received the award by next year.

Will ................................................................................................ ?

They will have finished their task before the sun sets.

When ................................................................................................ ?

**Future Perfect Continuous :**

I shall have been painting a landscape till Sunday morning.

What ................................................................................................ ?

They will have been working here for five years.

How long ................................................................................................ ?

**10. Write down the answers using different tenses as required :**

**Simple Present : [Structure : Base Verb only (Verb + '–s/–es')**

Do you write a letter?

Yes, ................................................................................................ .

No, ................................................................................................ .

Does he read any newspaper?

Yes, ................................................................................................ .

No, ................................................................................................ .

**Present Continuous : [Structure : am/is/are + (Verb + ing)**

What is your sister doing now?

She ................................................................................................ .

Who are playing cricket in the field?

The boys ................................................................................................ .

**Present Perfect : [Structure : has/have + Past Participle]**

Hasn't he attended the class?

Yes, ................................................................................................ .

No, ................................................................................................ .

Has the farmer sown the seed in the field?

Yes, ................................................................................................ .

No, ................................................................................................ .

Have the students noticed your presence?

Yes, ................................................................................................ .

No, ................................................................................................ .

Haven't you seen the 'Jurassic Park'?

Yes, ................................................................................................ .

No, ................................................................................................ .

**Present Perfect Continuous : [Structure : has been/have been + (Verb + ing)]**

How long have you been waiting for me?

I ................................................................................................ for you.

How long have you been learning English?

I ................................................................................................ .

Haven't foreign companies been putting a lot of money in Indian industry?

Yes, ................................................................................................ .

No, ................................................................................................ .

**Simple Past : [Structure : Past Form of Verb]**

When did you arrive here?

I ............................................................................................ .

Did you read the newspaper yesterday?

Yes, ..................................................................................... .

No, ...................................................................................... .

**Past Continuous : [Structure : was/were + (Verb + ing)]**

Was Bill driving his car very fast?

Yes, ..................................................................................... .

No, ...................................................................................... .

Where were they staying at the time of robbery?

They .................................................................................... .

**Past Perfect : [Structure : had + Past Participle]**

When had he finished his work?

He ....................................................................................... .

Had they performed well in the competition?

Yes, ..................................................................................... .

No, ...................................................................................... .

**Past Perfect Continuous : [Structure : had been + (Verb + ing)]**

What had your teachers been planning for you?

Our teachers ......................................................................... .

What had you been doing when the teacher entered the class?

I/we ...................................................................................... .

**Simple Future : [Structure : shall/will + Verb]**

Who will answer my questions?

I ............................................................................................ .

Where will you go now?

I/We ...................................................................................... .

Who will be helping us to organise the party?

Mithun ................................................................................... .

**Future Perfect : [Structure : shall have/will have + Past Participle]**

Will you have finished your homework by the evening?

Yes, ..................................................................................... .

No, ...................................................................................... .

When will they have consulted their family physician?

They .................................................................................... .

**Future Perfect Continuous : [Structure : shall have been/will have been + (Verb + ing)]**

What will you have been doing next Sunday?

I/we ...................................................................................... .

# 15 VERBAL NOUN, GERUND AND PARTICIPLE

## VERBAL NOUN

**"A verbal noun is noun and nothing more."—Nesfield**

**All Verbal Nouns are not Gerunds, but all Gerunds are Verbal Nouns.**

**A Verbal Noun is formed in two ways :**

(i) **by adding suffixes**, e.g., refuse + al = refusal; accept + ance = acceptance; judge + ment = judgement/judgment etc.

[Judgement/judgment; acknowledgement/acknowledgment—Both forms are correct.—**C.O.D.**]

(ii) **by adding -ing**, e.g., love + ing = loving; sleep + ing = sleeping; walk + ing = walking etc.

Now read the following sentences :

I like the reading of Geography. (Here 'reading' is a Verbal Noun formed from the Verb 'read')

A Verbal Noun is preceded by **'the'** and followed by **'of'** and it is a single part of speech having the force of a Noun only.

## GERUND

I like reading Geography—[Here 'reading' is a double part of speech—"A noun and verb combined." Hence, in the sentnce 'I like reading Geography' 'reading' is a 'Gerund'.

**A Gerund is that form of the Verb which ends in '-ing' and has the force of a Noun and a Verb.** Wren & Martin

**A Gerund is a double part of speech—a noun and verb combined.** Nesfield

## USE OF THE GERUND

A Gerund, being a verb-noun, may be used as :

[1] **Subject of a verb :**

Smoking is a bad habit.

Swimming is a good exercise.

Sleeping is necessary to life.

[2] **Object of a verb** :

He gave up smoking.

We enjoyed swimming in the river.

He enjoyed sleeping in the open air.

[3] **Complement of a verb** :

One of his bad habits is smoking.

What he likes best is fishing.

His constant habit was sleeping.

[4] **Object of a preposition** :

He gave up the habit of smoking.

May I request the favour of your granting me leave of absence?

On hearing the noise, the children rushed out of the school gate.

He was rebuked for swimming in a dirty pond.

He is tired of sleeping over hours.

He is fond of reading novels.

I think of retiring soon from service.

We are looking forward to seeing you again. ALD—**Hornby**

[5] **As a Compound Noun** : Walking stick ( = a stick for walking), a frying pan (= a pan for frying), a swimming costume (= a costume for swimming).

**Note** When a Gerund is preceded by a noun or a pronoun, it must be in the possessive form (Karim's, my, your, etc.) as the Gerund is, finally, a noun :

I hope you will excuse my leaving early. (correct)

I hope you will excuse me leaving early. (incorrect)

Remember, therefore, to use the **possessive case of nouns and pronouns before Gerunds** :

All depends on Urmila's passing the examination.

We rejoiced at her being promoted.

I ask the favour of your granting my prayer.

I insist on your being present there.

We left the place without anyone's knowing.

## GERUND AND INFINITIVE

As both the Gerund and the Infinitive have the force of a Noun and Verb, they have the same uses. Thus in many sentences either of them may be used without any special difference in meaning. **Wren & Martin**

**Note** In Modern Grammar the difference between Simple Infinitive and Gerundial Infinitive is not stressed as both of them may be transformed into a Gerund.

| Infinitive | Gerund |
|---|---|
| To walk is good for health. | Walking is good for health. |
| To find fault is easy. | Finding fault is easy. |
| He likes to play cards. | He likes playing cards. |
| We eat to live. | We eat for living. |

## PARTICIPLE

A **Participle** is that form of the Verb which is partly a Verb and partly an Adjective. **Wren & Martin**

A Participle is a **double part of speech**—a Verb and Adjective combined. **Nesfield**

## USE OF THE PARTICIPLE

Let us now see the uses of the Participle :

**PRESENT PARTICIPLE (Verb + ing) :**

[1] **A Participle can qualify a Noun** :

A rolling stone gathers no moss.

Don't try to get into a running train.

A blooming flower is beautiful to look at.

Don't put your hand in boiling water.

[The participles *rolling*, *running*, *blooming* and *boiling*, qualify the nouns *stone*, *train*, *flower* and *water*.]

[2] **Like an Adjective it can admit of degrees of comparison** :

Primary Education is the most pressing need of our time.

[The participle 'pressing' admits the degree of comparison by preceding 'most'.]

[3] **It may govern a Noun or a Pronoun** :

Hearing the noise, the boy woke up. [The noun 'noise' is governed by the participle 'hearing'.]

Seeing him fall from the tree, I rushed towards him.

[The pronoun 'him' is governed by the participle 'seeing'.]

[4] **It may be modified by an Adverb** :

Loudly knocking at the gate, he asked admission.

[The participle 'knocking' is modified by the adverb 'loudly'.]

All the above examples of Participles end in -ing and represent an action as going on. Hence this is called **Present Participle**.

**PAST PARTICIPLE (-d/-ed/-t/-n/-en) :**

Besides the **Present Participle**, there is another form of Participle called **Past Participle** which represents a completed action :

Deceived by his friends, he lost all hope.

Blinded by a dust-storm, they lost their way.

Driven by hunger, he stole a piece of bread.

The frightened child began to cry.

We saw the trees laden with fruit.

It is already widely circulated.

**PERFECT PARTICIPLE (Having + Past Participle)**

There may be a combined Participle (Present Participle + Past Participle) called Perfect Participle. It may be in the Active Voice or in the Passive Voice.

Having rested a while, we continued our journey. [Active Voice]

Having been notified by the court, he appeared before the judge. [Passive Voice]

**Note** [i] **Present Participle** with **Continuous Tenses** of the Verb **'Be'** :

I am doing the work. I was doing the work. I shall be doing the work.

[ii] Past Participle with Perfect Tenses of the Verb 'Have' :
I have loved. I had loved. I shall have loved.

[iii] Past Participle in the Passive Voice with tenses of Verb 'Be' :
I am loved. I was loved. I shall be loved.

[iv] Like an Adjective, a Participle may be modified by an Adverb :
We saw the man in an almost dying state.

[v] Like an Adjective, a Participle may have degrees of comparison :
I am more interested in the matter than you (are).
This is the most surprising news.

**Participles may qualify Nouns or Pronouns in the following ways :**

[i] Attributively (as an Adjective of a Noun) :
A rolling stone gathers no moss. A lost opportunity never returns. His tattered coat needs mending.

[ii] Predicatively (as a Predicate after Verb) :
The man seems worried. He kept me waiting.

[iii] Absolutely as a Nominative Absolute :

Nominative Absolute is such a Participial phrase whose Subject is different from that of the main part of the sentence, while the Subjects may be the same in case of other Perfect Participles.

The sun having risen, the fog dispersed. The fog having dispersed, the soldiers marched. The weather being fine, I went out.

## DIFFERENCES OF GERUND AND PRESENT PARTICIPLE

| Gerund | Participle |
|---|---|
| He is fond of playing cricket. | Playing cricket, he spent much time. |
| The old man is tired of walking. | Walking along the road, the old man is tired. |
| I don't like laughing so loud. | They went away laughing. |

## DIFFERENCES OF PRESENT PARTICIPLE AND GERUND (AS A COMPOUND NOUN)

| Present Participle (Verbal Adj.) | Gerund (Compound Noun) |
|---|---|
| A dancing girl. | A dancing hall. |
| A sleeping tiger. | A sleeping room. |
| A travelling party. | A travelling dress. |
| A swimming boy. | A swimming costume. |

## DIFFERENCES OF PARTICIPLE AND NOMINATIVE ABSOLUTE

| Participle | Nominative Absolute |
|---|---|
| Rising (Having risen) from bed he came out of the room. | The sun having risen, we began our march. |
| Being tired, he took rest for a while. | The match being over, they left the place. |

## ERRORS IN THE USE OF PARTICIPLES

As the Participle is a verb-adjective, it must be attached to some Noun or Pronoun. In other words, it must always have a proper 'subject-object' reference.

The following sentences are **incorrect** because in each case the Participle is left without **proper subject agreement** :

Being a very hot day, I remained in my tent. (incorrect)

It being a very hot day, I remained in my tent. (correct—Nom. Absolute)

Sitting on the gate, the teacher rebuked him. (incorrect)

Sitting on the gate, he was rebuked by the teacher. (correct)

Entering the room, the light was quite dazzling. (incorrect)

Entering the room, I found the light quite dazzling. (correct)

I saw a dead cow walking in the field. (incorrect)

I saw a dead cow while I was walking in the field. (correct)

[Or] While walking in the field, I saw a dead cow. (correct)

However, when there is no such confusion, usage permits such construction where the participle is left without a proper 'subject of reference' :

Frankly speaking, he is not fit for the job.

[Frankly speaking = If one speaks frankly.]

Roughly speaking, the post office is two miles away from here.

Considering his abilities, he should have done better.

Taking everything into consideration, the Magistrate was perfectly justified in issuing the verdict.

## EXERCISE

**1. Pick out the Gerunds and Participles in the following sentences :**

(i) I cannot go on doing nothing.
(ii) They found him playing in the garden.
(iii) We heard of his coming back today.
(iv) He prefers playing football to studying his lessons.
(v) Did you hear of his having won a prize?
(vi) They spend the afternoon in playing cards.
(vii) The boy was ashamed of being beaten in the class.
(viii) Walking on the grass is forbidden.
(ix) Hearing the noise she ran to the window.
(x) We saw a clown standing on his head.
(xi) The miser spends his time in hoarding money.
(xii) He has ruined his sight by reading small print.
(xiii) Praising all alike is praising none.
(xiv) Jumping over the fence, the thief escaped.
(xv) Asking questions is easier than answering them.

**2. Pick out the Participle in each of the following sentences and tell whether it is a Present Participle or a Past Participle :**

(i) I saw the storm approaching.
(ii) Having gained the truth, keep the truth.

(iii) Being disgusted, he resigned his position.

(iv) The rain came pouring down in torrents.

(v) The traveller, being weary, sat by the woodside to rest.

(vi) Generally speaking, we receive what we deserve.

(vii) Seizing by the arm, his friend led him away.

**3. Combine the following pairs of sentences by the use of a Participle. A few have been done for you :**

(i) We started early. We arrived in time. = Starting early, we arrived in time.

(ii) The gatekeeper opened the gate. We entered. = The gatekeeper having opened the gate, we entered.

(iii) We met a man. He was carrying a basket.

(iv) The hunter took up a gun. He went out to shoot the tiger.

(v) The girl was charmed to see the printed *sari*. She purchased it.

(vi) I had resolved on a certain course. I acted with vigour.

(vii) The steamer was delayed by a storm. So the steamer came late.

(viii) The letter was badly written. I had troubles in making out its contents.

**4. Rewrite the following sentences by changing the Participles into a Finite Verb. A few have been done for you :**

(i) Hearing the noise, I turned round. = As I heard the noise, I turned round.

(ii) Leaving the forest, we advanced into the open path. = We left the forest and we advanced into the open path.

(iii) Walking up to the front door, I rang the bell.

(iv) Mounting his horse, the robber rode away.

(v) Not knowing the way, he asked a policeman.

(vi) Walking on the roof, she slipped and fell to the ground.

(vii) I once saw a girl walking on a tight-rope.

(viii) Having no guide with us, we lost our way.

(ix) Winter coming on, the grasshopper had no food.

(x) Having failed in the first attempt, he made no further attempts.

**5. (a) Use Present Participles and Gerund and write some phrases in your own English. Here are some examples of Present Participles :**

[Present Participle (Verb + Adjective)]

A smiling face. The rising sun. The dying declaration.

[Gerund as a Compound Noun]

Living wages. A walking stick.

**(b) Write out some short sentences in your own English using Present Participles. Some have been done for you :**

Do not jump from a running train. The fishing boat capsized. I found him crying with pain. Just have a look at the sweet smile of the Divine Mother in the blooming flowers.

(c) **Write out some short sentences using Present Participles or Perfect Participles. Some have been done for you :**

Turning back, he called me. Having done the work, we went to play. He prevented the telegram being sent.

(d) **Write some phrases using Past Participles. Here are some examples of Past Participles :**

Sunken eyes. A deserted village. A bare-footed boy.

An out-spoken man. A ruined temple.

(e) **Write some short sentences using Past Participle. Here are some examples for you :**

At last we had to return with a broken heart.

He is so tired that he cannot walk.

I had the building constructed by two engineers.

**Note** that a Past Participle may be used attributively, predicatively and in passive voice.

(f) **Use the Gerunds and write some short sentences in your own English. Some have been done for you :**

It is worth buying. The girl burst out crying. Everybody is fond of being praised.

(g) **Use the Verbal Nouns and write some short sentences in your own English. Some have been done for you :**

Attention please. What is the cause of such poor attendance? I am now engaged in the reading of a novel.

# 16 MORE ABOUT ADVERBS AND ADVERBIALS

## WHAT IS AN ADVERB AND WHAT ARE ITS FUNCTIONS ?

**Read the following sentences and note the functions of Adverbs.**

1. An Adverb can modify a verb :
   The fox runs quickly. [quickly modifies runs, a verb]
2. An Adverb can modify an adjective :
   Lila is a very beautiful girl. [very modifies beautiful, an adjective]
3. An Adverb can modify another adverb :
   She sings extremely well. [extremely modifies well, an adverb]
4. An Adverb can modify a preposition :
   The bird flew exactly over our head. [exactly modifies over, a preposition]
5. An Adverb can modify a conjunction :
   I dislike him simply because he is a liar. [simply modifies because, a conjunction ]
6. An Adverb can modify a determiner :
   He has hardly any friends. [hardly modifies any, a determiner]
7. An Adverb can modify a phrase :
   The machine is completely out of order. [completely modifies a phrase 'out of order']
8. An Adverb can modify a whole sentence :
   Unfortunately, he could not continue his studies. [unfortunately modifies the whole sentence]

**An Adverb is a word used to qualify any Part of Speech except a Noun or Pronoun.** **J. C. Nesfield**

**An Adverb is a word which modifies the meaning of a Verb, an Adjective or another Adverb.** **Wren & Martin**

From the above-noted examples we can realise :

**An Adverb is a word used to modify any Part of Speech (except a Noun or Pronoun), or a whole sentence.** **P. C. Das**

**Note** As a general rule, an Adjective qualifies a Noun or a Pronoun, but some grammarians think that, in some exceptional cases, an Adverb may also modify a Noun or a Pronoun.

Even Rabindranath praised Saratchandra. (Even modifies Rabindranath—a noun)

Only he dared to enter the fire. (Only modifies he—a pronoun)

However, in our opinion, **these Adverbs modify a whole sentence** as the force of the Adverb 'even' is laid upon not only 'Rabindranath', the Noun, as the Subject, but also 'praised', the Verb of the sentence; similarly, the force of the Adverb 'only' is laid upon not only 'he', the Pronoun, as the Subject, but also 'enter', the Verb of the sentence.

**Note for Advanced Learners :**

The **Pocket Oxford Dictionary** gives an example of 'only' as an Adverb in the sentence "Only you, or, you only can guess." Some grammarians think that the word 'only' seems to qualify 'you' as an Adjective as the above-noted sentence means "You alone and none else, can guess". In a well-known book of English Grammar (by P. K. De Sarkar) we find the sentence "Only he promised to read the first chapter of the book", where 'only' is parsed as an Adjective qualifying the pronoun 'he'.

In such a context the Manager of the Oxford University Press opines "In the sentence 'Only you are to blame' one can paraphrase 'only' as 'solely' and, in such a context, 'solely' is clearly an adverb. Yet, equally obviously, it refers to and qualifies or modifies 'you'. It becomes clear, therefore, that to say that an adverb cannot qualify a pronoun (?) is to take too narrow a view. No doubt the current view that an adverb cannot do so has been taken over from Greek and Latin." A further discussion of the way in which adverbs may qualify pronouns may be found in **Advanced English Syntax** by **Onions** and the Syntax Volume of **Sweet's New English Grammar**.

**However, we may come to a logical conclusion that the Adverbs *even, only* etc. can modify a whole sentence as their force is laid upon not only the Noun or Pronoun, but also the Verb covering the whole sentence.**

## USES OF ADVERBS

Adverbs can be used in three ways :

**1. Attributive Adverb**

An Adverb is used attributively when it qualifies another word after it :

He did this work very badly. She shouted very loudly. It is entirely wrong.

**2. Predicative Adverb**

An Adverb is used Predicatively when, being placed in the Predicate part, qualifies 'It' in the Subject part and there is no other word after the Adverb to qualify or modify :

It is here. It is there. It is everywhere.

**3. Introductory Adverb**

When 'There' or 'Here' is placed at the beginning of a sentence as an introductory word, it is called Introductory Adverb :

There is no cloud in the sky. There are many boys in this class. There stands a house by the river. Here is a man waiting for you. Here is a telephone call for him.

**4. Adverb Particles**

Some Prepositions, such as, in, out, up, above, below, inside, outside, within, without, etc. may be used as Adverb. These are called '**Adverb Particles**' :

He raised his hands up. May I come in?

## KINDS OF ADVERBS

Adverbs are divided into three main categories.

ADVERB

Simple Adverb | Relative Adverb | Interrogative Adverb

### [A] SIMPLE ADVERBS

**Simple Adverbs are of eight kinds :** 1. Adverb of Time 2. Adverb of Place 3. Adverb of Manner 4. Adverb of Degree 5. Adverb of Reason or Purpose 6. Adverb of Affirmation and Negation 7. Intensifiers 8. Downtoners

**1. Time**

**When?** The train arrived late.
He came here yesterday.
**How long?** He seldom plays cricket.
Dhiraj frequently goes to Delhi.
**How often?** I have told you twice.

[**Such Adverbs are :** Now, then, before, since, ago, already, always, seldom, often, once, twice, thrice, again, soon, late, afterwards, yesterday, today, tomorrow, daily, early, formerly, frequently, presently, immediately, instantly etc.]

**2. Place**

**Where?** Stand here.
Go there.
Come in.
Is Mr. Das within?
The horse galloped away.
**Wherefrom?** This news has been collected locally.

[**Such Adverbs are :** Here, there, hither, thither, hence, thence, far, near, nearby, away, abroad, ahead, overhead, inland, locally, universally etc.]

**3. Manner**

**How?** Bhola reads clearly.
The child slept soundly.

The tortoise walks slowly.
The soldiers fought bravely.
**In what manner?** The boy has been badly treated.

[**Such Adverbs are :** Clearly, closely, correctly, bravely, badly, sadly, softly, steadily, slowly, soundly, swiftly, simply, suddenly, carefully, carelessly, easily, quickly, possibly, probably, luckily, fortunately, unfortunately, naturally, rightly, urgently, wrongly, widely, thus, well, etc.]

**4. Number**

**How many?** I take tea once a day.
He comes here twice a week.

**5. Degree**

**How much?** He is fully prepared.
He is good enough for his duties.
She is quite happy.
The fruit is almost ripe.
You are partly right.
**To what Extent?** I am rather busy.

[**Such Adverbs are :** Almost, quite, very, much, fully, partly, wholly, completely, strongly, totally, entirely, deeply, greatly, poorly, half, enough, somewhat, altogether, too, little, a little, rather etc.]

6. **Reason or Purpose**
   - **Reason**
     - He therefore left the school.
     - He is hence unable to deny it.
     - He is ill so he cannot go to school.
   - **Purpose**
     - He works hard so that he can succeed.

[**Such Adverbs are :** Hence, therefore, so, so that etc.]

7. **Affirmation and Negation**
   - **Affirmation**
     - Yes, I know him.
   - **Negation**
     - I do not know him.
     - I have never heard it.

[**Such Adverbs are :** Yes, not, never, etc. However, 'no' is an Adjective. He has no enemy etc.]

8. **Condition & Contrast**
   - **Condition** If you come, I'll go.
   - **Contrast** Although/Though he is rich, he is unhappy.

9. **Intensifier**
   - He would certainly go there.
   - Surely it is a pickpocket.
   - I really don't know.

[Such Adverbs intensify or emphasise the action of the Verb. These are : actually, certainly, surely, definitely, really, absolutely, thoroughly, utterly, very much, indeed etc.]

10. **Downtoner**
    - This is somewhat wrong.
    - I can hardly see it.
    - This soup is rather hot.

[Such Adverbs downtone the action of the verb. These are : hardly, barely, scarcely, nearly, rather etc.]

## [B] RELATIVE ADVERB & CONJUNCTIVE ADVERB

The Relative Adverb joins two sentences together and shows its relation to its antecedent expressed or understood.

A Relative Adverb is called Conjunctive Adverb when its antecedent is omitted.

A Relative Adverb makes a Relative Clause. But a Conjunctive Adverb makes an Adverbial Clause or a Noun Clause.

Do you know the man who came here last night? (Antecedent 'man') [Relative Clause with Relative Adverb 'who']

**Antecedent expressed**

- Show me the house where he was born.
  (Antecedent 'house') [Relative Clause with Relative Adverb 'where']
- Do you know the time when the Rajdhani Express arrives?
  (Antecedent 'time') [Relative Clause with Relative Adverb 'when']
- This is the reason why he left the meeting. (Antecedent 'reason')
  [Relative Clause with Relative Adverb 'why']

**Antecedent omitted**

- You may go where you like. ( Antecedent 'place' omitted)
  [Adverbial Clause with Conjunctive Adverb 'where']
- We shall go when he comes. ( Antecedent 'time' omitted)
  [Adverbial Clause with Conjunctive Adverb 'when']
- I do not know why he left the meeting. ( Antecedent 'reason' omitted)
  [Noun Clause with Conjunctive Adverb 'why']
- We do not know how it is done. ( Antecedent 'process' omitted)
  [Noun Clause with Conjunctive Adverb 'how']

A Relative Adverb, like a Relative Pronoun, relates or refers back to its Antecedent.
**Wren & Martin**

Such Relative Adverbs are always placed inside a sentence, and not at the beginning of a sentence.
**P. C. Das**

**'The' as a Relative Adverb :** 'The' is sometimes used as a Relative Adverb which is always followed by another Adverb of comparative degree :

The sooner, the better. The more they have, the more they want.

**[C] INTERROGATIVE ADVERBS** [For Wh-Questions]

When Adverbs are used in asking questions, they are called Interrogative Adverbs :

| | | | |
|---|---|---|---|
| Interrogative | Adverb | of Place | : Where is Rahman? |
| " | " | of Time | : When did he come? |
| " | " | of Reason | : Why are you late? |
| " | " | of Manner | : How did he do this? |
| " | " | of Number | : How many boys are there? |
| " | " | of Quantity | : How much milk would you take? |
| " | " | of Frequency | : How often are the pups born? |
| " | " | of Degree | : How far was the report true? |

[**Remember :** *Who, whose, whom, which* and *what* are Interrogative Pronouns. But *where, when, why, how, how many, how much, how often, how far, how long, how high* etc. are Interrogative Adverbs.]

## FORMATION OF ADVERBS

(i) Some words are **Basically Adverbs.**

These Adverbs are :

| | | | | | | | |
|---|---|---|---|---|---|---|---|
| ago | fast | often | rather | today | already | very | too |
| almost | late | once | seldom | yesterday | before | well | thus |
| afterwards | much | only | since | tomorrow | then | here | enough |
| always | now | quiet | soon | tonight | early | there | everywhere |

(ii) **Most of the Adverbs** are formed by adding **-ly** to an **Adjective** :

| Adjectives | + ly | Adverbs |
|---|---|---|
| bad | ly | badly |
| sad | ly | sadly |
| brave | ly | bravely |
| hard | ly | hardly |
| honest | ly | honestly |
| kind | ly | kindly |
| cruel | ly | cruelly |
| clever | ly | cleverly |
| certain | ly | certainly |
| clear | ly | clearly |

| Adjectives | + ly | Adverbs |
|---|---|---|
| correct | ly | correctly |
| quick | ly | quickly |
| quiet | ly | quietly |
| loud | ly | loudly |
| local | ly | locally |
| great | ly | greatly |
| soft | ly | softly |
| deep | ly | deeply |
| right | ly | rightly |
| partial | ly | partially |
| urgent | ly | urgently |
| poor | ly | poorly |
| proud | ly | proudly |
| strong | ly | strongly |
| sound | ly | soundly |
| slow | ly | slowly |
| sudden | ly | suddenly |
| sure | ly | surely |
| real | ly | really |
| instant | ly | instantly |
| private | ly | privately |
| present | ly | presently |
| former | ly | formerly |
| frequent | ly | frequently |
| fortunate | ly | fortunately |
| wrong | ly | wrongly |
| wide | ly | widely |
| total | ly | totally |
| definite | ly | definitely |
| actual | ly | actually |
| absolute | ly | absolutely |
| thorough | ly | thoroughly |
| utter | ly | utterly |
| careful | ly | carefully |
| cheerful | ly | cheerfully |
| hopeful | ly | hopefully |
| beautiful | ly | beautifully |
| meaningful | ly | meaningfully |
| careless | ly | carelessly |
| hopeless | ly | hopelessly |

(iii) **Adjectives** ending in **-le** : **e** is dropped and **-y** is added :

| Adjectives | + ly | Adverbs |
|---|---|---|
| single | ly | singly |
| double | ly | doubly |
| suitable | ly | suitably |
| horrible | ly | horribly |
| terrible | ly | terribly |
| possible | ly | possibly |
| probable | ly | probably |
| whole | ly | wholly |

(iv) A few **Adjectives** ending in **-ll** : only **-y** is added.

full + ly = fully

dull + ly = dully

(v) A few **Adjectives** ending in **-e** : **-e** is dropped and **-ly** is added.

| Adjectives | + ly | Adverbs |
|---|---|---|
| true | ly | truly |
| due | ly | duly |
| undue | ly | unduly |

(vi) **Adjectives** ending in **-y** change into **-i** and then **ly** is added.

| Adjectives | + ly | Adverbs |
|---|---|---|
| easy | ly | easily |
| lazy | ly | lazily |
| heavy | ly | heavily |
| happy | ly | happily |
| noisy | ly | noisily |
| lucky | ly | luckily |
| ready | ly | readily |
| satisfactory | ly | satisfactorily |

(vii) **Adjectives** ending in **ic** : **ally** is added :

| Adjectives | + ly | Adverbs |
|---|---|---|
| automatic | ally | automatically |
| economic | ally | economically |
| tragic | ally | tragically |
| **N.B.** public | ly | publicly |

(viii) Some **Adjectives** take **new words** as **Adverbs**.

**Good—Well** (He played **well**.) **Bad—Worse** (The situation is getting **worse**.) [There is no **good** in it.—**Noun**]

(ix) There is a class of **Adverbs** which are derived **from the Pronouns** :
He, who, that.

**ADVERBS DERIVED FROM PRONOUNS**

| Pronouns | Adverbs | | | | |
|---|---|---|---|---|---|
| | **Place** | **Motion to** | **Motion from** | **Time** | **Manner** |
| He | here | hither | hence | .......... | .......... |
| That | there | thither | thence | then | thus |
| Who | where | whither | whence | when | how |

(x) Some **Adverbs** are **compounded with Adjectives** :
Allclear, allround, alltime, everywhere etc.

(xi) Many of the above **Adverbs** are **compounded with Prepositions** :
Here > Hereby, herefrom, herein, hereupon, herewith, hereafter, hitherto; hence > henceforth, henceforward.
Herewith find a cheque of one thousand rupee.

There > Thereby, therefrom, therein, thereof, thereon, therewith, thereafter; thence > thenceforth, thenceforward.
Where > Wherein, whereon, whereof, wherefrom.

(xii) Some **Adverbs** are made up of a qualifying **Adjective** and **a Noun**.
sometimes, meantime, meanwhile, yesterday, midday, midnight, midway, always.

(xiii) Some **Adverbs** are a combination of a **Preposition** and a **Noun** :
away, along, ahead, abroad, aloud, asleep. [away = on way]
[Preposition 'on' weakened to 'a'. **Wren & Martin**]
behind, below, besides, today, tomorrow, overhead, overboard.

(xiv) **Two Adverbs** sometimes go together, **joined** by the Conjunction 'and' :
again and again (= I warned him again and again.)
far and near (= His fame has spread far and near.)
far and wide (= As a statesman he saw far and wide.)
far and away (= This is far and away the best course.)
now and then (= Now and then he writes to me.)
once and again ( = You must not read such trash once and again.)
through and through (= He has read Milton through and through.)
thus and thus (= Thus and thus only we shall succeed.)

**ADJECTIVES AND ADVERBS IN THE SAME FORM**

Some words are used sometimes as Adjectives and sometimes as Adverbs. The manner in which they are used identifies them :

| Words | Adjective | Adverb |
|---|---|---|
| early | He is an early-riser. | He started early. |
| enough | I have enough food. | She sings well enough. |
| fast | He is a fast runner. | He runs fast. |

| Words | Adjective | Adverb |
|---|---|---|
| hard | It is hard work. | He works hard all day long. |
| loud | He speaks in a loud voice. | Don't sing so loud. |
| much | There is much problem. | I am much pleased. |
| only | He is my only son. | He came here only once. |
| best | He is the best boy in the class. | Try your best. |
| well | I am well now. (Pred. Adj.) | He has done well. |

**Adverb with two forms :**

| close<br>closely | clear<br>clearly | deep<br>deeply | dear<br>dearly | easy<br>easily | fine<br>finely | direct<br>directly |
|---|---|---|---|---|---|---|
| hard<br>hardly | high<br>highly | late<br>lately | loud<br>loudly | near<br>nearly | pretty<br>prettily | tight<br>tightly |

**Usage :** I want to deal with him direct. He came to me directly for help.

I closed the door tight. She closed her lips tightly.

Biren speaks very loud. He sings very loudly. Time runs easy. Time runs easily.

**Two forms with different meanings :**

He works hard (very much). I have hardly any money (almost no). The prices of things are running high (up). I spoke highly of him (favourably). He arrived late (not early). I have not seen him lately (recently). Stand near (not far). Lila and Bela are nearly related (closely). I'm pretty sure of the fact (almost). She is prettily dressed (nicely).

## POSITION OF ADVERBS

[1] **Adverbs of Manner, Place and Time** are placed **after the intransitive verb** or **after the object of a transitive verb** :

It is raining heavily (Adverb of Manner). He will come here (Adverb of Place). I met him yesterday (Adverb of Time).

[2] **Adverbs of Frequency** which answer the question 'How often?' are **normally put before the verb or between the helping verb and the main verb** if there is any helping verb.

**Such Adverbs are :** always, often, never, seldom, rarely, usually, generally, sometimes, frequently etc.

He always speaks the truth. We usually have breakfast at eight in the morning. She has never seen a tiger. I have often told him to read clearly.

But the following Adverbs are always placed after the 'be' verb (i.e. is/am/are/was/were) :

He is always busy. He is usually busy. She is never late for school. She is often late for her school.

[3] **An Adverb is usually placed between a Helping Verb and a Main Verb :**

I shall certainly miss her. He is still waiting for me.

[4] When an **Adverb modifies an Adjective or another Adverb**, the Adverb usually comes before it :
The book is very interesting. The dog is quite dead. Donald is a rather lazy boy. I worked only two sums. Do not walk so fast.
But the Adverb 'enough' is always placed after the word it modifies :
You would be kind enough to grant me leave.

[5] An **Adverb** may be placed **at the beginning of a sentence** for **modifying a whole sentence**, for **emphasising** and for **asking questions** :
Fortunately, he was saved. Down went the Titanic. Where has he gone?

[6] When there are **two or more Adverbs** after a Verb, the **normal order** is : **Manner, Place and Time—[MPT]**

| | M | P | T |
|---|---|---|---|
| Runa sang | sweetly | in the town hall | last evening. |
| | M | T | |
| He worked | hard | yesterday. | |
| | P | T | |
| I shall go | there | early. | |

Now study the Adverbials :

**ADVERBIALS**

**Adverbs/Adverb Particles** | **Adverb Phrases** | **Adverb Clauses**

**Adverbials is a broad term. It includes :**

1. **Single word Adverb**—He came here yesterday.
2. **Adverb Phrase**—We reached there after the sunset. [Group of words, without Finite Verb]
3. **Adverb Clause**—Hawkins met his friends when he was released. [With F. Verb]

**Note** A Phrase is a group of words without a finite verb. A Clause is a part of larger sentence having a finite verb.

## ADVERBIAL PARTICLES

**Some Prepositions are used as Adverbs. They are called Adverbial Particles.**
[An Adverbial Particle is placed at the end.]

| | |
|---|---|
| He is in the house (Prep.). | May I come in (Adv.)? |
| Sit on the chair (Prep.). | Move on (Adv.). |

## DEGREES OF COMPARISON OF ADVERBS

Some Adverbs have three forms—**Positive**, **Comparative** & **Superlative**.

1. Some Adverbs of one syllable take -er for comparative and -est for Superlative degree :

| **Positive** | **Comparative** | **Superlative** |
|---|---|---|
| Fast | faster | fastest |
| Hard | harder | hardest |
| Late | later | latest, last |
| Long | longer | longest |

| Positive | Comparative | Superlative |
|---|---|---|
| Soon | sooner | soonest |
| Loud | louder | loudest |
| Quick | quicker | quickest |
| Near | nearer | nearest |

**2.** Adverbs ending in **-ly** form the comparatives adding **more** and superlatives by adding **most** :

| Positive | Comparative | Superlative |
|---|---|---|
| Beautifully | more beautifully | most beautifully |
| Clearly | more clearly | most clearly |
| Loudly | more loudly | most loudly |
| Quickly | more quickly | most quickly |
| Rapidly | more rapidly | most rapidly |
| Easily | more easily | most easily |
| Swiftly | more swiftly | most swiftly |
| Skillfully | more skillfully | most skillfully |
| Wisely | more wisely | most wisely |
| Exception : Early | earlier | earliest |

**3.** Some Common Adverbs form their Comparative and Superlative degrees **irregularly** :

| Positive | Comparative | Superlative |
|---|---|---|
| Ill/Badly | worse | worst |
| Far | farther, further | farthest, furthest |
| Little | less | least |
| Much | more | most |
| Well | better | best |

N.B. *Far, Much* and *Little* may be used both as **Adjective** and **Adverb**.

## INTENSIFIERS AND DOWNTONERS

[A] The Adverbs which modify Verbs, Adjectives, another Adverb or Prepositions by intensifying their effect are called **Intensifiers** :

### LIST OF INTENSIFIERS

| | | | |
|---|---|---|---|
| actually | really | highly | extremely |
| certainly | fully | perfectly | much |
| surely | greatly | utterly | very much |
| definitely | thoroughly | entirely | indeed |
| absolutely | positively | exactly | quiet, etc. |

**Examples :**

He is fully prepared for the examination. They are really pleased.

The clothes are totally out of fashion. The birds flew exactly over our head.

[B] The Adverbs which modify Verbs, Adjectives, another Adverb or Prepositions by toning down their effect are called **Downtoners** :

## LIST OF DOWNTONERS

| | | |
|---|---|---|
| almost | nearly | a bit |
| partly | hardly | a little |
| barely | scarcely | somewhat |
| slightly | rather | not at all |

Ruma speaks a bit quickly.

I am .......................................... busy.

He is ...................................... ill.

They are .................................. disappointed.

The bird flew .......................... over our head.

## APPLIED SECTION

**An Adverb is a word that generally answers the questions with How, When, Where etc.**

1. **Adverbs are generally placed after Verbs.** They are **formed by adding -ly with Adjectives.**

**Complete the chart :**

| Adjective | Adverb (= How?) |
|---|---|
| He is a slow walker. | He walks slowly. |
| He is a careless writer. | He writes carelessly. |
| The sum is easy. | The sum can be done easily. |
| Many students are slow readers. | .............................. |
| Sudha is a beautiful dancer. | .............................. |
| Upen is a careful driver. | .............................. |
| Are you a quick worker?  | Do you .................. |
| The story has a happy ending. | The story ends ........ |

2. We use **Prepositional Phrases as Adverbials** for answering questions with **'Where'** and **'When'**.

(i) **Answering questions with 'Where' :**

| | |
|---|---|
| Where should I go? | Come to the blackboard. Come to me. |
| Where should I sit? | Don't sit on the table. Sit on the chair. |

**Use phrases of place (where?) to complete the sentences :**

(a) Keep the pencil ...........................................................................

(b) Don't write your name ...............................................................

(c) Pakistan is ......................................................................... India.

**(ii) Answering questions with 'When' :**

| | |
|---|---|
| When do they have their breakfast? | They have breakfast at 8 a.m. |
| What do you do on Sunday? | I play and take rest on Sunday. |
| When do they play football? | They play football in the afternoon. |

**Use phrases of time (when?) to complete the sentences :**

Shrila gets up ..........................................................................

Our school will reopen ..........................................................................

We have our examination ..........................................................................

**3.** Study the **Mid-Position of Adverbs of Frequency :**

**Table 1 [Before the Verb]**

| **Subject** | **Adverb** | **Finite Verb etc.** |
|---|---|---|
| We | usually | get up early. |
| He | often | goes to bed late. |
| My mother | never | takes tea. |

**Table 2 [Between the Helping Verb and Main Verb]**

| **Subject** | **Helping Verb** | **Adverb** | **Finite Verb etc.** |
|---|---|---|---|
| We | have | usually | been at home on Sundays. |
| He | doesn't | often | go to bed early. |
| You | must | never | do that again. |

**Insert an Adverb given within brackets and rewrite the sentences :**

(a) Deben gets up early. (never)

(b) We meet our friends at the library. (often)

(c) I read novels before going to bed. (sometimes)

(d) You must look both ways before crossing a busy road. (always)

(e) What time do you get up in the morning? (usually)

**4.** Study the **End-position of Adverbs of Frequency :**

The buses run every ten minutes.

We have History class every other day.

Do you have games once a week?

**5.** Sometimes they may take the **Front-position** for emphasis :

Again and again I have warned you to be serious.

**6.** When the Adverbs make an Adjective or Adverb stronger or weaker, they are placed **before the Adjective or Adverb :**

Kishore sings very well. His school is too far to walk. It's quite cold in Darjeeling in winter.

Exception :

**Enough** (before a noun) Mr. Sen has enough books to read.
(after an adjective) He is not strong enough.
(after an adverb) He cannot work hard enough.

**Ever** (used mainly in question). Have you ever been to the Olympics?

7. **When there are two adverbials of place and time, the adverbial of time is usually placed at the end :**

| Subject & Verb | Adverbial of Place | Adverbial of Time |
|---|---|---|
| They are going | to London | next week. |
| Can you reach | Puri | in the evening? |
| He was swimming | in the Rabindra Sarobar | on Sunday morning. |

8. **When there are two adverbials of time or place, the shorter period of time or the smaller unit of place comes first :**

| Subject & Verb | Shorter Adverbial of Time/Place | Broader Adverbial of Time/Place |
|---|---|---|
| He arrived | at 9 o' clock | yesterday. |
| Mr. Roy lives | in a small village | in Birbhum. |

**But, for emphasis, broader point of time or place may come first.**

Yesterday he arrived at 9 o'clock. In Birbhum Mr. Roy lives in a small village.

9. Complete the sentences with **meaningful Adverbials :**

| Subject & Verb | Place | Frequency | Time |
|---|---|---|---|
| Can you come | here | once | a week? |
| She has been | .......... | .......... | .......... |
| He visits | .......... | .......... | .......... |
| Mr. Ghosh walks | .......... | .......... | .......... |

10. Complete the sentences with Adverbials in the order of **Manner, Place** and **Time (MPT)**. One has been done for you :

| Subject & Verb | Manner | Place | Time |
|---|---|---|---|
| Sharmila danced | beautifully | on the dais | last night. |
| He worked | .......... | .......... | .......... |
| She sang | .......... | .......... | .......... |
| They played | .......... | .......... | .......... |

**11.** Use the following **Adverbs** where you can : almost, already, also, even, soon, just, quite, never, hardly, yet :

| Subject | Helping Verb (+ not) | Adverb | Verbs etc. |
|---|---|---|---|
| I | have | already | finished my work. |
| We | have not | yet | visited Agra. |
| He | ............................... | ........... | changed his dress. |
| She | ............................... | ........... | come. |
| They | ............................... | ........... | tried to help him. |
| The rains | ............................... | ........... | started. |
| The students | ............................... | ........... | been to the cinema. |

**12.** Apply the following **Adverbs in Positive, Comparative and Superlative Degrees**. One of each type has been done for you :

Fast, soon, quick, badly, well, easily, early, skillfully.

**as + Adverb + as = Positive.**

Bithi runs as fast as Juthi.

**Comparative (-er / more) + than**

Kalpana runs faster than Alpana. Arpita does it more beautifully than Ankita.

**Superlative (-est / most) + of / in**

P. T. Usha runs fastest of all Indian women. She ran fastest in Asian Games. She did it most beautifully than any other.

**Note** 'The' is not placed before a Superlative Adverb although 'the' is placed before the Superlative Adjective. However, 'of' or 'in' may be placed as per sense after both the Superlative Adjective and Superlative Adverb.

**13.** Frame two pairs of sentences and apply the **Adverb form of 'good'**. [good > well] :

**Example :** Atanu is a good player.—**Adjective**
Atanu plays well.—**Adverb**

(i) ............................................................................ **Adjective**
............................................................................ **Adverb**

(ii) ............................................................................ **Adjective**
............................................................................ **Adverb**

**14.** **Most words ending in '-ly' are Adverbs. But a few words ending in '-ly' are Adjectives,** such as, friendly, lovely, lonely, likely, lowly, miserly, cowardly. They have no Adverb form. To make up this deficiency we use a similar Adverb or an Adverbial Phrase :

| | |
|---|---|
| likely (Adj.) | probably (Adv.) |
| friendly (Adj.) | in a friendly way (Adv. Phrase) |
| miserly (Adj.) | in a miserly manner (Adv. Phrase) |

Now use other words of this group in this manner.

**15. Apply the difference of the following pairs of Adverbs :**

high : The bird flew high.
highly : He was highly placed.

hard : ..........................................................................................
hardly : ..........................................................................................

late : ..........................................................................................
lately : ..........................................................................................

nearly : ..........................................................................................
nearly : ..........................................................................................

**16.** Note the difference of '**hardly**', '**barely**', '**scarcely**', '**rarely**' and '**seldom**' :
Hardly, barely and scarcely mean almost nothing or almost not at all. But rarely and seldom mean almost never.
**Fairly with favourable Adjectives :** Tom is fairly clever.

**17.** Note the difference of '**fairly**' and '**rather**' and use them properly :
**Fairly with favourable Adjectives :** Tom is fairly clever.
**Rather with unfavourable Adjectives :** Peter is rather stupid.

**Approval by using fairly :**
This soup is fairly hot. (= The speaker likes hot soup.)
**Disapproval by using rather :**
This soup is rather hot. ( = It is a little too hot for him.)—**Thomson & Martinet**
When 'rather' is used before favourable adjectives and adverbs, it becomes nearly equivalent to 'very' :
She is rather clever. (= She is very clever.)
'Rather' before comparatives means 'a little' :
The weather is rather worse than I expected.
'Rather' sometimes expressess preference :
I would rather stay here. (= I prefer to stay here.)
He would rather work than starve.—**Thomson & Martinet**.
Rather death than dishonour. (= Death is preferable to dishonour)

## EXERCISE

1. **How many kinds of Adverbs are there? What are they? Give two examples of each kind of Adverb.**
2. **Pick out the Adverbs and tell what they modify :**

   Each boy broke the stick easily. Read the story quickly. The boys did not quarrel again. The king looked at the garden carefully. The servants usually looked after them. They seldom saw their father. They almost knew the great epics by heart. The servants would go out and stay away for hours. Sir Asutosh was always the first boy in his class. The other students sometimes failed to answer correctly, but the boy's answers were always correct.
3. **Change the following Adjectives into Adverbs and use them meaningfully in the blanks :**

   brave, heavy, loud, complete, eager, perfect, probable.

   (i) I have ........................................................................ forgotten his name.
   (ii) She was breathing...................... when she came on the fourth floor.

(iii) He faced the difficulties ..........................................................................

(iv) The work has been ........................................................................ done.

(v) Do not read so ...............................................................................

(vi) I am ............................................................................ waiting for you.

(vii) ................................................ his father will come here tomorrow.

**4. Rewrite the following sentences after replacing italicized words with suitable Adverbs :**

(i) *It is possible* that he is ill.

(ii) *It is sure* that our team will win.

(iii) *It is certain* that there won't be any difficulty.

(iv) *It is obvious* that my father will depend on me after his retirement.

(v) *It was unfortunate* that no one could escape from the burning hut.

**5. Put the Adverbials in the brackets in the suitable positions in the sentences and rewrite them :**

(i) The boy stayed at school. (seldom, after the classes)

(ii) "It was chance, young man," Davy said. (mainly, modestly)

(iii) Kajal pushed her out of the room and bolted the door. (quickly, from outside)

(iv) He prepared his lecture carefully but could not deliver it. (very, unfortunately)

(v) The missiles are being thrown and these are damaging the people. (dangerously, in developed countries.)

**6. The Adverbials listed on the right are missing from the following passages. Insert them in the places marked ∧ :**

(i) Most people know what is right and what is wrong. ∧ however, when the time for action comes, they ∧ fail to act ∧. The trouble with them is that they are selfish and think ∧ of themselves, not of others. — often, only, rightly, unfortunately

(ii) ∧ one of the greatest problems is pollution. In our cities, the air is ∧ being polluted by smoke ∧ and from carbon monoxide gases emitted by motor vehicles. — constantly, from factories, in the 21st century

(iii) The warder who had fallen ∧ was in a ∧ critical situation, for he ∧ knew how to swim. Every second that passed increased his danger of being snapped up by one of these voracious creatures. ∧ one of the convicts, heeding his nobler feelings, threw himself into the water. — very, suddenly, hardly, into the river

(iv) Deaf education was ∧ introduced in Germany in the 19th century and it was not well ∧ to many concerned parents. — enough, first

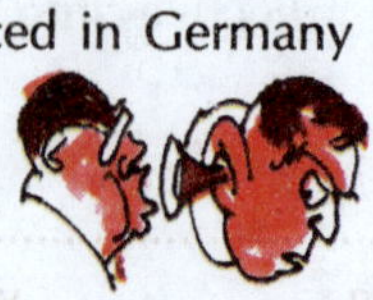

# 17 MORE ABOUT PREPOSITIONS

## WHAT IS A PREPOSITION ?

A preposition is a word placed before a noun or a pronoun or a noun-equivalent to show its relation to any other word of the sentence. The noun or pronoun or the noun-equivalent is called its object. **Nesfield**

Bob is coming with Bill. (Prep. before a Noun)
Anna is skilled in swimming. (Prep. before a Noun-equiv.)
What do you think of him/her? (Prep. before a Pronoun)

### READ THE SENTENCES IN THE FOLLOWING TABLE

| Put the cup | on | the dish. |
|---|---|---|
| The cows are | in | the field. |
| Michael goes | to | school. |
| He is fond | of | reading novels. |
| Lila lives | with | her parents. |
| You should stand | by | him/her. |
| The fan is moving (rotating) | over | our head. |
| The sky is | above | our head. |

In the above-mentioned sentences prepositions on, in, to, of, with, by, over and above show the relation of some nouns, noun-equivalents or pronouns to some other words in the sentences.

**Note** (a) **Prepositions may also govern some other parts of speech :**

He walks about from here to there. (Preposition governs an Adverb)
I have heard of this before now. (Preposition governs an Adverb)
This will last for ever. (Preposition governs an Adverb)
He is about to go. (Preposition governs an Infinitive)

(b) **Prepositions may govern phrases and clauses as well :**

He is ignorant of how to swim. (Preposition governs a Phrase)

I told everyone of what I have heard. (Preposition governs a Clause)

It depends on how you do your duty. (Preposition governs a Clause)

There are a few important Prepositions which are used in almost 80% sentences in English. They are : **to**, **by**, **with**, **for**, **from**, **than**, **of**, **in**, **at**.

| Preposition | Example |
|---|---|
| — | Arthur is a boy. [No preposition] |
| to | The boy goes to school. The book was given to Bob. |
| by (a person/a doer)<br><br>with (a thing/an instrument) | The snake was killed by Bill. [by a doer]<br>The cake was eaten by the dog. [by a doer]<br>Martha wrote the letter with a pen. [with an instrument] |
| for | I waited for him. |
| from, than | The apple fell from the tree.<br>He will not take less than ten rupees. |
| of | This is the book of poems. |
| in, at | He lives in Kolkata. I live at Gobindapur.<br>There is a lot of fish in the river. |

**Note** Although the **general rule** is **by a doer**, **with an instrument** there are some **exceptions**, such as—'blasted **by** an atom bomb', 'governed **by** the rules', 'died **by** poison', 'destroyed **by** fire' etc. In such cases '**by**' is used as appropriate preposition.

**Some more examples of Preposition :**

Mr. Bose is going to England.

The snake was killed by a hunter.

He killed a snake with a stick.

I have bought an umbrella for you.

He is coming home from school.

This is a leg of a broken chair.

I live at Gopdanga/Atghara (a name of a village).

He lives in Kolkata/Mumbai (a name of a city).

No man can live in a desert.

I live in a village. (But 'at' before the name of village)

## POSITION OF PREPOSITION

(i) **Normally Prepositions precede Nouns or Pronouns :**

I gave a book to the boy. The cat jumped on the rat.

I know nothing about him.

**(ii) When the object of the Preposition is an Interrogative Pronoun or a Relative Pronoun, the Preposition is placed at the end :**

What are you looking for? Where do you come from? Who (Whom) are you speaking to? This is the boy that I spoke of. This is the girl (whom) I spoke to. Here is the book that you asked for. Here is a chair to sit on (to sit on = to sit on which).

## KINDS OF PREPOSITION

**Prepositions may be arranged in six classes :**

(i) **Simple Prepositions :** at, in, by, of, for, on, over, under, up, to, from, out, with etc.

(ii) **Double Prepositions :** into, onto, within, without, from among, towards etc.

(iii) **Compound Prepositions :** These are formed usually prefixing a Preposition to a Noun, an Adjective or an Adverb :

across (= on + cross), along (= on + long),
behind (= by + hind), beneath (= by + neath)
beside (= by + side), underneath (= under + neath).
(a = on; be = by in such cases.)

(iv) **Phrase Prepositions or Prepositional Phrases :**

Groups of words used with the force of a single Preposition are called Phrase Prepositions or Prepositional Phrases :

He succeeded by dint of merit.
Please give me a pen instead of a pencil.
In course of time he found his mistake.

(v) **Participial Prepositions :**

Some Present or Past Participles are used as Prepositions :

What do you know regarding this proposal? Considering the quality, the price is not high. The river flows past the village.

(vi) **Disguised Prepositions :**

Sometimes a or o are used as Disguised Prepositions. [a' = on, o = of]

Potato sells ₹15 a kilo. She comes here once a week.

["Of can be changed into o as in 'four o'clock.'—**Nesfield**]

**Note** Several words are used sometimes as Adverbs or Adverbial Particles and sometimes as Prepositions. A word is a Preposition when it governs a Noun or a Pronoun. It is an Adverb when it does not. —**Wren & Martin**

[An Adverbial Particle is placed at the end while a Preposition is placed before a Noun or a Pronoun.]

| **Adverb/Adverbial Particle** | **Preposition** |
|---|---|
| Go, and run about. | Don't loiter about the corridor. |
| I could not come before. | I came the day before yesterday. |
| Has he come in? | Is he in the room? |
| Let us move on. | The book is on the table. |
| Raise your hands up. | Jack and Jill went up the hill. |
| The wheel came off. | The driver jumped off the car. |
| I have not seen him since. | I have not slept since yesterday. |

## RELATIONS EXPRESEED BY PREPOSITIONS

| | |
|---|---|
| **1. Place/Position**<br>at, about, above, across, against, among, before, behind, below, between, by, down, in, inside, near, of, on, over, under, upon, with, within | at the window, at his office (Vide—Hornby) a chain about his neck, above the sky, lying across the path, a barrier across the road, stood against you, among the boys, stood before him, behind the door, below the table, between you and me, stand by me, sitting by the woman, down the river, in/inside the room, near the (position) corner of the street, on the table, on your left, on the top of the hill, under the tree, with his friend, within the campus. |
| **2. Time**<br>at, after, before, by, during, from, for, in, on, since, till, until, within, throughout | at 10 a.m., at dawn, at noon, at night, at an early age, after 3 o'clock, after his arrival, before his arrival, before the 15th July, by 4 p.m., by surnrise, by night (we travelled by night), during five years, during the whole summer/the whole day, from 1st January, for a week/a month, in June 1995, in the morning/afternoon/evening, on Sunday, since he comes, within three months, throughout the year. |
| **3A. Direction/Movement**<br>at, away, across, down, for, from, into, off, over, out of, round, to, towards, up<br> | threw stones at the dogs, away from India, ran across the field, went down the hill, start for England, fled from home, jumped into the well, fell off the train, flew over my head, came out of the room/the cage, tour round the world, go to school, turn to the left, walk to the window, towards north/south, climb up the hill. |
| **3B. Special use of Direction**<br>(i) **In** denotes inside or within<br>(ii) **On** denotes on the border<br>(iii) **To** denotes outside | **Direction** { **In (inside)** / **On (on the border)** / **To (= outside)**<br>(i) Kashmir is in the north of India.<br>(ii) The Himalayas stand on the north of India.<br>(iii) Sri Lanka is to the south of India. |
| **4A. Agency/Instrument**<br>at, by, with, through, from<br> | at auction, killed by a man with a gun, by heart (Learn by heart), by force, by post, by poison, destroyed by fire, caused by flood, by bus, by tram, by air, by land, by sea, by (in) an accident. |

| | |
|---|---|
| **4B. Manner/Means**<br>by, with, through, from<br> | by tuition (He makes his living by tuition), paid by credit card, powered by electricity, by hand (These goods are made by hand.), by the ear (I pulled him by the ear.), by my watch (It's 5-30 by my watch.), taller by two centimetre.<br>with love, with courage, with ease, with difficulty, cut it with a blade, through an agent, through a friend, from gratitude. |
| **5. Reason/Purpose**<br>for, from, of, through, to, with | for the good of the people, died for the country, took medicine for a cold, died from fatigue, suffering from cold/fever, died of cancer/cholera/diarrhoea; lost his book through negligence, read to learn (purpose), trembles with fear, shivers with fever. |
| **6A. Possession**<br>of, with<br><br>**6B. Relationship** | the book of John, the factory of my father, the girl with blue eye, the woman with long hair, I have no money with me.<br>I live with my parents. Mix the flour with some milk. |
| **7. Standard/Rate/Value/Speed**<br>at, by | Bank charges interest at 17 percent (rate). Cloth is sold by the metre (standard). Rice is sold at Rs. 20 per kg (value). The train is running at 80 km per hour (speed). |

## SOME IMPORTANT PREPOSITIONS

### AT, IN

He is **at home** (denotes rest)
He is **at his office** (denotes 'on duty'/'at work') **A. L. D.—Hornby**
He is **in the office** (denotes 'inside the office')
**Oxford Guide to Eng. Grammar—Eastwood**

### DIFFERENCES OF 'AT' AND 'IN'

| [AT] | [IN] |
|---|---|
| (i) We use **at** for a position at a small space.<br>You can be at home/ at school/ at a hotel/ at the bus stop/ at Lalpur (village)/ at Arambagh (town).<br>"We were at the cafe." (expresses position)<br>**John Eastwood** | (i) We use **in** for a position in a large space.<br>You can be in Kolkata/ in Delhi/ in London (city)/ in Hooghly (district)/ in India (a country)/ in a forest/ in a desert.<br> |

| [AT] | [IN] |
|---|---|
| (ii) We use at office/library/cinema/theatre/building etc. when we are talking about the normal purpose of it.<br>He is at the office. (= on duty)<br>The Browns are at the theatre. (= watching a play).<br>"We were at the library." (= choosing a book)<br>**Oxford Guide to English Grammar—John Eastwood** | (ii) We use in office/in the office etc. when it denotes simply **inside the building or position within.**<br>He is in the office. (= inside the office)<br>He is not in office now. (= in position)<br>The Browns are in the theatre to meet someone.<br>"It was cold in the library. (= inside the building)" **Oxford Guide to English Grammar —John Eastwood** |
| (iii) We use **at** for a **point of time**.<br>You can meet me at 10 o'clock/at 8 a.m./at 4 p.m./at half past five/at breakfast (time)/at dawn/at noon (short span of time)/at that time/at the moment. We also use at with holiday periods of two or three days. at Christmas/at the weekend.<br>We go to the countryside at the weekend. | (iii) We use **in** for a **period of time**.<br>You can meet me in the morning/in the afternoon/in the evening/in the next few days/in the summer holidays/in spring/in July/in 2005.<br>He will come in an hour.<br>**Exception :** at night.<br>**Note :** We use **on** with a single day—on Sunday, on Tuesday afternoon, on that day, on the 7th August, on the evening of the 12th |
| (iv) "At is one-dimensional. We use it when we see something as a point in space."<br>**John Eastwood**<br>The car was waiting at the lights. There is someone at the door.<br> | (iv) "In is three-dimensional. We use it when we see something as all around."<br>I have five pounds in my pocket. There was a man sitting in the waiting room. **John Eastwood** |

**Now see some more examples in sentences :**

Manisha lives at Majpur (name of a village). Amal lives at Arambagh (at a small town). Shyamal lives in the district of Burdwan. Bimal lives in Kolkata (in a big city). Soma lives in a village. Uma lives in a town/in a city. Amina lives in India/in Asia/in Europe. Apu gets up at dawn. Mithu gets up at 6 a.m. Debu sings in the morning. Shibu built the house in a year.

**Some Time Phrases :** at dawn, at noon, at 6 a.m., at 5 p.m., but in the morning, in the afternoon, in the evening (Exception : at night, at midnight), in a week, in a month, in a year etc.

## SOME USAGES OF PREPOSITIONS

### AT

At present, at play, at work (I found them at play or at work.); at dinner, at hand (The examination is at hand; I do not expect such treatment at your hands); at page (Open your book at page ten.), at liberty (state or condition) at war or at peace; (The two countries are at war or at peace with each other); but, "Let me die in peace"; at a distance, at the door, at the age of eighty.

**Note** Never try to use 'in' in the place of 'at'. See the following sentences :

I was alarmed at the crash. I was astonished at your zeal. I was disgusted at his manners. Parents were displeased at the habit of the children. I am perturbed at my friend's business. I am aggrieved at this event. She got good marks at the hands of the teacher.

### IN

In arms (The two brothers are in arms against each other); in danger, in ruins (The historical building of Raja Rammohun Roy is in ruins now); in power (His party is in power now); in office (= in position). "He is not in office now", but, in the office = inside the office. "Is he in the office?"—at his office = on duty.—**Advanced Learners' Dictionary—Hornby**.

She is in bed (at rest), in haste; in cash or notes (but by cheque); in advance, in general, in ink (written in ink); in pain, in sorrow, in time, in his presence or absence; in a hurry (denotes state or condition); in the dark (I am in the dark about his purpose); in the sun (Do not run in the sun); in the shade (Keep the thing in the shade); in the army (occupation); in a few days; in a bad temper, dressed in silk, weak in history.

### ABOUT

(i) **In the sense of 'in' :** I have doubt about it.
(ii) **To mean 'near', 'probably' and 'almost' :** It is about 5 o'clock.
(iii) **To mean 'all prepared' :** I am about to go. He is about to write. She is about to be married.

### ABOVE

(i) **In the sense of 'over' or 'higher than' :** The hydrogen balloon rose above the clouds.
(ii) **To mean more than in number, quantity and degree :** There were above three thousand men. His expenses are above his means.
(iii) **To mean 'superior to' :** He is above the members of the Board.
(iv) **To mean 'beyond' :** He is above all suspicion.

### ACROSS

(i) **To mean 'on the opposite side' :** The beautiful villa stands across the river.
(ii) **To mean 'from one side to other' :** There is a bridge across the river.
(iii) **To mean 'on both sides' :** He took the load across his shoulders.

### AGAINST

(i) **To mean 'in opposition to' :** You should not act against the rule.
(ii) **To mean 'opposite to' :** Cycling against the wind is difficult.
(iii) **To mean 'vertically on' :** He is leaning against the wall.

(iv) **To mean 'with' :** The waves beat against the shore.

(v) **In relative term :** You are working against time. I know nothing against her character.

### ALONG

(i) **Following a line of a path, a road etc. :** He is walking along the road.

(ii) **To mean 'along with' :** The general left the town along with all the soldiers.

(iii) **To mean 'get along' :** He seems to be getting along well in the business.

### AROUND/ROUND

(i) **In the sense of 'round' :** The earth moves around/round the sun.

(ii) **To mean 'about' :** I will see you around 4 pm.

### BEFORE

(i) **To mean 'in front of'/'in presence of' :** They stood before the gate. The money was given before me. The case was brought before the magistrate.

(ii) **To mean 'earlier time' :** I take meal before going to school. She got training in computer before me.

**Note** There is difference between 'long before' and 'before long'. People of India knew farming long before the Europeans. My friend will come here before long. (soon)

### BELOW

(i) **To mean 'lower than' :** He is below age for service.

(ii) **To mean 'less than' :** The number of attendance was below 100.

(iii) **To mean 'inferior to' :** Her result is below expectation.

### BENEATH

(i) **To mean 'under' :** The treasure lies beneath the stone.

(ii) **To mean 'too low for' :** Your conduct is beneath the dignity of a gentleman.

### BEYOND

(i) **To mean 'at the farthest side of' :** There is a village beyond the hill.

(ii) **To mean 'surpassing' :** You are going beyond limits. What you want is beyond my capacity.

(iii) **To mean 'to get beyond' :** The robbers got beyond the reach of the police.

### BY

(i) **To mean 'by a doer' (with a thing) :** This letter was written by her with a pen.

(ii) **To denote a point of time :** I shall come back by 4 p.m.

(iii) **By a conveyance or to denote the way of travelling :** He goes by bus/by rail, by steamer/by aeroplane. He travels by land/by water/by air.

(iv) **To mean 'near' :** There is a lake by the township.

(v) **To mean 'by means of' :** You may send a letter by post. You may pay the bill by a cheque/draft. Cloth is sold by the metre. Sugar is sold by the kilogram.

(vi) **In some more different meanings :** I caught him by the neck. We can learn poems by heart. It happened by chance. You are older than I by three years. I swear by God. Work by day.

## FOR

(i) **To denote a period of time :** He has been suffering from flu for three days.

(ii) **For something** or **person :** The soldiers started for the battlefield. They fought for their motherland. My uncle has brought this nice present for me.

(iii) **To mean 'because of' :** They turned away for fear.

(iv) **To mean 'in spite of' :** For all his riches, he is not happy.

(v) **To mean 'in exchange of' :** What will you pay for this rare picture?

(vi) **To mean 'in comparison to' :** You look tall for your age.

(vii) **To mean 'to think' :** The bear in the story left the man for dead.

## FROM

(i) **To denote point of time :** She begins her work from day-break.

(ii) **To denote the point of leaving :** They started from home at 10 a.m.

(iii) **To denote motive or intention :** He did it from his sense of gratitude.

(iv) **To mean 'out of' :** Take some sugar from the jar.

## INTO

(i) **To denote inward motion :** The goat jumped into the well.

(ii) **To denote change :** The rich man fell into debt. Translate this story into French.

## OF

We often make mistakes in using 'from' or 'by' or 'about' in place of 'of'. See the correct usage of 'of' in the following sentences :

I am tired of talking too much. (not 'by'); The patient died of AIDS. (not 'by' or 'from'); I am afraid of dogs. (not 'from'); Beware of dogs. (not 'from'); This cloth is made of cotton. (not 'from'); I beg pardon of you. (not 'from'); They warned her of danger. (not 'about'); You should be careful of your dealings. (not 'about'); The neighbours spoke highly of him. (not about)

## ON

(i) **To indicate a point of time** (day or date) **:** We have arranged a picnic on Sunday/ on the 2nd June.

(ii) **On a subject :** He delivered a lecture on dowry system. There was a discussion on his action. He has authority on many subjects. [But] He has authority for saying or doing this.

(iii) **Some special usages of 'on' :** The naughty boy is bent on doing mischief. Our impression is based on facts. They are determined on going to Darjeeling.

## THROUGH

(i) **To mean across the interior of anything :** The boys bored a hole through the wall. He went through the jungle.

(ii) **To mean 'by means of' :** He got the post through my help.

## UNDER

(i) **To mean opposite of 'over' :** The traveller is taking rest under a tree.

(ii) **To mean 'less' :** He is under-age for service.

(iii) **To mean 'in the course of' :** The subject is under discussion. The building is under construction. A man under trial cannot escape.

(iv) **To mean 'according to' :** The miscreant was arrested under the warrant of the court.

## WITH

This is a peculiar preposition that denotes union, separation, agreement, opposition, etc.

(i) **To mean 'not to leave behind' :** The outcomer left the village with all his belongings.

(ii) **To mean 'agreement' or 'disagreement' :** I agree with (do not agree with) you on this point.

(iii) **To mean 'not to tolerate' :** A bad master always quarrels with his servants.

(iv) **In the sense of 'in the company of' :** All my friends came with me.

(v) **In the sense of 'with an instrument' :** He cuts his pencil with a knife. We hear with our ears.

## BY, WITH

**['By' a doer, 'with' an instrument]**

The tiger was killed by Bagha Jatin. The bird was killed by the hunter. The rat was killed by the cat. Sisir killed the snake with a stick. We see with our eyes and hear with our ears.

## ON, UPON, OVER, ABOVE

Put the book on the table. The cat sprang upon the table. The fan is moving over his head. The plane flew over Kolkata. The sky is above our head. The fan is moving just above my head.

(a) 'On' signifies contact with a thing at rest. [The TV is on the table.]

(b) 'Upon' speaks of things in motion. [Oil is floating upon the sea.]

(c) 'Over' refers to a point generally higher than a thing. [I hold the umbrella over my head]

(d) 'Above' refers to a point directly higher or far higher. [The sun is above the trees now.]

(e) 'Above' denotes 'more than' in quantity and degree. [His expenses are above his means.]

(f) 'Above' denotes 'superior to'. [He is above all the employees in the company.]

(g) 'Above' denotes 'beyond'. [He is a man above suspicion.]

## SOME OTHER USAGES OF 'OVER' AND 'ABOVE'

(a) "Above and over have sometimes similar meanings."

**John Eastwood—O.G.E.G.**

There was a clock above/over the entrance.

There's a picture over/above the door.

(b) "We do not normally use above to mean horizontal movement."

**John Eastwood**

[Over generally means a position or movement without contact.]

That plane flew low over the houses.

(c) "We do not use above for an area or surface." **John Eastwood**

[We use over for spreading something with or without contact.]

Thick black smoke hangs over the town.

Someone has spread a sheet over the body.

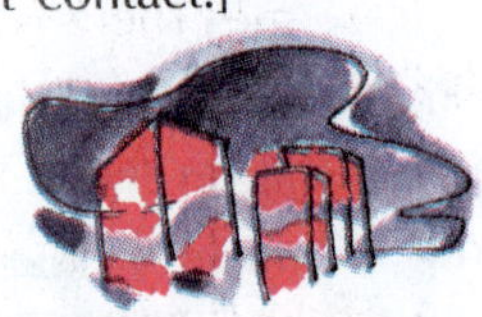

(d) "We prefer over before a number." **John Eastwood**

There are over fifty thousand people in the stadium.

(e) "We use above with a measurement, such as temperature."

Temperatures will rise above freezing.

(f) In the following example over has a special meaning.
The leaders discussed world affairs over lunch (= while having lunch).

(g) "We also use over for movement to the other side or position on the other side." **John Eastwood**
The horse jumped over the wall. Was the ball over the goal-line?

## SOME OTHER USAGES OF 'ON'

(a) **We use *on* with specific days and dates :**
She usually comes on Sundays.
We went to Darjeeling on New Year's Day.
Our school will open on the 2nd May.
The Examination will commence on the 13th March.

(b) **To denote contact :**
He is sitting on the chair. Some birds are on the tree.
The words are on the blackboard. The picture is hung on the wall.
She wears a ring on her first finger.

(c) **To denote subject :**
He wrote a book on chemistry. The story was on ghosts.
He delivered a lecture on Shakespeare's sonnets.
He dwelt at length on the subject.

(d) **To denote membership :**
Mr. Brown is on the committee. (not, in the committee)
I am on the Board of Studies. (not, in the Board of Studies)

(e) **To denote a special direction :**
Fortune smiled on him.
They launched an attack on our home.

(f) **To denote 'by means of' :**
They listened to it on the radio.
The cow lives on grass. (But, Mr. Sen lives by honest means.)
He lives on his father's income.

**Note** **on foot, on duty, on time** : The train runs on time. [Or] The train is running to time. [But] The train arrived in time.

## BESIDE, BESIDES

**[Beside = at the side of another. Besides = in addition to.]**

Sit beside me. There is a tree beside the river. He has none to help him besides you. He knows English besides Bengali.

## BETWEEN, AMONG

**['Between' two = 'Among' more than two]**

Divide the mangoes between the two brothers. Divide the mangoes among the boys. You must come between 7 a.m. and 8 a.m. The children quarrelled among themselves.

## AFTER, IN, WITHIN, BY

(a) **After** refers to

(i) Past period of time (not present or future period of time)

He came after a few days.

(ii) Point of time (in all tenses)

He comes/came/will come after 5 p.m.

(b) **In** refers to a future period of time to denote "at the end of some future time".

I shall go to Delhi in a week. (at the end of the week)

(c) **Within** denotes "sometime before the end of some future time."

I shall go to Delhi within a week.

(d) **By** refers to a point of future time

He will come back by/before 10 o'clock.

He will come back within 10 o'clock. (Incorrect)

(e) **By** refers to a period of time to denote 'during'.

We travelled by night.

I will come by tomorrow.

## AGO, BEFORE

(a) **Ago** is used to denote 'before now' :

He was our teacher two years ago. Many years ago the Portugese built this church.

(b) **Before** is used to denote 'before then' :

He had joined the office two years before his mother died.

(c) **Before** can also be used in future tense :

We must be ready before their arrival.

[**Oxford Guide to English Grammar—John Eastwood**]

## TO, IN, INTO

He is going to school. (to = movement towards); He is in the school. (in = inside); He jumped into the pool (inward movement); He fell into poverty (Change of state).

**'To'** denotes **motion**, **'in'** denotes position **within**, and **'into'** denotes motion **inward**. Moreover, **'into'** denotes some **change**.

## 'TO' INFINITIVE

I like to read the book. He does not like to go to school.

## 'TO' + VERBAL NOUN/GERUND

He is addicted to gambling. (not, addicted to gamble)

He is adverse to playing cards. (not, adverse to play)

## SOME OTHER USAGES OF 'TO'

(i) **To denote purpose :** I came to see you. We read to learn. He invited me to dinner.

(ii) **To denote limit and effect :** The army fought to the last. We shall pay to the last penny. He was beaten to death. To our disappointment he failed.

(iii) **To denote proportion :** Our team won by three goals to nil. The ratio of rice and pulse is two to one.

(iv) **To denote agreement :** The apple is sweet to taste.

(v) **To denote time :** It is ten to eight.

(vi) **To denote until :** The farmers work from dawn to dusk.

(vii) **To denote comparing :** He is junior/senior/inferior/superior to me.

(viii) **To denote attaching :** Stick the stamp firmly to the envelope.

(ix) **To denote facing :** The two sisters stood face to face.

(x) **For the indirect object :** Give it to me.

## BY, SINCE, BEFORE

You must be back by four o'clock.

He has been here since four o'clock.

He did not get back before four o'clock.

[ By, Since, Before—"These are all used for a point of time, not, for a period or space of time."—**Nesfield** ]

## SINCE, FOR, FROM

[**'Since' and 'From' = point of time; 'For' = period of time**]

He has been ill since Sunday last. He will begin English from next Sunday. I have not seen him from last week. I have not seen him for a week.

"Both (since and from) denote a point of time, not a space or period. But 'since' is preceded by a verb in some perfect tense, while 'from' can be used with any form of tense. Another difference is that 'since' can be used only in reference to past time, whereas 'from' can be used for present and future tense." **Nesfield**

### SOME MORE EXAMPLES OF SINCE AND FROM IN DIFFERENT TENSES

He has been here since/from Monday last.
(Present Perfect tense)

It has been raining since/from Sunday last.
(Present Perfect Continuous tense)

He began English since/from the age of ten/his boyhood.
(Simple Past tense)

He was tired as he had been working since/from dawn. (Past Perfect Continuous)

He begins English from (not since) today. (Present tense)

He will begin English from (not since) tomorrow. (Future tense)

*[However, "note that there is a difference between **last** and **the last**.

We say, 'I am here **since last week**' (**month, year etc.**) but 'I have been here **for the last week**'.

In the first sentence '**last week**' means a point of time about seven days ago. In the second sentence '**the last week**' means the period of seven days that has just finished."]

**A. J. Thomson & A. V. Martinet**

## PREPOSITIONAL PHRASES

At the top of—He shouted at the top of his voice.
By dint of—He won the prize by dint of hard work.
By means of—He got the prize by means of hard work.
By virtue of—He got the prize by virtue of hard work.
For the sake of—He sacrificed his life for the sake of his country.
In case of—In case of fire, call the Fire Brigade.
In consequence of—In consequence of fire, call the Fire Brigade.

In the event of—In the event of fire, call the Fire Brigade.
In course of—He told me this in course of conversation.
In comparison with—Sharmila is more beautiful in comparison with Urmila.
In compliance with—I can do this in compliance with your request.
In favour of—He said this in favour of his brother.
In front of—He is waiting in front of the school.
In lieu of—Give me this book in lieu of that.

In order to—He worked hard in order to win the prize.
In place of—He is working in place of his brother.
In search of—They went to the forest in search of a deer.
In spite of—He went to school in spite of his illness.
Instead of—He started a business instead of crying for a job.
In the midst of—He is in the midst of great troubles.
In the nick of time—The police arrived in the nick of time.
In the teeth of—He went on working in the teeth of strong opposition.
In view of—He agreed to do it in view of importance of the matter.
In accordance with—He did this in accordance with her request.
On account of—He could not attend school on account of his illness.
On behalf of—The Headmaster welcomed the visitors on behalf of the school.
On the eve of—He was given a farewell on the eve of his retirement.
Owing to—He could not attend school owing to his illness.
With an eye to—He did this with an eye to helping her. (not, to help)
With a view to—He did this with a view to helping his brother.
(not, with a view to help)

## APPLIED SECTION

**[1]** These figures will give you an idea of the **Prepositions of place or position :**

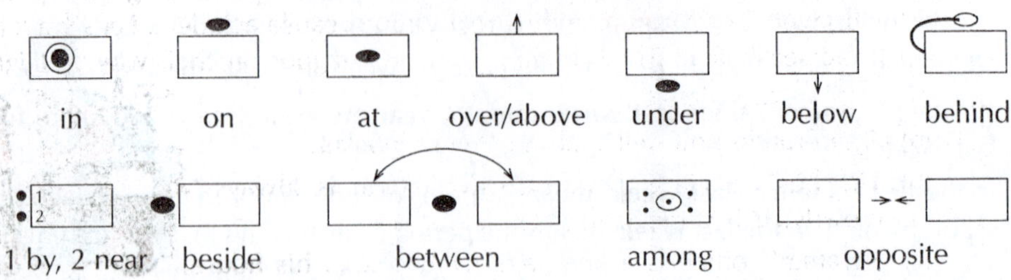

**Examples :**

at an exact place/at the station/at 22 Chowringhee Road etc.

in a country/city/continent/area/container/bed, e.g., in India/Kolkata/Asia; in a village or town (not the name)/a box/a bottle/a tea-pot etc.

on the chair/table, on the ceiling/figure, on the blackboard, a black spot on his shirt/on the Chowringhee Road etc.

under the tree/bridge/chair/table etc.

behind the bus-stand/bazaar/any person etc.

above the knee/average marks/60% marks etc.

below the knee/pass-marks/60% marks etc.

by the window/the gate/the ticket-counter etc.

near the school/the bank/the cinema etc.

opposite the bank/the post-office/the entrance etc.

between the two places/persons etc.

among the boys/girls/students/friends/people etc.

**Now fill in the blanks :**

(a) Parveen lives ........... College Street.

(b) She lives ........... 19/1 College Street.

(c) Mr. John lives ........... England.

(d) Medha lives ........... Mumbai.

(e) She has a flat ........... the second floor. Our flat is just opposite ........... hers.

(f) The little girl wanted to sit ........... the window ........... the compartment ........... the train. She likes to look ........... the green trees and the paddy field ........... the train.

(g) Apu likes to read story-books. He keeps his story-books ........... his pillow. He often reads them ........... night.

(h) Most of the students have scored ...... 20% marks. They have failed ......English.

[2] **These figures will give you an idea of the Prepositions of motion :**

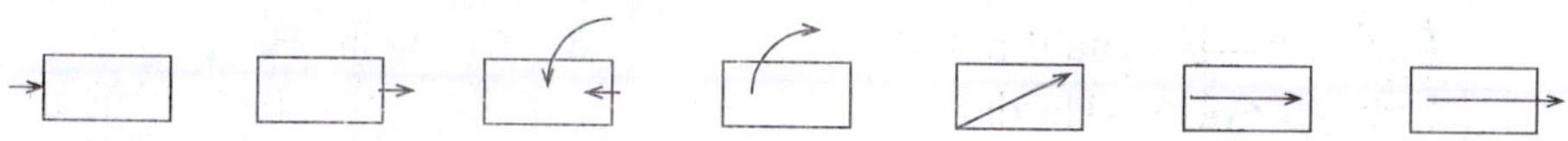

to/towards   from   into/onto   out of   across   along   through

**Examples :**

We are going to the cinema. They are going towards the station. He has been coming to school from January. Don't try to get into a running bus. The frog jumped into the well. The pet cat jumped onto her lap. Please get the purse out of the drawer. Don't run across the road. It may cause accident. Let's walk a mile along the sea beach. They drove through Kharagpur on their way to Digha.

**Now fill in the blanks :**

(a) A ten-rupee note fell ........... Pintu's pocket.

(b) The bus on Garerghat-Tarakeswar route is always crowdy. It is difficult to get ........... it.

(c) Shyamal's office is a kilometre away .......... his house.

(d) Don't walk ........... the garden. It is strictly prohibited.

(e) If you walk ........... the bank of the river ........... the south for a kilometre, you'll see a bridge ........... the river.

[3] These figures will give you an idea of the **Prepositions denoting a point of time and a period of time**.

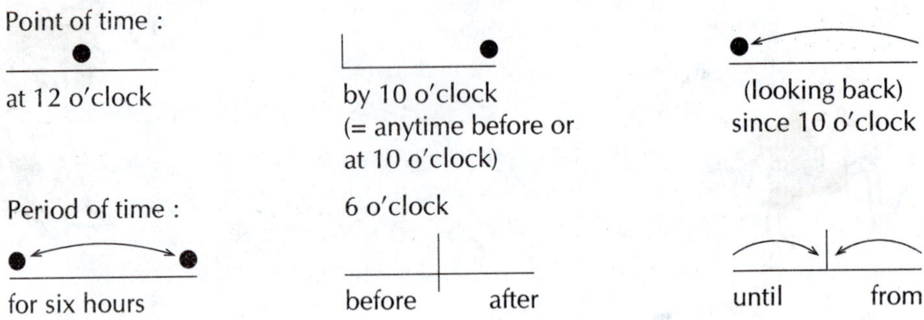


**Examples :**

Nipa will arrive here at 12 o'clock. Please do come by 12 o'clock. I have not seen her since 10 o'clock. He has been reading for six hours. Come here before 6 o'clock. Don't come after 6 o'clock. I'll wait for you until 4 p.m. I've been waiting for you from 4 p.m.

**Note** For is used for Period of time but since and from are used for Point of time. [**Nesfield**]

## SOME IMPORTANT USAGE OF 'AT', 'IN', 'ON'

**At** (5 a.m., 4 p.m., 12 o'clock, dawn, night, midnight)

**In** { 1992 / April / winter / the rainy season / the morning / the afternoon / the evening

**On** { Sunday / Sunday evening / the 5th August / the New Year's Day / the Christmas Eve

But we use 'during the night'. ('in the night' has the same meaning but it is not normally used.)

**Now fill in the blanks :** [ at, in, on, for, before, during ]

(a) You'll meet your friend .............. 7 p.m. .............. Saturday evening.

(b) Please see him anytime .............. 9 o'clock.

(c) The last time we met her was .............. May 1990.

(d) The Headmaster will not be .............. the school .............. the tiffin hours. [ in the school = inside the school; at the school = on duty—**Oxford Guide to English Grammar by John Eastwood** ]

(e) Is the Repubic Day .............. a Sunday this year?

(f) The school will remain closed .............. nearly a month during the summer.

**[4] Prepositions are sometimes omitted.**

Where have you been? (not 'Where have you been to'?)

Having finished my work, I went home. (not 'after having')

We did it last week. (not 'in last week')

Wait a minute. (not 'Wait for a minute')

**[5] Prepositions are sometimes wrongly omitted.**

| Incorrect | Correct |
| --- | --- |
| What use is it? | Of what use is it? |
| His conduct admits no excuse. | His conduct admits of no excuse. |
| The speaker referred his notes. | The speaker referred to his notes. |

## EXERCISE

**1. Match the prepositions (at, in, on, to, between) with the following :**

(a) ............... Sunday
(b) ............... January
(c) ............... 2008.
(d) ............... Monday morning
(e) ........... noon
(f) ............... night
(g) ............... dawn
(h) ............... the morning
(i) ............... the afternoon
(j) ............... 10 o'clock
(k) from dawn ........... dusk
(l) ........... 2 p.m. and 4 p.m.

**2. Complete the following sentences with appropriate prepositions :**

(a) Where do you come ................?
(b) What are you afraid ................?
(c) Please give him a chair to sit.............
(d) Please give me a pen to write.............

**3. Fill in the blanks with prepositional phrases given below:**

**[One has been done for you.]**

(i) He shouted at the top of his voice.
(ii) He got the prize ............. hard work.
(iii) There is a tall tree ............. our school.
(iv) He told me this ............. conversation.
(v) The police arrived ............. time.
(vi) He did not go to school ............. his illness.
(vii) He started a business ............. crying for a job.
(viii) He did this ............. helping his friend.
(ix) The bearer will receive the letter ............. me.
(x) He was given a farewell ............. his retirement.

[at the top of, on the eve of, by dint of, in the nick of, in course of, in front of, owing to, with a view to, instead of, on behalf of]

# 18 APPROPRIATE PREPOSITIONS

## WHAT IS APPROPRIATE PREPOSITION?

***According to English usage certain words are followed by particular Prepositions. These are called Appropriate Prepositions. Students should study the uses of Appropriate Prepositions carefully.***

**Abide by**—You should abide by the rules.
**Abide at (in)**—Now she abides at (in) a hotel.
**Abound in**—Fish abounds in this pond.
**Abound with**—The river abounds with fish.
**Absent from**—He was absent from school.
**Absorbed in**—He is absorbed in studies.
**Access to**—The public has no access to this garden.
**According to**—According to your order I went there.
**Accompanied by**—He was accompanied by his father.
**Accompanied with**—He has fever accompanied with headache.
**Acquainted with**—I am acquainted with him.
**Accused of**—He is accused of theft.
**Accustomed to**—I am accustomed to such a life.
**Acquit** (one) **of**—I acquit you of the charge.
**Add to**—Add this to that.
**Addicted to**—He is addicted to wine.
**Adjacent to**—His school is adjacent to his house.
**Admit of**—Your conduct/It admits of no excuse.

[*Admit* is followed by *of* only when it has an impersonal subject, i.e. *it* or *an abstract noun* (such as, *conduct*). But when the subject is personal, *admit* is not followed by *of*. I *admit* (accept) no excuse.]

**Admit to**—He was admitted to Class VI.
**Admit into**—He was admitted into the room.

**Affection for**—The teacher feels affection for every pupil.

**Affectionate to**—He is affectionate to me.

**Afraid of**—I am not afraid of ghosts.

**Agree with** (a person), **on** (a point), **to** (a proposal)
I agree with you on this point, but I cannot agree to all the proposals.

**Aim at**—He aimed his gun at the bird.

**Alarmed at**—We were alarmed at the news.

**Allot to**—One room has been allotted to him.

**Alternative to**—This question is alternative to that.

**Aloof from**—Keep yourself aloof from bad company.

**Ambition for**—He has no ambition for fame in life.

**Angry with** (a person), **for** (something), **at** (one's conduct)—He is angry with me for speaking against him. I am angry at your conduct.

**Annoyed with** (a person), **for** (something)—I was annoyed with him for being late.

**Anxious about**, **for**—I am anxious about your health. He is anxious for getting a job.

**Apart from**—Apart from the prize, he got a certificate.

**Appeal to** (a person), **for** (something) **against** (a wrong)—He appealed to the Headmaster for pardon. They appealed against the verdict of the lower court.

**Appetite for**—The patient has no appetite for food.

**Apply to** (a person), **for** (a thing)—He applied to the Secretary for the post.

**Aptitude for**—I have no aptitude for Mathematics.

**Arrive at**—We arrived at the station in time.

**Argue with** (a person), **for** or **against** (a thing)—I argued with him for (or against) the point.

**Assign to**—He assigned the task to me.

**Ashamed of**—He is not ashamed of his conduct.

**Ashamed for**—I feel ashamed for you. (**A.L.D.—Hornby**)

**Attend to**—Attend to your lesson.

**Attach to**—Attach this slip to the letter.

**Attend on** (upon)—She attends on (upon) her mother.

**Avail** (oneself) **of**—You must avail yourself of the opportunity.

**Aware of**—He is aware of the fact.

**Based on**—Your remarks are not based on facts.

**Beg** (a person) **for** (a thing)—He begged me for the favour.

**Beg** (a thing) **of** (a person)—He begged the favour of me.

**Believe in**—I do not believe in his honesty.

**Belong to**—This book belongs to me.

**Bent on**—He is bent on doing this.

**Beware of**—Beware of pickpockets.

**Blessed with**—He is blessed with (= possesses) good health.

**Blessed in**—He is blessed (= happy) in his children.

**Blind of**—He is blind of one eye.

**Blind to**—He is blind to his own faults.

**Blush with, for**—She blushed with shame.

[There is no cause to blush for me. (**COD**)]

**Boast of**—Do not boast of your wealth.

**Born of, in**—He was born of poor parents. He was born in poverty.

**Bound for**—The ship is bound for England.

**Brood on, over**—Do not brood over your misfortune.

**Burst into**—He burst into tears/laughter at the news.

**Burst out**—He burst out laughing at my joke.

**Busy with**—He is busy with his studies.

**Callous to**—He is callous to my suffering.

**Capable of**—He is capable of doing this alone.

**Capacity for**—He has capacity for hard work.

**Care for**—I do not care for you.

**Care of**—Take care of your health.

**Careful of**—He is careful of his money.

**Certain of**—He is certain of his ground.

**Charge** (a person) **with** (a fault), **on** or **against** (a person)—He was charged with theft. Theft was charged on (against) him.

**Close to**—The school is very close to our house.

**Clothed in, with**—He is clothed in wool. He was clothed with shame. [**A.L.D.**]

**Clue to**—Find out the clue to the mystery.

**Come of**—He comes of a noble family.

**Commence on**—Our examination commences on the 3rd July.

**Comment on**—He commented favourably on the point.

**Compare with** (similar things), **to** (dissimilar things)—Rabindranath may be compared with Shakespeare. Anger is compared to fire.

**Compete with** (someone), **for** (something)—I competed with him for the first prize.

**Complain to** (a person), **against** (another), **about** (a thing)—They complained (made a complaint) to the Director against the Manager about his behaviour.

**Comply with**—I shall comply with your request.

**Composed of**—Water is composed of Hydrogen and Oxygen.

**Confident of**—I am confident of success.

**Confined in** (a room), **to** (bed)—He is confined in a room for five days. He is confined to bed.

**Congratulate on**—I congratulate you on your success.

**Conscious of**—He is conscious of his weakness.

**Consist of**—This class consists of fifty boys./The committee consists of five members.

**Consist in**—Happiness consists in contentment.

**Consist with**—His statement does not consist with reason.

**Consistent with**—Your action is not consistent with the rules.

**Consult with** (a person), **on** or **about** (a thing)—I consulted with him on/about the matter.

**Contrary to**—His action is contrary to his words.

**Contribute to**—He contributed one thousand rupees to the Flood Relief Fund.

**Control over**—He has no control over his brother.

**Count for**—His advice counts for nothing (i.e. of no effect).

**Count upon**—I count upon your help for this work.

**Cure of**—He will be cured of the disease very soon.

**Cope with**—I cannot cope with the situation.

**Crave for**—He craves for wealth. (COD)

**Deaf of**—He is deaf of one ear. (COD)

**Deaf to**—He is deaf to my request.

**Deal in**—He deals in rice/clothes etc.

**Deal with**—He deals well with the customers.

**Dedicate to**—This book is dedicated to his father.

**Delight in**—He takes delight in music.

**Depend on**—Success depends on hard work.

**Deprived of**—He was deprived of his property.

**Desire for**—He has no desire for fame.

**Desirous of**—He is desirous of building a new house.

**Despair of**—Do not despair of success.

**Destined to**—He was destined to death.

**Devoid of**—He is devoid of common sense.

**Devote to**—He devotes much time to study.

**Die of** (a disease), **from** (an effect), **for** (a cause), **by** (poison), **in** (peace)—He died of cholera. He died from over-eating. He died for his country. He died by poison. Let me die in peace.

**Differ with** (a person), **on** (a point), **in** (opinion)—I differ with you on this point. They differ in their opinions.

**Differ from**—This thing differs from that.

**Difference between**—There is no difference between the two brothers.

**Different from**—This book is different from that.

**Diffident of**—I am diffident of success.

**Disgrace to**—He is a disgrace to his family./Slums are a disgrace to any city.

**Disgusted with** (a person), **at** (a thing)—I am disgusted with him at his conduct.

**Dislike for**—He has dislike for dogs.

**Displeased with** (a person) **at** (a thing)—I am displeased with him at his conduct.

**Dispose of**—He disposed of his books.

**Dispose off**—The old books were disposed off.

**Distinguish** one thing **from** (another)—A child cannot distinguish good from evil.

**Distinguish between**—Distinguish between a phrase and a clause.

**Divert from**—The loud music diverted my attention from study.

**Divide into** (parts)—It was divided into several parts.

**Divide between** (two), **among** (more than two)—Divide the mangoes between Ram and Shyam. Divide the mangoes among the boys.

**Due to**—His absence is due to illness./He is absent due to his illness.

**Dull of**—He is dull of understanding.

**Dull at**—He is dull at Physics/Mathematics etc.

**Eager for, about**—He is eager for promotion in service.
He is eager about the result. (**COD**)

**Eligible for**—He is eligible for the post.

**Encroach on**—Do not encroach on my land.

**End in**—All his plans ended in smoke.

**Endowed with**—He is endowed with talents.

**Engaged with** (a person) in (a work)—I was engaged with him in talk.

**Engaged to**—Lila was engaged to him.

**Enquire of** (a person), **into** (a matter)—He enquired of me into the matter.

**Enter into**—He entered into details. [But] He entered the room.

**Envy of**—I have no envy of him. (**POD**)

**Envious of**—I am not envious of his riches.

**Entitled to**—He is entitled to a reward for his honesty.

**Equal in** (rank), **with** (a person), **to** (a task)—Mr. Bose is equal in rank with Mr. Ghosh. He rose equal to the occasion.

**Escape from**—The man escaped from the prison.

**Escape by**—He escaped by a hair-breadth.

**Esteem for**—He has esteem for the superiors.

**Essential to**—Food is essential to health.

**Excel in**—He excels in painting. (**COD**)

**Excuse for**—He will not be excused for coming late.

**Excuse from**—They may be excused from complying with this regulation.

**Exempt from**—He was exempted from the fine.

**Faith in**—I have no faith in him./He has no faith in religion.

**Faith with** (break faith)—He broke faith with me.

**Faithful to**—The dog is faithful to his master.

**False to**—I cannot be false (unfaithful) to my friend.

**Famous for**—Radhanagar is famous for the birth-place of Raja Rammohun.

**Familiar with**—He is familiar with my brother.

**Fatal to**—The doctor's mistake proved fatal to the patient's life.

**Favour with**—Would you favour me with an early reply?

**(In) favour of**—He spoke in favour of his friend.

**Favourable to** (a person) **for** (something)—This situation is favourable to me for doing this.

**Feel for, in**—I feel for you in your trouble.

**Fit for**—He is not fit for the job.

**Fond of**—She is fond of sweets.

**Free from**—He is now free from danger.

**Fill with**—This tank is filled with water.

**Full of**—This tank is full of water.

**Glance at**—He glanced at me casually./Have a glance at the book.

**Good at**—He is good at tennis. [But, He is good for nothing.]

**Grateful to** (a person) **for** (something)—I am grateful to you for your help.

**Greed for**—He has no greed for wealth.

**Guess at**—Can you guess at her age?

**Guilty of**—He is guilty of murder.

**Hanker after**—Do not hanker after wealth.

**Hard at**—He is hard at work before examination.

**Hard of**—He is hard of hearing.

**Heir of** (a person), **to** (a property)—He is the heir of his uncle (to his uncle's property).

**Hope for**—Let us hope for the best.

**Hunger for**—His hunger for knowledge surprised us.

**Ignorant of**—He is ignorant of this rule.

**Ill with**—He is ill with fever.

**Impose on**—The task was imposed on me.

**Indebted to**—I am indebted to him for this help.

**Indifferent to**—He is indifferent to our problem.

**Indulge in**—Do not indulge in wine.

[But, Do not indulge him with your support.]

**Inform** (a person), **of** (something)—He informed the police of the murder.

**Inferior to**—This orange is inferior to that.

**Inquire of** (a person), **about, into** (a matter)—I inquired of him about (into) the matter.

**Insist on**—He insisted on my going home.

**Interest in**—He has a special interest in history.

**Interfere with** (a person), **in** (a matter)—Do not interfere with me in my business.

**Invite to**—I invited him to dinner.

**Involved in**—He is involved in the plot.

**Jealous of**—I am not at all jealous of his fortune.

**Jump at**—Do not jump at the offer.

**Jump to**—Do not hastily jump to a conclusion.

**Jump on**—The cat jumped on the table.

**Jump over**—He jumped over the fence.

**Junior to**—He is junior to me in service.

**Junior by**—He is junior to me by five years.

**Justification of/for**—There is no justification of (for) his conduct.

**Key to**—He has found out the key to his problem.

**Kind** (Noun) **of**—What kind of paper is it?

[So kind (= kindness) of you to see me.]

**Kind** (Adj) **to**—She is very kind to the children.

**Lack of**—I have no lack of friends.

**Lacking in**—He is lacking in courage.

**Lame of**—He is lame of one leg.

**Lament for**—She lamented for her child.

**Late in**—Why are you so late in coming?

**Laugh at**—Do not laugh at the poor.

**Lay by**—Lay by something for old age.

**Liable to**—He is liable to fine for his misconduct.

**Liking for**—She has a liking for music.

**Limit to**—You should have a limit to your demands.

**Limited to**—Invitation was limited to members only.

**Listen to**—Listen to me. Listen to the news on the radio.

**Live on** (food)—The cow lives on grass.

**Live by**—He lives by honest means.

**Live beyond, within**—He lives beyond his means.
He lives within his means.

**Live for** (an ideal)—He lives for fame.

**Look at**—Look at the moon.

**Look after**—There is none to look after her.

**Look for**—I am looking for a good job.

**Look into**—I am looking into the matter.

**Look over**—He is looking over the answer-papers.

**Look up**—Look up the word in the dictionary.

**Long for**—He longed for fame.

**Loyal to**—He is loyal to his master.

**Mad with**—He is mad with pain.

**Made of**—This ring is made of gold.

**Make for**—The ship made for England./Make for England at your earliest.

**Make out**—I cannot make out what you say.

**Marry to**—He married his daughter to a rich man. She was married to a rich man.

**Marry**—She married a Frenchman. (**A. L. D.—Hornby**)

**Mourn for, over**—Don't mourn for (over) the dead.

**Need for, of**—I have no need for more money. I am in need of money.

**Object to**—He objected to my proposal.

**Oblige** (a person) **with** or **by** (doing) something—He obliged me with a loan, or, by giving me a loan.

**Obliged to** (a person), **for** (a thing)—I am obliged to him for his kind help.

**Obsessed by, with**—He is obsessed by the idea./Why are people so obsessed with money?

**Obstacle to**—Poverty is often an obstacle to higher studies.

**Occupied with** (a business), **in** (doing a thing)—He is occupied with his studies. He is occupied in writing a letter.

**Occur to** (one's mind)—The idea never occurred to me.

**Occur in** (an essay, a poem etc.)—This line occurs in the poem 'The Cloud', written by Shelley.

**Offend against**—You have offended against good manners.

**Offended with** (a person) **at** (an action)—I am offended (displeased) with you at your conduct.

**Offensive to**—This acrid smell is offensive to me.

**Officiate for** (a person) **in** (a post)—He officiated for me in that post.

**Open to**—His plan is open to objection.

**Open at**—Open at page 20.

**Opportunity for, of**—I have no opportunity for (of) doing the work.

**Opposite to**—Your idea is opposite to mine. Our house is opposite to the park.

**Overcome with, by** (emotion etc.)—He was overcome with fatigue. He was overcome by anger. (**COD**)

**Owe to, for**—I owe my all to him./He still owes for the goods supplied to him.

**Parallel to**—This road is parallel to that.

**Part from** (a person), **with** (a thing)—He parted from his friend. She parted with the ring. (**COD**)

**Partial to**—He is partial to his son.

**Partiality for**—He has no partiality for his son.

**Pass for**—He passes for a clever man.

**Pass away**—He passed away last night.

**Persist in**—He persisted in disturbing me.

**Pity for**—Have pity for the poor.

**Play on**—He played on guitar.

**Plead with** (a person) **for** or **against** (something)—I pleaded with him for justice (against the wrong done to me).

**Pleased with** (a person) **at** (something)—I am pleased with him. I am pleased at the news.

**Polite in, to**—He is polite in his manners. He is polite to strangers.

**Poor in** (spirit)—Don't be poor in spirit. He is poor in Mathematics.

**Popular with**—He is popular with all for his good behaviour.

**Prefer** (one) **to** (another)—I prefer coffee to tea.

**Preferable to**—Death is preferable to dishonour.

**Preside over**—He presided over the meeting.

**Pretend to**—He does not pretend to high birth.

**Prevent** (one) **from** (doing something)—I prevented him from going there.

**Pride** (oneself) **on**, (take **pride in**)—He prides himself on (takes pride in) his high birth.

**Proud of**—He is proud of his position.

**Prior to**—Prior to that, he was in a wretched condition.

**Prohibit from**—I prohibited him from going there.

**Prompt in** (answers), **prompt at** (figures)—He is prompt in his answers. He is prompt at figures.

**Prone to**—He is prone to idleness.

**Proportionate to**—Punishment should be proportionate to offence.

**Provide against** (evil days), **for** (children), **with** (a thing)—You must provide against evil days for your children. I provide (supply) him with food.

**Qualified for**—He is qualified for the post.

**Quick at, of**—He is quick at figures. He is quick of understanding.

**Quarrel with** (a person) **for, over, about** (something)—They quarrelled with one another for (over, about) the property.

**Refer to**—Refer the matter to him for enquiry.

**Rejoice at, in**—Everyone rejoiced at (in) her success.

[**Nesfield** says "rejoice in one's own success", but "rejoice at the success of another." But **COD** does not make any such distinction]

**Relevant to**—Your remark is not relevant to the point.

**Rely on, upon**—You can rely on him./He can be relied upon for that kind of help.

**Remedy for**—There is no remedy for this disease. (**COD**)

[Nesfield says "remedy for or against snakebite."]

**Remind** (one) **of** (a thing)—I reminded him of his promise.

**Render into**—Render the passage into Hindi.

**Replace** (one thing) **with** another—Replace this chair with a new one. (**COD**)

["In a passive sentence where it is necessary to use 'by' to denote an agent, 'with' must be used before the name of the thing that is substituted."

—**Current English Usage by F. T. Wood**]

**Require** (a thing) **of** (a person)—I required a loan of him./What do you require of me?

**Resign** (oneself) **to**—I resigned myself to fate.

(In) **respect of** [in point of]—He is junior to me in respect of service.

(With) **respect to**—We are talking with respect to that matter.

**Respond to**—Nobody responded to my call.

**Responsible to** (an authority) **for** (an action)—He is responsible to the committee for his action.

**Rest with, upon**—The whole matter rests (depends) with you. I rest upon (rely on) your promise.

**Restore to**—Restore his property to him.

**Restrict to**—Admission was restricted to students.

**Retire from, on**—He retired from service on a pension.

**Rich in**—Bihar is rich in minerals.

**Rid of**—Get rid of bad company.

**Rob of**—Somebody robbed him of his purse.

**Sanguine of**—She is sanguine of her success.

**Satisfied with, of**—I am satisfied with him. I am satisfied of the truth.

**Satisfaction in, with**—I find satisfaction in gardening. Great was his satisfaction with his result.

**Search for**—Their search for the thing was of no avail.

(In) **search of**—They are in search of a singing bird.

**Sensible of**—She is sensible of the risk.

**Sensitive to**—She is sensitive to cold.

**Sentence to, for**—He was sentenced to death for murder.

**Senior to**—He is senior to me by four years. I am senior to him in service.

**Send for**—Send for a doctor immediately.

**Sick of, for**—I am sick of fever. I am sick of this idle life. He is sick for home.

**Similar to**—This pen is similar to that.

**Sink in** (mud), **into** (the sea, river etc.)—He sank in mud. The ship sank into the sea.

**Slow of** (speech), **at** (figures), **in** (doing something)—He is slow of speech. He is slow at figures. He is slow in writing.

**Smell of**—This glass smells of wine.

**Smile on**—Fortune smiled on him.

**Stare at**—She stared at me.

**Stick to**—He sticks to his decision.

**Subject to**—This is subject to approval of the committee.

**Succeed in**—He will succeed in life.

**Suffer from**—He is suffering from fever.

**Superior to**—This type of rice is superior to that.

**Supply** (a person) **with** (a thing), **to** (a person)—He supplied us with food. He supplied food to us.

**Sure of**—I am sure of success.

**Sympathy for**—I have no sympathy for him.

**Take after**—The boy takes after (resembles) his father.

**Talk to, with** (a person), **of, about, over** (a thing)—I am talking to (with) Mr. Roy of (about, over) the matter.

**Taste for**—She has no taste for music.

**Tell upon**—Over-eating tells upon health.

**Tide over**—He will soon tide over the difficulty.

**Tired of**—I am tired of doing the same thing day after day.

**Think of, about** (a person), **over** (something)—What do you think of (about) him? Think carefully over his advice.

**Tolerant of**—We must be tolerant of opposition.

**Triumph over**—Jim and Della triumphed over their poverty.

**True to**—He is true to his master.

**Trust** (a person) **with** (a thing), **to** (a person), **in** God—You may trust me with the work. You may trust the work to me. Trust in God.

**Unite with**—Be united with your friends.

**Useful to** (a person), **for** (some purpose)—This book is useful to us for examination.

**Vain of**—She is vain of her beauty.

**Vary from**—His opinion varies from his brother's.

**Vexed with** (a person), **for**, **at** (a thing)—He is vexed with me at my conduct. He is vexed with me for opposing him.

**Void of**—He is void of common sense.

**Wait for**—I waited for him for two hours.

**Wait on**—The nurse waited on (attended) the patient.

**Want of**—We have no want of money.

**Wanting in**—He is wanting in common sense.

**Warn of**—He warned me of the danger.

**Weak in**—He is weak in Mathematics.

**Weak of**—He is weak of understanding.

**Weary of**—He is weary of hard life.

**Wish for**—I do not wish for name and fame.

**Wonder at**—I wonder at his ignorance.

**Worthy of**—He is worthy of our praise.

**Yield to**—He yielded to his enemy.

**Zeal for**—He has a zeal for social work.

**Zealous for, in**—He is zealous for improvement in a good cause.

**Zest for**—She has no zest for music.

The Appropriate Prepositions are very difficult to remember. But if we arrange them in accordance with Prepositions, we can notice some sort of similarity and it becomes easy to learn. Moreover, our ear is tuned with the use of Prepositions.

## FOR

Study the words that take the Preposition 'for' after them. You have learnt the applications of the words. Now see them systematically.

## NOUNS : [FOR]

affection for
ambition for
anxiety for
apology for
appetite for
aptitude for
blame for
candidate for
capacity for
compassion for
compensation for
contempt for

craving for
desire for
dislike for
esteem for
fitness for
fondness for
greed for
guarantee for
hunger for
leisure for
linking for
match for

motive for
opportunity for
partiality for
passion for
pretext for
remedy for
reputation for
shame for
taste for
zeal for
zest for

## ADJECTIVES AND PARTICIPLES : [FOR]

anxious for
bound for
celebrated for
conspicuous for
customary for
designed for
destined for
distinguished for (something)
distinguished by (some action)

eager for
eligible for
eminent for
famous for
fit for
favourable for
good for
grateful for
necessary for
notorious for

penitent for
prepared for
proper for
qualified for
ready for
remarkable for
sorry for
sufficient for
useful for
zealous for

## VERBS : [FOR]

beg for
care for
clamour for
feel for

hope for
long for
lament for
make for

mourn for
pine for
pray for
stipulate for

start for
wait for
wish for
yearn for

## FROM

The following words take the Preposition '*from*' after them :

## NOUNS : [FROM]

abstinence from
descent from

digression from
escape from

exemption from
inference from

relief from
respite from

## ADJECTIVES AND PARTICIPLES : [FROM]

absent from
alienated from
apart from
disqualified from

distinct from
different from
precluded from
remote from

## VERBS : [FROM]

| | | |
|---|---|---|
| abstain from | differ from | prevent from |
| alight from | digress from | prohibit from |
| avert from | dissent from | protect from |
| cease from | dissuade from | quote from |
| debar from | elicit from | recoil from |
| derive from | emerge from | recover from |
| derogate from | escape from | refrain from |
| desist from | exclude from | result from |
| detract from | excuse from | retire from |
| deviate from | preserve from | vary from |

## IN

The following words take the Preposition 'in' after them :

### NOUNS : [IN]

complicity in (a crime)
concurrence in (a proposal)
confidence in (a person)
delight in (something)
experience in (doing something)
faith in (a person or thing)
jurisdiction in (a law suit)
laxity in (morals)
readiness in answering (a question)
temperance in diet

### ADJECTIVES AND PARTICIPLES : [IN]

absorbed in (study etc.)
accomplished in (art etc.)
accurate in (statistics etc.)
apt in (Mathematics etc.)
assiduous in (studies)
backward in (something)
bigoted in (opinion)
confirmed in (a habit)
correct in (a statement)
defective in (point of style)
deficient in (energy)
diligent in (business)
engaged in (business)
entangled in (a plot)
enveloped in (mist)
experienced in (something)
fertile in (resources)
foiled in (an attempt)
fruitful in (resources)
held in (esteem)
honest in (dealings)
impressed in (thought)
implicated in (a crime)
indebted in (a large sum)
interested in (a person or thing)
invested in (govt. paper)
involved in (difficulties)
late in (doing something)
lavish in (expenditure)
lax in (morals)
obstinate in (resistance)
polite in (manners)
poor in (spirit)
proficient in (any subject)
profuse in (offers)
remiss in (duties)
rich in (property)
skilful/slothful in (business)
slow in (doing something)
temperate in (habits)
veiled in (mystery)
versed in (any subject)
weak in (head)
zealous in (a cause)

## VERBS : [IN]

abound in (fish etc.)
arrive in (a country)
believe in (one's honesty)
consist in (facts or results)
dabble in (politics)
deal in (cloth etc.)
delight in (music etc.)
employ in (a work)
enlist in (the army etc.)
excel in (languages etc.)
fail in (an attempt)
fall in (love)
glory in (success)
increase in (wisdom)
indulge in (wine)
involve in (debt)
join in (a game)
labour in (a good cause)
originate in (a thing or place)
preserve in (an effort)
persist in (doing something)
rejoice in (own success)

## OF

The following words take the Preposition 'of' after them :

## NOUNS : [OF]

abatement of (the fever)
abhorrence of (ingratitude)
assurance of (help)
betrayal of (a secret)
cause of (troubles)
charge of (murder etc.)
consciousness of (guilt)
consideration of (a thing)
conviction of (guilt)
decision of (some dispute)
distrust of (a person or thing)
doubt of or about (a thing)
economy of (time)
endurance of (pain)
evasion of (a rule)
experience of (a thing)
failure of (a plan)
freedom of (action)
hatred of or for (a person)
heir of (a person)
hope of or for (better luck)
imputation of (guilt)
infliction of (punishment)
judge of (a matter)
proof of (guilt)
(in) pursuance of (an object)
relation of (one thing) to (another)
result of (a proceeding)
(in) search of (wealth)
tenacity of (purpose)
want of (memory)
witness of (an event)

## ADJECTIVES AND PARTICIPLES : [OF]

accused of (a crime)
acquitted of (a charge)
afraid of (death)
ambitious of (distinction)
apprehensive of (danger)
apprised of (a fact)
ashamed of (dullness)
assured of (the truth)
aware of (intentions)
bereft of (a child)
blind of (one eye)
born of (rich parents)
capable of (improvement)
careful of (money)

cautious of (anything)
certain of (success)
cognisant of (a truth)
commemorative of (a victory)
convinced of (a fact)
covetous of (goods)
cured of (a disease)
composed of (a material)
confident of (success)
conscious of (a fault)
convicted of (a crime)
defeated of (purpose)
deserving of (praise)
desirous of (success)
despondent of (success)
destitute of (money)
devoid of (common sense)
diffident of (success)
disappointed of (anything)
distrustful of (a man's motives)
dull of (understanding)
defrauded of (earnings)
depleted of (strength)
deprived of (something)
easy of (access)
empty of (contents)
envious of (another's success)
fearful of (something)
fond of (something)
full of (persons or things)
greedy of (riches)
guilty of (theft)
healed of (a disease)

heedless of (consequences)
hopeful of (success)
ignorant of (any subject)
impatient of (reproof)
inclusive of (extras)
independent of (parents)
indicative of (motives)
informed of (a fact)
innocent of (a charge)
irrespective of (consequences)
lame of (one leg)
lavish of (money)
neglectful of (interests)
negligent of (duties)
productive of (wealth)
proud of (position)
quick of (understanding)
receptive of (advice)
reckless of (expenditure)
regardless of (consequences)
repentant of (sin)
sanguine of (success)
sensible of (kindness)
sick of (waiting)
slow of (hearing)
subversive of (discipline)
sure of (success)
suspicious of (meaning)
thankful of (favours)
tired of (doing something)
vain of (fine dress etc.)
weary of (doing something)
worthy of (praise)

## VERBS : [OF]

accuse of (some misdeed)
acquit of (blame)
admit of (an excuse)
beware of (something)
boast of (something)
complain of (something)
consist of (materials)
convict a person of (a crime)
convince a person of (a fact)
cure a man of (a disease)
die of (a disease)
dispose of (property)

dream of (strange things)
fail of (a purpose)
heal of (a disease)
hear of (an event)
inform a person of (a thing)
inquire/enquire of (a person)
judge of or by (something)
purge the mind of (false notions)
repent of (misdeed)
smell of (fish)
suspect of (treachery)
taste of (salt)

## ON

The following words take the Preposition 'on' after them :

### NOUNS : [ON]

assault on (a person or thing)
attack on (a place)
authority on (a subject)
controversy on (a point)
decision on (some case)
dependence on (a person or thing)
imposition on (the public)
infliction on (the guilty)
influence on (a man's action)
lecture on (a subject)
load on (a person or thing)
onslaught on (a person)
operation on (a thing)
outlook on (a subject)
outlook from (a window)
parody on (a subject)
premium on (gold)
revenge on (a person)
slur on (his name)
subsistence on (rice)

### ADJECTIVES AND PARTICIPLES : [ON]

based on (something)
bent on (doing something)
conditional on (something)
entailed on (a person)
founded on (fact)
imperative on (a person)
consequent on (some cause)
determined on (doing a thing)
engraved on (the memory)
incumbent on (a person)
resolved on (doing a thing)
silent on (a point)

### VERBS : [ON]

calculate on (success)
decide on (something)
err on (the side of leniency)
encroach on (one's authority)
expatiate on (a subject)
fall on (the enemy)
fire on (a city)
gain on (someone in a race)
harp on (something)
hinge on (an event)
impose on (a person)
infringe on (someone's rights)
insist on (something being done)
intrude on (one's leisure)
lean on (a staff)
meditate on (some subject)
operate on (a patient)
ponder on (a subject)
pounce on (a thing)
prevail on (a person) to do something
pride oneself on (a thing)
smile on (a person)
speak on (a subject)
trample on (justice)

## TO

The following words take the Prepostion '**to**' after them :

### NOUNS : [TO]

access to (a person or place)
adherence to (a plan or cause)
allusion to (something)
alternative to (something)
antidote to (some poison)
antipathy to (a person or thing)
approach to (anything)
answer to (a letter/question)
attachment to (a person or thing)
attention to (study etc.)
attraction to (a thing)
concession to (a demand)
condemnation to (death)
conformity to (rule)
contribution to (a fund)
contrast to (a person or a thing)
disgrace to (a person)
dislike to (a person or thing)
drawback to (success)
duty to (a person)
exception to (a rule)
enmity to (a person) [**Wren & Martin**]
enmity with (a person) [**Nesfield**]
hostility to (a person or cause)
incentive to (industry)
indifference to (heat or cold)
invitation to (a dinner)
key to (a mystery)
leniency to (a person or rule)

likeness to (a person or thing)
limit to (a man's zeal)
menace to (the public health)
nomination to (a post)
obedience to (parents, orders etc.)
objection to (a proposal)
obstruction to (traffic)
opposition to (a person)
postscript to (a letter)
preface to (a book)
reference to (a person or a thing)
reply to (a letter)
repugnance to (wishes)
resemblance to (a person or a thing)
resignation to (fate)
resistance to (injustice)
responsibility to (the law)
But, responsibility for (an action)
sequel to (an event)
submission to (authority)
subscription to (a fund)
succession to (an estate)
supplement to (a book)
temptation to (an evil)
testimony to (one's character)
testimony against (one's character)
title to (an estate)
(A) victim to (oppression)
(The) victim of (oppression)

### ADJECTIVES AND PARTICIPLES : [TO]

abandoned to (his fate)
abhorrent to (his feelings)
acceptable to (a person)
accessory to (a crime)
accustomed to (riding etc.)
accessible to (strangers)
accountable to (a person)
adapted for (an occupation)
adapted to (his tastes)
adequate to (his wants)
addicted to (bad habits)
adjacent to (place)

adverse to (his interests)
affectionate to (a person)
agreeable to (his wishes)
akin to (a person or thing)
alien to (his character)
alive to (the consequences)

allied to (a thing)
allied with (a person or country)
amenable to (reason)
answerable to (a person)
answerable for (his conduct)
analogous to (a thing)
apparent to (anyone)
applicable to (a case)
appropriate to (an occasion)
astonishing to (a person)
averse to (hard work)
beneficial to (a person)
blind to (faults)
callous to (suffering)
close to (a person or thing)
common to (several persons or things)
comparable to (something else)
complaisant to (a person)
condemned to (death)
conducive to (success)
conformable to (reason)
congenial to (one's tastes)
consecrated to (a person)
contrary to (rule)
creditable to (his judgement)
deaf to (entreaties)
derogatory to (his character)
detrimental to (health)
devoted to (a person or cause)
disastrous to (a person etc.)
due to (some cause)
entitled to (a hearing)
equal to (the occasion)
essential to (something)

exposed to (danger)
faithful to (a master)
false to (his friends)
fatal to (his prospects)

favourable to (his prospects)
foreign to (the purpose)
hostile to (his endeavours)
hurtful to (health)
immaterial to (the point)
impertinent to (his master)
impervious to (water)
incidental to (a journey)
inclined to (laziness)
indebted to (a person)
indifferent to (heat or cold)
indigenous to (a country)
indispensable to (success)
indulgent to (his children)
indulgent in (wine)
inimical to (a person)
insensible to (shame)
inured to (some habits)
irrelevant to (a question)
liable to (error)
limited to (a certain area)
lost to (all sense of shame)
loyal to (the government)
material to (success)
natural to (a person)
necessary to (happiness)
obedient to (parents etc.)
obliged to (a person)
offensive to (a person)
opposed to (facts)
opposite to (a place)
painful to (one's feeling)
paramount to (everything else)
partial to (someone)
peculiar to (a person or thing)
pertinent to (a question)

pledged to (someone)
preferable to (something else)
polite to (strangers)
precious to (a person)
polite in (manners)
prefixed to (a title-deed)
prejudicial to (his interests)
preliminary to (an inquiry)
preparatory to (an inquiry)
preventive to (fever)
previous to (some event)
prior to (something else)
profitable to (an investor)
prone to (idleness)
reconciled to (a position)
reduced to (poverty)
reconciled with (an opponent)
related to (a person)
relevant to (a question)
repugnant to (his wishes)
repulsive to (his feelings)
requisite to (happiness)
requisite for (a purpose)
responsible to (a person)
restricted to (something)
sacred to (a man's memory)
sensitive to (blame)
serviceable to (a person)
similar to (a person or thing)
strange to (a person)
subordinate to (a person)
subject to (authority)
subsidiary to (trade)
subsequent to (another event)
suitable for (his income)
suited to (the occasion)
suited for (a post)
suited to (the occasion)
supplementary to (something)
true to (his convictions)
tantamount to (a falsehood)
vital to (health)

## VERBS : [TO]

accede to (a request)
accrue to (a person)
adapt to (cricumstances)
adhere to (a plan)
agree to (a proposal)
allot to (a person)
allude to (a fact)
answer to (a person)
answer for (conduct)
apologise to (a person)
apologise for (rudeness)
appeal to (a person)
appeal for or against (something)
appoint to (a position/situation)
ascribe to (a cause)
aspire to (an object)
assent to (one's terms)

attend to (a book or speaker)
attain to (a high place)
attribute to (a cause)
belong to (a person)
certify to (a man's character)
cling to (a person or thing)
compare to (a dissimilar thing)
communicate a thing to (a person)
conduce to (happenings)
concede to (some demand)
consent to (a proposal)
conform to (a rule)
contribute to (a fund)
correspond to (something)
demur to (statement)
defer to (a man's wishes)
devote one's time to (sport etc.)

dispute with (a person) on (a matter)
entitle anyone to (an estate)
explain to (a person)
impute blame to (a person)
invite a man to (dinner)
jump at (an offer)
jump to (a conclusion)
keep to (a point)
keep (abstain) from (wine)
listen to (something)
lead to (a place)
object to (a proposal)
occur to (one's mind)
occur in (a poem etc.)
prefer one thing to (another)
pretend to (omniscience)

proceed to (a business not yet started)
proceed with (a business already started)
refer to (a subject)
revert to (an appointment)
stoop to (something)
submit to (authority)
succumb to (difficulties)
supply a thing to (a person)
supply a person with (a thing)
trust in (a person—Intr. verb)
trust to (a man's honesty—Intr. verb)
trust a man with (money—Tran. verb)
turn to (a friend) for (help)
testify to (a fact)
yield to (some person or thing)

## WITH

The following words take the Preposition 'with' after them :

### NOUNS : [WITH]

accomplice with (a person)
accomplice in (some crime)
(In) accordance with (a rule)
acquaintance with (a person or thing)
alliance with (a person or thing)
bargain with (a person)
bargain for (a thing)
coheir with (a person)
collusion with (a person)
compact with (a person)
competition with (a person)
competition for (a thing)
comparison with (a person or thing)
(in) contrast with (a person or thing)
disagreement with (a person)
engagement with (a business)
engagement with (a person)
enmity with (a person)
familiarity with (a person or thing)
harmony with (anything)
identity with (a person or thing)
interview with (a person)
intercession with (a superior)
intercession for (a friend)
compliance with (a request)
concurrence with (a person)
concurrence in (a proposal)
conformity with (anyone's views)
conformity to (rule)
condolence with (a person)
contact with (something)
controversy on or about (something)
controversy with (a person)
conversation with (a person)
correspondence with (a person)
correspondence to (a thing)
connection with (a person or thing)
intercourse with (a person)
intimacy with (a person)
quarrel with (another person)
quarrel between (two persons)
rapport with (a person)

relations with (a person)
rupture with (a friend)
rupture between (two persons)
share with (a person)
share of (a thing)
(In) unison with (his character)

## ADJECTIVES AND PARTICIPLES : [WITH]

abounding with or in fish
acquainted with (a person or thing)
afflicted with (rheumatism)
aggravated with (a person)
aggravated at (a thing)
angry with (a person)
angry at (a thing)
annoyed at (a thing)
annoyed with (a person)
blessed with (good health)
beset with (difficulties)
busy with (his lessons)
charged with (a crime)
charged (loaded) with (a bullet)
charged to (his account)
collateral with (something else)
commensurate with (one's desires)
compatible with (one's temper)
compliant with (one's wishes)
compounded with (something else)
consistent with (honesty)
contemporary with (a person or event)
contented with (something)
contrasted with (something else)
conversant with (persons or things)
convulsed with (laughter)
delighted with (success)
deluged with (water)
disgusted with (a thing)
displeased with (a person)
distracted with (pain)
drenched with (water)
even (= equal) with ( a rival)
endowed with (natural ability)

exhausted with (labour)
familiar with (a person or thing)
fascinated with (a person or thing)
fatigued with (doing something)
flushed with (victory)
fraught with (danger)
gifted with (abilities)
honoured with (something)
identical with (anything)
ill with (fever)
indignant with (a person)
indignant at (something done)
imbued with (confidence)
infatuated with (a person)
infected with (chicken-pox etc.)
infested with (rats)
inspired with (hope)
intimate with (a person)
invested with (full powers)
mad with (disappointment)
occupied with (some work)
occupied in (reading a book)
overcome with (sorrow)
overwhelmed with (grief)
parallel with or to (anything)
popular with (some persons)
replete with (comfort)
satiated with (pleasure)
satisfied with (his income)
simultaneous with (an event)
stained with (crimes)
synonymous with (another word)
sympathetic with (sufferers)
touched with (anything)

## VERBS : [WITH]

accompany with (a thing)
accord with or to (a thing)
agree to (a proposal)
agree with (a person)
argue with (a person)
argue for or against (a point)
associate with (a person or thing)
bear with (a man's impatience)
clash with (one's meaning)
close with (an offer)
coincide with (one's opinion)
combat with (difficulties)
comply with (one's wishes)
concur with (a person)
content with (a person)
concur in (an opinion)
condole with (a person)
cope with (a person)
correspond with a person (write)
correspond to something (agree)
credit with (good intentions)
disagree with (a person or thing)
debit with (a sum of money)
deal with a person (behave)
deal with a subject (write on)
deal in rice etc. (trade in)
deluge with (water)
dispense with (a man's services)
entrust anyone with (a thing)
entrust a thing to (anyone)
exchange with (a person)
expostulate with (a person)
fill in or up (the blanks)
flirt with (a person)
furnish a person with (a thing)
grapple with (difficulties)
impress a person with (an idea)
impress an idea on (a person)
indorse/endorse with (a signature)
indulge oneself with (wine)
indulge in (wine)
interfere with (a person)
interfere in (some matter)
intersect with (each other)
inspire a man with (courage)
intrigue with (the opposite party)
menace with (punishment)
meddle with (other men's business)
overwhelm with (kindness)
part with (a person or thing)—**Nesfield**
participate with (a person)
participate in (something)
quake with (fear)
quarrel with (someone)
quarrel over or about (something)
reconcile with (an adversary)
remonstrate with (a person)
remonstrate against (some proceeding)
reason with (a person)
reason about (something)

reward a man with (something)
for (something done)
side with (a person) in (dispute)
sympathise with (a person) in
(his troubles)
trifle with (a man's feelings)
vie with (another person)

## SPECIALLY NOTABLE [FOR SIMILARITY]

**For :** affection for, ambition for, anxiety for, desire for, dislike for, etc.

**From :** differ from, escape from, preserve from, prevent from, prohibit from, protect from, quote from, recover from, refrain from, etc.

**In :** absorbed in, apt in, engaged in, backward in, defective in, etc.

**Of :** afraid of, ashamed of, blind of (one eye), lame of (one leg), deaf of (one ear), dull of (understanding), hard of (hearing), sure of, sanguine of, tired of, weary of, worthy of, etc.

## SPECIAL PREPOSITIONS

**Than :** 'Than' is usually a Conjunction, but it is sometimes used as a Preposition.

I cannot accept less than fifty rupees for this article. (than—Prep.) **Wren & Martin**

He is taller than I (am) [not me]. [Here 'than' is a Conjunction.]

**But :** As a rule 'but' is a Conjunction. When used as a Preposition 'but' means 'except' :

All is lost but honour. She returned all the gifts but one. None but the brave deserves the fair. Nobody will help you but me (**not I**). [but—Preposition]

'But' is a Conjunction where it does not mean 'except' :

The boy is intelligent but failed in the examination [but—Conjunction]

## SOME COMMON ERRORS IN PREPOSITION

We read English with him. (not, near him)

Give me a pen to write with. (not, write)

Keep the book with you. (not, near you)

Open the book at page 15. (not, page 15)

Ram was married to Sita. (not, with)

Give him a chair to sit on. (not, to sit)

He is angry with me. (not, upon me)

Where do you come from ? (not, from where)

He could not come to school on account of illness. (not, due to)

I went home. (not, 'to home' because in such a sentence, the word 'home' is just like an adverbial word here or there)

## EXERCISE

**1. Complete the following sentences with appropriate prepositions :**

(a) He is absent ......... school.

(b) He was admitted ......... Class VI.

(c) This book belongs ......... him.

(d) Are you busy ......... your studies?

(e) Take care ......... your health.

(f) He will comply ......... my request.

(g) He has no control ......... his son.

(h) The man is eligible ......... the post.

(i) They will not be excused .... coming late.

(j) She is familiar ......... my parents.

(k) He is not fit ......... the job.

(l) I am fond ......... sweets.

(m) I prefer sweets ......... meat.

(n) You can rely ......... him.

(o) He is senior ......... me.

(p) She is junior ......... him.

(q) This is superior ......... that.

(r) This is inferior ......... that.

(s) He is waiting ......... me.

(t) She waited ....... the patient.

**2. Insert suitable prepositions in the following passages :**

A list of prepositions to be inserted is given on the right column.

| | |
|---|---|
| (a) Mr. John is a European. He deals ............... umbrella. But he deals well ............ the customers. He is aware ............ good relations ........... the customers. He has invited some of them ............ dinner today. | of, in, to, with |
| (b) Karim died .......... cholera. But his friend, Abdul died ............ over-eating though he wished to die ............ his country. | for, from, of |
| (c) The man is blind ......... one eye. But he is not blind ......... his son's faults. He knows very well that his son is lame ............ one leg. He is also hard ........... hearing. However, he devotes much time ............ study. He hopes that fortune will smile ............ him. He is not ashamed ............ his physical deformity. He does not hanker ........ name or fame. | to, of, on, after |
| (d) I agree ............ you ............ this point. But I cannot agree ......... your previous proposal. However, you should not be angry ............ me ........... speaking ............ you. I am not at all angry ............ your conduct. | at, to, on, for, against, with |
| (e) He is fond ........ sweets. But I prefer fruit ......... sweets. In fact, fruit and honey are preferable ..... fish or meat. But my friend differs ............ me ..... this point. | to, on, of, with |
| (f) You should abide ............ the rules of the school and you should not be absent ............ school. Your school is adjacent ............ your house and so you will not be excused ............ coming late. | by, to, for, from |
| (g) She is proud ......... her wealth. But you should not take pride ........ your health or wealth. You should not be devoid ......... common sense. Moreover, you should not laugh ....... the poor and you should have zeal ............ social work. | at, in, of, for |

# 19 MORE ABOUT CONJUNCTIONS

## WHAT DOES A CONJUNCTION DO ?

**A Conjunction is a word used for joining :**

**[ 1 ] one word to another word**

**[ 2 ] one word to a clause**

**[ 3 ] one sentence to another sentence (i.e. one clause to another clause).**

### ONE WORD JOINED TO ANOTHER WORD

When two words are joined together by a Conjunction, each is usually of the similar part of speech.

Thus, a noun is joined to a noun or a pronoun; a verb to a verb; an adjective to an adjective; an adverb to an adverb; and a preposition to a preposition.

Noun to Noun—Ram and Rahim are two friends.

Noun to Pronoun—John and I do the work.

Pronoun to Pronoun—You and he are both wrong.

Verb to Verb—Lila sat down and wept.

Adjective to Adjective—They are sad but hopeful.

Adverb to Adverb—A cat moves slowly and silently.

Prep. to Prep.—He has read the book through and through.

**Note** '**And**' joins similar ideas, '**but**' joins opposite ideas; '**or**' denotes alternative ideas :

He is strong and brave. He is weak but brave.

Do or die. [= If you do not do, you will die.]

Do and die. [= If you do, you will die]

### ONE WORD JOINED TO A CLAUSE

[Clause = a group of words having a Finite Verb]

Adv. and Clause—He is so weak that he cannot walk.

Adv. and Clause—Such was her beauty that everybody loved her.

Adv. and Clause—No sooner had I sat down than they left the room.

Adv. and Clause—Hardly had I left the room when it began to rain.

Adv. and Clause—Scarcely had I left the room when it began to rain.

Adv. and Clause—She has none else than her mother. (**Nesfield**)

**Note** In a clause beginning with no sooner, hardly and scarcely the auxiliary verb precedes the subject.

Also note that no sooner takes than but hardly and scarcely take when as correlative.

## ONE CLAUSE JOINED TO ANOTHER CLAUSE

A clause is a shorter sentence within a bigger sentence.

Among those Conjunctions which join one clause or one sentence to another clause or another sentence, the most common can be seen from these examples :

| First part of sentence | Conjunction | Second part of sentence |
|---|---|---|
| My father says | that | this book is mine. |
| He works hard | that/so that | he may succeed. |
| I trust his word | because | he speaks the truth. |
| The girl will come | if | she is allowed to do so. |
| I wish to know | whether | he will come or not. |
| She walked slowly | lest | she should fall down. |
| He will do this | unless | he is stopped by you. |
| You may go out | as/since | the rain has stopped. |
| I wish to know | how | the sick man is now. |
| He left his bed | when | the sun peeped in the room. |
| No one could find out | where | the rogue was lying hid. |
| No one could tell | whence | the noise arose. |
| The mice will play | while | the cat is away. |
| You must wait here | till/until | your father comes back. |
| They could not tell | why | they were fined. |
| The girl is quick | and | (she) reads very well. |
| The girl is clever | but | (she) cannot do the work. |
| She went to bed | for/as | she felt very tired. |
| He closed the door | after | his friends had gone. |
| He had his house cleaned | before | his friends came. |
| I will trust you | provided | you sign your name. |
| He will not escape death | however | rich he may be. |
| He left the house | as soon as | the rain stopped. |
| He could not pass | though | he tried often. |
| Your uncle is older | than | your aunt (is). |
| It is a long time | since | I saw you last. |

## CORRELATIVES

There are some Conjunctions that go in pairs. They are called Correlatives : Both—and; either—or; neither—nor; not only—but also; so—that; such—that; no sooner—than; hardly—when; scarcely—when; else—than; rather—than; else—but.

Noun to Noun—He is both a fool and a knave.

Adjective to Noun—He is as busy as a bee.

Adjective to Adjective—He is both wise and good.

Adjective to Adjective—He is not only wise but also good.

Verb to Verb—He must either work or go. He would rather die than beg.

Adverb to Adverb—He behaved neither wisely nor kindly.

## KINDS OF CONJUNCTION FOR JOINING CLAUSES

**Conjunctions are of two types : (1) Coordinating (2) Subordinating.**

**Co-ordinating Conjunctions are of four types :**

- **(a) Cumulative**—and, both ... and, as well as, etc.
- **(b) Alternative**—or, either.....or, neither.....nor, etc.
- **(c) Adversative**—but, yet, still, etc.
- **(d) Illative**—so, therefore, etc.

**Subordinating Conjunctions denote** time, place, cause, effect, purpose, manner, condition, contrast, comparison (degree), apposition and concession.

## FUNCTIONS OF CONJUNCTIONS

**1. Subordinating Conjunctions have two main functions :**

**(a) To join a Principal Clause and a Subordinate Clause :**

(i) **To denote time :** I shall do it before father comes. He went out after he had finished his work. Don't leave the place till/until I come. When the sun rose, the fog disappeared. I was reading a book while she was singing a song. The thief fled away as soon as he saw the police.

(ii) **To denote cause :** You will be punished because you have done wrong. As you have done wrong, you will be punished. Since I am ill, I will not go out.

(iii) **To denote effect :** He is so weak that he cannot walk. He is such a fool that I cannot rely on him.

(iv) **To denote purpose :** He worked hard that/so that he could pass the examination. He tried hard in order that he might win the prize. He ran away lest he should be caught.

(v) **To denote manner :** Do as you like. He is honest as far as/so far as I know him. As you sow, so you reap. He behaves as though he were mad. She behaves as if she were a queen.

(vi) **To denote degree/comparison :** He loves you as much as I do. I am as tall as you (are). I am not so tall as you. I am taller than you. He is better than you (are).

(vii) **To denote condition :** I will go if the weather permits. He speaks as if he knows everything. In case you fail, I shall not fail to help you. You will not succeed unless you work harder. I shall help you provided you give up bad habits. Tell me whether you are interested in it.

(viii) **To denote contrast :** We lost the game though/although we tried our best. Though/Although it was difficult, he could do it. Poor as (= though) I am, I cannot beg.

(ix) **To denote apposition :** I made a promise that I would help him. He gave an assurance that he would give me a job.

(x) **To denote concession :** However strong you may be, you cannot do this. Whoever he may be, I cannot allow him here. Whatever may happen, I will help you. Notwithstanding that he was defeated, he did not give up fight.

**(b) As Relative Pronoun, Relative Adverb and Interrogative Adverb :**

He said that he was ill. I know that she is sick. I asked him if/whether he would go there. Tell me how you did it. Come when you like. Tell me why you are late. We found him where we had left him.

**2. Coordinating Conjunctions have four functions :**

**(a) To combine two independent clauses of the same type :**

He was a good boy and he stood first in the examination. Go where you like, only do not stay here. Both he and his brother are guilty.

**(b) To combine two independent clauses of the opposite type :**

He was intelligent but he failed in the examination. He is weak while I am strong. You are rich whereas I am poor. I gave you much help, yet you could not prosper. He earns much, still he is not contented. I don't hate him, on the contrary I love him.

**(c) To combine two independent clauses denoting effect or inference :**

You cannot live for ever, for man is mortal. I do not like him, for he is dishonest. He did not try, so he could not pass. He did not study, therefore he failed. He did not study, consequently he failed.

**(d) To combine two independent clauses to denote choice between two things :**

Work hard or you will suffer. Either come or go away. Neither you nor he knows it. Take the chance, otherwise you will repent.

## CONJUNCTIONS [LINKING WORDS]

**(i) Coordinating Conj.**

[**Joins clauses of equal ranks of a compound sentence**]

**And :** He played well and got a prize.

**Both.....and :** Both he and his brother will go.

**Or :** Read or you will fail.

**But :** She is sad but hopeful.

**As well as :** Dipu as well as his brother is honest.

**Still :** He worked hard, still he failed.

**Otherwise :** Try hard, otherwise you will fail.

**(ii) Subordinating Conj.**

[**Joins subordinate clauses to the principal clause of a complex sentence**]

**That :** He said that he would go.

**So that :** Shut the door so that the child may not go out.

**In order that :** He worked hard in order that he might pass the exam.

**If :** I'll go if you come.

**Though :** Though he is poor, he is honest.

**Although :** Although it was hard, he did it.

**As :** Do as you like.

As I am ill, I cannot go.

**As :** Poor as (= though) I am, I am honest.

**So :** He tried hard, so he could win the game.

**Yet :** Life is full of tears yet none wishes to die.

**While :** You failed while your brother passed.

**Whereas :** He is rich whereas his brother is poor.

**Not only .... but also :** Not only he but his brother also will go there. Jack plays not only drum but also flute.

**Either .... or :** Either do this or leave the room.

**Neither .... nor :** She will neither do this nor leave the room.

**Because :** He cannot go out because he is ill.

**When :** He came when I was there.

**Where :** You may go where you like.

**Since :** Since I am ill, I cannot go out.

**Before :** The patient had died before the doctor came.

**After :** He came after I had left the place.

**While :** Make haste while the sun shines.

**Till :** Wait till the train stops.

**Until :** Do not detrain until the train stops.

**Unless :** I shall fail unless you help me.

**Whether/If :** I asked him whether/if he would go there.

**Lest :** Work hard lest you should fail.

## SENTENCE LINKERS OR CONNECTORS

Some words provide link with different independent sentences to maintain a flow of expression. These words or expressions are called **Sentence Linkers** or **Sentence Connectors**.

Difference between the Conjunction or the Linking word, and the Sentence Linker :

| Conjunctions or Linking Words | Sentence Linkers or Sentence Connectors |
|---|---|
| (i) Join words, clause or sentences. | (i) Help in maintaining flow between consecutive sentences. |
| (ii) Used within a sentence. | (ii) Used between two sentences. |

**Examples of Sentence Linkers :**

[Full-stop or semicolon may be used between the sentences.]

| Sentence Linkers | Examples |
|---|---|
| **However / Nevertheless** | You are late. However/Nevertheless, you may start your action. |
| **Indeed** | He is honest. Indeed, he is respected by all. |
| **Besides** | He gave me a lodging. Besides, he provided me with a job. |
| **Therefore/Consequently** | He is ill. Therefore/Consequently, you should call in a doctor. |
| **Actually** | He got the first prize. Actually, he scored the highest marks. |
| **Naturally** | Her son died. Naturally, she is upset. |
| **Finally** | The police searched the house. Finally, they found the stolen goods. |

| Sentence Linkers | Examples |
|---|---|
| After all | You should not disregard him. After all, he is senior. |
| Anyway | It's too late now. Anyway, you can try. |
| For example | Pride begets fall. For example, Duryodhan was ruined. |
| In fact | I helped him. In fact, he is my relative. |
| As a result | He was ill. As a result, he could not score any goal. |
| Only | You may come. Only, make no noise. |
| Of course | Would you take a little more milk? Of course not. |
| On the whole | I could not answer all the questions. On the whole, it was satisfactory. |
| On the contrary | I do not hate him. On the contrary, I love him. |

## APPLIED SECTION

**These are some special situations for applying conjunctions**

**(i)** **Lest**, **till**, and **until** should not be followed by not :

Wait till/until the train stops. (Cor.)

Wait till/until the train does not stop. (Incor.)

Work hard lest you should fail. (Cor.) ['Should' is placed after 'lest'.]

Work hard lest you may not fail. (Incor.)

"The modern idiomatic construction after '**lest**' is **should**."—**Wren & Martin**

**(ii)** **So that, in order that** are followed by 'may' or 'might', 'shall' or 'should', but never by 'can' or 'could', or 'will' or 'would' :

He encouraged me so that/in order that I might not lose heart. (Cor.)

He encouraged me so that/in order that I would not lose heart. (Incor.)

**(iii)** Both **because** and **therefore** should not be used in the same sentence :

He could not go to school because he was ill. (Cor.)

Because he was ill, therefore he could not go to school. (Incor.)

**(iv)** **While** may be used as coordinating conjunction or subordinating conjunction according to its sense :

You failed while your brother passed. [while = but—(coordinate conjunction)]

Make haste while the sun shines. [while = till—(subord. conj.)]

**(v)** **As if, as though** should invariably be followed by a past conditional, not by a present form (would, not will; could, not can; did, not does; was/were, not is/are; had gone, not has gone; knew, not knows.)—**MEU**

**(vi)** **So that** denotes purpose. But, So ..... that denotes effect. **Such ..... that** also denotes effect.

So that : He works hard so that he may succeed.

So ..... that : He worked so hard that he fell ill.

Such ..... that : He is such a fool that I cannot rely on him.

**(vii)** **As ..... as** denotes comparison in the positive degree in an Affirmative sentence.

As ..... as : I am as tall as you (are).

**(viii)** **So ..... as** denotes comparison in the positive degree in a Negative sentence.

So ..... as : I am not so tall as you (are).

**(ix)** **Provided** denotes the sense of if.

Provided : I shall help you provided you obey me.

**(x)** **However, Whatever, Whoever** denote concession.

However : However strong he may be, he cannot do this.

Whatever : Whatever you may say, I do not believe you.

Whoever : Whoever you may be, I cannot allow you to come here.

## EXERCISE

**1. Pick out the Conjunctions in the following sentences and say which join words and which join sentences. If words are joined, say to what Parts of Speech they belong :**

(1) You and I are old friends. (2) Was it true or was it false? (3) He is poor but honest in his dealings. (4) If you wish, I will teach you to read. (5) I wish to read, but I dislike the trouble of reading. (6) Tell me, if you can, how I can learn to read without taking any trouble. (7) I can tell you that nothing can be learnt without trouble. (8) You must go on working till the sun goes down. (9) As soon as the sun goes down, you may stop work. (10) You should go home now as the sun has set. (11) They wept, for they had lost their mother. (12) You will miss the train unless you make haste. (13) I have never heard whether you missed the first train. (14) Do not get wet, lest you should catch cold. (15) I must punish both you and your brother for being absent, as neither of you asked for leave. (16) Although the sun is very hot today, you may go out for half an hour, provided you take an umbrella and wear a hat of some kind.

**2. Insert appropriate Conjunctions in the places left blank :**

(a) You must get up ............ the sun rises.

(b) You need not leave your bed ............ the sun rises.

(c) I could not find out ............ he lived.

(d) Wait here ............ I return.

(e) Take care ............ you should fall.

(f) You are much more idle ............ you used to be.

(g) Many years have passed ............ I saw you last.

(h) I wish to know ............ you have been so lazy as before.

(i) Tell me ............ you can ............ the clock has struck nine.

(j) A man must do his best ............ he may succeed.

(k) You should not despair ............ you have failed once.

(l) He who has failed once may succeed the second time, ............ he tries hard.

(m) You have neglected your work, ....... you know ....... you were doing wrong.

(n) I was afraid ............ he would not survive his illness.

(o) Either you ............ I must write that letter at once; ............ it must be sent within the next two hours.

(p) Gora sells both apples ............ oranges.

(q) Most insects have wings ............ most ants do not.

(r) Who sweeps the rooms, washes the clothes ............ cooks the meals?

(s) Gahar is hard-working ............ he is not an intelligent boy.

(t) Hashina is thin ............ tall, ............ her brother is fat ............ short.

(u) Will you meet me at 4 p.m. ............ 4.30 p.m.?

(v) The girls are helping their mother ..... the boys are flying kites.

(w) ........you keep on your habit, you may land up in jail.

# 20  ARTICLES AND DETERMINERS

## WHAT IS AN ARTICLE OR DETERMINER?

The words **a, an** and **the** are usually called **Articles**. They are called Articles as they have some special significance as the part of speech.

"They are really Demonstrative Adjectives." — **Wren and Martin**

But **a, an** and generalised **the**—to denote a class as a whole, are not Demonstrative Adjectives. Now, they are called **Determiners**. — **P. C. Das**

**Students often make mistakes in using Articles or omitting them. They should be aware of it.**

**There are two types of Articles :**

ARTICLE

1. **Definite Article—the** 2. **Indefinite Article—a, an**

1. If we wish to particularise the Noun, we use the Definite Article :

   Let us bathe in the river. (i.e. a particular river)

   The doctor came here. ('The doctor' means a particular doctor.)

2. If we wish to generalise the Noun, we use the Indefinite Article :

   A tiger lives in a forest (i.e. any tiger or tigers and any forest or forests—in general sense).

   An ox is running on the road. (Here an ox, that is not any particular ox, is running on a particular road.)

## USE OF ARTICLES

As a general rule, a Common Noun in the Singular Number must have an Article before it :

**We cannot say,** "I have seen boy."

**We must say,** "I have seen a boy, or the boy."

But a Common Noun in the Plural Number does not require the Definite Article 'the' unless we wish to particularise the Noun :

Boys (= boys generally) are fond of sweets. The boys (= those boys already referred to, or those boys before us) are playing football.

## INDEFINITE ARTICLE **A or AN** **Only for singular number but for all genders**

The choice between A and An is determined by sound.

**A is used before a word beginning with a Consonant sound** and **An is used before a word beginning with a Vowel sound.**

### VOWEL SOUND—a-e-i-o-u

| A<br>[A before **Consonant sound**] | | AN<br>[AN before **Vowel sound**] | |
|---|---|---|---|
| a boy | a lion | an ass | an elephant |
| a book | a mango | an ant | an inkpot |
| a bag | a student | an apple | an icecream |
| a cat | a woman | an arm | an idiot |
| a chair | a table | an egg | an ox |
| a dog | a tiger | an ear | an orange |
| a horse | a tree | an eye | an umbrella |

### SPECIAL USE

| **'A' before Vowel sounding as 'yu'/'wa'** | **'An' before Consonant sounding as Vowel** |
|---|---|
| a European | an hour ('h' silent) |
| a union | an honest man ('h' silent) |
| a university | an H.S. school |
| a U.S. plane | an M.A./MA |
| a useful book | an M.Sc./MSc |
| a unique scene | an M.P./MP |
| a one-rupee note | an M.L.A./MLA |
| a one-eyed deer | an S.D.O./SDO |
| a High/Higher Secondary school | an N.C.C./NCC |

**N.B. :** 'A' will be used in place of 'An' when 'h' sounds as 'haw', e.g. a hotel, a humble servant, a historical book etc. [ humble = not 'umble' but 'humble'—
**A.L.D.—Hornby** ]

### USES OF A/AN

**(i)** **A or An is used when it is mentioning someone or something (single countable noun) for the first time :**

I saw a man on the street. An old lady came to our house.

**(ii)** **A or An is used to indicate a unit :**

One hundred centimetres make a metre. An ounce is enough.

**(iii)** **A or An is used in the sense of 'one like'** (To make a Proper Noun a Common Noun) :

He thinks he is a Rabindranath. A Daniel has come to judgement (judgment). He seems to be an Indian.

**(iv) A or An is used before an unknown name or surname :**

A Jatin Babu called on you. A Mr. Sen came to see you. An Ikbal came here to collect the news.

**N.B.** Jatin Babu, Mr. Sen and Ikbal without A or An implies that the speaker knows them.

**(v) A or An is used in the sense 'of the same' :**

Birds of a feather flock together.

**(vi) A or An is used to denote profession, trade, class etc. :**

He is a businessman. He is an engineer. He is a lawyer.

**(vii) A is used before 'dozen', 'hundred', 'thousand', 'million' etc. :**

Here are a dozen of bananas. A hundred boys came out from school. There are a thousand people.

**(viii) A or An is used in the sense of 'each' or 'per' :**

He earns one thousand rupees a month. He drives the car at 50 kilometres an hour.

**(ix) A or An (also The) is used to indicate a class as a whole :**

A (The) cow has horns. (i.e. All cows have horns.)

—**Thomson & Martinet**

An (The) elephant never forgets.

**(x) A or An is used before some words and phrases :**

I have a headache. I am in a hurry. He had a bad cold. She had a cough. They take an interest in this.

**(xi) A or An is used in Exclamatory sentences beginning with 'What' :**

What a pity! What a pretty girl! What a nice bird it is! What an awful remark!

**(xii) A (and not The) is used before the superlative 'most' when it means 'very' :**

He saw a most wonderful sight. [(a most = a very) Oscar Wilde]

This is a most interesting story. (a most = a very)

**(xiii) A or An is used before 'few', 'little', 'lot of', 'good deal', 'great many', 'good many' etc. and sometimes after 'many' :**

Here is a lot of books. There is a little honey in the bottle. A great many soldiers entered the town. I saw a good many boys there. Many a flower is born to blush unseen. Many an admirer welcomed him. Give me a few books.

**Note** "It is also possible to say 'few apples', 'little water' but such constructions convey different meaning. They will mean 'not many', 'not much'."—**P. K. De Sarkar**

But really 'a few' and 'a little' mean 'not many' and 'not much'. 'Few' and 'little' without article mean 'almost nil'. —**P. C. Das**

"There is a great difference between few and a few (used for countables), and between little and a little (used for uncountables). A few and a little mean 'a small number' and 'a small amount'.

Few or little, on the contrary, denote scarcity or lack."

—**A. J. Thomson & A. V. Martinet**

## DEFINITE ARTICLE THE

**It is the same for singular and plural numbers and for all genders**

The Definitie Article '**THE**' is used :

**(i) To indicate a particular person(s) or thing(s) :**
Look at the boy/boys. He is/They are peculiarly dressed. I want 'The Golden Book of Treasures'. The book is out-of-print.

**(ii) Before a noun which has become definite by being mentioned a second time :** It is also called '**Familiar The**'.
There is a tree in the garden. The tree is an oak.

**(iii) Before a noun made definite by the addition of a phrase or clause :**
The girl with the white skirt is beautiful. The boy who came here is my friend. The pen which I bought from the market is not so good.

**(iv) Before a singular noun meant to represent a whole class :** It is called '**Generalising The**'.
The cow is a useful animal. The dog is a faithful animal. The rose is the sweetest of all flowers.
The banyan is a kind of fig tree. [Not "a kind of a fig tree". This is a common error.] **—Wren & Martin**

**Note** Two nouns 'man' and 'woman' used to denote the whole class never have any article :
Man is mortal. Woman is man's mate.

**(v) Before an Uncountable Noun to particularise it :**
The gold of the ring is very bright. The political wisdom of Nelson Mandela made him familiar as a popular leader in South Africa.

**(vi) Before a name of a thing which is only one in Nature :**
Look at the moon. The sun shines in the sky. The earth moves round the sun.

**(vii) Before a Noun denoting nation or race :**
The English are industrious. The Bengalees are intelligent but idle.

**Note** Such a Noun without 'the' indicates the language of the people :
English (= English language) is an international language. Bengali (= Bengali language) is a rich language.

**(viii) Before a name of Road, but not before a name of Street or Avenue :**
The bus is running on the Circular Road. The book is bought from College Street. This bat is available in a shop on Central Avenue.
[Not the before a road with a proper noun, e.g. Mahatma Gandhi Road]

**(ix) Before some nouns to indicate profession :**
He joined the Bar. He joined the Church.

**(x) Before the name of a musical instrument when one plays it. Otherwise not :**
He plays the flute. (But, he has a flute.)

**Note** 'The' is not applicable when 'play on' is a group verb.
He plays on flute. [or] He plays on *tabla*.

**(xi) Before ordinal numbers :**
Who is the first/the second boy? The 23rd January is a red-letter day (But, January 23).

**(xii) As a general rule a Porper Noun should not have any article before it. But some Proper Nouns take 'the' before them as exceptions :**

Before the names of holy books, newspapers, ships, trains, aeroplanes, spacecraft, famous buildings, rivers, seas, oceans, gulfs, mountain ranges, groups of islands, deserts and directions :

(a) **names of holy books :** the Bible, the Koran, the Ramayana.

**Note** If a book is called after its author, the article is not used. **—Nesfield**

Homer's Iliad, Valmiki's Ramayana. I have read Shakespeare. (= Shakespeare's books)

(b) **names of newspapers :** The Statesman, the Anandabazar.

(c) **names of ships :** the Titanic, the M. V. Akbar.

(d) **names of trains :** the Bombay Mail, the Rajdhani Express.

(e) **names of aeroplanes :** the Dakota, the Boeing 747.

(f) **names of spacecraft :** the Skylab, the Aryabhatta.

(g) **names of famous buildings :** the Taj Mahal, the Writers' Buildings, the Victoria Memorial.

(h) **names of rivers :** the Ganga, the Jamuna, the Danube.

(i) **names of seas :** the Arabian Sea, the Mediterranean Sea.

(j) **names of oceans :** the Indian Ocean, the Atlantic Ocean, the Pacific Ocean.

(k) **names of gulfs :** the Persian Gulf, the Bay of Bengal.

(l) **names of mountain ranges :** the Himalayas, the Alps, the Bindhyas.

(m) **names of groups of islands :** the Andamans, the West Indies, the Hebrides.

**Note** 'The' is not placed before the names of single mountains, single islands, nor before the names of capes, nor before the names of lakes. **—Nesfield**

Mount Abu, Mount Everest, Vesuvius (names of a single mountain).
Sri Lanka, Sicily, Java (names of a single island).
Cape Comorin, Cape of Good Hope.
Lake Chilka, Lake Sambar.

(n) **names of desert :** the Sahara, the Thar, the Gobi.
There are some trees on the oasis.

(o) **names of directions :** Go to the north and then turn to the south.

**(xiii) Before the names of a province having a descriptive geographical meaning :**

the Punjab, the Deccan.

**(xiv) Before the names of countries which are collectively formed :**

the U.S.A. (the United States of America.) the U.K. (the United Kingdom).
But not before India, England, America, etc.

**(xv) Before the plural names of families :**

The Boses are familiar with the Browns.

**(xvi) Before Proper Nouns for comparison to denote a type :**

Bankim is the Scott of Bengal. [Or] Scott is the Bankim of England.
Rabindranath is the Shakespeare of India in literary qualities.
Ahmedabad is the Manchester of India as an industrial belt.

**(xvii) Before a Proper Noun when it is qualified by an Adjective or Adjectival phrases or clauses :**

The great Caesar. The immortal poet Kalidas. I am the Suryakanta Sen who never stood second in the examinations.

**(xviii) Before some Common Nouns and Adjectives to express an abstract sense :**

All the mother (= motherly feelings) rose in her.

Check the beast (= beastly passion) in you.

Do not play the fool. (= foolishness)

Do not keep him in the dark. (= darkness)

He allowed the father (= his fatherly feelings) to be overruled by the judge (= his sense of duty as a judge) and declared his own son to be guilty.

**(xix) Before Adjectives to denote a particular part of a thing :**

I like the yellow of an egg. (the yellow)

He entered the thick (= the thick part) of the forest.

**(xx) Before a Common Noun as a substitute for the Possessive Adjective :**

He caught me by the arm. (the = my)

He struck you on the head. (the = your)

He pulled the cat by the tail. (the = its)

**(xxi) Before an Adjective to represent a whole class of persons :**

The rich (= rich men) are not always happy. The poor (= poor men) are not always dishonest. The virtuous (= virtuous people) are happy.

**Note** The rich are not always happy.

= Rich men are not always happy.

The rich man (= a particular rich man) is not always happy.

But not, The rich men are not always happy.

['The rich men' do not denote a whole class, but a particular group of persons.]

**(xxii) Before the Adjectives in Superlative degree and the words in the Superlative sense :**

He is the best boy in the class. She is the most beautiful girl. Even the darkest cloud has a silver lining. The Chief Minister/The Prime Minister has arrived here. He is the singer of the day. He is the man of the match.

**(xxiii) Before Comparatives as Adverbs :**

The sooner, the better. The more, the merrier. The more we have, the more we want.

## ZERO ARTICLE : OMISSION OF THE ARTICLES

We cannot but love flowers. (Generalisation with plural)

I can smell smoke here. (Uncountable Noun)

**The articles are not generally used :**

**(i) Before generalisation with plural or uncountable nouns :**

Birds can fly in the sky.

**Note** But we use 'the' when we talk about specific things or people.

Compare these sentences :

(a) Flowers really add beauty to a room. (No article is used before 'flowers' in general.)

(b) The flowers you bought me are lovely. ('The' is used before particular flowers.)

**(ii) Before Proper Nouns :**

Kolkata is the city of joy though there are many sufferings. Delhi is the capital of India for hundreds of years. Newton is a great scientist.

**Note** When the article is used before a Proper Noun, it becomes a Common Noun :

A Newton (= a scientist) cannot be a Milton (= a poet).

**(iii) Before Material Nouns :**

Gold is a precious metal. Iron and steel are useful metals. Coal is black but very useful to us. Cotton grows in India, Egypt and America.

**Note** 'The' is used before a Material Noun when it is particularly referred :

The coal of Jharia burns well.

**(iv) Before Abstract Nouns :**

Health is wealth. Honesty is the best policy. Kindness is a great virtue.

**Note** 'The' is used before an Abstract Noun when it is specified :

The kindness of Florence Nightingale has become a byword.

**An article is used before an Abstract Noun when it is preceded by an Adjective.** [Death is preferable to dishonour. (But) He died a peaceful death. What is the cause of the accident? (But) He met with a serious accident.]

**(v) Before a Common Noun preceded by the phrases—kind of, sort of, species of—in Interrogative sentences :**

What kind of flower is it?
What kind of/sort of man is he? } Interrogative
What species of mosquito is anopheles?

But we say, Malaria is caused by a species of mosquito. [Assertive]

The rose is a kind of flower. [ " ]

**(vi) Before school, college, church, bed, hospital, market, prison—when these places are visited or used for their primary purpose :**

| | |
|---|---|
| We go to school/college | (to learn) |
| Someone goes to church | (to pray) |
| " " to bed | (to sleep) |
| " " to market | (to sell or buy) |
| " " to prison | (as a punishment) |
| " " to hospital | (for treatment) |

**But when these places are visited or used for any other purpose *'the'* article is used :**

I went to the school to see the Headmaster. He went to the hospital to see his uncle. The bed is too dirty to use.

**(vii) Before man or woman in the sense of mankind and before father, mother, uncle, aunt, or baby when it expresses our father, our mother, our uncle, our aunt, our baby etc. :**

Man is mortal. Man and woman should go side by side.

Father is hungry. Mother is angry. Baby is crying.

Uncle is coming. Aunt is cooking.

**Note** However, in present-day English a man and a woman or men and women are more usual in general sense, e.g. A woman is more sensitive than a man. [Or] Women are more sensitive than men.

**(viii) Before 'home' when it means the home of the speaker, or the person spoken to :**

Go home. [Here 'home' is used as an Adverb.]

Stay at home. [Here 'home' is used as a Noun.]

But, "When home is followed by a descriptive phrase or clause, 'the' is necessary." **—Thomson & Martinet**

He returned to the home where he had been so happy. She was married in the home of her grandparents.

**(ix) Before the names of games and meals :**

We like to play football/cricket/hockey/tennis/badminton etc. We have dinner/breakfast at usual time.

**(x) Before names of seasons and festivals :**

Summer/winter/spring/autumn

[But, the rainy season]

Summer is the best time for picnic. The first time I went to Darjeeling was the summer.

Similarly festivals as : New Year's Day, Christmas etc.

**(xi) Before the names of squares, buildings, parks, streets, avenues etc. :**

Buckingham Palace, Curzon Park, Rashbehari Avenue, College Street.

**(xii) Before the words 'King' and 'Queen' if they are followed by the name of King or Queen and before title when they are used in apposition to a Noun :**

King George V, Queen Victoria.

Mr. Sen, Principal of our college, is a well-known figure.

**(xiii) Before Complement of a Transitive Verb :**

They made him President.

He was elected Chairman of the Board.

Mr. Sen became Principal of the college.

**(xiv) In certain Phrases consisting of a Transitive Verb followed by its Object :**

to catch fire, to take root, to give ear, to cast anchor, to set sail, to lose heart, to take offence etc.

**(xv) In certain Phrases consisting of a Preposition followed by its Object :**

at home, at dinner, at ease, at dawn, at daybreak, at sunrise, at sunset, at noon, at night, by day, by night, by name, by land, by water, by river, by air, by boat, by bus, by train, by steamer, by ship, on foot, underground, above-ground, from hand to mouth etc.

## REPETITION OF THE ARTICLE

**(i) When two or more Nouns or Adjectives refer to different persons or things, 'the' article is used before each Noun or Adjective :**

The Headmaster and the Secretary are coming. (two different persons)

He had a black and a white cat. (two different cats)

Give me a red and a blue pencil. (two different pencils)

(ii) **When two or more Nouns or Adjectives refer to the same person or thing, 'the' article is used before the first Adjective or Noun :**

The Headmaster and Secretary is coming. (one person)
He had a black and white cat. (one cat)
Give me a red-and-blue pencil. (one pencil)

(iii) **In a comparison, if two Nouns refer to different persons or things, 'the' article is used with each Noun. Otherwise not :**

He is a better statesman than a philosopher. (compared with different entity)
He is a better statesman than philosopher. (two qualities in the same person)

(iv) **Before Comparatives as Adverbs :**

The sooner, the better.

## DETERMINERS

In modern English grammar Articles and some Adjectives except Adjectives of Quality (i.e. Adjective of Quantity, Adjective of Number, Demonstrative Adjective, Distributive Adjective and Possessive Adjective) are called Determiners.

These are of two types—**Specific Determiners** and **General Determiners.**

**Specific Determiners/Definite Determiners.**

The Determiners used to refer to someone or something in a specific way are called Specific Determiners or Definite Determiners.

The boys are playing football. I want this pen and not that pen. These boys are dull but those boys are clever. The woman is looking after her child.

Here in the phrase 'the boys' the indicates that the boys are already known to the speaker.

Similarly this, these, her etc. are used to determine the persons or objects.

**List of Specific Determiners/Definite Determiners :**

| | | |
|---|---|---|
| the | my | |
| this | your | our |
| that | his | their |
| these | her | |
| those | its | |

**General Determiners/Indefinite Determiners :**

The determiners used to refer to someone or something in a general or indefinite way are called **General Determiners or Indefinite Determiners**.

A soldier is ready in his bunker. A boy is going to school. An owl is hooting. All men must die, but most men do not think of it. He did not eat any rice, but I ate some. Each candidate was asked to answer the question.

**List of General Determiners/Indefinite Determiners :**

| | | | |
|---|---|---|---|
| a | other | few | no |
| an | another | many | several |
| all | each | little | enough |
| any | every | much | such |
| some | either | more | one |
| both | neither | most | first etc. |

## GROUPS OF DETERMINERS

Now, we can classify the Determiners into three groups :

(i) **Th-type :** the, this, that, these, those.

(ii) **Possessive type :** your, my, our, his, their, its.

(iii) **Number/Quantity type :** a, an, each, every, any, another, little, some, enough etc.

## PREDETERMINERS

Some words are used before Determiners and function as combined structure. They are called **Predeterminers**.

I am not such a fool. [not 'a such fool']

All the girls wore white *sari*. [not 'the all girls']

Both the boys are equally guilty. [not 'the both boys']

What *a* beautiful bird it is!

**Note** Such, all, both, what—have been used before Determiners and have made a combined structure. So these are called Predeterminers.

## APPLIED SECTION

We cannot say : Boy is going to school. Ox is running.

We must say : A/The boy is going to school. An/The ox is running.

No Common Countable Noun can be used in a sentence without any article or determiner.

**Headlines again :**

**A is used :**

1. before a word beginning with a consonant :

   a bird, a flower, a lion.

2. before a vowel letter that sounds like a consonant :

   a European, a university (sound eu)

   a one-rupee note (sound o = wa)

**An is used :**

1. before a word beginning with a vowel :

   an ass, an orange.

2. before a consonant letter that sounds like a vowel :

   an M.A., an M.B., an S.D.O, an H.S. school

3. before a word beginning with a silent 'h' :

   an hour, an honourable person.

**Normally we do not use any article before Proper Nouns** (or Capital Letter Nouns), **Material Nouns** and **Abstract Nouns**. But other Determiners may be used before these words as necessary :

Kolkata is a big city. This Kolkata is a matter of pride to us.

Iron is a useful metal. Honesty is the best policy.

**But The is used :**

1. before names of rivers, mountain ranges, seas, deserts, important buildings etc. :
   The Ganges flows down from the Himalayas. The Bay of Bengal lies to the south of West Bengal. The Sahara is in Africa. The Thor is in Rajasthan. The Taj Mahal is one of the wonders of the world.

**Note** Though 'the' is not used before a Proper Noun, we can say :
The Boses are visting China. (Here The Boses = Mr. Bose and his family)
We also say—the U.S.A./the US (Short form of the United States of America)

2. before Nouns of which there is only one :
   The sun is shining in the sky.
3. before Nouns that refer to a class of things/people :
   The dog is a faithful animal.
   [But] Man is mortal.
4. to particularise the Noun :
   The book you mention is out-of-print.
   A farmer had three sons. The sons were lazy.
5. before the superlatives :
   He is the most intelligent boy.
6. as an Adverb with comparatives :
   The more the merrier. The sooner the better.
7. Normally we do not use any article or determiner in the following constructions :

| | | | |
|---|---|---|---|
| be in | bed | travel | by bus |
| go to | market | go | by car |
| sent to | church | come | by train |
| " | prison | " | by boat |
| " | hospital | " | by plane |
| be at | school/college | go | on foot |
| go to | university | " | on horseback |
| leave | home. | " | on bicycle |

## EXERCISE

**1. Fill in the blanks with A or An as required :**

| | |
|---|---|
| (a) ........... B.D.O. | (k) ........... university |
| (b) ............ S.D.O. | (l) ........... umbrella |
| (c) ........... D.M. | (m) ........... unique event |
| (d) ........... B.A. | (n) ........... uniform speed |
| (e) ........... M.A. | (o) ........... one-eyed man |
| (f) ........... F.R.C.S. | (p) ........... one-act play |
| (g) ........... ewe | (q) ........... opinion |
| (h) ........... union | (r) ........... historical play |
| (i) ........... European | (s) ........... honest man |
| (j) ........... H. S. school | (t) ........... High school |

**2. Fill in the blanks with suitable articles :**

It is ........... useful article. Animesh reads ........ Gita everyday. Gahar reads ........... Koran. This is ........... one-way road. Sri Lanka is ........ island. He is ........... Newton. He is ...........Newton of India. Bankimchandra is ........Scott of Bengal. He is ........ B.A., but his brother is ........... M.A. It is ........... unanimous decision. He lives in ........... U.K. but his sister lives in ........ U.S.A. This is ........... High School, but that is ........... H. S. School.

**3. Match the two parts of each sentence. Write 'the' where necessary and put a × where it is not necessary. [One has been done for you.]**

| | |
|---|---|
| (i) My father goes to (b) | (a) .............. school? |
| (ii) Does your sister go to | (b) ......×...... market. |
| (iii) Tourists in Delhi go to see | (c) ........... Park Street. |
| (iv) Tourists in Kolkata go to see | (d) ........ violin? |
| (v) Do you play | (e) ........ Delhi. |
| (vi) The U.B.I. is on | (f) ........... Australia. |
| (vii) The smallest continent is | (g) ........... Victoria Memorial. |
| (viii) His uncle lives in | (h) .............. Taj Mahal. |

**4. Put suitable articles and determiners in the following blanks. Choose the determiners from the given list. [ any, some, their, another, other, the, a ]**

(i) Our house is nearest to ........... house.

(ii) ...... man is sitting on ...... branch of ...... tree.

(iii) At night we stayed at ........ hotel.

(iv) I am not satisfied with this book. Could you supply me ........ book?

(v) Is there ...... difference between ...... two?

(vi) ........... Aryans were very proud of their high birth. They were afraid of getting mixed up with ........ tribals. It was ........ false pride.

**5. Complete the passages with suitable articles (a, an, the) :**

(i) Sarojini Naidu who was ........ Indian was born at Hyderabad in ........ Deccan, on ........ 13th February in 1879. Her father came of ........ Bengali family that was famous for learning, and she herself was ........ great scholar.

(ii) ........ Narmada is ........ name of ........ river in South India. It is ........ important river and is considered as a holy river in ........ South.

(iii) ........... gentleman walking with ........ stick in his hand is a very well-known person here. He is ........ professor in ........ university. He has just returned from ........ UK after a period of four years obtaining ........... Ph.D. from Oxford University.

**6. Put articles where it is required and put a cross (×) where it is not required :**

(i) "Is this ........ book you are telling me about?" "Yes, it is on ........ life of ........ Satyajit Roy, one of ........ greatest sons of ........ India.

(ii) Her sister is ...... musician. She plays ...... *sitar* and ...... guitar. But her brother has no interest in ...... music. He is ...... good sportsman. He plays ........ football and ........ hockey.

**7. The articles are missing in the following passages. Find where they are missing and insert them :**

(i) Do not look at me. Look above and see moon and stars. There are uncountable stars twinkling in sky at night. In morning they will disappear again.

(ii) One day old man was walking on road. He was carrying bagful of sugar in his hand. That man was secretary of school. I knew him to be honest person.

(iii) He saw most wonderful sight. Through little hole in wall children had crept in, and they were sitting in branches of trees. In every tree that he could see was little child.

(iv) High above city, on tall column, stood statue of Happy Prince. He was gilded all over with thin leaves of fine gold, for eyes he had two bright sapphires, and large red ruby glowed on his sword-hilt.

(v) Last one of this long procession of silent men and women was little wizened old man. Even he carried load of two baskets, slung on pole on his shoulder, same load of folded quilt, cauldron. Although load was light, it was too much for old man.

21 

# MODIFIERS

**[ Special stress has been given on the use of '-ing-phrase + by/without', '-ing/-ed within a clause', 'be + adj. + phrase' and 'be + adj. + to + verb'. ]**

Read the following sentences :

Anyone can learn a foreign language by practising it regularly. Without doing any physical exercise, you cannot keep good health. Doing homework at the right time is a good habit. A blooming flower is beautiful to look at. A growing child needs nutritious food. A sleeping lion cannot catch a prey. Don't put your hand in boiling water. Don't sit on a broken chair. The girl is nursing the wounded bird. They bade goodbye to the departed guest who came to visit them. We saw the men looking out hopelessly.

The words or phrases *by practising, without doing, doing, blooming, growing, sleeping, boiling, broken, wounded, departed* and *looking out hopelessly* are used here to modify the nouns. These are called **Modifiers**. These may be placed before or after the nouns. Hence these are also called **Noun Modifiers**.

There are two types of Modifiers :

**MODIFIERS**

1. **PREMODIFIER** 2. **POSTMODIFIER**

[1] A modifier which precedes a Noun is called **Premodifier**.

Example : A blooming flower. A broken chair.

[2] A modifier which follows a Noun is called **Postmodifier**.

Example : We saw the men looking out hopelessly.

## VARIOUS TYPES AND USES OF PREMODIFIERS

There are different types of Premodifiers :

[i] **Determiners as Premodifiers :**

The boys and girls are walking side by side.

Those boys and girls are very intelligent.

[ii] **Predeterminers as Premodifiers :**

All the boys were present in the class.

Both the books are out-of-print.

**[iii] Present participle (ing-participle) as Premodifiers :**

A darkening sky may bring showers.

The cloud brings showers for the thirsting (= thirsty) flowers.

A life of increasing labour and decreasing leisure is the characteristic of modern civilisation.

**[iv] Past Participle (ed/en-participle) as Premodifiers :**

The injured cat is limping.

A burnt child dreads the fire.

The ants eat their stored food in winter.

The worried man could not attend the guests.

After six deaths it became a haunted house.

**[v] Adjectives as Premodifiers :**

A lazy man cannot be an early riser.

A clever boy like you cannot do such a foolish work.

An intelligent girl worked out the sum in a few minutes.

**[vi] Noun for a Noun Modifier :**

The School Inspector came on a surprise visit.

I'm going to my country-house.

**[vii] Nominal Compound as Premodifiers :**

She is a record-breaking typist.

Mark the wheat-producing countries in the map.

Try to use this labour-saving method.

A low cost house is not easily available in Delhi.

## VARIOUS TYPES AND USES OF POSTMODIFIERS

There are different types of post-modifiers :

**[i] Present Participle phrases as postmodifier :**

The students saw their teacher coming into the class.

I found an old woman standing at the door.

I used to watch the flower plant growing everyday.

We saw the beggar looking out hopelessly.

The student working in the laboratory is very brilliant.

**[ii] Past Participle phrases as Postmodifier :**

I saw a man injured in an accident.

A tiger killed by the hunter was left in the jungle.

He has got the money sent by his father.

I have got the letter written by you.

**[iii] 'To' Infinitive phrase as Postmodifier :**

Here is a chair to sit on.

She got a nice bat to play with.

Fatima was surprised to hear the news.

I am the last man to leave the place.

Juthi was glad to know her SSC result.

**[iv] Adjective phrases as Postmodifier :**

Mr. Ali is experienced in teaching English.

A man with white beard came here yesterday.

He is a man of great honour.

**[v] Nominal Compound as Postmodifier :**

You should be aware of the Kolkata bus routes.

**[vi] Nominal clause as Appositive used as Postmodifier :**

The report that he was murdered is true.

Our hope that he would come back home proved false.

**[vii] Relative clause as Postmodifier :**

The boy who saved the girl is a scout.

This is the place where he was born.

This is the pen which I lost yesterday.

I want a car that I can drive.

## NOUN MODIFIERS AND HEAD NOUNS

Now, we see a **Noun** may be modified by :

[i] the words **before** the Head Noun—**Premodifiers**.

[ii] the words **after** the Head Noun—**Postmodifiers**.

| Premodifier | Head Noun | Postmodifier |
|---|---|---|
| (i) Predeterminers | | (i) Present Participle Phrases |
| (ii) Determiners | | (ii) Past Participle Phrases |
| (iii) Present Participles | ←O→ | (iii) 'To' Infinitive Phrases |
| (iv) Past Participles | | (iv) Adjective Phrases |
| (v) Adjectives | | (v) Nominal Clauses |
| (vi) Nouns | | (vi) Relative Clauses |
| (vii) Nominal Compounds | | |

## NOMINAL GROUP/NOUN CLUSTER

The whole group of words having the Head noun with its modifier(s) is called a **Nominal Group** or a **Noun Cluster** :

| | NOUN CLUSTER | REMAINING PART | |
|---|---|---|---|
| All those tall | girls | with long hair | danced in a big hall. |
| Premodifier | Head Noun | Postmodifier | |

## EXERCISE

**1. Fill in the blanks with 'ing'-participles which are used as Modifiers (Premodifier or Postmodifier) :**

Verbs to be used are given in the list below :

[ stand, walk, run, work, boil ]

(i) Don't try to get into a ......... train.

(ii) The farmers ......... in the field are very poor.

(iii) I found the girl ........... at the door.

(iv) We saw a girl ......... on the ropes.

(v) Only hard ........... students will succeed.

(vi) Don't put your hand in ......... water.

**2. Use Past Participle forms of the Verbs given in the list as Modifiers :**

[ burn, speak, read, wound, balance, break, worry ]

(i) A ......... diet is required for a growing baby.

(ii) Why have you such a ........... look?

(iii) They took the ......... man to hospital.

(iv) You should learn ......... English too.

(v) Good books ......... in childhood are the real guides.

(vi) Don't sit on a ......... chair.

(vii) A ......... child dreads the fire.

**3. Use appropriate words, phrases or clauses or infinitives as Modifiers. Root Verbs are given in the brackets :**

(i) Look at the cows (graze) in the field.

(ii) The girl came here (dance) joyfully.

(iii) If she catches you (read) her diary, she'll be furious.

(iv) The picture (paint) by the artist is wonderful.

(v) He advised me to apply for the post (vacate).

(vi) She is busy (write) some letters.

(vii) He fell down while (board) a bus.

(viii) We should avoid (waste) of money.

# 22 STRUCTURAL AND NON-STRUCTURAL WORDS

**WORDS**

Structural — Non-Structural

Words are the elements of a sentence. In Modern English Grammar words are divided into two broad groups—**[1] Structural Words or Minor Words, and [2] Non-Structural Words or Major Words**. Structural Words or Minor Words are also called **Grammatical Words**. Non-Structural Words or Major Words are also called **Class Words**.

**Differences between Structural words and Non-Structural words :**

(i) Structural words are used for forming the structure of a sentence. They have little meaning of their own.

But Non-Structural words or Major words play the important role in conveying the meaning of a sentence.

(ii) Only Structural words (a, an, the, this, as, on etc.) cannot make a sentence. But only a Major word (Non-Structural word) can make a sentence (Yes, No, Come, Stop, Well, Thanks etc.).

(iii) The same Structural word (a, an, the etc.) can be used more than once in a sentence. But a Non-Structural word (Major word) cannot be usually repeated in a sentence.

(iv) Structural words (a, an, the, in, on, to etc.) cannot take any prefix or suffix. But more and more new words can be formed by adding Prefixes or Suffixes with the Non-Structural words or Major words (e.g. normal > abnormal; greed > greedy etc.).

(v) Structural words (a, an, the, this, by, for etc.) have no inter-relationship while Non-Structural words or Major words or Class words have inter-relationship (e.g. happy > happiness > happily etc.).

| Structural Words or Minor Words | Non-Structural Words or Major Words or Class Words |
|---|---|
| (1) Determiners (a, an, the, this, my, his, our, etc.) | (1) Nouns (boy, girl, cat, bat, hat, etc.) |

| Structural Words or Minor Words | Non-Structural Words or Major Words or Class Words |
|---|---|
| (2) Intensifiers or Downtoners (very, much, too, little, rather, etc.) | (2) Pronouns (I, we, he, she, they, it, etc.) |
| (3) Auxiliaries (shall, will, can, may, etc.) | (3) Adjectives (good, bad, brave, weak, etc.) |
| (4) Prepositions (in, one, to, for, by, with, etc.) | (4) Main Verbs (be, have, do, eat, play, etc.) |
| (5) Conjunctions or Linkers (and, but, or, for, as, if, though, although, however, etc.) | (5) Adverbs (ago, always, fast, now, soon, here, there, well, enough, badly, bravely, hardly, quietly, etc.) |

## EXERCISE

1. **Fill in each blank with one word that fits in the context. Read through the text before you start filling in the blanks. Remember that all the words will be grammatical/structural word. One has been done for you :**

The sprawling lake at the Alipore Zoo is no longer a favourable haunt for thousands of migratory birds ...(i)... used to spend the winter months here. Even a couple ...(ii)... years ago the tumultuous cries ...(iii)... whistles of the "winter guests" from Siberia and ...(iv)... foothills of the Himalayas ...(v)... be heard. But this year there is silence ...(vi)... the lake. The Alipore Zoo has become a mere "transit" point in the migratory flight path of the birds. Experts believe that this can be explained by the fact ...(vii)... since last year about 6,000 birds from the Siberian region and the Himalayas ...(viii)... begun to visit the lake ...(ix)... about a week in November and ...(x)... fly away.

List of jumbled up words : that, and, in, had, that, could, for, of, the, then.
[Answer : (i) that]

2. **There are four numbered blanks in the passage given below. Fill in the blanks with the best alternatives from the lists provided. The numbers in the blanks correspond to the numbers of the lists concerned.**

**The best alternatives for the blank (i) is chosen for you :**

Baroda State in Western India had a reputation (i) ...... being progressive in many fields, not in the least in education and social reform. Sixty years ago the then Maharaja of Baroda invited an American to assist (ii) ......... the establishment of a complete, modern library system. That American, William Alanson Borden accepted the invitation and stayed (iii) .........as Director of State Libraries in Baroda (iv) ......... three years.

Example (i) (a) in, (b) for, (c) to, (d) about [Answer : (i) (b)]
(ii) (a) for, (b) by, (c) towards, (d) in
(iii) (a) on, (b) up, (c) out, (d) across
(iv) (a) after, (b) since, (c) for, (d) under

**3. Fill in the blanks with the structural words given in the list :**

Those who are responsible ...(i)...... teaching young people, have resorted, in different periods of history, to ......(ii)...... variety of means for making their pupils learn. The earliest of these was .........(iii)...... rule of the rod.

(i) (a) to, (b) for, (c) of

(ii) (a) an, (b) a, (c) the

(iii) (a) an, (b) a, (c) the

**4. Fill in the blanks with the structural words given below :**

I am annoyed ......(i)...... him for his behaviour. I refused ......(ii)...... play a second fiddle to him. He is ......(iii)...... man of strong principles. He will not swallow a camel easily.

(i) (a) with, (b) about, (c) on

(ii) (a) to, (b) for, (c) at

(iii) (a) an, (b) a, (c) the

**5. Fill in the blanks with the structural words given below :**

Mr. Bose is very strict ....(i)..... the children in his class. He is particularly strict (ii)....... punctuality. However, his relationship .......(iii)...... the children is ....... (iv)....... happy one.

(i) (a) on, (b) about, (c) with

(ii) (a) about, (b) with, (c) on

(iii) (a) an, (b) a, (c) with

(iv) (a) an, (b) a, (c) the

**6. Fill in the blanks with the appropriate structural words :**

Mr. Smith is ......European. He deals ......... umbrella but he deals ......... the customers very well. All Europeans are not ......... same.

# 23 NARRATION/REPORTING

**[ Special stress has been given not only on the use of statements, commands, requests, Yes-No Questions, Wh-Questions, but also on the use of Question Tags : Can/Can't they? Do they/Don't they? (Ali can speak English well, Can't he? ]**

We often need to report messages, speeches, comments, requests etc. of a person or persons to others.

**We may report the words of a speaker in two ways :**

[1] We may quote his actual words. This is called **Direct Speech**.

[2] We may report what he said without quoting his exact words. This is called **Indirect Speech** or **Reported Speech**.

Mrs. Smith says, "I am ill." (Direct Speech)

Mrs. Smith says that she is ill. (Indirect Speech)

## PUNCTUATION OF DIRECT SPEECH

The speech which is under Quotation marks or Inverted Commas in writing is called **Direct Speech** and the Verb by which it is expressed is called **Reporting Verb**.

**Three Features of Direct Speech :**

(i) In writing, the Direct Speech is put within **Inverted Commas** ("...") to mark-off the exact words of the speaker. Of course, in dialogues, Inverted Commas are often left out.

(ii) A **Comma** is used after Reporting Verb. Of course, in dialogues, Reporting Verb and Comma are not needed.

(iii) **The first letter** of the Direct Speech is a **Capital letter**.

Now read the following table :

**DIRECT SPEECH**

| Speaker | Reporting Verb | Direct Speech |
|---|---|---|
| Hanif | said, | "I am very busy". |

**INDIRECT SPEECH**

| Reporter | Reporting Verb | Linker | Reported Speech |
|---|---|---|---|
| Hanif | said | that | he was very busy. |

It will be noticed that, in changing the Direct Speech into Indirect, certain grammatical changes have been made :

(i) We have used the linker **'that'** before the Reported Speech or Indirect statement.

(ii) The pronoun **'I'** is changed to **'he'**.

(iii) The verb **'am'** is changed to **'was'**.

## RULES FOR CHANGING DIRECT SPEECH INTO INDIRECT

(i) We use a **linker** before the Indirect Speech :

Direct : He said, "I am busy."

Indirect : He said **that** he was busy.

**N.B.** The linker **that** is often omitted in Spoken English.

(ii) The **Pronouns** are changed according to sense :

Direct : Alam said, "**I** do not like milk in my tea."

Indirect : Alam said that **he** does not like milk in his tea.

Direct : Alam said to his friend, "**You** are ill."

Indirect : Alam told his friend that **he** was ill.

Direct : Alam said to me, "**You** will not play."

Indirect : Alam told me that **I** would not play.

Direct : I said to you, "**I** don't believe you."

Indirect : I said (that) **I** didn't believe you.

(iii) If the **Reporting Verb** is in the **Past Tense**, we must make the following changes :

### CHANGE OF TENSES

| Direct | | Indirect |
|---|---|---|
| a. Present Indefinite | becomes | Past Indefinite |
| b. Present Continuous | becomes | Past Continuous |
| c. Present Perfect Continuous | becomes | Past Perfect Continuous |
| d. Past Indefinite<br>e. Present Perfect<br>f. Past Perfect | becomes | Past Perfect |
| g. Past Continuous | becomes | Past Perfect Continuous |
| h. Future (shall/will) | becomes | Future (should/would) |

### Change in Time and Place expressions in Past Tense

| | | | | | |
|---|---|---|---|---|---|
| now | becomes | then | here | becomes | there |
| ago | " | before | hence | " | thence |
| today | " | that day | this | " | that |
| tonight | " | that night | these | " | those |
| tomorrow | " | the next day | thus | " | that way |
| yesterday | " | the previous day | thus | " | so |
| last night | " | the previous night | come | " | go (not always) |

**Note 1** Students often change **'it'** into **'that'** in the indirect. But that is wrong. It remains unchanged :

Direct : The boy said, "I'll do the work now."
Indirect : The boy said that he would do the work then.
Direct : He said, "I am glad to be here this evening."
Indirect : He said that he was glad to be there that evening.
Direct : He said, "I shall go to Delhi tomorrow."
Indirect : He said that he would go to Delhi the next day.
Direct : I said to him, "I may come to your office."
Indirect : I told him that I might go to his office.
Direct : He said, "I have never seen anything like it."
Indirect : He said that he had never seen anything like it.

**Note 2** The changes do not occur if the speech is reported during the same period or at the same place :

Speaker (at 10 a.m.) : The Inspector will visit our school today.
Reporter (at 10 a.m.) : He says that the Inspector will visit their school today.
Reporter (next day) : He said that the Inspector would visit their school that day.
Speaker (in Kolkata) : Sir Asutosh Mukherjee was born here.
Reporter (in Kolkata, but after a few days) :
He said that Sir Asutosh Mukherjee was born here.
Reporter (in Delhi) : He said that Sir Asutosh Mukherjee was born there.

## NARRATION OF ASSERTIVE SENTENCE [ STATEMENT ]

Direct : He said, "I do it."
Indirect : He said that he did it.
Direct : He said, "I am writing a letter."
Indirect : He said that he was writing a letter.
Direct : He said, "I have been suffering from fever".
Indirect : He said that he had been suffering from fever.

Direct : He said, "I wrote a letter."
Indirect : He said that he had written a letter.
Direct : He said, "I have passed the examination".
Indirect : He said that he had passed the examination.
Direct : He said, "I had passed the examination."
Indirect : He said that he had passed the examination.
Direct : He said, "I was playing football."
Indirect : He said that he had been playing football.
Direct : He said, "I shall play football."
Indirect : He said that he would play football.

**Note 1** In Assertive sentence **Linker 'that'** is used.

**Note 2** If the Reporting Verb is in the **Present** or **Future Tense**, the tense of the Verb of the Direct Speech is not changed at all :

Direct : The farmer says, "I am busy."

Indirect : The farmer says that he is busy.

Direct : The farmer will say, "I am busy."

Indirect : The farmer will say that he is busy.

**Note 3** In case of a **habitual truth** or **eternal truth**, no change of tense is required :

Bill said "I walk for an hour every morning".
Bill said that he walks for an hour every morning. } **Habitual truth**

The teacher said "The sun rises in the east".
The teacher said that the sun rises in the east. } **Eternal truth**

**Note 4** Normally, there are no changes in the Verb Forms of the **Modal Auxiliaries** like ***must***, ***ought to*** and ***should***; though ***should*** often becomes ***would*** for corresponding persons of the Subject and ***had to*** is often used in place of ***must*** :

Direct : "We ought to jump", she said.

Indirect : She said that they ought to jump.

Direct : "We must go", she said.

Indirect : She said that they must go/had to go.

Direct : Medha said to me, "I should be grateful if you help me."

Indirect : Medha told me that he would be grateful if I helped him.

But the 'should' of obligation is not changed.

Ayengar said to him, "You should be more careful."

Ayengar told him that he should be more careful.

**Note 5** Reporting Verb becomes 'say' where there is no Object and it becomes 'tell' where there is Object. In Indirect Speech, "said to him", "said to me" etc. before '*that*' are not good English. Write "told him", "told me" etc.

## EXERCISE I

**A. Report the following sentences in Indirect Speech :**

1. The teacher said to the boy, "You have forgotten the lesson."
2. The boy said, "I shall go out and play."
3. He said, "I am happy to be here today."
4. They said, "We shall play the game again tomorrow."
5. The boy said, "Two and two make four."
6. "I have lost my books and yours too," she told them.
7. The princess says, "I have lost my way."
8. They say, "We must keep our locality clean."
9. The girl says, "These books are theirs, but this one is mine."
10. The Happy Prince said, "I led the dance in the great hall."

**B. Use different forms of tenses of the verb 'write' as in the following example and then change the narration :**

| Tense | Direct | Indirect |
|---|---|---|
| Simple Present | Ayesha said, "I write a letter" | ..................... |
| Pr. Continuous | Ayesha said, "....................". | ..................... |
| Pr. Perfect | Ayesha said, "....................". | ..................... |
| Pr. Perfect Cont. | Ayesha said, "....................". | ..................... |
| Simple Past | Ayesha said, "....................". | ..................... |
| Past Continuous | Ayesha said, "....................". | ..................... |
| Past Perfect | Ayesha said, "....................". | ..................... |
| Simple Future | Ayesha said, "....................". | ..................... |

## NARRATION OF INTERROGATIVE SENTENCE

**Rules of Change :**

(i) If the Direct Speech is in Interrogative sentence, Reporting Verbs such as say, tell etc. are changed into ***ask, enquire, want to know*** etc. in the Indirect Speech and the Verb takes an Object.

(ii) If the Direct Speech begins with some 'Wh' Question word, such as ***who, what, where, why, how,*** etc., these are retained in the Indirect Speech.

(iii) But if the Direct Speech does not begin with such Question words, ***if*** or ***whether*** is used as the linker.

(iv) The order of words in the Indirect Speech is changed from the Interrogative construction to the Assertive construction and the note of Interrogation ( ? ) becomes Fullstop ( . ).

## QUESTIONS BEGINNING WITH DO/DOES/DID/IS/AM/ARE ETC.

### [ YES-NO QUESTIONS ]

Direct ; "Do you know the way to the station?" She said to Mahim.
Indirect : She asked Mahim if (whether) he knew the way to the station.
Direct : "Does she require any help?" the old man asked me.
Indirect : The old man asked me if she required any help.

Direct : I said to the boy, "Did you go to school?"
Indirect : I asked (enquired of) the boy if he had gone to school.
Direct : "Is not poverty a curse?" my father said to me.
Indirect : My father asked me if poverty was (is) not a curse.

Direct : "Are you weeping?" he asked her.
Indirect : He asked her if she was weeping.
Direct : "Have you brought a bat for me?" the girl said to her father.
Indirect : The girl asked her father if he had brought a bat for her.
Direct : "Can you see a woman seated at a table?" he asked her.
Indirect : He asked her if she could see a woman seated at a table.

Direct : "Would you sing for our visitors?" my mother said to my sister.

Indirect : My mother asked my sister if she would sing for our visitors.

Direct : "Do you suppose you know better than your own father?" jeered his angry mother.

Indirect : His mother angrily asked (enquired) whether he supposed that he knew better than his own father.

Direct : My brother said to me, "Will you not go to the show?"

Indirect : My brother asked me if I would not go to the show.

**Note** An Interrogative sentence beginning with ***shall*** takes the form ***would*** in the past tense in the Indirect Speech. But ***should*** is retained when it implies a matter of duty :

Direct : I said to him, "Shall I reach the village before dawn?"

Indirect : I asked him if I would reach the village before dawn.

Direct : The girl said, "Shall I go out for shopping?"

Indirect : The girl asked if she would go out for shopping.

[ But 'shall' will be changed into 'should' in the following sentence : ]

Direct : Imran said to me, "Shall I wait for you for an hour?"

Indirect : Imran asked me if he should wait for me for an hour.

## 'WH' QUESTIONS

Direct : I said to the man, "Who are you?"

Indirect : I asked the man who he was.

Direct : He said to me, "What are you doing?"

Indirect : He asked me what I was doing.

Direct : "Where do you live?" asked the stranger.

Indirect : The stranger asked (him) where he lived.

Direct : "Why are you weeping?" the Swallow asked the Prince.

Indirect : The Swallow enquired of the Prince why he was weeping.

Direct : "Why doesn't she talk to me any more?" I thought.

Indirect : I thought to myself why she did not talk to me any more.

Direct : "When will you come back?" the Prince said to the Swallow.

Indirect : The Prince asked the Swallow when he would come back.

Direct : "How did you do that?" they asked Edison.

Indirect : They asked Edison how he had done that.

Direct : He said to me, "Which book do you want?"

Indirect : He asked me which book I wanted.

Direct : "Who was the first man to fly in space?" the examiner asked the boy.

Indirect : The examiner asked the boy who was the first man to fly in space.

**Note** In the last sentence, the order of words has not been changed as the Interrogative word 'who' has been used as the Subject of the Clause.

## QUESTION TAGS

**Rules : Statement (Affirmative) → Question Tag (Negative)**
**Statement (Negative) → Question Tag (Affirmative)**

Direct : He said to me, "Ali can speak English well, can't he?"
Indirect : He asked me if Ali could speak English well and assumed *that he could*.
Direct : He said to me, "You are going to the playground, aren't you?"
Indirect : He asked me if I was going to the playground and assumed *that I was*.
Direct : He said to me, "You didn't cause much damage to the book, did you?"
Indirect : He asked me whether I had caused much damage to the book and assumed *that I had not*.

**Note** The main force lies in the first statement, not in the Tag Questions. It is used only for checking or confirming.

## EXERCISE II

**A. Report the following sentences in Indirect Speech :**

1. The boy said to me, "Will you accompany me?"
2. She said to me, "Shall I post these letters for you?"
3. He said to me, "Have you done your hometask?"
4. "Is it good or bad?" asked Rahim.
5. "Is there anybody there?" said the traveller.
6. "Are you coming with me?" he asked.
7. Hasina said to the man, "Do you know Mr. Ali?"
8. The man said to me, "Do you know where he lives?"
9. She said to me, "Did you write to me before?"
10. Lila said to me, "Can you tell me his address?"

**B. Report the following sentences in Indirect Speech :**

1. "Which animal are you going to kill?" he wanted to know.
2. "What do you think of it?" Edison asked John.
3. "Who are you and what do you want of us?" I said to them.
4. "Where had you been yesterday?" I asked her.
5. Father said to me, "When did you do it?"
6. I said to George, "Whose pen are you using?"
7. Mother said to the boy, "What is your father?"
8. They said to him, "Which fish did you catch?"
9. He said, "How could such a man be a teacher?"
10. I said to him, "Why have you failed?"
11. He said to me, "When will the Down train arrive?"
12. "Who was the first man to land on the moon?" asked the examiner.

**C. Change the following sentences into Indirect Speech :**

1. I said to him, "You are going home, aren't you?"
2. He said to me, "You didn't do your hometask, did you?"
3. Father said to me, "You have bought a pen from market for me, haven't you?"
4. My friend said to me, "You haven't read the Ramayana, have you?"
5. Mr. Kamat asked, "They didn't perform the job well, did they?"

## NARRATION OF IMPERATIVE SENTENCE

**[Commands, Requests etc.]**

**Rules of Change :**

(i) The Reporting Verb becomes ***order, request, advise, tell, ask*** etc. according to the sense. Hence the words ***'said to me', 'said to him'*** etc. becomes ***ordered me, requested him, advised him*** etc.

(ii) The Imperative mood is changed into the Infinitive. Hence ***to*** **is used before the main verb to make it Infinitive**.

(iii) Negative Imperative may be expressed by using ***not*** before the Infinitive in the Indirect Speech. The Reporting verb ***forbid, prohibit*** etc. may also be used without using not.

(iv) Such expressions as ***Please, Sir*** in the Direct are left out in the Indirect Speech and they are rendered by the Verb ***request*** or ***ask to be kind enough*** or by the Adverbs ***kindly, politely*** etc.

**Examples :**

Direct : The officer shouted to his men, "Halt!"
Indirect : The officer ordered his men to halt.
Direct : Father said to me, "Go home at once."
Indirect : Father ordered me to go home at once.
Direct : The teacher said to me, "Don't come here."
Indirect : The teacher ordered me not to go there.
[Or] The teacher forbade me to go there.
Direct : He said to me, 'Please open the door."

Indirect : He requested me to open the door.
[Or] He told me politely to open the door.
Direct : He said to me, "Please wait here till I return."
Indirect : He requested me to wait there till he returned.
Direct : I said to him, 'Please explain the passage."
Indirect : I requested him to explain the passage.
[Or] I asked him to be kind enough to explain the passage.
Direct : Mother said to me, "Don't run in the sun."
Indirect : Mother advised me not to run in the sun.
[Or] Mother forbade me to run in the sun.
Direct : He said to his master, "Pardon me, sir."
Indirect : He begged his master to pardon him.

When ***order, request, advise*** etc. are not clearly expressed, ***tell*** or ***ask*** may be used as the Reporting Verb :

Direct : He said to me, "Don't do it again."
Indirect : He told (asked) me not to do it again.
Direct : "Don't forget to give her the information," he said to you.
Indirect : He told (reminded) you not to forget to give her the information.
Direct : Rina said to him, "Sir, Don't go home now."
Indirect : Rina asked him politely not to go home then.

## IMPERATIVE BEGINNING WITH 'LET'

When Let in the Direct Speech expresses a proposal or suggestion, we may use ***should*** **for** ***Let*** **and change the Reporting Verb into** ***propose*** **or** ***suggest***. Moreover, the Imperative form is changed into Assertive form with the linker **'that'**.

Direct : Lila said to her friends, "Let us have a picnic."

Indirect : Lila proposed (suggested) to her friends that they should have a picnic.

Direct : He said to his companions, "Let us not miss this chance to see the last show."

Indirect : He proposed (suggested) to his companions that they should not miss that chance to see the last show.

But when ***Let*** does not express a proposal, it should be changed into ***might*** or ***might be allowed to***, or into some other form according to the sense :

Direct : We said, "Let him tell the story."

Indirect : We said that he might (or might be allowed to) tell the story.

Direct : She said, "Let him eat whatever he likes."

Indirect : She said that he might (or might be allowed to) eat whatever he liked.

Direct : He said, "Let me come in."

Indirect : He requested that he might be allowed to come in.

[Or] He requested to let him come in. [ **In Request, 'let' may be changed into 'to let'** ]

## IMPERATIVES WITH MUST, WOULD AND COULD

The Modal **must** is not normally changed in the Indirect Speech. You should also note that some sentences with ***would*** and ***could*** are Interrogative in form but Imperative in nature. So 'to' Infinitive is used in these cases :

Direct : He said to me, "You must leave the place."

Indirect : He told me that I must leave the place.

Direct : He said to me, "Would you help me to do the sum?"

Indirect : He requested me to help him to do the sum.

Direct : I said to her, "Could you give me a cup of tea?"

Indirect : I requested her to give me a cup of tea.

### EXERCISE III

**A. Report the following sentences in Indirect Speech :**

1. The master said to his servant, "Do as I told you."
2. The teacher said to the boys, "Don't make so much noise."
3. Kanika said to me, "Please lend me your pen."
4. He said, "Be quiet and listen to my words."
5. She said to her father, "Kindly excuse me this time."
6. The General said to his soldiers, "March forward!"

**B. Change the following Direct Speech into Indirect Speech :**

1. I said to the teacher, "Let me come in."
2. He said, "Let us wait for the award."
3. I said, "Let him do what he likes."
4. Father said to his son, "You must do this."
5. The hare said to the tortoise, "Let us run a race."
6. Rekha said to her mother, "Let me look out the window."

## NARRATION OF OPTATIVE SENTENCE

**[ Wishes, Prayers etc. ]**

**Rules of Change :**

Optative sentences express wish or prayer. So Reporting Verbs in such sentences are changed into ***wish, pray, desire, long for, yearn for*** etc. Moreover, the Optative form is changed into Assertive form with the linker ***that*** in the Indirect Speech.

**Nesfield**

**Examples :**

Direct : I said to him, "May you be happy."
Indirect : I wished that he might be happy.
Direct : Mother said to me, "May God bless you."
Indirect : Mother prayed that God might (would) bless me.
Direct : He said, "May his soul rest in peace."
Indirect : He prayed that his soul might rest in peace.
Direct : The girl said, "Oh, had I the wings of a dove!"
Indiect : The girl wished that she could have the wings of a dove.

### EXERCISE IV

**Report the following senences into Indirect Speech :**

1. I said to him, "May you live long."
2. Nilima said to me, "May you recover soon."
3. Mother said to him, "May God grant you a long life."
4. The holy man said, "May peace prevail."
5. She said, "May your son recover from illness soon."
6. He said, "Oh, If I could bring my departed friend back to life!"

## NARRATION OF EXCLAMATORY SENTENCE

**[ Sudden emotion ]**

**Rules of Change :**

(i) In Exclamatory Sentences, the Reporting Verb is changed into ***exclaim in*** (*with*) ***grief, exclaim in joy, exclaim in wonder*** etc. according to the sense of ***Alas, Hurrah*** etc. But in some cases, where one is not sure about the nature of exclamation, it is advised to change the Reporting Verb as ***cry out*** or ***exclaim*** only. Other forms of Reporting Verbs are ***swear, shout, applaud*** etc. in Exclamatory Sentences.

(ii) The Exclamatory Sentence is turned into a statement and Linker ***that*** is used in the Indirect Speech.

(iii) If the Exclamatory Sentence begins with ***What*** or ***How*** to denote extreme emotion, it becomes ***great*** or ***very*** according to sense. **Normally *great* is placed before a Noun and *very* is placed before an Adjective.**

(iv) In Indirect Speech, the sentence ends with a **full-stop ( . )** and not an **exclamation mark (!)**. It is applicable for all sorts of sentences as all these are Assertive Sentences or statements in Indirect Speech.

**Examples :**

Direct : The boys said, "Hurrah! We have won the match."
Indirect : The boys exclaimed in (with) joy that they had won the match.
Direct : He said to me, "Alas! I could not save you."
Indirect : He exclaimed in grief that he could not save me.
Direct : He said, "Alas! how foolish I have been!"
Indirect : He confessed with regret that he had been very foolish.
Direct : The boy said, "What a fool I am!"
Indirect : He exclaimed (cried out) that he was a great fool.
Direct : He said, "What a nice bird it is!"
Indirect : He exclaimed in wonder that it was a very nice bird.
Direct : He observed, "How dirty the house is!"
Indirect : He exclaimed that the house was very dirty.

## SOME SPECIAL USES OF EXCLAMATORY SENTENCES

Direct : "Help! Help!" shouted the woman.
Indirect : The woman shouted for help.
Direct : He said, "Good-bye, my friends!"
Indirect : He bade good-bye to his friends.
[Or] He bade his friends good-bye.
Direct : The teacher said, "Thank you, my boys!"
Indirect : The teacher thanked the boys.
Direct : He said, "By Jove! What a good news."
Indirect : He swore by Jove that it was a very good news.

Direct : She said to me, "Happy Christmas!"
Indirect : She wished me a Happy Christmas.
Direct : He said to them, "Bravo! You have done well."
Indirect : He applauded them saying that they had done well.
Direct : The old man said to him, "Fie! You are such a coward."
Indirect : The old man expressed his disgust and said that he was a coward.
[Or] : The old man exclaimed that it was shameful that he was such a coward.
Direct : He said, "Poor fellow! How changed you are."
Indirect : He pitied the man and exclaimed that he was greatly changed.
Direct : "So help me Heaven!" he cried, "I'll never do so again."
Indirect : He prayed to Heaven to help him and resolved not to do so (in that way) again.

Direct : He said, "Who knew that this would happen!"

Indirect : He said that none knew that (that) would happen.

Direct : He said, "Good Gracious! What a huge snake!"

Indirect : He exclaimed with wonder that it was a huge snake.

Direct : "Good Heavens! We have reached the peak," said the boys.

Indirect : The boys exclaimed with delight that they had reached the peak.

## EXERCISE V

**Report the following sentences in Indirect Speech :**

1. He said, "Alas! The war killed all my family."
2. He says, "Hurrah! My friend has come."
3. The teacher said to the boy, "Fie! You are a liar."
4. They cried out, "Bravo! It is a capital hit."
5. The girl said, "Ah! I am happy now."
6. The leader said to his men, "Good-bye, comrades!"
7. "How selfish I have been!" he said.
8. The girl remarked, "What a fine picture it is!"
9. The teacher remarked, "What a stupid fellow you are!"
10. Tom said to John, "How clever you are!"
11. "By God! What an interesting piece of painting," they said.
12. "So help me Heaven!" he cried, "I will never steal again."

## NARRATION OF VOCATIVES

**It is important** to note that conversion of Vocatives into ***Addressing as*** is now treated as '**Hackneyed English**.' **It should be avoided thus :**

Direct : He said to the officer, "Yes, sir, I shall do this."

Indirect : He told the officer politely that he would do that.

[If we write, Addressing the officer as sir, he told him that he would do that—it would be bad English.]

'Addressing as' should be used only when there is no other way to express vocatives.

**Vocatives may be omitted as** in the above example, or **may be dealt with as below :**

**Examples :**

Now study the conversion of the following Vocatives :

Direct : Father said, "Sunil, go to school."

Indirect : Father asked Sunil to go to school.

Direct : The teacher said, "Keep quiet, my boy!"

Indirect : The teacher asked the boy to keep quiet.

Direct : The teacher said, "Keep quiet, my dear boys!"

Indirect : The teacher affectionately asked the boys to keep quiet.

Direct : Bibhas cried, 'My friend, I always thought of you."

Indirect : Bibhas told his friend that he always thought of him.

Direct : "Jim, darling", cried Della, "Don't look at me that way."

Indirect : Addressing (Calling) Jim as her darling, Della implored him not to look at her that way.

## NARRATION OF QUESTION TAGS

Question Tags are short Interrogative clauses added like a tail to sentences, asking for confirmation :

**Affirmative Statement + Negative Question Tag [Expecting the answer 'Yes']**

Direct : We said, "We are late, aren't we?"

Indirect : We wanted to be confirmed that we were late.

Direct : I said to him, "You can speak French, can't you?"

Indirect : Expecting the answer 'yes', I asked him if he could speak French.

**Negative Statement + Affirmative Question Tag [Expecting the answer 'No']**

Direct : I said, "They will not go, will they?"

Indirect : Expecting the answer 'No', I asked if they would go.

Direct : I said, "They haven't any house, have they?"

Indirect : Expecting the answer 'No', I asked if they had any house.

**Note** The main force of affirmation or negation lies in the main clause, not in the Question Tag.

## REPORTING MIXED SENTENCES

**Rules of Change :**

(i) When the sentences of the same kind occur consecutively in the Direct Speech, the Reporting Verb becomes common and so it is to be used only once in the Indirect Speech. In such cases, the sentences are joined by the Linker 'and'.

(ii) When the sentences of different kinds are joined, different Reporting Verbs have to be used in the Indirect Speech.

(iii) A useful connective device is to use : then, added that, further said that or also said that.

**Examples :**

Direct : I said to him, "Who are you? What do you want?"

Indirect : I asked him who he was and what he wanted.

Direct : Shila said to me, "I have left my camera at home. Can you give me one to shoot with?"

Indirect : Shila told me that she had left her camera at home and asked me if I could give her one to shoot with.

Direct : Mr. Sen said to his friend, "What time is it? My watch has stopped."

Indirect : Mr. Sen asked his friend what time it was and added that (further said that/also said that) his watch had stopped.

Direct : Biman said, "Why are you still waiting here, Bipin? Go away now."

Indirect : Biman asked Bipin why he was still waiting there. Then he ordered (advised) him to go away.

## APPLIED SECTION

### (For Questions and Answers—'Yes' and 'No')

In changing 'Yes' or 'No' into Indirect Speech we should repeat the verb of the question or the common verb 'do' or the sense of the verb.

The ugly forms **'replied in the affirmative'** and **'replied in the negative'** are avoided nowadays :

The teacher said to the boy, "Are you ill?"

The boy replied, "No".

= The teacher asked the boy if he was ill, and the boy replied that he was not.

The host said to her, "Have all the guests arrived?"

She replied, "Yes".

= The host asked her if all the guests had arrived and she replied that they had.

Someone asked her, "Will you take some more *chapatis*?"

She said, "No". [= She refused to take any more *chapatis*.]

Someone asked him, "Did you break the glass?"

He said, "No, I didn't". [= He denied that he had broken it.]

[Or] He denied having done it.

Nikhil : 'Could you accompany me?'

Rakesh : 'No, I can't'. [= Rakesh told Nikhil that he could not do that.]

## REPORTING DIALOGUES/MESSAGES

Normally, in real-life situations, we do not report every word of the sentence. Many irrelevant points are intentionally omitted while reporting. Hence conversations and talks are reported in a summary form. Hackneyed expressions like **"Addressing him (his friend) by the name of Suren"** or **"replied in the negative"**, **"replied in the affirmative"** etc. **should be avoided**.

**Stress should be laid on reflecting the true mood of the dialogue or the message.**

**A dialogue can be reported in three ways :**

**(i) by the Speaker**, **(ii) by the Listener**, **(iii) by a Third Person**.

Study the following examples :

**EXAMPLE 1**

Bikash : Hello, Subhash, where are you going?

Subhas : I'm going to the playground to watch a basketball match. Why don't you accompany me?

Bikhash : I can't. I'm going to the station to receive my sister who is coming from Delhi by the Rajdhani Express.

Subhas : Then you must hurry up. I'll see you at your house this evening.

**(i) Now imagine you are Bikash and report the above dialogue :**

I greeted Subhas (not, I addressed Subhas by saying Hello) and asked him where he was going. Subhas replied that he was going to the playground to watch a basketball match and requested me to accompany him (not, asked me why I did not accompany him). I told him that I could not do that because I was going to the station to receive my sister who was coming from Delhi by the Rajdhani Express. Subhas asked me to hurry up and told me that he would see me at my house that evening.

**(ii) Now imagine you are Subhas and report the above dialogue :**

Bikash asked me where I was going and I replied that I was going to the play ground to watch a basketball match. I requested him to accompany me. Bikash told me that he could not do that because he was going to the station to receive his sister who was coming from Delhi by the Rajdhani Express. Then I asked him to hurry up and told him that I would see him at his house that evening.

**(iii) Now report the above dialogue as a third person :**

Bikhash greeted Subhas and asked him (Subhas) where he was going. Subhas replied that he was going to the playground to watch a basketball match. He also requested Bikash to accompany him. Bikash told him that he could not do that because he was going to the station to receive his sister who was coming from Delhi by the Rajdhani Express. Then Subhas asked him to hurry up and told him that he (Subhas) would see him at his house that evening.

**Note** In the three forms of the reporting, Pronouns should be carefully changed. Other rules are the same.

**EXAMPLE 2**

**Read the following conversation between a teacher and a student :**

Teacher : Why were you absent? The Headmaster is angry with you. Go to him and see him at once.

Student : I'm sorry, Sir. Now I'll go and pray to him to excuse me for the first time.

**(i) The student reports :**

The teacher asked me why I had been absent. He then informed me that the Headmaster was angry with me. So he advised me to go and see the Headmaster at once. However I apologised and told the teacher that I would go to the Headmaster and pray to him to excuse me for the first time.

**(ii) Report it as a third person :**

The teacher asked the student why he had been absent. He (the teacher) then informed him that the Headmaster was angry with him (the student). So he advised him to go and see the Headmaster at once. The student apologised and said that he would go to the Headmaster and pray to him to excuse him for the first time.

**EXAMPLE 3**

**Mala received a message from a messenger for her brother Dipu. The following was the conversation between them :**

Messenger : Hello! Is Dipu at home?

Mala : No, he's not. I'm his sister Mala.

Messenger : Could you tell him I've bought two tickets for 'Pather Panchali'? I'll be at the main gate of Nandan today at 1 p.m. sharp.

Mala : All right.

Messenger : Thank you, good-bye.

**Imagine you are Mala. You have to go out; so write a message for Dipu.**

[**Note :** he's = he is; I'm = I am; I'll = I will; I've = I have.]

**Ans.**

Dear Dipu,

Someone (possibly your friend) came to see you at our home. He told me that he had bought two tickets for 'Pather Panchali' and he would be at the main gate of Nandan today at 1 p.m. sharp.

Mala

**EXAMPLE 4**

**Read the following conversation :**

Prabir : Where are you going now?

Subir : To Durgapur.

Prabir : Why are you going there?

Subir : To meet the M.D. of the Steel Plant. He is my uncle.

Prabir : Where does he reside?

Subir : He resides in the officer's quarters of the Steel Plant.

(i) **Now study how the conversation can be reported in detail by another person after a few days :**

Prabir asked Subir where he was going. Subir replied that he was going to Durgapur. Prabir then asked him why he was going there. Subir replied that he was going there to meet his uncle who is the M.D. of the Steel Plant. Prabir further asked him where his uncle resided. In reply Subir told him that his uncle resides (resided) in the officer's quarters of the Steel Plant.

**Note** If Subir's uncle still resides in the officer's quarters of the Steel Plant, the Verb form will be in the Present Tense, not in the Past Tense.

(ii) **Now study how the conversation can be reported in a summary form :**

In reply to Prabir's queries Subir informed him that he was going to Durgapur to meet his uncle who was (is) the M.D. of the Steel Plant.

**EXAMPLE 5**

**Report the following :**

The traveller said, "Can you tell me the way to the nearest inn?"

"Yes," said the peasant, "do you want one where you can spend the night?"

"No", replied the traveller, "I only want a meal."

**Reported Speech :**

The traveller asked the peasant if he could tell him the way to the nearest inn. The peasant replied that he could, and asked whether the traveller wanted one where he could spend the night. The traveller answered that he did not wish to stay there, but only wanted a meal.

**Note** It will be noticed that we have avoided the ugly phrases '*replied in the affirmative*' and '*replied in the negative*' by using '*could*' and '*he did not wish to stay there*'.

**EXAMPLE 6**

**Report the following :**

"Who hath dared to wound thee?" cried the Giant; "Tell me that I may take my big sword and slay him."

"Nay!" answered the child : "but these are the wounds of Love."

"Who art thou?" said the Giant and a strange awe fell on him and he knelt before the little child.

**Reported Speech :**

The Giant angrily asked the child who had dared to wound him and requested him (the child) to tell him so that he might take his big sword and slay him. The child answered that no one had wounded him, but those were the wounds of love. The Giant wanted to know who he (the child) was as a strange awe fell on him, and he knelt before the little child.

**EXAMPLE 7**

**Report the following :**

'I am waited for in Egypt', said the Swallow. 'My friends are flying up and down the Nile, and talking to the large lotus-flowers. Soon they will go to sleep in the tomb of the great King.'

'Swallow, Swallow, little Swallow', said the Prince, 'will you not stay with me for one night, and be my messenger? The boy is so thirsty, and the mother so sad.'

**Reported Speech :**

The Swallow said that he was waited for in Egypt and added that his friends were flying up and down the Nile, and talking to the large lotus-flowers, and soon they would go to sleep in the tomb of the great King. The Prince earnestly requested (not, asked) the Swallow to stay with him for one night and be his messenger, and added that the boy was very (not, so) thirsty, and the mother very (not, so) sad.

**EXAMPLE 8**

**Report the following :**

Bishop : My dear, there's so much suffering in the world, and I can do so little, so very little.

Persome : Suffering, yes, but you never think of the suffering you cause to those who love you best, the suffering you cause to me.

Bishop : You, sister dear? Have I hurt you?

**Reported Speech :**

The Bishop told Persome affectionately that there was so much suffering in the world, and he could do so little. Persome admitted that there was suffering, but he never thought of the suffering he caused to those who loved him best, the suffering he caused to her. The Bishop was surprised at his sister's words and asked her if he had hurt her.

**EXAMPLE 9**

**Report the following :**

Davy : You have a trade, at present, Mr. Faraday?

Faraday : Yes Sir, I am a book-binder.

Davy : And you desire to change?

Faraday : Yes Sir, I am anxious to do so.

Davy : Why?

**Reported Speech :**

Davy asked Faraday if he had a trade. Faraday replied that he was a book-binder. Then Davy asked him whether he desired to change his trade. Faraday told him politely that he was anxious to do so. Davy wanted to know the reason.

### EXAMPLE 10

**Report the following :**

Sergeant : Stop. Didn't I tell you to stop? You cannot go there.

Man : Oh! Very well, it is a hard thing to be very poor. All the world is against the poor.

**Reported Speech :**

The Sergerant ordered the man to stop and reminded him that he had already asked him to stop. He (the Sergeant) warned him that he could not go there.

The man reluctantly admitted it and said (commented) that it was a hard thing to be very poor and that all the world was against the poor.

### EXAMPLE 11

**Report the following :**

Sergeant : You know him? Come back here. What sort of man is he?

Man : Come back, is it, Sergeant? Do you want me killed?

Sergeant : Why do you say that?

**Reported Speech :**

The Sergeant asked the man if he knew him. He further ordered him to go back there and asked him what sort of man he was. The man ironically asked the Sergeant if he (Sergeant) wanted him (to) go back to get killed. The Sergeant wanted to know the reason of saying that.

### EXAMPLE 12

**Report the following :**

Man : Can you cure a headache?

Chemist : (Thrusting a bottle under the man's nose) I am sure your headache is gone now.

Man : You fool! It is my wife that has got the headache, not me.

**Reported Speech :**

The man asked the chemist if he could cure a headache. Thrusting a bottle under the man's nose the chemist said that he was sure that the man's headache was gone (then). Then the man angrily called the chemist a fool and said that it was his wife who had got a headache, and not he.

### EXAMPLE 13

**Report the following :**

Hannah : Mrs. Meldon wants to know whether you'll come downstairs to tea or have it up here?

Corrie : Has she got back?

Hannah : Yes, Sir. She expected you to meet her at the station, Sir. She waited a long time in the cold, and then got Marshall to drive her up.

**Reported Speech :**

Hannah informed Mr. Corrie that Mrs. Meldon wanted to know whether he would go downstairs to tea or have it up there. Corrie wanted to know whether she had got back. Hannah politely replied that she had. She (Hannah) further informed him that she (Mrs. Meldon) had expected him to meet her at the station, that she had waited a long time in the cold, and then got Marshall to drive her up.

[**Note :** Hanna is a feminine character.]

**EXAMPLE 14**

**Report the following :**

Mrs. Meldon : It's all in your head?

Corrie : Yes, Yes. Don't keep on repeating yourself, but come and help to clear the mess you've made.

Mrs. Meldon : Henry, won't you do what I ask you?

**Reported Speech :**

Mrs. Meldon asked Corrie if it was all in his head. Corrie replied irritatingly and asked her not to keep on repeating herself, but to go and help to clear the mess she had made. Then Mrs. Meldon wanted to know from Henry if he would not do what she had asked him.

**EXAMPLE 15**

**Report the following :**

Mrs. Meldon : Henry, I beg you to destroy your invention.

Corrie : You what?

Mrs. Meldon : I beg you to destroy it. Let that be your memorial to Eddie!

Corrie : My dear Charlotte, I begin to believe that grief has unhinged your mind. Destroy my invention!

Mrs. Meldon : Your bomb will destroy life, Henry. I beg you to destroy it.

Corrie : Rubbish, woman, rubbish.

**Reported Speech :**

Mrs. Meldon called Corrie by his Christian name, Henry, and begged him to destroy his invention. Corrie wanted to be sure of what she begged . Mrs. Meldon repeated that she begged him to destroy the invention and let that be his memorial to Eddie. Corrie addressed Mrs. Meldon by her Christian name, Charlotte, and said that he began to believe that grief had unhinged her mind. It was unbelievable to him that he should destroy his invention. Mrs. Meldon reminded Corrie that his bomb would destroy life. So she begged of him to destroy it. Being irritated by the suggestion, Corrie addressed Mrs. Meldon as 'woman' and repeatedly called her suggestion 'rubbish'.

[**Note :** Here 'addressed ' should not be avoided, as Henry and Charlotte denote Christian names of Corrie and Mrs. Meldon, respectively.]

## EXERCISE VI

**[A] REPORT THE FOLLOWING DIALOGUES :**

1. Corrie : I'm sorry, Charlotte, I ought not to have talked about the war to you—especially today.

   Mrs. Meldon : I don't mind, Henry. And after all, the War Office is not the war.

**Imagine that you are**

(i) Corrie (ii) Mrs. Meldon (iii) a third person.

2. Corrie : What the hell are you doing?

   Mrs. Meldon : I'm destroying your foul invention.

   Corrie : (Laughing harshly) That won't destroy it. I've got it in my head. All that you've done, Charlotte, is to make a mess on my floor.

3. 'Mr. Faraday?' Davy put his hand out.
   'Yes, Sir Humphry', said Michael, jumping to his feet.
   'Let's sit down here and talk the matter over', began Davy.
4. Father : How do you feel, Schatz?
   Schatz : Just the same, so far.
   Father : Why don't you try to sleep? I'll wake you up for the medicine.

5. Schatz : About how long will it be before I die?
   Father : You aren't going to die. What's the matter with you?
   Schatz : Oh, yes, I am. I heard him say a hundred and two.
   Father : People don't die with a fever of one hundred and two. That's a silly way to talk.

6. Gandhi : You don't like vegetables?
   Fischer : I don't like the taste of these vegetables three days running.
   Gandhi : Ah, you must add plenty of salt and lemon.
   Fischer : You want me to kill the taste?
   Gandhi : (Laughing) No, enrich the taste.
   Fischer : (Jokingly) You're so non-violent you wouldn't even kill a taste!
7. Corrie : Oh, my dear Charlotte, I'm sorry, I did not meet you at the station.
   Mrs. Meldon : It doesn't matter, Henry. Only I thought you were coming— you said you would—and I waited a long time in the cold.
8. Hannah : Mrs. Meldon is not very happy today, sir.
   Corrie : Not happy! Why? I'm happy, aren't I?
   Hannah : Well, you see, sir, it's three years ago today since her son was killed in the war!
9. Corrie : I'm going to make war horrible, really horrible!
   Mrs. Meldon : Yes.
   Corrie : I've got something here, Charlotte, the formula for a bomb that will make war not only stupendously horrible, but will end it almost as quickly as it began.
   Mrs. Meldon : On that table?
   Corrie : Yes.
10. Passenger : Four tickets to Panaji, please.
    Booking clerk : What Class?
    Passenger : Second Class.
    Booking clerk : Won't you like to have First Class tickets for the sea part of the journey from Nagar Haveli?
    Passenger : What would be the difference in price between the two classes per ticket?
    Booking clerk : Some twenty-five rupees. Not much. But it will make your journey extremely enjoyable.

11. Son : Shall we take a taxi or a bus to go to the exhibition?

Father : It would be better we take a bus. It's really difficult getting a taxi at this rush hour. (hour = time)

Son : Shall we go to the next bus stop? That is the terminus. There we would get vacant seats.

Father : Yes, Yes: that's a good idea.

12. Mr. Holmes : Good morning, madam! My name is Sherlock Holmes. (Pointing out to Watson) This is my friend, Dr. Watson, before whom you can speak freely. But first I shall order you a cup of hot coffee, for I see that you are shivering.

Lady : (in a low voice) It is not cold which makes me shiver.

Mr. Holmes : What is it then?

Lady : It is fear, It is terror.

**[B] WRITE SOME DIALOGUES IN REAL-LIFE SITUATIONS AND REPORT THE SAME TO A THIRD PERSON :**

1. In a crowded bus you accidentally step on somebody's foot. Apologise.

You : ..............................................................................................

Somebody : ..............................................................................................

2. At a railway station you want to have a cup of tea but you have only a fifty-rupee note. What do you ask somebody there?

You : ..............................................................................................

Somebody : ..............................................................................................

3. Your neighbour's radio is very loud and you feel disturbed. You have knocked at his door. What do you say?

You : ..............................................................................................

Neighbour : ..............................................................................................

4. You meet a stranger in your town. He wants to go to the post office. He wants you to give him the direction.

The stranger : ..............................................................................................

You : ..............................................................................................

5. An old friend of yours has come to your town, and you meet him on the road. Invite him to come and spend the weekend with you.

You : ..............................................................................................

Your friend : ..............................................................................................

**[C] THIS IS A TELEPHONE MESSAGE THAT A P.A. (PERSONAL ASSISTANT) RECEIVED FOR MR. SEN, HIS BOSS. HOW WOULD HE REPORT IT TO HIS BOSS?**

P.A. : Hello!

Mr. Roy : Good afternoon. Mr. Roy speaking. Could I speak to Mr. Sen?

P.A. : I'm afraid, he has not yet returned from Mumbai. Possibly he'll be here tonight.

Mr. Roy : I telephoned at his home this morning, but couldn't get him. Would you give him a message from me, please? It's about our meeting on Friday. I have been suddenly called from the Head-office. It's better to postpone our meeting until next week.

P.A. : Yes, Sir, I'll give him the message.

Mr. Roy : Thank you, good-bye. (or, simply, Bye)

P.A. : Welcome, Sir.

Note that the first three lines do not come into the report. Begin like this :

Sir,

Mr. Roy rang up to speak to you. He telephoned at your home too, but couldn't get you. He informed that ..........................................................................

(Signature)

P.A.

# 24 VOICE CHANGE/ DESCRIBING A PROCESS

[ **Special stress has been given on the Passive mode to describe something in real-life situation, not wishing to specify the agent (e.g. The house was built in 1990.) including Quasi-Passive Voice (e.g. The room looks nice.)** ]

**What is 'Voice'?**

Voice is the form of the Verb which indicates whether the Subject does the work or something has been done to it.

There are **three kinds of Voices** :

(1) **Active Voice**, (2) **Passive Voice**, (3) **Quasi-Passive Voice**.

**Active Voice :** When the Subject of a sentence is the doer or actor, the Verb is in Active Voice. It is so because the Subject is active.

I do this work. He does this work. He did this work, etc. (Active voice)

**Passive Voice :** When the Subject of a sentence is acted upon, the Verb is in Passive Voice. It is so because the Subject is passive.

This work is done by me. This work was done by him, etc. (Passive Voice)

**Active-Passive Relation :**

| | Subject | Verb | Object |
|---|---|---|---|
| Active : | Manika | opened | the door |
| Passive : | The door | was opened | by Manika |

**Subject (or, Agent) + 'be' + P.P. of verb + Prep. & Object**

## RULES FOR CHANGING ACTIVE VOICE INTO PASSIVE

**Rule 1 :** The **Object of the Verb** in the Active Voice becomes the **Subject of the Verb in the Passive Voice**.

**Rule 2 :** The **Subject** of the Verb in the Active Voice becomes the **Object** in the Passive Voice, **generally preceded** by the preposition **by**.

**Rule 3 :** The **main Verb** is changed into the **Past Participle form** and it is preceded by the correct form of the Verb **'to be'** in Passive Voice.

**Rule 4 :** There are some Verbs with **two Objects**. In such cases either of the Objects (preferably the Personal Object) can be changed into the Subject and the other is retained as an Object. This Object is called **Retained Object**.

**Rule 5 : Double Passive should be avoided in a Simple Sentence or in a single Clause** as it is liable to give a wrong meaning. **But in changing the Voice of Complex Sentences the Voices of both the Principal and Subordinate Clauses should be changed if both of them have Transitive Verbs.**

## VERB PATTERNS OF PASSIVE VOICE

| Tenses | Verb 'to be' | Past Participle of the main Verb |
|---|---|---|
| Simple Present and Past | am<br>are<br>is<br>was<br>were | caught<br>killed<br>done<br>told<br>cured  |
| Continuous | am<br>are<br>is<br>was<br>were } being | caught<br>killed<br>done<br>told<br>cured  |
| Perfect | has<br>have<br>had } been | boiled<br>arrested<br>bought  |
| Future | shall<br>will } be | built<br>taught |

## TABLE OF TENSES IN ACTIVE AND PASSIVE

| Tenses | Active Voice | Passive Voice |
|---|---|---|
| Simple Present | buys | is/are bought |
| Simple Past | bought | was/were bought |
| Present Continuous | is/are buying | is/are being bought |
| Past Continuous | was/were buying | was/were being bought |
| Present Perfect | has/have bought | has/have been bought |
| Past Perfect | had bought | had been bought |
| Simple Future | shall/will buy | will be bought |
| Conditional | would buy | would be bought |
| Perfect Conditional | would have bought | would have been bought |

## OBJECTIVE FORMS OF PRONOUNS

| Subject Form | Object Form | Subject Form | Object Form |
|---|---|---|---|
| I | me | He | him |
| We | us | She | her |
| You | you | They | them |

## VOICE CHANGE OF ASSERTIVE SENTENCES

**Passive form : be (is, am, are, was, were, being, been) + Past Participle**

| Active | Passive |
|---|---|
| I do the work.  | The work is done by me.  |
| Ayesha types a letter. | A letter is typed by Ayesha. |
| Syed helped her. | She was helped by Syed. |
| Rabeya is singing a song. | A song is being sung by Rabeya. |
| She was singing a song. | A song was being sung by her. |
| He has called me. | I have been called by him. |
| They had seen the picture. | The picture had been seen by them. |
| You will play football. | Football will be played by you. |
| She would sing a song. | A song would be sung by her. |
| She would have read the book. | The book would have been read by her. |

**Note** **Adverbials** etc. **in the end position** in Active Voice **remains in the end position** in Passive Voice too.

He will finish the work in a week. → The work will be finished by him in a week.

## IMPERATIVE SENTENCES

If the Verb in the Active Voice expresses **orders**, **requests**, **advice** etc. the word '**Let**' **is usually placed at the beginning of the Passive Voice** and the '**be**' **Verb is placed before the Past Participle of the main Verb.** Another form of the Passive is with the Verb '**should**' + '**be**' or with '**Be**'/'**Get**' only. But if the sentences begin with '**Please**' in Active Voice, '**You are requested to**' is used in the Passive Voice. An Intransitive Verb may also be changed into Passive with '**You are requested to/advised to**', **etc.** Such **a Passive Voice of an Intransitive Verb** may be called an **Indirect Passive**.

**Passive : Let + Object + be + Past Participle of the Verb [ Or, (should) be/get + P.P.]**

| Active | Passive |
|---|---|
| Do this work. | Let this work be done. |
| Open the door. | Let the door be opened. |
| Shut the door. | Let the door be shut. |
| Tell him to go. | Let him be told to go. |
| Keep your word. | Your word should be kept. |
| Obey your teacher. | Your teacher should be obeyed. |
| Love the children. | The children should be loved. |

| Active | Passive |
|---|---|
| Prepare for the worst. | Be (Get) prepared for the worst. |
| Please do this work. | You are requested to do this work. |
| Please keep off the grass. | You are requested to keep off the grass. [or] The grass should be kept off. |
| Please go there. | You are requested to go there. |
| Please do not smoke. | You are advised not to smoke. |
| Go home. | You are advised to go home. |
| Do it at once. | You are ordered to do it at once. |

**Note** The Passive Voice of some Intransitive Verbs by adding 'you are advised to'/'you are ordered to'/'you are requested to' may be treated as 'Indirect Passive'.

## 'LET' IN ACTIVE AND PASSIVE

(i) **'Let'** may be used in both Active and **Passive Voice**.
(ii) **'Let' takes the** Objective-type of **Pronouns** (me, us, him, her, them).
(iii) **'Let'** may be replaced by 'may **be** allowed' in the Passive Voice.

| Active | Passive |
|---|---|
| Let him buy a camera. | Let a camera be bought by him. |
| **Let us forget the quarrel.** | Let the quarrel be forgotten (by us). |
| **Let him go.** | He may be allowed to go. |

## INTERROGATIVE SENTENCES

An Interrogative Sentence in Active Voice **keeps its Interrogative form in its Passive Voice**. If the Interrogative Sentence begins with the Auxiliary Verb **Do**, the process of changing is convenient by changing it into Assertive first and then into Interrogative. But if the Interrogative sentence begins with any other **Auxiliary Verb** or a **Wh-word**, it can be directly changed into Passive.

## YES-NO QUESTIONS

### [ BY PLACING THE HELPING VERB FIRST ]

Active : Do you see the bird?
[Assertive : You see the bird.—The bird is seen by you.]
**Passive : Is the bird seen by you?**
Active : Did you see the man?
[Assertive : You saw the man.—The **man** was seen **by you**.]
**Passive** : Was the man seen by you?
**Active : Has he done it?**
Passive : Has it been done by him?
Active : Have you read the book?
Passive : Has the book been read by you?

## 'WH' QUESTIONS

### [ BY PLACING THE WH-WORD FIRST ]

Active : Who gave you the icecream?
Passive : By whom were you given the icecream?

Active : Whom did you call?
Passive : Who was called by you?
Active : What do you want?
Passive : What is wanted by you?
Active : Why did the teacher punish you?
Passive : Why were you punished by the teacher?
Active : Which book do you want?
Passive : Which book is wanted by you?
Active : How did you do it?
Passive : How was it done by you?

## NEGATIVE SENTENCES

### [ BY PLACING 'NOT' BEFORE THE PAST PARTICIPLE OF THE VERB ]

Active : I do not like puffed rice.
Passive : Puffed rice is not liked by me.
Active : The boy did not break the glass.
Passive : The glass was not broken by the boy.
Active : I have not given him the letter.
Passive : The letter has not been given him by me. [' him'—Retained Object]
[Or] He has not been given the letter by me. ['the letter'—Retained Object]

[ In Interrogative—Negative 'not' after a Pronoun and 'not' before a Noun. ]

Active : Has he not seen the picture?
Passive : Has not the picture been seen by him?
Active : Had you not called him?
Passive : Had he not been called by you?
Active : Reba will not call you.
Passive : You will not be called by Reba. [ 'not' before 'be called' in future tense ]

## SPECIAL FORMS OF PASSIVE VOICE

We see that Objects are of five kinds—1. Direct; 2. Indirect (including Retained); 3. Cognate; 4. Factitive; 5. Reflexive.

**[1] Passive Voice of Intransitive Verbs with Cognate Object :**

We have so far noticed that the Transitive Verbs are generally converted into the Passive Voice as they have objects. The Intransitive Verbs having no objects cannot be converted into the Passive Voice. However, when an Intransitive Verb is used Transitively having a Cognate Object, it can be changed into the Passive Voice.

| Active | Passive |
| --- | --- |
| He ran a race. | A race was run by him. |
| He dreamt a dream. | A dream was dreamt by him. |
| The patient slept a sound sleep. | A sound sleep was slept by the patient. |
| I have fought a good fight. | A good fight has been fought by me. |

**[2] Intransitive Verb used Causatively :**

Active : The trainer walked the horse after the race.
Passive : The horse was walked by the trainer after the race.
Active : They have stood the table against the wall.
Passive : The table has been stood against the wall by them.

**[3] Passive Voice of Transitive Verbs with two Objects [one as Retained Object] :**

Some Verbs take double Objects—the Direct Object and the Indirect Object. In such cases any of the Objects may become the Subject. But the **Indirect Object** or **the Personal Object is preferred for the Subject. Another Object is retained. Hence it is Retained Object :**

Active : Mr. Sharma teaches us English.

Passive : (1) We are taught English by Mr. Sharma.
(2) English is taught (to) us by Mr. Sharma.

Active : David gave me a book.

Passive : (1) I was given a book by David.
(2) A book was given (to) me by David.

Active : My friend sent me a gift.

Passive : (1) I was sent a gift by my friend.
(2) A gift was sent (to) me by my friend.

Active : They handed him a gun.

Passive : (1) He was handed a gun by them.
(2) A gun was handed (to) him by them.

Active : Gahar offered me a seat.

Passive : (1) I was offered a seat by Gahar.
(2) A seat was offered (to) me by Gahar.

[Direct Object as Retained Object without 'to'—vide Nesfield, and with 'to'—vide Wren & Martin]

**[4] Factitive Objects : The Object of a Transitive verb used as a Complement :**

Active : They made him king. ['him'—Factitive Object or Objective Complement]

Passive : He was made king by them.
King was made him by them. (wrong)

Active : They elected him President.

Passive : He was elected President by them.
President was elected him by them. (wrong)

**[5] Reflexive Object : [Object formed with 'self']**

Reflexive Object cannot be changed into Subject.

Active : He hurt himself.

Passive : He was hurt by himself. (Not, Himself was hurt by him.)

**Note** But this Passive with Reflexive Object is not good English. The Active form should be preferred. According to '**Modern English Usage**' by **Fowler** "It is a familiar process. But it sometimes leads to bad grammar, false idiom or clumsiness."

**[6] Intransitive Verbs used as a Group Verb :**

Active : We should not laugh at a lame man.

Passive : A lame man should not be laughed at by us.

Active : We must listen to our teachers.

Passive : Our teachers must be listened to (by us).

Active : We talked of them.

Passive : They were talked of by us.

**Note** (i) The Preposition of the Group Verb in the Active Voice must be retained in the Passive Voice. (ii) Remember that He is gone, He is come or, you are welcome, etc. are not in the Passive Voice. They are merely alternative forms of He has gone, or, He has come, etc. But there is a slight difference in meaning between the two forms. In He has gone, emphasis is laid on the time of the action; but in He is gone, emphasis is laid on the state of the agent, i.e., his absence, and not on the time of the action. However, 'Come here' or 'Go there' may be converted into the Passive Voice in the following way :

Active : Come here.

Passive : You are requested to come here. [ Indirect Passive ]

Active : Go there.

Passive : You are requested (advised) to go there. [ Indirect Passive ]

**[7] Passive of Infinitives (to + verb)**

Active : There are lots of things to do.

Passive : There are lots of things to be done.

Active : There is no time to lose.

Passive : There is no time to be lost.

Active : You have to admit this.

Passive : This has to be admitted by you.

Active : I am to make a telephone call.

Passive : A telephone call is to be made by me.

Active : You are to make this arrangement.

Passive : This arrangement is to be made by you.

**[8] Verbs followed by Objects + Plain Infinitives/Bare Infinitives :**

Active : I saw him go to the garden. ('to' before 'go' is omitted)

Passive : He was seen to go to the garden. ['to' is used—Plain Infinitive]

Active : Martha made us laugh. ['to' is omitted—Bare Infinitive]

Passive : We were made to laugh by Martha. ['to' is used—Plain Infinitive]

**[9] Verbal Noun with Preposition and Object :**

Active : We went to see the launching of the ship.

Passive : We went to see the ship being launched.

**[10] Passive of doing/seeing etc. :**

Active : I don't like people telling me what to do.

Passive : I don't like being told what to do.

Active : She doesn't like people seeing her diary.

Passive : She doesn't like her diary to be seen by people (others).

Active : Mr. Miller hates people keeping him waiting.

Passive : Mr. Miller hates being kept waiting. —Raymond Murphy

**[11] Object understood in the Passive Voice :**

When the action is important, not the doer, or the doer is unknown, the Object or the doer with 'by' is understood :

| Active | Passive |
|---|---|
| I have lost my book. | My book has been lost. |
| Someone has stolen my car. | My car has been stolen. |
| Someone invited me to the party. | I was invited to the party. |
| The mason is building the house. | The house is being built. |

**Thus we say :**

The shed is burnt to ashes. [Doer is unknown.]

English is spoken all over the world. [Not the doer, but the action is important.]

The house was built in 1960. [Not to specify the doer or the agent.]

## QUASI-PASSIVE VOICE

A Quasi-Passive voice is **Active in form but Passive in sense**. It may be changed in the Passive Form in the followng way :

**[i] Verbs with a Complement :**

Active : Honey tastes sweet.

Passive : Honey is sweet when it is tasted.

Active : The rose smells sweet.

Passive : The rose is sweet when it is smelt.

Active : The stone feels rough.

Passive : The stone is rough when it is felt.

Active : This composition reads well.

Passive : This composition sounds well when it is read.

Active : Your blame counts for nothing.

Passive : Your blame is worth nothing when it is counted.

**[ii] Verbs without a Complement :**

Active : The trumpets are sounding.

Passive : The trumpets are being sounded.

Active : The drums are beating.

Passive : The drums are being beaten.

Active : The cow is milking. (= yielding milk)

Passive : The cow is being milked. Nesfield

**Note** 'The trumpets are sounding' or 'The drums are beating' is quite good; but 'The cow is milking' or 'The cows are milking well' [A.L.D.—Hornby] is not so common in use. However the following Quasi-Passive Voice cannot be changed into Passive forms :

A conch blows. [It expresses the quality of a conch.]

The room looks nice. [It expresses the condition of the room.]

[We cannot say, The room is nice when it is looked.]

Rice sells cheap. [It expresses the price of rice.]

[We cannot say, Rice is cheap when it is sold.]

## PASSIVE VOICE OF COMPLEX SENTENCES

In changing the voice of **Complex Sentences** the Voice of both the Principal and the Subordinate Clauses should be changed if they have Transitive Verb and Object/ Complement. **The Introductory 'It'** may also be sometimes used in such cases.

Active : We know that Columbus discovered America.

Passive : That America was discovered by Columbus is known to us.

[Or] It is known to us that America was discovered by Columbus.

Active : We hope that we shall finish the work in time.

Passive : It is hoped that the work will be finished in time.

Active : I cannot depend on what he says. [ 'what'—complement to 'say' ]

Passive : What is said by him cannot be depended on by me.

Active : We must endure what we cannot cure. ['what'—object to 'cure']

Passive : What cannot be cured must be endured.

**Note** Sometimes one Clause with Transitive Verb is turned into Passive and another with Intransitive Verb remains in Active Voice :

We know that the earth is round. → It is known to us that the earth is round.

I knew him when he came here. → He was known to me when he came here.

## SIMPLE PASSIVE TO COMPLEX PASSIVE

It is said that ......etc.

Simple Passive : She is said to be a hard-working lady.

Complex Passive : It is said that she is a hard-working lady.

Simple Passive : The boy is believed to be wearing a white shirt.

Complex Passive : It is believed that the boy is wearing a white shirt.

Simple Passive : The work is hoped to be finished in time.

Complex Passive : It is hoped that the work will be finished in time.

Simple Passive : The strike is expected to end soon.

Complex Passive : It is expected that the strike will end soon.

Simple Passive : He is alleged to have kicked a policeman.

Complex Passive : It is alleged that he kicked a policeman.

**Raymond Murphy**

**Note** **Double Passives in a Simple Sentence or in one Clause should be avoided,** as they are liable to give a wrong meaning :

Active : They proposed to hold a meeting.

Incorrect Passive : A meeting was proposed to be held by them.

Correct Passive : It was proposed by them to hold a meeting.

[Or] It was proposed by them that a meeting should be held.

Similarly :

The judge ordered the convict to be hanged. (Correct)

The convict was ordered to be hanged by the judge. (Incorrect)

## PASSIVE VOICE WITH DIFFERENT PREPOSITIONS

Active : His conduct shocked me.
Passive : I was shocked at his conduct. (not, by his conduct)
Active : Light filled the room.
Passive : The room was filled with light. (not, by light)
Active : Her manners pleased us very much.
Passive : We were very much pleased with her manners. (not, by her manners)
Active : The novels of Tolstoy interest me.
Passive : I am interested in the novels of Tolstoy. (not, by the novels of Tolstoy)

## SOME PECULIARITIES IN VOICE

Active : One should keep one's promise.
Passive : A promise should be kept. (by one—omitted)
Active : Someone has stolen my purse.
Passive : My purse has been stolen. (by someone—omitted)

Active : Circumstances obliged me to go.
Passive : I was obliged to go. (by circumstances—omitted)
Active : We can gain nothing without labour.
Passive : Nothing can be gained without labour. (by us—omitted)
Active : Why did they refuse him admittance?
Passive : Why was he refused admittance? (by them—omitted)
Active : We should not encourage indiscipline.
Passive : Indiscipline should not be encouraged. (by us—omitted)
Active : Mother looked after the boy. (look after—group verb)
Passive : The boy was looked after by mother. (prep. 'after' of the gr. verb retained)
Active : He has worked out the answer correctly. (work out—group verb)
Passive : The answer has been correctly worked out by him.
Active : Someone built this building in 1990.
Passive : This building was built in 1990. (by someone—omitted)
Active : Mr. Kapoor presided over the meeting.
Passive : The meeting was presided over by Mr. Kapoor.
Active : People consider me honest.
Passive : I am considered honest. (by people—omitted)
Active : We ought to help the poor.
Passive : The poor ought to be helped by us.

Active : People believe that you know.
Passive : It is supposed that you know.
Active : We will not admit children under ten.
Passive : Children under ten will not be admitted by us.
Active : It is time to do your duty.
Passive : It is time for your duty to be done.
Active : I know the fact. [Passive : The fact is known to me.—vide Wren & Martin]
Pseudo Passive : The fact is known to me. [vide—'A comprehensive Grammar of the English Language' by Quirk, Greenbaum, Leech & Svartvik]

## APPLIED SECTION

Students must remember that the ability to change the Active Voice into the Passive, and vice versa, is not sufficient. **They must know when to use the Active Voice and when to use the Passive** :

**Some sentences are always Active or always Passive :**

(a) I have (take) breakfast late on Sundays. [ **Always Active Voice** ]

(b) I was born on 18 April 1990. [ **Always Passive Voice** ]

**The Active Voice is used when the agent (i.e. the doer of the action) is to be made prominent; the Passive is used when the action is to be made prominent** . The Passive is, therefore, generally preferred when the Active form would involve the use of an indefinite noun or pronoun (someone, somebody, people, we, they etc.).

Hence, "My pen has been stolen" is preferable to "Someone has stolen my pen."

Modern English Grammar shows us categorically that the English Passives are generally formed from :

[1] **'Be' + Past Participle :**

A picture was bought from the market. Some acid is taken in a glass-jar.

[2] **Modal + 'Be' + Past Participle :**

It can be done in ten minutes. This may please be done. The luggage may be kept aside. The answers must be written in ink.

[3] **Get + Past Participle :**

Some furniture got damaged. (Quasi-Passive)

The plan got approved by the Corporation. (Full Passive)

### WHEN TO USE THE PASSIVE?

We use Passive Voice—

**(i) for describing a process :**

Describe how orange syrup is prepared :

First oranges are bought from the market. Then the rotten ones, if any, are rejected. After that the wholesome oranges are washed and peeled. Then the oranges are crushed in a specially designed bowl. Now the seeds are strained away. After that, sugar is added. Finally, the solution of sugar and orange juice is stirred and the orange syrup is ready.

**(ii) for narrating an incident/events :**

(a) An old man was knocked down by the bus and was taken to the hospital where it was declared that the poor fellow was dead.

(b) The Annual Sports meet of Delhi Public School was held on Sunday on the playground of the school under a sunny sky.

**(iii) for defining :**

(a) Short stories usually with animal characters and a moral are called fables.

(b) If the satellite is made to revolve at exactly the same speed as that of the earth, then the satellite will be called a 'geostationary' satellite.

**(iv)** **for impersonal scientific writing :**

Three flasks and a few brightly polished nails are taken. In the first flask three nails are dropped and water is poured. The flask is left uncorked.

**(v)** **for describing social and historical incidents :**

(a) A great battle was fought at Plassey (Palasi).

(b) Mr. Rajib Gandhi was murdered by some terrorists.

**(vi)** **for writing a notice :**

A meeting of the M.C. will be held in the school premises at 2 p.m. on 25 February. ...... All the members are requested to attend the meeting.

**(vii)** **for making announcement :**

The flight to Singapore will be delayed by three hours for foul weather.

**(viii)** **for classifying :**

Food can be classified into four groups—carbohydrates, vitamins, fats and proteins.

**(ix)** **for making requests and invitation :**

(a) You are cordially invited to visit the exhibition.

(b) You are requested to keep off the grass.

**(x)** **for giving warning, advice, suggestion etc. :**

(a) Smoking should be avoided.

(b) Answer-scripts may be cancelled for taking unfair means.

[**Note : Sometimes, an Active Voice is changed into the Passive according to sense.**]

Active : I have been able to spend Rs. 10/- only.

= (Active) I have spent Rs. 10/- only (according to sense).

Passive : Rs. 10/- only has been spent by me.

[Rs. 10/- is used here in collective sense. Hence the verb form is singular.]

## EXERCISE

**1. Use the Verb 'eat' in Active and Passive Voices in different Tenses in the following table. One has been done for you :**

| Tenses | Voice | Indefinite | Continuous | Perfect |
|---|---|---|---|---|
| Present | Active | I eat rice. | ........... | ........... |
| | Passive | Rice is eaten by me. | ........... | ........... |
| Past | Active | ......................... | ........... | ........... |
| | Passive | ......................... | ........... | ........... |
| Future | Active | ......................... | ........... | ........... |
| | Passive | ......................... | ........... | ........... |

**2. Rewrite the following sentences using the Passive Voice :**

A scientist invented penicillin in 1928. Someone built this school in 1990. I wrote a letter to you. Sumita will sing a song. Rakesh is drawing a picture. The girl was plucking a flower. He has read the book. Spring has forgotten the garden. He will give me a rupee. The Headmaster will punish the boy. They fought a good fight. The thief had stolen his bag. Mother looked after the children well. You should obey your parents. The Headmaster teaches us English. Please do this work. One must keep one's promises. We must endure what we cannot cure. Who has done this? I do not know why he has done this. Did you point out any defect? Prepare for the worst. Has anyone answered your question? May God bless you. Can I ever forget you? How many guests did you invite? It is now time to call over the names. I know that he did it. Do not laugh at the lame man. Do not look down upon the poor. Circumstances compelled me to go there. No one should take reference books out of the library. Somebody found your keys on the top of the almirah. They have increased the rate of taxation to thirty percent. They elected him President.

**3. Rewrite the following sentences using the Active Voice :**

This may please be done. He was elected President. The meeting was presided over by Mr. Sen. Let this work be done. You are requested to put off your shoes. Is the moon seen by you? The house has been repaired. English is spoken by them. Duties must be done. All the children should be loved. What is seen by him? My pen has been lost. A dream was dreamt by him. The thief has been caught by the police. The charge will be taken over tomorrow. It is known to us that the earth is round.

**4. Change the Voice of the following sentences :**

Grain stalks are cut and tied in bundles. Stalks are threshed to separate grain from stalk. Grain is stored in a grannery. The air is constantly being polluted by smoke. The ground is polluted by rotten rubbish. Water is also polluted by chemicals and other wastes from factories.

**5. Fill in the gaps, using the Passive Form of the Verbs given in the brackets for describing how tea is prepared for marketing :**

Leaves of tea plant ......... (pluck) and then ......... (take) to the factory. There they ......... (weigh) and ........... (prepare). First the leaves ......... (spread) on flat trays. These trays then ......... (take) to a heated room and ......... (keep) there for about twenty hours. The heat softens the leaves. Next the leaves ......... (pass) through a machine which curls and crushes the leaves. Then they ......... (place) in drawers and ......... (keep) there in layers of one or two inches thick. The drawers thereafter ......... (cover) with damp curtains. Here the leaves change their colour and look like bright copper. They also get their fine flavour here. Thus tea ......... (prepare) for marketing.

**6. Use Passive Voice in describing the following process. You should have an introductory sentence like this :**

The preparation of edible oil from mustard seeds goes through a number of steps :

Mustard Seeds collected and dried → dried seeds put into the hawler → a little water added for extracting oil ↓

oil cakes separated → oil collected in containers and sealed → now oil ready for use

**7. The following flow-chart describes how drinking water from Palta Water Works is supplied to Kolkata. Study the flow chart and describe the process. Have an introductory as well as a concluding sentence :**

Extraction of raw Ganga water → Purification by mixing alum → Reservation in a big tank → Filtration in filter beds → Super-purification in filter houses—chlorine charged → Testing → Taken into pressure house → Delivery/ Supply

**8. Study the hints and describe in Passive Voice how milk is processed in a dairy :**

Sending milk to factory ........... weighing and testing ........... separating cream and milk ...........heating at 72°C ........... cooling ........... packing ........... bottling ........... delivery.

# 25 PHRASES

**[ Special stress has been given on the use of NP (Sub) + Verb + NP + Infinitive; NP (Sub) + Verb + NP + Adj./Adv.; Verb + NP with 'how to' construction. ]**

Read the following sentences :

[i] This is a gold chain.

[ii] This is a golden chain.

[iii] This is a chain made of gold.

[iv] This is a chain which is made of gold.

All these sentences make the same meaning, but there is a difference of formation of the underlined words :

[i] 'gold chain' is a group of words (Noun + Noun) without any finite verb. It acts as a unit; so it is a phrase. Here it acts as a Noun; so it is a Noun Phrase (NP).

[ii] 'golden chain' is also a group of words (Adjective 'golden' takes a Noun 'chain') without any finite verb. But it is a natural construction of Adjective and Noun, not a unit or group. So it is not a Phrase.

[iii] 'made of gold' is a group of words without a finite verb and it acts as a unit. Moreover, it qualifies the preceding word 'chain'. Hence 'chain made of gold' is an Adjective Phrase.

[iv] 'which is made of gold' is also a group of words but it has a finite verb 'is'. Hence it is a Clause, not a Phrase.

So we can say :

**A Phrase is a group of words which acts as a unit and which has no finite verb.**
**A Clause is a group of words that has a finite verb.**

**Phrases are of eight kinds :**

PHRASES

- Noun Phrase
- Adjective Phrase
- Adverbial Phrase
- Prepositional Phrase
- Participial Phrase
- Phrase in Apposition
- Absolute Phrase
- Parenthetical Phrase

## NOUN PHRASES [ NP ]

Read the following sentences :

(i) The man wants something. [(Sub) + (Verb) + Noun]

(ii) The man wants something to eat. [(Sub + Verb) + NP with Infinitive]

(iii) Fatima took her supper. [(Sub + Verb) + Noun]

(iv) Fatima took her supper early. [(Sub + Verb) + NP + Adverb]

(v) Praising is a good virtue. [Noun as Sub + Verb]

(vi) Praising all is equal to praising none. [NP + Verb + Adjective + NP]

(vii) Mr. Ali showed his student a computer. [(Sub + Verb) + Noun]

(viii) Mr. Ali showed his student how to assemble a computer. [with 'how to']

In each of the above pairs of sentences, we first have a single Noun and then a group of words extending the same.

In the first sentence 'something' is a **Noun** and it is the object of the verb 'wants'.

In the second sentence 'something to eat' is also the object of the verb 'wants'. But it is a group of words and it acts as a Noun. It is, therefore, a **Noun Phrase**.

In the fourth sentence 'her supper early' is also the object of the verb 'took'. But it is a group of words and acts as a Noun. So, it is a **Noun Phrase**.

In the fifth sentence 'praising' is a **noun** and it is the subject of the verb 'is'.

In the sixth sentence 'praising all' is also the subject of the verb 'is'. But it is a group of words and it acts as a Noun. Hence it is a **Noun Phrase**.

In the eighth sentence 'how to assemble a computer' is also a **Noun Phrase**.

**A Noun Phrase is a group of words that acts as a Noun. It may be a Subject or Object/Complement of a Verb.** **P. C. Das**

Read the following Nouns and Noun Phrases :

| Nouns | Noun Phrases |
|---|---|
| Cricket is a good game. | Playing cricket is the style of the day. |
| Reading is a good habit. | Have you enjoyed reading this novel? |
| Your bed is ready. | Early to bed is a healthy habit. |
| Any prize is a prestigious thing. | To win a prize is not an easy task. |

**Note** **A Noun Phrase includes** the process of using **Infinitive**, **Verbal Noun** and **Gerund as subject or object /complement**.

## ADJECTIVE PHRASES

Read the following sentences :

(i) A boy met me yesterday.

(ii) A boy with blue eyes met me yesterday.

(iii) He tells a tale.

(iv) He tells a tale with the ring of truth in it.

In the first and third sentences, we have a Single Noun (a person or a thing), and in the second and fourth sentences we have a group of words describing that person or thing. These group of words act as an Adjective and are, therefore, **Adjective Phrases**.

So we can say :

**An Adjective Phrase is a group of words that acts as an Adjective for qualifying a noun or pronoun. It may be in the Subject part or in the Predicate part.**

**P. C. Das**

Read the following Adjectives and the Adjective Phrases that are same in meaning :

| Adjectives | Adjective Phrases |
|---|---|
| A blank page. | A page with no writing on it. |
| A heavy load. | A load of great weight. |
| A black coat. | A coat of black colour. |
| A golden crown. | A crown made of gold. |
| A white elephant. | An elephant of white colour. |
| A jungle track. | A track through the jungle. |
| The Indian flag. | The flag of India. |

Note **An Adjective Phrase includes some Prepositions and Participles that qualify a Noun.**

## ADVERBIAL PHRASES

Read the following sentences :

[i] The horse runs fast/quickly.

[ii] The horse runs with great speed.

[iii] He behaved rudely.

[iv] He behaved in a rude manner.

In the first and third sentences, we have a single Adverb and in the second and fourth sentences we have a group of words modifying in the same way. These groups of words in second and fourth sentences act as an Adverb and are, therefore, **Adverbial Phrases**.

So we can say :

**An Adverbial Phrase is a group of words that acts as an Adverb. It may generally modify a verb, an adjective or another adverb denoting manner, place or time.**

**P. C. Das**

Read the following Adverbs and the Adverbial Phrases that are same in meaning :

| | Adverbs | Adverbial Phrases |
|---|---|---|
| MANNER | bravely | in a brave manner/with bravery. |
| | carefully | with care. |
| | carelessly | without any care. |
| | fast/quickly | with great speed. |
| | beautifully | in a beautiful style. |
| PLACE | here | at this place/on this spot. |
| | there | at that place/on that spot. |
| | away | to another place. |
| | abroad | to (in) a foreign country. |
| | everywhere | in all places. |

| | Adverbs | Adeverbial Phrases |
|---|---|---|
| TIME | now<br>then<br>soon<br>formerly<br>recently | at this very moment.<br>at that time/moment.<br>before very long/at an early date.<br>in former times/once upon a time.<br>at present/at a recent date. |

## POSITION OF ADVERBIAL PHRASES

When there are two or more Adverbs or Adverbial Phrases after a Verb, the normal order is Adverb of **Manner**, **Place** and **Time—MPT**.

Soma sang sweetly in the town hall last evening.
(Manner) (Place) (Time)

**Note** An Adverbial Phrase includes some Adverbs with Prepositions called Adverbials that modify a verb, an adjective or another adverb.

## PREPOSITIONAL PHRASES

Read the following sentences :

(i) (a) He is ill. (b) He still works.
(ii) In spite of his illness, he works.
(iii) (a) He made a promise. (b) He kept it also.
(iv) Besides making a promise, he kept it.

In sentence (ii) 'In spite of' and in sentence (iv) 'Besides making' are groups of words beginning with a Preposition and act as a unit other than a Noun Phrase, an Adjective Phrase or Adverb Phrase. Such Phrases are called **Prepositional Phrases**.

**Note** Some Adjective Phrases and Adverbial Phrases also begin with a Preposition. But such an Adjective Phrase qualifies a Noun and such an Adverb Phrase modifies a Verb, Adjective or another Adverb, while a purely Prepositional Phrase keeps its main force on Preposition construction. However, in a broader sense, Prepositional Phrases include Adjective Phrase beginning with a preposition, Adverb Phrase beginning with a preposition and a purely Prepositional Phrase with its main force on preposition.

## PARTICIPIAL PHRASES

Read the following sentences :

(i) Hearing a noise, the boy woke up.
(ii) Driven by hunger, he stole a piece of bread.
(iii) Having rested a while, we continued our journey.

In sentence (i) 'Hearing a noise', in sentence (ii) 'Driven by hunger' and in sentence (iii) 'Having rested a while' are **Participial Phrases**. These Participial Phrases are formed by a Present Participle or a Past Participle or a Perfect Participle.

## PHRASES IN APPOSITION

Read the following sentences :

(i) (a) Shrila is my sister. (b) She is seriously ill.
(ii) Shrila, my sister, is seriously ill.

(iii) (a) Tom is my faithful dog. (b) I like him.

(iv) I like Tom, my faithful dog.

In sentence (ii) 'Shrila' and 'my sister' are the same person. In sentence (iv) 'Tom' and 'my faithful dog' are the same animal. The two groups of words 'my sister' and 'my faithful dog' are placed in apposition to the Noun 'Shrila' and 'Tom'. They are, therefore, **Phrases in Apposition**.

## ABSOLUTE PHRASES

Read the following sentences :

(i) (a) It was a holiday. (b) We went out for a picnic.

(ii) It being a holiday, we went out for a picnic.

(iii) (a) The war broke out. (b) The prices rose high.

(iv) The war having broken out, the prices rose high.

In sentence (ii) 'It being a holiday' and in sentence (iv) 'The war having broken out' are Nominative Absolute denoting the interdependence of these groups of words with the main parts of the sentences. Such groups of words of interdependence with separate subject and without finite verb are called **Absolute Phrases**.

## PARENTHETICAL PHRASES

Read the following sentences :

(i) He is, after all, an honest man.

(ii) I, to tell the truth, don't like this.

In each of the above examples, there are phrases thrown into the body of sentences without any structural relation between the phrase and the other part of the sentence. Such phrases are called **Parenthetical Phrases**.

## EXERCISE

**1. Pick out the Noun Phrases in the following sentences :**

(i) I hope to win the first prize.

(ii) To win a prize is my ambition.

(iii) He likes getting people into trouble.

(iv) He dislikes having to punish his servants.

(v) Shila invited her friends to join her birthday party.

(vi) She was happy to greet all her friends.

(vii) He refuses to answer the question.

(viii) She denied stealing the money.

(ix) To write such rubbish is disgraceful.

(x) Thinking good thoughts precedes good actions.

(xi) Travelling in a crowdy train can show you the present condition of the railway system.

(xii) Standing about in cold wind causes cough and cold.

**2. Fill in the blanks with suitable Noun Phrases :**

(i) I do not expect ..............................
(ii) I don't intend ..............................
(iii) My father hates ..............................
(iv) My brother loves ..............................
(v) ........................ surprised my mother.
(vi) ...................... gives me no pleasure.
(vii) .................................. is not so easy.
(viii) His sister promised ..............................
(ix) .................................. is disgraceful.
(x) The poor debtor ..............................

**3. Pick out the Adjective Phrases in the following sentences :**

(i) The Selfish Giant lived in a house built of stone.
(ii) Acharya P. C. Roy was a man with a kindly nature.
(iii) He is a person of very considerable renown.
(iv) Swami Vivekananda wore a turban made of saffron silk.
(v) He was a man of great versatility.
(vi) Nobody likes a man with a bad temper.
(vii) Arthur is a man with plenty of impudence.
(viii) He is a man without a friend.
(ix) He carried a sword stained with blood.
(x) They came to a path covered with mud.

**4. Replace the following italicized Adjective Phrases by Adjectives :**

(i) Mr. Birla is a man *of great wealth*.
(ii) None should throw stones, who lives in a *house built of glass*.
(iii) I like to see a *face with a smile on it*.

(iv) A wild beast *in* a *cage* is a sorry sight.
(v) He is a *man without a friend*.
(vi) I met a little *girl from a cottage*.
(vii) She was a *girl of great promise*.
(viii) The boys bore a banner *of peculiarity*.
(ix) The police arrested a man *of the tribes*.
(x) In a low voice he told the tale *of adventures*.

**5. Replace the following italicized Adjectives by Adjective Phrases :**

(i) A *grassy* meadow stretched before us.
(ii) I have passed a *sleepless* night.
(iii) He is a *professional* cricketer.
(iv) Mr. Varma is a *wealthy* man.
(v) Do you know which is the *longest* day in a year?
(vi) The poor beggar dwelt in a *wooden* hut.

(vii) How did he get such a *valuable* thing?

(viii) Lalu prefers an *earthen* pot for taking tea.

(ix) Netaji Subhas Chandra Bose is a *fearless* person.

(x) I admit that he is a *sensible* man.

**6. Pick out the Adverbial Phrases in the following sentences :**

(i) I stood under a great banyan tree.

(ii) He lived in the middle of a forest.

(iii) He fought to the last in the face of all obstacles.

(iv) He has painted it in proper colours.

(v) The gun went off with a loud sound.

(vi) The shepherd shouted at the top of his voice.

(vii) He tried with all his might to escape from the trap.

(viii) It must be done at any cost.

(ix) Mahatma Gandhi had his finger on the pulse of the nation.

(x) Honesty is written on her face.

**7. Replace the following italicized Adverbial Phrases by Adverbs :**

(i) Horses run *with great speed*.

(ii) You can buy it *in all places*.

(iii) Go *to that spot* and pay your fees.

(iv) Stop writing *from this very moment*.

(v) *At that moment* the queen arrived.

(vi) These posts are *without reserve*.

(vii) He has proved his fitness *to our satisfaction*.

(viii) I hope that you will come *at a very early date*.

(ix) This picture has not been painted *in the proper way*.

(x) He earms his living *by honest means*.

(xi) He shouted *at the top of his voice*.

(xii) It has been done *in an unwise manner*.

**8. Replace the following italicized Adverbs by Adverbial Phrases :**

(i) Do your homework *carefully*.

(ii) The bodies in the ill-fated bus were mangled *terribly*.

(iii) In the afternoon the wind blew *violently*.

(iv) *Formerly* he worked in a private company.

(v) The news has come to us *recently*.

(vi) He expects to get promotion *soon*.

(vii) The children are playing *cheerfully*.

(viii) The soldiers fought for the country *bravely*.

(ix) She binds her hair *beautifully*.

(x) He is preparing his best to go *abroad*.

(xi) He seems to have acted *properly*.

**9. Pick out the Phrases to say whether they are Noun Phrases, Adjective Phrases or Adverbial Phrases :**

(i) The accident occurred on this spot.
(ii) He left the place at that moment.
(iii) The cottage on the island was washed away.
(iv) I expect your answer at an early date.
(v) Cease-work is withdrawn from this very moment.
(vi) Is this the train to Bangalore?
(vii) The Headmaster announced the holiday in a loud voice.
(viii) He speaks like a born orator.
(ix) I do not expect such treatment at your hands.
(x) She gained our affection in spite of her many faults.

**10. Pick out the Participial Phrases and say whether they are formed by a Present Participle or a Past Participle or a Perfect Participle :**

(i) Hearing the noise, he rushed towards the spot.
(ii) Seeing him fall from the tree, I ran to him.
(iii) Loudly knocking at the gate, he asked admission.
(iv) Deceived by his friends, he lost all hope.
(v) Blinded by a dust-storm, they lost their way.
(vi) Sitting on the gate, he was rebuked by the teacher.
(vii) Entering the room, I found the dazzling light.
(viii) Walking in the field, I saw a dead cow.
(ix) Frankly speaking, he is not fit for the job.
(x) Considering his abilities, he should have done better.
(xi) Having rested a while, we started our work again.

**11. Pick out the Phrases to say whether they are Phrases in Apposition, an Absolute Phrase or a Parenthetical Phrase :**

(i) Maradona, a good player, was suspended.
(ii) The dinner being over, the party left the place.
(iii) Iqbal, a Punjabi poet, wrote many good poems.
(iv) Benaras (Varanasi), the city of temples, stands on the Ganga.
(v) Frankly speaking, I cannot admit your conduct.
(vi) It being a very hot day, we could not start our journey.
(vii) You are, to speak the truth, a scoundrel.
(viii) Akbar, the great emperor, was secular among the Muslim emperors.

**12. Join the following pairs of sentences by using a Noun Phrase :**

[A Noun Phrase includes the process of using Infinitive, Verbal Noun and Gerund as subject or object/complement.]

(i) The boy wants to eat. He wants something.
(ii) He is very weak. He cannot walk.
(iii) He has two sons. He has to teach them.

(iv) He has a cycle. He wishes to sell it.
(v) She works hard. She wants to pass the examination.
(vi) Early to bed is a good habit. It should be followed.
(vii) Swimming is a good exercise. Do you enjoy it?
(viii) We play cricket. We enjoy it.

**13. Join the following pairs of sentences by using an Adjective Phrase :**

[An Adjective Phrase includes some Prepositional phrases and Participles that qualify a Noun.]

(i) He was tired. He rested for a while.
(ii) He saw me come. He ran away.
(iii) The workers belong to a tribe. They are dwelling in the hills.
(iv) This is an axe. It is made of iron.
(v) There is a bird in the hand. It is worth two in the bush.
(vi) He told a tale. It was about his cruel deeds.
(vii) He tells a tale. There is a ring of truth in it.
(viii) Here is a boy. He is a boy of great promise.
(ix) He wore a turban. It is made of silk.
(x) He has done a deed. It is a deed of shame.

**14. Join the following pairs of sentences by using an Adverbial Phrase :**

[An Adverb Phrase includes some Adverbs and Prepositions called Adverbials that modify a Verb, an Adjective or another Adverb.]

(i) The train was late. That was usual.
(ii) She spoke the truth. She did not fear at all.
(iii) He fought alone. He was not helped.
(iv) He returned home. It was evening.
(v) The dead bodies were mangled. It was in a terrible manner.
(vi) Let us cease work. It should be from the very moment.
(vii) They succeeded. Their success came in the long run.
(viii) The wind blew. It blew with great violence.
(ix) He has proved his case. It is to my satisfaction.
(x) He may come. It may be at an early date.

**15. Join the following pairs of sentences by using a Prepositional Phrase :**

[A Prepositional Phrase begins with a Preposition and puts the main force on Preposition construction.]

(i) He won the prize. He could do it by dint of hard work.
(ii) He got the award. It was possible by means of hard labour.
(iii) He succeeded at last. It was possible by virtue of continuous labour.
(iv) He sacrificed his life. He did it for the sake of his country.
(v) Call the Fire Brigade. You may do it in case of fire.
(vi) He told me this. He told it in course of conversation.

(vii) He is waiting. He is standing in front of the school.

(viii) They went to the jungle. They went there in search of a deer.

(ix) He was poor. Still he donated a considerable amount in the fund for the flood-stricken people.

(x) The Headmaster welcomed the visitors. He did it on behalf of the school.

**16. Join the following pairs of sentences by using a Phrase in Apposition :**

(i) Alexander was a powerful king. He invaded India.

(ii) Ashoka was a great king. He loved his people dearly.

(iii) Akbar was the greatest Mughal emperor. He was secular among the Muslim rulers.

(iv) Kalidas wrote 'Shakuntala'. It is a play in Sanskrit.

(v) Bishnupur is a town of temples. It is situated in West Bengal.

**17. Join the following pairs of sentences by using an Absolute Phrase :**

(i) The sun rose. The fog dispersed.

(ii) The fog dispersed. The soldiers began to march.

(iii) The rain fell. The crops revived.

(iv) The sun set. We returned to our house.

(v) The war broke out. The prices rose high.

(vi) The bell rang. The students entered their class.

(vii) The treaty failed. The war broke out.

(viii) It was very hot. We could not get out of home.

(ix) It was a holiday. We went out for a picnic.

(x) The load-shedding occurs frequently. Business is suffering.

# 26 SENTENCES AND ITS CLAUSES/JOINING/SPLITTING

[ **Special stress on the use of Clauses : the place (Where)/the time (When); When/While/After + Future Clause; Though/Although + Clause; In order to (purpose); 1st conditional (if + Present Tense) + (will + Verb); 2nd conditional (if + Past Tense) + (would/could/might + Verb) etc.** ]

**Sentences according to structures are of three kinds :**

**[1] SIMPLE SENTENCE, [2] COMPLEX SENTENCE, [3] COMPOUND SENTENCE**

**[1] Simple Sentence :** A Simple Sentence is one that contains **only one subject and one finite verb**, expressed or understood. **J. C. Nesfield**

Example : He found his meal ready. He goes to school everyday.

***Note :** A simple sentence may also have one or more non-finite verb/verbs. e.g. He goes to school to read and write. Going home, he found his meal ready.

**Examples :**

| | |
|---|---|
| (a) Come. (Sub. omitted) | (d) The boy reads a book. |
| (b) Come here. (") | (e) The girl plucks a flower. |
| (c) Come to the blackboard. (") | (f) I shall not go to school. |

**[2] Complex Sentence :** A Complex Sentence is one that contains **one principal clause and one or more subordinate clause or clauses**. **Nesfield**

***Note.** A Complex Sentence may also have Subordinate Clauses joined with Conjunctions—*and, or, but, as well as*, etc.; e.g.—I left the room when my sister came and began to eat a ripe banana. I know that he is poor but honest.

**Examples :**

(a) I know — that he is honest.
Principal clause — Subordinate clause

(b) This is the boy — who did it.
Principal clause — Subordinate clause

(c) We waited — until he came.
Principal clause — Subordinate clause

**[3] Compound Sentence :** A Compound Sentence is one that contains **two or more independent clauses or coordinating clauses** joined together by coordinating conjunctions like *and, or, but, as well as, either...or, neither ... nor*, etc. **Nesfield**

**Examples :**

| | | |
|---|---|---|
| Salil is a good boy | and | he loves his brother. |
| Coord. clause | | Coord. clause |
| You may read the book | or | leave the class. |
| Coord. clause | | Coord. clause |
| He was late | but | he was not sorry. |
| Coord. clause | | Coord. clause |

## DIFFERENCE OF CLAUSE AND PHRASE

**A Phrase** is a group of words **which does not contain a finite verb.**
**A Clause** is a group of words **that contains a finite verb.** **Nesfield**

He gave me a gold chain. He gave me a chain which was made of gold.
Phrase — gold chain; Clause — which was made of gold

**Note** **Modern English Grammar**, however, has widened this view. It is now possible to talk of **Clauses with finite and non-finite Verbs** and **Verbless Clauses**. **However, a Clause is a shorter sentence within a bigger sentence :**

(a) I cannot tell *when he will come*. (Clause with a finite verb)

(b) *Wounded in the war*, he returned home. (Clause with a non-finite—Wounded in the war = When he was wounded in the war)

(c) *While walking in the field*, I saw a cow. (Clause with a non-finite—While walking = While I was walking)

(d) *When in England*, he saw a strange sight. (Verbless Clause—When in England = When he was in England)

So we should say :

**A Clause** is a group of words that **contains a finite verb** expressed or understood. **But a Phrase does not contain a finite verb** in any way. **P. C. Das**

## CLAUSES

**Clauses are of three kinds—[1] Principal Clause, [2] Subordinate Clause, [3] Coordinate Clause.**

The Subordinate Clauses are subdivided into three heads— (i) Noun or Nominal clause. (ii) Adjective or Relative Clause. (iii) Adverbial Clause.

A. **The Noun Clause** does the work of a Noun.

B. **The Adjective Clause** does the work of an Adjective.

C. **The Adverbial Clause** does the work of an Adverb.

### CLAUSES

| Principal Clause | Subordinate Clause | Coordinate Clause |
|---|---|---|
| I know that the boy is honest. | I know the boy who is honest. | The boy is honest and I know it. |

## SUBORDINATE CLAUSES

| Noun or Nominal Clause | Adjective or Relative Clause | Adverbial Clause |
|---|---|---|
| I know who he is. | I know the man who did it. | You may go where you like. |

## NOUN CLAUSE (NOMINAL CLAUSE)

A Noun Clause is used in a sentence in the same way as a noun may be used :
(i) **subject**, (ii) **object**, (iii) **object to a preposition**, (iv) **complement**, (v) **appositive**.

| Functions of a Noun Clause | Examples |
|---|---|
| **Subject** | What he said is true.<br>How he went there is known to all.<br>That he is honest is known to me.<br>When he will come is uncertain.<br>Whether he will succeed is uncertain. |
| **Object** | I know that he is honest. |
| **Object to a Preposition** | It depends on how he behaves.<br>I know nothing of what he will do. |
| **Complement** | This is what we expected. |
| **Appositive** to 'It' or a Noun | Our hope that he will come back proved false.<br>It is true that he has come. |

| Linking Words | Examples |
|---|---|
| that | He said that he would go. |
| who | I know who he is. |
| whose | Do you know whose book it is? |
| whom | I can guess whom you want to see. |
| what | No one knows what caused the accident. |
| which | Can you tell which one is Ram's? |
| where | I do not know where he was born. |
| when | I know when he will come. |
| how | I can tell how he stole your watch. |
| why | Could you explain why he did this? |
| whatever | I earn whatever I can. |
| if/whether | She asked me if/whether I would stay or not. |

**Note** 'that' is optional after : say, tell, think, believe; 'that' is obligatory after : declare, insist, mention, report, require, propose, suggest, state.

## SOME MORE EXAMPLES

[ **Note the Linkers** ]

(i) **Subject of a Verb :**
What he said is true. [**By joining :** He said this. It is true.]
Why she is sad is anybody's guess.

That you should say so surprises me.

That he is a good boy is known to us.

Who telephoned me is still a mystery.

When he will return is uncertain.

Why he left the place is a mystery.

Whatever he earns is spent lavishly.

Which he prefers is not known to me.

How he could assist his friend was his chief concern.

(ii) **Object of a Verb :**

We know that the earth is a planet.

[**By joining :** The earth is a planet. We know it.]

He hoped that it was true.

She denied that she had written the letter.

I cannot tell what has become of him.

I do not know when I shall return.

I asked the boy how old he was.

Tell me frankly why you did this.

Can you tell me what he requires?

Tell me where you live.

No one knows who he is.

I ask you what you want.

I know what he means.

(iii) **Object to a Preposition :**

There is no meaning in what you say.

[**By joining :** You say something. There is no meaning in it.]

I know nothing of what he will do.

Pay careful attention to what I say.

They had no complaint except that the day was too hot.

(iv) **Complement to a Verb :**

This is what we expected.

[**By joining :** This is the thing. We expected it.]

Life is what we make it.

My belief is that he will not come.

Our satisfaction is that we tried to the last.

My wish is that I may please you.

His request will be that he may be allowed to resign.

He says what he intends to be.

(v) **Object to a missing Preposition :**

The child was afraid that he would fall down. (afraid of)

[**By joining :** The child might fall down. He was afraid of it.]

They felt sorry that they lost the match. (sorry for)

The patient was sure that he would recover. (sure of)

She did not seem hopeful that he would arrive. (hopeful of)

**(vi) Apposition to a Noun or Pronoun :**

Your statement that you found the money in the street is correct.

[By joining : You found the money in the street. It is your statement. It is correct.]

There is a rumour that he is dead.

The fact that he is no more is painful to us.

It is true that the boy is honest.

It is feared that he will not come back.

It was unfortunate that you were absent.

His belief that someday he would succeed cheered me.

**Note** In a Noun Clause the Linking Word is usually that (Though some other linking words such as who, whose, what, which, how etc. are occasionally used.)

## SOME MORE JOINING WITH A NOMINAL CLAUSE

(a) You have solved the problem. No one knows the method.
[= No one knows how you solved the problem.]

(b) The student was absent yesterday. The teacher asked him the reason.
[= The teacher asked the student why he had been absent yesterday.]

(c) Mr. Rao is a great politician. This fact must be admitted.
[= This fact must be admitted that Mr. Rao is a great politician.]

(d) The Rajdhani Express will reach at a certain time. Do you know the time? [= Do you know when the Rajdhani Express will reach?]

(e) He passed the Final examination. He told me this.
[= He told me that he had passed the Final examination.]

(f) He did it. I do not know how. It is true.
[= It is true that I do not know how he did it.]

## ADJECTIVE CLAUSE (RELATIVE CLAUSE)

An Adjective Clause or Relative Clause is used as an Adjective **to qualify a Noun or Pronoun** or **it denotes relation to a Noun or Pronoun**. The Noun or Pronoun with which the Adjective clause is related is called its **Antecedent**. [An Adjective Clause or Relative Clause is placed just after its antecedent.]

| Functions of a Relative Clause | Examples |
|---|---|
| **Subject** | The boy who came here is my friend. |
| **Object** | The boy whom you know is my friend. |
| **Possessive** | The boy whose father is a doctor came here. |

## LINKING WORDS/LINKERS

| Relative Clause | Living | Non-living | Living and Non-living |
|---|---|---|---|
| Subject | who | which/that | that |
| Object | whom | which/that | that |
| Possessive | whose | of which | — |

**Some More Examples : [Note the Linkers]**

This is the boy who broke one of the windows.

[By joining : This is the boy. He broke one of the windows.]

The girl whom you saw last night is my sister.

= The girl is my sister. You saw her last night.

That's the man whose wife is an actress.

= That is the man. His wife is an actress.

The book which (that) I lent you belongs to my brother.

= I lent you the book. It belongs to my brother.

This is the chair of which one leg is broken.

= This is the chair. Its one leg is broken.

## NOUN CLAUSES AND ADJECTIVE CLAUSES SIDE BY SIDE

| Noun Clauses | Adjective Clauses |
|---|---|
| Tell me who did it. | I know the boy who did it. |
| Tell me where he lives. | Tell me the place where he lives. |
| Tell me when he will come. | Tell me the time when he will come. |
| I know why he said so. | I know the reason why he said so. |
| I know how he did it. | I know the way how he did it. |

## SOME MORE JOINING WITH A RELATIVE CLAUSE

(a) Something bright was moving across the sky. It was like a star.
[= Something which was bright like a star was moving across the sky.]

(b) Rabindranath Tagore was a great poet. We hold him in high esteem.
[= Rabindranath Tagore whom we hold in high esteem was a great poet./ Rabindranath Tagore who was a great poet is held in high esteem by us.]

(c) A body was found last week. The police are trying to identify the body.
[= The police are trying to identify the body which was found last week.]

(d) I went to see the doctor. The doctor told me to take rest for a few days.
[I went to see the doctor who told me to take rest for a few days.]

(e) Coal is found in West Bengal. It is a very useful mineral.
[= Coal which is a very useful mineral is found in West Bengal.]

(f) The Giant loved a little boy most. The boy was never seen again.
[= The little boy whom the Giant loved most was never seen again.]

(g) The gallery was crowded. It holds only one thousand people.
[= The gallery which holds only one thousand people was crowded.]

(h) The boy passed the Final examination. He told me this.
[= The boy told me the fact that he had passed the Final examination.]

(i) The house is under construction. It belongs to me.
[= The house which is under construction belongs to me.]

(j) This is the place. Rabindranath was born here.
[= This is the place where Rabindranath was born.]

(k) The book is very useful. Robert bought it yesterday.
[= Yesterday Robert bought a book which is very useful.
Or, The book which Robert bought yesterday is very useful.]

(l) The doctors and nurses are all thoroughly trained men and women. Their main purpose is to help the patients to get well as quickly as possible.
[=The doctors and nurses are all thoroughly trained men and women whose main purpose is to help the patients to get well as quickly as possible.]

## ADVERBIAL CLAUSE

**An Adverbial Clause** is used as an Adverb **to modify a Verb, an Adjective, another Adverb** etc. and usually denotes (i) **time** (ii) **place** (iii) **cause** or **reason** (iv) **effect** or **result** (v) **extent** (vi) **manner** (vii) **comparison** (viii) **contrast** (ix) **condition** (x) **purpose**.

| Functions of an Adverbial Clause | Linking Words | Examples |
|---|---|---|
| Time | when | Father came when I started for Delhi. |
| Place | where | You may go where you like. |
| Cause or reason | because | My friend will not come because he is ill. |
| | as | Or, My friend will not come as he is ill. |
| Effect or result | that | I am so tired that I cannot walk. |
| | | He worked so hard that he was tired. |
| Extent | as far as | As far as I know, the man is honest. |
| Manner | as | Ayenger plays as he usually does. |
| " | as if | He acted as if he were mad. |
| Condition | if | I shall help you if you come here. |
| Comparison | as, as | This boy is as brave as his brother (is). |
| | than | You are taller than I (am). |
| Contrast | though/ although | Though/Although he is poor, he is happy. |
| Purpose | that, in order that | We read that (in order that) we learn. |

**Note** **As (reason)** : As he is poor, he could not donate one thousand rupees.
**As (constrast)** : Poor as he is, he donated one thousand rupees.

## LINKERS OF ADVERBIAL CLAUSES

| | |
|---|---|
| (1) Adverbial Clause of Time | when, while, before, after, ere, till, until, since, whenever |
| (2) Adverbial Clause of Place | where, whence, wherever |

| (3) Adverbial Clause of Cause | as, because, since, that |
|---|---|
| (4) Adverbial Clause of Result | that, so...that, such...that |
| (5) Adverbial Clause of Purpose | that, in order that, so that, lest |
| (6) Adverbial Clause of Comparison<br>in the positive degree :<br>in the comparative degree : | <br>as...as, so...as, such...as<br>than |
| (7) Adverbial Clause of Condition | if, unless, in case, whether, on condition, provided (that), supposing that |
| (8) Adverbial Clause of Contrast | though, although |
| (9) Adverbial Clause of Extent | as far as, so far as, so...as |
| (10) Adverbial Clause of Manner | as, as if |
| (11) Adverbial Clause of Concession | whoever, whatever, whichever, however, whether, even if |

**Some more Examples :** [**Note the Linkers**]

Strike while the iron is hot.—Time
[**By joining :** The iron is hot. Strike it now.]
I shall go out to play when I finish my sums.—Time
[= I shall finish my sums. Then I shall go out to play.]
Mother put the fish where the cat couldn't reach it.—Place
It is many days since I saw you last.—Time
Sharmila did the work as it should be done.—Manner
Since you are ill, you need not come.—Reason
[Or] He could not come to school because he was ill.
They started early that they might reach early.—Purpose
He works hard in order that he may succeed.—Purpose
He is not as intelligent as his sister (is).—Comparison (of degree)
He is not so tall as his brother (is).—Comparison (of degree)
He loves you better than (he loves) me.—Comparison (of degree)
[Here 'than me' is compared with the object 'you'.]
He loves you better than I (love you).—Comparison (of degree)
[Here 'than I' is compared with the subject 'he'. Hence 'I' is in the subjective form]
I am not such a liar as you think.—Comparison (of degree)

The more, the merrier.—Comparison (of degree)
As you sow, so you will reap.—Comparison (of manner)
Although he studied hard, he could not pass the exam.—Contrast
So far as I know/As far as I know, he is honest.—Extent
Be so good as to help me (= as much as you can help me).—Extent
If you don't work hard, you won't pass the exam.—Condition

He held my hand lest I should fall.—Negative purpose

I shall wait for you till you come back.—Time (till/until)

The doctor had come before the patient died.—Time

When/While he will be in Dhaka, he will meet his old friends.—Time

You must do your duty ere you go out for a walk.—Time

In order to catch the train, you should start in the morning.—Purpose

**Adverbial Clause of Concession :**

Adverbial Clauses of Concession are introduced by whoever, whatever, whichever, however, whether, even if etc. :

Whoever he may be, he cannot be allowed.

Whatever you may say, I do not believe you.

You may take whichever you like.

However strong you may be, I am not afraid of you.

I shall support you whether (you are) right or wrong.

Even if I fail, I shall not give up hope.

## SPECIAL NOTES ON ADVERBIAL CLAUSE OF CONDITION

It is important to note that the **Future Tense is not used in the Conditional Clause. It may be used in the Main Clause if it is required** :

If you find the pen (not, If you will find the pen), I shall give it to you.

If I knew your number, I would/could/might telephone you.

**Conditionals are of three types :**

### Open Condition

| **If Clause** (Simple Present) | **Main Clause** (will/shall/can/may + verb) |
|---|---|
| If it rains, | I'll stay at home. |
| If you study hard, | you will get a first class. |
| If you find my money, | I shall give you an icecream. |
| If he runs all the time, | he can get there in time. |
| If her uncle arrives, | she may not come with you. |

### Unfulfilled Condition

| **If Clause** (Simple Past/Past Perfect) | **Main Clause** (would/should/could/might + Perfect) |
|---|---|
| If I had a degree, | I could get a job easily. |
| If I dropped the plate, | it would break. |
| If you had tried again, | you would have succeeded. |
| If I had studied hard, | I should have got a first class. |
| If I had seen him, | I could have saved him. |
| If you had come to me, | I might have helped you. |
| (If omitted) Had you taken the medicine, | you would have felt much better. |

### Improbable or Imaginary Condition

| If Clause (Past Subjunctive) | Main Clause (would/should/could/might + verb) |
|---|---|
| If I were the Chief Minister, | I'd abolish examinations. |
| If I were a bird, | I would sing cheerfully in the sky. |
| (If omitted) Had I been a bird, | I would sing to cheer you. |

We can also use 'unless' in the sense 'if...not', or 'in case' in the sense 'if by any chance' in the Conditional Clause :

Unless I hear from you, I'll go out for a week.

In case it rains, you should take an umbrella.

**Note** If you begin your sentences with a Conditional Clause, you must put a comma ( , ) at the end of the clause. But If you place the Conditional Clause after the Main Clause, there is no need of a comma.

If you study hard, you will get a first class.

[But] You will get a first class if you study hard.

## SOME MORE JOINING WITH ADVERBIAL CLAUSE

(a) He came to my house. I was not at home. (Use 'when' clause)
[= He came to my house when I was not at home.]

(b) He has been running temperature. He wishes to go to school. (Use 'though' clause).
[= Though he has been running temperature, he wishes to go to school.]

(c) He jumped out of bed. The bell rang then. (Use 'when' clause)
[= He jumped out of bed when the bell rang.]

(d) They learned the same things. They could help one another in the homework. (Join with a linker of reason.)
[= They could help one another in the homework as/because they learned the same things.]

(e) You are pardoned. You have confessed your crime. (Join with 'as' clause)
[= You are pardoned as you have confessed your crime.]

(f) I may grant your prayer. You shall have to ask for it. (Join with 'if' clause)
[= I may grant your prayer if you ask for it.]

(g) He is rich. I was in difficulty. He did not help me. (Use a time clause and a contrast clause.)
[= Though he is rich, he did not help me when I was in difficulty.]

(h) It is simple. A child can understand it. (Use so...that.)
[= It is so simple that a child can understand it.]

(i) He will not be able to pay off his debts. He is poor. (Use 'as' clause)
[= He will not be able to pay off his debts as he is poor.]

(j) I am his neighbour. He did not help me. (Use a clause of contrast.)
[= Though I am his neighbour, he did not help me.]

(k) He may come. Please request him to wait for me. (Use '**if**' clause)

[= **If** he comes, please request him to wait for me.]

(l) Don't get out of the train now. The train should stop at the station. (Use a **time** clause with '**till**'.)

[= Wait **till** the train stops at the station.]

## COORDINATING CLAUSES (COMPOUND SENTENCES)

Coordinating Clauses are **independent clauses or of the same order or rank. A Compound sentence must have two or more Coordinating Clauses** (Principal Clauses/Main Clauses). It may have a Subordinating Clause or may not have any Subordinating Clause. The Coordinating Clauses are joined by Coordinating Conjunctions or Connectives.

**Note** The sentence having two Coordinating Clauses is also called a **Double sentence** and the sentence having more than two Coordinating Clauses is called a **Multiple sentence**.

| Joining by Coordinating Conjunctions | Compound Sentences |
|---|---|
| **and** | I went there **and** found him ill. |
| **but** | He threw the stone **but** missed the dog. |
| **or** | I shall do it now **or** (I shall do it) **never**. |
| **so** | It is time to go; **so** let us start. |
| **Yet** | He is weak, **yet** he is working **hard**. |
| **both...and** | I **both** thanked him **and** rewarded him. |
| **either...or** | He is **either** mad **or** he has become a criminal. |
| **neither...nor** | He **neither** obtains success **nor** deserves it. |
| **not only...but also** | He is **not only** a knave **but** also a fool. |

**Note** '**And**' joins **similar** clauses of similar ideas, '**But**' joins **dissimilar** clauses having contrast, and '**Or**' joins alternative ideas.

## SOME MORE JOINING INTO A COMPOUND SENTENCE

(a) Ram is a student of this school. Rahim is also a student of this school.

[= Ram **and** Rahim are the students of this school.]

(b) The boy is intelligent. He stood first in the examination.

[= The boy is intelligent **and** he stood first in the examination.]

(c) The girl is intelligent. She failed in the examination. [= The girl is intelligent **but** she failed in the examination.]

(d) He was found guilty. He was hanged. [= He was found guilty, **so/therefore** he was hanged.]

(e) He stood first in the examination. He had been ill before.

[He had been ill before the examination; **yet** he stood first in it.]

(f) You may accept the offer. You may refuse it. [= You may accept the offer **or** refuse it./You may **either** accept the offer **or** refuse it.]

(g) I did not know anything of it. My brother also did not know anything of it.

[= **Neither** my brother **nor** I know anything of it.]

(h) You may turn to the left. You may turn to the right. [= You may turn **either** to the left **or** to the right.]

(i) John may come here. Mary may come here. But both of them will not come here at the same time. [= **Either** John **or** Mary may come here.]

**N.B. Either**......**or**, **Neither**......**nor** are placed just before the alternatives.

## CONTRACTED SENTENCES

**Compound sentences** often appear in a **contracted** or **shortened form**, so as to avoid the needless repetition of the same word. **J. C. Nesfield**

(a) When there are **two predicates to the same subject**, there is no need to mention the subject more than once :

(1) The sun rose and (the sun) filled the sky with light.

(2) He called at my house but (he) left soon.

(3) He is poor, but (he is) honest. (Adversative)

(4) He is diligent, and therefore, (he is) prosperous. (Illative)

(b) When there are **two subjects to the same predicate**, we need not mention the predicate more than once :

(1) He and you are guilty. (= He is guilty and you are guilty). (Cumulative)

(2) Either she did this or her parents (did this). (Alternative)

## DIFFERENT CLAUSES WITH THE SAME LINKER

Some Linking Words are used in different Clauses in different ways :

**That :**

(i) I know that he is honest. [Noun clause—Object to 'know']

(ii) I know the boy that stole the book. [Adj. cl.—qualifying 'boy']

(iii) He told me that he had got a prize. [Noun cl.—Object to 'told']

(iv) He told me the fact that he had got a prize. [Adj. cl.—qualifying 'fact']

(v) We read that we can learn. [Adv. cl.—modifying 'read' for purpose]

**Where :**

(i) I know where he lives now. [Noun clause—Object to 'konw']

(ii) I know the place where he lives now. [Adj. cl. qualifying the noun 'place']

(iii) The place where Fatima was born is Rajbari. [Adj. cl. qualifying 'place']

(iv) We shall go where he lives now. [Adv. cl. modifying the verb 'go']

**When :**

(i) I know when he will come back. [Noun clause—Object to 'know']

(ii) I know the time when he will come back. [Adj. cl. qualifying the noun 'time']

(iii) The time when he reached Dhaka was 4 p.m. [Adj. cl. qualifying 'time']

(iv) We shall go when he comes. [Adv. cl. modifying the verb 'go'.]

**Why :**

(i) I know why he looks so sad. [Noun clause—Object to 'know'.]

(ii) I know the reason why he looks so sad. [Adj. cl. qualifying the noun 'reason']

**Who :**

(i) Do you know who did it? [Noun clause—Object to 'know']

(ii) Do you know the boy who did it? [Adj. clause—qualifying the noun 'boy']

**Which :**

(i) Do you know which is what? [Noun clause—Object to 'know']

(ii) This is the pen which writes well. [Adj. Clause qualifying 'pen']

(iii) Which is preferable is not known to me. [N. clause—Subject to 'is known']

**Whether :**

(i) I asked her whether she would do it or not. [Noun clause—Object to 'ask']

(ii) I shall support you whether (you are) right or wrong. [Adv. cl.—modifying 'suppport']

## PARTICIPIAL PHRASES AND NON-FINITE CLAUSES

**In Modern Grammar** difference has been shown between a **Participial Phrase** and a **Non-finite Clause**. Modern Grammar deals with **a Non-finite Clause** which is a Subordinate Clause; but that Subordinate Clause does not contain a Finite verb. **It contains a Participle or an Infinitive where the Subject and Verb are understood. But a Participial Phrase itself becomes the Subject or the Object of a sentence.**

**In Chapter 20**, we have discussed how "-ing participle", "-ed/en participle" and Infinitives are used as **Premodifiers** or **Postmodifiers**.

Here we must note that such **Premodifiers with '-ing' or 'ed/en' participles are Participial Phrases.**

**But the Postmodifiers with '-ing' or '-ed/en' participles or Infinitives are Non-finite Clauses** as the omitted Subject and Verb can be easily inserted into such clauses. In fact, **Non-finite Clauses are shortened or reduced clauses.**

Now see the difference between a Non-finite Clause and a Participial Phrase :

| Non-finite Clause [Postmodifier] | Participial Phrase [Premodifier] |
|---|---|
| I found Gargi standing at the door. [= I found Gargi (who was) standing at the door.—Sub. and Verb may be inserted.] | A darkening sky may bring showers. ['darkening sky' is the Subject of the verb 'bring'. No other Subject and Verb can be inserted into the Participial Phrase.] |
| I saw a man injured in an accident. [= I saw a man (who was) injured in an accident.] | I saw some starving beggars. ['starving beggars' is the Object of the Verb 'saw'. No Subject and Verb can be inserted into the Phrase.] |
| He is the last man to leave the place. [= He is the last man (who is) to leave the place.]  | The injured boy was weeping. ['injured boy' is the Subject of the sentence and no other Subject and Verb can be inserted into it.] |

**Non-finite clause with '-ing' participle :** The sun having risen, the fog dispersed. Hearing the noise the boys sprang up.

[= When the boys were hearing the noise, they sprang up.]

Being absorbed in deep thought the boy could not answer the question.

**Non-finite clause with 'Having' + Past Participle :** The sun having risen, the fog dispersed.

Now see how Non-finite Clauses are used to reduce a Relative Clause or an Adverbial Clause :

(i) **Use of '-ing Participle' for reducing a Relative Clause :**

| Relative Clauses | Non-finite '-ing' Clauses (Reduced Relative Clauses) |
|---|---|
| Look at the boys who are running in the field. | Look at the boys running in the field. |
| Mr. Ali saw the children who were going with each other. | Mr. Ali saw the children going with each other.  |
| He saw the sailors who were hauling chests. | He saw the sailors hauling chests. |
| The boy who is working in the laboratory is studious. | The boy working in the laboratory is studious. |
| Can you see the kite which is flying high? | Can you see the kite flying high? |

(ii) **Use of '-ed/-en Participle' for reducing a Relative Clause :**

| Relative Clauses | Non-finite '-ed/-en' Clauses (Reduced Relative Clauses) |
|---|---|
| The picture which was painted by your brother is really beautiful. | The picture painted by your brother is really beautiful. |
| I got the letter which was written by you. | I got the letter written by you. |
| Lessons which are learnt easily are soon forgotten. | Lessons learnt easily are soon forgotten. |
| The book which was lent by the library is missing. | The book lent by the library is missing. |

(iii) **Use of '-ing/-ed Participle' for reducing an Adverbial Clause :**

| Adverbial Clauses | Non-finite '-ing/-ed' Clauses (Reduced Adverbial Clauses) |
|---|---|
| When he was wounded in the war he returned home. | Wounded in the war, he returned home.  |
| When he was in England, he saw a strange sight. | When in England, he saw a strange sight. |
| While I was walking in the field, I met a monk. | While walking in the field I met a monk. |
| When the plant was shaded, it stopped feeding. | Shaded (= Being shaded), the plant stopped feeding. |

(iv) **Use of 'to-infinitive' for reducing Relative Clauses :**

| Relative Clauses | Non-finite 'to-infinitive' Clauses (Reduced Relative Clauses) |
|---|---|
| Nurul was the last man who raised a protest. | Nurul was the last man to raise a protest [= Nurul was the last man (who was) to raise a protest.] |

| Relative Clauses | Non-finite 'to-infinitive' Clauses (Reduced Relative Clauses) |
|---|---|
| Ayesha was the girl **who arrived first**. | Ayesha was the girl **to arrive first**. [= Ayesha was the girl (who was) to arrive first.] |
| I have a nice pen **with which I can write**. | I have a nice pen **to write with**. [= I have a nice pen (that is) to write with.] |
| The next train **which is to arrive** is running three hours late. | The next train **to arrive** is running three hours late. |
| This is the work **which is to be done by us**. | This is the work **to be done** by us. |

**Note** A Non-finite Clause can be placed before, or, after a Main Clause, or in the middle of it.

## SOME MORE JOINING INTO SINGLE SENTENCE

(i) **Separate :** I saw him fall. I ran towards him. I feared the worst.

**Joined :** When I saw him fall, I ran towards him, fearing the worst. (Complex)

(ii) **Separate :** He rode his bicycle. He did not use his hands. That was a silly thing to do.

**Joined :** It was a silly thing that he rode his bicycle without using his hands. (Complex)

(iii) **Separate :** The man is very brave. You saw him. He once faced a tiger. He had only a stick in his hand.

**Joined :** The man you saw is so brave that he once faced a tiger with only a stick in his hand. (Complex)

(iv) **Separate :** A leopard saw me aim my gun towards it. It then sprang to one side into a bush. It was out of my view soon.

**Joined :** When a leopard saw me aim my gun towards it, it sprang to one side into a bush and was out of my view soon. (Compound)

(v) **Separate :** It was evening. Rahim Khan entred the hut. He saw the sparrows. They were twittering.

**Joined :** When Rahim Khan entered the hut in the evening, he saw that the sparrows were twittering. (Complex)

[Or] In the evening when Rahim Khan entered the hut, he saw the twittering sparrows. (Complex)

(vi) **Separate :** My brother is ill. You saw him the other day. So I cannot attend the meeting. You have called it.

**Joined :** As my brother whom you saw the other day, is ill, I cannot attend the meeting you have called. (Complex)

(vii) **Separate :** I held the card tight in my hand. I hurried to a lonely corner of the ship. I started reading it. My head reeled.

**Joined :** Holding the card tight in my hand, I hurried to a lonley corner of the ship and as I started reading it, my head reeled. (Compound)

(viii) **Separate** : I require a car. My friend is ready to help me with it. A man tells me this. He has just come.

**Joined** : The man who has just come tells me that my friend is ready to help me with a car which I require. (Complex)

(ix) **Separate** : A man may be poor. Yet he will win the love and respect of all. But he must be honest. My father says this.

**Joined** : My father says that however poor a man may be, he will win the love and respect of all if he is honest. (Complex)

(x) **Separate** : I got a scholarship. He heard this. He was very glad. He at once came to our house. He offered me his blessings.

**Joined** : When he heard that I had got the scholarship, he was so glad that he at once came to our house to offer me his blessings. (Complex)

## SPLITTING OF SENTENCES

A long sentence can be split up into some short simple sentences. In fact, it is just the opposite of Synthesis or Joining. Here are some examples. Pay special attention for supplying Subject and Verb in short sentences and maintain sequence of action :

(i) He took a pen and a piece of paper and wrote something on it.
= He took a pen. He took a piece of paper. He wrote something on it.

(ii) It is such a good news that I cannot believe it.
= It is a very good news. But I cannot believe it.

(iii) As you are a proved liar, I cannot believe you.
= You are a proved liar. So I cannot believe you.

(iv) Being tired by a long walk, the traveller sat under a tree.
= The traveller was tired by a long walk. So he sat under a tree.

(v) Habib was unhappy when he was punished and shown a red card by the referee.
= Habib was punished by the referee. He was also shown a red card by the referee. So he was unhappy.

(vi) This is Ayer who is not only my friend but also one of the best boys in the class.
= This is Ayer. He is my friend. He is also one of the best boys in the class.

(vii) Antony headed the ball that was floated into the penalty area by Akhtar, taken from a corner-kick.
= Antony headed the ball. It was floated into the penalty area by Akhtar. It was taken from a corner-kick.

(viii) The boy stood on the burning deck, from where everyone else had gone away.
= The boy stood on the deck. The deck was burning. Everyone else had gone away from there.

(ix) Men of science have proved that the sun does not move round the earth, but the earth moves round the sun.
= The earth moves round the sun. The sun does not move round the earth. Men of science have proved these facts.

(x) History says that Socrates, when he was given a cup of hemlock, continued to talk to his friends who were standing beside him.

= Socrates was given a cup of hemlock. He continued to talk to his friends. They were standing beside him. History says this.

## SEQUENCE OF TENSES

**RULE 1.**

| If the main clause is | the dependent clause may be |
|---|---|
| Present tense | 1. Present tense in any form. |
| Or | 2. Past tense in any form. |
| Future tense, | 3. Future tense in any form. |

Anna says that she can play the piano.

I hope he arrived safely.

They think she will come here tomorrow.

**RULE 2.**

| If the main clause is | the dependent clause may be |
|---|---|
| Past tense, | 1. Simple past |
| | 2. Past progressive |
| | 3. Past perfect |
| | 4. would/could/might + verb |

I saw her when she was in hospital.

He ran outside to see what was happening.

I hoped he had arrived safely.

She said that she would come soon.

He thought that he could win the prize.

He thought that he might do the work.

## APPLIED SECTION

**1. Join these Simple Sentences in A and B by using a Relative Clause :**
[Using who, whose, whom, which, what, that etc.]

| A<br>1st sentence | B<br>2nd sentence |
|---|---|
| (a) Columbus died in 1506. | He was the discoverer of America. |
| (b) Gravity is a force. | It attracts objects towards the centre. |
| (c) This is a tool. | It is used for cutting metal. |
| (d) English is a language. | It is spoken all over the world. |
| (e) This is the place. | There the poet Rabindranath was born. |
| (f) Report it to your friend | Nehru said this to his daughter. |
| (g) Rabindranath is a great poet. | He composed 'Gitanjali'. |
| (h) The fox saw some grapes. | Those were hanging from a vine. |
| (i) The air surrounds us. | It consists of various elements. |
| (j) You met the man last night. | He is a soldier. |

**2. Combine the part in A with a suitable Adverbial Clause in B :**

| A<br>1st part | B<br>2nd part (Choose suitable one) |
|---|---|
| (a) A plant will not grow<br>(b) Shila cut her finger<br>(c) The boy met with an accident<br>(d) What will happen to you<br>(e) They will reach here early<br>(f) Anne gave Helen a doll to hold in one hand | if they come by train.<br>while he was crossing the road.<br>if the roots are cut off.<br>while she was sharpening the pencil.<br>while she spelt 'doll' in the other.<br>if you take too much food? |

**3. Join the sentences using and, but, or, either...or, neither...nor :**

(a) John worked hard. He did very well in the exam.
(b) Edison is good at Mathematics. He is bad at English.
(c) Jahanara has read the story. She can't remember the title.
(d) Birbahadur started late. He reached school just in time.
(e) Is the red one your pen? Is the black one your pen?
(f) Shall I write to mother? Will you tell her?
(g) We may go to market. We may go to the playground.
(h) Bina does not take tea. She does not take milk too.
(i) Miss Helen Keller was highly sensitive to smell.
Dr. Tilney's sense of smell was not sharp.

## EXERCISE

1. **What is a Simple Sentence? Give two examples.**
2. **What is a Complex Sentence? Give three examples.**
3. **What is a Compound Sentence? Give three examples.**
4. **What is a Principal Clause and what is a Subordinate Clause?**
5. **What is a Coordinating Clause?**
6. **How many types of Subordinate Clauses are there in English? Give examples.**
7. **Classify the following sentences and name the clauses. One has been done :**

| Sentences | Classification of Sentences with Clauses |
|---|---|
| 1. If you listen, I shall tell you all. | 1. This is a complex sentence.<br>(a) I shall tell you all.—Pr. cl.<br>(b) If you listen—Sub. Adv. cl. |
| 2. If you speak, you will die.  | 2. ..........................................<br>(a) ..........................................<br>(b) .......................................... |
| 3. I know that he is honest. | 3. ..........................................<br>(a) ..........................................<br>(b) .......................................... |

| Sentences | Classification of Sentences with Clauses |
|---|---|
| 4. He is honest though he is poor. | 4. ........................................<br>(a) ........................................<br>(b) ........................................ |
| 5. He is poor but he is honest. | 5. ........................................<br>(a) ........................................<br>(b) ........................................ |
| 6. She must weep or she will die. | 6. ........................................<br>(a) ........................................<br>(b) ........................................ |
| 7. He came home and began to work. | 7. ........................................<br>(a) ........................................<br>(b) ........................................ |
| 8. He was the last man who went there. | 8. ........................................<br>(a) ........................................<br>(b) ........................................ |
| 9. When he reached the station, he saw that the train had started.  | 9. ........................................<br>(a) ........................................<br>(b) ........................................ |
| 10. He not only caned the boy but also fined him. | 10. ........................................<br>(a) ........................................<br>(b) ........................................ |

**8. Join the following pairs of sentences with a Nominal Clause :**

[Use that, who, whose, whom, what, which, when, where, how etc.]

(a) Where was he born? Do you know the place?
(b) He passed the examination. He told me this.
(c) You have made no mistake. I am sure of it.
(d) It will rain. I know that.
(e) She is an intelligent girl. We know this.
(f) Harish was weeping. Nobody knows the reason for his weeping.

**9. Join the following pairs of sentences with a Relative Clause :**

[Use who, which, where, what, that etc.]

(a) She told me the address. I wrote the address down on a piece of paper.
(b) The man answered the phone. He told me that you were out.
(c) I saw a car. It was rushing past the park.
(d) He is a soldier. He must show discipline.
(e) Where was Vidyasagar born? Do you know the place?
(f) Here is the pencil. You lost it yesterday.
(g) Teachers say something. Listen to those things.
(h) You saw the man the other day. He is Mr. Bose's nephew.

(i) Romario got the Gold Football Award. He was in the Brazil team.
(j) He gave me his textbooks. Those did me much good.
(k) The girl is a friend of mine. She is a good basketball player.
(l) Mr. Kapoor is my uncle. You saw him yesterday.
(m) A boy came to me yesterday. He is my classmate.
(n) Some frogs can fly. Those frogs generally live in trees.
(o) The Swallow was going to die. He bade goodbye to the Happy Prince.
(p) It was the day of prize-giving ceremony. A boy of Class IX bagged many prizes. I am familiar with the boy.

**10. Join the sentences with an Adverbial Clause :**

[By using if, though, although, as, because, unless, till, until, as soon as, when, where etc.]

(a) Garbage is dangerous to human health. It remains uncollected for a long period.
(b) Much work has been done in the field. The odour specialists have been unable to identify any primary smell.
(c) Walter was ready to stand under the tree. He wanted to save his father.
(d) He is poor. He cannot buy his books.
(e) I entered the room. Immediately I felt something was wrong.
(f) The plant was shaded. It stopped feeding.
(g) The clock struck five. He finished his work then.
(h) You should come. Otherwise I shall not go out.
(i) He has been running a high temperature. He wishes to go to school.
(j) He jumped out of bed. The bell rang then.
(k) I cannot compete with you. You are stronger.
(l) I left the meeting. There was awful noise there.
(m) He learnt the fact. He was then angry with himself.
(n) You may be powerful. I am not afraid of you.
(o) He stared at me long. He seemed never to have seen me before.

**11. Join the following pairs of sentences into a Compound Sentence :**

(a) Sharmila is a student of this school. Ayesha is also a student of this school.
(b) Rahaman is not a good student. He is a good player.
(c) You may accept the offer. You may refuse it.
(d) I did not know anything of it. My brother also did not know anything of it.
(e) You must pay the price. Otherwise you must return the goods.
(f) The gardener was old. He planted some mango trees in my uncle's garden.
(g) Rabin desired to help me in my difficulties. He was my sincere friend.
(h) The Headmaster thanked me. He rewarded me too.
(i) He is dishonest. Moreover he is wicked to the backbone.

**12. Join the following sentences by using '-ing', '-en', '-ed', Phrases or Infinitives :**

(a) He saw me come. He ran away.
(b) He was tired. He took rest for a while.
(c) A thief entered the room. He had found the room empty.
(d) He did not speak to me. He was angry with me.
(e) The Prime Minister addressed the meeting. He asked for everybody's cooperation.

(f) He wandered about from place to place. He had lost his way.
(g) I saw a tiger. It was wounded.
(h) He stood up to speak. He had determined to oppose the bill.
(i) He has many sons. He has to educate them.
(j) He has a car. He wishes to sell it.
(k) I have many friends here. They will stand by me.
(l) I went there. My object was to help him.
(m) He has a large family. He must maintain it.
(n) He is very weak. He cannot walk.
(o) I shall never do it again. I am determined.

**13. Shorten the following sentences by using '-ing', '-en', or '-ed' Phrases or Infinitives :** [The clause to be reduced is shown by Italics.]

(a) I saw the boy *who was injured*.
(b) The watch *which was stolen* was recovered at last.
(c) *As the boy was absorbed in deep thought* he could not answer my question.
(d) *When they heard the sound*, they sprang up.
(e) His misery is so great *that he cannot bear it*.
(f) He has a house *which he wishes to let*.

**14. Join the following sentences into single sentences :**

(a) I was ill. He heard of it. He at once went to the doctor. He did not wait for me.
(b) The boy was healthy. He was strong. It was not difficult for him to lift the load of forty kilograms.
(c) A meeting was held in the Town Hall. You were absent from the meeting. I am sorry at this.
(d) I heard a loud noise. It was like the bursting of a bomb. It came from a house close by.
(e) It was Sunday last. A fire broke out in the multi-storeyed building at Burrabazar. It broke out at midnight.
(f) I saw an old man. This was on my way to school. He was poor. He was also bent down with age.
(g) Hiroshima was a city of Japan. An atom bomb was dropped on it. The atom bomb destroyed it.
(h) He keeps some dogs. The dogs are well-trained. They will guard his house.

(i) The sky is cloudy. He should take an umbrella. It will be better for him.
(j) The book teaches me grammar. It is a new one. It was given by my father.

**15. Split up the following sentences into short simple sentences :**

(a) I am sorry to hear that you have failed, though I think that you deserved to pass.
(b) While he was speaking, a man entered and told him that the prince had suddenly died.
(c) Since he was a poor man, he said nothing of the bag full of one lakh rupees he had found, but left the country.
(d) Everybody knows that the boy who came to me for help is a liar and a cheat.

(e) I could not but feel sorry for the old man who, once very rich, was now deserted by all and was lying in sick-bed in his lonely hut.

(f) He taught us that it is the duty of every man to love his neighbours and help them to the best of his power.

(g) When I was in my native village during the summer vacation, I often went to the houses of the poor people to know their difficulties.

(h) Hearing that he was not able to accompany me because he was ill with fever, I gave up the idea of going to Darjeeling.

(i) We heard the cry and rushed to the spot to help the passengers who were trapped inside the bus that was overturned.

(j) I gave him my thanks for finding my purse and returning it to me without taking anything from it.

(k) I could not carry out his orders and did not inform him of my inability in time and so he was displeased with me.

(l) When the evening mist rose, he came to the cave, drew breath and looked down the valley.

(m) Not only he but his sister also went to Darjeeling where I often met them at the Mall, and we walked together.

(n) As I was young and you were old and experienced, I was afraid of your age and dignity and kept silent before you.

(o) Having lost my way I asked a policeman to direct me but he could not help me as he was new to his work.

(p) Homer, a great poet, was born somewhere but nobody knows the place of his birth.

(q) A drowning man shouted for help and hearing it the sailor plunged into the river to save the man's life.

(r) As you are still immature, your reaction of feeling elated at the praise of others is impractical.

(s) We waste our energies too often over trifles and we all make this mistake.

(t) Because of the want of opportunity in our course of study, we take it for granted that India had no culture, or next to none.

(u) When he was asked what river he had seen, that unfortunate boy, living at the confluence of the Ganges and Jamuna, replied that he had not seen any.

(v) The Hindu Code Law was duly passed but it did not provide beleaguered women respite from the violence that gripped their lives.

(w) When the Law was being hotly debated, we too arranged many meetings and gatherings among women and collected many signatures in its support.

(x) Johnny crashed through the garden gate and stormed down the path, demolishing some of his father's prize blooms with his trailing satchel.

(y) In urban areas, for instance, a minority of car owners cause massive pollution, congestion, noise, tension and accidents—all at the expenses of the public at large.

(z) Present trends of rapid groundwater tables in large parts of the country are utterly unsustainable, and call for urgent attention.

# 27 TRANSFORMATION OF SENTENCES

## WHY DO WE NEED TRANSFORMATION OF SENTENCES?

The conversion or transformation of sentences is an excellent exercise as it teaches variety of expression in writing English.

The transformation of sentences consists in changing a sentence from one form to another without any change of meaning.

### INTERROGATIVE TO ASSERTIVE SENTENCES

In some special types of Interrogatives, when the question is affirmative, a negative answer is implied; and when the question is negative, an affirmative answer is implied. Hence an Interrogative sentence is often changed into an Assertive sentence, and vice versa, **by affirmation or negation**.

Interrogative—What is the use of this statue?

Assertive—There is no use of this statue.

Interrogative—When can their glory fade? [Or] Can their glory ever fade?

Assertive—Their glory can never fade.

Interrogative—Is he not a great fool?

Assertive—He is a great fool.

Interrogative—Can anyone do this?

Assertive—No one can do this.

Interrogative—Can I ever forget you?

Assertive—I can never forget you.

### ASSERTIVE TO INTERROGATIVE SENTENCES

Assertive—Man cannot die better than facing fearful odds.

Interrogative—How can man die better than facing fearful odds?

Assertive—We bleed if you prick us.

Interrogative—If you prick us, do we not bleed? [vide **Nesfield**]

Assertive—It does not matter if I fail.

Interrogative—What does it matter if I fail?

Assertive—It does not matter much though we happen to be late.
Interrogative—What though we happen to be late? [vide **Wren & Martin**]
Assertive—Everybody loves his motherland.
Interrogative—Who does not love his motherland?
Assertive—He was a villain to do such a deed.
Interrogative—Was he not a villain to do such a deed?
Assertive—The beauties of Nature are beyond description.
Interrogative—Are not the beauties of Nature beyond description?
Assertive—There is no hope for me if you do not come.
Interrogative—What hope is there for me if you do not come?
[Or] Is there any hope for me if you do not come?
Assertive—Everyone wants to flee from a state of bondage.
Interrogative—Who does not want to flee from a state of bondage?

## EXERCISE I

**Transform the following sentences from Interrogative to Assertive, and vice versa :**

1. No one can bear an unprovoked insult.
2. No one ever saw a brighter daybreak than this.
3. If you tickle us, do we not laugh?
4. Who does not wish to be happy?
5. Shall I forget those happy days?
6. Is that the way a gentleman should behave?
7. Is this the kind of dress to wear in school?
8. Can anybody trust such a liar?
9. He was a fool to act thus.
10. Of what use is such an old thing?
11. Who does not know him?
12. Who can touch pitch without being defiled?

## EXCLAMATORY TO ASSERTIVE SENTENCES

In course of change from Exclamatory to Assertive sentences **'very'** is usually used **before an Adjective** and **'great' before a Noun**. Moreover, it can be changed by using the verb 'wish', 'exclaim in wonder' etc.

Exclamatory—What a fool you are!
Assertive—You are a great fool. [here 'fool' used as a Noun]
Exclamatory—How beautiful the night is!
Assertive—The night is very beautiful.
Exclamatory—How sweet the moonlight sleeps upon this bank!
Assertive—The moonlight sleeps very sweetly upon this bank.
Exclamatory—Oh, that I were young again!
Assertive—I wish that I were young again.
Exclamatory—Had I but a friend to support me!
Assertive—I wish I had a friend to support me.
Exclamatory—Good morning, Mr. Das.
Assertive—I wish you good morning, Mr. Das.

Exclamatory—Hurrah! My friend is coming.
Assertive—I rejoice that my friend is coming.
Exclamatory—Alas! The young man passes away.
Assertive—It is sad to think that the young man should pass away.
Exclamatory—What a nice bird it is!
Assertive—We exclaim in wonder that it is a very nice bird.
Exclamatory—What a dangerous thing a little learning is!
Assertive—A little learning is a very dangerous thing.
Exclamatory—Alas! Our beloved leader is dead.
Assertive—It is very sad that our beloved leader is dead.

## EXERCISE II

**Transform the following Exclamatory sentences into Assertive, and vice versa :**

1. Ah, what a (beautiful) sight was there!
2. What a piece of work is man!
3. How awkwardly he manages his bat!
4. What a delicious flavour these mangoes have!
5. Oh, that I were there at the time!
6. He seems to be very clever.
7. It is very beautiful to look at.
8. You have fallen very low.

## AFFIRMATIVE TO NEGATIVE SENTENCES

A Negative sentence is often formed by changing an Assertive sentence into an Interrogative, or vice versa. Moreover, a Negative form can be made by using **opposite words,** such as 'none but' for 'only', 'never' for 'ever', 'good' for 'bad', etc., or by **changing the degree of comparison** or by using a clause—'**It is not that**' etc.

Affirmative—He is a great fool.
Negative—Is he not a great fool?
Affirmative—Only a rogue can act thus.
Negative—None but a rogue can act thus.
Affirmative—The brave alone deserve the fair.
Negative—None but the brave deserve (deserves) the fair.
Affirmative—Can I ever forget you?
Negative—I can never forget you.
Affirmative—He always minds his lesson.
Negative—He never neglects his lesson.
Affirmative—I shall always remember you.
Negative—I shall never forget you.
Affirmative—He turned all the stones.
Negative—He left no stone unturned.
Affirmative—He is going to attend the meeting.
Negative—It is not that he is not going to attend the meeting.

Affirmative—You are the only person fit for the job.

Negative—No other person but you is fit for the job.

Affirmative—He is the best boy in the class.

Negative—No other boy in the class is as good as he.

Affirmative—I come here for the last time.

Negative—Never again shall I come here.

Affirmative—A fisherman's life is hard.

Negative—A fisherman's life is not easy-going.

Affirmative—Everybody will admit that I am right.

Negative—Nobody will deny that I am right.

Affirmative—Brutus loved Caesar.

Negative—Brutus was not without love for Caesar.

[Or] It is not that Brutus did not love Caesar.

Affirmative—It always pours when it rains.

Negative—It never rains but pours.

Affirmative—As soon as he saw the tiger, he fled.

Negative—No sooner did he see (had he seen) the tiger than he fled.

**Note** "None is a shortened form of not one. Yet it is commonly used with plural verbs." **Wren & Martin**

None but fools has/have ever believed it.

## EXERCISE III

**Transform the following sentences from Affirmative to Negative, and vice versa :**

1. I was doubtful whether it was you.
2. No one but a coward flees from his duty.
3. Learned men are not always judicious.
4. Great men are of no one nation, nor of one particular class.
5. As soon as he came, he made objections.
6. He is sometimes foolish.
7. Every man makes mistakes sometimes.
8. I care very little what he says about me.
9. There is nobody but believes in his honesty.
10. There is no smoke without fire.
11. It is not likely that he will ever see his home again.

## INTERCHANGE OF DEGREES OF COMPARISON

As the following examples show, it is possible to change the degree of comparison of an Adjective or Adverb in a sentence without changing the meaning of the sentence :

Positive—I am as brave as he.

Comparative—He is not braver than I (am).

Positive—He is as intimate to me as to you.

Comparative—He is not more intimate to you than to me.

Positive—There is no mystery so great as misery.
Comparative—Misery is greater than any other mystery.
Superlative—Misery is the greatest mystery of all.

Superlative—Everest is the highest peak of the world.
Positive—No other peak of the world is as high as Everest.
Comparative—Everest is higher than any other peak of the world.
Superlative—He is the best boy in the class.
Comparative—He is better than any other boy (all other boys) in the class.
Positive—No other boy in the class is as good as he.
Superlative—Iron is the most useful of all metals.
Comparative—Iron is more useful than any other metal.
Positive—No other metal is as useful as iron.
Superlative—Japan is one of the richest countries of the world.
Comparative—Japan is richer than most other countries of the world.
Positive—Very few countries of the world are as rich as Japan.
Superlative—This is one of the easiest subejcts.
Comparative—This is easier than many other (most other) subjects.
Positive—Very few subjects are as (so) easy as this. ['very few' in almost negative sense]

**Note** Positive—as.........as (as...as in all cases, but so...as only in negative sense.)
Comparative—.........than
Superlative—the.........in/ of

To change from Superlative to Positive or Comparative degree :
Positive—No/No other/Very few
Comparative—than any other/than many other things or persons

## EXERCISE IV

**Change the Degree of Comparison without changing the meaning :**

1. She is as intelligent as her brother.
2. She is the best girl in her class.
3. Gold is one of the most precious metals.
4. The cow is the most useful of all animals.
5. Mumbai is one of the richest cities in India.
6. Saraswati is better than any other girl in the class.
7. Akbar was one of the greatest emperors of India.
8. The Rajdhani Express runs faster than any other train.
9. Health is more valuable than wealth.
10. Very few countries are as (so) rich as America.

## ADVERB 'TOO'/JOINING BY 'TOO'

1. He is so honest that he will not accept a bribe. [Use 'too' in sense of 'not']
   = He is too honest to accept a bribe. [= He is very honest. He will not accept a bribe.]

2. I am so tired that I cannot walk.
   = I am too tired to walk. [= I am very tired. I cannot walk.]
3. The news is so good that it cannot be true.
   = The news is too good to be true. [= The news is too much good. It cannot be true.]
4. She is so proud that she cannot learn.
   = She is too proud to learn. [= She is very proud. She cannot learn.]
5. She is too clever not to see through your tricks. [Spl. use of both 'too' & 'not to']
   = She is so clever that she will see through your tricks. [vide **Wren & Martin**]

## EXERCISE V

**Rewrite the following sentences to avoid 'too' or to use 'too' :**

1. He is too proud to beg.
2. It is never too late to mend.
3. She was too late to hear the first speech.
4. The boy is too old for whipping.
5. He speaks too fast to be understood.
6. The fact is so evident that it does not require a proof.
7. Be not too eager for praise.
8. The sun is so hot for us that we cannot go out at present.
9. Too many cooks spoil the broth.
10. He reached the station too late to catch the train.

## SIMPLE SENTENCES TO COMPLEX SENTENCES

**(a) by expanding a word or a phrase into a Noun Clause :**

(i) Simple—He pleaded for his innocence.
Complex—He pleaded that he was innocent.

(ii) Simple—I know her name.
Complex—I know what her name is.

(iii) Simple—I am sure of her success in the examination.
Complex—I am sure that she will succeed in the examination.

(iv) Simple—I prayed for his recovery.
Complex—I prayed that he might recover.

(v) Simple—They confessed their guilt.
Complex—They confessed that they were guilty.

**(b) by expanding a word or a phrase into an Adjective (Relative) Clause :**

(i) Simple—He is a meritorious boy.
Complex—He is a boy who has his merit.

(ii) Simple—I lost this ball yesterday.
Complex—This is the ball which I lost yesterday.

(iii) Simple—I still remember the advice of my departed father.
Complex—I still remember the advice which was given by my departed father.

(iv) Simple—He is the last man to utter such a word.
Complex—He is the last man who can utter such a word.

(v) Simple—I want a car to drive.
Complex—I want a car that I can drive.

**(c) by expanding a word or a phrase into an Adverbial Clause :**

(i) Simple—Being rich he cannot understand the suffering of the poor.
Complex—As he is rich he cannot understand the suffering of the poor.

(ii) Simple—He is too weak to move out of doors.
Complex—He is so weak that he cannot move out of doors.

(iii) Simple—He is working day and night to finish the book.
Complex—He is working day and night so that he may finish the book.

(iv) Simple—We went to the station by taxi to avoid missing the train.
Complex— We went to the station by taxi lest we should miss the train.

(v) Simple—Nobody will be allowed to enter the hall without a ticket.
Complex—Nobody will be allowed to enter the hall unless he has a ticket.

(vi) Simple—In spite of being old he carried a load of heavy luggage.
Complex—Though he was old, he carried a load of heavy luggage.

(vii) Simple—She danced like an expert dancer.
Complex—She danced as if she were an expert dancer.

(viii) Simple—Your learning increases in proportion to your reading.
Complex—The more you read the more you learn.

## EXERCISE VI

**Transform the following Simple Sentences into Complex Sentences :**

(1) The news of his success has been published in the newspaper. (2) In the event of his failure he should take another chance. (3) He is not a man to tell a lie. (4) I do not know the name of this place. (5) I could not attend the class on account of my illness. (6) On going there I found him ill. (7) He is working hard to gain a prize. (8) He is too lazy to shine in life. (9) A lost moment is lost for ever. (10) It being a day of strike the children are playing on the street. (11) The success is always in proportion to hard work. (12) He was believed to be very honest. (13) Do you wish me to go? (14) They enquire the reason of his failure. (15) Uneasy lies the head wearing a crown. (16) It was a hard enough life. (17) They walked through the new capital. (18) They were too near death to see anything. (19) A rolling stone gathers no moss. (20) They need a friendly lead.

## COMPLEX SENTENCES TO SIMPLE SENTENCES

**(a) Converting a Noun Cluase into a word or a phrase :**

(i) Complex—I know where he was born.
Simple—I know his birthplace.

(ii) Complex—I do not know how long he will stay here.
Simple—The duration of his stay here is not known to me.

(iii) Complex—The truth is he was absent.
Simple—To tell the truth he was absent.

(iv) Complex—I expect that I shall get a prize.
Simple—I expect to get a prize.

(v) Complex—It is the scarcity of a thing that makes it treasured.
Simple—The scarcity of a thing makes it treasured.

**(b) Converting an Adjective Clause into a word or a phrase : [-ing/-ed/to etc.]**

(i) Complex—Only those boys who work hard will succeed.
Simple—Only hard-working boys will succeed.

(ii) Complex—They cannot forget the losses that they have suffered.
Simple—They cannot forget the losses suffered by them.

(iii) Complex—People who live in glass-houses ought not to throw stones.
Simple—People living in glass-houses ought not to throw stones.

(iv) Complex—The speaker, who was a man of eloquence, spoke in favour of the motion.
Simple—The speaker, a man of eloquence, spoke in favour of the motion.
[Or] The eloquent speaker spoke in favour of the motion.

(v) Complex—Give me some water that I may drink.
Simple—Give me some water to drink.

(vi) Complex—I always wonder when I look at the stars that shine in the sky.
Simple—I always wonder on looking at the shining stars in the sky.

**(c) Converting an Adverbial Clause into a phrase or a word :**

(i) Complex—The world must be made safe that the children may prosper.
Simple—The world must be made safe for the children to prosper.

(ii) Complex—He could not attend the function because he was ill.
Simple—He could not attend the function on account of his illness.

(iii) Complex—Though he got the news he was not happy.
Simple—In spite of getting the news he was not happy.

(iv) Complex—Spend your money carefully lest you should fall into poverty.
Simple—Spend your money carefully to avoid falling into poverty.

(v) Complex—They cried as loudly as they could.
Simple—They cried at the top of their voice.

## EXERCISE VII

**1. Convert the following Complex Sentences into Simple ones :**

(i) He asked where the girl was. (ii) In modern life it is the rolling stone that gathers the moss. (iii) Though the load was light it was too much for the old man. (iv) You need not ask who I am. (v) A law cannot be passed unless the Rashtrapati gives his assent to it. (vi) As the decision has been already taken, the arguments are useless. (vii) I finish the letter because I have no time left. (viii) He had such a little income that he cannot support his family. (ix) I shall buy it, what it may cost. (x) You are the first man who heard the news. (xi) He will not read the book unless he is compelled. (xii) That is the place where he was buried. (xiii) I have nothing that I can offer. (xiv) It is generally believed that he died by poison. (xv) The explanation they offered cannot be true.

**2. Join the Sentences with '-ing'/'-ed' words :**

(i) Standing on the seashore in Puri we saw waves. They were rolling furiously.
(ii) Many areas of India produce tea. Darjeeling is one of them.
(iii) He was angry with me. He did not help me.
(iv) He finished his work. He left the room.
(v) He had determined to oppose the bill. He stood up to speak.

**3. Shorten the following sentences by using '-ing'/'-en' :**

(i) It is really wonderful to look at the stars that shine in the sky.
(ii) Though I have a heart made of lead, yet I cannot choose but weep.
(iii) The scientists are recording the death pangs of a plant which is about to die.
(iv) Have you seen a fish which flies in the sky?
(v) Don't put your hand into the water which is boiling.
(vi) People who live in glass-houses cannot afford to throw stones.

**4. Fill in the gaps using '-en'/'-ed'/'-ing' ending of the following words within brackets : [weep, seal, rot, dry, sterilise] :**

(i) Have you seen any ........... girl on the street?
(ii) Milk is distributed to the consumers in bottles which are ......... and ..........
(iii) During sorting, the ......... oranges are thrown away.
(iv) Mother asked Ayesha to iron the ......... clothes.

## SIMPLE SENTENCES TO COMPOUND SENTENCES

**(a) by using Cumulative Conjunctions (and, also, both...and, as well as, not only...but also, etc.) :**

(i) **Simple**—Going to the garden Robert saw a red rose.
**Compound**—Robert went to the garden and saw a red rose.
(ii) **Simple**—Besides giving us advice he helped us with money.
**Compound**—He gave us not **only advice but also** money.
(iii) **Simple**—To add to his misfortune his father died.
**Compound**—His father died **and** this added to his misfortune.
(iv) **Simple**—Harris was present. Henry was present.
**Compound**—Harris **as well as** Henry was present.
(v) **Simple**—Ayesha likes tea. Rubina likes tea.
**Compound**—Both Ayesha **and** Rubina like tea.
(vi) **Simple**—He kept his promise.
**Compound**—He **not only** made a promise but (**but also**) kept it.

**(b) by using Adversative Conjunctions (but, still, yet, nevertheless, however, only, etc.) :**

(i) **Simple**—**In spite of** being old he was young at heart.
**Compound**—He was old **but** he was young at heart.
(ii) **Simple**—Notwithstanding her pitfalls I love her.
**Compound**—She has her pitfalls, **yet** I love her.

(iii) Simple—He had all the qualifications for the post except honesty.

Compound—He had all the qualifications for the post but he was not honest.

(iv) Simple—In spite of my annoyance, I kept quiet.

Compound—I was annoyed, still I kept quiet.

(v) Simple—In spite of his weakness, he works hard.

Compound—He is weak; nevertheless he works hard.

**(c) by using Alternative Conjunctions (either...or, neither...nor, or, otherwise, else, etc.) :**

(i) Simple—You must avoid fat to lose weight.

Compound—You must avoid fat or you will not lose weight.

(ii) Simple—He would have been insulted but for your timely intervention.

Compound—You had intervened timely, otherwise he would have been insulted.

(iii) Simple—Take another chance to avoid the peril of your life.

Compound—Take another chance, else your life will be at peril.

(iv) Simple—He feigns to be mad.

Compound—Either he is mad or he feigns madness.

(v) Simple—You should not be a borrower or a lender.

Compound—Neither a borrower nor a lender be.

**(d) by using Illative Conjunctions (therefore, then, so, and so, for, etc.) :**

(i) Simple—His work being unsatisfactory he was dismissed.

Compound—His work was unsatisfactory, so (therefore) he was dismissed.

(ii) Simple—He gained prominence by virtue of his sincerity.

Compound—He was sincere, and so he gained prominence.

(iii) Simple—Walking all day long he came back home.

Compound—He came back home; for he had walked all day long. vide **Nesfield**

## EXERCISE VIII

**Convert the following Simple Sentences into Compound ones :**

1. Going home he was very happy to see his mother.
2. The rain having stopped they started for their destination.
3. Being happy he agreed to a handsome donation.
4. In spite of being old he carried a heavy load.
5. Picking up a ruler he hit the boy.
6. In spite of bad weather he scaled the mountain.
7. Besides being honest he is sincere.
8. Notwithstanding several efforts he failed.
9. He must study hard to pass the examination.
10. He could not attend the meeting for his illness.

## COMPOUND SENTENCES TO SIMPLE SENTENCES

**(a)** by using a Participle : [-ing/-ed/-en, words] :

(i) Compound—They went home and found their brother.
Simple—Going home they found their brother.

(ii) Compound—Rita was very sorry and left for home early.
Simple—Being very sorry Rita left for home early.

(iii) Compound—Many areas of India produce tea and Darjeeling is one of them.
Simple—Darjeeling is one of the many tea-producing areas of India.

(iv) Compound—The clothes were dried and mother asked Runa to iron the clothes.
Simple—Mother asked Runa to iron the dried clothes.

(v) Compound—The oranges are being sorted. The rotten ones are thrown away.
Simple—During sorting, the rotten oranges are thrown away.

**(b)** by using a Prepositional Phrase :

(i) Compound—He was terribly unhappy but he did not blame the girl.
Simple—In spite of being terribly unhappy he did not blame the girl.

(ii) Compound—Dr. Roy was not only a physician but also a statesman.
Simple—Besides being a physician Dr. Roy was a statesman.

(iii) Compound—He indulges in tall talks but he is a scoundrel.
Simple—Notwithstanding his tall talks he is a scoundrel.

**(c)** by using an Infinitive :

(i) Compound—You must give up smoking or you will suffer.
Simple—You must give up smoking to aovid suffering.

(ii) Compound—His enterprises failed and this added to his worries.
Simple—To add to his worries his enterprises failed.

### EXERCISE IX

Convert the following Compound Sentences into Simple ones :

1. You must be personal, not abstract. (contracted compound)
2. Its familiarity is not its weakness but its supreme virtue.
3. He not only made a promise but kept it.
4. The Spring came all over but in the Giant's garden it was still Winter.
5. The train began to move and the soldier sank back on his seat.
6. He set his burden down with great gentleness and sank upon the ground.
7. I shall be back at the camp tonight and I'll write to everyone tomorrow.
8. Debu did not find the room suitable and moved to the first floor.
9. We must not be late, else we will miss the bus.
10. The judge found him guilty and sentenced him to three years' imprisonment.

## COMPLEX SENTENCES TO COMPOUND SENTENCES

**It can be done by using Coordinating Conjunctions—and, but, or, etc. :**

(i) Complex—Though he is poor, he is honest.
Compound—He is poor but he is honest.

(ii) Complex—If you do it, you will be punished.
Compound—Do it and you will be punished.

(iii) Complex—If you do not do it, you will be punished.
Compound—Do it or you will be punished.

(iv) Complex—I am sure that you are wrong.
Compound—You are wrong and of this I am sure (and I am sure of this).

(v) Complex—As he was ill, he could not go.
Compound—He was ill and so (therefore) he could not go.

(vi) Complex—Unless you do it, I shall fine you.
Compound—Do it or I shall fine you.

(vii) Complex—If you do not work hard, you will fail.
Compound—Work hard or you will fail.

## COMPOUND SENTENCES TO COMPLEX SENTENCES

**It can be done by omitting Coordinating Conjunctions and using Subordinate Clauses :**

(i) Compound—Work out the sum *or* you will be punished.
Complex—If you do not work out the sum, you will be punished.

(ii) Compound—One word more *and* I will turn you out.
Complex—If you utter one word more, I will turn you out.

(iii) Compound—I was angry but I did not punish him.
Complex—Though I was angry, I did not punish him.

(iv) Compound—He gives a command and it is immediately carried out.
Complex—As soon as he gives a command, it is carried out.

## EXERCISE X

**1. Change the following Compound Sentences into Complex ones :**

1. He is rich but he is miserly.
2. He made several attempts, yet he failed.
3. He is outwardly strict but lenient at heart.
4. United we stand and divided we fall.
5. Spare the rod and spoil the child.
6. Do or die./Do and die.
7. Study and you will learn.
8. A few more attempts and we succeed.
9. He is very weak and so he cannot sit (up) on bed.
10. He is very ill and so he is bound to lie in bed.

# 28

# WH-QUESTIONS

## DIFFERENCE BETWEEN SIMPLE QUESTIONS AND WH-QUESTIONS

**We ask questions to know something. These questions are of two types in English :**

**(1) Yes/No-Questions** [Seeking reply for 'Yes' or 'No']

**(2) Wh-Questions** [Beginning with Wh-words—Who, What, Why etc.]

Interrogative sentences formed with the Auxiliary Verbs Do, Have, Be and the Modals (shall, should, will, would, can, could, may, might) can be answered by 'Yes' or 'No'. But those formed with the help of Wh-words cannot be answered by 'Yes' or 'No'. They require some specific answers :

| Question | Answer |
|---|---|
| (1) Are you going to school? | Yes/No. |
| (2) Where are you going? | I am going to school. |

But we must remember that the rules of Interrogative patterns are the same in both the cases.

**Now let us see the rules of Interrogative patterns :**

**[1]** In Interrogative Sentence, 'Be' verb (is, am, are, was, were), 'Have' verb (has, have, had) and shall, should, will, would, can, could, may, might or must verb are used before the Subject :

| Assertive (Statement) | Interrogative (Question) |
|---|---|
| He is a good boy. | Is he a good boy? |
| He has a camera. | Has he any camera? |
| I shall go to Delhi. | Shall I go to Delhi? |
| Amar can do this work. | Can Amar do this work? |

**[2]** Besides those Verbs mentioned in Rule 1, if there is any other Verb, then 'Do' Verb will come before the Subject and 'Do' Verb will be changed according to Tense and Person, respectively.

| Assertive (Statement) | Interrogative (Question) |
|---|---|
| I play football.<br>He plays football.<br>He played football. | Do I play football?<br>Does he play football?<br>Did he play football? |

**[3]** If there is any interrogative word, i.e. who, whose, whom, which, what, why, when, where, how, how much, then it will be placed before both the places of above mentioned cases :

| Wh-Q. with 'Be'/'Have'/Modal etc. | Wh-Q. with 'Do' support |
|---|---|
| Who are you? | Whom do you want? |
| Whose book is this? | Where do you live (in)? |
| Which is your pen? | When does she sleep? |
| Who can run fast? | Why do you come here? |
| Where will you go? | How does he/she write? |
| How many sisters have you? | How much milk do you want? |
| Which one was absent? | Which school do you prefer? |

**Note** Wh-words are placed before both types of Verbs (be, have, shall, should, will, would, may, might and 'Do' Verbs) :

**Another important point :** If we like to make an Interrogative sentence Negative in non-contracted form, we should usually place '**not**' **before a Noun but after a Pronoun.**

Is not Amar going to school? ('not' before a Noun). Is he not going to school? ('not' after a Pronoun). However, the shortened form of verb + not (Don't/Doesn't/Can't, etc.) is always placed before a Noun or a Pronoun.

Doesn't/Can't John do this simple task? [Or] Doesn't/Can't he do this work?

**Note** Don't forget to put **Asking sign (?)** after Wh-question; otherwise the entire answer will be treated as wrong.

**Wh-words may be classified into three groups :**

**[1] Interrogative Pronouns :** Who, Whose, Whom, Which and What.

**[2] Interrogative Adjectives :** What, Which and Whose.

**[3] Interrogative Adverbs :** When, Where, How and Why.

These Wh-words are used to get information from a sentence.

## FRAMING WH-QUESTIONS

'Wh-questions' mean the questions that are framed with 'Wh'-words in the first place. The 'Wh'-words are who, whom, whose, which, what, when, where, why and how :

**Wh-WORDS**

| For Person | For Thing | For Choice | For Interrogative Adverbs |
|---|---|---|---|
| Who : Nominative | What : Nominative | [Both Person & Thing] | When : For Time |
| Whom : Objective | What : Objective | Which : Nominative | Where : For Place |
| Whose : Possessive | Which : Nominative | Which : Objective | Why : For Reason |
| | Which : Objective | | How : For Manner/ Quality/Quantity etc. |

**How to form Wh-Questions?**

RULES

**[1] The answer in the content must be left out.**

**[2] Wh-word will be placed in the first place.**

**[3] Maintain the following rules of forming Interrogative patterns :**

Rule A If there is any verb form of 'Be' (is, am, are, was, were, shall be, will be) or 'Have' (has, have, had, shall have, will have) such verb comes before the Subject :

['Be', 'Have' verb form + Subject + Wh-word]

| Wh-Pattern : (i) Wh-word + 'Be'/'Have' + Subject + other words |
|---|

Examples (a) Dr. Das is the author of this book.

Wh. Q. : Who is the author of this book?

(b) He has four children.

Wh. Q. : How many children has he?

Rule B If there is any Auxiliary/Modal (shall, should, will, would, can, could, may, might, must), such verb comes before the subject :

| Wh-Pattern : Wh-word + Aux./Modal + Subject + Main verb + other words |
|---|

Examples (a) The tree was very tall. Jagjit could not climb it.

Wh. Q. : *Why could not Jagjit climb the tree?

[Or] Why couldn't Jagjit climb the tree?

(b) The tree was very tall. He could not climb the tree.

Wh. Q. : Why could he not climb the tree?

[Or] Why couldn't he climb the tree?

*Note The word 'not' is occasionally used before a Noun but always after a Pronoun (as a Subject) in Negative questions. However, the shortened form of Verb + not such as can't, couldn't, etc. is always used before the Subject—'Why couldn't Ram/he climb the tree?' ["Do not the police really remain?" **Oxford English Grammar** by **Sidney Greenbaum**]

Rule C If there is no such verb form of 'Be', 'Have' or a Modal, the helping verb 'Do' comes before the Subject and the root form of the main verb is placed after the Subject. [Do, does, did—as per number, person and tense]

| Wh-Pattern : Wh-word + 'Do' verb + Subject + Main verb + other words |
|---|

Examples (a) I play cricket in the afternoon. [Subject—'I']

Wh. Q. : What do you do in the afternoon? [Subject—'you']

[Or] What game do you play in the afternoon?

(b) He starts for a morning walk at 5 a.m.

Wh. Q. : When does he start for a morning walk?

(c) He left his home in the morning.

Wh. Q. : When did he leave his home?

(d) You must go home now.

Wh. Q. : What shall I do now?

**Note** 1st person in the content becomes 2nd person and 2nd person in the content becomes 1st person in Wh-question (I → you; you → I etc.)

**Rule D** If 'Who', 'Which' or 'What' becomes the Subject, no helping verb is required :

| Wh-Pattern : Wh-word + Main verb + other words |
|---|

**Examples** (a) Mother prepared the breakfast.
Wh. Q. : Who prepared the breakfast?
(b) Mr. Ali could have thought it.
Wh. Q. : Who could have thought it?
(c) Here are some books. Among them this is my book.
Wh. Q. : Which is your book?
(d) A tumult. I want to know about it.
Wh. Q. : What is the matter?

## STRUCTURE OF WH-QUESTIONS

(i) Wh-Word + 'Be'/'Have' Verb + Subject + other words
(ii) Wh-Word + Helping Verb + Subject + Main Verb + other words
(iii) Wh-Word + 'Do' Verb + Subject + Main Verb + other words
(iv) Wh-Word + Main Verb + other words

## WH-QUESTIONS BY USING 'WHO', 'WHOSE', 'WHOM'

### WHO

1. Content : 'Arms and the Man' is a play. The author is G. B. Shaw.
Wh. Q. : Who is the author of the play 'Arms and the Man'?
2. Content : 'Macbeth' is a tragedy. William Shakespeare wrote it.
Wh. Q. : Who wrote the tragedy 'Macbeth'?
3. Content : Iswar Chandra Vidyasagar is a great man. Everybody is familiar with him.
Wh. Q. : *Who is not familiar with the great man Iswar Chandra Vidyasagar?
4. Content : Everyone loves his motherland.
Wh. Q. : *Who does not love his motherhand?

**Note** The word 'not' is used after the auxiliary verb (or the main verb where there is no auxiliary) if 'who' is placed in the Interrogative form for 'Everybody'/ 'Everyone' in the Affirmative form of the Assertive pattern.

### WHOSE

1. Content : This umbrella is mine.
Wh. Q. : Whose umbrella is this?
2. Content : Rohon's plan succeeded at last.
Wh. Q. : Whose plan succeeded at last?

### WHOM

1. Content : I want to see Mohan.
Wh. Q. : Whom do you want to see?
2. Content : Jahanara visited her mother in the village.
Wh. Q. : Whom did Jahanara visit in the village?

## WHOM WITH PREPOSITIONS

[To whom, By whom, With whom, For whom, In whom, On whom, etc.]

### TO WHOM

1. Content : They will address the letter to the Chairman.
   Wh. Q. : To whom will they address the letter?

### BY WHOM

2. Content : They can get this work done by some people.
   Wh. Q. : By whom can they get this work done?

### WITH WHOM

3. Content : He went to visit the Taj with his friends.
   Wh. Q. : With whom did he go to visit the Taj?

### FOR WHOM

4. Content : The church-bell tolls on Sunday for the Christians.
   Wh. Q. : For whom does the church-bell toll on Sunday?

### IN WHOM

5. Content : We should find the best qualities in the teenagers.
   Wh. Q. : In whom should we find the best qualities?

### ON WHOM

6. Content : We should put our trust on some people.
   Wh. Q. : On whom should we put our trust?

## WH-QUESTIONS BY USING 'WHAT'

### WHAT

1. Content : My name is Amal.
   Wh. Q. : What is your name?
2. Content : I am laughing on seeing the cartoon.
   Wh. Q. : What makes you laugh?
3. Content : I read story-books in the evening.
   Wh. Q. : What books do you read in the evening?
4. Content : I want to know his address.
   Wh. Q. : What do you want to know? [or] What is his address?

**Note** 1st person (I, we, me, us, my, our) in the content becomes 2nd person (you, your) in Wh-questions if the speaker and interrogator are different persons.

## 'WHAT' WITH PREPOSITIONS

[To what, By what, For what, What for, In what, On what, From what, What like, etc.]

### TO WHAT

1. Content : He is moving towards south.
   Wh. Q. : To what direction is he moving?

### BY WHAT

2. Content : His dishonesty was proved by evidence.
   Wh. Q. : By what was his dishonesty proved?

### FOR WHAT

3. Content : We shall take this risk for some gain.
   Wh. Q. : For what will you take this risk?

### WHAT FOR

4. Content : I am waiting here for some purpose.
   Wh. Q. : What are you waiting here for?
5. Content : It was thundering. He woke up.
   Wh. Q. : What did he wake up for? [Or] What made him wake up?
6. Content : I am looking for the word in the dictionary.
   Wh. Q. : What are you looking for in the dictionary?

### IN WHAT

7. Content : He is superior to me in physical force.
   Wh. Q. : In what (way) is he superior to me/you?

### ON WHAT

8. Content : I depend on authentic books for collecting data.
   Wh. Q. : On what do you depend for collecting data?

### FROM WHAT

9. Content : I got this information from 'The Telegraph'.
   Wh. Q. : From what did you get this information?

### WHAT LIKE

10. Content : He was too much agitated. He looked like a demon.
    Wh. Q. : What did he look like when he was too much agitated?

## WH-QUESTIONS BY USING 'WHICH'

### WHICH

1. Content : This red-coloured book is mine.
   Wh. Q. : Which is your book? [Or] Which book is yours?
2. Content : The elephant is the biggest of the animals.
   Wh. Q. : Which is the biggest of the animals?
3. Content : Among all the boys Sourav came first.
   Wh. Q. : Which of the boys came first?
4. Content : I like only Darjeeling tea.
   Wh. Q. : Which tea do you like? [Or] Which kind of tea do you like?
5. Content : Someone has committed the crime. I like to know the person.
   Wh. Q. : Which one has committed the crime?

## 'WHICH' WITH PREPOSITIONS

[To which, For which, From which, In which, Of which, etc.]

### TO WHICH

1. Content : Our nation is marching to a certain goal, specify it.
   Wh. Q. : To which goal is our nation marching?

### FOR WHICH

2. Content : He will plead for some of the accused. Name them.
   Wh. Q. : For which of the accused will he plead?

### FROM WHICH

3. Content : He can get help from his friends in his distress.
   Wh. Q. : From which can he get help in his distress?

### IN WHICH

4. Content : Her strength lies in her honesty and chastity.
   Wh. Q. : In which does her strength lie?

### OF WHICH

5. Content : One of the persons present there saved the boy's life. Tell us who is that person.
   Wh. Q. : Which of the persons present there saved the boy's life? [Of which = Which of]

## WH-QUESTIONS BY USING 'WHEN'

### WHEN

1. Content : The teacher will come in the classroom at 11 a.m.
   Wh. Q. : When will the teacher come in the classroom?
2. Content : The Higher Secondary Examination is over. The result will be out in three months.
   Wh. Q. : When will the result of the Higher Secondary Examination be out?
3. Content : I stopped at the door of the hut. The door was closed.
   Wh. Q. : When did you stop at the door of the hut?
4. Content : A violent storm rose. The workers left the place.
   Wh. Q. : When did the workers leave the place?
5. Content : The temple remains closed by day. You must visit in the evening.
   Wh. Q. : When shall I visit the temple?
6. Content : Still widely read by general readers. Saratchandra's fame can never wane.
   Wh. Q. : *When can Saratchandra's fame wane?
7. Content : Shakespeare is a great dramatist. His glory can never fade.
   Wh. Q. : *When can the glory of Shakespeare, the great dramatist, fade?

## WH-QUESTIONS BY USING 'WHERE'

### WHERE

1. Content : An old window. She wants to pass her life in a holy place.
   Wh. Q. : Where does the old widow want to pass her life?

2. Content : He went to the theatre. He saw the actress there.
   Wh. Q. : Where did he go to see the actress?
3. Content : There was an accident. It took place near the Howrah Bridge.
   Wh. Q. : Where did the accident take place?
4. Content : There was a car. The car was waiting in front of our house.
   Wh. Q. : Where was the car waiting?
5. Content : The man was killed last night. His dead body was found in a deserted house.
   Wh. Q. : Where was the dead body of the man found?
6. Content : You need a map. It can be purchased from a bookshop.
   Wh. Q. : Wherefrom can I purchase a map?
7. Content : He was in Hyderabad. He committed a crime there.
   Wh. Q. : Wherein did he commit a crime?

## WH-QUESTIONS BY USING 'WHY'

### WHY

1. Content : The manager was late. His car was in the traffic jam.
   Wh. Q. : Why was the manager late?
2. Content : He was arrested by the police. He was involved in a bank dacoity.
   Wh. Q. : Why was he arrested by the police?
3. Content : Heavy rainfall. I could not reach the station in (on) time.
   Wh. Q. : Why could you not reach the station in (on) time?

## WH-QUESTIONS BY USING 'HOW'

### HOW

1. Content : A tape recorder. It operates mechanically.
   Wh. Q. : How does a tape recorder operate?
2. Content : The workers moved through the town shouting out their demands.
   Wh. Q. : How did the workers move through the town?
3. Content : The convict fled away. He did so by breaking the iron bars of the prison.
   Wh. Q. : How did the convict flee away from the prison?
4. Content : He examined the answerscripts. He did it leniently.
   Wh. Q. : How did he examine the answerscripts?
5. Content : The silken shari of the woman caught fire. A stove burst.
   Wh. Q. : How did the silken shari of the woman catch fire?
6. Content : The Indians are mostly farmers. They earn their livelihood by the sweat of their brow.
   Wh. Q. : How do the Indian farmers earn their livelihood?

## 'HOW' WITH ADVERB PARTICLES

[How much, How many, How long, How tall, How far, How often, etc.]

### HOW MUCH

1. Content : I like a teaspoonful of sugar in my tea.
   Wh. Q. : How much sugar do you like in your tea?

**HOW MANY**

2. Content : Only two hundred people attended the meeting.
   Wh. Q. : How many people attended the meeting?

**HOW LONG**

3. Content : We shall take five hours to do the job.
   Wh. Q. : How long will you take to do this job?

**HOW TALL**

4. Content : The man who visited us yesterday is 5′6″ tall.
   Wh. Q. : How tall is the man who visited you yesterday?

**HOW FAR**

5. Content : This is our house. It's 3 km from our school.
   Wh. Q. : How far is your house from your school?

**HOW OFTEN**

6. Content : I visit my friend's house once a week.
   Wh. Q. : How often (How many times) do you visit your friend's house?

**[1] INTERROGATIVE PRONOUNS [WHO, WHOSE, WHOM, WHICH, WHAT]**

Who construction (Who, Whose and Whom).

Who, Whose and Whom are the Interrogative with the same form in singular and plural. Who and Whose do not require any Auxiliary Verb as they themselves become the Subject of the Verb. There is an only exception when who is placed instead of everyone or everybody.

If 'everyone' or 'everybody' is used in the affirmative, it becomes negative in the Interrogative form. Hence the Auxiliary Verb 'do' is used to make it negative.

**Now study the examples :**

[Who, Whose or Whom is used only in case of person]

**SOME MORE EXAMPLES**

**WHO**

**[ No 'do' support is required where the Subject is 'Who' ]**

Statement : My mother prepared breakfast.
Question : Who prepared breakfast?
Statement : Your sister danced well on the stage.
Question : Who danced well on the stage?
Statement : The gardener is watering the garden.
Question : Who is watering the garden?
Statement : I am an ex-student of this school.
Question : Who are you? ['you' used here in place of 'I' because the speaker and the interrogator are two different persons]
Statement : The doctor will visit me today.
Question : Who will visit you today? ['you' used here in place of 'me' because the speaker and the interrogator are two different persons]

Statement : I shall go to the hospital to see my ailing brother.

Question : Who will go to the hospital to see your ailing brother? ['your' used here in place of 'my' because the speaker and the interrogator are two different persons and the verb must be 'shall' in place of 'will'. ]

Statement : I have a beautiful and portable garden-chair.

Question : Who has a beautiful and portable garden-chair?

Statement : The French stormed Ratisbon.

Question : Who stormed Ratisbon?

Statement : Yuri Gagarin was the fist man in space.

Question : Who was the first man in space?

Statement : Shakespeare wrote 'Macbeth'.

Question : Who wrote 'Macbeth'?
[Or] Who is the author of 'Macbeth'?

Statement : I was requested by my friend to do so.

Question : Who requested you to do so?

[Note : Here the sentence has been changed from Active to Passive voice.]

Statement : Someone is our friend and someone else is our enemy.

Question : Who is our friend and who is our enemy?

Statement : Someone may give me the correct number.

Question : Who can give you the correct number?

['Me' changed into 'you' because the speaker and the interrogator are different.]

Statement : Somebody may give me the correct number. Let me know about him.

Question : Who can give me the correct number?

['me' needs no change because the speaker and the interrogator are the same person]

Statement : Some person is allied to some other person. Tell me about them.

Question : Who is allied to whom?

Statement : Everyone is familiar with the name of Netaji.

Question : Who is not familiar with the name of Netaji?
[Or] Who does not know the name of Netaji?

Statement : Everyone loves his motherland.

Question : Who does not love his motherland?

Statement : Everybody knows his background.

Question : Who does not know his background?

[Auxiliary Verb 'do' may be required to change from everyone or everybody to Negative Interrogative.]

[No need of such type of change if there is 'No one' or 'Nobody' in a Statement]

Statement : No one could have thought of it.

Question : Who could have thought of it?

Statement : Nobody knows what will befall this country.

Question : Who knows what will befall this country?

Statement : No one would believe that he is a Chinese.

Question : Who would believe that he is a Chinese?

## SPECIAL USE OF WHO

Statement : I ask you to declare your identity.

Question : Who are you?

Statement : You have no authority to suggest this.

Question : Who are you to suggest this?

## 'WHO' IN PLACE OF 'WHOM'

Statement : I am afraid of somebody. Tell me about him.

Question : Who are you afraid of?

Statement : I am talking to Mr. Sen.

Question : Who are you talking to?

**Note :** In Modern English **'Who'** is used in place of **'Whom'**, especially when it is the Subject as well as an Object of a Preposition.

## WHOSE

[**A question starting with Whose does not need any Auxiliary verb.**]

Statement : This book is mine.

Question : Whose is this book? [Whose—Int. Pronoun]

[Or] Whose book is this? [Whose—Int. Adjective as it qualifies 'book'.]

Statement : These are my brother's trousers.

Question : Whose are these trousers? [ Whose—Int. Pronoun ]

[Or] Whose trousers are these? [ Whose—Int. Adj. ]

Statement : The queen's dress is the most beautiful.

Question : Whose is the most beautiful dress? [ Whose—Int. Pronoun ]

[Or] Whose dress is the most beautiful? [ Whose Int. Adj. ]

**Note** 'Whose' as Int. Adjective is more frequent in usage.

## WHOM

[**Auxiliary verb required where Subject is different in a Q. starting with Whom.**]

Statement : I want to see Lipika.

Question : Whom do you want to see? [Or] Who do you want to see?

Statement : Rekha visited her mother in the village.

Question : Whom did Rekha visit in the village?

Statement : The mad dog bit her brother.

Question : Whom did the mad dog bite?

Statement : I shall call somebody and somebody will be my messenger. Suggest the person.

Question : Whom shall I call and who will be my messenger?

[The speaker and the interrogator are same]

**Note : In Modern English 'Who' in place of 'Whom' is used as a pseudo Subject.**
**Wren & Martin**

## WHOM WITH PREPOSITIONS

**To whom, by whom, with whom, for whom, in whom, on whom, etc. :**

Statement : We shall address the letter to the chairman.

Question : To whom shall we address the letter?

[Speaker and interrogator remain same]

[Or] To whom will you address the letter?

[Speaker and interrogator remain different]

Statement : We are not responsible to anybody but to ourselves.

Question : To whom are we responsible (but to ourselves)?

Statement : We can get the work done by some people. Tell me their names.

Question : By whom can you get this work done?

['You' stands in place of 'I' or 'we' where 'tell me' appears after Statement.]

Statement : You went to visit the Taj with somebody. Let us know about him.

Question : With whom did you go to visit the Taj?

['You' appears in Question where 'I' or 'We' stays in Statement. If there is 'you' in Statement, then it should be 'you' in question.]

Statement : The church-bell tolls on Sunday for the Christians. Let us know about them.

Question : For whom does the church-bell toll on Sunday?

Statement : We should put our trust on some people.

Question : On whom should we put our trust?

Statement : We should trust in God.

Question : In whom should we trust?

Statement : You are pleading for somebody. Tell me his name.

Question : Whom are you pleading for?

Statement : You are pleading against someone. Tell me his name.

Question : Whom are you pleading against?

Statement : You are associated with somebody in this business. Tell me his name.

Question : Whom are you associated with in this business?

(with whom = whom ...... with)

## WHICH-CONSTRUCTIONS

**['Which' as an Interrogative Pronoun and as an Interrogative Adjectives]**

'Which' is used instead of objects or inanimate things (not persons). But when 'which' refers to selection or choice, it may be used for both persons and objects. Another important point is that when 'which' stands for the Subject of a Verb, no Auxiliary Verb is required. However, when there is another Subject, the Auxiliary Verb is needed.

### WHICH

Now study the examples :

Statement : This sky-coloured house is ours.

Question : Which is your house? [Which—Int. Pronoun]

Statement : This is Mr. Patel's car.
Question : Which is Mr. Patel's car? [Which—Int. Pronoun]
Statement : Martha is the best student in the class.
Question : Which one is the best student in the class? [Which—Int. Adj.]
[Here 'which' in place of Person comes to make anyone understand the selection.]
Statement : Of the ten boys, one came before all others. Point out the boy.
Question : Which one came first? [Which—Int. Adj.]
Statement : I like only Darjeeling tea.
Question : Which tea do you like? [Which—Int. Adj.]
[Here Auxiliary Verb 'do' used because 'you' appeared in place of 'which' as a subject of verb 'like'.]
Statement : The girl prefers sweet dishes.
Question : Which (kind of) dishes does the girl prefer? [Which—Int. Adj.]
['Which' turned into Interrogative Adjective where 'which' used with Noun.]

### WHICH WITH PREPOSITIONS

**To which, for which, from which, in which, of which** (= **which of** )

Statement : Our nation is marching to a certain goal. Specify it.
Question : To (= towards) which goal is our nation marching?
Statement : He will plead only for some of the accused. Name them.
Question : For which of the accused would he plead?
Statement : You conclude from some evidence that this is a case of suicide. Tell us about the evidence.
Question : From which (By which) evidence do you conclude that this is a case of suicide?
Statement : Her strength lies in her honesty and chastity. Tell us where her strength lies.
Question : In which characteristics does her strength lie?
Statement : One of the persons present there saved the boy's life. Tell us who is that person.
Question : Which of you saved the boy's life? [Of which = Which of .........]
Statement : Between you two, one will accompany me. Point him out.
Question : Which one of you will accompany me?

### WHAT-CONSTRUCTIONS ['What' as an Interrogative Pronoun]

The Interrogative Pronoun 'what' asks for **(i) a specific answer.** It also asks for **(ii) a choice or selection.** It may also ask idiomatically a variety of questions connected with the two above. Moreover, 'ever' may be added to 'what' to make a strong form of 'what' (what + ever = whatever) which is often used in spoken English, e.g., Whatever can be his intention in this matter?

Another point is that some prepositions are added to 'what' *e.g.*, to what, by what, for what, from what, in what and on what. So, all such uses of 'what' should also be remembered.

'What' does not require any Auxiliary verb when it stands for a subject. But when there is another subject of a verb, an Auxiliary verb is needed. However, no Verb is required, sometimes, in Spoken English :

**WHAT**

Now study the examples :

Statement : Olga has brought a box with her. It is a geometry box.
Question : What is this?

Statement : I am laughing on seeing the cartoon.
Question : What makes you laugh?
Statement : Infection on her vocal chord. She was silent.
Question : What made her silent?
Statement : Something makes it rather difficult to start. Let us know about it.
Question : What makes it so difficult to start?
Statement : There is no use running so fast.
Question : What is the use of running so fast?
[Question should be Affirmative when Statement is Negative.]
Statement : Jacob wants to know what he can do.
Question : What can Jacob do? [If you are Jacob, then, 'What can I do?']
Statement : I am sure of success.
Question : What about your success? [There is no verb.]
Statement : You seem to be in haste. Something must have happened.
Question : What happened to you?
Statement : Illness prevented me from attending the meeting.
Question : What prevented you from attending the meeting?

Statement : Heavy rain delayed the function today.
Question : What delayed the function today?
Statement : He left the place as he felt unwell.
Question : What did he do as he felt unwell?
Statement : Tell me your opinion.
Question : What am I to tell you? [Here the speaker and the interrogator are different. Otherwise 'What is your opinion?']
Statement : It matters little if the man from Mumbai fails to turn up.
Question : What matters if the man from Mumbai fails to turn up?
Statement : Something prompted you to come here this morning.
Question : What prompted you to come here this morning?
[Or] What brought you here this morning?

Statement : I am nothing but an ordinary player.
Question : What am I but an ordinary player? [Here the speaker and the interrogator are same.]
Statement : You have written something in reply. Let us know about it.
Question : What have you written in reply?

Statement : Gobinda got a prize for his hard work.
Question : What did Gobinda get for his hard work?
[Here Auxiliary Verb is 'do' because Gobinda is a Subject]
Statement : People will say bad things if you behave like this.
Question : What will people say if you behave like this?
[In this Statement, Auxiliary Verb is 'will' because People is a Subject]
Statement : You must mean something. Let us know about it.
Question : What do you say? [Here also, 'do' verb is applied because 'you' is a Subject]

**'WHAT' TO DENOTE PROFESSION**

Statement : My father is a teacher/doctor/farmer.
Question : What is your father?
Statement : He is a businessman.
Question : What is he?

Note carefully the following distinctions :

**(a)** **Who is he?**—enquires about the name or parentage of the person. The answer of such a quesion should be : He is Mr. Bimal Dasgupta; or, He is Bimal Babu, my neighbour; or, He is a Dasgupta; or, He is Sharmila's uncle, etc.

**(b)** **What is he?**—enquires about the profession or social status. The answer of such a question should be : He is a doctor; or, He is a businessman, etc.

**(c)** **Which is he?**—refers to selection or choice. The answer should be : He is the man on the left; or, He is the man with the hat on his head; or, He is the boy who stood first in the examination, etc.

**'WHAT' WITH PREPOSITIONS**

**To what, by what, for what, from what, in what, on what etc. :**

Statement : He is moving towards the south.
Question : In what (Towards which) direction is he moving?
Statement : His dishonesty was proved by evidence.
Question : By what was his dishonesty proved?
Statement : We shall take this risk for some gain.
Question : For what (gain) will you take this risk?
Statement : You are waiting still for some purpose. Tell us about it.
Question : What for are you waiting still? [What for = For what?]
Statement : You are here with a purpose. Let me know it.
Question : What are you here for?
[departing from sentence, preposition posted at the end]
Statement : You are looking for the word in the dictionary.
Question : What are you looking for in the dictionary?
[look for (group verb)]

Statement : She is looking at the moon.
Question : What is she looking at?

Statement : We are really poor in some matters.

Question : In what are we really poor?

Statement : He is being considered superior to me.

Question : In what (way) is he superior to me?
[Or] In what (way) am I inferior to him?

Statement : India is regarded 'backward' by some foreigners. Tell us the criteria of judgement.

Question : In what respects is India regarded 'backward' by some foreigners?

## SOME IDIOMATIC USES OF 'WHAT'

Statement : Something would follow the event. I ask about that.

Question : What next?

Statement : You have come. You have brought some news. Please tell us about it.

Question : What news?

Statement : We offered a proposal. We want to know how it is to be considered.

Question : What about our proposal?

Statement : It matters little that we are not rich.

Question : What though we are not rich?
[Or] So what?

Statement : You are suggesting something. It seems absurd. Let us know about it.

Question : What on earth are you suggesting?

Statement : You may tell us if there be any other meaning of the word.

Question : What else is the meaning of the word?

## [2] INTERROGATIVE ADJECTIVES [WHAT, WHICH AND WHOSE]

Sometimes what, which and whose are used with Nouns to ask questions. In that case, what, which and whose become Interrogative Adjectives instead of Interrogative Pronouns, as they qualify the Nouns following them.

### WHAT-CONSTRUCTIONS ['What' as an Interrogative Adjective]

Statement : I read story-books.

Question : What kind of books do you read?

Statement : I follow English newspapers.

Question : What kind of newspapers do you follow?

Statement : We prefer folding umbrellas.

Question : What kind of umbrellas do you prefer?

Statement : A peaceful agreement was signed between the two parties.

Question : What sort of agreement was signed between the two parties?

Statement : Dr. Sen is a man of disciplined manner.

Question : What kind of man is Dr. Sen?

Statement : No good will be served by his speech. [Here 'good' used as Noun]

Question : What good will be served by his speech?

Statement : It will not serve any good purpose really.
[Here 'good' used as Adjective]

Question : What good purpose will it serve really?

Statement : A good Honours qualification is needed for this post.
Question : What qualification is needed for this post?

**Note** that all these whats in the above sentences are Interrogative Adjectives as they qualify the Nouns following them.

### WHICH-CONSTRUCTIONS [Which as an Interrogative Adjective]

[No need of Auxiliary verb where Noun itself is a Subject added with 'which']

Statement : Mr. Sen is driving the red car.
Question : Which car is Mr. Sen driving?
[Which—Int. Adj. as it qualifies 'car']
Statement : The young girls are dancing.
Question : Which girls are dancing?
Statement : Only the best boy will be given a prize.
Question : Which boy will be given a prize?
Statement : The town has many parts. All parts are not clean. Mention the parts that are clean.
Question : Which parts of the town are clean?
Statement : Several items of food are there. Some are nutritious for the child. Point them out.
Question : Which items of food are nutritious for the child?
Statement : We want only Darjeeling tea.
Question : Which tea do you want? [Here 'you' is the subject of 'want' verb in place of 'which tea' and thus Auxiliary verb 'do' is used.]
Statement : The boys will play only the fast games.
Question : Which games will the boys play? [Here 'the boys' is the subject of 'play' verb in place of 'which games' and thus Auxiliary verb 'will' is used.]
Statement : I met Mr. Roy, the clerk.
Question : Which one did you meet? [Although 'which' used in relation with substance, yet it can be used in relation with person in respect of selection or choice.]

### WHOSE-CONSTRUCTIONS [Whose as an Interrogative Adjective]

[The interrogative sentences which are made of 'whose' need no Auxiliary Verb except Main Verb. When 'whose' has no Noun is called Interrogative Pronoun, but it will be treated as Interrogative Adjective when Noun is present because in that case it qualifies the Noun]

Statement : This book is Ramen's.
Question : Whose is this book? [Whose—Int. Pronoun]
[Or] Whose book is this? [Whose—Int. Adjective]
Such constuction as 'Whose book is this?' is preferred in usage.
Statement : It is somebody's house. Let us know the name of the owner.
Question : Whose house is this?
Statement : He is a competitor of someone. Let us know about him.
Question : Whose competitor is he?
Statement : This handwriting is by somecone. Let us know about him.
Question : Whose handwriting is this?

### [3] INTERROGATIVE ADVERBS [WHEN, WHERE, WHY AND HOW]

[When, Where, Why and How—within these Interrogative Adverbs, Auxiliary Verb is necessary to form interrogative questions with When. In case of Where, Why and How, sometimes it needs Main Verb, sometimes it needs Auxiliary Verb in different Subjects. Example—Where is the post-office? Where do you live? How are you? How did you get it?]

**When is an Interrogative Adverb of Time.**

**Where is an Interrogative Adverb of Place.**

**Why is an Interrogative Adverb of Reason or Purpose.**

**How is an Interrogative Adeverb of Degree, Manner etc.**

**WHEN**

Content : It was morning. He left for his home.
Question : When did he leave for his home?
Statement : The teacher will come soon.
[Or] The teacher will come in the afternoon.
Question : When will the teacher come?
Statement : The train will start at 13.20 hours (= 1.20 p.m.).
Question : When will the train start?
Statement : Nikhilesh goes to office daily at 9.30 a.m.
Question : When does Nikhilesh go to office daily?
Statement : He will return from office at 5 p.m.
Question : When will he return from office?
Statement : I don't remember having mentioned such a funny thing.
Question : When did I mention such a funny thing?
Statement : We shall not see his like again.
Question : When shall we see his like again?
Statement : The visitors left the place before sunset.
Question : When did the visitors leave the place?
Statement : We three shall meet again, Let us decide the definite time of meeting.
Question : When shall we three meet again? ['Macbeth' ; William Shakespeare.]
[Here the speaker and the interrogator are same persons.]
[Or] When will you three meet again? [Here speaker and interrogator are different.]
Statement : We are going to see the patient. Tell us the time.
Question : When are you going to see the patient?
Statement : We shall visit the Museum. Let us fix the time for it.

Question : When shall we visit the Museum?
Statement : Please tell us the date of your next birthday.
Question : When is your next birthday?
Statement : Such a happy day is unlikely to come again.
Question : When will such a happy day come?
Statement : The government is likely to withdraw the emergency rule. We want to know the possible time.

Question : When will the government withdraw the emergency rule?

Statement : His salary has been stopped with effect from last January. Let us know the date.

Question : Since when has his salary been stopped?

Statement : The modern period of history begins from a certain time. Let us know the date.

Question : From when does the modern period of history begin?

**WHERE**

Statement : My father is at home.

Question : Where is your father? [Here speaker and interrogator are different]

Statement : Atom bombs were dropped on Hiroshima and Nagasaki during the Second World War.

Question : Where were the atom bombs dropped during the Second World War?

Statement : Shelley is a great poet. He was born in England.

Question : Where was Shelley born?

Statement : The ONGC is to look for oil-fields in the Sundarban area.

Question : Where is the ONGC to look for oil-fields?

Statement : We want to know the location of the Cape of Good Hope.

Question : Where is the Cape of Good Hope?

Statement : There is no logic in his statement.

Question : Where is logic in his statement?

Statement : I don't find you here. Please respond if you are here.

Question : Where are you? [Speaker and Interrogator are different]

Statement : Just now we are at a particular place. I would like to know its exact location.

Question : Where are we now? [Speaker and Interrogator are same]

Statement : I am going to Mumbai tonight.

Question : Where are you going tonight. [Speaker and Interrogator are different]

Statement : I read a nice poem in 'Golden Treasury'. Someone asks the source.

Question : Where did you read such a nice poem? [Here, Auxiliary 'do' verb is needed because 'you' is a different Subject and the Main verb is 'read'.]

Statement : He comes from Assam. Let us know the place of his origin.

Question : Where does he come from?

Statement : It hampers our interests in certain points. Let us know the points.

Question : Where does it hamper our interest?

Statement : The kitten was hiding in a bush. My brother brought it from there.

Question : Where did your brother bring the kitten from?

Statement : It touches our national interests in certain matters. Let us know them.

Question : Where does it touch our national interest?

Statement : You will not find him anywhere just now.
Question : Where will you find him just now? [If Statement is negative, Question should be affirmative.]
Statement : In India, lions can be found in Gujarat.
Question : Where can lions be found in India?
Statement : People may reject our plea. I would like to know our position in that case.
Question : Where shall we stand if people reject our plea?

## 'WHERE' WITH PREPOSITIONS

Statement : I like to know the source of your strength.
Question : Wherein lies your strength?
Statement : You will recognise him in the crowd by the red shirt.
Question : Whereby will you recognise him in the crowd?
Statement : She is in a happy mood. Tell us the reason.
Question : Wherefore is she so happy? [Wherefore = for what reason]
Statement : Tuhina came from Assam.
Question : Where did Tuhina come from?

## WHY

Content : The tree was tall. He could not climb up it.
Question : Why could he not climb up the tree?
Statement : I am pale because I was sick.
Question : Why are you so pale?
Statement : The Manager was late because he was caught in the traffic jam.
Question : Why was the Manager late?
Statement : I just came to see you.
Question : Why did you come?
Statement : We honour him for his honesty.
Question : Why do you honour him?
Statement : I want to know the reason of his saying so.
Question : Why did he say so?
Statement : I like to know the purpose of your meeting the secretary.
Question : Why did you meet the secretary?/ Why will you meet the secretary?
Statement : I like to know the reason of your being too late.
Question : Why are you so late? ['so' in place of 'too']
Statement : I want to know the reason of their disturbing our studies everyday.
Question : Why are they disturbing our studies everyday?
Statement : Since you are poor you need not pay the money.
Question : Why need I not pay the money?
[Or] Why am I not to pay the money?

Statement : She saw a snake. She was frightened.
Question : Why was she afraid? [Or] Why was she frightened?

## HOW

Statement : Tell me about the condition of your health.
Question : How are you?
[Or] How do you do?
Statement : Let us know if the player is out (especially in a cricket match)
Question : How's that? [How is that? = Is the player out or not?]

Statement : I want to know the price of fish in the market.
Question : How much is fish (in the market)?
Statement : I am getting along well with my boss.
Question : How are you getting along with your boss?
Statement : He came to office by a car.
Question : How did he come to office?
Statement : He speaks French fluently.
Question : How does he speak French?
Statement : I caught the fox by its tail.
Question : How did you catch the fox?
Statement : We finished the work in time by hard labour.
Question : How did you finish the work in time?
Statement : I would like to know the process of operation of a telephone.
Question : How does a telephone operate?
Statement : Mohun Bagan played the match like a champion.
Question : How did Mohun Bagan play the match?
Statement : You were very rude. This cannot be expected of you.
Question : How could you be so rude?
Statement : Wars are caused because of men's greed.
Question : How are wars caused?

## HOW MUCH, HOW MANY, HOW LONG, ETC.

**How much; how many; how long; how tall; how far; how small; how good; how bad; how soon; how quickly; how often; how awkward; how inconvenient :**

Statement : We expect some help from him. Tell me the extent of your expectation.
Question : How much help do you expect from him?
Statement : There are two kgs of sugar in this pot.
Question : How much sugar is there in this pot?
Statement : Only a small number of people attended the meeting.
Question : How many people attended the meeting?

Statement : There are five thousand books in this library.
Question : How many books are there in this library?
Statement : This has been going on for several years.
Question : How many years has this been going on?
Statement : This is a 200 metre track for running the race.
Question : How long is the track for running the race?

Statement : This man is 160 cm tall.
Question : How tall is this man?
Statement : We shall take some time to do this job. Tell me the duration of time.
Question : How long will you take to do this job?
Statement : He is studying medicine. He will take five years to complete his study.
Question : How long will he take to complete his study of medicine?
Statement : This is my house. It is 3 km from our school.
Question : How far is your house from your school?
Statement : The river is two km from our house.
Question : How far is the river from your house?
Statement : I cannot believe all his words.
Question : How far is he believable?
Statement : His contribution was very small. Let us know its extent.
Question : How small was his contribution really?

Statement : I would like to know the utility of this machine.
Question : How good (useful) will this machine be?
Statement : His health is not so good. Let us know to what extent it is so.
Question : How bad is his health nowadays? [ 'not so good' > 'bad' ]
Statement : You are expected to come soon. Tell us when you are coming.
Question : How soon will you come?
Statement : You should complete the task quickly. Let me have an idea about it.
Question : How quickly can you complete the task?
Statement : You should take medicine twice daily.
Question : How many times should I take medicine?
Statement : I visit my friend's house once a week.
Question : How often do you visit your friend's house?
Statement : My position was awakward in the meeting. Tell us its extent.
Question : How awkward was your position in the meeting?
Statement : It is very inconvenient to stay with me in such a small room.
Question : How inconvenient is it to stay with you in such a small room?

**Note** If there is 'I' or 'we' in a statement, then 'you' will be used in Question, but if there is 'you' in the Statement, then 'I' or 'we' will be used in Question.

## WH-QUESTIONS FOR TWO OR MORE SENTENCES

Sometimes there are two or more sentences as content and from that content students are asked to form Wh-questions. In such cases we should form Wh-questions to get specific answers from two or more sentences as a whole :

1. **Wh-word** : Why
   Content : A street accident. He arrived late at his office.
   Ans. (for Q.) : Why did he arrive late at his office?

2. **Wh-word** : Who
   Content : 'Arms and the Man' (a play). The author is G. B. Shaw.
   Ans. (for Q.) : Who is the author of 'Arms and the Man'?
3. **Wh-word** : What
   Content : The boys won the match. They were shouting in joy.
   Ans. (for Q.) : What were the boys shouting for?
4. **Wh-word** : What
   Content : A bank robbery. His prompt action prevented it.
   Ans. (for Q.) : What prevented the bank robbery?
5. **Wh-word** : How
   Content : Rice sells at Rs. 20.00 a kilo. He wants to buy two kilos.
   Ans. (for Q.) : How much rice does he want to buy at Rs. 20.00 a kilo?
6. **Wh-word** : When
   Content : Extensive load shedding. The bus accident took place.
   Ans. (for Q.) : When did the bus accident take place?

7. **Wh-word** : Why
   Content : Rough weather. The traveller had to stop walking.
   Ans. (for Q.) : Why was the traveller compelled to stop walking?
   [Or] Why had the traveller stopped walking?
8. **Wh-word** : How
   Content : Management studies. The candidates will take two years to complete their studies.
   Ans. (for Q.) : How long (How many years) will the candidates take to complete their Management studies?
9. **Wh-word** : When
   Content : The sun sets. The birds home their way. ['home' as verb]
   Ans. (for Q.) : When do the birds home their way?

10. **Wh-word** : Why
    Content : The LPG leaked from the tanker. The police cordoned-off the area.
    Ans. (for Q.) : Why did the police cordon-off the area?
11. **Wh-word** : How
    Content : The doctor used a scooter. The doctor attended on the patients punctually.
    Ans. (for Q.) : How did the doctor attend on the patients puncutally? (Here the answer is—The doctor used a scooter.)
    [Or] : How did the doctor attend on the patients? (Here the answer is—punctually.)
12. **Wh-word** : Where
    Content : My friend collected the book from the college mart. He could not find it elsewhere.
    Ans. (for Q.) : Where did your friend collect the book?

13. **Wh-word** : Why
Content : Torrential rain last night. All pools are full to the brim.
Ans. (for Q.) : Why are all pools full to the brim?

14. **Wh-word** : What
Content : Sudden outbreak of enteric disease. He died.
Ans. (for Q.) : What did he die of? [Or] What is the cause of his death?

15. **Wh-word** : What
Conent : Drenched through and through. He was absent from the meeting.
Ans. (for Q.) : What made him absent in the meeting?
[Or] What was the cause of his absence from the meeting?

16. **Wh-word** : Why
Content : She was upset at the news. She could not speak.
Ans. (for Q.) : Why couldn't she speak?

17. **Wh-word** : Which
Content : The elephant is an animal. It is the biggest animal on land.
Ans. (for Q.) : Which ('Which' Int. Pron.) is the biggest animal on land?
[Or] : Which animal ('Which' Int. Adj.) is the biggest on land?

18. **Wh-word** : What
Content : My brother made a good result. I am happy.
Ans. (for Q.) : What made you happy?

19. **Wh-word** : Whose
Content : There is a house by the side of the river. It is Mr. Paul's.
Ans. (for Q.) : Whose house is by the side of the river?

20. **Wh-word** : Where
Content : He got a job. He left for Delhi.
Ans. (for Q.) : Where did he leave for after getting a job? (leave for—group verb)
[When Q. Word is 'Why'—Why did he leave for Delhi?]

21. **Wh-word** : Why
Content : Purnima was late for school. She missed the bus.
Ans. (for Q.) : Why was Purnima late for school?

22. **Wh-word** : What
Content : Nita was angry. The girl behind her gave her a push.
Ans. (for Q.) : What made Nita angry?

23. **Wh-word** : How
Content : The boy sprained his ankle. He was playing football.
Ans. (for Q.) : How did the boy sprain his ankle?

24. **Wh-word** : What
Content : He came to my place. He sought my help.
Ans. (for Q.) : What did he seek when he came to your place?

25. **Wh-word** : How
Content : He came in time. He did not know the coach number. So he missed the train.
Ans. (for Q.) : How did he miss the train though he came in time?

26. **Wh-word** : Why
Content : Reading trash is useless. We must not waste time in it.
Ans. (for Q.) : Why should we not waste time in reading trash?
(Here 'we' remains 'we' because it is a generalised statement.)

27. **Wh-word** : How
Content : Ghosts visit the house every now and then. The house is deserted.
Ans. (for Q.) : How often do the ghosts visit the deserted house?

28. **Wh-word** : When
Content : There was once a prediction about the British Empire. The sun would never set on it.
Ans. (for Q.) : When was the prediction about the British Empire that the sun would never set on it?

29. **Wh-word** : Where
Content : An immigrant differs from an emigrant. The difference lies in their meanings.
Ans. (for Q.) : Where does the difference between an immigrant and emigrant lie?

30. **Wh-word** : How
Content : I did the work in a particular way. You want information about it.
Ans. (for Q.) : How did you do the work?

31. **Wh-word** : What
Content : I may fail to turn up in time. It does not matter much.
Ans. (for Q.) : What does not (doesn't) matter much?

32. **Wh-word** : What
Content : He is wearing a shirt. It is brown.
Ans. (for Q.) : What coloured shirt is he wearing?

33. **Wh-word** : Which
Content : I want to see Mr. Patil. He is the Deputy Director.
Ans. (for Q.) : Which one do you want to see?
[Or] : Which Mr. Patil do you want to see?

34. **Wh-word** : How
Content : The house was destroyed. A tidal wave swept over it.
Ans. (for Q.) : How was the house destroyed?

35. **Wh-word** : How
Content : He comes here. Thrice a week.
Ans. (for Q.) : How often does he come here?

## EXERCISE

**[A] Ask questions to the answers given below with *Wh*-words at the beginning :**

1. An earthquake rocked the city at dead of night. (when)
2. There was none in the room. (who)
3. There is no logic in his statement. (where)
4. Everybody loves his motherland. (who)
5. I want to know his address. (what)
6. Since you are poor you need not pay the fees. (why)
7. The train runs at seventy kilometres per hour. (how)
8. They waited for their friends for four hours. (how)
9. I am sure of my success. (what)
10. They reached the place in the evening. (when)
11. There were sixty passengers in the bus. (how)
12. The students aim at passing the examination. (what)
13. This book belongs to my sister. (whom)
14. This umbrella belongs to my father. (whose)
15. I would like to know the next point. (what)
16. Such a happy day is unlikely to come again. (when)
17. It is difficult to find him out, he is so elusive. (where)
18. I do not expect you to be so rude. (how)
19. We shall never see his like again. (when)
20. I was speaking to Mr. Das. (whom/who)
21. The market is just a few minutes' walk. (how)
22. There is no sense in it. (where)
23. It matters little that we are not rich. (what)
24. Tell me your opinion. (what)
25. None can conquer death. (who)
26. No one could have done it. (who)
27. There is no use running so fast. (what)
28. Everybody knows that two and two make four. (who)
29. Tell me the condition of your father's health. (how)
30. His uncle is a business admininstrator. (what)
31. The man is 160 cm tall. (how)
32. This is a hundred metre track to run the race. (how)
33. I visit my friend's house once a month. (how)
34. She purchased a Baluchari saree. (which)
35. He usually goes to school by bus. (how)
36. They made him the President last year. (when)
37. He goes to St. Xavier's School. (which)
38. The boy has been working for four hours. (how)

39. Shakespeare's glory can never fade. (when)
40. He left the place as he felt unwell. (what)
41. I can't remember having mentioned such a funny thing. (when)
42. The girl prefers sweet dishes. (which)
43. This book is mine. (whose)
44. There are many books. The red book is mine. (which)

**[B] Frame *Wh*-questions for the content of two sentences :**

1. Content : 'Gulliver's Travel' is a novel. Swift wrote it.
   **Who** :
2. Content : 'Arms and the Man' (a drama). The author is G. B. Shaw.
   **Who** :
3. Content : 'Pride and Prejudice' (a novel). The writer is Jane Austen.
   **Who** :
4. Content : They are three brothers. This boy is the eldest.
   **Which** :
5. Content : Here are two books. I would like to get this one.
   **Which** :
6. Content : Here is my brother. He is an engineer.
   **What** :
7. Content : The train will arrive. They are waiting for it.
   **What** :
8. Content : His hairs are all white. He looks like an old man.
   **What** :
9. Content : He could not attend the meeting. The reason was his illness.
   **What** :
10. Content : He should withdraw from the contest. He proposed this.
    **What** :
11. Content : The train leaves Howrah. The time of departure is 2.20 p.m.
    **What** :
12. Content : I have come here with a purpose. I want some money.
    **What** :
13. Content : Foul weather. They postponed the journey.
    **Why** :
14. Content : The teacher arrived in the class. The students stood up.
    **When** :
15. Content : He killed the wild boar. He did so with a gun.
    **How** :
16. Content : A smart young man. He is just 18.
    **How** :
17. Content : The load was too heavy for him. He could not lift it.
    **Why** :

18. Content : A beautiful house. I want to know the name of its owner.
    **Whose** :
19. Content : He knew my difficulty. Still he sought my help.
    **What** :
20. Content : He didn't know the train number. So he missed it.
    **How** :
21. Content : His failure made him give up his study. You want to know the reason.
    **Why** :
22. Content : The Statesman is a newspaper. She reads it daily.
    **Which** :
23. Content : He was in Delhi. He came to Kolkata.
    **Where** :

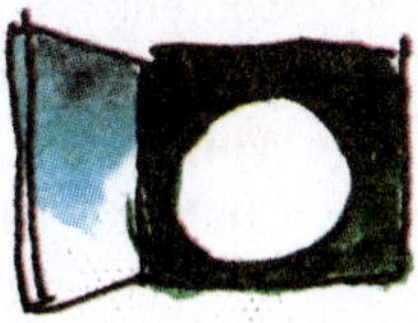

24. Content : A silver disc. The full moon looks like it.
    **What** :
25. Content : It was thundering. I woke up.
    **What** :
26. Content : A smart young lady. She is just eighteen.
    **How** :
27. Content : Reading trash is useless. We must not waste time on it.
    **Why** :
28. Content : Police firing. There was great commotion.
    **What** :
29. Content : Heavy rainfall. He could not reach the station in time.
    **Why** :
30. Content : He received an urgent message. He left suddenly.
    **What** :
31. Content : The road was slippery. He broke his leg.
    **How** :

32. Content : I was very upset at the news. I could not speak.
    **Why** :
33. Content : A serious accident. His prompt action prevented it.
    **What** :
34. Content : My sister fell ill. She could not sit for the examination.
    **Why** :
35. Content : The Oscar Award. A famous film-maker received it.
    **Who** :
36. Content : The boy was playing football. He broke his leg then.
    **When** :
37. Content : Only a small number of people attended the meeting. I want to know the number.
    **How** :

38. Content : The solar eclipse will occur. Tell me the date.
**When** :

39. Content : He has been called an 'outsider'. I want to know the yardstick of judgment. ['judgment' and 'judgement'—both are correct]
**What** :

40. Content : He comes here. Twice in a week.
**How** :

41. Content : He met with an accident. He gave up sports.
**What** :

42. Content : Rahul loves a girl dearly. You want to know her name.
**Whom** :

43. Content : My preference was for the last chapter of the book. You want to know the fact.
**Which** :

44. Content : The train runs at seventy kilometres per hour. You want to know the speed.
**How** :

45. Content : He reads English in the morning. You want to know the time.
**When** :

46. Content : It occurred near Hyderabad. You want to know the place.
**Where** :

47. Content : I shall help you to do the sum. You want to know the nature of help.
**How** :

48. Content : Here are some pens. Let me know about these.
**Whose** :

49. Content : He is expected to come soon. Tell us when he is coming.
**How** :

50. Content : The train leaves Howrah. It is at 10 a.m.
**What** :

51. Content : My friend is a journalist. You want to know his profession.
**What** :

52. Content : He likes to change his service for a better pay-scale. You want to know the reason of it.
**Why** :

53. Content : They talked about their childhood days so wistfully. You want to know the theme of their talking.
**What** :

54. Content : A stranger. He comes from London.
**Where** :

55. Content : A gold medal. The scholar won it in the competition.
**How** :

56. Content : Great noise. The teacher left the class in rage.
**Why** :

57. Content : Still widely read. Tagore's glory can never fade.
When :

58. Content : Old age prevented him from doing the work. You want to know the fact.
What :

59. Content : The difference begins from this point. You want to know the difference.
Where :

60. Content : Tell me the process in which the disease was cured. You want to know the process.
How :

61. Content : An earthquake rocked the city at dead of night. You want to know the time.
When :

62. Content : They invited Mr. Ghosh to preside over the meeting. You want to know the person.
Whom :

63. Content : Failure due to negligence. He could not pass the examination.
Why :

64. Content : Smooth operation of a machine. We are going well with the new washing machine.
How :

65. Content : Great excitement. They watched the football match between Argentina and Spain.
What :

66. Content : No watch with me. I want to know the time.
What :

67. Content : I am a student. No one knows it.
Who :

68. Content : I saw Kunwar Singh. He was lying on the bare mud floor.
Whom :

69. Content : Very idle. He failed in the examination.
What :

70. Content : Many mangoes on the table. He ate five mangoes.
How :

71. Content : There is a house on the top of the hill. It is Mr. Chhetri's.
Whose :

72. Content : This is a tool. This is used for boring.
What :

73. Content : A price has been put on his head. He has committed a lot of crimes.
Why :

74. Content : He snores. He disturbs others' sleep.
How :

75. Content : Inclement weather. They had to break the journey.

[Hint : Why had they to break the journey? This is not good English. Why were they compelled/bound to break the journey?]

**Why** :

76. Content : Skill, strength and stamina. China bagged many Olympic Gold Medals.

**How** :

77. Content : Marathon load-shedding. The theft was committed.

**When** :

78. Content : This is a cup. It is made of glass.

**What** :

79. Content : Here are some books. Show me yours.

**Which** :

80. Content : The Cape of Good Hope. I want to know the location.

**Where** :

81. Content : The boy takes exercise in the morning. I want to know the time.

**When** :

82. Content : He has been working for five hours. I want to know the period of time.

**How** :

83. Content : Subhas is my brother. He is a doctor.

**What** :

84. Content : 'As You Like It' (a play). The author is William Shakespeare.

**Who** :

85. Content : The market is just a few minutes' walk. You want to know the distance.

**How** :

86. Content : We suffer much. There is no reason behind it.

[Hint : Why do we suffer much for nothing? Here 'we' remains unchanged.]

**Why** :

87. Content : Seven hours. He can read at a stretch.

**How** :

88. Content : The owner of this house. He is unknown.

**Whose** :

89. Content : Extremely rough weather. He kept indoors all day long.

[Hint : Why was he kept ............? In such cases Wh-sentences should be made in passive voice.]

**Why** :

90. Content : Neil Armstrong. He was the first man to land on the moon.

**Who** :

91. Content : His friend was seriously ill. He went to his house.

[Hint : What made him go to ......? Not 'What did he go']

**What** :

92. Content : Excellent performance. Bibhas achieved great success.
    **What** :

93. Content : Homer's Eliad. It is a world-famous Greek epic.
    **What** :

94. Content : 'Gitanjali' written by Tagore. It brought him the Nobel Prize.
    **What** :

95. Content : The farmer toiled hard. He succeeded in producing plenty of wheat.
    **What** :

96. Content : 'Rabindra Sangeet' is an academic discipline. Kanika excels in it.
    **Which** :

97. Content : Rash driving. The driver met with an accident.
    **How** :

98. Content : Maradona scored a marvellous goal. His fans went into raptures over him.
    **What** :

99. Content : Kapil Dev scored a century. He did it graciously.
    **How** :

100. Content : Tsunami 2004. It caused devastation in South-East Asia.
    **What** :

# 29  FORMATION OF WORDS/ANTONYMS

## HOW CAN WE FORM ONE WORD FROM ANOTHER?

You may compile a good Dictionary of your own if you learn formation of words in English.

**Such words are fomed in two ways : [1] Primary, and [2] Seocndary Derivatives.**

### [1] PRIMARY DERIVATIVES

**Primary Derivatives** are those Derivatives that form words by making some change in the body of the simple word.

**[a] Formation of Nouns from Verbs**

| Verbs | Nouns | Verbs | Nouns |
|---|---|---|---|
| advise | advice | bind | bond |
| bite | bit | bless | bliss |
| break | breach | choose | choice |
| chop | chip | dig | ditch |
| float | fleet (warships) | fly | flea (**Wren & Martin**) |
| gape | gap | grieve | grief |
| live | life | lose | loss |
| prove | proof | sing | song |
| sit | seat | speak | speech |
| strike | stroke | stick | stitch (**Wren & Martin**) |
| strive | strife | wake | watch (**Wren & Martin**) |
| weave | web | weave | web (**Wren & Martin**) |

**[b] Formation of Nouns from Adjectives**

| Adjective | Noun | Adjective | Noun |
|---|---|---|---|
| hot | heat | proud | pride |

**[c] Formation of Adjectives from Verbs and Nouns**

| Verbs | Adjectives | Nouns | Adjectives |
|---|---|---|---|
| float | fleet (swift) | milk | milch |
| lie (**Wren & Martin**) | low | wit (**Wren & Martin**) | wise |

### [d] Formation of Verbs from Nouns

| Nouns | Verbs | Nouns | Verbs | |
|---|---|---|---|---|
| bath | bathe | glass | glaze | (**Wren & Martin**) |
| belief | believe | gold | gild | (″) |
| blood | bleed | grass | graze | (″) |
| brood | breed | knot | knit | (″) |
| breath | breathe | price | prize | (″) |
| cloth | clothe | sale | sell | (″) |
| dog | dodge (**Martin**) | sooth | soothe | (″) |
| drop | drip | tale | tell | (″) |
| food | feed | wreath | wreathe | (″) |

### [e] Formation of Verbs from Adjectives

| Adjectives | Verbs | Adjectives | Verbs |
|---|---|---|---|
| cool | chill | hale (healthy) | heal |
| full | fill | fresh | frisk |

**Note** The change in the body of a verb for forming Tense is not a Derivative as there is no change of meaning of the word.

## [2] SECONDARY DERIVATIVES

**Secondary Derivatives** are those Derivatives that form words by an addition to the beginning or to the end of a word.

An addition to the beginning of a word is a **Prefix** and an addition to the end is a **Suffix**.

Danger (N.) > En + danger = Endanger (V.) [En—Prefix]

Glad (Adj.) > Glad + en = Gladden (V.) [En—Suffix]

**Prefix** : Pre (= before) fix = that which is fixed before a word in order to form a new word.

### PREFIXES

| Prefix (with meaning) | Base word | Formation of new words |
|---|---|---|
| a (= on, in) | bed | abed (= on bed)  |
| | board | aboard (= on board) |
| | shore | ashore (= on the shore) |
| | side | aside (= on side)  |
| | sleep | asleep (= in sleep) |
| | way | away (= on the way) |
| a (= off, out, from, up) | rise | arise |
| | rouse | arouse |
| | wake | awake |
| | shamed | ashamed |

| Prefix (with meaning) | Base word | Formation of new words |
|---|---|---|
| a (= not, without) | theist<br>theism<br>pathy | atheist (= not theist)<br>atheism<br>apathy (= without pathy) |
| ab (= bad, away, not) [opposite] | use<br>normal | abuse (= bad use)<br>abnormal (= not normal) |
| ac (to) | count | account |
| ad (to) | join | adjoin (= to join) |
| all > al (= all) | one<br>most<br>ready<br>together | alone (= all one = only)<br>almost (= all most)<br>already (= all ready)<br>altogether (= all together) |
| ap (= to) | point | appoint |
| ante, anti (= before)<br>anti (= against) [opposite] | date<br>chamber<br>cipation<br>pathy<br>dote<br>social<br>septic<br>climax | antedate (= before date)<br>antechamber<br>anticipation<br>antipathy<br>antidote<br>antisocial<br>antiseptic<br>anticlimax |
| arch (= chief) | bishop | archbishop |
| auto (= self)  | graph<br>mobile<br>biography | autograph<br>automobile<br>autobiography |
| be (= by)<br>be (= make)<br>be (= cut off) | side<br>fool/little<br>head | beside (= by the side)<br>befool/belittle<br>behead |
| bi (= two)<br>co (= with) | cycle<br>lateral<br>exist<br>operate<br>education | bicycle<br>bilateral<br>coexist<br>cooperate<br>coeducation  |
| contra, counter (= against, with) | diction<br>action<br>part | contradiction<br>counteraction<br>counterpart |
| de (= down, reversal) | scend<br>merit<br>train | descend<br>demerit<br>detrain |

| Prefix (with meaning) | Base word | Formation of new words |
|---|---|---|
| di (= twice) | oxide | dioxide |
| dia (= through) | meter | diameter |
| dis (= apart, not) [opposite] | allow<br>join<br>honour | disallow<br>disjoin<br>dishonour |
| en (= in, on) | act<br>cage | enact (= on action)<br>encage (= in the cage) |
| ex (= out of, former) | tract<br>student | extract<br>exstudent |
| extra (= beyond) | ordinary | extraordinary |
| il, im, in, ir (= not) [opposite] | legal<br>possible<br>ability<br>regular | illegal<br>impossible<br>inability<br>irregular |
| inter (= among, within) | school<br>link<br>change | inter-school (= among the schools)<br>interlink<br>interchange |
| fore (= before) | cast<br>tell<br>father | forecast<br>foretell<br>forefather |
| hemi (= half) | sphere | hemisphere |
| homo (= like)<br>hyper<br>(over, beyond) | geneous<br>acidity<br>sensitive | homogeneous<br>hyperacidity<br>hypersensitive |
| hypo (= under) | acidity<br>thesis | hypoacidity<br>hypothesis |
| mal (= bad, ill) [opposite] | practice<br>nutrition | malpractice (= bad practice)<br>malnutrition (= ill-nutrition) |
| mis (= bad, less) [opposite] | conduct<br>fortune<br>fire<br>use | misconduct<br>misfortune<br>misfire (= failure to go-off)<br>misuse (= bad use) |
| mono (= single) | logue | monologue |
| non (= not) [opposite] | sense<br>stop | nonsense<br>non-stop |

| Prefix (with meaning) | Base word | Formation of new words |
|---|---|---|
| pan (= all) | theism | pantheism |
| post (= after) | mortem<br>war | postmortem<br>postwar |
| pre (= befoe) | fix<br>Independence | prefix<br>Pre-Independence |
| peri (= round) | meter | perimeter |
| re (= again) | build<br>consider | rebuild<br>reconsider |
| retro<br>(= backwards) | grade<br>spect | retrograde<br>retrospect |
| semi (= half) | circle<br>final<br>vowel | semicircle<br>semifinal<br>semivowel |
| sub (= under) | way<br>committee | subway<br>subcommittee |
| super<br>(above, beyond) | fine<br>man<br>natural | superfine<br>superman<br>supernatural |
| sym (= with) | pathy | sympathy |
| to (= this) | day<br>night | today<br>tonight |
| tres, trans<br>(= across) | pass<br>form<br>plant | trespass<br>transform<br>transplant |
| ultra<br>(= beyond) | modern<br>liberal<br>violet | ultramodern<br>ultraliberal<br>ultraviolet |
| un (= not)<br>[opposite] | able<br>armed<br>willing<br>worthy | unable<br>unarmed<br>unwilling<br>unworthy |
| vice<br>(= in the place of) | president<br>principal<br>chancellor | vice-president<br>vice-principal<br>vice-chancellor |

## SUFFIXES

### [ FORMING NOUNS ]

[1] **Denoting agent or doer** :

| Suffix | Formation of words |
|---|---|
| -er, -eer (doer) | reader, driver, maker, hunter, painter, fighter, speaker, worker, writer, ruler, convener, producer; auctioneer, mountaineer |
| -ar (doer) | beggar, liar, scholar, etc.  |
| -or (doer) | donor, sailor, vendor, supervisor |
| -yer (doer) | lawyer |
| -ess (feminine doer)<br>-an, -en, -on (doer) | actress, hostess, authoress, poetess, waitress,<br>artisan, citizen, surgeon |
| -ist (doer)  | dentist, dramatist, typist, novelist, atheist, theist, anarchist, terrorist, pragmatist, optimist, pessimist, antagonist, moralist, egoist, scientist, royalist, socialist |
| -ee (agent) | addressee, allottee, desiree, nominee, absentee, payee, trainee, examinee |

[2] **Denoting state, action, result of an action, condition, being, etc.**

| | |
|---|---|
| -age | bondage, breakage, leakage, marriage, carriage, postage, bandage, package, stoppage, etc. |
| -al | arrival, denial, approval, recital |
| -ance | abundance, appearance, assistance, brilliance, endurance, disturbance, repentance, utterance, etc. |
| -ence | obedience, absence, excellence, presence, prudence, innocence, difference, dependence |
| -cy | accuracy, fancy, lunacy, bankruptcy, decency, emergency, frequency, urgency, etc. |
| -ice | service, cowardice |
| -ion | action, union, revision, opinion |
| -ity, -ty | ability, electricity, sensibility, falsity, unity, reality, visibility, flexibility, cruelty, frailty, safety |
| -ist | artist, chemist, dramatist, essayist, novelist, etc. |
| -ation, -tion, -ion, -sion  | creation, formation, information, confirmation, reformation, examination, reflection, opposition, translation, agitation, starvation, stagnation, redemption, confession, compulsion, illusion, inclusion, extension, procession, confusion, conversion |

| Suffix | Formation of words |
|---|---|
| -ism | barbarism, criticism, hooliganism, patriotism, socialism |
| -logy | biology, ecology, geology, physiology, zoology |
| -ment | acknowledg(e)ment, argument, agreement, arrangement, improvement, judgement, punishment, fulfilment, merriment, bereavement |
| -mony | parsimony, matrimony, testimony |
| -ness | boldness, darkness, goodness, kindness, happiness, sharpness, sweetness, etc. |
| -red | kindred, hatred |
| -ship | hardship, friendship, lordship, membership, partnership, scholarship, etc. |
| -th | health, wealth, growth, length, breadth, stealth, etc. |
| -tion | dictation, conviction, botheration, translation, etc. |
| -tude | fortitude, magnitude, servitude |
| -hood | boyhood, childhood, brotherhood, manhood, womanhood |
| -dom | freedom, kingdom, martyrdom, wisdom |

[3] **Forming diminutives** :

| | |
|---|---|
| -let, -et | booklet, leaflet, cutlet, anklet, brooklet, streamlet, rivulet, locket, lancet |
| -ling | sapling, duckling, stripling (= young one), darling < dear |
| -kin, -en | lambkin, napkin, chicken < cock, kitten < cat, maiden < maid |
| -ock | hillock, bullock |

[4] **Denoting place** :

| | |
|---|---|
| -ary, -ery, -ry | dispensary, library, nunnery, treasury |

**N.B.** *acknowledgement/acknowledgment and judgement/judgment—both forms are correct—COD

## SUFFIXES

### [ FORMING ADJECTIVES ]

| | |
|---|---|
| -al | legal, royal, mental, fatal, mortal, national, brutal, official, political, physical, frontal, final, tidal, educational, optional, fictional, natural, horizontal, coastal, cultural, functional, provincial, provisional, vital, etc. |

| Suffix | Formation of words |
|---|---|
| -ic, -ical | angelic, cynic, historic, historical, tragic, tragical, Miltonic, Platonic, democratic, energetic, telegraphic, comic, comical, domestic, patriotic, economic, economical, musical, classical, biological, geological, philosophical, critical, mechanical, satirical, stoical, technical, etc. |
| -ish | Irish, Turkish, Polish, Swedish, selfish, boyish, childish, blackish, foolish, hellish, devilish, feverish, slavish, bookish, snobbish, yellowish, whitish |
| -istic | characteristic, fantastic, antagonistic, optimistic, pessimistic, sarcastic |
| -id | humid, vivid, lucid |
| -ile | fragile, juvenile, servile |
| -ine | feminine, canine, feline, divine |
| -ive | active, attentive, sportive, creative, attractive, productive, affirmative, negative, talkative, formative, constructive, conservative, instinctive, intuitive |
| -ian, -an | Indian, Italian, American, Russian, Tibetan, African, Egyptian, Victorian, etc.  |
| -ar | familiar, regular |
| -ary | contrary, customary, honorary, necessary, documentary, etc. |
| -ate | fortunate, obstinate, temperate |
| -ed | gifted, talented, learned, cultured, spotted, salted, spiced, coloured, moneyed, wretched |
| -en | wooden, earthen, leaden, golden, brazen, silken, woollen |
| -able | laughable, eatable, drinkable, movable, lovable, formidable, answerable, reliable, preferable, breakable, forgettable, separable, charitable, reasonable, choicable, arguable, objectionable, comfortable, suitable, culpable, valuable, pitiable, inflamable |
| -ible | admissible, divisible, sensible, indelible, intelligible, audible, incorrigible, possible, visible |
| -fold | two-fold, three-fold, manifold |
| -full > full | beautiful, hopeful, joyful, fearful, fruitful, aweful, helpful, handful, forgetful, cheerful, dutiful, grateful, faithful, merciful, spoonful, thoughtful, useful, etc. |
| -less | fearless, cheerless, helpless, hopeless, faithless, merciless, shameless, senseless, boundless, meaningless, nameless, countless, reckless, soundless, lifeless, restless, penniless, tireless, aimless, lawless, thoughtless, useless, etc. |

| Suffix | Formation of words |
|---|---|
| -ly | manly, godly, saintly, sickly, lowly, friendly, earthly, heavenly, lively, leisurely, miserly, cowardly, weekly, bi-weekly, fortnightly, monthly, yearly |
| -y  | healthy, wealthy, greedy, needy, dirty, thirsty, noisy, bloody, airy, bony, handy, fishy, fatty, choosy, mossy, rocky, sandy, leafy, sunny, stormy |

## SUFFIXES

### [ FORMING VERBS ]

| -ate | assassinate, captivate, exterminate, annihilate |
|---|---|
| -en  | broaden, gladden, lengthen, shorten, fatten, thicken, blacken, darken, deepen, harden, soften, strengthen, moisten, loosen, sharpen, widen |
| -er | chatter, clutter, fritter, flutter, glitter, glimmer |
| -ish | publish, nourish, punish, banish |
| -ise, -ize | civilise, civilize, organise, organize, apologise, apologize, realise, realize, legalise, legalize, penalise, penalize, mechanise, mechanize, fertilise, fertilize, popularise, popularize, victimise, victimize etc. |
| | [**N.B.** 's' not 'z' in advertise, despise, surprise as there is no Suffix] |
| -se | cleanse, rinse, etc. |
| -fy  | amplify, beautify, certify, classify, fortify, Frenchify, identify, modify, magnify, rectify, signify, simplify, satisfy, speechify, sanctify, terrify, vilify |

## SUFFIXES

### [ FORMING ADVERBS ]

Most Adverbs are formed by adding **-ly** to Adjectives :

| -ly | badly, sadly, madly, boldly, clearly, oddly, deeply, shortly, softly, actively, thinly, entirely, fully, partly, partially, exactly, absolutely, initially, directly, passively, precisely, evidently, slowly, forcefully, fortunately, sharply, bluntly, angrily, possibly, quickly, happily, hopefully, hopelessly, livingly, smilingly, curiously, historically, widely, etc. |
|---|---|
| -wise | clockwise, likewise, otherwise |
| ward(s) | backwards, homewards, towards, upward(s), downward(s) |

## ANTONYMS

### [ OPPOSITE WORDS ]

**Antonyms** or **opposite words may be formed in three ways :**

[1] **by adding a prefix like**—un, non, dis, mis, anti, de, il, im, in, ir

[2] **by adding a suffix like**—less; full > ful

[3] **by using a new word.**

**[1] Antonyms formed by adding prefixes :**

| Prefix | Base words | Opposite words/Antonyms |
|---|---|---|
| | able  | unable  |
| | armed | unarmed |
| | kind | unkind |
| | common | uncommon |
| | fit | unfit |
| | fortunate | unfortunate |
| **un** | conscious | unconscious |
| | developed | undeveloped |
| | controlled | uncontrolled |
| | pleasant | unpleasant |
| | popular | unpopular |
| | wise | unwise |
| | social | unsocial |
| | sense | nonsense |
| **non** | stop | nonstop |
| | violence | nonviolence |
| | agree | disagree |
| | allow | disallow |
| | comfort | discomfort |
| | honest | dishonest |
| | honesty | dishonesty |
| **dis** | honour | dishonour |
| | like | dislike |
| | obey | disobey |
| | obedient | disobedient  |
| | please | displease |
| | appear | disappear |
| **mal** | practice | malpractice |
| | nutrition | malnutrition |

| Prefix | Base words | Opposite words/Antonyms |
|---|---|---|
| mis | conduct | misconduct |
| | fortune | misfortune |
| | interpret | misinterpret |
| | lead | mislead |
| | happening | mishap |
| | use | misuse |
| | understand | misunderstand |
| anti | dote | antidote |
| | climax | anticlimax |
| | sympathy | antipathy |
| | septic | antiseptic |
| | social | antisocial |
| | toxin | antitoxin |
| de | control | decontrol |
| | merit | demerit |
| | hoard | dehoard |
| | code | decode |
| | entrain | detrain |
| | enthrone | dethrone |
| il | legal | illegal |
| | legible | illegible |
| | logical | illogical |
| | liberal | illiberal |
| | literate | illiterate |
| im | balance | imbalance |
| | partial | impartial |
| | possible | impossible |
| | patient | impatient |
| | personal | impersonal |
| | potent | impotent |
| | probable | improbable |
| | pure | impure |
| | moral | immoral |
| | mortal | immortal |
| | mature | immature |
| | mobile | immobile |
| | movable | immovable |
| | measurable | immeasurable |

| Prefix | Base words | Opposite words/Antonyms |
|---|---|---|
| in | ability | inability |
| | active | inactive |
| | capable | incapable |
| | animate | inanimate |
| | accurate | inaccurate |
| | credible | incredible |
| | attentive | inattentive |
| | decent | indecent |
| | definite | indefinite |
| | distinct | indistinct |
| | divisible | indivisible |
| | discipline | indiscipline |
| | justice | injustice |
| | sensible | insensible |
| | separable | inseparable |
| | stability | instability |
| | sufficient | insufficient |
| | valid | invalid |
| | visible | invisible |
| ir | rational | irrational |
| | regular | irregular |
| | relevant | irrelevant |
| | repairable | irrepairable/irreparable |
| | recoverable | irrecoverable |
| | resistible | irresistible |
| | responsible | irresponsible |
| | resolute | irresolute |

**[2] Antonyms formed by adding Suffix :**

| Prefix | Base words | Opposite words/Antonyms |
|---|---|---|
| full (= ful) & less | careful | careless |
| | colourful | colourless |
| | hopeful | hopeless |
| | fearful | fearless |
| | cheerful | cheerless |
| | faithful | faithless |
| | merciful | merciless |
| | useful | useless |

**[3] Antonyms by using new words :**

| Base words | Opposite words/Antonyms |
|---|---|
| above | below |
| accept | reject |
| big | small |
| bold | timid, coward |
| cold | hot |
| cool | warm |
| different | similar |
| drowsy | wakeful |
| dead | alive |
| early | late |
| entirely | partially |
| exposed | concealed |
| expanding | contracting |
| fat | thin |
| forget | remember |
| general | specific |
| growing | decaying |
| hard | soft |
| hope | despair |
| humble | proud |
| humorous | serious |
| kind | cruel |
| long | short |
| lend | borrow |
| life | death |
| liberty | bondage |
| meek | proud |
| minor | major |
| motion | stillness |
| masculine | feminine |
| old | young |
| oppose | support |
| optimism | pessimism |
| peevish | genial |
| pleasure | pain |
| professional | amateur |
| quick | slow |

| Base words | Opposite words/Antonyms |
|---|---|
| reduce | increase |
| reveal | conceal |
| rude | polite |
| rich | poor |
| right | wrong |
| strict | lenient |
| strong | weak |
| survive | die |
| tall | dwarf |
| top | bottom |
| touchy | genial |
| ugly | beautiful |
| unity | diversity |
| vague | clear |
| war | peace |
| weal | woe |
| wither, decay | flourish, thrive |

## HOMOGRAPH

**Homographs** are the words of same spelling but different in pronunciaton and meaning.—**Oxford ALD**

**Example :** Bow (bou—a device for shooting arrows), and bow (bau—bend to show respect).

## HOMONYMS

**Homonyms** are "two or more words having the same spelling and pronunciation but different meanings and origins." **Compact Oxford Dictionary by Catherine Soanes**

**Examples :** Can (pot or container) and Can (ability);

Bat (equipment for playing cricket) and Bat (a kind of flying mammal);

Cricket (a kind of game) and Cricket (a kind of insect that makes a shrill sound);

Kite (a bird of prey of the hawk family) and Kite (a toy-framework made to fly);

Right (correct) and Right (opposite to left).

## HOMOPHONES

**Homophones** are "Each of two or more words having the same (almost same) pronunciation but different meanings, origins or spelling." e.g. Dear (favourite) and Deer (a kind of animal) **Compact Oxford Dictionary by Catherine Soanes**

**Examples :**

| PAIRS | MEANINGS |
|---|---|
| 1. **Accept** | Agree to take |
| **Except** | Besides/excluding |
| 2. **Access** | A way of a approaching |
| **Excess** | The amount beyond due limits |

| PAIRS | MEANINGS |
|---|---|
| **3. Affect** | Act badly |
| **Effect** | Result |
| **4. Birth** | Origin/parentage |
| **Berth** | A bunk in a ship or train |
| **5. Career** | Progress through life/occupation |
| **Carrier** | One that carriers something |
| **6. Cite** | Quote or mention as an example |
| **Site** | The place where a building stands or an event takes place |
| **7. Check** | Control/check the motion |
| **Cheque** | A written order to a bank to pay |
| **8. Canvas** | Coarse cloth for tents, painting, etc. |
| **Canvass** | Plead for goods, votes etc. |
| **9. Cast** | throw/emit something |
| **Caste** | division of social classes, especially in Hinduism |
| **10. Cease** | Come or bring to an end |
| **Seize** | Take hold of a thing forcibly or by legal right |
| **11. Coarse** | Rough or crude in texture or manner |
| **Course** | The direction taken or intended |
| **12. Council** | A group of persons to advise or organize something |
| **Counsel** | Advice or suggestions |
| **13. Complement** | (Gr.) the word(s) added to a verb to complete the predicate |
| **Compliment** | Formal greetings/a gift |
| **14. Dairy** | A place where milk products are processed |
| **Diary** | A daily record of personal events or thoughts |
| **15. Decease** | death |
| **Disease** | Faulty functioning of a bodily process |
| **16. Die** | Cease to be alive |
| **Dye** | Colour, esp. by dipping in a liquid |
| **17. Eligible** | Regarded as suitable |
| **Illegible** | Not legible/hard to read |
| **18. Fare** | The price charged for travelling |
| **Fair** | An exhibition of commercial goods |
| **19. Farm** | An area for raising crops |
| **Firm** | A commercial establishment/steady or securely fixed |
| **20. Lose** | Cease to have something |
| **Loose** | Not rigidly fixed |
| **21. Lever** | A device on a fixed point |
| **Liver** | An organ secreting bile |
| **22. Massage** | Rubbing and kneading the body to lesson stiffness |
| **Message** | A spoken or written communication |

| PAIRS | MEANINGS |
|---|---|
| **23. Peace** | A state of harmony |
| **Piece** | One of the portions of a thing |
| **24. Plane** | A flat or level surface/an aeroplane |
| **Plain** | Easy to see or understand/not intricate |
| **25. Pole** | A long piece of wood or metal used as a support/either end of the earth's axis |
| **Poll** | Voting at an election |
| **26. Principal** | First in rank or importance |
| **Principle** | A general rule of conduct |
| **27. Quiet** | Free from disturbance or sound |
| **Quite** | Completely/entirely |
| **28. Root** | Supporting part of a plant/source or basis |
| **Route** | The course or way to get to a place |
| **29. Sole** | One and only |
| **Soul** | The spiritual or immortal element of a peson |
| **30. Steal** | Take othe person's things secretly and without right or permission/move secretly |
| **Steel** | A very strong alloy of iron and carbon |
| **31. Tail** | The hindermost hanging part of an animal |
| **Tale** | A narrative or story |
| **32. Way** | A path or road |
| **Weigh** | Measure the weight of something |

**Note** See the usage of HOMOPHONES in Chapter 32.

## WORDS EXPRESSING THE CRIES OF ANIMALS

Learn carefully the following verbs which denote the cries of some of the lower creatures

1. The apes gibber
2. The asses bray
3. The bears growl
4. The bees hum
5. The birds chirp, twitter
6. The buffaloes bellow
7. The bulls bellow
8. The calves low
9. The camels grant
10. The cats mew
11. The cattle low
12. The cocks crow
13. The cows low
14. The crows caw
15. The cuckoos coo
16. The doves coo
17. The ducks quack
18. The dogs bark
19. The eagles scream
20. The elephants trumpet
21. The flies buzz
22. The frogs croak
23. The geese cackle
24. The goats bleat
25. The hawks scream
26. The hens cackle/cluck

27. The horses neigh
28. The jackals howl/yell
29. The kittens mew
30. The lambs bleat
31. The lions roar
32. The monkeys chatter, gibber
33. The pigs grunt
34. The owls hoot
35. The oxen low/bellow
36. The parrots screech
37. The peacocks scream
38. The pigeons coo
39. The serpents hiss
40. The sheep bleat
41. The squirrels squeak
42. The sparrows chirp, twitter
43. The vultures scream
44. The wolves howl

## WORDS INDICATING YOUNG ONES OF ANIMALS

Read carefully the following words for the young ones of animals :

| | | |
|---|---|---|
| 1. Bear — Cub | 6. Dog — Puppy | 11. Lion — Cub/Whelp |
| 2. Cat — Kitten | 7. Goat — Kid | 12. Sheep — Lamb |
| 3. Cow — calf | 8. Goose — Gosling | 13. Stag — Fawn |
| 4. Deer — Fawn | 9. Hen — Chicken | 14. Tiger — Cub |
| 5. Duck — Duckling | 10. Horse — Foal | 15. Wolf — Cub |

## SINGLE WORD FOR A GROUP OF WORDS

### [A] Words denoting professions or trades

| | |
|---|---|
| One who keeps accounts for business | **Accountant** |
| One who plans and draws the designs of building | **Architect** |
| One who takes up legal profession | **Advocate** |
| One who foretells things by the stars, planets, etc. | **Astrologer** |
| One who studies heavenly bodies | **Astronomer** |
| One who travels in space | **Astronaut** |
| One who studies the evolution of mankind | **Anthropologist** |
| One who sells or prepares medicine | **Apothecary** |
| One who writes books | **Author** |
| One who sells things at public auction | **Auctioneer** |
| One who is interested in ancient buildings and relics | **Archaeologist** |
| One who cuts people's hair, shaves beard, etc. | **Barber** |
| One who bakes bread, cake, etc. | **Baker** |
| One who lives on alms | **Beggar** |
| One who sells meat | **Butcher** |
| One who mends shoes | **Cobbler** |
| One who makes furniture | **Carpenter** |
| One who draws maps | **Cartographer** |
| One who sets types in a printing press | **Compositor** |
| One who sells sweets and pastries | **Confectioner** |
| One who sells cloth | **Draper** |

| | |
|---|---|
| One who sells drugs | **Druggist** |
| One who deals in cattle | **Drover** |
| One who treats the teeth | **Dentist** |
| One who deals in fish | **Fishmonger** |
| One who walks on ropes | **Funambulist** |
| One who sells flowers | **Florist** |
| One who studies rocks and soils | **Geologist** |
| One who sells rice, dal, etc. | **Grocer** |
| One who reads the palm | **Palmist** |
| One who collects postage stamps | **Philatelist** |
| One who carves on stone | **Sculptor** |
| One who travels for selling articles | **Hawker** |
| One who rides the horses in races | **Jockey** |
| One who writes for the newspaper | **Journalist** |
| One who takes care of a building | **Janitor** |
| A person in charge of a museum | **Curator** |
| A person in charge of a library | **Librarian** |
| The head of a town Council or Corporation | **Mayor** |
| One who builds houses with bricks | **Mason** |
| One who imitates the voice, gestures etc. of another | **Mimic** |
| One who fights for money | **Mercenary** |
| One who writes novels | **Novelist** |
| One who attends the diseases of the eye | **Oculist** |
| One who tests eyesight and sells spectacles | **Optician** |
| One who flies an aeroplane | **Pilot** |
| One who mends waterpipes | **Plumber** |
| One who makes earthen pots | **Potter** |
| One who carries burden for hire | **Porter** |
| One who treats diseases by operation | **Surgeon** |
| One who writes in shorthand | **Stenographer** |
| One who converts raw hide into leather | **Tanner** |
| One who lends money at a very high interest | **Usurer** |
| One who sells small articles | **Vendor** |
| One who deals in wine | **Vintner** |
| One who makes wheels for carriages and carts | **Wheelwright** |

**[B] Persons with some special features**

| | |
|---|---|
| One who is a diplomat of a government in other country | **Ambassador** |
| One who rules with absolute power | **Autocrat** |
| One who shoots with bows and arrows | **Archer** |
| One who fishes with rod (angle) | **Angler** |

| | |
|---|---|
| One who atacks first | **Aggressor** |
| One who lives in a country without citizenship | **Alien** |
| One who belongs to a foreign country | **Foreigner** |
| One who gives up one's religion | **Apostate** |
| One who gives up the religious faith | **Renegade** |
| One who neglects duty or the law | **Delinquent** |
| One who sticks to a small point obstinately | **Stickler** |
| One who changes the party or principle | **Turncoat** |
| One who breaks into a house to steal | **Burglar** |
| One who eats human flesh | **Cannibal** |
| One (an animal) feeding on flesh of others | **Carnivorous** |
| One who is skilled in dealing with people in business or politics | **Diplomat** |
| A person who pays too much care to his clothes etc. | **Dandy** |
| One who is entitled to act on behalf of others | **Delegate** |
| One who thinks or speaks too much of himself | **Egoist** |
| One who eats too much | **Glutton** |
| One who holds opinions contrary to the established religious faith | **Heretic** |
| One who cheats others by deceptive talk or behaviour | **Humbug/Hypocrite** |
| One who belongs to a wandering race | **Gypsy** |
| One who follows extreme line | **Extremist** |
| One who causes terror, esp. for political purposes | **Terrorist** |
| One who wishes to destroy government | **Anarchist** |
| One who undertakes an enterprise | **Entrepreneur** |
| One who occupies other's premises forcibly | **Encroacher/Squatter** |
| One who enters other's place without permission | **Intruder/Trespasser** |
| One who believes too easily | **Credulous** |
| One who is hard to please | **Fastidious** |
| One who deals in medicinal herbs | **Herbalist** |
| One who plays or acts for pleasure and not as a profession | **Amateur** |
| One who has the same name as another | **Namesake** |
| One who does not take any intoxicating drinks | **Teetotaller** |
| One who behaves disloyally or betrays one's country | **Traitor** |
| One who finds pleasure in inflicting pain on others | **Sadist** |
| A person between 60-69 years | **Hexagenarian** |
| A person between 70-79 years | **Septugenarian** |
| A person between 80-89 years | **Octogenarian** |
| A person between 90-99 years | **Nonagenarian** |
| A person who is 100 years old or more | **Centenarian** |
| One who is banished from his own country | **Exiled** |
| One who spends lavishly | **Extravagant** |

| | |
|---|---|
| One who breaks images | **Iconoclast** |
| One who is loved and respected | **Idol** |
| One who pretends to be what he is not | **Impostor** |
| One who is versed in many languages | **Linguist** |
| One who speaks many languages | **Polyglot** |
| One who dies for a noble cause | **Martyr** |
| One who pretends illness to escape duty | **Malinger** |
| One who looks at the bright side of things | **Optimist** |
| One who looks at the dark side of things | **Pessimist** |
| One who loves one's own country | **Patriot** |
| One who goes on foot | **Pedestrian** |
| One who journeys to a holy place | **Pilgrim** |
| One who foretells events to come | **Prophet/Soothsayer** |
| One who makes a vain display of learning | **Pedant** |
| One who knows many subjects | **Polymath** |
| One who spends too little | **Miser** |
| One who spends too much | **Spendthrift** |
| One who comes before another | **Predecessor** |
| One who comes after another | **Successor** |
| One living at the same time with another | **Contemporary** |
| One who bears pain and discomfort without any complaint | **Stoic** |
| One who receives something | **Recipient** |
| One who takes refuge in a foreign country | **Refugee** |
| One who flies abandoning the alloted duty | **Truant** |
| One who walks in sleep | **Somnambulist** |
| One who hates women | **Misogynist** |
| A messenger sent in great haste | **Courier** |
| One who has long experience | **Veteran** |
| One who thinks to know everything | **Wiseacre** |

**[C] Words denoting places**

| | |
|---|---|
| A place where animals are slaughtered for the market | **Abattoir** |
| A place of study or training in a specific field | **Academy** |
| A place where bees are kept | **Apiary** |
| A place where birds are kept | **Aviary** |
| A place where fishes are kept | **Aquarium** |
| A place where government papers are kept | **Archives** |
| The space in the roof of a house | **Attic/Garret/Turret** |
| A place for production of bread | **Bakery** |
| Underground dwelling place of an animal | **Burrow** |
| Wheeled home of a person, esp. a gypsy | **Caravan** |
| A place where soldiers are housed | **Barrack/Cantonment** |

A shelter or shed for cows **Cowshed**
A place or ground for burial of dead bodies **Cemetery**
The living place of the wild beasts **Den/Lair**
A place where goods are stored **Depot**
A place for production and treatment of milk **Dairy**
A place where medicines are compounded **Dispensary**
A place for keeping motor cars **Garage**
The normal abode of an animal **Habitat**
A place where grains are stored **Granary**
A room or hall with instruments for physical exercise **Gymnasium**
The house of an Eskimo **Igloo**
A place for keeping aeroplanes **Hangars**
A place for flying or landing of aeroplanes **Aerodromes/Airport**

A small house unfit to live in **Hovel**
A house of shelter for a dog **Kennel**
A house for keeping books **Library**
A place of discharge from the bowels **Lavatory**
A place where scientific experiments are carried on **Laboratory**
A place for keeping, or a collection of wild animals, esp. for a show **Menagerie**
A place where treasures of art & curios are kept **Museum**
A place where money is coined **Mint**
A place where astronomical observations are taken **Observatory**
A place in the desert where water is found and some plants grow **Oasis**
A place where orphans are kept **Orphanage**
A house or shelter for a confined cow **Pen**
A place where batting of cricket ball takes place **Pitch**
A landing place of ships or a place where ships are loaded and unloaded **Quay**

A place where horses are kept **Stable**
A place where films are produced **Studio**
A place where patients slowly recover from illness **Sanitarium**
A place where leather is tanned **Tannery**

## [D] Miscellaneous

Subjects to be discussed in a meeting **Agenda**
People who come to see theatre, concert, lecture, etc. **Audience**
Not bearing the name of a writer **Anonymous**
A book with a collection of photographs, postage stamp, etc. **Album**
A medicine to nullify the effect of poison **Antidote**
A short account of an interesting incident **Anecdote**
The science of body-structure of an animal **Anatomy**
Animals living both in land and water **Amphibian**
Animals or plants living in or near water **Aquatic**

| | |
|---|---|
| A plant which does not bear fruit | **Acarpous** |
| One who kills secretly | **Assassin** |
| A mixture of two or more metals | **Alloy** |
| The legendary art of turning base metals into gold | **Alchemy** |
| Co-existence of opposite forces in a person | **Ambivalence** |
| Life-story of oneself | **Autobiography** |
| Life of a person | **Biography** |
| Animals that suckle their young | **Mammal** |
| An animal having two feet/A two-footed animal | **Biped** |
| An animal having four legs | **Quadruped** |
| A disease affecting many people at the same time | **Epidemic** |
| A short speech or poem made at the end of the play | **Epilogue** |
| An inscription on a monument in memory of the dead | **Epitaph** |
| A brief summary of a book | **Epitome** |
| A course of study in a school, college or university | **Curriculum** |
| A silly, dull-witted fool | **Booby** |
| One who persecutes the weak | **Bully** |
| A large number of soldiers | **Battalions** |
| A general pardon for political offence | **Amnesty** |
| A number of travellers across desert/A vehicle equiped for living in | **Caravan** |
| A brief pithy saying | **Aphorism** |
| The original one from which others are copied | **Prototype** |
| An estate inherited from ancestors | **Patrimony** |
| An assembly of viewers | **Spectators** |
| A collection of passages from literature, especially poems | **Anthology** |
| The scientific study of mankind, esp. of origins, customs, etc. | **Anthropology** |
| The study of the supposed influence of stars on human affairs | **Astrology** |
| The scientific study of the stars and planets and their movements | **Astronomy** |
| The study of birds of different categories | **Ornithology** |
| A missile that returns to the thrower | **Boomerang** |
| A roundabout way of expression | **Circumlocution** |
| A mass of snow with ice and rock descending from mountain | **Avalanche** |
| Using undue influence to place one's own relatives in lucrative posts | **Nepotism** |
| An unmarried man | **Bachelor** |
| An unmarried woman | **Maiden/Spinster** |
| A previous act taken as an example of later acts | **Precedent** |
| A number of warships under the guidance of one commander | **Fleet** |
| Continuous discharge of fire arms | **Fusillade** |
| An agreement to cease fire for a time | **Armistice** |
| One's own handwriting, especially signature | **Autograph** |

| | |
|---|---|
| An official counting of all the people in a country | **Census** |
| A stretch of open grassy land | **Lea** |
| Household staff of little or no value | **Lumber** |
| A partial or total loss of memory | **Amnesia** |
| A remedy for all diseases | **Panacea** |
| A scanty allowance or share | **Dole** |
| A medicine that kills insects | **Insecticide** |
| Cruel and indiscriminate killing of many human beings | **Massacre** |
| Great slaughter or killing of many people | **Carnage** |
| Deliberate destruction of a racial or political group | **Genocide** |
| A horrible dream | **Nightmare** |
| Garments worn to protect clothes | **Apron** |
| The practice of having one wife | **Monogamy** |
| The practice of having two wives or husbands at a time | **Bigamy** |
| The practice of having two or more than two wives | **Polygamy** |
| A pithy well-known saying of the wise men | **Proverb** |
| A film show in the afternoon | **Matinee** |
| One who does not believe in God | **Atheist** |
| One who believes in the existence of God | **Theist** |
| Doctrine that there is only one God | **Monotheism** |
| Belief in many gods | **Polytheism** |
| One who has narrow religious views | **Bigot** |
| One who is not sure of God | **Agnostic** |
| A disbeliever in religion | **Infidel** |
| A child whose parents are dead | **Orphan** |
| A name taken specially by an author, instead of his real name | **Pseudonym** |
| Sentimental yearning for the past | **Nostalgia** |
| A person or thing that is supposed to bring good luck | **Mascot** |
| A group of plants or animals that are of the same kinds | **Species** |
| A stream-like sliding mass of ice | **Glacier** |
| A violent whirlpool | **Maelstrom** |
| The long hair on the neck of the horse or lion | **Mane** |
| Boys and girls between thirteen and nineteen | **Teenagers** |
| Any drink except water | **Beverage** |
| The recipient of a benefit | **Beneficiary** |
| A person of fastidious taste | **Epicure** |
| Food for horses and cattle | **Forage** |
| Dried food, hay etc. for farm animals, horses etc. | **Fodder** |
| Wrting in praise of something | **Eulogy** |
| One who is all-powerful | **Almighty/Omnipotent** |

| | |
|---|---|
| One who knows or sees everything | **Omniscient** |
| One who is present everywhere | **Omnipresent** |
| A person appointed by two parties to settle a dispute | **Arbitrator** |
| One leaving his native country to settle in another | **Emigrant** |
| One coming to a foreign land to settle there | **Immigrant** |
| One who is able to use both hands alike | **Ambidexter** |
| One free from national prejudices | **Cosmopolitan** |
| A pleasure trip by a newly married couple | **Honeymoon** |
| A path followed by a planet or a satellite round another body | **Orbit** |
| A heavenly body or a mechanical device moving round a planet | **Satellite** |
| Racial discrimination between the white man and the black man | **Apartheid** |
| Use of judgement according to the situation | **Discretion** |
| A sense of feeling humiliated or wounded | **Mortification** |
| Supply of water for agriculture by means of ditches or channels | **Irrigation** |
| A planned activity to gain a special object | **Campaign** |
| A drug that puts one to sleep | **Tranquilizer/Sedative** |
| Scattered fragments of something wrecked | **Rubble/Debris** |
| A period of 10 years | **Decade** |
| A period of 100 years | **Century** |
| A period of 1,000 years | **Millennium** |
| An insect or plant that lives on another | **Parasite** |
| One who collects stamps | **Philatelist** |
| One trying to do good to mankind | **Philanthropist** |
| One who hates mankind | **Misanthropist/Misanthrope** |
| One always doubting or who doubts about everything | **Sceptic** |
| One who speaks for others | **Spokesman** |
| Indifference to pain or pleasure | **Stoicism** |
| One unable to pay one's debts | **Insolvent, Bankrupt** |
| One unable to read and write | **Illiterate** |
| Something contrary to law | **Illegal** |
| Destitute of knowledge | **Ignorant** |
| Beyond the power of nature | **Supernatural** |
| Characterised by dull uniformity | **Monotonous** |
| A paper written by hand | **Manuscript** |
| Capable of being seen through | **Transparent** |
| Murder of one's own self | **Suicide** |
| Murder or murderer of a man | **Homicide** |
| Murder or murderer of an infant | **Infanticide** |
| Murder or murderer of one's father | **Patricide** |
| Murder or murderer of one's mother | **Matricide** |

| | |
|---|---|
| Murder or murderer of one's brother or sister | **Fratricide** |
| Murder or murderer of a king | **Regicide** |
| Operation (on living things) for scientific research | **Vivisection** |
| A journey by river or sea | **Voyage** |
| Artificial covering of hair for one's head | **Wig** |
| Persons who work in the same rank in an office | **Colleagues** |
| A dead body of a human being | **Cadaver, Corpse** |
| The dead body of an animal | **Carcass** |
| A human being much below the oridinary size | **Dwarf** |
| A person having physical or mental defect | **Handicapped** |
| A sleeping room with many beds | **Dormitory** |
| The art practised by a statesman | **Diplomacy** |
| A public official who carries out the punishment by death | **Executioner** |
| A person to speak and act on other's behalf | **Representative** |
| One to whom some property is entrusted for the benefit of others | **Trustee** |

**[E] Words denoting qualities—Adjectives**

| | |
|---|---|
| On the go | **Active** |
| Relating to sound or sense of hearing | **Acoustic** |
| Capable of being reached | **Accessible** |
| Capable of more than one meaning | **Ambiguous/Equivocal** |
| Capable of being admitted | **Admissible** |
| Engaged to be married | **Affianced/Betrothed** |
| Capable of being applied | **Applicable** |
| Without the name of the author | **Anonymous** |
| Liable to answer | **Answerable** |
| Concerning the north pole | **Arctic** |
| Concerning the south pole | **Antarctic** |
| Suitable for ploughing | **Arable** |
| Capable of being heard | **Audible** |
| Capable of being believed | **Believable/Credible** |
| Twice a week | **Bi-weekly** |
| Liable to break easily | **Brittle** |
| Of middle class or having conventional ideas and tastes | **Bourgeois** |
| Happening once in a hundred years | **Centennial** |
| Of the same age | **Coeval** |
| Catching or conveyed by contact | **Contagious** |
| Relating to body | **Corporal** |
| Pretending to be shy | **Coy** |
| A period of ten years | **Decade** |
| Recurring in ten years | **Decennial** |

| | |
|---|---|
| Relating to statistics of birth | **Demographic** |
| That which produces the desired effect | **Efficacious** |
| Believing in the principle of equality | **Egalitarian** |
| Of the production of fine offspring | **Eugenic** |
| Not admitting something else | **Exclusive** |
| Delivered without previous thought or preparation | **Extempore** |
| Excessively zealous in religion | **Fanatic** |
| Of unbelievable excellence | **Fantabulous** |
| That which causes death | **Fatal** |
| Careful not to waste | **Frugal** |
| (Animals) feeding on flesh of others | **Carnivorous** |
| (Animals) feeding on grass | **Graminivorous** |
| (Animals) living in flocks or herds | **Gregarious** |
| (Animals) living on herbs | **Herbivorous** |
| (Animals) living on all kinds of food | **Omnivorous** |
| One living on vegetables | **Vegetarian** |
| Given to tall talk | **Grandiloquent** |
| Differing in kinds | **Heterogeneous** |
| Of the same kind | **Homogeneous** |
| With work of honour but without remuneration | **Honorary** |
| One who does not know how to read or write | **Illiterate** |
| Not qualified to be elected or selected under rules | **Ineligible** |
| Not to be doubted or questioned | **Indubitable** |
| That which cannot be blotted | **Indelible** |
| Not fit to be eaten | **Inedible** |
| That which cannot be cured | **Incurable** |
| Incapacity to produce the result desired | **Inefficacy** |
| Incapable of being penetrated | **Impenetrable** |
| Incapable of being done or incapable of happening | **Impossible** |
| Incapable of being passed along | **Impassable** |
| Not liable to perish easily | **Imperishable** |
| Not likely to happen | **Improbable** |
| Incapable of being moved | **Immovable** |
| Incapable of being reached | **Inaccessible** |
| Incapable of being applied | **Inapplicable** |
| That which cannot be compared | **Incomparable** |
| Incapable of being comprehended | **Incomprehensible** |
| Incapable of being conceived | **Inconceivable** |
| Incapable of being disputed | **Indisputable** |
| Incapable of being tired | **Indefatigable** |

| | |
|---|---|
| Incapable of being defended | **Indefensible** |
| Incapable of being expressed | **Inexpressible** |
| Incapable of being exhausted | **Inexhaustible** |
| Incapable of being read | **Illegible** |
| Incapable of being heard | **Inaudible** |
| Incapable of being seen | **Invisible** |
| Incapable of being approached | **Inaccessible** |
| Incapable of being admitted | **Inadmissible** |
| Incapable of being believed | **Incredible** |
| Incapable of being resisted | **Irresistible** |
| Incapable of being corrected | **Incorrigible** |
| Incapable of being divided | **Indivisible** |
| Incapable of being perceived | **Imperceptible** |
| Incapable of being imitated | **Inimitable** |
| Liable to be easily kindled | **Inflammable** |
| Incapable of being solved | **Insoluble** |
| Incapable of being surmounted | **Insurmountable** |
| Incapable of being touched | **Intangible** |
| Incapable of being conquered | **Invincible** |
| Incapable of being altered | **Unalterable** |
| Incapable of being questioned | **Unquestionable** |
| That without which one cannot do | **Indispensable** |
| That which cannot be explained | **Inexplicable** |
| That which cannot be avoided | **Inevitable** |
| Incapable of committing mistakes | **Infallible** |
| Incapable of being limited | **Illimitable** |
| Incapable of being repaired | **Irrepairable/Irreparable** |
| That which cannot be reconciled | **Irreconcilable** |
| That which is not to the point | **Irrelevant** |
| That which cannot be changed | **Irrevocable** |
| Easily excited to anger | **Irritable** |
| That which cannot be satisfied | **Insatiable** |
| That which cannot be scrutinised | **Inscrutable** |
| Capable of being understood | **Intelligible** |
| That which cannot be hurt | **Invulnerable** |
| Capable of being justified | **Justifiable** |
| Capable of being read | **Legible** |
| Relating to the region lying along the coast | **Littoral** |
| Liable to be easily bent | **Maleable/Flexible** |
| Easily moved to tears | **Maudlin** |

| | |
|---|---|
| Fit to be remembered | **Memorable** |
| (Something) long and dull | **Monotonous** |
| Capable of being moved | **Movable** |
| Liable to die | **Mortal** |
| Left after all deductions | **Net** |
| Not having any sense | **Nonsense** |
| Incapable of being seen through | **Opaque** |
| Having contradictory meanings | **Paradoxical** |
| Likely to happen | **Probable** |
| Occurring after one's death/Born after death of father | **Posthumous** |
| Published after the death of the author | **Posthumous** |
| Showing extreme care to carry out duties | **Punctilious** |
| Pertaining to the countryside/village | **Rural** |
| Pertaining to the town/city | **Urban** |
| That which is beyond nature | **Supernatural** |
| Capable of being touched | **Tangible** |
| Capable of being seen through | **Transparent** |
| Slightly intoxicated | **Tipsy** |
| Not capable of being altered | **Unalterable** |
| Not capable of being answered | **Unanswerable** |
| Not capable of being questioned | **Unquestionable** |
| Leading a wandering life | **Vagrant** |
| Capable of being seen | **Visible** |
| Working on one's own will | **Voluntary** |
| Liable to be easily hurt or wounded | **Vulnerable** |

**[F] Words denoting action—Verbs**

| | |
|---|---|
| Help someone to do something wrong or illegal | **Abet** |
| Lie concealed in wait to attack by surprise | **Ambush** |
| Destroy completely | **Annihilate** |
| Shut out from society | **Boycott/Ostracize** |
| Unite into one body | **Coalesce** |
| Devise a plan often for an evil purpose | **Concoct** |
| Work with someone in order to achieve something | **Collaborate** |
| Recall the memory of a person by a solemn act | **Commemorate** |
| Make something impure | **Contaminate** |
| Regain health gradually | **Convalesce** |
| Travel in an unknown country for knowing it thoroughly | **Explore** |
| Invent or make up often with an evil motive | **Fabricate** |
| Make love insincerely | **Flirt** |
| Move by jumping with all feet together | **Hop** |

| | |
|---|---|
| Carry away a person forcibly | **Kidnap** |
| Learn by heart | **Memorise** |
| Sleep for a short while | **Nap** |
| Give a gentle push | **Nudge** |
| Pass slowly a soft liquid through small openings | **Ooze** |
| Shut out from society | **Ostracize** |
| Pick up food with the beak | **Peck** |
| Declare beforehand | **Predict** |
| Walk with an air of superiority | **Swagger** |
| Push something suddenly or violently | **Thrust** |
| Change the form or outward appearance | **Transform** |
| Encroach upon the rights or property of another | **Trespass** |
| Walk with tired and heavy steps | **Trudge** |

## APPLIED SECTION

**1. Form words by choosing appropriate Prefixes [one has been done for you] :**

| | Phrases | Words with Prefixes | Prefixes |
|---|---|---|---|
| (i) | exist side by side | coexist | co |
| (ii) | former Secretary | .............. | anti |
| (iii) | to consider again | .............. | bi |
| (iv) | appearing twice a week | .............. | ex |
| (v) | determined beforehand | .............. | im |
| (vi) | depending on each other | .............. | in |
| (vii) | used against enemy aircraft | .............. | inter |
| (viii) | that which cannot be measured | .............. | pre |
| (ix) | between two or more schools | .............. | re |
| (x) | Incapable of being corrected | .............. | |

**2. Use appropriate Sufixes with the words in the bracket and fill in the gaps with appropriate words :**

(i) Ashoke ruled over a vast ........... (king).

(ii) The old man passed away .............. (peace).

(iii) Leprosy can nowadays be ........... (complete) cured.

(iv) The news gave us great ........... (please).

(v) They are going in the wrong ........... (direct).

(vi) You should be ........... (care) about your ........... (move).

(vii) As it is a ......... (danger) task, you should deal with it very......(care).

(viii) In his ........... (boy) he was very .............. (greed).

(ix) The Shah of Persia jumped over the ........... (enclose).

(x) Some ......... (mystery) power impelled Sudha to dance ......... (grace).

## EXERCISE

**1. Use the prefixes given in the list to form new words with the following words :**

List of Prefixes : ab, ac, ante, anti, auto, contra, dis, ex, il, im, in, ir

| | | | |
|---|---|---|---|
| (i) | ........... legal | (vii) | ........... honour |
| (ii) | ........... use | (viii) | ........... student |
| (iii) | ........... count | (ix) | ........... possible |
| (iv) | ........... graph | (x) | ........... active |
| (v) | ........... diction | (xi) | ........... dote |
| (vi) | ........... regular | (xii) | ........... chamber |

**2. Use the suffixes given in the list to form new words with the following words :**

List of Suffixes : er, ar, or, ist, ee, age, al, ence, ity, tion, ment, ish, ness, hood

| | | | |
|---|---|---|---|
| (i) | beg ......... | (viii) | arrive ......... |
| (ii) | speak ........... | (ix) | translate ........... |
| (iii) | type ........... | (x) | child........... |
| (iv) | carry ......... | (xi) | merry ......... |
| (v) | absent ........... | (xii) | able ........... |
| (vi) | present ........... | (xiii) | happy ........... |
| (vii) | sail ........... | (xiv) | brother ........... |

**3. Write the opposite words or Antonyms of the following words :**

| | Words | Antonyms | | Words | Antonyms |
|---|---|---|---|---|---|
| (i) | able | .............. | (xi) | legal | .............. |
| (ii) | active | .............. | (xii) | literate | .............. |
| (iii) | above | .............. | (xiii) | moral | .............. |
| (iv) | careful | .............. | (xiv) | mature | .............. |
| (v) | common | .............. | (xv) | partial | .............. |
| (vi) | conscious | .............. | (xvi) | practice | .............. |
| (vii) | comfort | .............. | (xvii) | regular | .............. |
| (viii) | conduct | .............. | (xviii) | useful | .............. |
| (ix) | fortune | .............. | (xix) | violence | .............. |
| (x) | honest | .............. | (xx) | visible | .............. |

**4. Write a single word for each of the following groups of words :**

(i) One who collects postage stamps ..............
(ii) One who attends the diseases of the eye ..............
(iii) One who treats fidrsdrd by operation ..............
(iv) One who lends money at a very high interest ..............
(v) A person in charge of a museum ..............
(vi) The head of a town Council or Corporation ..............
(vii) One who pretends illness to escape duty ..............
(viii) One who looks at the bright side of things ..............

(ix) One who looks at the dark side of things ..............
(x) One who loves one's own country ..............
(xi) One who journeys to a holy place ..............
(xii) One who foretells events to come ..............
(xiii) One who lives in a country without citizenship. ..............
(xiv) One who is entitled to act on behalf of others ..............
(xv) One who enters other's place without permission ..............
(xvi) One who behaves disloyally or betrays one's country ..............
(xvii) One living at the same time with another ..............
(xviii) One who takes refuge in a foreign country ..............
(xix) One who flies abandoning the allotted duty ..............
(xx) Animals living both in land and water ..............

# 30 WORD-FAMILY FROM ONE PART OF SPEECH TO OTHERS

## HOW TO ENRICH OUR WORD-FAMILY?

In most cases we can change one Part of Speech to another. In fact, English vocabulary has been enriched by changing one Part of Speech to others. If you develop the habit of forming such different Parts of Speech, you may have a good deal of stock of words, rather a good dictionary of your own.

Now read the following charts :

### NOUNS CORRESPONDING TO OTHER PARTS OF SPEECH

| Noun | Verb | Adjective | Adverb |
|---|---|---|---|
| anger | anger (V.) | angry | angrily |
| art / artist | — | artistic | artistically |
| awe (N.) | awe (V.) | awful | awfully |
| base (N.) | base (V.) | { basic | { basically |
| base (N.) | debase (V.) | baseless | baselessly |
| beauty | beautify | beautiful | beautifully |
| beautician | " | " | " |
| beautifier | " | " | " |
| beautification | " | " | " |
| belief | believe | believable | believably |
| biology | — | biological | biologically |
| blood | bleed | bloody | — |
| book (N.) | book (V.) | bookish | bookishly |
| care (N.) | care (V.) | careless | carelessly |
| " | " | careful | carefully |
| centre | centralize | central | centrally |
| ceremony | — | ceremonial | ceremonially |
| character | characterize | characteristic | characteristically |
| charity | — | charitable | charitably |

| Noun | Verb | Adjective | Adverb |
|---|---|---|---|
| class | classify | classified | classifically |
| colony | colonize | colonized<br>colonial | — |
| colour (N.) | colour (V.) | colourful | colourfully |
| comfort (N.) | comfort (V.) | comfortable | comfortably |
| commerce | commercialize | commercial | commercially |
| company | accompany | companionable | — |
| condition | condition (V.) | conditional | conditionally |
| convenience | — | convenient | conveniently |
| courage | encourage | courageous | courageously |
| credit (N.) | credit (V.) | creditable<br>credible | creditably<br>credibly |
| credulity | — | credulous | credulously |
| crime | crime (V.) | criminal | criminally |
| critic | criticize | critical | critically |
| curiosity | — | curious | curiously |
| danger | endanger | dangerous | dangerously |
| debate (N.) | debate (V.) | debatable | debatably |
| democracy | democratize | democratic | democratically |
| discipline | discipline (V.) | disciplinary | — |
| drama | dramatize | dramatic | dramatically |
| duty | — | dutiful | dutifully |
| ease | ease (V.) | easy | easily |
| economy | economize | economic<br>economical | —<br>economically |
| education | educate | educative | — |
| effect | effect (V.) | effective | effectively |
| energy | energize | energetic | energetically |
| envy (N.) | envy (V.) | enviable | enviably |
| event | — | eventful<br>eventual | eventfully<br>eventually |
| excellence | excel (V.) | excellent | excellently |
| favour (N.) | favour (V.) | favourite<br>favourable | —<br>favourably |
| fear (N.) | fear (V.) | fearful | fearfully |
| facility | facilitate | facilitating | facilitatingly |
| figure (N.) | figure (V.) | figurative | figuratively |
| fool | befool | foolish | foolishly |

| Noun | Verb | Adjective | Adverb |
|---|---|---|---|
| force (N.) | force (V.) | forceful<br>forcible | forcefully<br>forcibly |
| form (N.) | form (V.) | formal | formally |
| friend | befriend | friendly | — |
| fright | frighten | frightful | frightfully |
| fruit | fruit (V.) | fruitful<br>fruitless | fruitfully<br>fruitlessly |
| glory (N.) | glory (V.)<br>glorify | glorious | gloriously |
| grace | grace (V.) | graceful<br>graceless | gracefully<br>gracelessly |
| grammar | grammaticise | grammatical | grammatically |
| habit | habituate | habitual | habitually |
| happiness | — | happy | happily |
| heart | hearten | hearty | heartily |
| history | historicise/historify | historical | historically |
| honour (N.) | honour (V.) | honourable | honourably |
| horror | horrify | horrible | horribly |
| humour | humour (V.) | humorous | humorously |
| idiot<br>idiocy | — | idiotic | idiotically |
| industry | industrialise | industrial<br>industrious | industrially<br>industriously |
| interest | interest (V.) | interesting | interestingly |
| joy | enjoy | joyful<br>joyous | joyfully<br>joyously |
| king | — | kingly<br>royal | royally |
| labour (N.) | labour (V.) | laborious | laboriously |
| law | — | lawful<br>legal | lawfully<br>legally |
| luck | — | lucky | luckily |
| matter | materialize | material | materially |
| measure (N.) | measure (V.) | measurable | measurably |
| memory | memorize | memorable | memorably |
| method | methodize | methodical | methodically |
| mind (N.) | mind (V.) | mindful<br>mental | mindfully<br>mentally |

| Noun | Verb | Adjective | Adverb |
|---|---|---|---|
| nature | naturalise | natural | naturally |
| need (N.) | need (V.) | needful | needfully |
| | | needless | needlessly |
| | | needy | — |
| office | officiate | official | officially |
| origin | originate | original | originally |
| organ | organise | organic | organically |
| pain | pain (V.) | painful | painfully |
| patron | patronize | patronizing | patronizingly |
| person | personify | personal | personally |
| picture (N.) | picture (V.) | pictorial | pictorially |
| progress (N.) | progress (V.) | progressive | progressively |
| quarrel (N.) | quarrel (V.) | quarrelsome | quarrelsomely |
| rest (N.) | rest (V.) | restful | restfully |
| | | restless | restlessly |
| silence | silence (V.) | silent | silently |
| sleep (N.) | sleep (V.) | asleep | — |
| | | sleepless | sleeplessly |
| strength | strengthen | strong | strongly |
| substance | substantiate | substantive | substantively |
| | | substantial | substantially |
| success | succeed | successful | successfully |
| system | systematize | systematic | systematically |
| sympathy | sympathize | sympathetic | sympathetically |
| theory | theorize | theoretical | theoretically |
| vigour | envigorate | vigorous | vigorously |
| victim | victimize | victimised | — |
| violence | — | violent | violently |
| vitality | vitalize | vital | vitally |
| vivacity | — | vivacious | vivaciously |
| voice | voice (V.) | vocal | vocally |

## VERBS CORRESPONDING TO OTHER PARTS OF SPEECH

| Verb | Noun | Adjective | Adverb |
|---|---|---|---|
| accept | acceptance | acceptable | acceptably |
| act | action | active | actively |
| activate | activity | | |
| accelerate | acceleration | accelerated | — |
| add | addition | additional | additionally |
| admire | admiration | admirable | admirably |

| Verb | Noun | Adjective | Adverb |
|---|---|---|---|
| admit | admission | admissive | — |
| | | admissible | admissibly |
| adventure (V.) | adventure (N.) | adventurous | adventurously |
| advise | advice | advisable | advisably |
| agree | agreement | agreeable | agreeably |
| allow | allowance | allowable | allowably |
| appreciate | appreciation | appreciable | appreciably |
| attend | attention | attentive | attentively |
| | attendance | | |
| attract | attraction | attractive | attractively |
| authorise | authority | authoritative | authoritatively |
| bury | burial | buried | — |
| celebrate | celebration | celebrated | — |
| | celebrity | | |
| choose | choice | chosen | — |
| | | choosable | |
| close | closure | closed | — |
| clean | cleanness | clean | cleanly |
| cleanse | cleanliness | cleanly | — |
| commit | commitment | committed | — |
| compel | compulsion | compulsive | compulsively |
| | | compulsory | compulsorily |
| comprehend | comprehension | comprehending | — |
| conceive | conception | conceivable | conceivably |
| conclude | conclusion | conclusive | conclusively |
| confide | confidence | confident | confidently |
| | | confidential | confidentially |
| congratulate | congratulation | congratulatory | — |
| conquer | conquest | conquerable | — |
| consider | consideration | considerable | considerably |
| consist | consistence | consistent | consistently |
| | consistency | | |
| conspire | conspiracy | conspiring | conspiringly |
| consturct | construction | constructive | constructively |
| continue | continuity | continuous | continuously |
| cooperate | cooperation | cooperative | cooperatively |
| deceive | deception | deceptive | deceptively |
| decide | decision | decisive | decisively |
| define | definition | defined | definitely |
| | | definite | |

| Verb | Noun | Adjective | Adverb |
|---|---|---|---|
| defy | defiance | defiant | defiantly |
| derive | derivation | derivative | derivatively |
| describe | description | descriptive | descriptively |
| destroy | destruction | destructive | destructively |
| detect | detection/detective | detective/detectable | — |
| determine | determination | determined | — |
| devote | devotion | devotional | devotionally |
| differ | difference | different | differently |
| digest | digestion | digestive | digestively |
| divide | division | divisional<br>divisible | divisionally<br>divisibly |
| dominate | domination | dominant | dominantly |
| edit | edition | editorial | — |
| educate | education | educational | educationally |
| elect | election | elective | electively |
| employ | employment<br>employee | employed | — |
| engage | engagement | engaged | — |
| establish | establishment | established | — |
| excavate | excavation | excavated | — |
| excel | excellence | excellent | excellently |
| exist | existence | existent | existently |
| extend | extention | extensive | extensively |
| fail | failure | failed | — |
| fix | fixation | fixed | — |
| forget | forgetfulness | forgetful | forgetfully |
| generate | generation | generative | generatively |
| govern | government | governmental | governmentally |
| grade | gradation | gradual | gradually |
| guide | guidance | guided | guidedly |
| hesitate | hesitation | hesitant | hesitantly |
| hope (V.) | hope (N.) | hopeful<br>hopeless | hopefully<br>hopelessly |
| help (V.) | help (N.) | helpful<br>helpless | helpfully<br>helplessly |
| identify | identification | identified | — |
| ignore | ignorance | ignorant | ignorantly |
| illuminate | illumination | illuminative<br>illuminating | —<br>illuminatingly |

| **Verb** | **Noun** | **Adjective** | **Adverb** |
|---|---|---|---|
| imitate | imitation | imitative | imitatively |
| imply | implication | implied | impliedly |
| implicate | implication | implicit | implicitly |
| inaugurate | inauguration | inaugural | — |
| include | inclusion | inclusive | inclusively |
| inform | information | informative | informatively |
| inherit | inheritance | inherited | — |
| insist | insistence | insistent | insistently |
| instruct | instruction | instructive<br>instructional | instructively<br>instructionally |
| invent | invention | inventive | inventively |
| join | joint (N.) | joint (Adj.) | jointly |
| know | knowledge | knowledgeable | knowledgeably |
| laugh | laughter | laughable | laughably |
| manage | management | manageable | manageably |
| marry | marriage | marriageable | — |
| marvel (V.) | marvel (N.) | marvellous | marvellously |
| measure | measurement | measurable | measurably |
| mix | mixer<br>mixture | mixed | mixedly |
| move | movement | movable | movably |
| moisten | moisture | moist | moistly |
| navigate | navigation | navigable | navigably |
| neglect | negligence | negligent<br>negligible | negligently<br>negligibly |
| obey | obedience | obedient | obediently |
| oblige | obligation | obliging<br>obligatory | obligingly<br>obligatorily |
| observe | observation<br>observance<br>observancy | observant<br>observational | observantly<br>observationally |
| occupy | occupation | occupant<br>occupational | —<br>occupationally |
| offend | offence | offensive | offensively |
| operate | operation | operational | operationally |
| oppose | opposition | opposite | oppositely |
| organise | organisation | organised | organisedly |
| oust | — | ousted | out |
| pack | package<br>packet | packed | —<br>— |

| Verb | Noun | Adjective | Adverb |
|---|---|---|---|
| pass | passage | passed/passable | passably |
| perform | performance | performed<br>performable | — |
| permit | permission | permissible | permissibly |
| persist | persistence | persistent | persistently |
| persevere | perseverance | persevering | perseveringly |
| persuade | persuasion | persuable | persuably |
| please | pleasure | pleasant<br>pleasurable | pleasantly<br>pleasurably |
| pollute | pollution | pollutant<br>polluted | pollutantly |
| practise | practice | practical | practically |
| prefer | preference | preferable<br>preferential | preferably |
| present | presentation | presentable | presentably |
| prescribe | prescription | prescriptional | prescribingly |
| prevent | prevention | preventive | preventively |
| proclaim | proclamation | proclamatory | — |
| produce | production<br>product<br>producer<br>productivity | productive<br>produced | productively |
| provide | provision | provisional | provisionally |
| purify | purification | purified | — |
| qualify | qualification | qualified | — |
| quote | quotation | quotable<br>quoted | — |
| reason (V.) | reason (N.) | resonable | reasonably |
| receive | receipt<br>reception<br>receptivity | receptive<br>receivable | receptively<br>receivably |
| reduce | reduction | reducible<br>reducibly | reduced |
| refer | reference | referential<br>referable | referentially<br>referably |
| reflect | reflection | reflective | reflectively |
| relate | relation | relative<br>related | relatively |

| Verb | Noun | Adjective | Adverb |
|---|---|---|---|
| rely | reliance<br>reliability | reliant<br>reliable | reliantly<br>reliably |
| remember | remembrance<br>rememberer | rememberable | rememberably |
| resent | resentment | resentful | resentfully |
| resume | resumption | resumable | resumptively |
| retard | retardation | retardant | — |
| rotate | rotation | rotational | rotationally |
| satisfy | satisfaction | satisfactory | satisfactorily |
| see | sight | visual | visually |
| select | selection | selective | selectively |
| separate | separation | separable | separably |
| settle | settlement | settled | — |
| speak | speech | spoken | speakingly |
| solve | solution | solvable | — |
| study (V.) | study (N.) | studious | studiously |
| suffer | suffering | sufferable | sufferably |
| suffice | sufficiency | sufficient | sufficiently |
| suggest | suggestion | suggestive | suggestively |
| suppose | supposition | supposable | supposably |
| succeed | success | successful | successfully |
| suspect | suspicion | suspicious | suspiciously |
| surprise (V.) | surprise (N.) | surprised<br>surprising | surprisingly |
| thank | thanks | thankful<br>thankless | thankfully<br>thanklessly |
| tolerate | toleration<br>tolerance | tolerant<br>tolerable | tolerantly<br>tolerably |
| translate | translation | translational<br>translatable<br>translated | translationally<br>translatably |
| trust (V.) | trust (N.)<br>trustee | trustful<br>trustworthy | trustfully<br>trustworthily |
| use (V.) | use (N.)<br>usefulness<br>uselessness<br>usability | —<br>useful<br>useless<br>usable | —<br>usefully<br>uselessly<br>usably |
| value | valuation<br>value (N.) | valuable<br>valueless | valuably<br>valuelessly |

| Verb | Noun | Adjective | Adverb |
|---|---|---|---|
| vary | variation<br>variance<br>variability | variant<br>various<br>variable | variantly<br>variously<br>variably |
| verify | verification<br>verifier | verified<br>verifiable | verifiably |
| wash | wash (N.)<br>washing (N.)<br>washer (N.) | washable<br>washing<br>washy | washably<br>—<br>washily |

## ADJECTIVES CORRESPONDING TO OTHER PARTS OF SPEECH

| Adjective | Verb | Noun | Adverb |
|---|---|---|---|
| able | enable | ability | ably |
| bright | brighten | brightness | brightly |
| broad | broaden | breadth | broadly |
| busy | busy (V.) | business | busily |
| curious | — | curiosity | curiously |
| deep | deepen | depth | deeply |
| false | falsify | falsehood | falsely |
| glad | gladden | gladness | gladly |
| happy | — | happiness | happily |
| intense | intensify | intensity | intensely |
| innocent | — | innocence | innocently |
| just | justify | justification<br>justness | justly |
| local | localize | locality | locally |
| quiet | quieten | quietness | quietly |
| patient | — | patience | patiently |
| particular | particularize | particulars | particularly |
| poor | — | poverty | poorly |
| steadfast | — | steadfastness | steadfastly |
| strong | strengthen | strength | strongly |
| sure | ensure | surety | surely |
| vital | vitalize | vitality | vitally |
| voluntary | volunteer (V.) | volunteer | voluntarily |
| weak | weaken | weakness | weakly |
| wide | widen | width | widely |
| wise | wisen | wisdom | wisely |

## APPLIED SECTION

1. **Change the Parts of Speech of the following words as directed and frame a sentence with each of them :**

able (into Noun), choice (into Verb), courage (into Adjective), belief (into Verb), base (into Adjective), beauty (into Verb), colour (into Adverb), energy (into Adjective), duty (into Adjective), fool (into Verb), enjoy (into Noun), mind (into Adjective), sleep (into Adjective), accept (into Noun), admire (into Noun), attend (into Adjective), compel (into Noun), provide (into Adjective), speak (into Noun), false (into Noun), wise (into Noun).

2. **Fill in the Parts of Speech Columns with proper forms of the words given in the 'Noun' column and then make sentences with each of them :**

| Noun | Verb | Adjective | Adverb |
|---|---|---|---|
| awe | | | |
| base | | | |
| beauty | | | |
| care | | | |
| class | | | |
| danger | | | |
| drama | | | |
| glory | | | |
| habit | | | |
| labour | | | |
| matter | | | |
| origin | | | |
| success | | | |
| voice | | | |

3. **Fill in the Parts of Speech columns with proper forms of the words given in the 'Verb' Column and then make sentences with each of them :**

| Verb | Noun | Adjective | Adverb |
|---|---|---|---|
| act | | | |
| accept | | | |
| admit | | | |
| advise | | | |
| compel | | | |
| consist | | | |
| decide | | | |
| differ | | | |
| divide | | | |
| elect | | | |
| excel | | | |

| Verb | Noun | Adjective | Adverb |
|---|---|---|---|
| fail | | | |
| grade | | | |
| include | | | |
| marvel | | | |
| obey | | | |
| permit | | | |
| practise | | | |
| relate | | | |
| suspect | | | |
| use | | | |
| value | | | |

**4. Fill in the Parts of Speech Columns with proper forms of the words given in the 'Adjective' Column and then make sentences with each of them :**

| Adjective | Verb | Noun | Adverb |
|---|---|---|---|
| able | | | |
| busy | | | |
| broad | | | |
| glad | | | |
| false | | | |
| local | | | |
| pleasant | | | |
| patient | | | |
| strong | | | |
| sure | | | |
| vital | | | |
| weak | | | |
| wide | | | |
| wise | | | |

## EXERCISE

**1. Make sentences by changing the forms of the words as directed :**

(i) Anger → (as an adjective) : ____________

(ii) Beauty → (as a verb) : ____________

(iii) Centre → (as an adjective) : ____________

(iv) Crime → (as an adjective) : ____________

(v) Danger → (as an adjective) : ____________

(vi) Duty → (as an adjective) : ____________

(vii) Drama → (as an adverb) : ____________

(viii) Education → (as a verb) : ____________

(ix) Fear → (as an adverb) : ____________

(x) Fool → (as a verb) : ____________

(xi) Force → (as an adverb) : ____________

(xii) Glory → (as an adjective) : ____________

(xiii) Grace → (as an adverb) : ____________

(xiv) Habit → (as an adjective) : ____________

(xv) Honour → (as an adjective) : ____________

(xvi) Horror → (as an adjective) : ____________

(xvii) Humour → (as an adverb) : ____________

(xviii) Law → (as an adjective) : ____________

(xix) Value → (as an adjective) : ____________

(xx) Wise → (as a noun) : ____________

**2. Put the words given in the brackets meaningfully to fill in the following blanks :**

(a) It was a ......... (memory) day when Independence was won. (b) He follows ......... (blind) what others do. (c) The child was under bad influences during the ......... (form) years of his life. (d) Men may die, but their works are not ......... (destroy). (e) After months of ......... (negotiate), the two sides have been ......... (quiet) and ......... (please). (f) The ......... (manage) is trying to reach an ......... (agree) with several ........... (separation) unions. (g) A passage of ........... (describe) writing is very difficult to ........... (summary).

**3. Fill in the blanks in the following passage with the appropriate forms of the words given below :**

[flow, eloquence, once, occupy, mythology, pollution, suppose, ultimate, view, worship]

Whether ......... as a river or ......... as a goddess, the Ganges ......... an important position in Hindu .......... While the Rigveda mentions the Ganges only ........., the later texts grow increasingly ......... about it. It ......... across the whole country and ......... mingles in the Bay of Bengal. The water of the Ganges is ......... to be holy, although the degree of its ......... is very high.

**4. Rewrite the sentences changing the form of the underlined words as directed :**

(i) He is not able to do it. [Change into noun]

(ii) She has an appearance that pleases all. [Change into adjective]

(iii) He is a man of wisdom. [Change into adjective]

(iv) These things have no uses. [Change into adjective]

(v) Explain your behaviour whether it is just or not. [Change into verb]

(vi) Father treated the boy with kindness. [Change into adverb]

# 31  SAME WORD USED AS DIFFERENT PARTS OF SPEECH

## HOW AND WHY DO WE USE THE SAME WORD DIFFERENTLY?

**What is the difference between a schoolmaster and a stationmaster?** A schoolmaster **trains** (V.) the mind (N.) but a stationmaster **minds** (V.) the train (N.)!

Some words may belong to different **Parts of Speech** according to the way in which they are used. Always remember that it is the function or use that determines to which **Part of Speech** a word belongs in a given sentence.

Now study the use of the following words in different **Parts of Speech**:

### ABOVE

Noun : Our blessing comes from **above**.
Adjective : Read the **above** sentence carefully.
Adverb : The heavens are **above**.
Preposition : The moral law is **above** the civil law.

### AFTER

Adjective : **After ages** will sing his glory.
Adverb : **After** a while they arrived.
Preposition : She takes **after** her mother.
Conjunction : They arrived **after** the train had left the station.

### ALL

Noun : He lost his **all** in a hurry.
Pronoun : **All** spoke in his favour.
Adjective : **All** men are mortal.
Adverb : He was **all** alone at that time.

### ANY

Pronoun : Does **any** of you know anything about it?
Adjective : Is there **any** witness?

### AS

Adverb : He ran **as** fast as he could.
Conjunction : I helped him **as** he was poor.

### BEFORE

Adverb : I have seen you before.
Preposition : He came before the appointed time.
Conjunction : He went away before I came.

### BETTER

Noun : Give place to your betters.
Adjective : I think yours is a better plan.
Adverb : I know him better.

### BUT

Rel. Pronoun : There is no one but likes him. = There is no one who does not like him.
Adverb : It is but (= only) right to admit our faults.
Preposition : None but (= except) the brave deserves the fair.
Conjunction : We tried hard but did not succeed.

### DOWN

Noun : He has seen the ups and downs of life.
Verb : Try to down him.
Adjective : The down train has left the station.
Adverb : Down went the Royal George.
Preposition : She came down the hill.

### EITHER

Pronoun : Ask either of them.
Adjective : He is watching either side of the river.
Conjunction : You must either work or starve.

### ENOUGH

Noun : I have had enough of this.
Adverb : You know well enough what I mean.

### EVEN

Verb : Let us even the ground.
Adjective : The chances are even.
Adverb : Does he even suspect the danger?

### FOR

Preposition : I can do it for myself.
Conjunction : He cannot do this now for he is ill.

### HEAD

Noun : Head is the vital part of the body.
Verb : He headed the ball in right time.

### HONOUR

Noun : He is a man of great honour.
Verb : Everyone honours him.

### LESS

Noun : He wants one hundred rupees for that book. He won't be satisfied with less.

Adjective : You are paying less attention.

Adverb : The soil of Purulia is less fertile than that of Hooghly.

### LIKE

Noun : We shall not see his like again.

Verb : Children like sweets.

Adjective : They are men of like build and stature.

Preposition : Do not talk like that.

### LITTLE

Noun : I want but little.

Adjective : There is little danger in going there.

Adverb : She eats very little.

### MORE

Pronoun : More of us die in bed than out of it.

Adjective : We want more men like him.

Adverb : You should talk less and work more.

### MUCH

Pronoun : Much of it is true.

Adjective : There is much sense in what he says.

Adverb : He boasts too much.

### NEAR

Verb : The time nears.

Adjective : He is a near relation.

Adverb : Draw near and listen.

Preposition : The school is near the post office.

### NEITHER

Pronoun : It is difficult to negotiate where neither will trust.

Adjective : Neither statement is true.

Conjunction : Give me neither poverty nor riches.

### NEXT

Noun : Who is your next?

Adjective : I shall go to Delhi next Sunday.

Adverb : What next?

Preposition : He was sitting next to her.

### NO

Noun : I'll not take a no.

Adjective : It is no joke.

Adverb : He is no more.

## OIL

Noun : Oil is a fatty substance.
Verb : Oil your own machine.

## ONCE

Noun : Please help me for once.
Adverb : You were young once.
Conjunction : Once he hesitates, he will fall.

## ONE

Noun : One would think he was mad.
Pronoun : The little ones cried in joy.
Adjective : One day I met him in the street.

## ONLY

Adjective : It was his only chance.
Adverb : He was only (= simply) foolish.
Conjunction : Take what I have, only let me go.

## OVER

Noun : In one over he took four wickets.
Adverb : Read it over carefully.
Preposition : At forty a change came over him.

## RIGHT

Noun : It is a matter of right.
Verb : It is such a fault that will right itself.
Adjective : He is the right man for the job.
Adverb : Serve him right.

## ROUND

Noun : The boy played well in the first round.
Verb : They rounded the temple silently.
Adjective : A square peg in a round hole.
Adverb : At last he came round to their belief.
Preposition : The earth moves round the sun.

## SHOWER

Noun : Heavy shower is harmful to crop.
Verb : Honours were showered upon him.

## SINCE

Adverb : I have not seen him since.
Preposition : I have not seen him since Monday.
Conjunction : It is many days since I saw you last.

## SO

Adverb : I am so sorry.
Conjunction : He was ill, so he could not come to school.

## SOME

Pronoun : Some say one thing and others another.
Adjective : We must find some way out of it.
Adverb : Some twenty guests were there.

## STILL

Noun : He heard a shrill cry in the still of night.
Verb : Mothers still their babies with a lulling song.
Adjective : Mosquitoes lay eggs in still water.
Adverb : He is still in idleness.

## SUCH

Pronoun : Such was not my intention.
Adjective : Don't do this in such a hurry.

## THAT

Pronoun : That is what I want.
Adjective : What is that noise?
Rel. Pronoun : The evil that men do remains after them.
Conjunction : He works hard that he may succeed.

## THE

Article : The boy who came here is my brother. (Demon. Adjective)
Adverb : The sooner the better.

## TILL

Preposition : He will stay here till tomorrow.
Conjunction : Do not start till I give the order.

## UP

Noun : Every man has ups and downs in life.
Adjective : The next Up train will leave at 8 p.m.
Adverb : Prices of essential commodities are going up.
Preposition : He went up the hill.

## WATER

Noun : None can live without water.
Verb : She is watering the plant.

## WELL

Adjective : I am well. [Predicative Adj.]
I hope you are now well.
Adverb : He played well.
[Or] Well begun is half done.—**Wren & Martin**
Interjection : Well, you may go.

## WHAT

Interrogative Pronoun : What do you want?
Interrogative Adjective : What book do you want?
Relative Pronoun : Give me what you can.
Interjection : What ! You don't mean to say so?

### WHILE

Noun : Sid down and rest a **while**.
Verb : They **while** away their time in idleness.
Conjunction : **While** a great poet he is a greater dramatist.

### WHY

Noun : I don't know the **why** and wherefore of it.
Interrogative Adverb : **Why** did he come here?
Relative Adverb : I know the reason **why** he did it.
Interjection : **Why**, it is surely Suren!

### YET

Adverb : There is more talk **yet** to be told.
Conjunction : He is unable, **yet** willing.

## EXERCISE

**A. What Part of Speech is each of the marked words?**

1. He is the **right** man in the **right** position. 2. There is **much** truth in what he says. 3. Don't eat too **much**. 4. It matters **little** what he says. 5. She is **little** known here. 6. A **little** learning is a dangerous thing. 7. He spoke in a **loud** voice. 8. Don't speak so **loud**. 9. It is **hard** to understand. 10. He is **hard** of hearing. 11. You must work **hard** to succeed in life. 12. **Some** ten boys are present. 13. I'll take **some**, but not all. 14. He rises **early** in the morning. 15. The **early** bird catches the worm. 16. **All** is fair in love and war. 17. **All** that glitters is not gold. 18. We shall lie **all** alike in our graves. 19. She did her **best**. 20. I like this **best**. 21. This is the **best** book. 22. He is **but** a child. 23. **But** for his help I couldn't have done it. 24. I change, **but** cannot die. 25. The paths of glory lead **but** to the grave.

**B. Make sentences with the following words as directed :**

(i) Above → (as a noun) : ____________________
(ii) Above → (as a preposition) : ____________________
(iii) After → (as an adverb) : ____________________
(iv) After → (as a conjunction) : ____________________
(v) Better → (as an adjective) : ____________________
(vi) Better → (as an adverb) : ____________________
(vii) Down → (as a noun) : ____________________
(viii) Down → (as an adverb) : ____________________
(ix) Head → (as a noun) : ____________________
(x) Head → (as a verb) : ____________________
(xi) Honour → (as a noun) : ____________________
(xii) Honour → (as a verb) : ____________________
(xiii) Little → (as an adjective) : ____________________
(xiv) Little → (as an adverb) : ____________________
(xv) Much → (as an adjective) : ____________________
(xvi) Much → (as an adverb) : ____________________
(xvii) Right → (as a noun) : ____________________
(xviii) Right → (as an adverb) : ____________________
(xix) Well → (as an adjective) : ____________________
(xx) Well → (as an adverb) : ____________________

# 32 WORDS COMMONLY CONFUSED

## WORDS COMMONLY CONFUSED IN SPELLING

**Here is a list of words which are commonly misspelt. This list has been prepared on the basis of frequency of usage :**

### [A]

abundance
access
accident
achieve
admission
adequate
adolescence
advice (N)
advise (V)
aggression
amateur
aerial
aggregate
ancestor
alter
anniversary
announce
anxiety
anxious
apology
apparent
appeal
appearance
appetite
approach
appropriate
appreciation
approximate
arthritis
autumn
average

### [B]

balloon
banner
banquet
barrage
barrier
bias
beggar
behaviour
belief (N)
believe (V)
benefit
beneath
beware
bewilder
bloom
blossom
blush
bona fide
bonus

### [C]

cancer
canteen
canvas
canvass
carrier
career
catalogue
cattle
cease
seize
celebrate
cemetery
cenotaph
century
ceremony
certain
ceiling
cigarette
cinema

circle
circus
coffee
college
collision
colleague
commission
committee
competition
conceal
conscience
conscientious
conquer
consensus
conscious
consecutive
consent
courage
curse
curtain
custom
cyclone
culture
convenience
conveyance

**[D]**

danger
debt
decision
deceive
development
design
diarrhoea
disease
discipline
division
doubt
due
duly
dyke
dynasty
dysentery

**[E]**

earnest
element
elementary
embarrass
endeavour
engineer
enormous
entrance
envelope
enough
enthusiasm
equity
equivalent
erroneous
essential
esteem
ether
etiquette
exaggerate
excellent
except
exception
exhibition
existence
explosion

**[F]**

failure
fascinate
fascism
fatigue
favourite
festoon
fibre
field
fiery
forcibly
foreign
forfeit
foul
fowl
fulfil
furniture
fusillade
fusion
fuss
future

**[G]**

gaiety
gallant
gallery
gazette
genius
gesture
goddess
gorgeous
grammar
grateful
grief (N)
grieve (V)
grievance
guarantee
guard
guardian
guess
guide

**[H]**

hammer
height
heiress
hindrance
humour
hygiene

**[I]**

illegal
illiterate
illustration
inconvenience

indecent
indigenous

indispensable
individual
influential
initial
ingenious
ingenuous
innocence
irresistible
intelligent
interfere

interview
island

**[J]**

jealous
jealousy
jester
jewellery
journey
journalist
jubilee
judgement
judgment
jugglery
juicy
junction

**[K]**

kerosene
kindergarten

knack
knave
kneel
knife
knob
knock

knot
knit
knowledge

**[L]**

laboratory
leisure
leopard
leper
licence (N)
license (V)
lieutenant
liquid
liquor
lily
literacy
literate
literature
litterateur
livelihood
loose
lose
lustre
luxury
lyre
lyric

**[M]**

machine
machinery
maintain
maintenance
manageable
mansion
marriage
marvellous
material
mathematics
measure
mechanical
millionaire
miscellaneous
mischief
monotonous
moustache
museum
musician
mystery

**[N]**

nasal
necessary
necessity
neighbour
neutral
niece
ninth
nonsense
noticable
numerous

**[O]**

obedience
obedient
observe (V)
observance (N)
obvious
occasion
occupation
occur (V)
occurred (P/PP)
occurrence (N)
odour
offence (N)
offensive (Adj)
offered

offering
omelette
omitted
operation

opportunity
orator

**[P]**

pamphlet
parallel
parliament
parlour
partial
particular
patient

pavilion
peasant
peculiar
pencil
pension
permanent
permission
persuade
persuasion
petroleum
physique
pigeon
planetarium
pleasant
pleasure
polygamy
popular
portion
previous
primary
privilege
profession
programme
proprietor
protein
psychology
psycological
punctual

[Q]

quarrel (V)
quarrelled (P/PP)
quarter
question
queue
quiet
quite
quinine
quote (V)
quotation (N)

[R]

rabbit
radius
railing
realm
receipt (N)
receive (V)
recommend (V)
recur (V)
recurrence (N)
refer (V)
referred (PP)
reference (N)
referee (N)
regret (V)
regrettable (Adj)
relief (N)
relieve (V)
religion (N)
religious (Adj)
remember (V)
remembrance (N)
reminiscence
repetition
reservoir
resistance
restaurant
root
route
routine

[S]

saviour
scarcity
scene
scenery
schedule
scheme
scholar
science
scientific
scissors
sculptor
sculpture

seize
sense
session
separate
servant
several
shield
shrewd
shy
sign
significance
skilful
society
soldier
shoulder
solemn
source
square
sovereign
stadium
successful
sufficient
suggestion
summer
superior
surgeon

[T]

technical
technique
telephone
temperature
theatre
theme
theoretical
thorough
through
thief
tolerance
tongue
tournament

tranquility
transferred
treasure
tremendous
tributary
truly
tuition
twelfth
twilight
tycoon
tyre
typhoid
typhoon

**[U]**

umbrella
unconscious
unintelligible
unmistakable
unique
universal
university
until
usually
usury
utensil
utter (V)
utterance (N)

**[V]**

vacancy
vaccinate
valley
variety
variance
vegetables
ventilator
veil
vicious
victory
victual
vigorous
visitor
vivacity
voluntary
volunteer
vulgar

**[W]**

wealth
weather
welcome
wield
wilful
witness
wolf
woollen
wreath
wreck
writing
written

**[X]**

xerox
X-mas
X-ray

**[Y]**

yawn
yearling
yellow
yield

**[Z]**

zeal
zebra
zest
zinc
zoology

## WORDS COMMONLY CONFUSED IN MEANING

### HOMOPHONES

**In English there are some words which have similarity in sound but bear some difference in spelling and meaning. The following pairs of words are often confused and misused : [See Notes on HOMONYMS and HOMOPHONES in Chapter 29]**

| Pairs | Examples |
|---|---|
| 1. Accecpt | Accept the proposal. |
| Except | All except you are guilty. |
| 2. Access | There is no easy access to success. |
| Excess | I shall not give you any excess payment. |
| 3. Adapt | Try to adapt to the new customs. |
| Adopt | Mr. Roy adopted a son. |
| 4. Addition | Some additions and alternations have been made in this book. |
| Edition | The latest edition of the book is good. |

| Pairs | Examples |
|---|---|
| 5. Advice | Listen to my advice. |
| Advise | The teacher advised the students. |
| 6. Affect | Smoking affects health. |
| Effect | What is the effect of such bad habit? |
| 7. Air | Walking in open air is a healthy habit. |
| Heir | Who is the heir of this estate? |
| Hair | Grey hair indicates old age. |
| Here | Here is an umbrella. |
| 8. Altar | An altar has been made for the goddess. |
| Alter | I have altered my plan. |
| 9. Alternate | You should take this medicine on alternate days. |
| Alternative | Is there any alternative? |
| 10. Ascent | His career is on the ascent. |
| Assent | I gave assent to his proposal. |
| 11. Amend | You must amend your ways. |
| Emend | The first part of the book has been emended. |
| 12. Bare | He came here bare-footed. |
| Bear | I cannot bear such a burden. |
| 13. Bath | Have a bath in the bathroom. |
| Bathe | He is bathing in a pond. |
| 14. Berth | He had a reserved berth. |
| Birth | Where is your birthplace? |
| 15. Beside | His house is beside the bank. |
| Besides | They got a commission besides their salary. |
| 16. Boar | The hunter shot a wild boar. |
| Bore | They bore a hole in the soil to bring out oil. |
| 17. Born | He was born in 1980. |
| Borne | The burden should be borne. |
| 18. Breath | A man cannot live without breath. |
| Breathe | He is breathing deeply. |
| 19. Canvas | The artist used this canvas. |
| Canvass | What are you canvassing now? |
| 20. Cast | Cast your vote. |
| Caste | Caste is no bar to success. |
| 21. Career | Try to build your career. |
| Carrier | The mosquito is the carrier of malaria. |
| 22. Cent | A cent is a small American coin. |
| Sent | They sent a letter to the publisher. |
| Scent | The scent of these flowers is pleasing. |

| Pairs | Examples |
|---|---|
| 23. Certain | Death is certain to all. |
| Curtain | Do not keep behind the curtain. |
| 24. Cease | Hiroshima ceased to exist. |
| Seize | All the goods have been seized. |
| 25. Cite | He cited an example. |
| Site | This is the site for the hospital. |
| Sight | He went out for sight-seeing. |
| 26. Check | Check your passport. |
| Cheque | Here is a cheque of Rs. 5,000. |
| 27. Coarse | I don't like such coarse cloth. |
| Course | Have you finished your course? |
| 28. Crops | The farmer is reaping the crops. |
| Corpse | Corpses are either burnt or buried. |
| 29. Complement | Some verbs take complements. |
| Compliment | A good work deserves compliment. |
| 30. Conscience | Have a clear conscience. |
| Conscious | He was conscious of his guilt. |
| Conscientious | A conscientious person cannot do this. |
| Consensus | At last they came to consensus. |
| 31. Council | He has applied to the H. S. Council. |
| Counsel | You need a good counsel. |
| 32. Credible | He is not at all credible. |
| Creditable | He has achieved a creditable career. |
| 33. Dairy | We get milk from Mother Dairy. |
| Diary | He has the habit of writing diary. |
| 34. Decease | The deceased person has no heir. |
| Disease | Cancer is a fatal disease. |
| 35. Defer | The resolution was deferred. |
| Differ | I differ from you on this point. |
| 36. Deference | In deference to his father's memory, we postponed the banquet. |
| Difference | There is difference of opinion on this. |
| 37. Dependant | Look after your dependants. |
| Dependent | Children are dependent on parents. |
| Defendant | The lawyer argued for the defendant. |
| 38. Desert | After three days we deserted the desert. |
| Dessert | The party was served with apples and sweets as dessert. |
| 39. Die | The soldier died for the country. |
| Dye | Why are you dyeing your cloth? |
| 40. Dew | The day passed like a dewdrop. |
| Due | He came here in due time to pay his dues. |

| Pairs | Examples |
|---|---|
| 41. Dual | Some persons have dual personality. |
| Duel | They fought a duel and one was severely injured. |
| 42. Eligible | You are eligible for the post. |
| Illegible | His handwriting is illegible. |
| 43. Emigrant | He is an emigrant from India to Bangladesh. |
| Immigrant | He is an Indian immigrant in the U.S.A. |
| 44. Eminent | He is an eminent professor. |
| Imminent | Be careful of the imminent danger. |
| 45. Eruption | Volcanic eruption ruined the city. |
| Irruption | The Mughal irruption was fatal to India. |
| 46. Expand | Now we have to expand the office. |
| Expend | You should not expend beyond your limit. |
| 47. Extant | It is the extant rule. |
| Extent | He has been relieved to a large extent. |
| 48. Fair | A fair-looking girl is running to the fair. |
| Fare | How much is the bus fare? |
| 49. Farm | He possesses a big agricultural farm. |
| Firm | Be firm if you wish to work in a foreign firm. |
| 50. Farther | Mumbai is farther from Delhi than Varanasi. |
| Further | Proceed further. Thus far and no further. |
| 51. Floor | He is sitting on the floor. |
| Flour | I like *chapatis* of flour. |
| 52. Foul | Don't go out in such foul weather. |
| Fowl | Here is a dish of fowl curry. |
| 53. Hail | We hailed the hail after the summer. |
| Hale | Be hale and hearty. |
| Hell | It is the gateway to hell. |
| 54. Haven | Terrorists now find a safe haven in W.B. |
| Heaven | It is better to reign in hell than to serve in heaven. |
| 55. Holy | Muharram is a holy festival. |
| Wholly | I wholly agree with your decision. |
| 56. Human | To err is human. |
| Humane | He was given humane treatment. |
| 57. Ingenious | He has an ingenious mind. |
| Ingenuous | His ingenuous nature attracts us. |
| 58. Jealous | Don't be jealous of other's fortune. |
| zealous | He is a zealous worker. |
| 59. Lane | It is a narrow lane. |
| Loan | Repay your loan. |
| Lone | Play a lone hand. |

| Pairs | Examples |
|---|---|
| 60. Leopard | A leopard has spots on its body. |
| Leper | A leper has scars on his body. |
| 61. Lever | A heavy load can be lifted easily with a lever. |
| Liver | The liver is an important organ to consume food. |
| 62. Lighting | There was a good lighting at the pandal. |
| Lightening | He is lightening my burden. |
| Lightning | See the flash of lightning in the sky. |
| 63. Literature | I am fond of English literature. |
| Litterateur | G. B. Shaw is a famous litterateur. |
| 64. Loose | Loose your belt before eating. |
| Lose | She loses her purse very often. |
| 65. Luxuriant | The tree bears luxuriant leaves. |
| Luxurious | He lives a luxurious life. |
| 66. Main | It is the main gate. |
| Mane | The lioness has no mane. |
| Mean | What do you mean by a mean character? |
| 67. Massage | He takes body massage regularly. |
| Message | Have you any message for me? |
| 68. Moral | He bears a good moral character. |
| Morale | The leaders should have high morale. |
| 69. Ordinance | The President has issued an ordinance today. |
| Ordnance | He is appointed in the ordnance factory. |
| 70. Paint | Make a picture using paint. |
| Pent | She is now in a state of pent-up anger. |
| 71. Peace | Let me die in peace. |
| Piece | Please give me a piece of paper. |
| 72. Piety | He is famous for his piety. |
| Pity | Have pity on him. |
| 73. Personal | It is my personal matter. |
| Personnel | Where is the electoral personnel? |
| 74. Persecute | The Jews were persecuted by the Nazis. |
| Prosecute | Trespassers will be prosecuted. |
| 75. Physic | No physic can cure if you are careless. |
| Physique | He has a fine physique. |
| 76. Plane | He travels by plane./Football is played on plane land. |
| Plain | I love plain cooking/plain dress. |
| 77. Popular | He is a popular teacher. |
| Populous | Kolkata is a populous city. |

| Pairs | Examples |
|---|---|
| 78. Pore | Sweat comes from the pores of skin. |
| Pour | Pour some water on his head. |
| 79. Portable | I have bought a portable T.V. |
| Potable | The water of this pond is not potable. |
| 80. Practice | Spitting is a bad practice. |
| Practise | Do you practise what you preach? |
| 81. Pray | Pray to God. |
| Prey | The tiger is a beast of prey. |
| 82. Precedent | Is there any precedent about it? |
| President | He is the President of the G.B. |
| 83. Prescribe | The doctor prescribed a very costly medicine. |
| Proscribe | 'Pather Dabi' was proscribed by the British Government. |
| 84. Principal | Dr. Pal is the Principal of the college. |
| Principle | He is a man of strong principle. |
| 85. Quiet | Be calm and quiet. |
| Quite | He is not quite happy. |
| 86. Rain | A heavy rain cooled the people. |
| Reign | It is better to reign in hell than to serve in heaven. |
| Rein | When the reins were pulled, the horse stopped. |
| 87. Raise | Raise your hands. |
| Rays | The rays of the sun is too hot at noon. |
| 88. Refuge | He took refuge in the slum. |
| Refuse | He refused to do it. |
| 89. Right | Might is right. Turn to right is not always right. |
| Rite | The religious rites are done. |
| Write | Write 'right' on the right side. |
| 90. Root | What is root of this evil? |
| Route | This is the short route to go to hell. |
| Rout | The morale of the enemy was very low because of its rout. |
| 91. Sculptor | He is a famous sculptor. |
| Sculpture | Everyone praises his sculpture. |
| 92. Seize | The police seized the good. |
| Siege | The army laid siege to the city. |
| Size | What is the size of your belly/sweater? |
| 93. Soldier | He is a brave soldier. |
| Shoulder | He shoulders the burden on his broad shoulder. |
| 94. Sole | She is the sole heir to the estate. |
|  | Get the sole of the shoes changed. |
| Soul | Let her soul rest in peace. |

| Pairs | Examples |
|---|---|
| 95. Sore | He got a throat **sore**. |
| Soar | The bird **soared** higher and higher. |
| 96. Stair | Step on the **stair** of the staircase. |
| Stare | He **stared** hard at the knave. |
| 97. Staff | The **staff** of the school do not carry a staff in hand. |
| Stuff | It is made of indigenous **stuff**. |
| 98. Stalk | The tiger is **stalking** its prey. |
| Stock | He is clearing his **stock**. |
| 99. Stationary | The sun is **stationary** and the planets move round it. |
| Stationery | He deals in **stationery** goods. |
| 100. Steal | To **steal** is a crime. |
| Steel | There is a **steel** plant at Durgapur. |
| Still | Is the mosquito **still** alive in the **still** water? |
| 101. Suit | This **suit** does not **suit** him. |
| Suite | They rented a **suite** in the hotel. |
| 102. Tail | Don't pull the **tail** of the dog. |
| Tale | Listen to the **tale** of the greedy dog. |
| 103. Tall | How **tall** is the tree? |
| Tell | **Tell** me a tall tale of the cunning fox. |
| 104. Tamper | He tried to **tamper** the deed. |
| Temper | Don't lose your **temper**. |
| 105. There | Who is **there** and what is **there**? |
| Their | There lies **their** purse. |
| 106. Vain | She poses to be **vain** in **vain**. |
| Vein | The surgeon cut his **vein** while he was talking in a light **vein**. |
| 107. Voluntary | This is a **voluntary** job. |
| Volunteer | The **volunteers** should keep quiet. |
| 108. Wave | The **waves** of the sea rolled on the shore./He **waved** goodbye. |
| Waive | The judge **waived** the injunction. |
| 109. Way | Is there any **way** to go to heaven? |
| Weigh | **Weigh** yourself in the scale of justice. |
| 110. Warm | They gave him a **warm** reception. |
| Worm | The **worm** has consumed the book. |
| 111. Weak | The old man is too **weak** to walk. |
| Week | Please come once a **week**. |
| Wick | Please trim the **wick** of the lamp. |

## WORDS COMMONLY CONFUSED [IN USAGE]

**Here is a list of words which have some similarity in meaning but a distinction in usage. The following words are frequently confused and misused :**

| Pairs | Examples |
|---|---|
| Admit | I admit your claim. |
| Confess | He confessed his guilt. |
| Apt | He is apt to get into the business. |
| Liable | You will be liable for damages. |
| Anxious | We are anxious about your health. |
| Eager | We are eager to know the results. |
| As [Linker], Like | Do as you like. |
| Like [Prep] | Do not behave like a child. |
| Artisan | A carpenter is a good artisan. |
| Artist | Jamini Roy was a great artist. |
| Audience | The speaker bored the audience. |
| Spectators | The spectators were bored to see the play. |
| Better | He is better today than a week ago. |
| Well | Now I am well. |
| Between | Divide the mangoes between the two. |
| Among | Divide the mangoes among the boys. |
| Bring | Bring some butter from the shop. |
| Take | Take your pen. |
| Can | I can work out the sum. |
| May | May I come in?/It may rain today. |
| Childish | I do not like such childish talk. |
| Childlike | His childlike behaviour attracts us. |
| Climate | The climate of India is hotter than that of England. |
| Weather | Do not go out in such foul weather. |
| Compliment | A good work deserves compliment. |
| Compliment | Please pay my compliments to your parents. |
| Complement | An Intransitive verb may trake a complement. |
| Couple | The couple went out for the honeymoon. |
| Pair | Have a new pair of shoes. |
| Despise | Do not despise the poor. |
| Detest | I detest the modern fashion. |
| Each other | These two brothers love each other. |
| One other | All these boys are familiar with one other. |
| Formally | I have informed him formally. |
| Formerly | Formerly he was a professor. |
| Fewer | There are fewer students in the class. |

| Pairs | Examples |
|---|---|
| Less | Why are you paying less attention to it? |
| Habit | Give up your bad habit. |
| Custom | Dowry is an evil social custom. |
| Later | This is the later edition of the book. |
| Latter | Between the two boys the former is strong and the latter is weak in English. |
| Latest | This is the latest edition of the book. |
| Last | He is the last boy in the class. |
| Legible | Your hand writing should be legible. |
| Readable | This book is not readable. |
| Many | Here are many books on History. |
| Much | I do not like much sugar in tea. |
| Tasteful | The tasteful decoration of the house attracted the guests. |
| Tasty | The new cook has prepared a tasty dish. |

## AMERICAN AND BRITISH ENGLISH

| British | American | British | American |
|---|---|---|---|
| Aeroplane | Airplane | Queue | Line |
| Angry | Incensed | Railway | Railroad |
| Fellow | Guy | Rubber | Eraser |
| Film | Movie | Rubbish | Garbage |
| Flat | Apartment | Shop | Store |
| Ground floor | First floor | Sweets | Candy |
| Lift | Elevator | Tap | Faucet |
| Lorry | Truck | Taxi | Cab |
| Mad | Crazy | Timetable | Schedule |
| Main road | Highway | Tin | Can |
| Pavement | Sidewalk | Toilet | Restroom |
| Petrol | Gas/Gasoline | Torch | Flashlight |
| Post | Mail | Trousers | Pants |
| Monday to Sunday | Monday through Sunday | Underground | Subway |

## AMERICAN AND BRITISH SPELLING

| British | American | British | American |
|---|---|---|---|
| Analyse | Analyze | Litre | Liter |
| Catalogue | Catalog | Metre | Meter |
| Centre | Center | Paralyse | Paralyze |

| British | American | British | American |
|---|---|---|---|
| Cheque | Check | Practise (v) | Practice (v) |
| Colour | Color | Programme | Program |
| Defence | Defense | Realise | Realize |
| Grey | Gray | Skilful | Skillful |
| Honour | Honor | Theatre | Theater |
| Jewellery | Jewelry | Traveller | Traveler |
| Labour | Labor | Tyre | Tire |

## EXERCISE

**1. Show the difference of meaning of each pair of words with examples :**

| Pair of Words | Examples |
|---|---|
| [1] Accept<br>Except | |
| [2] Access<br>Excess | |
| [3] Adapt<br>Adopt | |
| [4] Advice<br>Advise | |
| [5] Affect<br>Effect | |
| [6] Altar<br>Alter | |
| [7] Bath<br>Bathe | |
| [8] Beside<br>Besides | |
| [9] Cast<br>Caste | |
| [10] Career<br>Carrier | |
| [11] Cite<br>Site | |
| [12] Cease<br>Seize | |
| [13] Corps<br>Corpse | |

| Pair of Words | Examples |
|---|---|
| [14] Complement<br>Compliment | |
| [15] Council<br>Counsel | |
| [16] Credible<br>Creditable | |
| [17] Decease<br>Disease | |
| [18] Defer<br>Differ | |
| [19] Die<br>Dye | |
| [20] Dew<br>Due | |
| [21] Eligible<br>Illegible | |
| [22] Emigrant<br>Immigrant | |
| [23] Expand<br>Expend | |
| [24] Farther<br>Further | |
| [25] Fair<br>Fare | |
| [26] Jealous<br>Zealous | |
| [27] Loose<br>Lose | |
| [28] Personal<br>Personnel | |
| [29] Peace<br>Piece | |
| [30] Popular<br>Populous | |
| [31] Practice<br>Practise | |
| [32] Soldier<br>Shoulder | |

| Pair of Words | Examples |
|---|---|
| [33] Stair<br>Stare | |
| [34] Steal<br>Steel | |
| [35] Tail<br>Tale | |
| [36] Voluntary<br>Volunteer | |
| [37] Way<br>Weigh | |
| [38] Wave<br>Waive | |
| [39] Weak<br>Week | |
| [40] Warm<br>Worm | |

# 33 GROUP VERBS/ PHRASAL VERBS

## DIFFERENCE BETWEEN SIMPLE VERBS AND GROUP VERBS

**Read the following sentences :**

Lila laughs. Lila laughed at the poor.

Finite Verb — Group Verb

In the first sentence the verb laughs has its simple meaning. But in the second sentence the verb laughed at is a compound verb and it means ridiculed—which is an idiomatic meaning. So you see :

**When a Verb takes a Preposition or an Adverbial Particle after it and as a Compound Verb gives idiomatic meaning, it is called a Group Verb or a Prepositional Verb or a Phrasal Verb.**

## SOME GROUP VERBS WITH ILLUSTRATIVE SENTENCES

### ACT

**Act on or upon** (affect)—Such hard work will act upon your health.

**Act under** (act in obedience to)—He acted under the orders of the Headmaster.

**Act up to** (act according to)—He always acts up to my advice.

### ASK

**Ask for** (pray for)—He asked for a loan of one thousand rupees.

### BEAR

**Bear away, off** (win)—He bore away (off) four prizes in the Annual Sports.

**Bear on** (relate to)—His remark does not bear on this subject.

**Bear out** (support)—His evidence does not bear out the charge.

**Bear up** (sustain)—His patience bore him up in that crisis.

**Bear with** (tolerate)—I cannot bear with such insult.

### BLOW

**Blow off** (emit)—The engine blows off carbon dioxide.

**Blow out** (extinguish)—Blow out the lamp.

**Blow up** (destroy by explosion)—The soldiers blew up the bridge.

## BREAK

**Break away** (get away)—The convict broke away from the prison.

**Break down** (decline)—His health broke down by hard work.

**Break in, on** (interrupt)—You should not break in (on) our conversation.

**Break into** (enter by force)—The robber broke into the house at midnight.

**Break off** (stop studdenly)—The speaker broke off in the middle of his speech.

**Break out** (spread suddenly)—Cholera broke out in the village.

**Break through** (get through by force)—The soldier broke through the enemy's line.

**Break up** (close)—Our school breaks up at 4 p.m.

**Break with** (quarrel)—He has broken with his friend.

## BRING

**Bring about** (cause to happen)—He tried to bring about a quarrel between them.

**Bring down** (reduce)—The good harvest brought down the price of rice.

**Bring forth** (produce)—The timely rain brings forth good crops.

**Bring in** (yield)—His property brings him in Rs. 5,000 a year.

**Bring off** (rescue)—He brought off the passengers of the wrecked ship.

**Bring out** (publish)—The publisher has brought out a new book.

**Bring through** (cure)—The new medicine has brought the patient through.

**Bring up** (rear)—She is brought up by her mother.

## BURST

**Burst into** (express emotion)—She burst into tears to see her dead son.

**Burst out** (begin suddenly)—He burst out laughing.

## CALL

**Call at** (visit)—He called at my office yesterday.

**Call for** (demand)—He called for an explanation from me.

**Call forth** (use)—You have to call forth all your energy in the ensuing examination.

**Call in** (send for)—Please call in a doctor.

**Call off** (withdraw)—The strike was called off.

**Call on upon** (meet)—He called on (upon) me in my office.

**Call out** (shout)—He called out for help.

**Call over** (read out)—The teacher called over the names of his pupils in the class.

**Call up** (remember)—I cannot call up your name.

## CARRY

**Carry away** (remove)—The wounded man was carried away to hospital.

**Carry away** (cause death to)—He was carried away by the current.

**Carry off** (cause death to)—Cholera has carried off one hundred people this year in the village.

**Carry off** (win)—He carried off all the prizes.

**Carry on** (continue)—He will carry on the business/his studies.

**Carry out** (obey)—You must carry out my order.

**Carry over** (take forward)—This amount should be carried over to the next page.

**Carry through** (bring success)—His hard labour will carry him through.

**Carry with** (cause to agree)—He carried the audience with him.

## CAST

**Cast about** (move about)—He is casting about for an opportunity.

**Cast aside** (throw off)—He cast aside (or, cast away, or cast off) his old shoes.

**Cast out** (reject)—As he is my friend, I shall not cast him out.

## CATCH

**Catch at** (take the opportunity)—A drowning man catches at a straw.

**Catch up** (come up with)—India is trying to catch up with the advanced countries.

## COME

**Come about** (happen)—How did the accident come about?

**Come across** (meet)—I came across the lame man on the way.

**Come at** (come up within the reach of)—The fox tried to come at the grapes but failed.

**Come by** (get)—How did you come by this picture?

**Come down** (decrease)—The price of rice has come down.

**Come of** (to be born)—He comes of a respectable family.

**Come off** (take place)—Our annual sports came off yesterday.

**Come out** (be known)—The result will come out soon.

**Come round** (recover)—The patient will come round soon.

**Come to** (amount to)—His income comes to Rs. 1,000 a month.

**Come up** to (be equal to)—His work did not come up to our expectation.

## CRY

**Cry down** (decry)—Do not cry down anything without considering the pros and cons of it.

**Cry for** (demand)—They are crying for a master plan for the prevention of flood.

**Cry out** (shout)—He cried out for help.

## CUT

**Cut down** (reduce)—Try to cut down your budget.

**Cut off** (dislocate)—The robbers cut off the telephone connection.

## DO

**Do away with** (abolish)—We should do away with our bad habits.

**Do for** (serve the purpose of)—This cloth will do for a flag.

**Do up** (put into order)—He had to do up many rooms everyday.

**Do with** (deal with)—He has to do with all sorts of people.

**Do without** (manage without)—I cannot do without the help of my assistant.

## DEAL

**Deal in** (carry on business)—He deals in rice.

**Deal with** (behave)—He deals with me very well.

## DRAW

**Draw away** (divert)—His attention was drawn away by the noise.

**Draw back** (retreat)—The army is now drawing back.

**Draw in** (reduce)—Try to draw in your expenditure.

**Draw off**—(pull off)—She drew off her gloves.

**Draw on** (approach)—The festival is drawing on.

**Draw out** (sketch)—Will you draw out a scheme?

## DRIVE

**Drive away** (turn out)—He was driven away from the village.

## FALL

**Fall at** (show disappointment)—His face fell at the news.

**Fall among** (happen to come among)—He fell among the thieves.

**Fall back upon** (have recourse to)—Having lost his job he fell back upon agriculture.

**Fall in with** (agree with)—I cannot fall in with his views.

**Fall from** (come out)—Not a word fell from his lips.

**Fall off** (decline)—The quality of goods has fallen off.

**Fall on** (attack)—The robbers fell on the passerby.

**Fall out** (quarrel)—Do not fall out with your friend.

**Fall through** (fail)—All his plans fell through.

## FILL

**Fill in, up** (complete)—Fill in (up) the gaps.

## FIND

**Find out** (detect)—He is always busy to find out others' faults.

## GET

**Get at** (reach)—The apples are hanging high up and I can't get at them.

**Get away** (escape)—The thief could not get away with the necklace.

**Get by** (pass)—Please let me get by.

**Get down** (descend)—He got down from the train/bus.

**Get into** (ascend)—He got into the train.

**Get off** (escape)—The thief got off safely.

**Get on** (proceed)—How are you getting on with your studies?

**Get out** (got out)—Get out of the class.

**Get out** (come out)—The secret got out at last.

**Get over** (overcome)—He will soon get over the difficulties.

**Get through** (succeed)—He got through the examination.

**Get up** (rise)—He gets up at 5 a.m. everyday.

## GIVE

**Give away** (make over)—The president gave away the prizes.

**Give in** (yield)—The enemies gave in at last.

**Give off** (send out)—The cooking coal gives off a lot of smoke.

**Give out** (disclose)—He will never give out the truth.

**Give over** (make over)—He will give over the charge tomorrow.

**Give over** (stop)—The rain will soon give over.

**Give up** (abandon)—Try to give up your bad habit.

## GO

**Go about** (move about)—He goes about canvassing his goods.

**Go away** (leave the place)—He has gone away with all his belongings.

**Go after** (follow)—The dog went after the thief.

**Go against** (oppose)—This goes against the interest of the people.

**Go back on** (withdraw)—He won't go back on his word.

**Go beyond** (exceed)—You have gone beyond your limit.

**Go by** (act according to)—I have to go by the rules.

**Go forth** (be issued)—The order went forth for the public yesterday.

**Go in for** (sit for)—He is going in for the W.B.C.S. Examination.

**Go off** (be fired/be thrown)—The gun (The arrow) went off by accident.

**Go on** (continue)—Go on with your studies.

**Go out** (extinguish)—The light has gone out.

**Go over** (change)—He went over to the other party.

**Go through** (read)—He has gone through the book.

**Go through** (bear)—He has gone through many hardships.

**Go up** (increase)—The cost of living has gone up.

**Go with** (agree)—He will not go with you in this matter.

**Go without** (live without)—They have to go without from time to time.

## HAND

**Hand over** (place someone or something at the custody of some other)—The thief was handed over to the police.

## HANG

**Hang about** (remain near)—The girl always hangs about her mother.

**Hang by** (put to death by hanging)—The murderer was hanged by the neck.

**Hang down** (lower)—Father had to hang down his head in shame for his son's misconduct.

**Hang for** (put to death by hanging)—He was hanged for murder.

**Hang on** (depend upon)—What is the use of hanging on others for a job?

**Hang up** (put up)—Hang up your coat. (Or) The Headmaster asked him to hang up the notice on the wall.

**Hang up** (delay)—The plan has been hanging up for a long time.

## HOLD

**Hold back** (hide)—You need not hold back the secret from me.

**Hold in** (check)—You should hold in your temper.

**Hold off** (keep away)—Please hold off your dog.

**Hold on** (passive)—The meeting will be held on the 5th of May.

**Hold out** (offer or promise)—He held out a helping hand to me.

**Hold over** (postpone)—This item has been held over till the next meeting.

**Hold up** (delay)—The train was held up for two hours.

## KEEP

**Keep at** (stick to)—The girl kept at her mother in the kitchen.

**Keep away** (remain at a distance from)—Keep yourself away from evil company.

**Keep down** (control)—He could not keep down his anger.

**Keep in** (prevent from going out)—They were kept in by rain.

**Keep in with** (keep good terms)—I can't keep in with you any longer.

**Keep off** (remain at a distance)—Keep off the fire.

**Keep on** (continue)—He kept on shouting.

**Keep up** (maintain)—He always tries to keep up his reputation as a good teacher.

**Keep up with** (keep pace with)—Try to keep up with the changing world.

## LAY

**Lay aside** (keep apart)—Try to lay aside something for your old age.

**Lay before** (place something)—He laid the facts before the committee.

**Lay by** (save)—You must lay by something for the future.

**Lay down** (sacrifice)—He laid down his life for the sake of his country.

**Lay in** (store)—The potatoes were laid in for the off-season.

**Lay off** (dismiss temporarily)—The workers were laid off for two months.

**Lay on** (apply)—He laid on the paint on the doors.

**Lay on** (put)—He laid his hand on my shoulder.

**Lay out** (invest)—He laid out a large amount of money in National Savings Certificates.

**Lay up with** (be confined to bed)—He was laid up with pneumonia.

**Lay with** (cover)—He laid the floor with a carpet.

## LOOK

**Look at** (gaze)—He is looking at the moon.

**Look after** (take care of)—Mother looked after her child.

**Look down upon** (hate)—Do not look down upon the poor.

**Look for** (search)—He is looking for a job.

**Look forward** (expect eagerly)—They look forward to your help.

**Look into** (examine)—I asked him to look into the matter.

**Look on, upon** (consider)—I look upon (on) him as my best friend.

**Look over** (examine)—I have looked over your papers.

**Look through** (inspect carefully)—The auditor looked through the account.

**Look up** (find out)—Look up the word in the dictionary.

**Look up** (rise in price—**C.O.D.**)—The price of goods is looking up nowadays.

### MAKE

**Make after** (run after)—The police made after the thief.

**Make away** (kill)—He made away with himself.

**Make for** (move towards)—The ship made for London.

**Make of** (compose of)—This ornament is made of gold.

**Make off** (escape)—The thief made off with the ornaments.

**Make out** (understand)—I can't make out your words.

**Make over** (transfer)—He has made over the charge to the secretary.

**Make up** (complete)—I still need rupees one hundred to make up the loss.

**Make up for** (compensate)—I must make up for the lost time.

**Make up one's mind** (resolve)—He made up his mind to go there.

### PASS

**Pass away** (die)—The patient passed away peacefully.

**Pass by** (pay no attention to)—He passed by these mistakes.

**Pass by** (go alongside)—He passed by our house.

**Pass for** (be regarded as)—He passed for a scholar in the village.

**Pass off** (to be over)—The ceremony passed off smoothly.

**Pass on** (proceed)—He passed on from this to that.

**Pass over** (overlook)—We may pass over the unnecessary details.

**Pass through** (to gather experience)—He had to pass through many difficulties.

### PUT

**Put away** (leave)—He put away all ideas of being a doctor.

**Put by** (lay by)—Put by something for your old age.

**Put down** (write)—Put down your name on the blackboard.

**Put down** (suppress)—The king put down the revolt.

**Put off** (take off)—Put off your shoes.

**Put off** (postpone)—The meeting was put off.

**Put off** (get rid of)—You must put off your doubts.

**Put on** (wear)—Put on your dress.

**Put on** (pretend)—He puts on an air of innocence.

**Put out** (extinguish)—He put out the lamp.

**Put up** (hang up)—The Headmaster put up a notice.

**Put up with** (tolerate)—I cannot put up with such insults.

### RUN

**Run after** (chase)—The villagers ran after the thief.

**Run away** (flee)—The boys ran away on seeing the police.

**Run away with** (steal)—The thief ran away with all the valuables.

**Run into** (fall into)—He ran into danger.

**Run into** (to be involved in)—He ran into heavy debts.

**Run on** (continue)—The troubles will run on for a few days.

**Run out** (become exhausted)—His patience is running out.

**Run over** (knocked down)—The old man was run over by a car.

## SEE

**See off** (to bid goodbye)—I went to the station to see off my friend.

**See through** (understand)—I have seen through his plan.

## SEND

**Send for** (summon)—Please send for a doctor.

**Send up** (recommend for competition)—Fifty candidates have been sent up for the examination.

## SET

**Set about** (begin)—He set about his work early in the morning.

**Set apart** or **aside** (reserve)—He set apart (aside) a part of his income for charity.

**Set aside** (ignore)—Let us set aside all formalities.

**Set against** (go against)—Public opinion is setting against the proposal.

**Set-back** (stop progress of)—Public opinion is setting back the programme.

**Set by** (lay by)—Set by something for old age.

**Set forth** (start)—They set forth early in the morning.

**Set in** (begin)—The rains have set in.

**Set out** (start)—He set out for London.

**Set up** (establish)—The villagers have set up a school in the village.

**Set upon/on** (advance to attack)—She had been set on (upon) by a dog.

## SIT

**Sit for** (appear in)—He sat for the Final Examination.

**Sit up** (continue to sit)—His mother sat up the whole night.

## STAND

**Stand against** (oppose)—They stood against their common enemy.

**Stand by** (support)—Always stand by your friends.

**Stand for** (contest for)—He stood for Presidentship in the last election.

**Stand for** (symbolise)—The judge stands for justice.

**Stand up for** (support the cause of)—The strong should stand up for the weak.

**Stand out** (be prominent)—His work stands out from others.

**Stand over** (be postponed)—Let this matter stand over till the next meeting.

**Stand to** (stick to)—He stands to his promise.

**Stand to** (abide by)—It stands to reason that the best boy will get the best prize.

## TAKE

**Take after** (resemble)—She takes after her mother.

**Take back** (withdraw)—She will not take back her words.

**Take by** (catch)—He took the man by his neck.

**Take down** (write down)—Take down the note in short.

**Take for** (consider)—I took him for a saint.

**Take off** (put off)—Take off your coat.

**Take over** (accept)—The new secretary will take over the charge.

**Take to** (addict)—He has taken to drinking in his youth.

**Take up** (occupy)—This work will take up too much time.

**Take up** (undertake)—He will take up the problem and try to solve it.

### TALK

**Talk over** (discuss)—They are talking over the matter.

### TELL

**Tell of** (describe)—He told of his plan in details.

**Tell on/upon** (affect)—Over-eating may tell on (upon) your health.

### TURN

**Turn aside** (deviate from)—We should not turn aside from the path of virtue.

**Turn against** (become hostile)—They soon turned against us.

**Turn away** (keep away)—He turned away in disgust.

**Turn down** (reject)—He turned down our proposal.

**Turn into** (change into)—Turn this passage into English.

**Turn off** (stop)—Turn off the switch.

**Turn on** (let it work)—Turn on the switch.

**Turn out** (drive out)—He was turned out from the school.

**Turn to** (engage oneself)—I advised him to turn to the study of medicine.

**Turn up** (appear)—He has not turned up yet.

### WORK

**Work at** (be engaged in)—He is working at the statue.

**Work on** (continue working)—He worked on throughout the night.

**Work out** (solve)—He could not work out the sum.

**Work up** (excite)—Antony worked up the feelings of the Roman mob by his speech.

## APPLIED SECTION

### Some substitution of Group Verbs for Single Verbs

| Single Verb | Group Verb |
|---|---|
| 1. Over-exercise affected his health. | 1. Over-exercise told upon his health. |
| 2. The boys arrived in good number. | 2. The boys turned up in good number. |
| 3. They abolished the custom. | 3. They did away with the custom. |
| 4. They have established a school. | 4. They have set up a school. |
| 5. We expected his help. | 5. We looked forward to his help. |
| 6. He has demanded an explanation. | 6. He has called for an explanation. |

| Single Verb | Group Verb |
|---|---|
| 7. The plan failed for want of funds. | 7. The plan fell through for want of funds. |
| 8. The meeting was postponed. | 8. The meeting was called off. |
| 9. Save something for old age. | 9. Lay by something for old age. |
| 10. Do not hate the poor. | 10. Do not look down upon the poor. |
| 11. She resembles her mother. | 11. She takes after her mother. |
| 12. The old man died yesterday. | 12. The old man passed away yesterday. |
| 13. Extinguish the lamp. | 13. Put out the lamp. |
| 14. He wears white dress. | 14. He puts on white dress. |
| 15. I cannot tolerate such an insult. | 15. I cannot put up with such an insult. |
| 16. The villagers chased the thief. | 16. The villagers ran after the thief. |
| 17. He supported me. | 17. He stood by me. |
| 18. Please summon a doctor. | 18. Please call in a doctor. |
| 19. He visited my office. | 19. He called at my office. |
| 20. He could not understand the passage. | 20. He could not make out the passage. |

## EXERCISE

**A. Replace each of the italicised words by using the Group Verb given in brackets :**

[1] They *discussed* the matter. (talk over)
[2] The meeting was *postponed*. (put off)
[3] The two boys *quarrelled* over the purse. (fall out)
[4] He will soon *overcome* his difficulties. (get over)
[5] You should not *hate* the poor. (look down upon)
[6] Lila *met* her old friend. (come across)
[7] The patient *died* peacefully. (pass away)
[8] The price of rice is *decreasing*. (go down)
[9] He has *won* the first prize. (bear away)
[10] The strike was *withdrawn*. (call off)
[11] The light has been *extinguished*. (put out)
[12] He *started for* Paris. (set out)
[13] He *rises* early in the morning. (get up)
[14] He *met* me in my office. (call on)
[15] You should not *incur* debts. (run into)
[16] Our school *closes* at 4 p.m. (break up)
[17] The rains have *begun*. (set in)
[18] He *behaved* with me very well. (deal with)
[19] Have you *got* an article? (come by)
[20] It *happened* in this way. (come about)

[21] I have *read* the book. (go through)

[22] Try to *find* out the word in the dictionary. (look up)

[23] I have *examined* the matter carefully. (look into)

[24] I have *understood* your words. (make out)

[25] Please *continue* your studies. (go on with)

[26] He *saved* something for his old age. (lay by)

[27] *Mother took* care of her child. (look after)

[28] He is *regarded* as a great scholar. (pass for)

[29] She *resembles* her mother. (take after)

[30] I have *demanded* his explanation. (ask for)

**B. Replace each of the italicised words by using a Group Verb from the list given below :**

[1] He *removed* his shoes before entering his house.

[2] Overwork has *affected* his health.

[3] The boys and girls *entered* the carriage.

[4] The robber forcibly *entered* the house.

[5] I can *solve* the problem easily.

[6] I cannot *endure* such an insult.

[7] He is *considered* (as) a scholar.

[8] The villagers *followed* the thief.

[9] The patient will soon *recover*.

[10] The President *distributed* the prizes.

[11] You should *control* your anger.

[12] Try to *maintain* your reputation.

[13] Don't *quarrel* with your brother.

[14] I could not *remember* your name.

[15] I will soon *overcome* my difficulties.

**List of Group Verbs :**

[ Tell upon, put up with, put off, run after, break into, get into, work out, pass for, come round, fall out, keep down, give away, get over, call up, keep up. ]

**C. Fill in the blanks appropriately :**

Mr. Roy deals ........... umbrella but he does not deal well ........... his customers. Our school breaks ........... at 4 p.m. Overwork tells ........... his health. We should not look down ........... the poor. His proposal was turned ........... and he was turned ......... of the room. Try to work ........... the sum.

**D. Insert the correct Group Verb in the gap of the following sentences :**

[1] His health has ......for hard labour.

(a) broken away, (b) broken down, (c) broken up, (d) broken out

[2] You should ......your bad habit of smoking.

(a) get down, (b) give in, (c) give up, (d) go up

[3] There is none to ...... the orphan.
(a) look at, (b) look after, (c) look into, (d) look upon

[4] Such hard work will ...... your health.
(a) act upon, (b) bear upon, (c) bring about, (d) break out

[5] The patient will ...... soon.
(a) come of, (b) come off, (c) come down, (d) come round

[6] Don't ...... with your friend.
(a) fall at, (b) fall out, (c) draw back, (d) give over

[7] Try to ...... something for bad days.
(a) keep on, (b) keep down, (c) keep up, (d) lay by

[8] The student could not ...... what the teacher said.
(a) look for, (b) look out, (c) make out, (d) put out

[9] He could not ...... the sum.
(a) take after, (b) take up, (c) turn out, (d) work out

[10] At last the strike was ......
(a) worked on, (b) stood for the, (c) run out, (d) called off

# 34  PHRASES AND IDIOMS

## WHAT IS THE DIFFERENCE BETWEEN A PHRASE AND AN IDIOM?

**A Phrase is a group of words without a Subject and a Finite Verb. But it is used as a 'Part of Speech' in a sentence. However, an Idiomatic Phrase or Idiom expresses a special meaning beyond its literal meaning.**

**ABC** (primary knowledge)—He does not know even the ABC of music.

**Above all** (more than anything else)—Above all, be careful of your health.

**Above board** (beyond doubt)—His activities are open and above board.

**A bag of bones** (a very thin and lean person or animal)—The beggar is nothing but a bag of bones.

**A bite at the cherry** (an opportunity)—He expected to have a bite at the cherry.

**A bull in a china shop** (a person who behaves awkwardly in a fashionable place)—By handling delicate articles awkwardly and breaking a few of them, he acted like a bull in a china shop.

**A clean sheet** (a clean or creditable record)—Our Company has maintained a clean sheet in its budget.

**A close shave** (a narrow escape)—It was a close shave for him, for, the bullet only grazed his shoulder.

**A dead duck** (a plan or an event that has totally failed to function and not worth discussing)—The proposal for merging the two political parties is now a dead duck.

**A dog in the manger** (one who does not allow others to enjoy things which he himself cannot use)—Don't be a dog in the manger and please allow your old camera to be used by your friend.

**A double-edged sword** (something that has been advantages and disadvantages)—Urban life is a double-edged sword.

**A far cry from** (very difficult form)—The new government is a far cry from the earlier one.

**A feather in one's cap** (an award, a credit)—This victory will surely add a feather in his cap.

**A fly in the ointment** (a person or thing that spoils an enjoyment or an occasion)—The only fly in the ointment was the noise of the loudspeaker in the function.

**A fly on the wall** (a person who watches others secretly)—The members were busy talking, and didn't notice the fly on the wall.

**A fool's paradise** (a sense of happiness based on an illusion)—If you think that all men will be honest, you're living in a fool's paradise.

**A house of cards** (a plan or project that will break down easily)—His fancy / friendship with the filmstar fell through like a house of cards.

**A jack of all trades** (one who does many kinds of job, but cannot perform any of them well)—Our assistant is a jack of all trades, but master of none.

**A lame duck** (a person or organization that is in trouble and needshelp)—Once a very prosperous Company has turned into a lame duck now. > (a government whose period of office will end soon)—The lame duck government placed its last budget.

**A leap in the dark** (a step taken without knowing its results)—Having decided to go abroad without a job in hand, he is taking a leap in the dark.

**A lone wolf** (one who prefers to live alone)—He is a lone wolf and shuns our company.

**A losing game** (a cause or issue that is sure to fall)—He knows that he is playing a losing game, but he won't give it up.

**A mare's nest** (an invention that seems interesting, but proves to be bogus)—The magic cure for cancer turned out to be a mare's nest.

**A needle in a haystack** (something impossible to find out)—How can you find the scrap of paper in the piles of files. It's a needle in a haystack.

**A peg to hang something on** (a plea or a pretext)—His illness is nothing but a peg to hang his irregularity on.

**A pretty kettle of fish** (an awkward situation)—He has lost his passport in the airport. That's a pretty kettle of fish, indeed!

**A prime mover** (one who has the most effective influence on something done)—Rammohun Roy was the prime mover in the abolition of *sutteedaha*.

**A race against the clock** (an attempt to do something too fast)—To finish the construction of the bridge within a mouth is really a race against the clock.

**A rat race** (an aggressive competition for success)—Children are now put to a rat race in schools.

**A red alert** (a serious warning for an immediate danger)—After the blast in Mumbai, all the cities in the country were put on a red alert./On the forecast of a cyclone, a red alert was notified in the coastal area.

**A red rag to a bull** (something that enrages a person furiously)—Any mention of his involvement in the scam is like a red rag to a bull.

**A rule of thumb** (a rough estimate or measurement)—I guessed the amount by a rule of thumb./I think it's one hundred yard long by a rule of thumb.

**A sacred cow** (something that is greatly regarded)—The constitution of a country is a sacred cow to the countrymen.

**A shot in the dark** (a guess)—His comment about the President was a shot in the dark.

**A sleeping partner** (a business partner who only invests money but does not participate in running the business)—He is just a sleeping partner and hardly takes the trouble of running the business.

**A square peg in a round hole** (a person or thing that is misfit in a particular situation)—The newcomer felt like a square peg in a round hole in this job.

**A storm in a tea cup** (a great fuss over an unimportant matter)—The heated debate on who took the larger part of the cake is nothing but a storm in a tea cup.

**Achilles' heel** (weak point)—Hankering for votes is the Achilles' heel of the so-called leaders of our country.

**After all** (in spite of everything)—After all, he is a patriot.

**Ahead of** (in advance)—He is ahead of us all in the class./His ideas are well ahead of his time.

**All and sundry** (everyone)—All and sundry of the locality came to see the function.

**All at once** (suddenly)—All at once he accepted my proposal.

**All but** (nearly)—The poor villagers are all but ruined.

**All flesh** (all human beings and animals; the animal world)—Goutam Buddha felt compassion for all flesh.

**All in all** (supreme)—Mr. Sen is all in all in his office.

**All on (of) a sudden** (suddenly)—All on (of) a sudden a tiger came out of the bush.

**All the best** (expression of good wishes when one departs)—All the best. Take care.

**An eye for an eye and a tooth for a tooth** (retaliation against somebody in the same way as somebody was treated)—He doesn't believe in the policy of an eye for an eye and a tooth for a tooth.

**An honest penny** (money earned honestly)—I always depend on my honest penny for my livelihood.

**An ivory tower** (a state or place detached from the realities of life)—He thinks to be a poet and hardly descends upon reality from his ivory tower.

**An open secret** (something that is supposed to be a secret, but known to people)—His love affair is now an open secret.

**And all that jazz** (and all other similar things)—It's a shop that sells papers, books, pens and all that jazz.

**Apart from** (except for)—Apart from the poor boy, all others were dressed neatly. > (in addition to that)—Apart from the prize, he got a certificate.]

**Apple of discord** (matter of dispute)—The paternal property has become an apple of discord between the two brothers.

**Apple of one's eye** (a person or thing that is most dearly loved)—The young boy is the apple of his mother's eye.

**As if** (as it would be)—He swims so beautifully as if he is the water-god.

**As it were** (like)—The sun is, as it were, the lamp of the universe.

**As usual** (habitually)—He is late as usual.

**At a loss** (puzzled)—He was at a loss and sought help from me.

**At a low ebb** (declining)—His fame is at a low ebb now.

**At a stretch** (without break)—He can run ten kilometres at a stretch.

**At all** (primarily)—He does not know French at all.

**At all events** (in all cases)—I shall stand by him at all events.

**At arm's length** (at a distance)—Try to keep the bad boy at arm's length.

**At bay** (in a tight corner)—The tiger was at bay in the bush.

**At beck and call** (always ready to obey)—He is at his employer's beck and call.

**At close quarters** (very near)—They heard a hue and cry at close quarters.

**At daggers drawn** (at enmity)—The two brothers are now at daggers drawn.

**At home** (skilled, comfortable)—He is at home in Mathematics. (Or) I feel at home in your house.

**At hornet's nest** (a troubled situation of hot quarrelling)—His article in the newspaper stirred up a hornet's nest.

**At large** (free)—The antisocials are still at large.

**At last** (in the long run)—I got my missing book at last.

**At least** (at the lowest)—At least a hundred boys will come to school today.

**At one's beck and call** (obedient)—He is always at my beck and call.

**At one's finger-tips/ends** (ready at hand)—All these facts are at his finger-tips/ends.

**At one's own sweet will** (according to one's wishes)—He still does it at his own sweet will.

**At one's wit's end** (puzzled)—He was at his wit's end and turned to me for help.

**At random** (without any aim)—He hit the ball at random.

**At sixes and sevens** (scattered)—All the furniture in the room were at sixes and sevens.

**At stake** (in danger)—His life is at stake now.

**At the eleventh hour** (at the last moment)—The doctor came to the patient at the eleventh hour.

**At the heels of** (following closely)—The police are at the heels of the suspected man.

**Bad blood** (ill-feeling)—Now there is bad blood between the two brothers.

**Bag and baggage** (with all belongings)—He left the place bag and baggage. [not, with bag and baggage]

**Bare bones** (the basic or essential facts)—I want only the bare bones of the story.

**Be all eyes** (to be watching eagerly)—She is all eyes at her computer.

**Beat about the bush** (do something pointlessly / talk irrelevantly)—Please come to the point without beating about the bush.

**Beat black and blue** (beat severely)—They beat the thief black and blue.

**Bed of roses** (comfortable condition)—Life is not a bed of roses.

**Beggar description** (cannot be described)—The beauty of the Taj beggars description.

**Behind bars** (in prison)—The antisocial elements are now behind bars.

**Below the belt** (unfair)—It's unfair to attack someone below the belt.

**Between the devil and the deep blue sea** (caught in a dilemma)—The poor fellow has been caught between the devil and the deep blue sea.

**Bid fair** (have the possibility of prospering)—He bids fair to be a good doctor.

**Big gun** (a leading man)—He is a big gun of our locality.

**Bird's-eye view** (a over-all / rough idea)—He took a bird's-eye view of the flood-stricken area from an aeroplane./He took a bird's-eye view of the project.

**Birds of a feather** (persons of similar nature)—Birds of a feather flock together.

**Black sheep** (person of bad character)—He is a black sheep in the family.

**Blow hot and cold** (to change one's opinion or mood too often)—He blows hot and cold almost in the same breath.

**Bolt from the blue** (some sorrowful event quite unexpected)—The news of his father's death came to him as a bolt from the blue.

**Bone of contention** (matter of dispute)—The paternal property is the bone of contention between the two brothers.

**Bookworm** (one who always reads books only)—Don't be a bookworm; try to enjoy life on all sides.

**Bosom friend** (intimate friend)—Salil is my bosom friend.

**Break the ice** (to start things or talk to feel relaxed and easy)—He cut jokes to break the ice in the meeting.

**Break the news** (to make an important news known to a person)—When I broke the news to him yesterday, he felt very disturbed.

**Breathe one's last** (die)—The old man breathed his last on Sunday last.

**Bring to book** (punish)—He should be brought to book for his misconduct.

**Bring to light** (make open)—At last all the facts were brought to light.

**Build castles in the air** (indulge in idle vision)—Don't idle away your time in building castles in the air.

**Burning question** (matter of strong debate)—The problem of the dowry system is the burning question of the day.

**Bury the hatchet** (to stop quarrelling and become friends again)—Let's burry the hatchet from this day.

**By (in) virtue of** (because of, by means of)—He succeeded by virtue of perseverence. /The president by virtue of his office, enjoys this privilege.

**By all means** (in all possible ways)—Try to do it by all means.

**By and by** (soon)—He will come here by and by.

**By and large** (mostly)—People in our village are, by and large, farmers.

**By chance** (by accident)—I met him on the way by chance.

**By fair means or foul** (in any way good or bad)—He was eager to get it by fair means or foul.

**By far** (in all respects)—He is by far the best boy in the class.

**By fits and starts** (irregularly)—He works by fits and starts.

**By hook or by crook** (by fair means or foul)—You must do this work by hook or by crook.

**By leaps and bounds** (very rapidly)—The population of India is increasing by leaps and bounds.

**By no means** (in no way)—I shall by no means call on him.

**By the bye/By the by** (in course of talking)—By the bye/By the by I came to know that he was ill.

**Call a spade a spade** (to speak plainly)—I have no hesitation in calling a spade a spade.

**Call in question** (doubt)—No one can call his honesty in question.

**Call to mind** (remember)—I cannot call your name to mind.

**Carry the day** (win victory)—Amal, the best player of the school, carried the day in the annual sports.

**Catch red-handed** (catch with the stolen articles)—The thief was caught red-handed.

**Cats and dogs** (rain very heavily)—It was raining cats and dogs.

**Child's play** (a task that is too easy to perform)—Cooking is not a child's play, mind you.

**Chip of the old block** (a worthy son of a worthy father)—Mr. S. P. Mukherjee is a chip of the old block.

**Close at hand** (not far away, nearby)—There is a cafe close at hand.

**Close by** (not far away, at a short distance)—My uncle lives close by.

**Close fisted** (miserly, thrifty)—You can't expect donation from such a close fisted person.

**Close to the bone** (candid as to cause uneasiness)—His comment about her age was so close to the bone that she felt embarassed.

**Close-mouthed** (reserved, unwilling to open out)—He is a close-mouthed fellow and you won't be able to know what he wants.

**Cock and bull story** (absurd story)—Who will believe your cock and bull story?

**Cold feet** (nervourness)—Don't show your cold feet when facing an interview.

**Cold-hearted** (lacking warmth or affection)—She greeted me with a cold-hearted smile.

**Come off with flying colours** (win a victory)—Our school-team came off with flying colours.

**Come to light** (become known)—Their private talk has come to light at last.

**Crocodile tears** (pretended cry)—He shed crocodile tears at our misery.

**Cry for** (to ask for something impossible)—Be sensible, and don't cry for the moon.

**Cry over split milk** (to worry over something that has already been spoiled)—You can't undo it now; so it's no use crying over split milk.

**Crying need** (urgent need)—Mass education is the crying need of India.

**Cupboard love** (show of love or affection in order to get something)—Try to differentiate between cupboard love and selfless love.

**Curry favour** (be favourite through flattery)—He knows how to curry favour with officers.

**Curtain lecture** (a wife's private advice)—Very often husbands are influenced by curtain lectures.

**Cut a sorry figure** (make bad results)—He cuts a sorry figure in the examination.

**Cut and dried** (fixed or settled)—It's not a cut and dried policy and any suggestion is welcome.

**Cut no ice with** (to have little or no effect)—His efforts cut no ice with the members.

**Cut to the bone** (to reduce something to the bare minimum)—He was compelled to cut his monthly expenses to the bone.

**Cut to the quick** (be hurt)—I was cut to the quick by this words.

**Dance attendance on** (to do one's best to please somebody)—He keeps himself busy dancing attendance on his boss.

**Dance to someone's tune** (to do or act as someone dictates)—I'm not a man to dance anybody's tune.

**Dare devil** (one who enjoys doing dangerous things)—You're a dare devil, I see!

**Dark horse** (a person with unexpected qualities and little known to others)—He is a dark horse whose skill was unknown to us.

**Day in and day out** (all day)—The mike blared out day in and day out. > (everyday for a long time)—Day in and day out this tedious thing went on.

**Days are numbered** (the end of a thing or death of a person is not far away)—He is suffering from liver cancer and his days are numbered.

**Dead against** (bitterly against)—I am dead against this proposal.

**Dead language** (a language which is no longer in use)—Latin / Sanskrit is a rich language, but it is now a dead language.

**Dead of night** (midnight)—The wolves began to howl at dead of night.

**Die in harness** (die while in service)—Dr. Sen died in harness.

**Do yeoman's service** (render valuable service)—Raja Rammohun Roy has done yeoman's service to our country.

**Down-at-heel** (shabby)—How can you dare to join our club in this down-at-heel dress?

**Down-to-earth** (practical and sensible)—He is a down-to-earth person and so he is a good adviser.

**Early bird** (a person who gets up very early in the morning or starts work early)—He is an early bird and has no problem in catching a morning train. / An early bird catches the worm.

**Easy on the eye** (ear) (pleasant to look at or listen to)—Her look is easy on the eye. / Her music is easy on the ear.

**Eat like a pig** (eat voraciously)—Having eaten like a pig, he now feels very uneasy.

**Ebb and flow** (the rise and fall in a repeated way)—The ebb and flow of business / of seasons / of mood is quite natural.

**Elbow one's way** (to move forward by pushing people with the elbow)—He elbowed his way through the crowd.

**End in smoke** (fail)—All his plans ended in smoke.

**Ever and anon** (occasionally)—He comes here ever and anon only.

**Every inch** (wholly)—He is every inch an idealist.

**Every nook and cranny/corner** (all parts of a place)—We searched every nook and cranny/corner for the missing file.

**Fair and square** (honestly)—He likes to get the job fair and square. > (honest)—He believes in a fair and square policy.

**Fair sex** (women in general)—We must be fair to the fair sex.

**Fair-weather friend** (a false friend)—Beware of the fair-weather friends.

**Fall flat** (have no effect)—My advice fell flat on him.

**Fall foul of** (to be in conflict with)—He fell foul of his neighbours in a petty affair.

**Fall short of** (to be inadequate)—The fund fell short of his need. > (to fail to reach up to a distance)—The missile fell short of the target.

**Far and near** (everywhere)—His fame as a scholar spread far and near.

**Far and wide** (everywhere)—His fame as a scholar spread far and wide.

**Fast friend** (a close friend)—Only my fast friends know me intimately.

**Fast living** (a life of pleasure in a hurried way)—He hates the style of fast living.

**Fat cat** (a rich and influential person)—Such privileges are enjoyed by the fat cats only.

**Fat in the fire** (turmoil)—I think there's some fat in the fire./Your comment will act like fat in the fire.

**Feast for the eyes** (enough good sights)—Kashmir presents a feast for the eyes.

**Feast one's eyes** (to look at something with great pleasure)—On a clear morning we had the opportunity to feast our eyes on the Tiger Hill.

**Feather one's nest** (to get rich or make money by selfish means)—I'm the last person to feather my nest in this way.

**Feet of clay** (the fault or weakness in one's character)—Your opponents are looking for your feet of clay.

**Few and far between** (happening very infrequently)—He visits his country-house few and far between.

**Fight shy** (avoid)—Why do you fight shy of your teacher?

**Fish in troubled waters** (take advantage of disturbed situation)—He made a lot of money by fishing in troubled waters.

**Fish out of water** (in an uneasy situation)—When he came to the village, he felt like a fish out of water.

**Fit as a fiddle** (quite healthy)—Don't worry. I'm fit as a fiddle now.

**Flesh and blood** (human body)—Flesh and blood cannot bear with such insults.

**Flog a dead horse** (to waste one's energy on a lost case)—It's no use to flog a dead horse. This club has no chance of revival.

**For good** (for ever)—He left the country for good.

**French leave** (absence from work without permission)—You mustn't take French leave too often.

**Fresh blood** (new members in an organizaton)—Our Company looks for fresh blood now.

**From A to B** (from the starting point to the end or to the destination)—I enjoyed the sights from A to B.

**From A to Z** (over the entire range)—He knows the subject from A to Z./He has read the book from A to Z.

**From hand to mouth** (live by hard labour)—The poor man lives from hand to mouth.

**From pillar to post** (continually from one place or person to another)—He is going from one pillar to post for a job.

**Gala day** (a day of festivity)—The *'Holi'* is a gala day to the Indians.

**Gala dress** (dress of festivals)—They are on their gala dress on the *'Id'*.

**Get rid of** (be free from)—Try to get rid of that rogue/nuisance.

**Gift of the gab** (power of delivering speech)—An advocate should have the gift of the gab.

**Go to the dogs** (to go astray)—The young man has gone to the dogs in recent years.

**Green in one's eye** (a sign of credulousness)—There was no **green in her eye** even after your long speech.

**Green-eyed monster** (jealousy)—The **green-eyed monster** was aroused in him when I beat him in the competition.

**Hair-breadth escape** (narrow escape)—Thank God! I was saved by a **hair-breadth escape**. / I'm so lucky of my **hair-breadth escape**.

**Hand and glove/Hand in glove** (working together)—The two groups are working **hand and glove/hand in glove** against the secretary.

**Hand in hand** (close together)—Illiteracy and poverty go **hand in hand**.

**Hard and fast** (rigid)—There is no such **hard and fast** rule in this matter.

**Hard cash** (coins and notes, not bankrafts or cheques)—The workers want **hard cash**, and not cheques for wages.

**Hard line** (a very strict policy)—The government has decided to adopt a **hard line** on corruption.

**Hard nut to crack** (a difficult problem)—The problem of adult education is really a **hard nut to crack**.

**Have a finger in every pie** (to meddle in too many matters)—Those who try to **have a finger in every pie**, are not liked by others.

**Head and ears** (completely)—He is over **head and ears** in debt.

**Head and shoulders** (better or superior to a considerable degree)—He is **head and shoulders** above his classmates in performance.

**Head over heels** (absolutely, completely)—He is **head over heels** in love when he was in college. > (topsy-turvy)—After the scuffle, everything in the room was **head over heels**.

**Heart and soul** (with all energy)—Try **heart and soul** and you will succeed.

**Herculean task** (very difficult tusk)—It is a **Herculean task** to solve the unemployment problem in our country.

**High and dry** (in a difficult financial condition)—The slump in the share market has left the company **high and dry**. > (in a difficult situation)—The boat was left **high and dry** on the sandbank.

**High and low** (people of all classes/rank and file)—He is popular among **high and low**.

**High and mighty** (insolent, arrogant)—Money and power have made him **high and mighty**.

**High in spirits** (in a jovial mood)—He has done well in the game and so he is **high in spirits**.

**High time** (the time without allowing any further delay)—It is **high time** to take steps against inflation.

**Hit-and-run** (causing damage and escaping fast)—The terrorists took the **hit-and-run** policy.

**Hold good** (apply)—This rule will not **hold good** here.

**Hold one's tongue** (to keep silent)—He hurled abuses on me but I **held my tongue**.

**Hold water** (be effective)—This policy will not **hold water** in this situation.

**Hot potato** (a very tough subject; a controversial matter)—High production and low price, or low production and high price is a **hot potato** for us.

**Household word** (familiar name)—Mickey Mouse has now become a household word.

**Hue and cry** (a noise)—The villagers raised a hue and cry to see the thief.

**Hush money** (bribe money)—He offered a hush money to suppress the murder.

**In a fix** (in a difficult position)—He is in a fix and does not know what to do.

**In a hurry** (very quickly)—Don't do the work in a hurry.

**In a nutshell** (very briefly)—Tell the story in a nutshell.

**In black and white** (in writing)—Put down the statement in black and white.

**In cold blood** (without provocation)—He committed this murder in cold blood.

**In fine** (in conclusion)—In fine he declared his plan.

**In force** (in activity)—This law is in force now.

**In full swing** (in full activity)—The school is now in full swing./The fan is moving in full swing.

**In hot pursuit** (following someone very closely)—The police were in hot pursuit of the gang of robbers.

**In lieu of** (instead of)—Give me this pen in lieu of that.

**In no time** (soon)—He will finish the work in no time.

**In one's bones** (ingrained deeply)—The sense of gratitude is in his bones.

**In one's teens** (between thirteen and nineteen years of age)—She is yet in her teens.

**In order to** (with the object of)—He came here in order to meet my brother.

**In the buff** (naked)—A little boy is in the buff.

**In the dark** (nothing known or ignorant about something)—I'm still in the dark about his whereabouts.

**In the event** (as it turned out)—I thought the iterview would be very tough. But in the event it was so easy.

**In the event of** (if something happens)—In the event of a defeat the whole team would be disheartened.

**In the face of** (confronted with difficulties)—He showed great presence of mind in the face of danger.

**In the flesh** (in person, in the actual state)—People rushed in thousands to see the filmstar in the flesh.

**In the long run** (ultimately)—You will have to suffer in the long run.

**In the meantime** (in the time between)—Lila will come here tonight. In the meantime you should get her room ready.

**In the nick of time** (in right time)—The school team arrived in the nick of time.

**In the picture** (associated or involved in a matter)—Who may be in the picture for this doing or wrong-doing?

**In the same breath** (simultaneously)—He can blow hot and cold in the same breath.

**In the teeth of** (in the face of; through all difficulties)—He stood firm in the teeth of all opposition.

**In time** (in proper time)—He reached the station in time.

**Ins and outs** (full details)—I know the ins and outs of the matter.

**Instead of** (in exchange of)—Give me this book instead of that.

**Irony of fate** (by bad luck)—He could not succeed by irony of fate.

**In vain** (fruitless)—All his attempts were in vain.

**In vogue** (in fashion/in practice)—Polygamy is not in vogue now.

**Jump out of one's skin** (to be greatly frightened)—The child jumped out of its skin at the clap of the thunder.

**Keep mum** (to keep silent)—She went on making allegations, but I kept mum.

**Kiss the dust** (to submit humbly)—At last he gave up the arms and kissed the dust.

**Kiss the rod** (to accept humiliation and punishment without protest)—He made a blunder and so had to kiss the rod.

**Kith and kin** (near relatives)—He has no good relation with his kith and kin.

**Lame excuse** (bad/weak plea)—This lame excuse will not do.

**Leave no stone unturned** (try every possible means in order to achieve something)—They left no stone untruned to get a job.

**Leave someone in the lurch** (to leave someone in danger without help)—Leaving his friend in the lurch he went away.

**Lend an ear to** (to listen to someone or something patiently)—The students should lend an ear to their teachers/their teacher's advice.

**Lick someone's boots** (to show too much obedience to someone)—However poor he is, he won't lick anybody's boots.

**Lion's share** (major part)—He took the lion's share of the profit.

**Loaves and fishes** (offers to tempt people to do immoral work)—I never hankered after loaves and fishes.

**Maiden speech** (first speech)—His maiden speech fell flat on the audience.

**Make a clean breast of** (to confess something wrong)—He made a clean breast of what wrong he has done.

**Make a pig's ear** (to do something clumsily)—She made a pig's ear of the knitting.

**Make believe** (to pretend innocently)—Children often make believe that they are adults.

**Make both ends meet** (live within means)—I cannot make both ends meet with my small income.

**Make good** (to compensate)—I will surely make good for your loss.

**Man of letters** (a scholar)—Sir Ashutosh Mukherjee was a man of letters.

**Man of straw** (a man of little importance / worthless man)—Why should I care a man of straw like you?/We care a fig for a man of straw like him.

**Moot point** (an undecided matter)—Dowry system is still a moot point in India.

**Move heaven and earth** (to make great efforts to achieve something)—He moved heaven and earth to get a job.

**Music to one's ears** (very pleasant to hear)—The news of her success was music to our ears.

**Nip in the bud** (destroy in the initial)—All his hopes were nipped in the bud.

**Not worth the candle** (not worthy of taking trouble)—The task you've undertaken is not worth the candle.

**Now and then** (occasionally)—He comes here now and then.

**Null and void** (ivalid)—The deed has been null and void now.

**Odds and ends** (small and unimportant things)—The odds and ends are left in the corner of the room.

**Of course** (certainly)—Of course, you know what that means.

**Of easy virtue** (a woman ready to have sex with anybody)—She is a woman of easy virtue and it's better to avoid her.

**Off and on** (occasionally, not frequently)—She comes here off and on.

**On a razor's edge** (in a very critical situation)—We are on a razor's edge now and any small mistake may ruin us.

**On account of** (because of)—He could not attend his office on account of illness.

**On all fours** (on one's hands and knees)—He crawled on all fours to look for the coin.

**On ice** (postponed)—The project will be on ice so long it is granted by the government.

**On the carpet** (being taken to task by the authority)—He was on the carpet for being late off and on.

**On the contrary** (just opposite)—I do not hate him; on the contrary, I love him.

**On the face of it** (apparently, as it stands)—On the face of it, his decision seems to be justified.

**On the go** (working in a constant motion)—He's always on the go and hardly takes rest. > (on the move)—The machine is on the go.

**On the horns of dilemma** (to be caught in a dilemma)—I was on the horns of dilemma as I was caught between the contesting manager and the director.

**On the other hand** (on the other side)—I like him very much; on the other hand I can't ignore his shortcomings.

**On the spur of the moment** (under the impulse of the moment)—He did it on the spur of the moment.

**On the wane** (declining)—His fame is on the wane now.

**On the whole** (generally speaking)—On the whole, his conduct is good.

**Once bitten, twice shy** (an unpleasant experience makes somebody too careful)—Once he abused a girl and she slapped him. Once bitten, twice shy.

**Once in a blue moon** (scarcely)—He comes to his country house once in a blue moon.

**One jump ahead** (ahead of one's rivals)—In the last phase I was one jump ahead of my rival.

**One's salad days** (a period when one is young and have too little experience/green age)—I made too many mistakes in my salad days.

**Out and out** (to the full range)—He is out and out a fool/a liar/an idiot.

**Out at elbows** (ragged and wretched)—He helped a man who is out at elbows. > (worn-out)—The coat is out at elbows.

**Out of breath** (feeling uneasy in breathing)—I feel out of breath if I walk too fast.

**Out-of-date** (out of fashion)—This fashion is now out of date.

**Out of doors** (outside)—It is rather cold out of doors.

**Out of gear** (out of order)—The machine has gone out of gear. > (out of control)—Don't let your emotions go out of gear.

**Out of order** (defective)—This car is out of order.

**Out of pocket** (having much less money or no money)—I couldn't pay the bill as I was out of pocket.

**Out of sight** (beyond sight)—Out of sight, out of mind.

**Out of sorts** (not well)—He is out of sorts now.

**Out of temper** (angry)—He is out of temper now.

**Out of the frying pan into the fire** (from a bad to worse situation)—He left his old job and setting the new one he found his condition out of the frying pan into the fire.

**Out of the picture** (not associated or involved)—Don't count him in the competion. He's out of the picture.

**Out of the wood** (free from danger)—He is not yet out of the wood.

**Over and above** (in addition)—He received his salary and over and above a bonus.

**Part and parcel** (an integral part)—Discipline is part and parcel of administration.

**Pay lip-service** (to show that you support a cause but do nothing)—Political leaders are paying only lip-service to pollution control/to check corruption.

**Pay someone back in one's own coin** (to take revenge on someone by treating accordingly)—Those who do not obey discipline, must be paid back in their own coin.

**Pay the price for** (to suffer for something done by oneself)—You will have to pay the price for your mistakes.

**Pay through the nose** (to pay undue prices for something)—In the city we have to pay through the nose for everything.

**Penny wise and pound foolish** (thrifty in small expenditure, but wasteful of big amounts)—He mends his shoes many times, but doesn't mind to meet an accident. He's really penny wise and pound foolish.

**Pick holes in** (to find fault with)—He is in the habit of picking holes in other's work.

**Play fast and loose** (to behave insensibly not caring about others' feelings)—It's very unkind to play fast and loose with a girl's sentiments.

**Play second fiddle** (to have a less important position than someone)—I wasn't born to play second fiddle to someone.

**Play to the gallery** (to behave in a manner that will attract people's attention)—Playing to the gallery doesn't always prove one's capability.

**Point of no return** (the situation when it is not possible to change one's decision)—He has already signed the document, and it is now a point of no return.

**Point of order** (a point of protest)—A member of the opposition raised a point of order in the parliament.

**Poles apart** (completely different)—The two persons are poles apart as regards political views.

**Pour oil on troubled waters** (to try to settle a dispute and make the situation calm)—There were hot exchanges and he tried the pour oil on troubled waters.

**Pros and cons** (details)—You should consider the pros and cons of the system.

**Pull someone's leg** (to harass someone by telling something jokingly)—Don't be angry with me. I was only pulling your leg in joke. > (to do something from behind to harass someone)—Don't believe him. He can pull your leg at any time.

**Put flesh on the bones** (to develop an idea by adding data and details)—He gave me the basic idea and I put flesh on the bones.

**Put someone in the picture** (to make someone informed of a matter)—How can I comment on the matter till you put me in the picture?

**Put the cart before the horse** (to do something in the reverse order)—You've selected a tutor before getting your baby born. You're really putting the cart before the horse.

**Rain cats and dogs** (to rain very heavily)—It has been raining cats and dogs for nearly an hour.

**Rank and file** (common men)—We should pay attention to the rank and file of the country. > (the ordinary members of an organisation)—The real strength of a Company is the support of the rank and file.

**Read between the lines** (understand the inner significance )—Try to read between the lines of the letter.

**Red letter day** (memorable day)—The 15th August is a red letter day in the history of India.

**Red tape** (official formalities)—Red tapism causes delay in official work.

**Rise to the occasion** (tackle a difficult situation)—He faced a tough opponent, but rose to the occasion and beat him.

**Rope of sand** (a security that is delusive)—The support you are expecting from your rich friend may prove a rope of sand.

**Round the clock** (twenty-four hours)—He is working round the clock.

**Run riot** (to behave violently)—The students ran riot in the classroom in absence of the teacher. > (of imagination, ideas, etc.—to go uncontrolled)—The poet's imagination runs riot in this poem./True education does not encourage us to go the ideas run riot into our brain.

**Salt of the earth** (a very worthy person)—Raja Rammohun Roy was the salt of the earth.

**See eye to eye with** (to agree)—In the matter of modern art I don't see eye to eye with her.

**Set free** (liberate)—The prisoners were set free by a special rule.

**Sleep like a dog** (sleep deeply)—She slept like a dog and had no idea when the thief did his work.

**Slip of the pen** (slight mistake in writing )—This mistake is due to a slip of the pen.

**Slip of the tongue** (a slight mistake in speaking)—This is a slip of the tongue; don't lay much stress on it.

**Slow coach** (one who is lazy)—You cannot expect much from a slow coach like him.

**Small fry** (unimportant person)—We don't care for a small fry like him.

**Smell a rat** (to suspect something wrong)—I smelt a rat when I found them peeping into the room.

**Sow one's wild oats** (to enjoy one's life wildly when one is young)—He sowed his wild oats even when he was not even twenty.

**Square meal** (full meal)—He is too poor to have a square meal everyday.

**Steer clear of** (avoid)—You must **steer clear of** evil company.

**Stone's throw** (within a very short distance)—Our school is at a **stone's throw** from our house.

**Take heart** (to feel encouraged)—The boy **took heart** from his teacher's encouraging words.

**Take one to task** (rebuke)—He was **taken to task** for negligence of duty.

**Take to heart** (cut to the quick)—He **took** his remark **to heart**.

**Take to one's heels** (to run away)—The thieves **took to their heels** to see the police.

**Take with a grain of salt** (to accept by reducing the odds)—To be safe, you should **take** his story **with a grain of salt**.

**Talk of the town** (the interesting subject of common gossip)—The new film 'Three Idiots' was the **talk of the town** then.

**The call of nature** (a need to pass urine or stool)—Now I must respond to **the call of nature**.

**The cat's whiskers** (a very fine or excellent person or thing)—He thinks himself as if he is **the cat's whiskers**.

**Three R's** (elementary education)—The majority of our people have not yet learnt the **three R's**—READING, WRITING, ARITHMETIC.

**Through thick and thin** (through all difficulties)—Sita followed her husband **through thick and thin**.

**Tit for tat** (repayment of harm or injury in almost the same way)—He abused me and I slapped him on the face. It's **tit for tat**.

**To and fro** (hither and thither)—Being unable to make up his mind the man is walking **to and fro**.

**To the backbone** (to the core)—The boy is wicked **to the backbone**.

**To the contrary** (against what someone had said)—In the court he said nothing **to the contrary**.

**To the letter** (in all details)—He followed my advice **to the letter**.

**Tooth and nail** (strongly)—He fought **tooth and nail** against his enemy.

**Top brass** (very important people)—All the **top brass** of the city were present in that occasion.

**Turn a deaf ear to** (pay no attention)—He **turned a deaf ear to** my advice/proposal.

**Turn down** (refuse)—He **turned down** my proposal.

**Turn over a new leaf** (begin a new phase of life)—After he joined the circus, the monkey **turned over a new leaf**.

**Under cover** (in disguise)—The detective was **under cover**.

**Under one's belt** (already achieved)—Two awards are already **under his belt**.

**Under one's nose** (very close to one although not aware of it)—The crime was committed **under the nose** of the police.

**Under someone's thumb** (under someone's control)—The club is **under the thumb** of a political leader.

**Under the carpet** (things that are kept hidden)—Don't let the things out that are **under the carpet**.

**Under the circumstances** (in this situation)—Under the circumstances I'd like to resign from the post.

**Up and doing** (active )—Be up and doing and then you will succeed in life.

**Up to one's elbows** (deeply involved in something, head and ears in something)—He is upto his elbows in debt.

**Ups and downs** (rise and fall)—There are ups and downs in everyone's life.

**Weal and woe** (joy and sorrow)—Human life is full of weal and woe.

**Wear and tear** (the damage due to long and constant use)—The furniture of good-quality wood can stand up to the wear and tear.

**Wet blanket** (a person who spoils enjoyment or merrymaking)—He is a wet blanket and is avoided by all picnic-goers.

**White elephant** (a costly but unprofitable undertaking)—At last the department proved to be a white elephant.

**White lie** (a harmless lie)—I won't mind telling a white lie in order to avoid hurting her.

**Widow's mite** (small contribution of a poor man)—A widow's mite is no less important than a large contribution of a rich man.

**Wild goose chase** (useless pursuit)—Do not waste time in wild goose chase.

**With bated breath** (in great suspense)—We waited with bated breath for the results of the cricket match.

**With flying colours** (very successfully)—He came out of the competition with flying colours.

**Writing on the wall** (signs of impending misfortune)—He failed to read the writing on the wall, and so faced the disaster.

**Young blood** (a young member of an organization)—A young blood is predictably lacking in experience.

## EXERCISE

**A. Put the meanings of the following phrases/idioms and make sentences with them :**

[1] ABC : ____________________

[2] Above board : ____________________

[3] Bad blood : ____________________

[4] Black sheep : ____________________

[5] Big gum : ____________________

[6] Curry favour : ____________________

[7] Die in harness : ____________________

[8] End in smoke : ____________________

[9] Fight shy : ____________________

[10] Gala Day : ____________________

[11] Hush money : ____________________

[12] Irony of fate : ____________________

[13] Lame excuse : ____________________

[14] Man of letters : ____________

[15] Moot point : ____________

[16] Null and void : ____________

[17] Out of date : ____________

[18] Pros and cons : ____________

[19] Ups and downs : ____________

[20] White elephant : ____________

**B. Replace the italicised word or words by idiomatic expressions :**

(1) His activities are *beyond doubt*. (2) The paternal property is the *matter of dispute* among the brothers. (3) The sun is *like* the lamp of the universe. (4) His popularity is *declining*. (5) The two brothers are now *at enmity*. (6) He feels *comfortable* at his friend's house. (7) He is *skilled* in Mathematics. (8) He is beating the bush *without any aim*. (9) He reached there *at the last moment*. (10) He left the place *with all belongings*. (11) The beauty of the Taj *cannot be described*. (12) He will come here *soon*. (13) Lila dances *irregularly*. (14) The price of rice is increasing *rapidly*. (15) The dowry system is the *matter of strong debate* nowadays. (16) Mass education is the *urgent need* of India. (17) I do not know why he *avoids* me. (18) Nobody can believe such *absurd story*. (19) Tell me the story very *briefly*. (20) He comes here *occasionally*.

# 35 NOMINAL COMPOUNDS

## WHAT IS A NOMINAL COMPOUND ?

Sometimes a **Noun** and a **Noun-equivalent** or a **Noun-phrase** are joined in a compact manner in order to express clearly and precisely a person or a thing. This is called a **Nominal Compound.**

## FORMATION OF NOMINAL COMPOUNDS

| NOUN + NOUN | EXPANSION |
|---|---|
| **[ A ]** | |
| **Adult literacy** | [literacy for adults] |
| **Air-condition** | [a system to control temperature] |
| **Air hostess** | [a hostess to attend the air-passengers] |
| **Airman** | [a man (crew) of an aircraft] |
| **All clear** | [a signal clearing all dangers] |
| **Armchair** | [a chair with arms for comfort] |
| **Ashtray** | [a tray to put tobacco ash] |
| **Atom bomb** | [a bomb with atomic power] |
| **[ B ]** | |
| **Bathtub** | [a tub for bath] |
| **Battleground/field** | [a field or ground for battle] |
| **Bedroom** | [a room for sleeping on bed] |
| **Bedtime** | [time to go to bed] |
| **Birthday** | [a day to celebrate one's birth] |
| **Boatman** | [a man who controls a boat] |
| **Boat-racing** | [racing by boat] |
| **Bodyguard** | [a guard on duty for protection of anybody] |
| **Box camera** | [a camera looking like a box] |
| **Box-office** | [an office (a counter) to sell tickets] |
| **Bookbinder** | [a binder of books] |

| NOUN + NOUN | EXPANSION |
|---|---|
| **Book fair** | [a fair to display and sell books] |
| **Book-stall** | [a stall for books] |
| **Bookstore** | [a store for keeping books] |
| **Bookworm** | [a man (worm) fond of (reading) books] |
| **Brain child** | [a child (thought) out of one's brain] |
| **Brainwash** | [a wash to wipe out old thoughts of a brain] |
| **Briefcase** | [a case (suitcase) for carrying briefs (records, money) etc.] |
| **Bus fare** | [fare for travelling by bus] |
| **Bus journey** | [a journey by bus] |
| **Business-man** | [a man who lives on business] |
| **Business deal** | [a deal (transaction) of a business] |
| **Buttonhole** | [a hole to push in a button] |

[ C ]

| NOUN + NOUN | EXPANSION |
|---|---|
| **Ceiling fan** | [a fan hanging from ceiling] |
| **Census report** | [a report containing census] |
| **City life** | [life spent on city] |
| **City park** | [a park in a city] |
| **Chair-person** | [a person presiding on chair] |
| **Chessboard** | [a board for playing chess] |
| **Chargesheet** | [a sheet (papers) for some charges] |
| **Cotton textiles** | [textiles made of cotton] |
| **Cottage industry** | [industry running in a cottage] |
| **Country cottage** | [a cottage in a country] |

[ D ]

| NOUN + NOUN | EXPANSION |
|---|---|
| **Daydream** | [a dream dreamt in daytime] |
| **Daybreak** | [the time when a day breaks, i.e. dawn] |
| **Daylight** | [light during daytime] |
| **Day school** | [a school held in daytime] |
| **Death bed** | [a bed in which a person is dying] |
| **Death trap** | [a trap causing death to someone] |
| **Doormat** | [a mat at the door] |
| **Doorbell** | [a bell on the door for the visitors] |
| **Dust heap** | [heap of dust] |
| **Dustbin** | [a bin used for throwing dust and rubbish] |
| **Dust storm** | [storm blowing dust] |

[ E ]

| NOUN + NOUN | EXPANSION |
|---|---|
| **Eardrop** | [a drop of medicine into ears] |
| **Earring** | [a ring for wearing on ear as an ornament] |
| **Earphone** | [a phone (hearing aid) worn on the ear] |

| NOUN + NOUN | EXPANSION |
|---|---|
| **Earthquake** | [a quake shaking earth's surface] |
| **Education system** | [a system to conduct education] |
| **Election fever** | [feverish sensation during election] |
| **Election fund** | [a fund for conducting an election] |
| **Evening show** | [a show showed in the evening] |
| **Evening star** | [a star (a planet—Venus) seen in the evening sky] |
| **Eyeglass** | [glasses to help the eyesight] |
| **Eyesore** | [a sore (an unpleasant thing) to see by the eye] |
| **Eyewitness** | [a person who saw the incident] |
| **[ F ]** | |
| **Fact finding** | [finding of fact] |
| **Farm house** | [a house built in the farmyard] |
| **Fault finding** | [finding of fault] |
| **Ferry boat** | [a boat to ferry persons/things] |
| **Fibreglass** | [glass in the form of fibre] |
| **Fieldwork** | [a work done in the practical field] |
| **Film producer** | [a producer of film] |
| **Fire brigade** | [a brigade to fight fire] |
| **Fireplace** | [a place for a fire in a room] |
| **Fire station** | [a station for a fire brigade] |
| **Fishplate** | [a plate for joining railway lines] |
| **Flower vase** | [a vase for keeping flower] |
| **Flower show** | [a show of flowers] |
| **Football match** | [a match played with football] |
| **Football club** | [a club with an object of playing football] |
| **Footpath** | [path for walking on foot] |
| **Fortune hunting** | [hunting of fortune] |
| **[ G ]** | |
| **Gas cylinder** | [cylinder full of gas] |
| **Gas oven** | [oven lit by gas] |
| **Glasshouse** | [a house made of glass] |
| **Goods train** | [a train for carrying goods] |
| **Guest-room/house** | [a room/house for receiving guest] |
| **[ H ]** | |
| **Health centre** | [a centre offering health care] |
| **Heart attack** | [an attack on heart] |
| **Heat wave** | [wave for hot weather] |
| **Home comfort** | [comfort felt at home] |

| NOUN + NOUN | EXPANSION |
|---|---|
| **[ I ]** | |
| **Icebag** | [a bag full of ice] |
| **Ink bottle** | [a bottle containing ink] |
| **Iron determination** | [determination as strong as iron] |
| **Iron gate** | [a gate made of iron] |
| **Iron safe** | [a safe made of iron] |
| **Ivory tower** | [a tower made of ivory] |
| **[ L ]** | |
| **Law court** | [a court for deciding a case by law] |
| **Landslide** | [sliding of a mass of land, rock, etc.] |
| **Letter-box** | [a box for getting letters into] |
| **Lifetime** | [time throughout life] |
| **Life insurance** | [insurance covering risk of life] |
| **Lunchbox** | [a box containing lunch] |

| NOUN + NOUN | EXPANSION |
|---|---|
| **[ M ]** | |
| **Machine cloth** | [cloth made by machine] |
| **Marble palace** | [a palace made of marble] |
| **Mountain streams** | [streams in the mountains] |
| **Moonlight** | [light of the moon] |
| **Mudguard** | [a guard over a wheel to reduce mud] |
| **[ N ]** | |
| **Necktie** | [a tie worn round the neck] |
| **News bulletin** | [bulletin for news] |
| **Newspaper** | [paper for news] |
| **Night club** | [a club to enjoy a night] |
| **Nursery rhyme** | [rhyme for reading in nursery] |
| **[ O ]** | |
| **Oil lamp** | [a lamp lit with oil] |
| **Opera house** | [a house for performing operas] |

| NOUN + NOUN | EXPANSION |
|---|---|
| **[ P ]** | |
| **Paper merchant** | [a merchant dealing in paper] |
| **Paper bag** | [a bag made of paper] |
| **Paper mill** | [a mill for manufacturing paper] |
| **Picture book** | [a book containing pictures] |
| **Pleasure trip** | [a trip for pleasure] |
| **Pocket book** | [a book short enough to keep in a pocket] |
| **Postman** | [a man for delivering postal articles] |
| **Post-office** | [an office of the Postal Department] |
| **Potato chips** | [(fried) chips of potato] |
| **Poverty line** | [line marking poverty] |

| NOUN + NOUN | EXPANSION |
|---|---|
| **[ R ]** | |
| Radio programme | [a programme on the radio] |
| Routine work | [work regulated by routine] |
| **[ S ]** | |
| Safety razor | [a razor with guard for safety] |
| Sea-sickness | [sickness while travelling on sea] |
| Science fiction | [a fiction on science] |
| Sportsman | [a man skilled in sports] |
| Steam engine | [engine worked by steam] |
| Stone wall | [a wall made of stone] |
| Summerday | [a day in summer] |
| **[ T ]** | |
| Tea cup | [a cup for taking tea] |
| Tea garden | [a garden of tea plants] |
| Tea-stall | [a stall for serving tea] |
| Tear drop | [a drop of tear] |
| Tear gas | [gas causing tear] |
| Telephone operator | [an operator operating a telephone-exchange] |
| Toothpaste | [paste used for tooth] |
| Toy train | [a train enjoyed as a toy] |
| TV serial | [a serial on TV] |
| **[ W ]** | |
| Warship | [a ship used in war] |
| Windmill | [a mill driven by wind] |
| Wristwatch | [a watch for wearing on wrist] |
| **[ Y ]** | |
| Youth hostel | [a hostel for the youth] |

| NOUN + VERB/VERBAL NOUN | EXPANSION |
|---|---|
| Boat-racing | [racing by boat] |
| Bus stop | [a spot where buses stop] |
| Clay modelling | [modelling on clay] |
| Daybreak | [the time when a day breaks, i.e. dawn] |
| Data processing | [processing of data on a computer] |
| Fact finding | [finding of fact] |
| Fault finding | [finding of fault] |
| Folk dance/song/tale | [a dance/song/tale traditional to the rural folk] |
| Fortune hunting | [hunting of fortune] |

| NOUN + VERB/VERBAL NOUN | EXPANSION |
|---|---|
| **Loudspeaker** | [an instrument by which one can magnify sound] |
| **Oil-painting** | [painting with oil colour] |
| **Rainfall** | [falling of rain] |
| **Record breaking** | [that which breaks the record] |
| **Sunrise** | [rising of the sun] |
| **Snake-bite** | [biting of a snake] |
| **Sword-fighting** | [fighting with sword] |
| **Tax-payer** | [one who pays tax] |

| VERB/VERBAL NOUN/PARTICIPIAL + NOUN | EXPANSION |
|---|---|
| **Breakfast** | [a tiffin that breaks fasting overnight at daybreak] |
| **Burial ground** | [the ground where burial is done] |
| **Burning ghat** | [a ghat for burning dead bodies] |
| **Dining table** | [a table for dining on] |
| **Dotted graph** | [a graph that is recorded with dots] |
| **Driving Licence** | [licence for driving a vehicle] |
| **Fishing boat** | [a boat for fishing] |
| **Flashback** | [a part of a play flashing (showing) back] |
| **Flying fish** | [a fish that flies, i.e. jumps out of water] |
| **Frying pan** | [a pan for frying food] |
| **Hunger-strike** | [a strike carried by fasting] |
| **Pickpocket** | [one who picks somebody's pocket] |
| **Shuddering reaction** | [reaction that causes shuddering] |
| **Watch dog** | [a dog that watches] |
| **Withered violet** | [a violet that is withered] |

| ADJECTIVE + NOUN | EXPANSION |
|---|---|
| **Blackboard** | [a board painted black] |
| **Blue blood** | [one born of an aristocratic family] |
| **Common room** | [a room for common students/teachers] |
| **Common sense** | [a sense gained by common experience] |
| **Daily routine** | [a routine of work followed daily] |
| **Darkroom** | [a room for photo processing in darkness] |
| **Deadline** | [a line (limit) not to cross] |
| **First aid** | [aid given first before going to a doctor] |
| **Full moon** | [the moon appearing in full form] |
| **Hot pot** | [a pot to keep food hot] |
| **Juvenile court** | [a court trying juveniles (young ones)] |
| **Leaden heart** | [heart that is made of lead] |

| ADJECTIVE + NOUN | EXPANSION |
|---|---|
| **Magic lantern** | [a lantern used for projecting pictures on slides] |
| **Magic show** | [a show displaying magic] |
| **Main spring** | [a spring which operates the main function] |
| **Metal money** | [money made of metal] |
| **Red card** | [a card to warn an errant player] |
| **Solar energy** | [energy emitting from the sun] |

## NOMINAL COMPOUND CONSISTING OF MORE THAN TWO WORDS

| | |
|---|---|
| **Aircraft-control system** | [a system that controls aircraft] |
| **Birthday party** | [a party to celebrate birthday] |
| **Jute-producing areas** | [[areas that produce jute] |
| **Kolkata bus routes** | [routes for buses in Kolkata] |
| **Labour-saving method** | [a method that saves labour] |
| **Low cost house** | [a house made at a cost that is low] |
| **Machine-made clothes** | [clothes made by machine] |
| **One-parent family** | [a family consisting of one parent] |

## SOME MORE NOMINAL COMPOUNDS

| | |
|---|---|
| **Noun + Adjective** | : eco-friendly |
| | snow-white |
| **Noun + Preposition** | : lock-up |
| **Pronoun + Noun** | : he-goat |
| **Reflexive Pronoun + Noun** | : self-control |
| " " | : self-confidence |
| " " | : self-sufficiency |
| " " | : self-respect |
| **Reflexive Pronoun + Nominal** | : self-seeker |
| " " | : self-supporting |
| **Reflexive Pronoun + Verb** | : self-help |
| **Reflexive Pronoun + Adjective** (derived from verb) | : self-taught |
| " " " | : self-employed |
| " " " | : self-willed |
| " " " | : self-centred |
| **Adjective + Noun** | : easychair |
| **Adjective + Nominal** | : bestseller |
| **Adjective + Adjective** | : blue-black |
| **Adjective + Verb** | : shortcut |
| **Adjective + Verb** | : whitewash |
| **Adjective + Preposition** | : leftover |

| | |
|---|---|
| **Verb + Noun** | : washbasin |
| **Verb + Pronoun** | : holdall |
| **Verb + Verb** | : hearsay |
| **Verb + Adverb** | : knowhow |
| **Verb + Preposition** | : make-up |
| " " | : cover-up |
| " " | : turnover |
| " " | : walkout |
| **Adverb + Adverb** | : wherever, whenever |
| **Preposition + Noun** | : overtime |
| " " | : over-production |
| " " | : by-law |
| " " | : by-pass |
| " " | : offprint |
| " " | : overcoat |
| " " | : oversight |
| " " | : overwork |
| " " | : over-exercise |
| " " | : outgrowth |
| **Preposition + Verb** | : overflow |
| " " | : outcry |
| " " | : outlet |
| " " | : outlook |
| " " | : uplift |
| " " | : uproar |
| " " | : upstart |

## APPLIED SECTION

### Writing procedure for Nominal Compound

**(i) Some Nominal Compounds are written with hyphen mark (-) :**

over-flow, over-production, know-how, pen-friend, self-centred, self-control, self-respect etc.

**(ii) Some Nominal Compounds are written without a hyphen mark and with a little space between the words :**

football match, pocket book, film star, radio programme, post office etc.

**(iii) Some Nominal Compounds are written with either a hyphen mark or a space between the words :**

mountain-stream/mountain stream; flower-vase/flower vase; ink-bottle/ink bottle; ivory-tower/ivory tower; ice-bag/ice bag

**(iv) A few Nominal Compounds are written without a hyphen mark or a space between the words i.e. in a compact way, making a single word :**

postman, birthday, newspaper, boatman, necktie, breakfast, wherever, whenever etc.

**(v) A few Nominal Compounds having more than two words are written with hyphens between first two words and with space between later words :**

one-parent family, jute-producing area etc.

**(vi) A few Nominal Compounds having more than two words are written without hyphens but the first two words as a single word and the later words with a little space :**

birthday party, breakfast table etc.

## EXERCISE

**1. Make Nominal Compounds from the following :**

| Meaning | Nominal Compounds |
|---|---|
| (a) a wall made of stone | |
| (b) a method that saves labour | |
| (c) clothes made by machine | |
| (d) streams in the mountains | |
| (e) a serial on TV | |
| (f) a programme on the radio | |
| (g) a path for walking on foot | |
| (h) a train enjoyed as a toy | |
| (i) a man skilled in sports | |
| (j) a party to celebrate birthday | |
| (k) a report containing census | |

**2. Write down the meanings of the following Nominal Compounds :**

| Nominal Compounds | Meaning |
|---|---|
| (a) jute textile | |
| (b) ceiling fan | |
| (c) teaspoon | |
| (d) frying pan | |
| (e) gas stove | |
| (f) swimming pool | |
| (g) bosom friend | |
| (h) science fiction | |
| (i) tear gas | |
| (k) film producer | |
| (l) traffic police | |
| (m) book fair | |
| (n) wheat-producing countries | |
| (o) aircraft-control system | |

**3. Use the following Nominal Compounds in your own sentences. One has been done for you :**

| Nominal Compound | Sentence |
|---|---|
| book-binder | He is an excellent book-binder. |
| book shelf | |
| gas cylinder | |
| cottage industry | |
| poison gas | |
| tea garden | |
| film star | |
| telephone operator | |
| birthday party | |
| bus fare | |
| breakfast | |

**4. Shorten the following sentences by using '-ing' or '-ed' words or phrases :**

(a) Have you ever seen a fish that flies?

(b) A child that has been fed well will be healthy.

(c) The angel saw the dead swallow in the heap of dust.

(d) The violet which was withered lay on the table.

(e) It is a table meant for dining.

(f) When a little poison is added, the plant shows its reaction with shuddering.

**5. Use Nominal Compounds to avoid Relative Clauses :**

(a) These streams which are flowing from mountains are following in the sea.

(b) Bring me the bag that is full of ice.

(c) This is a mill which is driven by wind.

(d) The children are riding a train which is enjoyed as a toy.

(e) Go to the room which is meant for sleeping on bed.

(f) We should give due importance on industry running in cottages.

(g) He deserves praise as one who pays tax.

(h) The man is famous as he charms snakes.

# 36  PUNCTUATION AND CAPITALIZATION

## WHAT IS PUNCTUATION?

Rathin said, "Jayeeta is a fool."
"Rathin", said Jayeeta, "is a fool."

The word order is the same. But see how a fool is exchanged by punctuation.

So **PUNCTUATION** is **PAUSES IN SPEECH** to make a new meaning or change the meaning of a sentence.

> "Punctuation (derived from the Latin *punctum*, a point) means the right use of putting in points or stops in writing." **Wren & Martin**

"When we speak, we naturally make pauses and stops for an unbroken stream of words tends to become a mere unintelligible gabble. In writing we make these natural pauses by means of stops." **L. Tipping**

The following are the marks or stops used in writing :

| | | | |
|---|---|---|---|
| **[1] Full Stop** | [ . ] | **[7] Apostrophe Comma** | [ ' ] |
| **[2] Comma** | [ , ] | **[8] Dash** | [ — ] |
| **[3] Semicolon** | [ ; ] | **[9] Hyphen** | [ - ] |
| **[4] Colon** | [ : ] | **[10] Inverted Commma** | [' '], [" "] |
| **[5] Note of Interrogation** | [ ? ] | **[11] Brackets** | [ ( ) ] |
| **[6] Note of Exclamation** | [ ! ] | **[12] Asterisk** | [ * ] |

**[1] The Full Stop represents the greatest pause.**

**A Full Stop is used :**

(i) To mark the end of an **Assertive** or an **Imperative** or an **Optative** sentence :

Shrila is a good girl. (Assertive sentence)

Come to the blackboard. (Imperative sentence)

May you live long. (Optative sentence)

(ii) To mark **abbreviations** :

B.Sc., M.Sc., B.D.O., S.D.O., B. C. Roy, Dr. Das, 300 B.C., 1990 A.D., 5 a.m., 9 p.m., U.K. (United Kingdom), U.S.A. (United States of America), etc.

**Note** In current English Mr. and Mrs. occur without a full stop (as Mr and Mrs) as these have come to be regarded as the full spellings. **—Wren & Martin**

U.K., U.S.A. etc. are also used nowadays as UK, USA, etc.

**[2] The Comma represents the shortest pause.**

**A Comma is used :**

(i) To separate three or more words or phrases of the same class when the last two are connected by 'and' :

Afia, Yaw and Kofi are going to school.

(ii) To separate each pair of words connected by 'and' :

High and low, rich and poor, wise and foolish, must all die.

(iii) After a Nominative Absolute :

The sun having set, the lotuses closed their eyes.

(iv) To mark off a Noun or Phrase in Apposition :

Milton, the great poet of England, was blind.

(v) To mark off the Vocative :

Bipin, come here.

**Note** But when the Vocative is emphatic,
we use the note of exclamation. **—Wren & Martin**

Oh my child! Don't do that.

(vi) To separate Introductory Yes or No :

Yes, he will come here. No, he will not go there.

(vii) Before and after Parenthesis—words, phrases or clauses inserted into the body of a sentence :

He did not, however, gain his object. He is, after all, an honest man. The boy, who stood first, got a prize.

(viii) After an Adverbial Clause if it is placed first :

When he arrived, it was too late.

If it rains, I shall not go out. [But] I shall not go out if it rains.

(ix) Before a Quotation mark :

Father said to him, "Go to school."

**[3] The Semicolon represents a greater pause than the Comma and shorter pause than the Full Stop.**

**A Semicolon is used :**

(i) Between two clauses of a Compound sentence when they are not joined by a coordinating conjunction :

To err is human; to forgive divine.

(ii) Between Coordinating Clauses joined by and, but, still, yet etc., when the subjects are different :

The music came to an end; and the musician was greeted heartily.

**[4] The Colon represents a longer pause than the Semicolon.**

**A Colon is used :**

(i) Before listed items that are introduced by such words as follows, the following, thus, etc. :

His virtues are as follows : sincerity, punctuality and truthfulness.

(ii) To separate two sentences of which the second explains more fully the meaning of the first :

I know Dr. Sena very well : We (we) lived together for a long time.

(iii) To separate the speaker and the formal quotation :

Mary : Isn't the soup boiling yet?

**[5] The Note of Interrogation or Question mark is used :**

(i) After sentences which ask direct questions :

Who are you? Have you done the work?

But the Note of Interrogation is not used after an indirect question when it is used as the Noun clause.

I don't know who stole the watch. Tell me whether it is good or bad.

(ii) In brackets to express a doubt.

His father died in 1990 (?).

**[6] The Note of Exclamation is used after Interjections and after Exclamatory Phrases or sentences expressing sudden emotion or wish :**

Alas! The man is no more. What a nice bird it is! If I were a bird! What a fool you are!

**[7] The Apostrophe Comma is used sometimes with s as 's :**

(i) To form the Possessive Case of a Singular Noun if it is animate :

This is Rambo's desk. Father is blind to his son's fault.

Keats' poem. [Only apostrophe Comma (') where is 's' with the Singular noun]

(ii) Only Apostrophe Comma is used to form the Possessive of a Plural Noun where the Plural Number is formed with s or es :

Biltu reads in a boys' school. Bina reads in a girls' school.

(iii) To form the Possessive Plural noun, where there is no s or es in the Plural form :

Here is a women's college. This is a children's garden.

(iv) Only Apostrophe is used to indicate the omission of a letter or letters in a word :

I'm (= I am), You're (= you are), He's (= He is), They're (= They are), isn't (= is not), haven't (= have not), can't (= cannot), won't (= would not), Hon'ble (= Honourable) etc.

(v) To form Plurals of letters and figures :

There are four M.A.'s in our school. Cut your t's and dot your i's. There are 10 ten's in a hundred.

**[8] The Dash is used :**

(i) To indicate a break or abrupt turn in a sentence :

If my wife were alive—but why should I lament for the past?

(ii) To indicate a significant pause :

The hero of the story is rich, clever, charming but—a gambler.

(iii) To resume a list of subjects :

Friends, companions, relatives—all deserted him.

(iv) To indicate the repetition of an idea :

This is an ideal school—perhaps the best.

**[9] The Hyphen or a shorter line than the Dash is used :**

(i) **To connect the parts of a compound word :**

Brother-in-law, mother-in-law, passers-by etc.

(ii) **To connect the parts of a word divided at the end of a line :**

The chocolate-soldier went to the battle-field but the situation was clear-ly not favourable to him.

**Note** Though the hyphen is shown as a punctuation mark, it is not at all a mark of pause, rather the reverse.

**[10] The Inverted Commas or Quotation marks are used :**

(i) **To indicate quotation in a sentence :**

"Who are you?" he asked. The teacher said, "Come here, my boy." He said, "I am a Chinese/a Japanese/ an Indian".

**Note 1** If a quotation occurs within a quotation, it is marked by single inverted commas :

"You might as well say", added the teacher, "that 'I like what I get' is the same thing as 'I get what I like'."

**Note 2** The full stop, the comma, the question mark or the note of exclamation comes inside Quotation Marks.

(ii) **To indicate the title of books, poems, stories etc. and to draw attention to a word :**

'Macbeth' is written by Shakespeare. 'I' is a pronoun.

**[11] Brackets are used :**

(i) **To introduce an explanation as is done by the Dash :**

I have lost all I had in my purse (ten rupees).

(ii) **To enclose a Parenthesis like a pair of commas or dashes :**

He learnt, such is the power of a genius, the whole alphabet in one day.

[Or] He learnt—such is the power of a genius—the whole alphabet in one day.

[Or] He learnt (such is the power of a genius) the whole alphabet in one day.

(iii) **To separate a word from a sentence :**

**Note** that 'Or' is in brackets in the above sentences. It may be used in a first bracket or third bracket (Or), [Or]. The **1st bracket** ( ) is the **British style** and the **3rd bracket** [ ] is the **American style**.

**[12] One Asterisk** is used to draw some special attention and **three Asterisks** or **dots** are used to denote that some words or phrases or clauses have been intentionally left out :

*Punctuation is very important in writing.

The woman *** at last confessed the crime.

[Or] The woman ... confessed the crime.

## USE OF CAPITAL LETTER

A **Capital Letter** is used :

(i) To begin a sentence—Next to mother's smile books are the best.

(ii) To begin each line of a poem :

He prayeth best who loveth best
All things both great and small.

(iii) To begin the first word of a quotation in a sentence or a Direct Speech—Father said to me, "Go to school."

(iv) To begin a Proper Noun and an Adjective derived from it—We know Delhi is the capital of India. Is there any Chinese hotel?

(v) For abbreviation of the names of the countries, official ranks, academic degrees etc.—U.S.A., U.K., B.D.O., S.D.O., B.A., M.A., M.B. etc.

(vi) For God and for the pronoun relating to Him—God is good and He is kind to all. Pray to God for His blessings. (But 'g' for plural—'gods')

(vii) To write the Pronoun 'I' in all places—I can do this work. It is I who can do this work.

(viii) To personify an object—The Harmattar Wind rattled on his roof. The voice of Envy whispered in her ear.

(ix) To write the first word and all Nouns in salutation—Dear Sir, My dear Mother, My dear Uncle, etc.

(x) To write the title or designation of distinction—The Headmaster, The Principal, The President, The Secretary, etc.

## EXERCISE

**Rewrite the following sentences using Capital Letters and Punctuation Marks where necessary :**

(a) he is too selfish she said

(b) uncle podger said do you think I'm a fool

(c) she said sweet my child I live for thee

(d) i had it in my hand a minute ago

(e) this is a delightful spot he said we must ask the hail on a visit

(f) the second cricket match between india and england started at eden gardens on 31st december

(g) on the first day india won the toss and decided to bat the opening batsman batted well but england bowled very well also

(h) the weather was not good on the second day the game had to be stopped before time the indian batsmen were batting very well and they had already scored a good total

(i) the game was a very slow one on the third day and cricket lovers were unhappy they wanted good cricket

(j) the soyabean is a plant with great food value but neither the farmers nor the common people knew very much about it

(k) we can either drink milk or use it for making tea coffee and other drinks other milk products are sandesh pudding and dahi

(l) the soviet union and the united states have made great progress in exploring outer space the USSR was the first to launch a satellite

(m) whos there whos there i say am i to get no sleep tonight

(n) how did you get here child whose baby are you the man asked

(o) the convict said they have made me a thief god curse them all

(p) hallo mr crocodile why are you lying in the sun arent you feeling hot

(q) boys you know the need for planting trees we want to start a tree planting project

(r) the boys turned up the soil added fertiliser after they had planted the saplings and watered them well

(s) with which game are sourav ganguli and sachin tendulkar associated

(t) how do you greet your teacher when he enters the class in the morning

(u) what is the most important quality of a student

(v) how many members are there in your family who are they please introduce them

(w) suddenly i heard a howl just behind me my cousin cried out help help

(x) we saw the thief being chased by the guards they caught the thief and beat him badly

(y) the wind was very angry he said to the sun men always prefer you to me that is why you have succeeded

(z) the sun smiled and said no mr jealous i am really stronger than you are though i never brag men like good behaviour most so i am successful

# 37 COMMON ERRORS/ CORRECT USAGE

We very often commit grammatical errors while making a sentence. These errors are called **common errors**. Errors may be due to **wrong use of article**, **number**, **gender**, **noun**, **pronoun**, **verb**, **adverb**, **adjective**, **preposition**, **conjunction**, **tense**, etc.

If we are acquainted with such common errors and its correct forms, we will acquire self-confidence in speaking and writing correct English.

## CORRECT USAGE OF ARTICLES

| | Incorrect | Correct |
|---|---|---|
| **1.** | (a) He travelled by an US plane. | He travelled by a US plane. |
| | (b) He is an European. | He is a European. |
| | (c) It was an unique sight. | It was a unique sight. |
| | (d) This is an useful book. | This is a useful book. |
| | (e) He is an university professor. | He is a university professor. |

**Note** ***US***, ***European***, ***unique***, ***useful*** and ***university*** begin with **'-yu'** sound. Therefore **'a'** is used before them.

| | Incorrect | Correct |
|---|---|---|
| **2.** | (a) This is an one-act play. | This is a one-act play. |
| | (b) There is an one-eyed deer. | There is a one-eyed deer. |

**Note** ***One*** begins with **'wa'** sound. Hence **'a'** is used before it.

| | Incorrect | Correct |
|---|---|---|
| **3.** | (a) I have a X-ray plant. | I have an X-ray plant. |
| | (b) They run a NGO. | They run an NGO. |
| | (c) He is a NCC officer. | He is an NCC officer. |
| | (d) My friend is a MP. | My friend is an MP. |
| | (e) His father is a MLA. | His father is an MLA. |
| | (f) He is a MA. | He is an MA. |
| | (g) His brother is a SDO. | His brother is an SDO. |

**Note** X-ray, NGO, NCC, MP, MLA, MA and SDO begin with **'e'** sound which is a vowel sound. Therefore, **'an'** is used before them.

| Incorrect | Correct |
|---|---|
| **4.** (a) They got into train. | They got into a train. |
| (b) Everybody needs holiday. | Everybody needs a holiday. |
| (c) I often ride horse. | I often ride a horse. |
| (d) I had lesson yesterday. | I had a lesson yesterday. |
| (e) You must give answer. | You must give an answer. |
| (f) He wants to become politician. | He wants to become a politician. |
| (g) Kolkata is big city. | Kolkata is a big city. |

**Note** ***Train, holiday, horse, lesson, answer, politician*** and ***city*** are singular countable nouns. Therefore, **'a /an'** is used before them as per consonant or vowel sound. However, no article is used in such phrases as : ***by train***, ***by bus***, etc.

| | |
|---|---|
| **5.** (a) He came here by the car. | He came here by car . |
| (b) She goes there by the bus. | She goes there by bus . |
| (c) They travel by the train. | They travel by train . |

**Note** ***'By car/bus/train/plane/ship/air/water'*** etc. are idioms and article is not used before them.

| | |
|---|---|
| **6.** (a) I play piano. | I play the piano. |
| (b) She plays on the piano. | She plays on piano. |
| (c) He learns guitar. | He learns the guitar. |
| (d) She likes harmonium. | She likes the harmonium. |

**Note** If the verbs ***play, like, learn*** are followed by the name of any musical instrument, **'the'** should be used before it. But the group verb ***play on*** does not take any article before its object.

| | |
|---|---|
| **7.** (a) This is a smallest TV set. | This is the smallest TV set. |
| (b) It was not a best model. | It was not the best model. |
| (c) That is biggest creature. | That is the biggest creature. |
| (d) It was most wonderful scene. | It was the most wonderful scene. |

**Note** **'The'** should be used before the superlative degree of adjective.

| | |
|---|---|
| **8.** (a) The most people like it. | Most people like it. |
| (b) The most of the people like it. | Most of the people like it. |

**Note** If **'most'** or **'most of'** is followed by a noun, **'the'** is not used before 'most'.

| | Incorrect | Correct |
|---|---|---|
| **9.** | (a) Poor always suffer. | The poor always suffer. |
| | (b) Rich are seldom happy. | The rich are seldom happy. |
| | (c) He is collecting money for blind. | He is collecting money for the blind. |

**Note** There are some adjectives before which **'the'** is always used and they have plural meaning as ***the poor***, ***the rich***, ***the blind***, ***the deaf***, ***the sick***, ***the old***, ***the dead***, ***the unemployed***, ***the handicapped, etc. are a class of people*.**

| | Incorrect | Correct |
|---|---|---|
| **10.** | (a) All the mankind should be happy. | All mankind should be happy. |
| | (b) We enjoyed the beauty of the nature. | We enjoyed the beauty of nature. |
| | (c) We should live in the society. | We should live in society. |
| | (d) The man is mortal. | Man is mortal. |

**Note** If ***mankind***, ***nature***, ***society*** and ***mortal*** are used in general sense, no article should be used before them.

| | Incorrect | Correct |
|---|---|---|
| **11.** | (a) He had the rank of a captain. | He had the rank of captain. |
| | (b) He accepted the job of the headmaster. | He accepted the job of headmaster. |
| | (c) He was given the post of the director. | He was given the post of director. |

**Note** Article should not be used before a noun preceded by the ***post/job/rank/position***.

| | Incorrect | Correct |
|---|---|---|
| **12.** | (a) Nile is a fine river. | The Nile is a fine river. |
| | (b) Ganga is a holy river. | The Ganga is a holy river. |
| | (c) Geeta is a sacred book. | The Geeta is a sacred book. |
| | (d) Himalayas are the highest mountains. | The Himalayas are the highest mountains. |

**Note** **'The'** is used before the name of a famous ***river/mountains/book***.

| | Incorrect | Correct |
|---|---|---|
| **13.** | (a) Sports make body strong. | Sports make the body strong. |
| | (b) Games make arms strong. | Games make the arms strong. |

**Note** **'The'** is used before the ***body*** or the ***parts of the body***.

| | Incorrect | Correct |
|---|---|---|
| **14.** | (a) My friend is in Army. | My friend is in the Army. |
| | (b) He joined a Navy. | He joined the Navy. |
| | (c) He retired from Air Force. | He retired from the Air Force. |

**Note** **'The'** is used before the name of armed forces.

| | Incorrect | Correct |
|---|---|---|
| **15.** | (a) I have a homework to do. | I have homework to do. |
| | (b) He is in a good health. | He is in good health. |
| | (c) I have received a news. | I have received news. |
| | (d) The culprit asked for a mercy. | The culprit asked for mercy. |

**Note** No article is used before ***homework***, ***health***, ***news*** **or** ***mercy***.

| | Incorrect | Correct |
|---|---|---|
| **16.** | (a) We reached the home. | We reached home. |
| | (b) He returned from the home. | He returned from home. |
| Note | Article is not used before ***home***. | |
| **17.** | (a) I go to the school everyday. | I go to school everyday. |
| | (b) He goes to the college everyday. | He goes to college everyday. |
| | (c) He goes to the hospital for treatment. | He goes to hospital for treatment. |
| Note | When we go to ***school/college*** for reading or teaching purpose or ***hospital*** for treatment, no article is used before them. | |
| **18.** | (a) We had a breakfast at five. | We had breakfast at five. |
| | (b) He invited me to the lunch. | He invited me to lunch. |
| | (c) He was invited to the dinner. | He was invited to dinner. |
| Note | Article is not used before the names of meals. | |
| **19.** | (a) He tells lie. | He tells a lie. |
| | (b) He speaks truth. | He speaks the truth. |
| Note | Article **'a'** and **'the'** is used before ***lie*** and ***truth***. | |
| **20.** | (a) He works in morning. | He works in the morning. |
| | (b) He plays in afternoon. | He plays in the afternoon. |
| | (c) He rests in evening. | He rests in the evening. |
| Note | **'The'** is used before morning/afternoon/evening. | |
| **21.** | (a) The sun shines by the day. | The sun shines by day. |
| | (b) The stars shine by the night. | The stars shines by night. |
| | (c) We reached there at the night. | We reached there at night. |
| | (d) He came here on the foot. | He came here on foot. |
| Note | ***By day***, ***by night***, ***at night***, ***on foot*** are accepted phrases and no article is used with them. | |
| **22.** | (a) He gets a good pay. | He gets good pay. |
| | (b) We write on a paper. | We write on paper. |
| | (c) We like to have a perfect safety. | We like to have perfect safety. |
| | (d) I like a comfortable travel. | I like comfortable travel. |
| | (e) It was a bad weather. | It was bad weather. |
| Note | No article is used with ***pay***, ***paper***, ***safety***, ***travel*** and ***weather***. | |

## CORRECT USAGE OF NOUNS

| Incorrect | Correct |
|---|---|
| **1.** (a) I have not a single money. | I have not a single rupee/dollar. |
| (b) I have no rupees/dollars. | I have no money. |
| (c) He has lots of rupees/dollars. | He has lots of money. |

**Note** ***Rupee*** or ***dollar*** is a countable noun and ***money*** is an uncountable noun.

| Incorrect | Correct |
|---|---|
| **2.** (a) He got three breads. | He got three loaves of bread. |
| (b) I want a bread. | I want a piece of bread. |

**Note** ***Bread*** is an uncountable noun, therefore, ***a piece of/loaf of*** is used.

| Incorrect | Correct |
|---|---|
| **3.** (a) He gave me good advises. | He gave me good advice. |
| (b) I took some foods to eat. | I took some food to eat. |
| (c) I sold my furnitures. | I sold my furniture. |
| (d) Please give me all the informations. | Please give me all the information. |
| (e) I need some equipments. | I need some equipment. |

**Note** ***Advice, food, information, furniture and equipment*** are uncountable nouns. They are not used as plural.

| Incorrect | Correct |
|---|---|
| **4.** (a) Ten peoples were in the garden. | Ten people were in the garden. |
| (b) Cattles are grazing in the field. | Cattle are grazing in the field. |

**Note** ***People*** and ***cattle*** are plural nouns but they do not take -s after them.

| Incorrect | Correct |
|---|---|
| **5.** (a) The news are true. | The news is true. |
| (b) The wages of sin are death. | The wages of sin is death. |

**Note** ***News*** and ***wages*** are singular nouns and they take verb in singular form.

| Incorrect | Correct |
|---|---|
| **6.** (a) The goods was sent. | The goods were sent. |
| (b) This premises looks very big. | This premises look very big. |
| (c) The police is watching the house. | The police are watching the house. |

**Note** ***Goods, premises, police, scissors, sleaves*** and ***trousers*** are always plural.

| Incorrect | Correct |
|---|---|
| **7.** (a) A bundle of sticks are not easy to break. | A bundle of sticks is not easy to break. |
| (b) A group of people were there. | A group of people was there. |
| (c) A herd of cattle were stolen. | A herd of cattle was stolen. |
| (d) A team of players have arrived. | A team of players has arrived. |

**Note** ***A bundle of/A group of/A herd of/A team of*** etc. before plural nouns take a verb in singular form.

| | Incorrect | Correct |
|---|---|---|
| **8.** | (a) He has a lot of opportunity. | He has a lot of opportunities. |
| | (b) Some of the boys is ill. | Some of the boys are ill. |
| | (c) There are plenty of rice. | There is plenty of rice. |
| | (d) Most of the salt are used. | Most of the salt is used. |
| | (e) Most of the apples is rotten. | Most of the apples are rotten. |

**Note** ***A lot of, plenty of, a great deal of, most of*** and ***some of*** are singular or plural according to the nouns after them.

| | Incorrect | Correct |
|---|---|---|
| **9.** | (a) One of the boys were ill. | One of the boys was ill. |
| | (b) Each of the girls are clever. | Each of the girls is clever. |

**Note** ***One of*** or ***each of*** placed before a plural noun, takes a singular verb.

| | Incorrect | Correct |
|---|---|---|
| **10.** | (a) This pair of shoes are mine. | This pair of shoes is mine. |
| | (b) That pair of scissors belong to him. | That pair of scissors belongs to him. |

**Note** ***A pair of*** or ***This pair of*** is considered singular and it takes a singular verb.

## CORRECT USAGE OF PRONOUNS

| | Incorrect | Correct |
|---|---|---|
| **1.** | (a) One must do her work. | One must do one's work. |
| | (b) One should love his country. | One should love one's country. |

**Note** If ***one*** is the subject of any sentence, ***one's*** should be used, not ***his*** or ***her*** in possessive case.

| | Incorrect | Correct |
|---|---|---|
| **2.** | (a) I and he liked it. | He and I liked it. |
| | (b) He and you went there. | You and he went there. |
| | (c) I and you have done it. | You and I have done it. |
| | (d) John, I and you ate sweets. | You, John and I ate sweets. |

**Note** The **personal pronouns** should be arranged thus : **2nd**, **3rd** and **1st** or 231. But it is reverse in case of confessing blame 132 (e.g.) **I**, **he** and **you** are to blame.

| | Incorrect | Correct |
|---|---|---|
| **3.** | (a) These two boys help one another. | These two boys help each other. |
| | (b) These three boys help each other. | These three boys help one another. |

**Note** ***Each other*** for two persons and ***one another*** for three and more persons.

| | Incorrect | Correct |
|---|---|---|
| **4.** | (a) Any of these two girls is your sister. | Either of these two girls is your sister. |
| | (b) Either of the five boys will do it. | Any of the five boys will do it. |

**Note** '**Either of**' for two persons. '**Any of**' for three or more persons.

| | Incorrect | Correct |
|---|---|---|
| **5.** | (a) Neither of the six can succeed. | None of the six can succeed. |
| | (b) None of the two girls is very tall. | Neither of the two girls is very tall. |

**Note** ***Neither of*** for two persons or objects, ***none of*** for three or more persons or objects.

| | Incorrect | Correct |
|---|---|---|
| 6. | (a) Let he do this. | Let him do this. |
| | (b) This is between you and I. | This is between you and me. |
| | (c) You should not depend on he. | You should not depend on him. |

**None** **Objective case** is used after ***let***, ***between*** and any **preposition**.

| | | |
|---|---|---|
| 7. | (a) Your's truly/faithfully | Yours truly/faithfully |
| | (b) Your's is the best painting in the class. | Yours is the best painting in the class. |
| | (c) The climate of India is hotter than England. | The climate of India is hotter than that of England. |

**Note** Use ***yours*** instead of ***your's***. The climate of India is compared to the climate of England, not with England. So ***that of*** should be placed before 'England'.

## CORRECT USAGE OF ADJECTIVES

| | | |
|---|---|---|
| 1. | (a) We have any books. | We have some books. |
| | (b) He has not some books. | He has not any books. |
| | (c) Do you need some salt? | Do you need any salt? |

**Note** '**Some**' is used in affirmative sentences while '**any**' is used in negative sentences and questions.

| | | |
|---|---|---|
| 2. | (a) I am the younger in the family. | I am the youngest in the family. |
| | (b) Your painting is worst than mine. | Your painting is worse than mine. |
| | (c) Which is the better of the three methods? | Which is the best of the three methods? |

**Note** Comparative degree is used between two and superlative is used among three or more persons or objects.

| | | |
|---|---|---|
| 3. | (a) Preeti is taller from her sister. | Preeti is taller than her sister. |
| | (b) The weather is warmer as last week. | The weather is warmer than that of last week. |

**Note** In comparative degree '**than**' is used.

| | | |
|---|---|---|
| 4. | (a) This is more safer place. | This is a safer place. |
| | (b) He is comparatively better today. | He is better today. |
| | (c) The most busiest hour is 10 o'clock. | The busiest hour is 10 o'clock. |

**Note** Double comparative or double superlative should not be used.

| Incorrect | Correct |
|---|---|
| **5.** (a) He is inferior than me. | He is inferior to me. |
| (b) You are superior of all. | You are superior to all. |
| (c) I am senior than you. | I am senior to you. |

**Note** Use **'to'** in place of **'than'** or **'of'** before the words—***inferior***, ***superior***, ***senior***, ***junior***.

| Incorrect | Correct |
|---|---|
| **6.** (a) My brother has not much book. | My brother has not many books. |
| (b) Is there many sugar in the bag? | Is there much sugar in the bag? |

**Note** '**Much**' denotes quantity; '**many**' denotes number.

| Incorrect | Correct |
|---|---|
| **7.** (a) Health is more preferable than wealth . | Health is preferable to wealth. |
| (b) Knowledge is preferable than riches. | Knowledge is preferable to riches. |

**Note** Before '**preferable**' use '**to**' in place of '**than**'.

| Incorrect | Correct |
|---|---|
| **8.** (a) Patna is larger than any city in Bihar. | Patna is larger than any other city in Bihar. |
| (b) Mumbai is richer than any city in India. | Mumbai is richer than any other city in India. |

**Note** '**Other**' should be used after '**any**' in comparative degree.

## CORRECT USAGE OF VERBS

| Incorrect | Correct |
|---|---|
| **1.** (a) We shall discuss about it. | We shall discuss it. |
| (b) He has married with Rekha. | He has married Rekha. |
| (c) Viki will pass in the examination. | Viki will pass the examination. |
| (d) I am awaiting for your reply. | I am awaiting your reply. |

**Note** ***Discuss***, ***marry***, ***pass*** and ***await*** are transitive verbs and after these verbs comes the object, not a preposition.

| Incorrect | Correct |
|---|---|
| **2.** (a) He was looking me. | He was looking at me. |
| (b) I am waiting you. | I am waiting for you. |
| (c) He didn't reply me. | He didn't reply to me. |
| (d) It may result trouble. | It may result in trouble. |
| (e) She succeeded her examination. | She succeeded in her examination. |

**Note** ***Look***, ***wait***, ***reply***, ***result***, ***succeed***, etc. are intransitive verbs and they will be followed by a preposition, not an object.

| Incorrect | Correct |
|---|---|
| **3.** (a) I enjoyed at the party. | I enjoyed myself at the party. |
| (b) I enjoyed myself the fresh air. | I enjoyed the fresh air. |
| (c) I enjoyed during the holidays. | I enjoyed myself during the holidays. |

| Incorrect | Correct |
|---|---|
| (d) Did you avail the opportunity? | Did you avail yourself of the opportunity? |

**Note** With ***avail myself, yourself*** etc. ***of*** is used, but ***of*** is not used with ***enjoy*** something.

| Incorrect | Correct |
|---|---|
| **4.** (a) I said ~~to~~ him goodbye. | I said goodbye to him. |
| (b) I bade ~~to~~ him goodbye. | I bade him goodbye. |
| (c) He ~~said~~ me to come in. | He told me to come in. |
| (d) He ~~told~~ to me, 'Come in'. | He said to me, 'Come in'. |

**Note** ***Say*** is an intransitive verb, but ***bid*** and ***tell*** are transitive verbs.

| Incorrect | Correct |
|---|---|
| **5.** (a) He ~~told to~~ me that he was coming. | He said to me that he was coming. |
| (b) He ~~told to~~ open the door. | He told someone to open the door. |

**Note** The verb ***tell*** is a transitive verb. It takes an object. ***to*** is not used after it.

| Incorrect | Correct |
|---|---|
| **6.** (a) The murderer was caught and ~~hung~~. | The murderer was caught and hanged. |
| (b) He ~~hanged~~ the picture on the wall. | He hung the picture on the wall. |

**Note** The past participle forms of ***hang—hung*** and ***hanged*** are used in different senses.

| Incorrect | Correct |
|---|---|
| **7.** (a) Columbus ~~invented~~ America. | Columbus discovered America. |
| (b) Edison ~~discovered~~ the gramophone. | Edison invented the gramophone. |
| (c) He ~~gave~~ the examination. | He appeared at the examination. [Or] He sat for the examination. |
| (d) The man ~~gave~~ a speech. | The man made a speech. |
| (e) He ~~made~~ a lecture. | He delivered/gave a lecture. |

**Note** It is **discovered** if something was there, but it is **invented** if there was nothing like it. **Appear at** the examination or **sit for** the examination is used. **Make a speech**, and **deliver/give a lecture** is set expressions.

| Incorrect | Correct |
|---|---|
| **8.** (a) He ~~denied~~ to take the money. | The boy refused to take the money. |
| (b) He ~~refused~~ that he was guilty. | He denied that he was guilty. |

**Note** '**Deny**' means to say that something is not approved but '**refuse**' means not to accept or do or give.

(a) She **refused** his offer. [ not 'denied' ]

(b) She **refused** him even a kiss. [ not 'denied' ]

(c) Can you **deny** the truth of his statement? [ not 'refuse' ]

| Incorrect | Correct |
|---|---|
| **9.** (a) He said me a cheat. | He called me a cheat. |
| (b) He admitted his son into a school. | He got his son admitted into a school. |

**Note** When we address someone, '**call**' is used. We use '**get**' someone admitted into an institution.

| Incorrect | Correct |
|---|---|
| **10.** (a) I like to learn English. | I like learning English. |
| (b) They enjoy to watch T.V. | They enjoy watching T.V. |
| (c) He avoids to speak to me. | He avoids speaking to me. |
| (d) He has finished to study. | He has finished studying. |
| (e) I don't mind to open the window. | I don't mind opening the window. |

**Note** (i) The '**-ing**' is added to verbs to form verbal nouns, gerund and present participles.

Excuse my **interrupting**.

I like the **reading** of novels.

I really appreciate **having** time to relax.

**Sleeping** is necessary to life.

A **rolling** stone gathers no moss.

(ii) The **verb** + '**ing**' form can be used in the following cases also :

To burst out **crying**/**laughing**.

To go **swimming**/**shopping**.

To spend money/waste time **doing** something.

To keep (on) **doing** something.

(iii) After ***need***, ***require*** and ***want***, '**-ing**' is added in passive sense :

Your hair needs **cutting** (= to be cut).

Does your suit require **pressing**, Sir?

The car wants **servicing**.

## CORRECT USAGE OF ADVERBS

| Incorrect | Correct |
|---|---|
| **1.** (a) He seems happily. | He seems happy. |
| (b) She looks sadly. | She looks sad. |
| (c) The food tastes bitterly. | The food tastes bitter. |
| (d) The rose smells sweetly. | The rose smells sweet. |

**Note** The verbs '***feel***, ***seem***, ***look***, ***appear***, ***sound***, ***taste***' and '***smell***' take a predicative adjective, not adverb.

| Incorrect | Correct |
|---|---|
| **2.** (a) He **quickly ran**. | He **ran quickly**. |
| (b) They **immediately disappeared**. | They **disappeared immediately**. |

**Note** If an adverb qualifies an intransitive verb, it should be kept after the verb.

| Incorrect | Correct |
|---|---|
| **3.** (a) He **eagerly wishes** to do it. | He **wishes eagerly** to do it. |
| (b) She **danced** last night **beautifully**. | She **danced beautifully** last night. |

**Note** An **adverb** should be kept near the word it qualifies.

| Incorrect | Correct |
|---|---|
| **4.** (a) He comes always late. | He always comes late. |
| (b) She did it never. | She never did it. |
| (c) We went often there. | We often went here. |
| (d) I visit him frequently while in Delhi. | I frequently visit him while in Delhi. |

**Note** ***Always***, ***never***, ***often***, ***generally***, ***sometimes***, ***quiet***, ***hardly***, ***nearly***, ***frequently***, ***almost***, ***just***, ***usually***, ***scarcely*** are kept between subject and principal verb.

| Incorrect | Correct |
|---|---|
| **5.** (a) He always is early. | He is always early. |
| (b) She never has been early. | She has never been early. |
| (c) They often will go there. | They will often go there. |

**Note** ***Always***, ***never***, ***often***, ***generally***, ***sometimes***, ***usually***, ***already***, ***almost***, ***just***, ***nearly***, ***quite***, ***hardly***, ***scarcely*** are used after verb to be (am, is, are...) or auxiliaries.

| Incorrect | Correct |
|---|---|
| **6.** (a) The water of the river is too pure. | The water of the river is very pure. |
| (b) He is very blind to read small print. | He is too blind to read small print. |

**Note** The adverb '**too**' has a negative force and should not be used instead of '**very**' or '**much**'.

| Incorrect | Correct |
|---|---|
| **7.** (a) The news is much interesting. | The news is very interesting. |
| (b) The picture was very admired. | The picture was much admired. |
| (c) The result was very much surprising. | The result was very surprising. |

**Note** '**Very**' modifies present participle and '**much**', modifies past participle.

| Incorrect | Correct |
|---|---|
| **8.** (a) I do not know to swim. | I do not know how to swim. |
| (b) I know to make omelettes. | I know how to make omelettes. |
| (c) She does not know to dance. | She does not know how to dance. |

**Note** An infinitive (***to swim***, ***to dance***, ***to make***) should not usually follow '**know to**'. Therefore we use ***know how to***. However, modern English permits both 'learn to swim' and 'learn how to swim', etc.—A.L.D.

## CORRECT USAGE OF PREPOSITIONS

| | Incorrect | Correct |
|---|---|---|
| 1. | He insists me to do it. | He insists on my doing it. |
| 2. | He accused me for cheating him. | He accused me of cheating him. |
| 3. | The prisoner was accused for murder. | The prisoner was accused of murder. |
| 4. | My sister is afraid for dogs. | My sister is afraid of dogs. |
| 5. | Father was angry at his son. | Father was angry with his son. |
| 6. | I was angry for his conduct. | I was angry at his conduct. |
| 7. | I must admit of a feeling of shame. | I must admit to a feeling of shame. |
| 8. | We arrived to school in time. | We arrived at school in time. |
| 9. | I arrived at here early. | I arrived here early. |
| 10. | This is different than the other. | This is different from the other. |
| 11. | Your suggestions were very helpful for us. | Your suggestions were very helpful to us. |
| 12. | He is very interested with my story. | He is very interested in my story. |
| 13. | We are proud for our new car. | We are proud of our new car. |
| 14. | I shall return before a week. | I shall return in a week. |
| 15. | This question is difficult for me. | This question is difficult to me. |

## CORRECT USAGE OF CONJUNCTIONS

| | Incorrect | Correct |
|---|---|---|
| 1. (a) | He had hardly heard the news than he wept aloud. | He had hardly heard the news when / before he wept aloud. |
| (b) | He had scarcely gone than his friend arrived. | He had scarcely gone when his friend arrived. |

**Note** '**When**' or '**before**' (not '**than**') is used after '**hardly**' or '**scarcely**'.

| | Incorrect | Correct |
|---|---|---|
| 2. (a) | No sooner had he returned but he was off again. | No sooner had he returned than he was off again. |
| (b) | No sooner had the rain started but we left the place. | No sooner had the rain started than we left the place. |

**Note** '**Than**' (and not 'but') is used after '**no sooner**'.

| | Incorrect | Correct |
|---|---|---|
| 3. (a) | Unless you do not work hard, you will fail. | Unless you work hard, you will fail. |

| Incorrect | Correct |
|---|---|
| (b) ~~Unless~~ you have no objection, I shall see you tomorrow. | If you have no objection. I shall see you tomorrow. |

**Note** '**Unless**' means '**if not**'; therefore '**no**', '**not**' should not be used after it.

| Incorrect | Correct |
|---|---|
| **4.** (a) ~~Until~~ you work hard, you will improve. | So long as you work hard, you will improve. |
| (b) Wait here ~~as long as~~ five o'clock. | Wait here until five o'clock. |
| (c) ~~Until~~ it rains, I won't go. | As long as it rains, I won't go. |

**Note** '**Until**' denotes point of time; '**as long as/so long as**' denotes period of time.

| Incorrect | Correct |
|---|---|
| **5.** (a) I have no other friend ~~but~~ you. | I have no other friend than you. |
| (b) There is no one else ~~than~~ you. | There is no one else but you. |

**Note** '**Other**' is paired with '**than**', and '**else**' with '**but**'.

| Incorrect | Correct |
|---|---|
| **6.** (a) Because he is rude, ~~therefore~~ he is punished. | Because he is rude, he is punished. |
| (b) Because you are poor, ~~therefore~~ I shall help you. | Because you are poor, I shall help you. |

**Note** Both '**because**' and '**therefore**' are not used together in a sentence.

| Incorrect | Correct |
|---|---|
| **7.** (a) Come here between ten ~~or~~ twelve. | Come here between ten and twelve. |
| (b) Both Ram ~~as well as~~ Hari were there. | Both Ram and Hari were there. |

**Note** '**And**' is used after '**between**'/'**both**'.

| Incorrect | Correct |
|---|---|
| **8.** (a) Walk slowly, lest you ~~shall not~~ fall. | Walk slowly, lest you should fall. |
| (b) Work hard, lest you ~~may not~~ fail. | Work hard, lest you should fail. |

**Note** '**Lest**' signifies negative purpose and '**should**' is used with it.

| Incorrect | Correct |
|---|---|
| **9.** (a) Though he is poor, ~~but~~ he is happy. | Though he is poor, he is happy. |
| (b) Although he is rich, ~~but~~ he is unhappy. | Although he is rich, he is unhappy. |

**Note** '**But**' is not used with '**though**'/'**althogh**'.

| Incorrect | Correct |
|---|---|
| **10.** (a) If you do not labour, ~~then~~ you cannot pass. | If you do not labour, you cannot pass. |
| (b) When he saw the tiger, ~~then~~ he was afraid. | When he saw the tiger, he was afraid. |
| (c) As he entered the room, ~~then~~ he met me. | As he entered the room, he met me. |
| (d) As he was ill, ~~so~~ he could not come. | As he was ill, he could not come. |

**Note** '**So**' or '**then**' is not used with '**as**', '**when**', '**if**'.

| Incorrect | Correct |
|---|---|
| **11.** (a) Either he will obey me or take the consequence. | Either he will obey me or he will take the consequence. |
| (b) Either the step taken was right or wrong. | The step taken was either right or wrong. |
| (c) He not only cheated me but also my friend. | He cheated not only me but also my friend. |
| (d) He was both strong in power and will. | He was strong in both power and will. |

**Note** **Either ... or, neither ... nor, both ... and, not only ... but also** are correlatives. They are placed just before the alternatives or the related words.

| Incorrect | Correct |
|---|---|
| **12.** (a) I have neither written to her or spoken to her. | I have neither written nor spoken to her. |
| (b) He has either a pen nor a pencil. | He has either a pen or a pencil. |
| (c) He neither speaks English or French. | He speaks neither English nor French. |

**Note** '**Neither**' is always paired with '**nor**'; '**either**' with '**or**' and it is always placed just before the alternatives.

## CORRECT USAGE OF TENSE

| Incorrect | Correct |
|---|---|
| **1.** (a) I am born in India. | I was born in India. |
| (b) He has been born in a village. | He was born in a village. |
| (c) She has been born in a town. | She was born in a town. |

**Note** '**Was born**' is idiomatic and 'am born' or 'has born' is incorrect.

| Incorrect | Correct |
|---|---|
| **2.** (a) I have gone there yesterday. | I went there yesterday. |
| (b) He has done it last night. | He did it last night. |
| (c) She has come here three days ago. | She came here three days ago. |
| (d) They have built a house last year. | They built a house last year. |

**Note** If in a sentence ***yesterday***, ***ago***, ***last year/month/week*** etc. are used, the verb should be in past indefinite. But if the period of time has not come to an end, present perfect is used.

(i) I **have read** two books this week. (week not yet finished)

(ii) He **has seen** her this morning. (morning not yet finished)

| Incorrect | Correct |
|---|---|
| **3.** (a) I am here since 1990. | I have been here since 1990. |
| (b) I am waiting here since 7 o'clock. | I have been waiting here since 7 o'clock. |
| (c) He doesn't write to you for a week. | He hasn't written to you for a week. |
| (d) We study here for the last three years. | We have been studying here for the last three years. |
| (e) This was my ideal since a long time. | This has been my ideal for a long time. |

**Note** If '**for**' or '**since**' is used, the verb of the sentence will be in present perfect or present perfect continuous. '**Since**' denotes point of time while '**for**' denotes period of time.

| Incorrect | Correct |
|---|---|
| **4.** (a) I haven't seen him since I have been a child. | I haven't seen him since I was a child. |
| (b) Viki hasn't written to us since he has left home. | Viki hasn't written to us since he left home. |

**Note** The verb of the '**since**' **clause** will be in simple past tense.

| Incorrect | Correct |
|---|---|
| **5.** (a) I didn't yet see him. | I haven't yet seen him. |
| (b) She finished her work now. | She has finished her work now. |
| (c) He already gave me a book. | He has already given me a book. |
| (d) They just came here. | They have just come here. |
| (e) They came here not yet. | They have not yet come here. |

**Note** ***Yet, now, already, just, not yet*** are adverbials and present perfect is used with them.

| Incorrect | Correct |
|---|---|
| **6.** (a) We shall look forward to seeing you. | We look forward to seeing you. |
| (b) I shall accept your invitation with pleasure. | I accept your invitation with pleasure. |

**Note** Don't use a future tense when a present meaning is really intended.

| Incorrect | Correct |
|---|---|
| **7.** (a) He will come when he will be ready. | He will come when he is ready. |
| (b) She will do it if she will have time. | She will do it if she has time. |
| (c) They will telephone as soon as they will arrive home. | They will telephone as soon as they arrive home. |

**Note** ***When, as soon as, if, after, before, until, till*** are temporal conjunctions. Do not use future tense after them.

| | Incorrect | Correct |
|---|---|---|
| **8.** | (a) He looks as if he is mad. | He looks as if he were mad. |
| | (b) He talks as if he is my boss. | He talks as if he were my boss. |
| | (c) He speaks as if he knows the subject well. | He speaks as if he knew the subject well. |
| | (d) She walks as though she is going away. | She walks as though she were going away. |

**Note** **Past subjunctive** is used after **'as if'**, **'as though'**.

| | Incorrect | Correct |
|---|---|---|
| **9.** | (a) I am hating him for his vanity. | I hate him for his vanity. |
| | (b) You must be knowing Mr. Sen. | You must know Mr. Sen. |

**Note** Some verbs are not used with **-ing**. Examples :

| | | | | | |
|---|---|---|---|---|---|
| see | hear | feel | seem | taste | smell |
| know | think | believe | forget | like | love |
| hate | hope | mean | need | prefer | want |
| recognize | remember | understand | | | |

| | Incorrect | Correct |
|---|---|---|
| **10.** | (a) It is necessary that the weather is dry. | It is necessary that the weather should be dry. |
| | (b) It is necessary to do your duties properly. | It is necessary that you should do your duties. **Or** It is necessary that your duties should be done properly. |

**Note** Verb **'should'** is used after **'It is necessary that'**.

## SEQUENCE OF TENSE

| Incorrect | Correct |
|---|---|
| 1. He asked me what I am reading. | He asked me what I was reading. |
| 2. She said that she will come soon. | She said that she would come soon. |
| 3. He thought that he can win the prize. | He thought that he could win the prize. |
| 4. I asked her what she has done. | I asked her what she had done. |
| 5. He ran outside to see what is happening. | He ran outside to see what was happening. |

**Note** (i) If the principal clause is in past tense, the subordinate clause should also be converted into past tense.

(ii) If the verb of the principal clause is in present or future tense, the verb of the subordinate clause can be in any tense.

**Examples :** Jack says that John is ill. Jack says that John was ill. Jack thinks that John will go home.

## SUBJECT-VERB AGREEMENT

| | Incorrect | Correct |
|---|---|---|
| **1.** (a) | The wages of sin are very hard. | The wages of sin is very hard. |
| (b) | The news of the accident are shocking. | The news of the accident is shocking. |
| (c) | Mathematics are not easy to learn. | Mathematics is not easy to learn. |
| (d) | Politics are a dirty game. | Politics is a dirty game. |
| (e) | All his money are kept in the bank. | All his money is kept in the bank. |

**Note** ***Wages***, ***news***, ***mathematics***, ***politics***, ***money*** are singular nouns and they take singular verbs. But ***games*** and ***sports*** are plural nouns with plural verbs.

| | Incorrect | Correct |
|---|---|---|
| **2.** (a) | A number of boys is absent. | A number of boys are absent. |
| (b) | The number of pupils are increasing. | The number of pupils is inceasing. |

**Note** '**The number**' is singular and singular verb is used with it. '**A number of**' is plural and plural verb is used with it.

| | Incorrect | Correct |
|---|---|---|
| **3.** (a) | The bag, together with the books, are lost. | The bag, together with the books, is lost. |
| (b) | A man, besides his sons, were there. | A man, besides his sons, was there. |

**Note** 'The bag' and 'A man' are real singular subjects, hence singular verb.

| | Incorrect | Correct |
|---|---|---|
| **4.** (a) | Gulliver's Travels are a good book. | Gulliver's Travels is a good book. |
| (b) | The United States have a big army. | The United States has a big army. |

**Note** Title of a book and name of a country are treated as singular nouns.

| | Incorrect | Correct |
|---|---|---|
| **5.** (a) | **Many a things** are used for the show. | **Many a thing** is used for the show. |
| (b) | **Many a men** want to be rich overnight. | **Many a man** wants to be rich overnight. |

**Note** Both subject and verb should be singular after '**many a**'.

| | Incorrect | Correct |
|---|---|---|
| **6.** (a) | Two miles are not a long distance. | Two miles is not a long distance. |
| (b) | Four hundred rupees are not a big sum. | Four hundred rupees is not a big sum. |
| (c) | Ten years are a long time. | Ten years is a long time. |

**Note** **Two miles**, **Ten years**, **Four hundred rupees** have been used as single units. Therefore the verb in singular form is used.

| Incorrect | Correct |
|---|---|
| **7.** (a) One of the books are lost. | One of the books is lost. |
| (b) One of the boys have done it. | One of the boys has done it. |

**Note** If the subject of a sentence is **'one of'**, the verb will be singular.

| Incorrect | Correct |
|---|---|
| **8.** (a) He is one of those boys who is wicked. | He is one of those boys who are wicked. |
| (b) I have lost one of the books which was costly. | I have lost one of the books which were costly. |

**Note** Here **'who'** and **'which'** relate not to **'one of'**, but to **'boys'** and **'books'** that are plural. Therefore the verb in the Relative Clause will also be in plural form.

| Incorrect | Correct |
|---|---|
| **9.** (a) Each of them were happy. | Each of them was happy. |
| (b) Everyone of them are here. | Everyone of them is here. |
| (c) Every boy and every girl are present today. | Every boy and every girl is present today. |
| (d) Each man and each woman have a soul. | Each man and each woman has a soul. |

**Note** (i) Here the real subject is **'each'** and **'everyone'** and so the verb will be singular in form.

(ii) If two subjects are modified by **every** or **each**, the verb will be singular.

| Incorrect | Correct |
|---|---|
| **10.** (a) Either of these girls have a book. | Either of these girls has a book. |
| (b) Neither of the two boys are tall. | Neither of the two boys is tall. |
| (c) Either Hari or Moti have done it. | Either Hari or Moti has done it. |
| (d) Neither the boy nor the girl were there. | Neither the boy nor the girl was there. |

**Note** (i) If a sentence begins with **either of**, **neither of**, verb will be singular.

(ii) If two singular subjects are joined by **either...or** or **neither...nor**, the verb will be singular.

## MISCELLANEOUS ERRORS

| Incorrect | Correct |
|---|---|
| **1.** (a) You were absent at the meeting. | You were absent from the meeting. |
| (b) He did one mistake in dictation. | He made one mistake in dictation. |
| (c) A boy's hat is different from a girl. | A boy's hat is different from a girl's. |
| (d) Are you alone or married? | Are you married or single? |
| (e) You are coming with me, isn't it? | You are coming with me, aren't you? |

| Incorrect | Correct |
|---|---|
| **2.** (a) He is my cousin brother. | He is my cousin. |
| (b) She did not see me or my friend. | She saw neither me nor my friend. |
| (c) We look forward to see you. | We look forward to seeing you. |
| (d) Be careful not to lose your money. | Be careful of your money. |
| **3.** (a) He came by foot/walking. | He came on foot. |
| (b) He went there by horse. | He went there on a horse. |
| (c) Walking through a jungle, a snake bit him. | As he was walking through a jungle, a snake bit him. |
| (d) I think his grandfather is died. | I think his grandfather died/ is dead. |
| (e) The whole people were in panic. | All the people were in panic. |
| **4.** (a) India has a Shakespeare of his own. | India has a Shakespeare of her/its own. |
| (b) I have just met a lady which I saw last week. | I have just met a lady whom I saw last week. |
| (c) I have an account on this bank. | I have an account at/with this bank. |
| (e) There was a house **at two mile's distance**. | There was a house **at a distance of two miles**. |
| **5.** (a) You had better to go home. | You had better go home. |
| (b) They were in doubt in it. | They were in doubt about it. |
| (c) My house is changed in a hospital. | My house is changed into a hospital. |
| (d) Please execuse me to be so late. | Please excuse me for being (so) late. |
| **6.** (a) He did nothing but to laugh. | He did nothing but laugh. |
| (b) He is better able to walk than to run/to read rather than to write. | He is better able to walk than run/ to read rather than write. |
| (c) The boy entered into the class. | The boy entered the class. |
| (d) He entered the details. | He entered into the details. |
| **7.** (a) He is our mutual friend. | He is our common friend. |
| (b) What is the fresh news? | What is the latest news? |
| (c) I shall leave by the latest train. | I shall leave by the last train. |

| | Incorrect | Correct |
|---|---|---|
| | (d) My all friends are well off. | All my friends are well off. |
| | (e) Her both brothers are doctors. | Both her brothers are doctors. |
| | (f) He spent whole the day in play. | He spent the whole day in play. |
| | (g) The whole india mourned the death of Mahatma Gandhi. | The whole of India mourned the death of Mahatma Gandhi. |
| **8.** | (a) He has many works to do. | He has much (a lot of) work to do. |
| | (b) I need two dozens oranges. | I need two dozen oranges. |
| | (c) The road is closed for repair. | The road is closed for repairs. |
| | (d) If I were him, I should help you. | If I were he, I should help you. |
| | (e) She cannot bear my separation. | She cannot bear separation from me. |
| | (f) My camera is superior to your. | My camera is superior to yours. |
| | (g) One should do his duty. | One should do one's duty. |
| | (h) Good night! I am so glad to meet you. | Good evening! I am glad to meet you. |
| **9.** | (a) The slave hid himself in a cave. | The slave hid in a cave. |
| | (b) He qualified himself as a doctor. | He qualified as a doctor. |
| | (c) The teacher will take us a test tomorrow. | The teacher will give us a test tomorrow. |
| | (d) I did not see him for a long time. | I have not seen him for a long time. |
| | (e) What make you laugh? | What makes you laugh? |
| | (f) Our hen has given two eggs. | Our hen has laid two eggs. |
| | (g) Stop to write. | Stop writing. |
| | (h) He shook my hand. | He shook hands with me. |
| **10.** | (a) Sulekha works hardly. | Sulekha works hard. |
| | (b) The deer runs fastly. | The deer runs fast. |
| | (c) It is nothing else than pride. | It is nothing else but pride. |
| | (d) This book is much interesting. | This book is very interesting. |
| | (e) I came directly from Delhi. | I came direct from Delhi. |
| | (f) She gave up her studies two years before. | She gave up her studies two years ago. |
| | (g) I have good many things to do. | I have a good many things to do. |

| | Incorrect | Correct |
|---|---|---|
| **11.** | (a) Can I come in, sir? | May I come in, sir? |
| | (b) I am too weak that I cannot walk. | I am too weak to walk. |
| | (c) I am so weak that I may not walk. | I am so weak that I cannot walk. |
| | (d) Tell me what is your name. | Tell me what your name is. |
| | (e) Do you know who is he ? | Do you know who he is ? |
| | (f) I cannot help but think that you are wrong. | I cannot help thinking that you are wrong. |
| | (g) I cannot but thinking that you are wrong. | I cannot but think that you are wrong. |
| | (h) I laid in bed till 7 a.m. | I lay in bed till 7 a.m. |
| | (i) The river has overflown its blanks. | The river has overflowed its banks. |
| | (j) The boy was sunk in the river. | The boy was drowned in the river. |
| | (k) The ship was drowned in the sea. | The ship sank in the sea. |
| | (l) The doctor saw my pulse. | The doctor felt my pulse. |
| | (m) Baichung gave a goal. | Baichung scored a goal. |
| | (n) See the word in the dictionary. | Look up the word in the dictionary. |
| | (o) He went asleep. | He fell asleep. |
| | (p) The murderer has been hung. | The murderer has been hanged. |
| | (q) He says good English. | He speaks good English. |
| | (r) Don't speak a lie. | Don't tell a lie. |
| | (s) He threw a pot of milk. | He split a pot of milk. |
| | (t) She gave me a visit. | She paid me a visit. |
| | (u) You have kept pass-marks. | You have got/obtained pass-marks. |
| | (v) I admit my guilt. | I confess my guilt. |
| | (w) I confess your point. | I admit your point. |
| | (x) The matter was informed to him. | He was informed of the matter. |
| | (y) He is seeing the TV now. | He is watching the TV now. |
| | (z) The scientist migrated to the USA. | The scientist emigrated to the USA. |

## EXERCISE

**A. Find the errors and correct them in the following sentences :**

1. He advices me to wait.
2. I am senior than him.
3. You are junior than him.
4. This book is preferable than that.
5. Your informations are false.
6. I will inform to your father.
7. The rain has stopped yesterday.
8. I am confident to win.
9. This book is preferable than that.
10. One ought to love his country.
11. A number of boys has come.
12. He is a M.A./M.Sc.
13. Ganga is a sacred river.
14. Where you are going?
15. He is more taller than his sister.
16. The sceneries of the hillside are lovely.
17. He has passed last year.
18. He said that he will go after a week.
19. He says English fluently.
20. It is the most unique thing.
21. She resembles with my daughter.
22. Five rupees are a small sum.
23. He gave me the book I want.
24. She availed of the offer.
25. He as well as I am guilty.
26. Either you or I are wrong.
27. I know to speak English.
28. He is taller than her.
29. He gave a good speech.
30. His health is too good.
31. Do not speak lie.
32. The man is mortal.

**B. Correct the following sentences :**

1. He said me this.
2. I past my driving test.
3. I believe upon God.
4. He called me as a fool.
5. Let me write by a pen.
6. He gave a most perfect answer.
7. He is comparatively better today.
8. This mango tastes sweetly.
9. I have rang the bell.
10. He wrote a best book.
11. He does not know to swim.
12. He is ill since a week.
13. Debu said that he will do it.
14. He had come here yesterday.
15. He is my cousin brother.
16. He and I am neighbours.
17. Quote the poem from heart.
18. Every man are mortal.
19. He is an European.
20. The gold is yellow.
21. Tell me what is your name.
22. He prevents me to go there.
23. He is a worst student in the class.
24. Sunil is a NCC cadet.
25. Does he speaks English?
26. He was hung for murder.
27. He has died yesterday.
28. We had a picnic tomorrow.
29. Columbus invented America.
30. All the furnitures were lost.
31. Physics are not easy to learn.
32. He is best of the two boys.
33. Each of the students were punished.
34. Either of the three teams might win.
35. Either he or I are to blame.
36. We read grammar near our Headmaster.

# 38 FIGURES OF SPEECH

## WHAT IS A FIGURE OF SPEECH ?

A figure of speech is ornamental use of words. It is used to increase the effectiveness of words in a sentence. For example, if we say, 'There are four pillars in this building', the word 'pillars' is used in its ordinary sense. But when we say, 'Failure is the pillar of success', the word 'pillar' is used in figurative sense.

Here are simple illustrations of the important figures of speech commonly used :

### SIMILE [ From Latin Similis ]

It is a figure of comparison in which two dissimilar things are compared explicitly for a point of similarity. The simile is usually introduced by such words as: ***like***, ***as***, ***such***, ***as***, ***just as***:

1. He ran like a hare down the street.
2. Errors, like straws, upon the surface flow.
3. She sways like a flower in the wind of the music.
4. Your face is as a book where man can read strange letters.
5. As flies to wanton boys are we to the gods. (Shakespeare)
6. Drive my dead thoughts over the universe
   Like withered leaves to quicken a new birth. ( Shelley)

### METAPHOR

A metaphor is an implicit comparison without using words such as: ***like***, ***as***, ***just as***, ***such as***. In it, the two objects of completely different nature are identified.

1. The camel is the ship of the desert.
2. The ship ploughs the sea.
3. Our eldest son is the star of the family.
4. He has a heart of stone. [ = He has a heart like stone. ]
5. Life is a tale told by an idiot.
6. What joyance rains upon me !
7. We must be guided by the light of nature.

### ALLEGORY

An allegory has been defined as a sustained metaphor.

## METONYMY

In this figure a thing is called, not by its name, but by its user.

The pen (i.e. the writer) in mightier than the sword (i.e. the soldier).

## PERSONIFICATION

In personification, inanimate (lifeless) objects and abstract ideas are spoken of as having life and intelligence:

1. Death lays its icy hand on everyone.
2. The sea that bares her bosom to the moon.
3. Let no ambition mock their useful toil.
4. Her patience, to prevent that murmur, soon replies.

## TRANSFERRED EPITHET

This is a figure of speech where an epithet or an adjective is transferred from a living-being to a non-living one.

1. I passed a sleepless night.
2. He lay all night on his sleepless pillow.
3. The ploughman homeward plods his weary way.

## APOSTROPHE

By this figure the speaker addresses some inanimate things or some abstract ideas directly.

1. O Death! Where is thy sting?
2. O World! O Life! O Time!
3. Frailty, thy name is woman!

## INVERSION/ANASTROPHE

This is a figure of speech that refers to an inversion or change of usual order of words for emphasis or special effect.

1. Many a foreign dawn has he seen.
2. Much have I travelled in the realm of gold.
3. Come I may, but go I must.
4. Silver and gold have I none.

## ALLITERATION

This consists in the repetition of the same sound or syllable at the beginning of two or more words :

1. An Austrian army awfully arrayed.
2. A load of learning lumbering in his head.
3. A reeling road, rambles round the shine.
4. A strong man struggling with the storms of fate.
5. Slowly silently now the moon/Walks the night in her silver shoon.
6. Wilful waste makes woeful want.

## HYPERBOLE OR EXAGGERATION

In hyperbole a statement is made emphatic by overstatement. Such expression is not meant to be taken literally:

1. Ten thousand saw I at a glance.
2. She shed an ocean of tears.
3. All the perfumes of Arabia will not sweeten this little hand.

## OXYMORON

It is a figure of speech which combines two seemingly contradictory elements :

1. He is regulary irregular.
2. This is like a living death.
3. And having nothing, he had all.
4. The kind cruelty of the surgeon's knife.
5. Our sweetest songs are those that tell of saddest thoughts.

## EUPHEMISM

By this figure of speech we speak rude things in gentle and favourable terms.

1. He was gathered to his forefathers (= he died).
2. He was Her Majesty's guest (= in prison) for three years.
3. How sleep the brave who sink to rest (= escape from battle).

   [Thus 'Queen' is a modern euphemism for 'homosexual']

## CLIMAX [ Latin and Greek 'Klimax' ]

This is a Greek word signifying a ladder. This figure raises the sense by successive steps to what is more and more important and impressive:

1. I came, I saw, I conquered.
2. I laugh, I run, I leap, I sing, I dance for joy.
3. We planned, we laboured, we succeeded in our mission.

## ANTICLIMAX OR BATHOS

This is just opposite to climax and signifies a ludicrous descent form the higher to lower level:

1. He lost his wife, his daughter, his son and his pet cat.
2. The woman said, "I do have a prestigious husband and a pair of shoes."
3. Here, thou great Anna! Whom three realms obey. Dost sometimes take counsel—and sometimes tea.

## PARADOX

A paradox is a statement which appears to be outwardly contradictory but conveys inner significance:

1. Failures are the pillars of success.
2. He that loses his life shall save it.
3. There is plenty in poverty.
4. The child is the father of the man.
5. There is no one so great a donor as a wealthy miser.

## ANTITHESIS

This means the setting of one thing against another. This figure of speech is an explicit statement of an implied contrast:

1. Man proposes, God disposes.
2. To err is human, to forgive divine.
3. Speech is silver, but silence is golden.
4. A bird in the hand is worth two in the bush.

## PUN

A pun is a figure of speech that consists in a play on the various meanings of a word and is mostly used in humorous sense :

1. Is life worth living ? That depends on the liver.
2. Yes, the leopard changes its spots, whenever it goes from one spot to another.
3. Not on thy sole but on thy soul, harsh Jew,
   Thou maks't thy knife keen. (Shakespeare)

## IRONY

An Irony is a figure of speech to make a statement more emphatic in mockery by the use of words denoting the opposite of what is really meant:

1. She speaks of her unlawful sisters as 'the jewels of our father'.
2. Yet Brutus says he is ambitious and Brutus is an honourable man.

## EPIGRAM

The epigram is a figure of speech that is marked by wit and brevity :

1. We all have sufficient strength to endure the misfortunes of others.
2. Hypocrisy is the homage, vice pays to virtue.
3. Treason doth never prosper; what is the reason?
   Why, if it prospers, none dare call it treason.
4. Vision is the art of seeing things invisible.

## SYNECDOCHE

By this figure of speech a less comprehensive term is used for a more comprehensive one.

1. Ring out the narrowing lust of gold. [Here the less comprehensive term 'gold' is used for more comprehensive 'wealth and riches'.]
2. And take from seventy springs a score/It only leaves me fifty more. [Here the less comprehensive term 'springs' is used for more comprehensive 'years'.]

## ONOMATOPOEIA

It is a figure of speech consisting such words that echo their sense through their sound effect:

1. And beauty born of murmuring sound.
2. The murmurous haunt of flies on summer eves.
3. The curfew tolls the knell of parting day.
4. Grunt, grunt goes the hog.
5. Our echoes roll from soul to soul.

## SOME MORE SIMILES/COMPARISON PHRASES

1. As black as coal
2. As bright as day
3. As brave as a lion
4. As brisk as a butterfly
5. As brilliant as stars
6. As busy as a bee
7. As careless as the wind
8. As cautious as a fox
9. As cheerful as a lark
10. As clear as day/as crystal
11. As clever as a crow
12. As cold as ice
13. As cool as cucumber
14. As cosy as the nest of a bird
15. As cunning as a fox
16. As dirty as a hog
17. As distant as the horizon
18. As dumb as a statue
19. As fair as a rose
20. As faithful as a dog

21. As fast as a hare/as mind
22. As fat as a pig
23. As flat as board
24. As fierce as a tiger
25. As frail as glass
26. As free as air (a bird)
27. As fresh as dew/as a rose
28. As gay as a lark
29. As gentle as a lamb
30. As good as gold
31. As grave as a judge
32. As greedy as a wolf
33. As green as grass
34. As hard as stone
35. As harsh as truth
36. As hasty as fire
37. As heavy as load
38. As hoarse as a crow
39. As hot as fire
40. As hungry as a hawk/a wolf
41. As invisible as the air
42. As light as a feather
43. As loud as thunder
44. As mute as a fish
45. As nervous as a mouse
46. As obstinate as a mule
47. As patient as the hills
48. As playful as a kitten
49. As pointed as a needle
50. As poor as a church-mouse
51. As proud as a peacock
52. As quick as thought/lightning
53. As quiet as a lamb
54. As rapid as lightning
55. As red as blood
56. As sharp as a razor
57. As silent as a grave
58. As silly as a sheep
59. As soft as butter/wax
60. As steady as a rock
61. As stupid as a donkey
62. As sure as death
63. As sweet as honey
64. As swift as an arrow
65. As timid as a hare
66. As tricky as a monkey
67. As true as steel
68. As ugly as a toad
69. As useful as a cow
70. As uncertain as the weather
71. As vain as a peacock
72. As warm as wool
73. As weak as a kitten
74. As wise as a saint
75. As white as snow

## EXERCISE

**A. Point out the figures of speech in the following sentences :**

1. Childhood is like a passing dream.
2. Variety is the spice of life.
3. Truth sits upon the dying man.
4. There is dagger in thy words.
5. He is a man of iron will.
6. Swiftly flies the feathered death.
7. The more haste, the less speed.
8. Rana Pratap was the lion of India.
9. Hitler's mad policy let lose the dogs of war.
10. The soldiers were swifter than eagles and stronger than lions.
11. The chair collapsed under the weight of the philosopher.
12. The midday sun is a mystic dog with paws of fire.
13. A thousand years are as yesterday where it is lost.
14. Hope is the poor man's bread.
15. Poverty is a blessing in a good many situations.

**B. Make sentences with the following Similes or Comparison Phrases :**

1. as busy as a bee : ..........
2. as cheerful as a lark : ..........
3. as clever as a crow : ..........
4. as cunning as a fox : ..........
5. as dirty as a hog : ..........
6. as dumb as a statue : ..........
7. as fast as a hare : ..........
8. as fat as a pig : ..........
9. as gentle as a lamb : ..........
10. as greedy as a wolf : ..........
11. as hard as stone : ..........
12. as hungry as a hawk : ..........
13. as light as a feather : ..........
14. as loud as thuder : ..........
15. as mute as a fish : ..........
16. as nervous as a mouse : ..........
17. as old as the hills : ..........
18. as proud as a peacock : ..........
19. as ugly as a toad : ..........
20. as wise as a judge : ..........

# PART II

# COMPOSITION

# 1  LETTER WRITING

## WHY AND HOW TO WRITE A LETTER?

In modern times every educated person should know how to write a clear and readable letter. Everyone sometimes feels the necessity of writing Official letters or Business letters of some sort, and may have to face the problem of writing an important Personal letter that would vitally mould his interests in life. Hence letter writing is a necessity and it is also an art. But whenever we sit down to write a letter, we realize that writing a good letter is not an easy job and needs careful practice.

**Letters may be divided into the following classes :**

[1] **Private letters and telegrams**

[2] **Social letters**

[3] **Business letters**

[4] **Official & Demi-official letters**

[5] **Letters in response to advertisements**

[6] **Letters to the editor of a newspaper**

[7] **Circular letter or Notice and Draft**

**Private letters, Social letters, Business letters and Official letters or Demi-official letters** may be broadly divided into two groups—[i] **Letters of information and proposal**, [ii] **Reply letters**.

Each of the Official letters, Business letters, Private letters etc. has its own particular form. But in all kinds of letters there are six parts that must be attended to :

1. The heading consisting of the writer's address and the date
2. The courteous greeting or salutation
3. The communication or message—the body of the letter
4. The subscription or courteous leave-taking
5. The signature
6. The superscription or outside address

**Now see a model of a Private letter with all the six parts discussed above :**

## MODEL OF A LETTER

**[ A Private Letter about Progress in Studies ]**

**[1. Heading ]**

10 Kathleen Avenue
London

**[2. Salutation ]**

My dear Father,

**[3. Body of the letter ]**

I got your letter in time. You know our examination is knocking at the door. I think, you are very anxious to know about my progress in studies. Please don't worry about it. You will be glad to know that I have made satisfactory progress in all the subjects. Yet I shall devote more time in studying French as French is a foreign language. But still, I hope, I may fare well in the examination. I am pretty well now.

Nothing more for the present.

**[4. Subscription ]** Yours affectionately,

**[5. Signature ]** ***Andrew***

**[6. Superscription ]**

Stamp

**Stuart Davis**
270 Catherine Court, Chase Rd.
South Gate, London, N14 4RB

**Note** The first letter of Father, Mother, Uncle, Aunt, etc. are capitalised in salutation. No full stop or punctuation mark is used after signature. Nowadays, no punctuation mark is used even after Salutation and Subscription or Courteous Leave Taking in American style while comma ( , ) is used after Salutation and Leave Taking in the British style. However, **the British style has been followed in this book**.

**Now write a letter in your mother tongue. Then write it in your own English :**

## PRIVATE LETTERS

**[1] A letter to a friend who has recently lost his father.**
**Or, A letter of condolence to a bereaved person.**

1 Maequari Street
Past Circular Quay
Sydney, Australia

Dear friend,

I can hardly believe that your father is no more. The news came to me as a bolt from the blue. Only a month ago I received a very affectionate letter from your father and he offered me much good advice. But death snatched him away so cruelly! I know he had a mild stroke last year. But he looked so cheerful and fit. He was so kind to me that I feel it as a personal loss to myself. May his soul rest in peace.

You know, what is lotted cannot be blotted.

Yet words, I know, are poor comforters. "The heart knoweth its own sorrow", and in all such situations we are always alone. But it is not mere words when soul speaks to soul. I can only trust to the healing effect of time and pray to God for the strength that will help you to bear the misfortune.

Yours ever,
*Steven*

| Stamp |
|---|
| John Smith<br>1088 Burrard Street, Vancouver<br>British Columbia V 67, Canada |

**[2] Reply to the above**

Vancouver
Canada

My dear Steven,

Thank you very much for your kind and sympathetic response. You say that words are poor comforters. But the sympathy of a true freind is a great comfort in time of sorrow; and I am grateful to you for your cordial letter.

Some say death by stroke is a boon to him who dies rather unknowingly, though it is painful to his kith and kin. My father suffered no prolonged illness. He passed away suddenly and quietly in his sleep. His end came peacefully.

Father's death is a great shock to me though I do not fully realize it even yet.

He was fond of you, and spoke of you several times towards the end.

However, I may be excused from writing more at present. I don't feel equal to it.

Yours sincerely,
*John Smith*

**Stamp & address of the receiver**

**[3] A letter of congratulation on success in the Final Examination.**

Kalkaji
New Delhi, India
April 19, 2010

My dear Abhijit,

I have just heard of your result of the Final Examination. I convey my heartiest congratulations on your brilliant success. To secure star marks and letters in five subjects is no easy achievement. All your friends and relatives must be proud that you have won such distinction. We are specially happy that you performed so well even though you had fallen ill just before the examination.

I am sure this result will encourage you to do better in your higher studies. If you come out successfully in the Joint Entrance Examination, I hope you will choose either Science or Engineering course. If it is Computer Science, you should prefer Kanpur to Delhi.

I think you are now being flooded with letters from your friends and relatives.

I wish you a still more glorious future.

Yours ever,
*Preeti*

**Stamp & address of the receiver**

**[4] Reply to the above.**

Indiranagar
Bangalore, India
April 26, 2010

My dear Preeti,

Your sweet letter has anchored in the shore of my heart. It is so pleasant that it is like receiving a rare prize from you. Many people have congratulated me on my success. But a line from you is much more to me. I value your friendship more than anything else. Your letter will give me strength and courage to work with diligence in my life.

I am yet to decide which course I should take up because any mistake now will cause a disappointment later. I hope father will talk to me about taking a final decision. With love to you,

Yours truly,
***Abhijit***

**Stamp & address of the receiver**

**[5] A letter of invitation to join a birthday party.**

Herney Bay
Auckland City, New Zealand
March 7, 2010

My dear Kim,

You will be glad to learn that my fourteenth birthday comes off on the 10th instant. All our near and dear ones are expected to join the celebration. Mother asks me to invite you to come and dine with us that evening. There will be a lot of fun and merry-making on that day.

So be sure to come. With love to you,

Yours sincerely,
***George***

**Stamp & address of the receiver**

**[6] Reply to the above letter accepting invitation.**

Seol
South Korea
March 8, 2010

My dear George,

I am glad to receive your invitation on the occasion of your fourteenth birthday celebration. I don't like to miss your loving company on that occasion. You may rest assured that I'll reach your home to add to your enjoyment on that day. I think there will be a lot of fun and amusement.

With best wishes to you,

Yours truly,
***Youngun Kim***

**Stamp & address of the receiver**

**[7] Reply to the above letter apologising for having failed to join the birthday party.**

Seol
South Korea
March 11, 2010

My dear George,

I am really very sorry for having failed to join the birthday party with you. I can well imagine how angry you are. But believe me, I had no way out.

Yesterday evening, as I was getting ready for attending your birthday party, I got a telephone from Anirvan. Probably you remember him. He is an old friend of ours. He informed me that his mother was seriously ill. So I had to rush out at once to his house. Thank God, timely help saved her life. I tender my apology for having failed to keep my appointment with you. I am sure you missed me very much.

Happy birthday to you,

Yours truly,
***Youngun Kim***

**Stamp & address of the receiver**

**[8] A letter to a friend inviting him to spend the summer vacation with you.**

Simla, India
April 10, 2010

My dear Vijaylakshmi,

A lot of thanks for your sweet letter.

You wrote to me that your school will be closed for summer vacation from the 20th May. I will be very glad if you spend the vacation with us at Simla. After a long confinement in the city, I am sure, you will feel happy in the hillside. The cool weather will refresh your mind and restore your energy. The apple orchards in the hillsides are special attractions here. Besides, my parents will be very glad to have you with us. Please do come.

Your loving friend,
***Rahul***

**Stamp & address of the receiver**

**[9] Write a reply to the above accepting the invitation.**

Madurai
Tamil Nadu, India
April 18, 2010

Dear Rahul,

Many thanks for your invitation for spending a few days with you in the hillside. My parents have permitted me to accept your cordial invitation. It will refresh my body and mind as I shall be away from the drudgery of city life for a few days. I think we will have lot of fun and amusement, and sight-seeing too. I hope I'll reach your home around 12 noon on the 30th instant.

With love and best wishes,

Yours ever,
***Vijaylakshmi***

**Stamp & address of the receiver**

**[10] Write a reply to the above declining the invitation.**

Madurai
Tamil Nadu, India
April 18, 2010

Dear Rahul,

Many thanks for your cordial invitation. But I am sorry to inform you that my parents have already fixed another programme to spend the holidays at Goa. I shall accompany them and stay there till the end of summer vacation. But I don't like to miss your loving company in the hillside.

I hope to visit your place during the Puja holidays.

With best love to you and regards to your parents,

Your loving friend,
*Vijaylakshmi*

**Stamp & address of the receiver**

**[11] A letter to a friend in a hospital.**

Gandhinagar
Gujarat, India
April 28, 2010

Dear Gahar,

I have only just heard from your mother that you have broken your leg in a cycle accident and you have been lying in bed in hospital for a week. I am very sorry. If I had known it, I should have met you in the hospital. And now I'm going to Bangalore for an urgent piece of business. However, I am glad to know that it is a case of simple fracture and, you are now much better. I hope you will be all right and come out of this mishap as smart and jolly as you were.

As soon as you can, please write to me and let me know how you are.

Yours ever,
*Hanif*

**Stamp & address of the receiver**

**[12] A letter to a friend about a street accident.**

Bangalore
India
April 28, 2010

My dear Shreedhar,

You have possibly noticed the shocking news in today's newspaper. I witnessed the same yesterday before my very eyes.

That accident took place at about 10 a.m. yesterday. A school-boy of 15 was run over by a private bus at the crossing of the Brigade Road and the M G Road. A bus was coming up at a break-neck speed along the M G Road. The ill-fated boy was crossing the road at that moment. Unfortunately a book dropped from his school-bag and he stooped to pick it up. The passersby raised shouts of alarm. The driver tried his best to stop, but he could not check the speed in time. The boy was run over by the bus and his body became a lump of flesh in a pool of blood. Still he was taken to the Medical

College hospital where he was declared DOA (dead on arrival). This pathetic sight moved every heart and some of them who were there could not check tears.

Now I am not in a position to write any more. More when we meet.

Yours ever,

***Kamakshi***

**Stamp & address of the receiver**

**Note** 'The' is not used before the name of a street, but it is used before the name of a Road or Avenue.

**[13] A letter to your younger brother advising him not to neglect his studies by watching TV—the 'idiot-box'.**

.....................

.....................

(Sender's address & date)

Dear Tessa,

It has been quite a long since we have not written to each other. I hope everything is going fine at your side.

Of late, Mum seems to be worried about you. The other day I overheard Mum saying that you spend a lot of time on TV. If this is true, I should advise you that it is high time you need to concentrate more on your studies. Here you may think differently that TV is not entirely for foolish entertainment as it is commonly known as the 'idiot-box'. I do agree with you that it is also a medium that gives us ample opportunity to learn, for example, from the channels for programmes on 'Discovery channel', 'Milo Quiz Contest' and some others. However, at this vital moment you should be able to distribute your timings between your studies for the exams and others.

Before I actually put a full stop, I must tell you that I am quite confident that you will be sincere to your studies and make all of us proud.

With love to you,

Your loving brother,

***Kamal***

**Stamp & address of the receiver**

## LETTERS TO PEN-FRIENDS

**[1] Imagine the following to be your pen-friend. Now write a letter to him.**

Ranjan Krishnamurty

69 Eleventh Main Road, Molleswaram

Bangalore 560 055

He wants to know about your English Examination.

Write a letter to him focussing on the following points :

(i) the three sections in the question paper

(ii) how you like each section

(iii) how you think you have fared in each of them

(iv) your final impression of the paper.

Salt Lake, Kolkata
March 22, 2010

My dear Ranjan,

I have just received your letter. You are eager to know about my English paper in the Final Exam. There are three sections in our English question paper—Reading Skill, Writing Skill and Grammar & Vocabulary. I like Reading Skill the most. But I face some difficulty in Writing Skill as I am afraid of writing my puny English. I am also afraid of Grammar & Vocabulary, especially Grammar as we have read it in our textbooks in a homeopathic dose without its rules and proper usage. So I have to overcome a lot of hurdles in that section.

However, I have fared well in the English paper on the whole. I think our English paper is a mixture of easy and difficult questions for the common and brilliant students.

I must stop now with a hope of having a chance to meet you in near future.

Yours ever,

***Rahul***

**Stamp & address of the receiver**

**[2] A letter to a pen-friend in England about your difficulty in learning English.**

Bhagalpur
Bihar, India
March 12, 2010

My dear Brown,

It is so good of you to expect frequent letters from me. But I fight shy of writing in English as, I think, a foreign language is really a hard nut to crack. I face difficulty in every step of learning English. Articles puzzle me. If this is 'an umbrella', why that should be 'a university'? Pronunciation is also a problem. 'U'-sounds in 'bus', 'bush' and 'busy' are not the same! The use of prepositions also misleads me. He resides 'at Bhagalpur', but his office is 'in Patna'! Tenses are other hurdles. To use them properly in sentences puts me on tension.

How do I dare write oftener?

Yours truly,

***Ranvir Singh***

**Stamp**

R. P. Brown
15 Downing Street
London, U.K.

**Note :** Instead of 'Yours truly', you may also write 'Truly yours'

**[3] Read the following advertisement that came out in 'The Telegraph' :**

> Wanted an Indian pen-friend, a boy or a girl, interested in travelling and reading comics. Write to :
> Miss Sophia Erono
> 31 Ellius Road
> London N.W. 12

**Now write a letter to your pen-friend intimating**

(i) How you got her name and address
(ii) Why you want to have a pen-friend
(iii) The name of your institution and the class you study in
(iv) Something about your background, i.e. yourself, family, hobby etc.

Petersplat Z
Switzerland
March 24, 2010

Dear Sophia,

I have got your name and address from the advertisement that came out in 'The Telegraph' dated 3rd March 2010.

You have wanted an Indian pen-friend interested in travelling and reading comics. This advertisement has drawn my attention as I am also interested in these two things. Of course, it is not possible to travel around the world but we can have pen-friends all over the world, collect news from them and be intimate to them.

Now let me give some details about myself and my family background. I study in Class X in an Academy in our town. My favourite hobby is reading comics. My father is a carpenter and he is proud of the dignity of his labour.

However, I am eager to have a sketch of your family and yourself by return of post.

With love and best wishes,

I remain
Yours sincerely,
***Mirrian Watts***

Stamp

Miss Sophia Erno
31 Ellius Road
London N.W. 12

**[4]** **Imagine that you have a British pen-friend who wants to know how different life and customs are in India from those in his/her country. Write in an informal manner covering the following points :**

| BRITISH | INDIAN |
|---|---|
| (a) small family—parents and children | (a) joint family |
| (b) old people do not expect support from the young ones | (b) old people expect the young ones to support them |
| (c) marriage not arranged | (c) arranged marriages |
| (d) relationship with relatives/ friends rather formal—can't visit without notice | (d) informal relationship with friends/relatives—can visit without notice |
| (e) very polite—'Thank You' and 'Please' common | (e) polite but not in the same manner |
| (f) life appears to move fast | (f) slower movement—though getting faster |

Chandigarh
India
March 23, 2010

Dear John,

Your sweet note has just anchored in the shore of my heart. You are eager to learn how different life and customs are in India from those in yours.

You must admit that each country has its own way of life. In England, as you well know, people live in a small family consisting of parents and children. But in India we generally live in a joint family where even grandparents and grandsons live together. In your country, old people do not expect support from their young ones. But in India the case is reverse.

In England, marriages are not arranged by parents, but in India the custom is in vogue. In your country, relationship with relatives or friends is rather formal. They can't visit without notice. But in India they come whenever they like. You, the English people, are very polite in manners and often say, 'Thank You' and 'Please' for any kind of help. We Indians are also polite in manners but our greetings are different. In England life appears to move at a fast pace but our people are accustomed to slower movement—though life is getting faster nowadays.

Yours ever,
*Preetam*

**Stamp & address of the receiver**

## SOCIAL LETTERS

Social letters of invitation may be **formal** or **informal**. Formal invitations are generally issued in cards and the informal ones in letters.

**[1] A formal letter of invitation :**

> **Mr. and Mrs. P. C. Sen** [**Or, Mrs and Mr P. C. Sen**]
> request the pleasure of the company of **Mr. and Mrs. N. N. Bose**
> at the party to be held on the occasion of their daughter's marriage
> at 53 Rafi Marg at 8 pm on April 18, 2010
>
> *Prakash Ch. Sen* and *Sumita Sen* [**Or**] *Sumita Sen* and *Prakash Ch. Sen*

**[2] A formal letter of acceptance :**

Mr. & Mrs. N. N. Bose have much pleasure in accepting the kind invitation of Mr. & Mrs. P. C. Sen at the wedding party of their daughter at 8 pm on April 18, 2010.

*N. N. Bose*

**[3] A formal letter of Regret :**

Mr. & Mrs. N. N. Bose thank Mr. & Mrs. P. C. Sen for their kind invitation to the wedding party on April 18, 2010, but very much regret that they are unable to attend it on account of a previous engagement.

*N. N. Bose*

**Note** A formal invitation is generally written in the third person and should contain no heading, no salutation and no complementary close. The writer's name and address should appear in the body of the letter. The reply should also be in the third person and in the same manner.

**[4] An informal letter of invitation :**

53 Rafi Marg, New Delhi
April 10, 2010

My Dear Mrs. and Mr. Bose,

Would you please give us the pleasure of your company on the auspicious occasion of the wedding of our daughter at 8 pm on 18 April, 2010 at our residence?

[Or] We look forward to your warm company on the auspicious occasion of the wedding of our daughter at 8 pm on 18 April, 2010 at our residence.

Yours truly,

***Sumita Sen***

and

***Prakash Chandra Sen***

**Note** Nowadays some prefer to place Mrs. before Mr.

**[5] An informal letter of acceptance :**

AE Block
Salt Lake, Kolkata 700 064
April 10, 2010

My dear Mr. and Mrs. Sen,

Thank you very much for your kind invitation. We'll be highly glad to be with you on the auspicious occasion of your daughter's marriage on the 18th April.

Yours sincerely,

***N. N. Bose*** and ***Mrs. Bose***

**[6] An informal letter declining invitation :**

AE Block, Salt Lake
Kolkata 700 064
April 10, 2010

My dear Mr. and Mrs. Sen,

Thank you very much for your kind invitation. But we regret to say that we won't be able to attend it on account of a previous engagement. We'll be out of the town/ city on that day.

Yours sincerely,

***N. N. Bose*** and ***Mrs. Bose***

**Note** The frequent practice of writing the date with numbers only such as 10.04.10 may be sometimes confusing. In England the order is—first date, then month, then year. But in America the order is—first month, then date, then year. Therefore, 10.4.10 will mean April 10, 2010 to an Englishman, but October 4, 2010 to an American! Hence the dates should be written in full form.

## BUSINESS LETTERS

Such letters begin with **Dear Sir / Sirs**, and end with **Yours truly / faithfully**. Your address and date should be put in the left hand corner below the letter.

**[1] Write a letter to a book-seller complaining that the books supplied by them do not conform to the order placed.**

To
New Central Book Agency (P) Ltd.
Ansari Road, Dariaganj, New Delhi

**Sub : Replacing books as per order**

Dear Sirs,

I received the packet of books sent by you per VPP on the 5th May, but I regret to inform you that the books sent to me by parcel do not conform to the order placed by me. They are of old editions and they will not serve my purpose. So I am returning them to you.

Please replace the books of the latest editions by return of post.
I hope I may count upon your active cooperation.
Thanking you,

Yours faithfully,
***M. M. Pillai***

Dated :
Model Town
Delhi, India
15 May, 2010

**Note** Messers is not used before impersonal title of a Company. Hence Messers Mondal & Sons etc. is right but Messers New Central Book Agency is wrong. It should be only New Central Book Agency.

**[2] Reply to the above letter :**

New Central Book Agency (P) Ltd.
Ansari Road, Dariaganj, New Delhi

Ref. No. ........... Dated..............

Dear Sir,

In reply to your letter dated May 15, 2010, I beg to say that the books sent to you per VPP. on the 5th May are really of old edition. I am extremely sorry for that (our inadvertent oversight), and the books of the latest edition are despatched herewith.

Thanking you,

Yours faithfully
***A. Sen***
(Managing Director)

**Note 1** In replying to a Business letter, always quote the number of reference (if any) and the date of the letter you are answering. If a clerk signs a Business letter on behalf of his/her employer, he/she puts the letter **p.p.** (Latin **per pro** = on behalf of) before the name of the company and writes his/her own name below or above that.

**Note 2** **In American style the Leave-taking and Signature are used in left hand side, but in the British style these are used in right hand side.**

**[3] Write a letter to the Manager/Branch Manager of a Bank for a Bank Draft.**

To
The Branch Manager
State Bank of India
Kota, Rajasthan

**Sub : Issuing a Bank Draft**

Dear Sir,

I shall be highly obliged if you would supply me with a Bank Draft of Rs. 2,000/- (Rupees Two Thousand only) in favour of "Unit Trust of India", Mumbai.

Please debit the amount to my current account.

Thanking you in anticipation,

Yours faithfully,
***Geeta Chouhan***

Dated : 23 June, 2010
29 Sanjay Nagar
Kota, Rajasthan

**[4] Reply to the above letter :**

State Bank of India
June 24, 2010

Ref. No. ........... Dated : ...........

Dear Sir,

In reference to your letter (No. Nil dated June 23, 2010) we enclose a Bank Draft of Rs. 2,000 (Rupees Two Thousand only) herewith as required by you. We have debited your account for the same.

This may please be acknowledged.

Yours faithfully,
..............
(MANAGER)

**[5] Suppose, you want to travel with your friends to the hills this summer. You have read the following advertisement in a newspaper. Now write to the Manager requesting him to book room(s) for you. Your letter should contain enquiry about type and number of rooms you require, charges, number of days and other information you need.**

| Snow-View Hotel, Darjeeling—quiet surroundings—comfortable rooms—24-hr. water—sight-seeing facilities—moderate charges. **Manager** |
|---|

To
The Manager
Snow-View Hotel, Darjeeling

**Sub : Booking rooms in your hotel**

Dear Sir,

With reference to your advertisement in the newspaper I am to inform you that I want to go with my friends to Darjeeling this summer. I request you to book two four-seated rooms in your hotel for me and my friends from the 5th to the 11th of June.

Please let me know the type of rooms, the charges for 7 days and the sight-seeing facilities and expenses thereof in details. It is known from your advertisement that there is 24-hr water supply. But what about electric supply, especially when there are frequent power-cuts?

Awaiting your early reply,

Yours faithfully,
..........................
..........................
(Date and Address)

....................
(Full Signature)

## OFFICIAL AND DEMI-OFFICIAL LETTERS

Such letters begin with the very formal **Sir /Madam** (or **Dear Sir /Dear Madam** with the same rank), but not 'My dear Sir/My dear Madam'.

**[1] Write a letter to the O.C. of your local police station reporting that you lost your bicycle. Refer to the following points :**

(i) Date and time of the loss. (ii) Name of the place wherefrom it was lost. (iii) Details of the cycle. (iv) Condition of the cycle.

To
The O.C.
Lornui P.S.
Bilaspur, Chattisgarh

**Sub : A bicycle lost or theft**

Sir,

This is to inform you that my bicycle was stolen at 10 a.m. on the 7th May at Lornui Supermarket. I set my cycle aside against a light post in front of the market. But after my shopping from a stationery shop I found my cycle missing. I searched every nook and corner but failed to trace it. It was a 'Hero' bicycle of green colour and it was almost in a new condition as I bought it only a month ago. Of course, I regret to say that I do not remember the long number engraved on the cycle.

Please look into the matter and do the needful.

........................ Yours faithfully,
........................ *Rajib Jha*
(Date and Address)

**Note** In Official letter, Yours faithfully must be written before Signature and nowa-days, no need of Comma (,) after it.

**[2] Write a letter to the Postmaster of your zone complaining of the faulty delivery of your letters.**

To
The Postmaster
Gaya Junction, Bihar

**Sub : Faulty delivery of letters etc.**

Sir,

I regret to bring to your notice that the irregularity in the delivery of letters etc. of our family has been causing a lot of trouble quite for some time. They are either not being delivered in time or not being delivered at all! The postman for delivering letters in our locality seems to be negligent in his duty. He visits the locality casually. Sometimes he hands over the important letters to the children playing about here and there. Sometimes the delivery of registered letters, parcels, money-orders and even telegrams are delayed!

Would you kindly look into the matter and warn him to set him right?

........................ Yours faithfully,
........................ ........................
(Date and Address) (Full Signature)

**[3] Write a letter to the Chairman of your municipality drawing his attention to the problems of your locality infested with flies and mosquitoes for the junk of garbage and for the cut-fruits (causing malaria, jaundice etc.).**

To
The Chairman
Municipal Corporation, Nabi Mumbai, India

**Sub : Problems of flies and mosquitoes for the junk of garbage**

Sir,

On behalf of the people of our locality I would like to draw your kind attention to a serious problem faced by the people of our area. For the last few months in the rainy season the whole area has been infested with flies and mosquitoes causing hardship to the people of the locality. What more, it poses a serious health hazard for the people in general and children in particular. In this connection, let me also point out that the wayside drains are not cleaned regularly. As a result, the drains get choked and waterlogged and become the breeding grounds of mosquitoes.

Similarly, piling of garbage near the market leads to the breeding of flies. The number of houseflies in and around the locality has gone up alarmingly. To make the situation worse, the vendors go on selling cut-fruits merrily. All these help in spreading jaundice, enteritis and malaria.

Would you take proper steps for regular clearance of garbage and cleaning of drains? Of course, people of the locality should also join the cleaning operation. I request you to come forward with a comprehensive programme.

Yours faithfully,

........................

........................ ........................

(Date and Address) (Full Signature)

**[4] Write a letter to the Director, Jal Board complaining about the scarcity of drinking water in your area.**

To
Director
Jal Board
Samastipur, Bihar, India

**Sub : Scarcity of drinking water**

Sir,

We, the villagers of Samastipur, beg most respectfully to state that we live in a flood-stricken area and we are facing great hardship for want of pure drinking water after the recent flood.

More than five thousand people live in our locality. All the tubewells are submerged in flood-water and, as a result, the drinking water has become unhygienic. But no step has yet been taken by the Panchayet for sinking new tubewells. Even halogen tablets have not yet been supplied by the workers of the Health Department for making the drinking water pure and free from pollution! As a result, an epidemic may break out at any time.

We hope that you would take necessary steps to solve this problem as early as possible.

Yours faithfully,
X
Y
Z

Samastipur, Bihar, India
10 August, 2010

**[5] Write an application to the H.M. of your school for leave of absence for your illness.**

To
The Headmaster/Headmistress
..................................School.

**Sub : Leave of absence for illness**

Sir/Madam,

With due respect I beg to state that I could not attend school from the 10th to the 15th instant as I was laid up with fever.

Kindly grant me leave of absence for those days only. (I shall be much obliged if you kindly grant me leave of absence for those days only.)

Yours obediently,

..............

(Full Signature)

Dated........... Class ..........., Roll No. ...........

**Note** In letters to the H. M. you should write 'Yours obediently', instead of 'Yours faithfully', etc., especially if you are a student.

**[6] Write an application to the H.M. of your school for leave of absence for the marriage ceremony of your sister.**

To
The Headmaster/Headmistress
.................................. School.

**Sub : Leave of absence for sister's marriage ceremony**

Sir/Madam,

Most respectfully I beg to state that as the wedding ceremony of my sister comes off tomorrow, I shall not be able to attend school for three days from today.

I shall be much obliged if you grant me leave of absence for these days only.

Yours obediently,

..............

(Full Signature)

Dated ......... Class ..........., Roll No. .........

**[7] Write an application to the authority of a school for sick leave.**

To
The Secretary
..................... School/Institution
P.O.................., Dist...............

> No Punctuation mark is now used after the Designation in the Heading.

**Sub : Sick leave for six days**

Sir,

With due respect I beg to state that I could not attend school from the 10th to the 15th instant, both days inclusive, on account of my illness. Now I am fit to join.

A medical certificate is attached herewith for your kind consideration.

May I request the favour of your granting me sick leave with full average pay for the period stated above?

Yours faithfully,

Date ...........

....................

(Full Signature)

Asst. Teacher

## APPLICATION FOR EMPLOYMENT

**[1] Write an application for the post of a clerk-cum-typist in LIC**

> **Situation Vacant**
>
> Wanted 15 clerk-cum-typists in LIC. Office, Howrah. Apply with full bio-data within 15 days to the Divisional Manager, L.I.C. of India, Howrah Division.
>
> **The Telegraph** (23.6.2010)

To
The Divisional Manager
LIC of India, Howrah Division

**Sub : Application for the post of a clerk-cum-typist**

Sir,

In response to the advertisement in 'The Telegraph' dated 23rd June for the post of clerk-cum-typists in your office, I beg to offer myself as a candidate for the same and furnish the following particulars for your kind perusal.

As regards my qualifications, I beg to state that I passed the H.S. Examination in 2nd Division in 2008. Then I joined a Commercial College to learn Computer and completed the one-year course. My age as per Madhyamik certificate is now 22. My full Bio-data and other relevant particulars in the prescribed form is enclosed herewith.

If you favour me with an opportunity, I shall spare no pains to serve you up to your satisfaction.

June 30, 2010 *Apurba Dey*

**[2] Write an application in response to the following advertisement with full bio-data.**

> Wanted an Asst. Teacher (M.A. in English) preferably B.Ed. in deputation vacancy for Model High School, Ahmedabad, Gujarat. Apply to the Secretary, stating qualifications, age and experience, if any, within 10 days.

To
The Secretary
Model High School
Ahmedabad, Gujarat

**Sub : An Asst. Teacher in deputation vacancy**

Sir,

In response to the advertisement in The Statesman dated 3rd July for the post of an Asst. Teacher in deputation vacancy in your school, I beg to offer my candidature for the same.

The following bio-data are furnished for your kind consideration :

| | |
|---|---|
| Name | : Ishan Mathur |
| Father's Name | : Late Jagdish Mathur |
| Date of birth | : 3rd June 1980. |
| Academic Qualifications | : B.A. Hons. (Eng.)—1st Class<br>B.Ed.—1st Class |
| Co-curricular activities | : Drama, debate & recitation |
| Experience | : 10 months in a deputation vacancy |

The marksheets and testimonials are enclosed herewith.

If you favour me with your selection for the post, I shall try my best to perform my duties to the utmost satisfaction of the authority.

Dated : April 7, 2005
15 Sardar Patel Road
Sabarmati, Ahmedabad

Yours faithfully,
*Ishan Mathur*

## LETTERS IN RESPONSE TO ADVERTISEMENTS

**[1]** You may want to learn something to keep yourself engaged while waiting for the results of the Madhyamik Examination. Go through the following advertisements. Then choose one that suits you and write an application in about 60 words. Ask in your letter for some more information that you may need.

(a) Learn computer in your spare time. Join 'Stepping Stone Commercial School' (Branches all over West Bengal). Open from 8 a.m.-8 p.m. Apply Box 4585, The Statesman.

(b) Learn to cook delicious dishes—Indian, Chinese, Continental. Classes will begin soon. Limited seats. Apply Box 3888, The Telegraph.

(c) Learn to make artistic life-like plants and trees. 3 p.m. to 6 p.m. Apply Box 245, The Statesman.

**Letters in response to the Advertisements :**

**[a]** To

The Principal/Advertiser
Stepping Stone Commercial School
Box 4585
The Statesman, Kolkata, India
Pin 700 001

**Sub : Basic Computer**

Sir,

With reference to your advertisement in The Statesman, I would like to inform you that I am interested in the computer course and so I like to engage myself as a student of your school in my spare time.

I shall be highly obliged if you let me know the duration of the course and the fees to be paid. I would like to know if the certificate issued by your institution is recognized by the State Government.

Please send me an enrolment form at an early date.

Yours faithfully,

Dated ............ ..............

(Date & Address of the student) (Signature of the student)

**[b]** To

The Advertiser
Box 3888
The Telegraph, Kolkata, India
Pin 700 001

**Sub : Course of cooking delicious dishes**

Dear Sir,

With reference to your advertisement in The Telegraph, I would like to inform you that I am interested in cooking in my spare time and so I would like to learn how to cook delicious dishes. My preference goes to Chinese type of cooking. I may mention here that I can cook some Indian dishes, of course.

I shall be highly obliged if you let me know the duration of the course, the days and time of the classes and the fees to be paid for the course.

Awaiting an early reply,

Yours faithfully,

Dated .............. .................

(Date and Address of the applicant) (Signature of the applicant)

**[c]** To
The Advertiser
Box 245
The Statesman, Kolkata, India
Pin 700 001

**Sub : Artistic life-like plants and trees**

Dear Sir,

In response to your advertisement in the Statesman, I would like to inform you that I am keenly interested in tree planting and gardening. I like to learn how to make artistic life-like plants and trees in a garden.

I shall be highly obliged if you let me know the duration of the course, the days and time of the classes and the fees to be paid for the course.

Awaiting an early reply,

Yours faithfully,

Dated .............. ..............................

(Date and Address of the applicant) (Signature of the applicant)

**[2] Read the following advertisement carefully :**

> **BANGA SANSKRITI SAMMELAN, Kolkata**
> will organise a Cultural Competition in the Maidan for the students of Class X. Apply through the head of your institution to The Secretary 4 Elgin Road, Kolkata 20—**The Telegraph** (15. 04. 2005)

**You want to take part in the competition. Write to the Secretary requesting him/her to inform you of the time, place, items, etc.**

To
The Secretary
Banga Sanskriti Sammelan
4 Elgin Road, Kolkata 20
Through
The Headmaster/Headmistress
.........................................
(The name of your school)

**Sub : Participation in the cultural competition**

Sir/Madam,

I came to know from the advertisement in The Telegraph dated 15 April, 2010 that a cultural competition will be organised by Banga Sanskriti Sammelan in the Maidan for the students up to Class X.

I want to take part in the competition. I am a student of Class X and have a special liking for recitation.

So I request you to inform me the time and exact location of the competition. Please also let me know the items of the cultural competition at an early date.

Awaiting your reply,

I remain,

Yours faithfully,

.........................................

.........................................

.........................................

(Date & Address of the applicant) (Full Signature of the applicant)

**[3] Here is an advertisement :**

| **HOUSES AND FLATS TO LET** |
|---|
| Area—Kalkaji, New Delhi |
| 2/3 Bed-Roomed Modern Flats |
| Box No. 5302, The Hindustan Times |

**Read the advertisement and write a suitable letter to the advertiser requesting him to supply the following information :**

(i) Total floor space, (ii) Monthly rent, (iii) Distance from the nearest Bus/Train stop, (iv) Convenient date and time for visiting the site.

To
The Advertiser
Box No. 5302
The Hindustan Times
New Delhi, India
Pin 110 001

**Sub : A flat in New Delhi**

Dear Sir,

I have gone through the advertisement in The Statesman dated..............

I am in need of a flat at Kalkaji in New Delhi. A 2-bed-roomed flat will suit me fine.

Please inform about the total floor-space and monthly rent. Please also let me know the distance from the nearest bus stop and the convenient date and time for visiting the site.

Awaiting an early reply,/Waiting for an early reply,/Looking forward to an early reply, /Looking forward to receiving an early reply,

I remain,

Yours faithfully,

..............................

..............................

(Date & Address) (Full Signature)

**Note** **Awaiting an early reply** and **Waiting for an early reply**—both are correct as **'await'** is a transitive verb and **'wait'** is an intransitive verb. Of course, **'wait'** may be used transitively in such usage—**"wait a minute"**.

—**vide 'Advanced Learner's Dictionary'—Hornby**

**Looking forward to receiving** an early reply (not **'to receive'** as an infinitive, but **'to receiving'** as a gerund) is, however, a correct but complicated form. ["We are looking forward to seeing you again." ***A.L.D.—Hornby***]

## LETTERS TO THE EDITOR OF A NEWSPAPER

**[1] Write a letter to the editor of a newspaper about communal harmony.**

To ['To' may be omitted.]
The Editor [Punctuation mark, Comma (,) after 'The Editor', etc. is now omitted.]
The Hindustan Times
New Delhi, India
Pin 110 001

**Sub : Communal harmony**

Sir,

[Through the columns of your esteemed daily I venture to voice my views about the present threat on Indian secularism.]

From long long ago to the present times, India offers unity in diversity. It is always a peaceful country to every religion. There is not a single country in the globe which can demand so versatility in religion like India. Yet there is always a peaceful co-existence among all of them.

But now this communal harmony is going through an ordeal. Several political parties use religion as their capital for vote. But it is not a just way to win the election. However, there is a silver lining that, along with this evil game, some other liberal parties are trying to maintain amity in the society. A point to be noticed here is that there is no quarrel between the people of two major religions. It is a noble sign indeed.

So we hope that India will be far more firmly united in the coming years as the common people are neglecting the bigoted propaganda of the political parties.

Let us learn from the history of various countries—United we Stand, Divided we Fall.

Dated : 3 May, 2005 Yours faithfully,
Gol Market *Asif Hussain*
New Delhi

**Note** 'Through the columns......etc. may be omitted in Direct approach.

**[2] Write a letter to the editor of a newspaper about the problem of drug addiction.**

To
The Editor
The Hindu
Chennai, India

**Sub : Problem of drug addiction**

Sir,

[Through the columns of your esteemed daily I venture to voice my views about the problem of drug addiction.]

Drug addiction has now become a major problem of our social life. Many young men and women are falling victims to this dreadful curse. Hashish, Heroin, Brown Sugar, L.S.D., and other narcotics are smuggled into the country by the dishonest traders. These traders operate underground and the young ones look onto these drugs for temporary pleasure. These drugs are nothing but death traps. Initially the drugs stimulate but slowly they lead to death. As a result the rosy possibilities of our youths are nipped in the bud.

It is high time to take effective steps to control drug addiction. I hope that the right-thinking people will come forward to raise public opinion against this deadly curse of our social life. We should take the pledge—'Let us unite for a drug-free world'. On behalf of the citizens, I fervently request you to publish an editorial comment on the subject to draw the attention of the public.

Sarbana Nagar
Chennai
April 14, 2010

Yours faithfully,
*K. Srinibasan*

**[3] Write a letter to the editor of a newspaper about the evils of dowry system.**

To
The Editor
Decan Herald
Kochi, India

**Sub : The evils of Dowry System**

Sir,

[Through the columns of your esteemed daily I venture to voice my views about the dowry system—one of the most vicious evils of our society.]

Dowry reduces the sacred sacrament of marriage to a business deal. It turns the brides into cattle. The parents of the brides are put to inhuman pressure for a handsome dowry. In many cases young brides are murdered or pushed to suicide by the husband and the in-laws so that the groom can marry again and endanger the life of another innocent girl! That is why the birth of a daughter is looked upon as an unwelcome evil by many poor parents.

It is high time for us to take necessary steps against this curse of our social life. The only way to root it out is to motivate public opinion against it and, at the same time, to enforce the strict laws to punish the offenders. I hope that the right-thinking people will come forward to raise their voice against this social crime.

25C Beach Road
Kochi
4 May, 2010

Yours faithfully,
*A. V. Narayanan*

**[4] Write a letter to the editor of a newspaper complaining against the misuse of microphones.**

To
The Editor
The Indian Express
Lucknow, India

**Sub : The misuse of microphones**

Sir,

[Please allow me to focus my concern through the columns of your esteemed daily on the inconveniences created by the thoughtless use of microphones.]

Nowadays indiscriminate use of microphones on all occasions has become a torture to public life. There may be merry-making within the limit, but when mikes blare out nothing but cheap film songs round the clock, it becomes a nuisance to all and sundry. It disturbs the students and patients in the neighbourhood and most people are compelled to pass sleepless nights.

I think the police should take necessary steps to stop this careless use of microphones. Moreover, a strong public opinion should be created through your editorial.

Aminabad
Lucknow
22 April, 2010

Yours faithfully,
*Sanjib Rastogi*

**[5] Write a letter to the editor of a newspaper complaining against the high price of essential commodities.**

To
The Editor
The Hindustan Times
New Delhi, India
Pin 110 001

**Sub : The high price of essential commodities**

Sir,
[Through the columns of your esteemed daily I venture to voice my views against the soaring price of essential commodities.]

The rcecent price-rise has become a headache to most of the people and it is now impossible for people to make both ends meet. It has hit hard the low and middle class people. The day-labourers and the fixed salaried people are the worst sufferers. Not to speak of meat or fish, even the prices of vegetables are increasing every day. The white coloured water in the name of milk sells at Rs. 15/- a litre! The prices of rice, clothes, kerosene, medicine and other essential commodities are also increasing by leaps and bounds!! All these have made the life of common people miserable.

Hence, I think that the Government—both State and Centre should take effective steps to control the price of essential commodities without any further delay.

Vasant Kunj
New Delhi
26 April, 2010

Yours faithfully,
***Garima Malik***

**[6] Write a letter to the editor of a newspaper about the necessity of planting more trees in the country/afforestation in the country/social forestry programmes in the country.**

To
The Editor
The Hindu
Bangalore, India

**Sub : The necessity of planting more trees**

Sir,
[Through the columns of your esteemed daily I venture to point out about the necessity of planting more trees in the country.]

We know there is an eternal bond between man and trees. Trees help us in many ways. They supply us fresh oxygen. Trees give us food, fruits, fuel, wood, timber, medicine and many other useful things. The trees check soil erosion. They are also the harbingers of rain to produce crops in a cyclic order—trees bring clouds, clouds bring rain and rain brings harvest. Moreover, they give us shelter and shade. They protect the wildlife. The absence of trees creates desert. Trees help us fight against environmental pollution. It is interesting to note that 33·3% (1/3rd) land is required as forests in any country to maintain the ecological balance. We cannot think of life without trees. So we must all grow more trees and stop deforestation.

I think that the Government should take drastic measures to check the cutting down of the forests and, at the same time, social forestry programmes should be given high consideration.

C. V. Ramannagar
Bangalore, India
25 May, 2010

Yours faitfhfully,
***Vinod Kumar***

**[7] Write a letter to the editor of a newspaper about the bad condition of the hospital in your locality.**

To
The Editor
The Pioneer
New Delhi, India

**Sub : Bad condition of local hospital**

Sir,

[Through the columns of your esteemed daily, I would like to express my views about the bad condition of the hospital in our locality.]

The standard of service of the hospital has gone down and most people think it to be the gateway to death! The outdoor patients have to wait for a long time. Very few doctors and trained nurses are available to attend the patients. Food served to the patients is of poor quality. Dogs share beds with patients in the hospital! Beds are always dirty. Patients don't have even the life-saving drugs! Yet the authorities are trying to impose fees even for the outdoor patients and higher charge for the paying beds and cabins. An unhygienic atmosphere prevails everywhere.

Under the circumstances, the Government should immediately take necessary steps to improve the over-all situation. Public opinion should also be raised through your editorial column.

Gaziabad
U.P., India
8 May, 2010

Yours faithfully,
***Megha Pathak***

**[8] Write a letter to the editor of a neswpaper against the antisocial activities in your locality.**

To
The Editor
The Decan Chronicle
Hyderabad, India

**Sub : Antisocial activities in our locality**

Sir,

[Through the columns of your esteemed daily, I would like to warn your readers about the problem of anti-social activities in our locality.]

For the last several years some antisocial elements are in operation in this area. They rob the passersby of their valuables at dagger-point. Sometimes they wander with revolvers and bombs and raid shops, houses and banks. Often they turn violent and destroy public and private properties for flimsy issues. Even the local police—the so-called protector of law and order—play an idle role, as if, there is a nexus between the police and the criminals.

In a word, unrest and violence are spreading in every walk of life and the people of the area are under constant panic.

I, therefore, request you to write an editorial note to create a strong public opinion against such anti-social activities in this locality.

Sultan Bazar Road
Hyderabad, India
10 May, 2010

Yours faithfully,
***Urmila Rao***

**[9] Write a letter to the editor of a newspaper about the bad condition of the roads and reckless driving in your area.**

To
The Editor
Bihar Times
Patna, India

**Sub : Bad condition of local roads and reckless driving**

Sir,

[Through the columns of your esteemed daily, I draw the readers' attention to the bad condition of roads and reckless driving in our area.]

The condition of the High Road near Bhagalpur is so deplorable with so many pits on it that it is always a danger to the traffic. But the buses, lorries, taxies and mini-buses are running at break-neck speed causing terror to the passersby. The drivers very often try to overtake other buses and lorries and collide with one another. Hardly a day passes without a serious accident. The death toll is increasing day-by-day.

I feel that the authorities should take necessary steps to repair the roads and stop reckless driving at the same time.

A public opinion should also be raised through your editorial column.

15 Nehru Nagar
Patliputra Colony, Bihar, India
March 10, 2010

Yours faithfully,
***Prakash Jha***

**[10] Write a letter to the editor of a newspaper about the problem of traffic jam in Bangalore.**

To
The Editor
The Dean Herald
Bangalore, India

**Sub : Problem of traffic jam in Bangalore**

Sir,

[Allow me to focus my concern through the columns of your esteemed daily on the unbearable problem of traffic jam in the streets of Bangalore.]

We have been hearing from time to time about several schemes to improve the transport system of the city. But so far there has been no considerable improvement. We must admit that traffic jam has become a daily occurence in Bangalore, mostly because of the enormous increase in the number of private cars, two-wheelers, buses, lorries, mini-buses etc. But we should pay attention to another important point of traffic jam. Almost every day long processions are brought out which dislocate the traffic system and put the people to much harassment by paralysing normal city life. Such long processions in the city, especially in office hours, should be totally banned.

If the authorities really want to have a better and safer transport and traffic system in Bangalore, they should extend the Metro Railways and withdraw the slow-moving vehicles from the busiest part of the city. Moreover, there should be strict enforcement of traffic rules with severe penal measures for the law-breakers in order to avoid daily traffic jam.

It is high time to create strong pubic opinion through your editorial column in this regard.

14 Queen's Road
Bangalore, India
May 6, 2010

Yours faithfully,
***Shila Rahaman***

**[11] Write a letter to the editor of a newspaper complaining agaisnt the late running of trains.**

To

The Editor

The Hindu

Chennai, India

**Sub : The late running of trains**

Sir,

Allow me please to focus my concern through the columns of your esteemed daily on the inconvenience caused to the people on account of late running of trains.

Late running of trains has become a regular feature nowadays. The daily commuters are the worst sufferers. Thousands of daily passengers are late for offices, schools and colleges. Many of them are compelled to cancel appointments and miss urgent pieces of business. Sometimes ailing patients cannot be hospitalised in time on account of late running of trains. The railways are virtually the arteries of suburban life and people have to depend on train services almost at every step. A train delayed or cancelled means a lot of hardship to them. For the long-distance-trains also, it is equally painful for the passengers. In spite of repeated assurance of the railway authorities, no improvement is in sight. On the contrary, the situation is drifting from bad to worse! I hope that the authorities will come forward to mitigate the sufferings of the people by ensuring that trains run in time.

Chennai, India
May 12, 2010

Yours faithfully,
***G. S. Priya***

**[12] Write a letter to the editor of a newspaper about the problem caused by the hawkers on the footpath.**

To
The Editor
The Times of India
New Delhi, India

**Sub : Problem caused by the hawkers on the footpath**

Sir,

[I venture to voice my views on the problem caused by the hawkers on the footpath, through the columns of your esteemed daily.]

The problem posed by the hawkers is growing graver day-by-day. The hawkers use the footpath as tax-free and rent-free open spaces for their stalls. These stalls obstruct free movement of the passersby because of the narrowing of space. The passersby are sometimes compelled to walk on the road instead of on the footpath and endanger their life! The roads too become crowded causing accidents and traffic jams.

It has become a nuisance to public life and this nuisance must be stopped at any cost. Of course, the Government should set up Hawkers' Corner so that the hawkers are not thrown out of employment.

Faridabad

Hariyana, India

March 14, 2010

Yours faithfully,
***Sakshi Singh***

**[13] Write a letter to the editor of a newspaper appealing to the public for the victims of a flood.**

To
The Editor
The Samaja
Bhubaneswar, Orissa, India

**Sub : Appeal for flood-relief**

Sir,

[Could you allow me a vital space in your esteemed paper to appeal to the public to help the victims of flood?]

The recent flood around Bhadrak in Orissa is one of the most devastating one ever witnessed by the people of the areas. Hundreds of people were carried away by the flood's fury. It is estimated that thousands of villagers were rendered homeless. Some of them are living in temporary shelters and many of them are suffering from lack of food and clothing. The State Government is doing what it can but that is not enough.

I, therefore, strongly appeal to the generous public to rise to the occasion and help in rehabiliation and relief work started by the State Government.

Yours faithfully,
***Sanket Mahapatra***

**Stamp & address of the receiver**

## CIRCULAR LETTER OR NOTICE AND DRAFT

**[1] Suppose you are the Secretary of the Students' Excursion Committee of your school. Write a notice for the participants of the next excursion to Digha.**

Mention the following points :

(i) Duration of the excursion.
(ii) Time, date and place of assembly.
(iii) Expected date and time of return.
(iv) Last date for the submission of applications by intending participants.
(v) Amount of money to be deposited.
(vi) Things to be taken in kit bags.
(vii) The guardian's consent letter to be submitted.

### NOTICE

**[ Educational Excursion ]**

It is hereby notified that an excursion to Digha has been arranged by the Students' Excursion Committee of our school. The excursion will be for four days. All the participants are to be assembled at 6 a.m. on the 15th May in our school campus. It is expected that we shall return from Digha at 8 p.m. on the 19th May.

Don't forget that the last date for the submission of application by the intending participants is the 10th May. All the applicants must deposit Rs. 100/- (Rupees One Hundred only) with their applications.

Please take two sets of clothings, a toothbrush, a torch and a towel in your kit bag. The guardian's consent letter is also to be submitted along with the application.

Countersigned ..............................

..................... (Full Signature)

(Counter Signature of the HM) Secretary

Date ...................... Students' Excursion Committee

**[2] Write a notice using the points given below for the school notice-board announcing that the school is organizing a Literacy Drive Programme during the summer vacation :**

(a) An appeal pointing out the importance of the programme.
(b) How and when to enlist.
(c) The time they would be required to spend each day.
(d) The area to be covered.
(e) Any other relevant point.

**NOTICE**

**[ Literacy Drive Programme ]**

It is known to all that illiteracy is a social curse. Our school is going to organise a Literacy Drive Programme during the summer vacation. The students of Class IX are hereby requested to act as student volunteers in the programme. They should meet the undersigned and enlist their names from 1 p.m. to 4 p.m. on or before next Saturday. They are required to spend two hours in the afternoon each day for the programme during the vacation. The village adjacent to our school is to be covered by the programme. But we should keep in mind that it should be a continuous process even after vacation though we may not afford such hours at that time.

Date ...................... ...........................
(Counter Signature of the HM) (Full Signature)
(Name of the school) Organiser, Literacy Drive Progamme

**[3] Your school is going to publish its Annual Bilingual Magazine. Suppose you are the Student Editor of the Magazine Sub-committee. Write a notice inviting contribution from the students. Your notice should contain the following :**

(i) last date of submission, (ii) Types of articles and word limit, (iii) size of manuscript paper and quality of handwriting.

Get your notice countersigned by the Head of your school.

**NOTICE**

**[ School Magazine ]**

It is hereby notified that the Annual Bilingual Magazine of the school will be published this year too just after the summer vacation. The students are, therefore, requested to submit their articles to the undersigned by the 20th May at the latest.

Articles should be written either in Bengali or in English. Essays, stories etc. should not exceed 300 words and poems should not exceed the limit of 100 words.

All should be written on one side of foolscap papers in legible handwriting.

Looking forward to your active co-operation,

Date ................. (Full Signature)
(Counter Signature of the HM) Student Editor
(Name of the school) Magazine Sub-committee

**[4] Suppose you are the Secretary of the Students' Welfare Committee. Write a notice with the following points :**

(i) free distribution of textbooks to deserving students
(ii) time, date and place
(iii) prior intimation to the committee office necessary.

## NOTICE

**[ Free Distribution of Textbooks ]**

It is hereby notified that a lot of textbooks will be distributed to the deserving poor and meritorious students free of cost at 2 p.m. on the 7th May in the school campus. All concerned should be aware that prior intimation with the names of textbooks is necessary. It should be submitted to the undersigned in the committee office by the 5th instant. The decision of the Students' Welfare Committee is final in this regard.

.................................... ....................................

(Counter Signature of the HM) (Full Signature)

.................................... Secretary

(Date & Name of the school) Students' Welfare Committee

**[5] Suppose you are the Secretary of a club. You want the members of your club to take cholera inoculation. Write a notice for the notice-board of the club giving time and date when interested members may take inoculation.**

## NOTICE

**[ Cholera Inoculation ]**

You are aware that cholera has broken out in our locality. Arrangements have been made for the members of the club and the villagers at large for getting inoculated. Those who are interested may take inoculation on 20.6.08 at 3 p.m. in the club premises.

.................................... ....................................

(Date and Address of the club) (Signature of the Secretary)

**[6] Nobody likes dirt but we find it everywhere. What do we do about it? Usually, nothing! Don't you think it will be nice to live in clean and beautiful surroundings? Write out a Draft about it.**

## DRAFT : CLEAN SURROUNDINGS

Nobody likes dirt but we find it everywhere. We think that it will be nice to live in clean and beautiful surroundings. We usually keep our homes clean. But we do not take care of keeping our public places clean! The parks are sometimes made dirty by indiscriminate throwing of garbage. The streets, railway stations, buses and market places are full of torn papers, cigarette ends, banana skins etc.! We spit here and there in public places!! This shows we are more careful about our own things than public property.

But dirty surroundings breed germs and insects. It affects our health and hygiene. Sometimes it causes accidents and annoys people. On the other hand, clean surroundings look nice and we feel happy. Therefore it is important that we keep our surroundings clean.

**[7] Read the following hints about SMOKING and write out a Draft about it :**

(a) Physical problems :

(i) breathing troubles

(ii) proneness to be attacked with cough, T.B., Cancer.

(b) Wastage of money

(c) Public annoyance :

(i) Bus/Tram/Railway compartments

(ii) Offices (iii) Cinema (iv) Market.

Give up the habit yourself and help others :

(i) Bus/Tram/Railway compartments

(i) Advise individually (ii) Seminars (iii) Group discussions.

## DRAFT : GIVE UP SMOKING

Smoking is a deplorable habit. It causes a number of problems. The physical problems are breathing troubles and proneness to be attacked with cough, Tuberculosis (T.B.) and Cancer. It is nothing but wastage of money too. Moreover, it creates public annoyance in bus, tram, railway compartments, office, cinema and market-places.

To give up the habit means better health by means of free breathing. It promotes longer life too. Besides, it causes more saving of money for better living and decent future. And in view of the recent (October 2008) Central Government warning on smoking in all public places—you may save a fine of Rs. 500/- too!!

So, give up the habit yourself and help others to follow. For this purpose, you should advise individually and also seminars and group discussions may be arranged.

**[8] Write out a Draft for 'Nirmal Gram Puraskar' launched by the Mininstry of Rural Development of India for rural sanitation.**

## DRAFT : RURAL SANITATION

Providing sanitation facilities in rural areas is one of the most important developmental challanges for our country. We cannot hope to build a nation unless such basic amenities are provided to our population. The Ministry of Rural Development Programme has launched a Total Sanitation Campaign (TSC) and is presenting the 'Nirmal Gram Puraskar' on February 24, 2005, for promoting sanitation and hygiene in rural areas. It is certainly a milestone in the whole rural sanitation drive.

## TELEGRAMS

### How to write a telegram?

A telegram is a very short messege. So full grammatical sentences may not be required. **The address and the message should be written in Block Capital Letters.**

**[1] ON ILLNESS :** Suppose, you are Arghya. Your mother is ill. You want to send a telegram to your brother in Delhi to come home at once :

| TO<br>APURBA SARKAR<br>356 NAI SARAK<br>DELHI 110 006 | |
|---|---|
| MOTHER ILL(.) COME SHARP<br>Date.................. | (From) ARGHYA |
| [ Not to be Telegraphed ] | [Sender's Signature and Address] |

**[2] ASKING FOR MONEY :** Suppose, you are Juthi. You are in urgent need of money for paying examination fees. Send a telegram to your father for that :

| TO<br>BILASPATI RAO<br>10 JUNGPURA, NEW DELHI | |
|---|---|
| SEND RS. ONE HUNDRED FOR EXAM FEES<br>Date.................. | (From) JUHI |
| [ Not to be Telegraphed ] | [Sender's Signature and Address] |

**[3] AN INVITATION :** Suppose, you are Ayan. Send a telegram to your friend inviting him to attend your sister's marriage ceremony :

| |
|---|
| TO<br>TANBIR AHMED<br>BARAMULLA<br>KASHMIR |
| SISTER'S MARRIAGE(.) SIXTEENTH JUNE(.) COME POSITIVELY<br>Date.................. (From) AYAN |
| [ Not to be Telegraphed ] [Sender's Signature and Address] |

**[4] EXCURSION :** Sudip Roy requests his friend Arush Saksena, 25 Mukherjee Nagar, New Delhi, to join thin club excursion to South India on the 24th instant. He wants to send a telegram. Write the telegram or an SMS.

| |
|---|
| TO<br>ARUSH SAKSENA<br>25 MUKHERJEE NAGAR<br>NEW DELHI |
| CLUB EXCURSION(.) SOUTH INDIA(.) TWENTY FOURTH(.) JOIN<br>Date.................. (From) SUDIP |
| [ Not to be Telegraphed ] Sudip Roy<br>13 Chittaranjan Park<br>New Delhi 110 019 |

**[5] EXPRESSING INABILITY :** Biman Bose has decided to send a reply telegram to his friend expressing his inability to join the excursion. Imagine that you are Biman Bose and write a telegram. State in the telegram that you will send him a letter too :

| |
|---|
| TO<br>SUDIP ROY<br>13 CHITTARANJAN PARK<br>NEW DELHI 110 019 |
| SORRY(.) UNABLE TO JOIN EXCURSION(.) LETTER FOLLOWS.<br>Date ..................... (From) ARUSH |
| [ Not to be Telegraphed ] Arush Saksena<br>25 Mukherjee Nagar<br>New Delhi |

Now write out the letter that should follow your telegram. Your letter should contain the following points :

(i) Apology (ii) Reasons (iii) Good wishes for the trip.

## REPLY LETTER

25 Mukherjee Nagar
New Delhi
May 5, 2010

My dear Sudip,

You must have received my telegram. However, I tender my apology for my inability to join the proposed excursion to South India on the 24th instant. Believe me, I have no way out. Father is away from home and my mother is in sick-bed. There is none else to look after her.

So, please do not misunderstand me.

Hope that your trip to South India will be very happy and thrilling.

Yours ever
Arush Saksena

Stamp

Sudip Roy
13 Chittaranjan Park
New Delhi 110 019

**Some Important Guidelines for the beginning and ending of a Private Letter :**

**Beginning :**

(a) Your letter is just to hand.
(b) Many thanks for you sweet letter.
(c) I have not heard from your for a long time.
(d) I have not received any letter from you for about a month.
(e) I received your letter only the other day.
(f) Why have you not written to me for about a fortnight?
(g) Thank you very much for your kind and sympathetic letter.
(h) I am delighted to hear of your success. (Congratulation)
(i) I was deeply grieved to learn ......... (Condolence)
(j) I am glad to receive your invitation ...... (Invitation)

**Ending :**

(a) Thanking you
(b) Wishing you all success
(c) Hoping you are quite well/doing fine
(d) Awaiting an early reply/Waiting for an early reply/Looking forward to an early reply/Looking forward to receiving an early reply
(e) With sincere regards to you
(f) With love and best wishes
(g) Yours truly/Yours sincerely/Your loving friend/son, daughter

**Some common Errors in Letter-writing :**

| Incorrect | Correct |
|---|---|
| [1] Your letter is to my hand.<br>[2] I have received your letter yesterday. | [1] Your letter is to hand.<br>[2] I received your letter yesterday. |

| Incorrect | Correct |
|---|---|
| [3] Please write to me how you are? | [3] Please write to me how you are. |
| [4] Your sincerely. | [4] Yours sincerely [In private letters] |
| [5] Your's faithfully. | [5] Yours faithfully[In official letters] |
| [6] Your ever. | [6] Yours ever |
| [7] Yours loving friend. | [7] Your loving friend |
| [8] Mr./Shri/Prof./Capt./Col. (name) and Esq. | [8] Use either of the two and name. |
| [9] Dr. (name) and Ph.D./ D.Sc./D.Lit./M.D. | [9] Use either of the two and name. |
| [10] M. N. Dutta and Co. | [10] Messers M. N. Dutta and Co. |
| [11] Messers Calcutta Publishers. | [11] Calcutta Publishers. [Messers is not used in case of the impersonal name of the company] |
| [12] I shall be glad if you grant me medical leave and oblige. | [12] Please grant me medical leave and oblige. [or] Please be kind enough to grant me medical leave and oblige. |

**Note** Do not use "and oblige" at the end of the letter unless 'and' connects 'oblige' with a verb in the Imperative or Infinitive mood.

## DO IT YOURSELF

- **PRIVATE LETTERS (with hints) :**

**[1] Write a letter to your friend inviting him to visit Darjeeling in the Summer/ Puja Vacation.**

[**Hints :** affectionate letter; is just to hand; commence; amidst the beauty of nature; spend time well]

**[2] Write a reply-letter accepting invitation.**

[**Hints :** My parents have permitted me/have given me permission; inform you the exact date; the climate of your area]

**[3] Write a reply-letter declining invitation.**

[**Hints :** kind invitation; I am sorry to tell you; look after; next opportunity; loving company]

**[4] Write a letter to your friend expressing your views about the recent nuclear explosions in India and Pakistan.**

[**Hints :** recent nuclear explosion; reaction at different levels; neighbouring countries; allround development; hinder; danger-signal; making deadlier weapons; eradicating disease and poverty; below the poverty-line; have two square meals a day; for wrong treatment or without treatment; It is needless to say; human welfare; direct energies; warmonger; suicidal policy]

**[5] Write a letter to your friend stating your role in the Literacy Drive Programme taken up in your school.**

[**Hints :** Literacy Drive Programme; school performance; neighbouring area; illiterate people; three R's; novice hands]

- **OFFICIAL LETTERS (with hints) :**

**[6] Write a letter to the H.M. of your school praying for early leave.**

[**Hints :** Most respectfully; I beg to let you know/inform you; feel out of sorts; have a severe headache; cannot attend to my lessons in the classroom; under such circumstances; You would be kind enough to grant me early leave and oblige.]

**[7] Write an application for a job with full bio-data.**

[**Hints :** In response to the advertisement; I beg to offer myself as a candidate for the same. The following bio-data are furnished for your kind perusal; The attested copies of marksheets and testimonials are enclosed herewith.]

- **LETTERS TO THE EDITOR (with hints) :**

**[8] Write a letter to the editor of a newspaper expressing your views about the child-labour in our country.**

[**Hints :** editorial note; round the clock; nutritious food; free time (leisure); deprived; wages; profession; minor age; economic reform; poverty line; spread of literacy; high time; exploitation]

## NOTICE

**[9] Suppose you are the Secretary of your local club. Write a notice for the members of the club for keeping the surroundings clean.**

[**Hints :** importance of clean surroundings; public places; responsibility; seminar; All the members are requested to attend the meeting.]

**[10] Write a notice inviting contributions for the school magazine on behalf of the student-editor.**

[**Hints :** It is hereby notified; bring out; interested; creative writing; student-editor; submit; on reverse side; neat and clean. foolscap paper; active cooperation]

## EXERCISE

- **PRIVATE LETTERS**

1. Write a letter to your friend congratualating him on his success in the Madhyamik Pariksha.
2. Write a letter to your friend consoling him for his failure in the Final Examination.
3. Write a letter of consolation to a friend who has recently lost his mother.
4. Write a letter to your friend inviting him to join your birthday celebration.
5. Write a letter to your friend to join your sister's marriage celebration.
6. Write a letter to your friend accepting/apologising the invitation.
7. Write a letter to a friend for arranging an excursion together.
8. Write a letter to your cousin requesting the loan of a camera during your holidays.
9. Write a letter to your friend asking him to spend a few days during the Puja vacation.
10. A boy is in a boarding school. He wants to write a letter to his mother telling her that he dislikes the life of a boarder. Write out the letter.

11. Write a letter to your friend about a street accident.
12. Write a letter to your brother advising him to take regular physical exercise.
13. Write a letter to your sister to read a leading newspaper regularly.
14. Write a letter to your sister who is in hospital wishing her speedy recovery.
15. Write a letter to your younger brother not to neglect studies by watching TV—the 'Idiot Box'.

## • LETTERS TO PEN-FRIENDS

1. Imagine that a pen-friend of yours has sent you a Diwali card. Thank him/her for it and also tell him how you had spent the time. Also enquire about his/her family.
2. Write a letter to your pen-friend in England thanking him/her for a present sent to you on your birthday.
3. Write a letter to your pen-friend in America telling her the purpose of setting up of Model Schools (Nabodaya Vidyalayas) in India.
4. Write a letter to a South Indian friend about the Literacy Campaign in your district. Mention the merits, hindrances and achievements of the scheme.

## • SOCIAL LETTERS—FORMAL AND INFORMAL

1. Write a formal letter of invitation for Shri and Smt. Dasgupta wishing the company of Shri and Smt. P. L. Banerjee at daughter's marriage ceremony.
2. Write a formal letter of acceptance/refusal.
3. Write an informal letter of invitation on the occasion of a dinner party.
4. Write an informal letter of acceptance/refusal.

## • BUSINESS LETTERS

1. Write a letter to a shop-keeper ordering goods as per your requirement.
2. You are interested in buying a L. P. Gas oven.

   Write a letter to the local gas company enquiring about :

   (a) special features of the oven, (b) price of the oven, (c) mode of payment, (d) delivery arrangement, (e) after-sales service.
3. Write a letter to a landlord asking certain repairs to be done to your rented house.
4. Write on behalf of your father to the Manager of a housing complex about a suitable flat stating clearly your requirements.
5. Here is an advertisement published in 'The Times'. Go through it carefully and write a letter to the publisher requesting him to send you a copy of the book by V.P.P.

**PENGUIN BOOKS, India**

**Announcing**

The advent of the first great detective Feluda full of crime and suspense.

**Satyajit Ray**

**THE ADVENTURES OF FELUDA**

**272 PAGES Rs. 60.00**

6. Suppose you have bought a T.V. set which is found faulty. Write a letter to the Manager of the company asking for service.
7. Write a letter to the Manager of a hotel for booking rooms during your tour.

## • OFFICIAL AND DEMI-OFFICIAL LETTERS

1. Write a letter to the B.D.O. requesting him to arrange to sink some tubewells for pure drinking water in your locality.
2. Write an application for the post of a depot-assistant for a milk depot in your area in Kolkata.
3. Write an application for the post of a Junior Clerk in a company.
4. Write an application to the Secretary of a High School for the post of a clerk/ an Asst. Teacher.
5. Write to the Chairman of the Municipality complaining about selling of cut-fruits on the footpaths causing enteric diseases and malaria.
6. Write to the civic authority on the necessity of a public park in a crowded city.
7. Suppose you have read the following advertisement and you want to respond.

> **FOR IIT AND JOINT ENTRANCE XAVERIAN STUDY CENTRE**
>
> [ CORRESPONDENCE DIVISION ]
>
> Applications are invited for admission. Those who applied earlier need not apply again. For form and prospectus send a self-addressed envelope along with M.O. of Rs. 50/- in favour of Principal, Xaverian Study Centre (Correspondence Division) 3/C Sarat Chatterjee Avenue, Kolkata 700 020

Now write out the letter in response to the advertisement.

## • LETTERS TO THE EDITOR OF A NEWSPAPER

1. Write a letter to the editor of a newspaper complaining against bad condition of roads in your locality/reckless driving.
2. Write a letter to the editor of a newspaper about the problem caused by the hawkers on the footpath.
3. Write a letter to the editor of a newspaper about the problem of traffic jam in Kolkata.
4. Write a letter to the editor of a newspaper complaining against late running of trains.
5. Write a letter to the editor of a newspaper complaining against scarcity of milk supply/inadequate supply of municipal water in your area.
6. Write a letter to the editor of a newspaper about the necessity of a drug-free world.
7. Write a letter to the editor of a newspaper about the necessity of literacy campaign in our country.
8. Write a letter to the editor of a newspaper appealing for funds to relieve the sufferers in a flood-stricken area.
9. Write a letter to the editor of a newspaper complaining against the high price of essential commodities.
10. Write a letter to the editor of a newspaper about the necessity of afforestation in the country.
11. Write a letter to the editor of a newspaper about growing anti-social activities.

## • CIRCULAR LETTER OR NOTICE

1. Your school is going to arrange its wall magazine. Suppose you are the student-editor of that magazine. Write a Notice inviting creative writing from students.
2. Suppose you are the Secretary of the Students' Welfare Committee. Write a Notice with the following points :

   (i) Inoculation programme in the school. (ii) Time, date and place for each class. (iii) Prior intimation to the committee office if already inoculated.

3. Imagine that your school team has become District Champion by winning the football match organised by the D.S.S.A., Bankura. As the captain of your school team write a Notice requesting the students to join the victory procession which will be taken out today. Mention the time and place of assembly.
4. Suppose the people of your area are suffering from enteric diseases. Write a Notice for caution against bad uses of ponds in your locality. Also tell them : (a) enteric diseases spreading easily, (b) causing death, (c) seeking doctor's advice, (d) taking preventive measures, (e) advising others.
5. Write a Notice prohibiting plastic bags and plastic cups in your school campus.
6. Suppose you are the Secretary of the students' union. Write a Notice for raising fund from your school to help the victims of Tsunami 2004.

## • TELEGRAMS

1. Suppose, your father is ill. You want to send a telegram to your uncle in Mumbai to come home at once.
2. You are in urgent need of money for buying textbooks. Send a telegram to your father for such.
3. Write out a telegram that Abhijit should send to Anirvan instead of writing the following letter :

> FE-520, Salt Lake City, Sector-3
> Kolkata-700 106
> May 13, 2014
>
> Dear Anirvan,
> Here is a happy news. Maya's marriage is fixed on the 7th instant. We are awaiting you eagerly.
> With love and best wishes,
>
> Truly yours,
> ***Abhijit***

4. Suppose your friend is waiting to hear whether/when you are coming to spend a holiday with him/her. But you have broken your leg. Send a telegram.
5. Write out a telegram to a close friend acknowledging the receipt of a gift which arrived yesterday.
6. Write out a telegram to your friend/brother/cousin congratulating him/her for doing very well in the Madhyamik Pariksha.
7. Here are a few telegrams. First write out the complete forms of the sentences and then write out the content in the form of a letter :
   (i) BROTHER ILL. WANTS TO SEE YOU. SUPARNA
   (ii) MONEY STOLEN. SEND HUNDRED RUPEES. YOUTH HOSTEL. BIMAN.
   (iii) STOOD FIFTH IN MADHYAMIK. INFORM FATHER. RUMA.
8. Send a telegram informing your mother that you safely arrived Bangalore and you are busy with examination and not to worry.
9. Send a telegram to the Manager of a hotel informing the change of date for booking a room.
10. Suppose, one of your relatives is a government officer in Car Nicobar. Write a telegram enquiring how he is after Tsunami 2004.

# 2 NARRATING EVENTS/ REPORTS

## HOW TO NARRATE OR REPORT EVENTS?

(a) The Report should always be provided with a **Heading** or **Caption**. It should be brief but clear. It should sum up the total information.

(b) The Report should be **logical**. It should be written in simple, lucid and graceful language so that common readers can follow it.

(c) **It should be written in Indirect Speech**.

(d) **The name of the place** and the **date** on which the Report is sent should be given at the top of the Report. It may be on the same day or on the following day.

(e) If it is a **Newspaper Report**, it should be written **'By a Staff Reporter'** or **'From our Special Correspondent'**, etc.

## SPECIMENS OF REPORTING EVENTS

### [1] ARMED ROBBERY IN TRAIN

Use the following information to write a short Report about an armed robbery in a train :

| | |
|---|---|
| Date | : 24.11.2010 |
| Place | : Between Kharagpur and Jakpur |
| Time | : 10 pm |
| Vehicle | : Local train, South-Eastern Railway |
| Results | : Purse containing Rs. 50,000/- from a businessman and wristwatches and ornaments from other passengers were snatched |

Kharagpur, November 25

An armed robbery, according to a local source, took place between Kharagpur and Jakpur stations of the South-Eastern Railway yesterday. As soon as the train left Kharagpur and gained speed, a band of robbers consisting of five armed men brought out their revolvers and daggers. They threatened the passengers in a second class compartment of the running train at about 10 p.m. They ordered the passengers at the point of dagger and revolver not to raise an alarm or pull the alarm chain but quickly surrender their valuables and cash. The passengers were simply bewildered.

The raiders snatched a purse containing Rs. 50,000 from a businessman. They also took the wrist-watches from other passengers and ornaments from women amounting to Rupees fifty thousand or more. All the passengers were under panic and the whole incident took place within a few minutes. The raiders jumped from the train as soon as it slowed down its speed approaching Jakpur station and escaped within a twinkle of an eye. The passengers pulled the alarm chain. The train stopped at Jakpur station. But the raiders could not be traced. [ **By a Staff Reporter** ]

## [2] METRO LINKS DELHI WITH GURGAON

Use the following information and write a Report about 'Metro links Delhi with Gurgaon' [You may use additional information, if necessary] :

| | |
|---|---|
| Date | : 3 September, 2010 |
| Place | : New Delhi |
| Occasion | : The Central Secretariate-Qutub Minar corridor of the Delhi Metro opened |
| Some details | : 12·53 km stretch of the Metro, a part of the Jehangirpuri-HUDA City Centre (Gurgaon) line commuting between Delhi and Gurgaaon become quicker, comfortable and economical—the longest line of the metro railway and passes through some of the most congested parts of the city—expected 2 lakh passsengers to travel by 2011—34 stations from Jehangirpuri in North Delhi to HUDA City Centre in Gurgaon—the authorities plan to run 36 to 40 trains on this corridor |

New Delhi, September 4

The long-awaited Central Secretariate-Qutub Minar Corridor of the Delhi Metro railway connecting the heart of the capital with the bustling suburb of Gurgaon was inaugarated and opened to the public on Friday.

With the opening of this 12·53 km stretch, which is a part of the Jehangirpuri-HUDA City Centre (Gurgaon) line, commuting between Delhi and Gurgaon has became quicker, comfortable and economical. The corridor, passing through some of the most densely populated parts of South Delhi, is expected to offer a convenient travel option and help reduce congestion on the roads.

Though the footfalls on the first day were relatively low, the Metro authorities expect the ridership to go up substantially in the coming days.

One of the officials of the Metro authority said, "This is the longest line of the Metro railway and passes through some of the most congested parts of the city. With the trains going all the way to Gurgaon, it is expected, 2 lakh passengers may travel on this line by 2011."

However, for most of the commuters, it was sheer curiosity and the excitement of travelling on a new line that drew them to the Metro stations. There are 34 stations from Jehangirpuri in North Delhi to HUDA City Centre in Gurgaon. The authorities plan to run 36 to 40 trains on this corridor. Union Urban Development Minister S. Jaipal Reddy, who inaugurated the Central Secretariat-Qutub Minar line, admitted that some of the stations on the upcoming lines were not yet ready. And he hoped the works will be completed well ahead of the Commonwealth Games in October.

[Based on the reports of the Hindu]

### [3] 25 INJURED IN KASHMIR CLASHES

Use the following information and write a report about '25 injured in Kashmir clashes' [You may use additional information, if necessary.] :

| | |
|---|---|
| **Date** | : 3 September, 2010 |
| **Place** | : Srinagar |
| **Incidents** | : After four days, curfew was lifted in Anantnag—elsewhere, life returned to normalcy after the hard-line Hurriyat Conference suspended the portest for the day, the last Friday of Ramzan. 25 people injured in clashes between protesters and security forces in the Kashmir Valley—the troops opened fire to disperse stone-throwers on Friday—5 persons injured in police firing at Baramulla, 55 km from Srinagar |
| **Cause** | : removing two 'objectionable' flags from atop a communication tower by the Army personnel—attacked by stone-throwers |
| **Result** | : two of the seriously injured referred to Srinagar—a woman injured by stone-throwing during the clash |

**Srinagar, September 4**

After four days, curfew was lifted in Anantnag. Elsewhere, life returned to normalcy after the hard-line Hurriyat Conference suspended the protest for the day, the last Friday of Ramzan.

25 people were injured in clashes between protesters and security forces in the Kashmir Valley, where the troops opened fire to disperse stone-throwers on Friday. Among them 5 persons were injured in police firing at Baramulla, 55 km from Srinagar.

The incident took place when a group of Army personnel, removing two 'objectionable' flags from atop a communication tower, were attacked by stone-throwers. Initially, the troops fired warning shots, but as the mob refused to disperse, they opened fire in self-defence.

Two of the seriously injured were referred to Srinagar hospital. A woman was also injured when she was hit by a stone during the clash.

### [4] CELEBRATION OF 'ID' IN HYDERABAD

Use the following information to make a short Report on the celebration of Id in Hyderabad :

**Date** : 11 September, 2010
**Place of assemblage** : Charminar Square
**Leader of the prayer** : The Imam of Jama Masjid
**Objectives** : Peace and amity among people of all communities
**Message from the Governor and the Chief Minister** : special appeal to people for rooting out malice and strengthening brotherhood among all the communities

**Hyderabad, September 12, 2010**

'Id' was celebrated in Hyderabad yesterday with due solemnity and grandeur. A big assemblage was organised at Charminar Square in the morning. Thousands of devout Muslims attended it. The Imam of Jama Masjid led the prayer. In his prayer he wished that people of all communities may live in peace and amity. The Governor and the Chief Minister of Andhra Pradesh greeted the Muslims and sent their goodwill messages. They made special appeal to the people for rooting out malice and strengthening brotherhood among all the communities of Andhra Pradesh and India.

### [5] KALI PUJA IN KOLKATA

Write a short report about Kali Puja in Kolkata with the help of the following information :

> **Date** : Wednesday, 5 October 2010
> **Puja Pandals** : Decorated Puja Pandals with dazzling illuminations
> **Number of Pandals** : 2,372 community Puja Pandals
> **Special attractions** : Kalighat, Dakshineswar, Belur Math and Thanthania Kalibari—Novel plans of pandals—Bhawanipur resembled Dakshineswar, Church-like pandal on Keshab Sen Street and Pagoda-like pandal at Paikpara—34 feet (10 meter/metre) image at a pandal at Pathuriaghata
> **Police Control** : Large number of police engaged for crowd-control

Kolkata, October 6, 2010

With crackers bursting amid dazzling illuminations, Kali Puja was celebrated in Kolkata on Wednesday. Decorative lamps glittered inside the community-Puja Pandals and candles were lit in almost every house, adding to the grandeur. Though the puja was offered around midnight, the festive mood was visible from the evening. In some places, animals were sacrificed in accordance with traditional rituals. According to the police 2,372 community pujas were held this year in the city. Streams of people visited the attractive pandals in the evening. There was a staggering crowd at Kalighat, Dakshineswar, Belur Math and Thanthania Kalibari. Some of the community pujas in the city had novel pandal and image designs. A pandal in the Bhowanipur area resembled the Dakshineswar temple. A pandal on Keshab Sen Street was designed after a church and a pagoda-like pandal was set up at Paikpara. A 34-feet (10 meter/metre) image was worshipped at a pandal at Pathuriaghata. A large number of police were engaged in crowd-control at the gorgeous pandals.

**Note** British spelling : metre; American spelling : meter

### [6] CLOUD BURSTS RAVAGE LEH—133 DEAD

Use the following information to write a short Report about Leh ravaged by cloudbursts [You may use additional information, if necessary] :

| | |
|---|---|
| Date | : 6 August, 2010 |
| Place | : Ladakh's Leh area situated at a height of 11,500 feet |
| Time | : Thursday night and Friday morning |
| Causes | : two cloudbursts and heavy downpour |
| Casualty | : 113 dead, 400 injured, 500 missing |
| Other loss | : the BSNL building, the ITBP camp, the AIR building, a government hospital, a school, hotels, etc. |
| Rescue operations | : under the state police, paramilitary personnel and the Army |
| Help to the victims | : a disaster management cell including medical officers, tents, etc. |

Leh, August 7

In one of the worst rain-related calamities to strike the Himalayan region, two cloudbursts hit Ladakh's Leh area late on Thursday night and Friday morning. It washed away large parts of the historic town and wreaked havoc in the surrounding villages. Authorities confirmed 113 deaths aand said 400 others were injured and around 500 missing. With rescue teams yet to reach the site, the toll is bound to increase.

The ecologically fragile region witnessed an enormous mud creep, with loose soil, softened further on account of torrential rains. It broke off a huge chunk of land, virtually carrying off an entire village before it rammed Leh, situated at a height of 11,500 ft. Houses were washed away and important buildings of the tourist town were demolished by the fury of the moving mass of slush.

The BSNL building, the ITBP camp, the AIR building, a government hospital, a school and hotels, besides a Tibetan market with around 200 shops have suffered massive damage. Two buildings of the housing offices of the Union Home Ministry were also affected. The centre is rushing a 140-member team of National Disaster Relief Force along with doctors and paramedical staff in an aircraft to Leh for relief and rescue operations. Meanwhile rescue operations are under the management of the state police, paramilitary personnel and the Army. One of the officials said many civilians including foreign tourists, were stranded at various places and efforts were on to rescue them. He said the affected areas stretched from Prang village on Rohtang-Leh highway upto Leh-Srinagar highway, a distance of more than 150 km.

Tents capable of use at high altitudes are also being dispatched. ITBP troops have converted their 121-bed barracks into a temporary camp and are using its auditorium as a disaster ward for blood victims.

### [7] FLOOD IN NORTH BENGAL AND ASSAM

Study the following chart and write a Report on Flood in North Bengal and Assam :

**Date** : July 26, 2010

**Place** : Century's worst flood in North Bengal and Assam. Situation marginally improved with the water level of all rivers receding

**Amount of loss** : Crops washed away; mud-built huts collapsed; residents of pucca houses lost all their belongings; Eight lakh people affected; Death toll touches 188.

**Rescue Operation** : Three helicopters and thirty five speed boats. About 3,75,000 people rescued by the army and civil authorities. Army in action in four districts of Assam

**Relief Work** : Woefully inadequate, State Govt. relief 100 grams of chira, half liter (litre) of kerosene and a sprinkling of mustard oil per family

**Communication** : Communication links between Jalpaiguri and Alipurduar and between Cooch Behar and Alipurduar restored

**Chief Minister's Visit** : Aerial survey and promises of all sorts of help

**Alipurduar, July 27**

The century's worst flood has hit Alipurduar, Jalpaiguri and Cooch Behar in West Bengal and Hailakandi, Karimganj, Kokrajhar and Dhubri in Lower Assam. The situation has marginally improved with the water level of all rivers receding. Crops of the vast areas have been washed away. Thousands of mud-built houses have collapsed and residents of pucca houses have lost all their belongings. Eight lakh people have been affected in Jalpaiguri and eight lakh six thousand people in Cooch Behar. Meanwhile, the death toll in the floods in North Bengal rose to 188 including 97 in Cooch Behar and 91 in Jalpaiguri. Three helicopters and 35 speed-boats were pressed into service of rescue operation and about 3,75,000 people have been rescued by the army and civil authorities. Meanwhile, the army was in action in the four worst-hit districts of Assam—Hilakandi, Karimganj, Kokrajhar and Dhubri. However, the woefully inadequate State Government relief of 100 grams of chira, half liter (litre) kerosene and a sprinkling of mustard oil per family reached the flood-stricken people. The streets were crowded by hundreds of naked children and men and women in torn clothing, waiting for relief materials to be brought by clubs and voluntary organisations. In the meantime, communication links between Jalpaiguri and Alipurduar and between Cooch Behar and Alipurduar have been restored. The Chief Minister has made an aerial survey of the flood-areas and promised all sorts of help from the State to relieve the sufferings of the flood-stricken people.

**Note** British spelling : litre; American spelling : liter

## [8] TSUNAMI IN ANDAMANS, INDONESIA etc.

Study the following chart and write a Report on 'Tsunami in Andamans, Indonesia, etc. :

> *Tsunami*, a Japanese word—it means tidal waves due to quake at the bottom of the sea—occurred on 26 December 2004—continued for about two hours in the morning; 30 metres (100 feet) high tidal waves at the speed of 500 km per hour; epicentre of the quake near Sumatra in Indonesia; measurement of the quake at 9 on the Richter Scale; areas affected : Andamans, Car Nicobar, Chennai, Andhra Pradesh, Kerala in India; Indonesia, Thailand, Sri Lanka, Myanmar, Maldwip outside India; casualties of about 1·5 lakh people; innumerable people without food, drink and shelter; offering hands from India, America, UK, Australia, Japan etc.

Bureau Report, December 27, 2004

*Tsunami* is a Japanese word. It means gigantic tidal waves due to quake at the bottom of the sea. The greatest tragedy of Tsunami in recent times occurred on 26 December 2004 and it continued for about two hours in the morning. The epicentre of the quake was at the bottom of the sea near Sumatra in Indonesia. The quake was measured at 9 on the Richter scale. The tidal waves were as high as about 30 metres (100 feet) at the speed of 500 km per hour. It smashed vast areas including the Andamans, Car Nicobar, Chennai, Andhra Pradesh, Kerala in India and Indonesia, Thailand, Sri Lanka, Mayanmar, Maldwip outside India—so many countries in South-East Asia! It caused casualties of about 1.5 lakh people and innumerable people are without food, drink and shelter now. However, offering hands from India, America, Great Britain, Australia, Japan etc. have come forward to help the Tsunami-stricken people.

## [9] THE MOON IMPACT PROBE 2008

Study the following chart and write a newspaper report on 'The Moon Impact Probe 2008'. You may add some detailed information.

> Successful attempt to put India's first signature on the moon—the Moon Impact Probe began functioning at about 8·07 pm on 13 November—the first-ever-close-up pictures of a range of highlands called Malpert mountains—the MIP struck the ground at a speed of 1·5 km per second—the Chandrayaan-I spacecraft continues to go around the moon in a circular orbit 102 km above the surface—observations to generate a map of the moon including minerals and sites for future missions.

New Delhi, November 14, 2008

The Chandrayaan I put India's first signature with the tricolour national flag on the moon in a planned successful attempt on November 13. During its 24 minute dive that began at about 8·07 pm the Moon Impact Probe began to capture images of the lunar surface, including the first-ever-close-up pictures of a range of highlands called Malpert mountains. The scientists said that the MIP would have struck the ground at a speed of 1·5 km per second and its electronic inwards (innards) scattered on the lunar landscape. "We are all in a jubilant mood", said R. Venkata Ramanan, a scientist from the Vikram Sarabhai Space Centre. The Chandrayaan-I spacecraft with its other 10 scientific payloads continues to go around the moon in a circular orbit 102 km above the surface. It is expected to begin 2 years of observations to generate a map of the moon in unprecedented detail, look for minerals and identify sites for future missions.

### [10] TSUNAMI IN NORTH-EAST JAPAN

Write a newspaper report on the 'Tsunami' in Japan with the help of the following chart.

> Tsunami struck Japan's north-east coast on Friday, 11 March—magnitude of 8·9 on the Richter scale—seawaves rising upto 33 ft high—floodwater engulfed Sendai Airport, 300 km from Tokyo—swept away boats, cars, trains and homes—cities, towns and villages along 2100 km stretch of coastline shaken by tremors—death toll about 1000 and 349 missing as per first hand report and the number soaring more—fearing blast in the nuclear power plants.

**Sendai, 12 March, 2011**

The devastating tsunami struck Japan's north-east coast on Friday, 11 March. It was triggered by one of the largest earthquakes ever recorded, with a magnitude of 8·9 on the Richter scale. The seawaves rose upto 33 ft high, and floodwater engulfed even Sendai Airport, 300 km from Tokyo. It swept away boats, cars, trains and thousands of homes. The cities, towns and villages along 2100 km stretch of coastline were shaken by tremors of the earthquake. The death toll was about 1000 along with 349 missing as per first hand report. The number is likely to continue soaring more in the disaster. It is feared that the blast in the nuclear power plants in Japan may occur following the tsunami and the earthquake.

### [11] LAXMAN BATS INDIA TO VICTORY

Use the following information and write a report about the victory of India against Sri Lanka : [You may add some more information, if necesssary.]

> **Date** : 6 August, 2010
>
> **Place** : Colombo
>
> **A remarkable happening in cricket** : India wins pursuing 257, to five wicket over Sri Lanka
>
> **Credit to Laxman** : a marvellous unbeaten 103 facing 149 deliveries and 12 boundaries. This one the 35-year old right-hander's 16th Test hundred—declared the man of the match
>
> **Partnership** : Beginning the day at 53 for three, India lost Ishant Sharma (4) early, but a determined Sachin (54) and an aggressive Suresh Raina (41 not out) figured in crucial partnerships with Laxman—Laxman and Tendulkar added 109 for the fifth wicket—then Laxman and Raina put on 87 unbeaten runs
>
> **Sri Lanka missed** : a vital opportunity when Dilshan dropped Tendulkar, on 18, at short-leg off Randiv

**Colombo, 7 August, 2010**

A marvellous unbeaten 103 from V.V.S. Laxman guided India, pursuing 257, to a five-wicket win over Sri Lanka on the final day of the third test at Colombo on Saturday. This is India's fourth highest successful chase in Test Cricket.

The victory enabled India the three-match Micro-max series 1-1. The last occasion when India drew a Test series in Sri Lanka was in 1997. India lost by an identical 2-1 margin to Sri Lanka in both 2001 and 2008.

Laxman, who faced 149 deliveries and struck 12 boundaries, displayed great character. Despite being troubled by a spasm on his back, he continued to bat with wonderful timing and poise. This was the third 35-years old right-hander's 16th Test hundred. Laxman was declared the man of the match.

Beginning the day at 53 for three, India lost Ishant Sharma (4) early, but a determined Sachin Tendulkar (54) and an aggressive Suresh Raina (41 not out) figured in crucial partnerships with Laxman. Laxman and Tendulkar added 109 for the fifth wicket. Then, Laxman and Raina put on 87 unbeaten runs.

However, Sri Lanka missed a vital opportunity when Dilshan dropped Tendulkar, on 18, at short-leg off Randiv.

## [12] WORLD CUP SEMIFINAL 2011

[India vs. Pakistan]

Write a newspaper report on 'World Cup Semifinal 2011' with the help of the following chart. You may add the details.

> Mohali, March 30—Team India with the captain Mahendra Singh Dhoni beat Pakistan by 29 runs—Sachin Tendulkar's chancy 85 powered India to 260-9 against Pakistan—Sehwag's 38 out of 25 balls with a brisk start helped a handsome total—India beat Pakistan by 29 runs—Prime Minister Manmohan Sing and his Pakistani counterpart Yusuf Razza Gillani shook hands with the two teams in Mohali.

**Mohali, 30 March, 2011**

India beat Pakistan by 29 runs and marched to Mumbai (Final) from Mohali (Semifinal) today, blazing the trial to the cricket World Cup final on the back of a team effort in which the bowlers threw up pleasant surprises one after another.

Earlier, Sachin Tendulkar's chancy 85 powered India to 260-9 against Pakistan. Sehwag's 38 out of 25 balls may have failed to blossom, but his innings provided India with a brisk start which helped for a handsome total.

Just when it seemed nothing can stop the 37 years old prolific run-getter from scoring his 100th international century, Afridi caught Sachin to restrict him making the milestone.

Suresh Raina's (36 not out) middle order helped India past the 250 mark.

Pakistan could not do well in batting. Munaf Patel took two valuable wickets, so did Harbhajan Singh, Ashis Nehra and Yuvraj Singh. Zaheer Khan also took two.

Manmohan Singh, the Prime Minister of India and his Pakistani counterpart Yusuf Razza Gillani shook hands with the two teams in Mohali giving a green signal to promote friendly relation between two neighbouring countries.

## [13] WORLD CUP FINAL 2011

[India vs. Sri Lanka]

Write a newspaper report on 'World Cup Final 2011' with the help of the following chart. You may add the details.

> Wankhede Stadium, April 02—set 274 to win after Jayawardene scored a sublime 103 off 88 balls—India stumbled as Sehwag trapped LBW—Tendulkar racing to 18—Goutam Gambhir and Virat Kohli set about rebuilding the innings—enter Dhoni—when the chips were down, he conquered the world Cup Final scoring 277/4 with 10 balls to spare—Dhoni man of the match.

Wankhede Stadium, 02 March, 2011

After a wait of 28 years, India is once again crowned world champion. Mahendra Singh Dhoni and his team now stand atop a pedestal hitherto occupied only by Kapil's Devils. No team had ever won a World Cup on home ground, no side had ever successfully chased a target in excess of 250 in a World Cup final.

Sri Lanka set 274 to win after Jaywardene had scored a sublime 103 off 88 balls. India stumbled as Sehwag was trapped LBW by Malinga. Sachin Tendulkar looked in sublime touch, racing to 18 only. He walked off to a standing ovation. A few hours later, he would be carried around, all teary-eyed, to a rapturous reception. The gusty Goutam Gambhir and Virat Kohli then set about rebuilding the innings, while ensuring the asking rate never got out of hand. But the match still hung in the balance when Kohli fell to a superb return catch by Dilsan, with the score at 114/3. Dhoni entered at the crucial moment. The Indian skipper had struggled through the tournament. But when the chips were down, he made his statement of intent, by scoring 277/4 with 10 balls to spare. Finally, Dhoni was declared the man of the match.

## DO IT YOURSELF

### [1] ANNUAL SPORTS OF A SCHOOL

Use the following information to write a Report on the Annual Sports of a school :

> Date : January 25, ...
>
> Place : Name of the school.
>
> Events : Flat race, relay race, hurdle race, spoon race, high jump, long jump, pole-vault, discus throw, javelin throw, throwing the cricket ball etc.
>
> The most interesting event : The tug-of-war between the students and the teachers.
>
> President of the function : The B.D.O. of the concerned Block.

Fill in the blanks to make it a complete Report :

.................... (place), January 26, ..........................

The Annual Sports meet of .......................... was held on .......................... in the playground of the school under a sunny sky. It was ........................ (attend) by the students and a crowd of spectators and it ............................ (continue) almost from ............................ to sunset. There ............................ as many as ......................... sporting events, such as—flat race, relay race, hurdle race, spoon race, high jump, long jump, pole-vault, discus throw, javelin throw, throwing the cricket ball etc. In each of these there ................................. good many participants. All the events .............................. very interesting. But the most interesting of all ................................. the tug-of-war between the students and the teachers. The ................................. presided over the funciton. He ................................. (give away) the prizes and .................................

a brief but neat speech befitting the occasion. All those who were present had a jolly day with a lot of fun. The Annual Sports of the school ................................ (come) to an end with a vote of thanks to the Chair.

## [2] THE PRIZE-GIVING CEREMONY OF A SCHOOL

Use the following information to write a short Report on the Prize-giving Ceremony of your school. Write the Report after two days.

**Date** : Saturday, March 13, ................
**Time** : ........................
**Place** : School campus, ............................................................................
**President of the function** : ..........................................................................
**Details of the function** : Recitations, songs and drama staged by the students —Annual Report by the Headmaster—distribution of prizes—Presidential Address—vote of thanks.

**Fill in the blanks to make it a complete Report :**

................. (place), March 15, ...........

The Annual Prize-giving Ceremony of our school ........... (come off) the day before yesterday. The school building ........... (decorate) with flags and flowers on that occasion. The function ........... (start) at 3 p.m. and ........... (last) for ........... hours. The ........... presided over the function. It was the day of days for the students. There ........... recitations, songs and the drama in which as many as ........... students ........... (take part). As soon as the recitations and songs ........... over, our Headmaster ........... (read out) the Annual Report describing the work and the progress of the school in various directions. After that the President ........... (give away) the prizes and ........... (deliver) a short but neat speech. Then the ceremony ........... (come) to an end with a vote of thanks to the President, the Chief Guest and all other visitors.

## [3] A FRIENDLY FOOTBALL MATCH

Use the following information to write a short Report on a friendly football match :

**Date** : Saturday, August 15, ................
**Time** : 3 p.m.
**Place** : Playground at ...............................................
**Contesting parties** : ..................................................................................
**Results** : No score in the fist half but an impressive goal scored by the ........... team in the second half—Then a goal by a corner shot by the centre-forward of the ........... team—The game ended in a draw.

**Fill in the blanks to make it a complete Report :**

.............. (place), August 16, ...........

Last Saturday, the boys of ........... High School ........... (play) a friendly football match with the boys of ........... High School on the playground at ........... Many spectators ........... (come) to ........... the game. It was a keenly contested game. In the first half of the game there ........... no score. But in the second half the ........... High School team scored an impressive goal. The spectators ........... (cheer) them heartily. They .............. (become) hopeful of winning the game. But soon the table ........... (turn) and the centre-forward of the .............. High School team .............. (score) a splendid goal by a swerving corner shot. This .............. (inspire) the players very much. But in spite of their earnest efforts the players of either side ................. (fail) to score any more goal. Thus the game .............. (end) in a draw.

**Note** British spelling : centre; American spelling : center

### 4. FLOOD AT MADHEPURA

Use the following information to make a short Report about flood at Bihar :

**Date** : August 30, ......
**Place** : Madhepura, Bihar
**Position of the river** : The river Koshi crossed the danger level at 10 p.m. on August 30
**Amount of loss** : Crops washed away; mud-built houses collapsed
**Shelter** : Shelter on the roads and in the school and college buildings
**Relief work** : Packets of dry food dropped from helicopters; Ramakrishna Mission and Bharat Sevashram Sangha in relief work
**Communication** : Widespread damage to roads and communication cut off at several places
**Chief Minister's visit** : Aerial survey and promises of all sorts of help

**Fill in the blanks to make it a complete Report :**

Madhepura, August 31, ........

The district of Madhepura in Bihar ........... is flooded. The river Koshi ........... the danger level ........... 10 p.m. ......... August 30. Stretches of miles are under ........... now. Crops of vast areas are ......... away. Hundreds of ......... houses and even some of the brick-built ........... on the river-side have collapsed. A large number of men, women and children ........... shelter on the roads and in ........... buildings. Some of them ........... (starve) for 48 hours! Packets of dry food ......... (drop) from helicopters. Ramakrishna Mission and Bharat Sevashram Sangha ........... (do) their commendable best in relief work. There ........... widespread damage to roads and communication ................. (cut off) at several places. The Chief Minister ........... an aerial survey of the flood-areas and ........... (promise) all sorts of help from the State to relieve the ........... of the flood-stricken people.

## EXERCISE

1. **Use the information given in the following chart to write a Report for the Newspaper in about 120 words. Use a headline of the Report :**

| Incident | Severe earthquake |
|---|---|
| Where? | Wide areas in the Garhwal and Kumaon regions of U.P. |
| Date & time | Early hours—20th October |
| Casualties | 415 people died, 1,200 injured |
| Results | 2,000 houses damaged; 5,000 houses destroyed<br>Water and power supply affected 200 pilgrims stranded |
| Relief work done | Air Force planes (food & necessary articles) Govt. grants sanctioned Rs. 55·50 lakhs—Uttarkashi; Rs. 13·60 lakhs—Tehri Garhwal |

2. **Write a Newspaper Report on a Bus accident in about 120 words on the basis of the following points. Use a headline of the report :**

| Date & Time | Place | Cause | Casualty | Measures taken |
|---|---|---|---|---|
| 6th May at 4 p.m. | Banshibari | A minibus collided with a private bus | 5 died on the spot (incl. 2 women & 2 children), 15 wounded, 3 seriously | (1) removed to Kalidighi hospital (2) 7 let-off after first aid (3) the rest hospitalised |

3. **Write a Report on a serious Train accident in about 100 words using the following information :**

Date and time : September 20, 13-35 hours
Place of accident : Near Bankura Rly Station
Cause of accident : Derailment
Vehicle involved : Howrah-Chakradharpur Passenger train (appr. Howrah)
Casualty : One (name not known)
Injured : Thirtyfive (serious)
Where admitted : Bankura Medical College Hospital

4. **Write a Report about the Independence Day celebration in your school this year. Use the following points :**

Participants : Students, teachers, non-teaching staff, guardians
President : B.D.O.
Chief Guest : Sabhapati of the Panchayet Samity
Programmes : Flag Hoisting; Opening song; Recitations; Speeches by senior students, Headmaster/Headmistress and others; closing song

5. **A school-boy is missing. Write a Report for the school Notice-Board incorporating the following information :**
Name and age—school address—home address—date and time—dress—height and complexion—any special identification mark—where to inform.

3 

# PARAGRAPHS

## WHAT IS A PARAGRAPH AND HOW TO WRITE IT ?

"A Paragraph is a number of sentences grouped together and relating to one topic; or a group of related sentences that develop a single point."—**Wren & Martin**

A Paragraph must have a **Heading** or **Caption** usually **CAPITALISED**. All the relevant points should be dealt with in its body. It should have an **Introductory Sentence** and a **Concluding Sentence**.

**[In the New Syllabus Paragraphs comprise Description of Places, Persons and Objects.]**

## PARAGRAPHS ON PLACES

### [1] A RAILWAY STATION

Study the following information-table about 'A Railway Station' and write a Paragraph on it :

A buzzing sound at Howrah Station—Queues to collect tickets—Passengers, hawkers and porters—Cries of vendors—Getting down from and getting into the train—Gymnastic skills—Departure of the train.

There is always a buzzing sound at Howrah Station. The passengers stand in queues to collect tickets in front of the ticket counters. The station is alw ays crowded with the passengers, hawkers and porters. There are stalls of pedlars and book-sellers and there are waiting rooms in such large stations. Vendors shout their trade cries. Who has not heard the trade-cry 'Cha-garam' or 'Thanda Pani' in the railway station? When a train reaches the station, the passengers hurry to get off the train. At the same time, passengers waiting for the train want to get into the train. As a result, a collision of two groups of passengers takes place. Sometimes it requires some gymnastic skills to get into the train. Ultimately, when the time of departure of a train arrives, the signal nods and the train leaves the station. The whistling sound of the departing train creates a sense of vacuum in the minds of the passengers.

## [2] A VILLAGE FAIR

Read the following information-table abut 'A Village Fair' and write a Paragraph on it :

> The place of the fair—The occasion of the fair—Fair-going people—Stall for selling various articles—Special attraction of the fair—Breaks monotony—Adds joy.

A fair is held every year at Krishnanagar on account of *Rasjatra*. I visited the fair this year. I saw a stream of people on the road to the fair. When I reached there, I saw a sea of human heads moving to and fro on the fair-ground. There were hundreds of stalls for selling various articles, such as toys, dolls, balloons, ribbons, wooden utensils, earthen pots, household goods, baskets etc. There were a large number of sweetmeat stalls and they tempted the buyers, especially the children—more than any other thing. The chief objects of attraction were two circus parties. They beat their drums every now and then to attract the spectators. The people who came to visit the fair came from all ranks of society and all were clad in gala dress. The life of the villagers is usually dull and monotonous. Once a year the fair breaks the monotony and adds joy to their life. It creates a ripple of joy all around. It is also a meeting ground for the old and the young, the rich and the poor.

## [3] THE RIVERS IN THE RAINY SEASON

Read the following information-table about 'The Rivers in the Rainy Season in West Bengal' and write a Paragraph on it :

> Monsoon rain—Rivers furious in size and volume—Strong current—Overflows the banks—Crops are washed away by flood water—Many domestic animals die—Many people become homeless—Dams are made on some of the rivers—Sometimes a curse and sometimes a boon.

Fed by the monsoon rain the rivers become furious in size and volume in the rainy season in West Bengal. At that time water runs down from hills and mountains and strong currents overflow the banks of the rivers. Sometimes crops are washed away by flood water on both sides of the rivers. When the flood becomes more furious, some domestic animals are drowned and many people become homeless. They are bound to starve for a number of days. The whole system of economy of the rural Bengal is miserably hampered by the floods in the rivers. Dams are erected on some of the rivers to check such devastating floods. When the volume of water is controlled through dams, flood is stopped and it causes good harvest by the useful use of the river water. Thus sometimes the rivers become a curse and sometimes a boon in the rainy season.

## [4] A MEMORABLE DAY

Write a paragraph on 'A Memorable Day' in your life with the help of the following outlines :

> The occasion—how and why memorable in your life—your mental reaction.

Human life is a mixture of weal and woe, smiles and tears. However, what would have been a memorable day of pleasure turned to be the saddest day of my life. I can still remember the day. The awful examination was over and we were as free as birds. We planned for a picnic with all our classmates. We decided to go to the Botanical Gardens and our picnic spot was on the bank of the Ganga. We reached there at about 11 a.m. and after the cooking was completed, we made up our mind to take a bath in the Ganga. Our class teacher warned that only those who knew swimming would be alowed to bathe in the river. Rajesh, our youngest classmate, did not know how to swim. But he came unnoticed and tried to imitate us in the river. And it happened what was feared. Rajesth was drowned. We tried to rescue him but in vain. After a long search we recovered the body. The sight made us dumb and tears trickled down our cheeks. It still haunts me whenever I am alone.

### [5] A BOAT JOURNEY

Read the following information-chart about 'A Boat Journey' and write a Paragraph on it :

Date and time : In the morning on Sunday last.
Description : Gentle morning breeze welcomed; the sights on either side very charming; green paddy fields touching the horizon; birds flying overhead; fishermen at work; some boats sailing up and down; a steamer passed by; the bathing ghats; the evening scene on the river.

We started our journey by boat from Bagbazar to Haldia in the morning on Sunday last. The gentle morning breeze welcomed us when we stepped into the boat. The sun was peeping from the horizon. The sights on either side of the river were very charming and these were a feast for our eyes. Our mind leaped in joy when we saw the vast green paddy-fields touching the horizon. The birds were flying over our head now and then. The fishermen were at work here and there. We saw some boats, big and small, sailing up and down the river. When a steamer passed by, it caused big waves and all the boats nearby tossed violently. At the bathing ghats men and women were bathing and children were swimming about. This touch of life added a beauty to the river. But the river became loveliest in the evening when the waves danced and sparkled under the crimson rays of the setting sun. We recalled the poetic line of Keats :

"The day so soon has glided by
Even like the passage of an angel's tear."

### [6] A JOURNEY BY TRAIN

Read the following information-chart about 'A Journey by Train' and write a Paragraph on it :

Destination : Puri
Purpose of journey : To spend a few days during the Puja vacation.
Name of the train : Puri Express.
Time of departure : Half an hour after the scheduled time.
Name of the starting station : Howrah Station.
Description of the station : The crowd was not so great as it was expected for pre-Puja rush.
Experience inside the compartment : The compartment was full of passengers and frightful piles of luggage.
Scene outside the train : Vast open paddy fields and *Sal* and *Mahua* forests on either side; houses and trees slip back from the moving train.
Time of arrival : In the morning on the following day.
Feelings : Mixed.

We had a journey by train as we wished to spend a few days at Puri during the Puja vacation. We travelled by the Puri Express which left Howrah Station half an hour after the scheduled time. We expected the usual pre-Puja rush of passengers. But when we arrived at the station, we noticed that the crowd was not so great. After getting into the train, we found that the compartment was full of passengers and frightful piles of luggage including pots and pans. Thus I had a sad experience inside the compartment but outside it there was a feast for our eyes. I was thrilled to see the vast open paddy fields and *Sal* and *Mahua* trees on either side in the moonlit night. It was amusing to see houses and trees slip back from the moving train. The train arrived at Puri in the morning on the following day. Though we had a pleasant experience on the whole, yet we felt weary with the heat and dust and the cries of the crowd. So I was happy to get rid of it at last.

### [7] A VISIT TO A PLACE OF INTEREST

**Suppose, you visited a place of historical interest. Write a Paragraph on it with the help of the following information-chart :**

> Place of visit : Delhi and Agra.
>
> Where did you stay there?—Uncle's house.
>
> Who accompanied you?—Parents.
>
> Sights seen in Delhi : The Red Fort, the Moti Masjid, the Jumma Masjid, the Qutub Minar, the Parliament House, the Jantar Mantar, the Shantiban, the Rajghat and the Bijoyghat.
>
> Sights seen at Agra : The Taj Mahal—one of the wonders of the world—built by Shahjahan in memory of his beloved wife Mumtaj—feelings after visiting it.

Last summer I had a wonderful time in Delhi. I stayed there at my uncle's house with my parents. Delhi, especially Old Delhi, is a place of historical interest. I visited the Red Fort, the Moti Masjid and the Qutub Minar. I also saw the Parliament House, the Jantar Mantar, Shantiban, the Rajghat and the Bijoyghat. One day we went to Agra to visit the Taj Mahal, one of the Seven Wonders of the world. It was built by Shahjahan in memory of his beloved wife Mumtaj on the bank of the river Jamuna. In fact, it looks like a dream in marble in a moonlit night. The majestic beauty of the Taj will ever remain imprinted on my mind.

### [8] A BOOK FAIR

**Write a Paragraph on 'A Book Fair' with the help of the given keynotes :**

> A book fair in the 'Maidan' opposite to Park Street—More than 500 stalls—Opportunity of choice of books—Display of books—Crowd of book-lovers (bibliophiles)—Temptation to buy a lot of books—Collection of a few books and a lot of catalogues.

Amongst all the fairs, the book fair is of recent origin. Book fairs are now frequently held in towns and cities. A few years back I visited a book fair in the 'Maidan' opposite to Park Street. There were more than five hundred stalls of so many books. It was a great opportunity of having a varied choice of books in the book fair. The main point about a book fair is not sale but the vast display of books on different subjects. Book-lovers crowded there to make their choice and buy books from the stalls. I was tempted to buy a lot of books but my purse did not permit me. As a result I bought a few books and collected a lot of catalogues to buy books at the next opportunity. Here we hear the books talking to each other. However, a book fair spreads the message that books are our best friends and companions that enlarge our vision and make our life more meaningful.

### [9] SCENE IN AN EXAMINATION HALL

Study the following information-chart and write a Paragraph on the 'Scene in an Examínaiton Hall' :

| Time→ | 9-45 A.M. | 10 A.M. | 12-45 P.M. | 1 P.M. |
|---|---|---|---|---|
| Action→ | Warning-bell rings. Students take their seats. | Question Papers are distributed. Invigilators moving up and down. Examinees found busy. | Warning-bell rings. Students busier than before. Some revise their answers. Some increase their speed. | Answer-scripts are taken back. Students step out of the hall. |

The scene in the examination hall is full of typical suspense. To a student the examination hall is like a Greek amphitheatre where he is open to attacks from even unexpected quarters. But the student has no other instrument to fight with than his pen. When the warning bell rings at 9.45 a.m., students take their seats. Question papers are distributed to them at 10 a.m. sharp. Invigilators start moving up and down the hall to keep watch over the candidates. Very soon the examinees are found busy writing answers in the scripts. Some look bright and some look vacant; a few students try to adopt unfair means. Time rolls on. When the warning bell rings at 12-45 p.m., students are busier than before. Some begin revising their answers while others increase their speed to finish. When the final bell rings at 1 p.m., answer-scripts are taken back and the students step out of the hall. They feel a sense of relief after passing the three serious hours in the examination hall.

## PARAGRAPHS ON PERSONS

### [10] A HAWKER

Write a Paragraph about a hawker with the help of the following information :

> A common sight—Various kinds of things for sale—Various tricks to attract the attention of the buyers—Sometimes funny and sometimes irritating—Small goods at a cheaper rate—A moving shop and a salesman combined—Hard labour for living from hand to mouth.

A hawker is a common sight on a street of a city or a town or in a compartment of a train. He carries his wares sometimes on his head, sometimes in his hands, sometimes in a bag and sometimes in a small hand-cart. He sells various kinds of small goods including sweets, drinks, books, pens, medicines and what not. He uses various tricks to attract the attention of the buyers. Sometimes he starts singing or even starts acting. Sometimes he is funny and sometimes irritating. He sells his wares at a cheaper rate than that of the settled shopkeepers. It is possible as he has not to pay any rent for a shop or salary to a salesman. He is, as if, a moving shop and a salesman combined. But it is a pity that he has to do such hard labour for living from hand to mouth.

## [11] THE POSTMAN

Write a Paragraph about the postman in your locality with the help of the following information-chart :

> A familiar figure—Essential service to the community—Link between a locality and the outside world—Delivers letters, telegrams, parcels, moneyorders etc.—Responsibility of his work—Misdelivery or delay in delivery may cause serious loss—Mingled feelings of joy and tears—A friend of our society.

The postal system is, as if, the nervous system of a country. The postman is a familiar figure in this system. He renders essential service to a community. In fact, he is an important link between a locality and the outside world. He comes door-to-door in his daily rounds of duties and delivers letters, telegrams, parcels, moneyorders etc. to proper persons. He holds a responsible job. An interview letter or an appointment letter of a person may be cancelled for misdelivery or late delivery. He brings happy news to someone and sad news to some other. Thus he carries mingled feelings of joy and tears. It is a pity that he is still ill-paid though he has a great responsibility of work. However, we must admit that he is a good friend of our society.

## [12] THE MAN YOU ADMIRE MOST

### M. K. GANDHI

Write a Paragraph on 'The Man you Admire Most' with the help of the following outlines :

> Name of the man you admire most—Why do you admire him—his activities—his impression in your individual life and in national or international aspect.

The man I admire most is M. K. Gandhi. His full name is Mohandas Karamchand Gandhi. He was attributed 'Mahatma' for his glorious life. He was born at Porebandar in Gujarat (India) on 2 October, 1869. After completing education in India he went to England in order to study Law. He obtained the degree in Law and returned to India and began to practise in Mumbai Highcourt at first and then in South Africa. While he was there, he started a new era of non-violence movement to reduce the oppression of the Europeans against the natives of South Africa. The movement became famous as *Satyagraha* and when he came to India again he used this method against the British rule. It was strengthened in Non-cooperation Movement in 1921 and Quit India Movement in 1942. He became the leader of the people giving his clarion call—"Do or die'. After a long struggle under his leadership India won her independence on 15 August in 1947. He was shot dead on 30 January, 1948 by a derailed young man. But his life and message are still the source of inspiration not only in the national field, but also in the international field.

## [13] YOUR FAVOURITE AUTHOR/POET

### RABINDRANATH TAGORE

Write a Paragraph on 'Your Favourite Author/Poet' with the help of the following outlines :

> Name of your favourite author—Place of Birth—Boyhood—Versatile genius—Some of his best books of poems, novels, drama and songs—Educationist—Conclusion.

Mother India produced a galaxy of geniuses in the 19th century and Rabindranath Tagore is perhaps the brightest among them. He is my favourite author/poet. He was born at Jorasanko in Kolkata on the 7th May 1861. He had no regular school education. But his education was not neglected. Under the personal care of his father Maharshi Debendranath Tagore, and the tutors at home, he gained a deep knowledge in Bengali, Sanskrit and English. From his boyhood he began to write poems of great merit and charm. He was a versatile genius. In later life he became a poet, a dramatist, a story-writer, a novelist, a critic and an essayist. Some of his best poems are found in the 'Gitanjali', 'Sonar Tari', 'Kheya', 'Kalpana', 'Balaka' etc. For his English version of the 'Gitanjali' he was awarded the Nobel Prize in Literature in 1913. His novels and plays are of high order. His songs named as Rabindra Sangeet are yet very popular in our country. He was a great educationist too. He had unique ideas of open-air educational institution and freedom from the fear of examination. He blended ancient Indian type of teaching with modern ideas of education. The students found a new meaning of life with their all-round development. He established a school at Santiniketan in 1901 and afterwards founded the University of Visva-Bharati in 1921. I love him because he was a great poet as well as a great thinker and educationist of international reputation. He left this earth on the 7th August 1941 but still he is remembered as the poet-laureate all over the world.

## [14] LORD BUDDHA

**Write a Paragraph on 'Lord Buddha' with the help of the following points :**

> Birth in Kapilavastu (now Nepal) in 563 BC and death in 483 BC—father King Suddhodan and mother Queen Maha Maya (Mayadevi)—mother died at his birth—brought up by his mother's sister Maha Pajapati—infant name Siddhartha and family name Goutama—at the age of 16, his father arranged his marriage to a cousin named Yasodhara—gave birth to a son named Rahula—spent 29 years as a prince in Kapilavastu—felt that material wealth was not life's ultimate goal—left his palace for the life of a mendicant—seated under a peepal tree (known as Bodhi tree) in Bodh Gaya, India—attained 'Enlightenment' and known to his followers as 'Buddha' or 'Awakened one'—realised complete insight into the cause of sufferings and the steps necessary to eliminate it—these discoveries known as the 'Four Noble Truths'—through these truths, a state of supreme liberation or 'Nirvana' possible for any being—reached 'Parinirvana' or the final deathless state at the age of 80.

Lord Goutam Buddha was a spiritual preacher from ancient India who founded Buddhism. The time of birth and death of Lord Buddha is uncertain. However, most of the historians believe his lifetime to be 563 BC to 483 BC. He was born at Lumbini in Kapilavastu (now Nepal). His father was King Suddhodana and mother Queen Maha Maya (Mayadevi). His infant name was Siddhartha and family name Goutama. His mother died at his birth and he was brought up by his mother's sister Maha Pajapati. When he attained the age of 16, his father arranged his marriage to a cousin named Yasodhara. He gave birth to a son named Rahula and spent 29 years as a prince in Kapilavastu. Although his father provided Siddhartha with everything he could want or need, he felt that material wealth was not life's ultimate goal. At the age of 29 he left his palace for the life of a mendicant. Some days after being seated under a peepal tree (known as Bodhi tree) in Bodh Gaya, India, he attained 'Enlightment' and thereafter he was known as 'Buddha' or 'Awakened One' to his followers. He realised complete insight into the cause of suffering and the steps necessary to eliminate it. These discoveries became known as the 'Four Noble Truths'. And through these truths, a state of supreme liberation or 'Nirvana' is possible for any mortal being. He himself, reached 'Parinirvana' or the final deathless state at the age of 80, according to the Buddhist scriptures.

### [15] JESUS CHRIST

**Write a Paragraph on Jesus Christ with the help of the following information :**

> Birth and lifetime 7(?) BC—30(?) AD—central figure of Christianity—born at Bethlehem, Judea in Roman empire—mother vergin Mary—A Jew preacher and healer—crucified in Jerusalem on the orders of Roman Prefect of Judea, Pontius Pilate—most Christians regard him as the incarnation of Son of God—the four cano-nical gospels—the Old Testament and the New Testament

Jesus Christ [7(?) BC—30(?) AD] is the central figure of Christianity. He was born at Bethlehem, Judea in Roman empire and his mother was Mary. The Christians traditionally believe that Jesus was born of a virgin, performed miracles and founded an independent religious movement. The majority of Christians worship Jesus as the incarnation of Son of God, one of three divine persons of a Trinity. A few Christian groups, however, reject Trinitarianism, partly or wholly, taking it to be non-scriptural. The principal sources of information regarding Jesus are the four canonical gospels, and most critical scholars find them useful for reconstructing the life and teachings of Jesus. Some scholars believe apocryphal texts such as the Gospel of Thomas and the Gospel of the Hebrews are also relevant. Later on the Bible has been divided into two parts—the Old Testament (before Christ) and the New Testament, containing the life of Jesus and principles of Christianity. In Islam, Jesus (transliterated in Arabic as Isa) is considered one of God's important prophets, and the product of a virgin birth; but do not believe that he was God incarnate.

Most of the historians agree that Jesus was a Jew regarded as a preacher and healer, and was crucified in Jerusalem on the orders of the Roman Prefect of Judaea, Pontius Pilate, on the charge of sedition against the Roman Empire.

### [16] MUHAMMAD

**Write a Paragraph on 'Muhammad' with the help of the following information. You may add some relevant points too :**

> Born in the month of 'Rabi'al-awwal' in 570 AD in the Arabian city of Mecca—orphaned at an early age and brought up under the care of his uncle Abu Talib—joined trading journeys to Syria—met a Christian monk named Bahira—married Khadijah, a 40-year-old widow at the age of 25, and later on 12 other women—meditation in a cave on Mount Hira near Mecca—after three years of spiritual practices began preaching monotheism or 'God is one'—not to worship idols or associate other deities with God (Allah)—the Quran, the holy scripture of Islam—died on Monday, 8 June, 632 in Medina at the age of 63.

Muhammad, the founder of the religion of Islam was born in the month of 'Rabi'al-awwal' in 570 AD in the Arabian city of Mecca. He was orphaned at an early age and brought up under the care of his uncle Abu Talib. He worked as a shepherd as well as a merchant. He joined trading journeys to Syria and met a Christian monk named Bahira. At the age of 25 he married Khadijah, a 40-year-old widow, and later on 12 other women. Discontented with this life, he retreated to a cave on Mount Hira near Mecca for meditation. After three years of spiritual practices, he started preaching monotheism or 'God is one' and advised not to worship idols or associate other deities with God (Allah). He proclaimed that he himself was a prophet and messenger of God. At first he gained only a few followers and was met with hostility from some mecca tribes. Thereafter, he and his followers migrated to Medina in the year 622. This event, the *Hijra,* marks the beginning of the Islamic (*Hijri*) calender. In Medina Muhammad united the conflicting tribes, and after eight years of fighting with the Meccan tribes, conquered Mecca. Muhammad died on Monday, 8 June, 632 at the age of 63. His preaching are contained in the Quran, the holy scripture of Islam.

## [17] GURU NANAK

**Write a Paragraph on 'Guru Nanak' with the help of the following points. You may add some details.**

> Founder of the religion of Sikhism and the first of the ten Sikh Gurus—born on 15 April, 1469 into a Bedi (*Kshatriya*) family in a Muslim village of Rai Bhoi de Talwandi, now called Nankana Sahib near Lahore—father Mehta Kalyan Das Bedi, popularly shortened to Kalu Mehta and mother Tripta Devi—at the age of 5 voiced interest in divine subjects and at the age of 7 enrolled at the village school—followed her elder sister to Sultanpur to live with her and her husband at the age of 16 years—married to Mata Sulakhni at about 19 years of age—at the age of 30 he had a vision and disappeared—after three days reappeared—spoke about God's path—made four major journeys—preached 'God is the Doer and without God there is no other'—died on 22 September, 1539 in Kartarpur at the age of 69.

Guru Nanak was the founder of the religion of Sikhism and the first of the ten Sikh Gurus. He was born on 15 April, 1469 into a Bedi (*Khastriya*) family in a Muslim village of Rai Bhoi di Talwandi, now called Nankana Sahib near Lahore. His father was Mehta Kalyan Das Bedi, popularly shortened to Kalu Mehta and his mother was Tripta Devi. At the age of 5 he voiced his interest in divine subjects. At the age of 7 he was enrolled at the village school. He followed her elder sister to Sultanpur to live with her and her husband Daulat Khan at the age of 16 years. He was married to Mata Sulakhni at about 19 years of age. At the age of 30 he had a vision and disappeared from the village. After three days he reappeared and spoke about God's path—"There is neither Hindu nor Musalman, so whose path shall I follow? I shall follow God's path." He said that he had been taken to God's court. There he was offered a cup filled with amrit (nectar) and given the command—"This is the cup of the adoration of God's name. Drink it...I have bestowed the gift of my name upon you. Let this be your calling." He made four major journeys—first, towards Bengal and Assam, second, towards Tamil Nadu, third, towards Kashmir, Ladakh and Tibet, and the final tour towards Bagdad, Mecca and Medina on the Arabian Peninsula. At Mecca, Guru Nanak was found sleeping with his feet towards the Kaaba Mosque. Kazi Rukan-ud-din observed this and angrily objected. Guru Nanak said, "Please turn my feet in a direction where there is no house of God." The Kazi understood the meaning that "God is everywhere" and was struck with wonder. Guru Nanak preached "God is the Doer and without God there is no other." He advised his followers to practise his teachings in three ways :

[1] *Naam Japna* : Chanting the Holy name, [2] *Kirat Karo* : Earning a living honesty, [3] *Vand Chakko* : helping those with less who are in need.

Guru Nanak expired on 22 September, 1539 in Kartarpur at the age of 69.

## [18] SRI RAMAKRISHNA

Write a Paragraph on 'Sri Ramakrishna' with the help of the following points :

> Birth and parentage—early name and early life—at the temple-garden of Dakshineswar—marriage with Saradadevi—God-intoxication (*sadhana*)—association with Narendranath Dutta (Swami Vivekananda)—last days and expiry from mortal body.

Sri Ramakrishna, the God-man of modern India, was born on 18 February, 1836 at Kamarpukur in the Hooghly district in India. His parents Khudiram and Srimati Chandramoni were exceptionally devoted persons and earned the love and respect of the villagers for their charity, truthfulness and kindness. Sri Ramakrishna's early name was Gadadhar or Gadai. He learnt some lessons in the village pathshala but he was not very much interested in it. Gadadhar was seven years old when his father died. At the age of sixteen Gadadhar came to Calcutta (now Kolkata) with his elder brother Ramkumar, who wished his assistance in his priestly duties. At that time a rich widow named Rani Rasmani founded a temple to the goddess Kali on the eastern bank of the Ganga at Dakshineswar. Being invited by Rasmani, Ramkumar with his brother Gadadhar came to the sacred temple-garden and Gadadhar found greater opportunities to pursue his spiritual practices. To Sri Ramakrishna the image of Kali was not an inert stone, but the Mother herself. Rani Rashmani was greatly attracted to Sri Ramakrishna, for she felt that his strange behaviour was for the fullness of devotion to goddess Kali. Sri Ramakrishna had a catholic spirit from the very beginning and he made no distinction between one form of God in Hinduism to another in Islam or Christianity. In the meantime Sri Ramakrishna was married to Sarada Devi and practised a spiritual life at Dakshineswar. To spread his message to the world around Sri Ramakrishna needs a strong instrument. And such an instrument was found in Narendranath Dutta, his beloved Naren, later known to the world as Swami Vivekananda. The last days of Sri Ramkrishna were with his devoted disciples. And on 15 August, 1886 he breathed his last leaving behind his preachings and godliness for the whole world.

## [19] MARTIN LUTHER KING JR.

Write a Paragraph on 'Martin Luther' with the help of the following points. You may add some details :

> Birth : 15 January, 1929 in Atlanta, Georgia in America—parentage : Reverend Martin Luther King, senior and Alberta William—early life and education—his contribution in religion, politics and social reforms—influence of M. K. Gandhi on him in point of non-violence—Nobel Peace Prize in 1964—assassinated on 4 April, 1968 in Memphis, Tennesse—posthumously awarded the Presidential Medal of Freedom in 1977 and Congressional Medal in 2004—Martin Luther King's birthday established as a US federal holiday since 1986

Martin Luther King, Jr. was born on 15 January, 1929 in Atlanta, Georgia in America. His father was Reverend Martin Luther King, Senior and mother Alberta Williams. His early life was spent in Atlanta. As a precocious student, he skipped both the ninth and twelfth grade and entered Morehouse College at the age of fifteen without formally graduating from High School. In 1948 he graduated from Morehouse with a Bachelor of Arts degree in sociology, and enrolled in Crozer Theological Seminary in Chester, Pennsylvania from which he graduated with a Bachelor of Divinity degree in 1951.

He began doctoral studies in systematic theology at Boston University and obtained the degree of Doctor of Philosophy in 1955. As a Baptist minister he became a Protestant and founded the Southern Christian Leadership Conference in 1957. He was the prominent leader in the African-American Civil Rights Movement. He is best known for being an iconic figure in the advancement of civil rights in the United States and around the world, using the non-violent methods following the teachings of Mahatma Gandhi. He believed that the non-violent resistance is the most potent weapon available to oppressed people in their struggle for justice and human dignity. He delivered his famous speech 'I have a Dream' in 1963 in Washington. Thereon he expanded liberal American values against the colour-blind society. His notable efforts were on ending poverty from the society and stopping the Vietuam War. In 1964 he was the youngest recipient of the Nobel Peace Prize for his work to end racial segregation through civil disobedience and other nonviolent means. He was assassinated on 4 April, 1968 in Memphis, Tennessee. He was post-humously awarded the Presidential Medal of Freedom in 1977 and Congressional Gold Medal in 2004. Martin Luther King Jr. Day (15 January) is observed as a US Federal Holiday since 1986.

## [20] ABRAHAM LINCOLN

**Write a Paragraph on 'Abraham Linolu' with the help of the following points. You may add some details.**

Born on 12 February, 1809 in Hardin (now Laure) County in Kentucky—father Thomas Lincon, a skilled carpenter, mother Nancy Hanks—Lincolns moved to Indiana in 1816—little school education—left Indiana for Illinois in 1830—military interlude in the Black Hawkwar (1832) and captain of his volunteer Company—married Mary Todd in 1842—served one term (1847-49) as a member of the US House of Representatives—opposed the Mexican War—won the Presidential election as the 16th President of the US and his inauguration in March 1861—taking vigorous measures in the Civil War—naturally anti-slavery—endorsed the 13th Amendment to the Constitution abolishing slavery—Wilkes Booth, a Negrophobe shot Lincoln on 14 April, 1865.

Abraham Lincoln, the 16th President of the United States, guided his country through the most devastating experience in its national history—the Civil War. He is considered by many historians to have been the greatest American President. He was born on 12 February, 1809 in Hardin (now Laure) county in Kentucky. His father Thomas Lincoln was a skilled carpenter and his mother was Nancy Hanks. Lincolns left Kentucky and moved to Indiana in 1816. There little Lincoln attended some schools for less than a year altogether. Lincolns left Indiana for Illinois in 1830. In 1831 Lincoln left home for New Salem and served briefly in the Black Hawk War (1832). The military interlude was uneventful except that he was elected Captain of his volunteer Company. In 1842 he married Mary Todd. He served one term (1847-49) as a member of the US House of Representatives where he opposed the Mexican War as unnecessary and unconstitutional. He had been indifferent about the annexation of Texus, already a slave territory, but he opposed any expansion that would allow slavery into new areas, gained as a result of the Mexican War. He expressed his view that the nation would become "either all slave or all free". He won the Presidential election as the 16th President of the US and his inauguration was held in March, 1861. He was soon noted for taking vigorous measures in the Civil War sometimes at odds with the Constitution and often at odds with the ideas of his military commanders. He was naturally anti slavery. He endorsed the 13th Amendment to the Constitution abolishing slavery and thus charged the racial future of the United States. But it agitated a section of the white people. John Wilkes Booth, a Negrophobe shot Lincoln while he attended a performance at Ford's Theatre in Washington on 14 April, 1865. Lincoln's achievements for saving the Union and freeing the slaves, and his martyrdom just at the war's end assured his continuing fame forever.

### [21] NELSON MANDELA

**Write a Paragraph on 'Nelson Mandela' with the help of the following points :**

> Born on 18 July, 1918—Mandela's father Gadla Henry Mphakanyiswa served as chief of the town of Mvezo—upon alienating the colonial authorities, moved his family to Qunu—Mandela was born to his third wife Nosekeni Fanny—Mandela was the first member of his family to attend a school—his teacher Miss Mdingane gave him the English name 'Nelson'—after the election-victory of the Africaner-dominated National Party in 1948, Mandela began actively participating in politics—Mahatma Gandhi influenced Mandela's approach and the methods of South African anti-apartheid activities—in 1959 the ANC lost its support from Ghana and broke away to form the PAC—the leader of the ANC's armed wing in 1961—on 5 August, 1962 Mandela was arrested—on 11 February, 1990 Mandela was released from Victor Verster Prison—on 27 April, 1994 South Africa's first multi-racial elections—on 10 May, 1994 Mandela became the first black President of the country—Mandela married three times and fathered six children—retired in 1999—received many South African and international honours including the Nobel Peace Prize in 1993.

Nelson Mandela was born on 18 July, 1918. His father Gadla Henry Mphakanyiswa served as chief of the town of Mvezo. Upon alienating the colonial authorities, he moved his family to Qunu. Mandela was born to his third wife Nosekeni Fanny. However, he was the first member of his family to attend a school. His teacher Miss Mdingane gave him the English name 'Nelson'. After the election-victory of the Africaner-dominated National party in 1948, Mandela began actively participating in politics. Mahatma Gandhi had influenced Mandela's approach and the methods of South African anti-apartheid activities. In 1959 the ANC (African National Congress) lost its support from Ghana and broke away to form the PAC (Pan Africanist Congress). In 1961 Mandela became the leader of the ANC's armed wing. On 5 August, 1962 he was arrested and stayed behind bars for 28 years. During his years in prison his reputation grew steadily and he was widely accepted as the most significant black leader in the anti-apartheid movement in South Africa. On 11 February, 1990 he was released from Victor Verster Prison. South Africa's first multi-racial elections were held on 27 April, 1994 and Mandela became the first black President of the country on 10 May, 1994. Mandela married three times and fathered six children. He retired from the Presidentship in 1999. He received many South African and international honours including the Nobel Peace Prize in 1993.

### [22] RAJA RAMMOHUN ROY—A SOCIAL REFORMER

**Write a Paragraph on 'Raja Rammohun Roy—A Social Reformer' with the help of the following information :**

> The pioneer of modern India—Two-fold role as a reformer—a religious reformer as well as a social reformer—Society of his times—Out and out a humanist—Challenge against the 'Satidaha' system—Successful in his attempt with the help of Lord Bentinck—The first beacon light of Renaissance in Bengal as well as in India.

Raja Rammohun Roy was the pioneer of modern India. He was born at Radhanagar in the district of Hooghly on 22nd May 1772. From his boyhood he showed his spirit. His role as a reformer was two-fold. He was a religious reformer as well as a social reformer. He revolted against idolatry and laid the step-stone of the Brahma Samaj. On the other hand he tried heart and soul to remove the evil customs of the society of his times such as caste-prejudice, early marriage, widow-burning etc. He was greatly shocked at the deplorable condition of the society as these evil customs were eating into the vitals of the society. He was out and out a great humanist. He ceaselessly challenged the 'Satidaha' system and in the long run in 1829 he was successful in his attempt with the help of the-then Governor-General Lord William Bentinck. The name of Raja Rammohun and the abolition of the cruel 'Satidaha' system are inseparable from each other. He wished to spread modern culture and education into the conservative fabric of our society. In fact, he was the first beacon-light of Renaissance in Bengal as well as in India. He passed away at Bristol in England on 27 September 1833 and we say, "The sun of the East went on setting in the West."

## [23] SWAMI VIVEKANANDA

**Write a Paragraph on 'Swami Vivekananda' with the help of the following information :**

> Brith and parentage—Education—Curiosity about God and Religion—contact with Sri Ramakrishna—Tour over India—Misery of the masses—Parliament of Religions at Chicago—Establishment of the Belur Math and the Ramakrishna Mission—Call to his countrymen—An idol of youth and nationalism.

Swami Vivekananda is one of the greatest religious heroes and social reformers of India. His earlier name was Narendranath Dutta. He was born in Kolkata on 12th January in 1863. His father, Biswanath Dutta, was a pleader and his mother Bhubaneswari Debi was a pious lady. He was a bright student at school and he passed the B.A. examination with Honours in philosophy from Scottish Church College. He had a strong curiosity about God and religion and this was satisfied only after his contact with Sri Ramakrishna. On the passing away of Ramakrishna (1886) he went about touring all over India on foot. During his tour he came in close touch with the misery of the masses. He went to the Parliament of Religions in 1893 at Chicago and delivered his speeches on the greatness of Hindu religion. Coming back to India he established the Belur Math and Ramakrishna Mission in 1897. He breathed his last on 4th July, 1902. But his clarion call "Let the poor be your gods" is a never-ending source of inspiration to his countrymen. In fact, he is the idol of youth and nationalism of modern India.

## [24] SISTER NIVEDITA

**Write a Paragraph on Sister Nivedita, with the help of the following hints :**

> **Real Name** : Margaret Elizabeth Nobel
> **Date of birth** : 28 October, 1867
> **Early education** : Normal School in Kolkata.
> **Place of birth** : Vanganon, Ireland
> **Parents** : Samuel Richmond Nobel, Mary Isabel Hamilton
> **Various types of shocks in life** : Sudden death of her father and grandmother—brought up by her maternal grandfather.

After completing education : Took up the vocation of a teacher.
Turning point in life : Meeting with Swami Vivekananda in England in 1895—came to India on 28 January in 1898—to spread education and serve humanity—renamed Nivediata.
Famous books : The master as I saw him, Notes of Some Wanderings with Vivekananda.
Death : 13 October, 1911

The real name of Sister Nivedita is Miss Margaret Elizabeth Nobel. She was born at Vanganon, Ireland on 28 October, 1867. Her father Samuel Richmond Nobel was a priest and mother Mary Isabel Hamilton was a pious lady. Her family heritage was enriched with not only the religions bent, but also a sense of burning patriotism. Her life was going on easily and happily till the sudden death of her father and grand-mother. After the shock she received in her life she was brought up by her maternal grandfather. And when she completed her education, she took up the vocation of teaching in a school. However, the turning point in her life came when she met Swami Vivekananda in England in 1895. Miss Nobel responded to the call of Swami Vivekananda and she came to India on 28 January in 1898. She was renamed as Nivedita (dedicated) and inspired by Vivekananda to spread education and serve humanity in India. Her famous books are *The Master as I saw him* and *Notes of some wanderings with Vivekananda*. She breathed her last on her death-bed at Darjeeling on 13 October, 1911. Her parting word still conveys a source of inspiration to us—"The boat is sinking, but I shall see the sunrise."

## [25] AMARTYA SEN, THE NOBEL LAUREATE

**Write a Paragraph on Amartya Sen, the Nobel Laureate, with the help of the following hints :**

Born on 3rd November 1933—Parentage : Dr. Asutosh Sen & Amita Sen—Education : Santiniketan, Presidency College, Calcutta University, and Cambridge—Activities : Professor of Economics, Jadavpur University 1956-58; Delhi University 1963-71; London School of Economics 1971-77; Oxford 1977-80; Master of Trinity College since 1997—Some of his best books : Choice of Techniques, 1960; Growth Economics, Collective Choice and Social Welfare, 1970; Poverty and Famines, 1981; Choice, Welfare and Measurement, 1982; On Ethics and Economics, 1987; The Political Economy of Hunger 1990-91; India : Economic Development and Social Opportunity, 1995—Honours and Awards : Hon. D. Litt. from a number of universities; Agnelli Internet Prize 1990; World Hunger Award 1990; Nobel Prize in Economics 1998 for his contribution to 'Welfare Economics.'

Nobel Laureate Amartya Sen was born on November 3 in the year 1933. He is the grandson of Pandit Kshitimohan Sen. His father Dr. Asutosh Sen was a reputed figure in agricultural science and his mother Amita Sen was a disciple of Rabindranath Tagore at Santiniketan. He was named 'Amartya' by Rabindranath himself. He studied at Santiniketan up to the Intermediate Examination and then in Presidency College, Calcutta University, and Cambridge, having Economics as his favourite subject. Later on he became the Professor of Economics in Jadavpur University 1956-58, Delhi University 1963-71, London School of Economics 1971-77, Oxford 1977-80. He has been holding the prestigious post of Master of Trinity College since 1997. He is reputed for his vast knowledge in Economics and Philosophy. Some of his best books in the field of Economics are 'Choice of Techniques' 1960, 'Growth Economics' and 'Collective Choice and Social Welfare' 1970, 'Poverty and Famines' 1981, 'Choice, Welfare and Measurement' 1982, 'On Ethics and Economics' 1987, 'The Political Economy of Hunger' 1990-91, 'India : Economic Development and Social Opportunity' 1995. Honours and awards are showered on him from different corners of the world. He obtained Hon. D. Lit. from a number of universities of India and abroad. He received Agnelli Internet Prize and World Hunger Award in 1990. He was awarded the prestigious Nobel Prize in Economics in 1998 for his contributions to Welfare Economics. He is the sixth Indian to get a Nobel and the first Asian winner in the field of Economics. He has made a good many noteworthy contributions to central field of economic science and opened up new fields of study—especially on famine and poverty—for subsequent generations.

## PARAGRAPHS ON OBJECTS

### [26] TELEVISION

**Write a Paragraph on 'Television' with the help of the following information-table :**

> One of the wonderful inventions of modern science—Invented by John Baird—Combination of the radio and the cinema—Medium for mass education and recreation—Instrument for advertisement—Still a costly thing—Dark sides of TV.

The word 'television' comes from the Greek word '***tele***' which means distant and the Latin word '***visio***' which means vision. It is one of the most wonderful inventions of modern science. It was invented by John Baird, a Scottish scientist, in 1925. After the Second World War (1939-1945) it has become very popular all over the world. It is an audio-visual instrument and excellent medium for mass education and recreation. Moreover, it is an important medium for advertisement. We also enjoy drama, cinema, sports, quiz and many other important events on television. It puts before our eyes the objects and persons thousands of kilometers (kilometres) away with their pictures, sounds and voices. Thus it has brought the outer world into our drawing room. But still it is a costly thing and we hope that the price of television will come down soon so that the common people can enjoy television—the magic baby of modern science. It has great possibilities in future. But TV has its dark sides too. It has made people unsocial to some extent. Guests feel embarrassed and unwelcome when they pay visit to someone while a hot programme is on the screen. Children are tempted to spend valuable study hours watching TV serials. The adult members of the family should be cautious of it.

**Note** British spelling : Kilometres; American spelling : Kilometers

### [27] NEWSPAPER

**Write a Paragraph on 'Newspaper' with the help of the following information-table :**

> The newspaper is the mirror of the world—Helps to acquire general knowledge—A dainty dish of varieties such as the news of current affairs, trade and commerce, films, games and sports etc.—Views of scholars on different subjects—A great blessing of modern civilisation—Not to be blindly influenced.

"Newspaper is the people's parliament".The newspaper plays a vital role in modern civilisation. It is said to be the mirror of the world. We must have the habit of reading a newspaper daily. It helps us acquire general knowledge which is essential for our education. Nobody can keep contact with the world outside without reading a newspaper. Mere bookish knowledge is not sufficient in the struggle of life. A man who does not read a newspaper daily is like a frog in a narrow well. Being ignorant of current topics, he cannot take part in the talks and discussions in an enlightened society and seems like a fish out of water in it. The newspaper is a dainty dish of varieties, such as the news of current affairs, trade and commerce, films, games and sports etc. Moreover, views of scholars on different subjects are discussed in it. All these have some educative value and we must have the habit of reading a newspaper regularly as it is a great blessing of modern civilisation.

But one should bear in mind that newspapers bear comments of diverse nature and interests by the reporters and critics from various angles. We should not be blindly influenced by these comments but should keep an open mind to judge the facts and problems in our country and abroad.

## [28] YOUR FAVOURITE HOBBY

**Write a Paragraph on 'Your Favourite Hobby' with the help of the following outlines :**

Name of your hobby—What do you do for your favourite hobby?—Special feature of your hobby—Reason of following a hobby.

A hobby is a favourite subject which a man follows not because it is his main business but because it gives him pleasure. In fact, it is the way of using one's leisure with pleasure. There are so many fashionable hobbies such as stamp-collecting, coin-collecting, photography etc. But my favourite hobby is gardening. I dig the land, sow the seeds and water the plants in my garden. It involves hard work but it is not tiresome, because it is love's labour. I can sit for hours in my garden, watching the buds come up, and the branches nodding in the breeze. I feel that the plants and flowers are no mute insensate things. They have a language of their own which I understand. Although a hobby is a source of pleasure, not of profit, my hobby combines the two. My mother looks upon it very kindly, as a part of my garden serves as a kitchen garden. My friends often ask me why I have chosen gardening as my hobby when there are so many fashionable hobbies. Frankly speaking, we hardly know why we have chosen our hobbies. Possibly our character draws us to it, for a hobby is an index to a man's character.

## [29] DISCIPLINE IN STUDENT LIFE

**Write a Paragraph on 'Discipline in Student Life' with the help of the following outlines :**

Discipline means obedience to some rules—To obey parents and superiors at home and teachers in school—Condition of effective teaching—Players should obey the rules of the game—Many students are ill-behaved—Results of such behaviour.

Discipline means obedience to some general rules of conduct. It is essential in student life as it is the seedtime of life. A student should obey his parents and superiors at home and teachers in school. No institution can run successfully if its students are not disciplined. Effective teaching is not possible in the class if the students are not disciplined. Even the players should obey the rules of game in the playground. They must obey the orders of the captain or the referee of the game. So, at home, in school and in the playground too—discipline is essential. But it is a matter of pity and regret that some students are ill-behaved. They take it as a symbol of heroism. But a day will come when they will be grown up and the young ones will pay them back in their own coin and that also with compound interest!

## [30] STUDENTS AND SOCIAL SERVICE

**Write a Paragraph on 'Students and Social Service' with the help of the following information :**

> Man is a social being—Social service is a must in a system of man-making education—Kinds of social service—to remove illiteracy—to remove bad customs—to inform the poeple the laws of health and sanitation—to dig wells—to repair bad roads—to clean dirty ponds—Emergency relief work—To organise cultural functions—Fellow-feeling and organising capacity.

Man is a social being and social service is a must in a system of man-making education. There are so many kinds of social service and students have a lot of work to do in this field. They have some duties to remove illiteracy. They can hold night schools for the illiterate adults and give them lessons on the three R's. They can remove bad customs and inform the people of the laws of health and sanitation. They can dig wells, repair bad roads and clean dirty ponds. In times of emergency such as flood, famine and earthquake, they can take an active part in bringing relief to the sufferers. In times of normalcy they can organise cultural functions for the poor villagers as we know that poverty is depressing but drudgery is killing. It is true that the studies of students will be affected somewhat if they turn their attention to social service. But, on the whole, they will be gainer as social service will promote their fellow-feeling, increase their love for the country and develop their organising capacity.

## [31] TRAVELLING AS A PART OF EDUCATION

**Write a Paragraph on 'Travelling as a Part of Education' with the help of following outline :**

> Curiosity to see the unseen and to know the unknown—Educative value—Provides pleasure too—Breaks the monotony of life—A good training in the struggle of life.

To see the unseen and to know the unknown is inherent in human nature. And this curiosity leads men to travel from one place to another. Besides this, travelling has a great educative value. Books provide us with only bookish knowledge but travelling can make it perfect. It brings us into contact with different people and different ways of life. We read of the majesty of the Himalayas, the vastness of the ocean and the beauty of the Taj from books. But we can know much more of them if we see those with our own eyes. It makes Geography, History and some other subjects throbbing with life. Travelling gives us pleasure too. It breaks the monotony of life and fills the mind with joy. Moreover, travelling teaches us to bear hardship, and thus it is a good training for success in the struggle of life.

## [32] TICKETLESS TRAVELLING

**Make a Draft on 'Ticketless Travelling' :**

> The Railway Department invited all to think and join an Essay Competition on Ticketless Travelling. Join the competition and make a draft on the topic.

From time to time we read in the newspapers about people travelling by railway without tickets. They are fined or imprisoned for the offence. Ticketless travel has been increasing day by day. It has become a major crime in our society. In fact, it is an anti-social activity. When the ticketless travellers occupy seats in the compartment, the honest travellers who pay full fares are deprived of it and face a lot of troubles. The Railways are a Government undertaking. Its income is a part of our national income. So when a man travels without a ticket, he is actually stealing a part of the national income. The railway has an estimate of annual income. It has to cover the loss caused by ticketless travellers by raising railway fares. So ticketless travellers do harm to the honest travellers by causing the continuous rise in railway fare.

## [33] FAMILIARISING SCIENCE OR MAKING SCIENCE POPULAR

From the points given below write a Paragraph on the importance and need of 'Familiarising Science' :

> Science—Its blessings in different fields of our life—A new era—The spirit of Science—Its necessity—How best of it can be achieved.

This is an age of science. In every stage of our life today we depend on science. Science has blessed us with so many gifts. With the help of science man has become the master of the whole universe. In agriculture, commerce, industry, communication, household appliances, medicine, transport, entertainment—in all departments of life—science and technology have ushered us into a new era of hope and prosperity. But in spite of all these, has science really changed the basic attitude towards the problems of our life? Probably not. Superstitions, false notions and baseless beliefs predominate in many areas of our social and economic life. Therein comes the question of pupular science. We have to take science to every door and develop a scientific outlook in all of our deeds. Everyone must imbibe the spirit of science before enjoying the fruits of science. By familiarising science among the common people, we may bring in a new social order. Science must go deep within our social system and change our attitude from within and thus we can achieve the best of science.

## [34] IMMUNIZATION WORLDWIDE

Develop the information given in the following chart and write a Paragraph comparing the Immunization Programme in different continents :

**PERCENTAGE OF WORLD'S CHILDREN IMMUNIZED IN THE FIRST YEAR OF LIFE**

| | BCG | DPT | POLIO | MEASLES |
|---|---|---|---|---|
| Africa | 34% | 24% | 21% | 42% |
| America | 53% | 58% | 71% | 39% |
| South-East Asia | 24% | 33% | 14% | 1% |
| Europe | 77% | 76% | 81% | 74% |

BCG (**B**acillus **C**almette-**G**uerin) immunizes against Tuberculosis (TB).
DPT immunizes against **D**iphtheria, **W**hoo**P**ing Cough and **T**etanus.

The worldwide immunization programmes are brought about to prevent some dreadful diseases. The children of the world are expected to be immunized against six common infant diseases—Tuberculosis, Diphtheria, Whooping Cough, Tetanus, Polio and Measles. The percentage of world's children immunized in the first year of life is different in different continents. From the above chart it is clear that Europe is the continent with the most developed immunization programme. Next is the position of America. South-East Asia has the least developed programmes. Africa stands a bit higher than that, except only in DPT. All the diseases deserve more attention to be immunized—especially in South-East Asia and Africa. But Polio deserves the most attention world-over.

### [35] COMPUTERS IN VILLAGES

Write a paragraph on 'Computers in Villages' with the help of the following chart :

> Computer, an indipensable tool—Wide range of activities—Efficient data storage and recovery—Is it relevant to rural economy?—Advantages for farmers, village artisans and Gram Panchayets—Accurate information about day-to-day weather and the market condition.

Computers are becoming an indispensable tool in the modern society. Now it is engaged in a wide range of activities—from railway reservations to the operation theatre. Computers help difficult things to be done in quick and accurate ways. They allow the scope for efficient data storage, transfer and recovery. But some persons doubt whether they are relevant for a village economy. Would it be really effective for farmers, village artisans, Gram Panchayets and other village folk to invest in such a sophisticated technology as a computer? We can say that computers once connected to the internet can allow farmers to get quick and accurate information about the day-to-day weather and the market conditions of their products. The village artisans too would be able to collect information about the potential markets. They can also use the internet to show their special talents and capabilities. Other village folk can also take the help of the internet to find and create suitable opportunities. The Gram Panchayets similarly can receive and transmit relevant information from the State and Central government to the people. Of course, all of these require a lot of enterprise and enthusiasm, from among the villagers and from the Central and the State governments. Hopefully, over the years, our country have been striving to achieve these goals.

## AUTOBIOGRAPHY

### [36] AUTOBIOGRAPHY OF A RUPEE

I am an old one-rupee coin and have been passing a busy life for many, many years. Now I have become worn and the lettering on my back has been almost faded out with rough use. But still I can remember my birth when I was issued from the Mint. Then I was shining and the lettering on my back was very distinct. I was then very proud of my smart appearance. However, my active life began when I was paid over the counter of a bank, along with other coins and notes, to a gentleman. I was jingling in his pocket, but I did not stay there for long as he gave me to a shop-keeper. Next I came to a little girl when she bought a dot pen from the shop and got me as the balance of a five-rupee note. She exclaimed, "Ah! I have not seen a new coin for a pretty long time." She brought me home and kept me in her drawer with a lot of other coins. There I found a number of rupees of my own rank, but none so new and bright as I was. I began to hate them as they were dull and worn. At this, most of the coins became jealous, but one very old rupee was kind to me. He advised me that I should honour old rupees too as a rupee is always a rupee, however old and worn. I can't remember when I came out of the drawer and began to pass over to a new master and then again to another; but I feel it is better to roll and to be worn than to be locked up in the strong-box of a miser.

## DO IT YOURSELF

### [1] YOUR NATIVE VILLAGE

Try to answer the following questions and with the help of them write a Paragraph on 'Your Village'. Fill in the blanks to make it a Complete Paragraph :

What is the name of your village? Where is it situated? How long and how broad is it? Is there any metalled road? Are there cornfields around your village? How many people live in your village? What are their occupations? Is there any arrangement of daily market? Is there any primary school? Is there any post office? Is there any college? Is there any special attraction? How do you feel for your village?

The name of our village is ........... It is a small quiet village in the district of ........ It is about .........long and ........... broad. A metalled road.........(run) by the side of it and buses and lorries ply on the road. There ........... large green cornfields around our village. The population of our village ......... about............ Most of them ........... farmers. There ........... doctors and teachers too. A daily market is held in the morning in the market place where we ......... all the necessary things. We ........... also a Primary School, a High School, a Post office, and a Degree college in our village. But the special object of pride of our village is ........... I am very proud of being a son of such a village.

## [2] YOUR SCHOOL

Fill in the blanks and make it a complete Paragraph :

The name of our school is ......... It is one of the most reputed schools in the district of ........ in West Bengal. It was established in ............ It is a ........ building. There are ......... classrooms, a library room, a teacher's ........... and the Headmaster's room. There is a large playground ........ our school where the students ........ when they get time for that. There are ......... pupils and ......... teachers in our school. The teachers ........ well-qualified. They teach us ......... They are good and loving. We ........ our teachers like our parents. The results of our school ........ satisfactory. We are proud ........ such a school of high reputation.

## [3] THE SCHOOL LIBRARY

Write a Paragraph on 'The School Library' with the help of the given keywords or outlines. Fill in the blanks to make it a Complete Paragraph.

Textbooks only are not sufficient—Books in a library—Mighty minds of old—Journals and periodicals—Current knowledge—Essential part of the school—Conclusion.

The library........... an important role in a school. No ideal school can run without a good library. The few books which we ........ as texts in our classes ........ not sufficient for our mental food. To widen our knowledge and to broaden our outlook, we ........ many other useful books. A school library helps us here. In the library we ........ (come across) 'the mighty minds of old'. Moreover, by ........ (read) journals and periodicals we can ........ (know) how the world ........ (move) around us. Books also provide us with joy. They comfort us in sorrow and cheer us up in distress. They ........ our never-failing friends. A well-stocked and properly organised library ........ therefore an essestial part of a school. In the words of Carlyle—"A true university of these days is a library of books".

## [4] YOUR FAVOURITE PLAYER

Write a Paragraph on 'Your Favourite Player' with the help of the following outlines :

Name of your favourite player—Various new records—Records of highest Test centuries—total highest runs in Test cricket—The technique and temperament—A run-machine—One of the best gems in the field of world cricket.

My favourite player is ......... He ......... one of the greatest cricketers of the world and as a batsman he is a class by himself. He is......... (love) by all for his bright performance. He always ......... to enjoy himself in making various new records. He .........(have) the records of ......... and so on. The sound technique and temperament which ......... the key of success of a cricketer ...... fully present in him. He ......... (regard) as a run-machine by the critics of cricket. Most of his strokes ......... (be) of copy-book style. He surpasses anybody else except Bradman in score and in style of batting. He gives pleasure and gets pleasure in ......... (play) the game. For all these reasons I ......... (think) him as one of the best gems in the field of the world cricket.

### [5] MOTHER TERESA

Write a Paragraph on 'Mother Teresa' with the help of the following information-chart.

**Year and place of birth** : Born on 26 August in 1910 at Skopje, a small village in Yugoslavia. Parents Albanian

**Earlier name** : Agnes Gonxhas Bojaxhin.

**Arrival in India** : Came to India in 1928 as a nun and thereafter an Indian citizen—Albanian by chance, Indian by choice.

**First activities in Kolkata** : A teacher in a Loretto Convent school.

**Later activities** : 'Nirmal Hriday' at Kalighat, the shelter of the sufferers—various other activities all over the world.

**Recognition of her work** : Nobel Prize in 1979, 'Bharat Ratna Award' in 1980, 'Angel of Peace' on her visit to African countries.

**Death** : 5th September 1997

Mother Teresa .........another dedicated soul like Sister Nivedita. Both of them ...... (be) originally foreigners but ......... (make) this country their home. Teresa ......... born of Albanian parents on 26 August in 1910 at Skopje, a small village in Yugoslavia. Her earlier name ......... was .......... At eighteen she decided to ......... (become) a nun and so she .........(come) to India in 1928 and thereafter she ......... (become) an Indian citizen. Thus, though she was Albanian by chance, she ......... (become) an Indian by choice. She ......... (start) her life in Kolkata as a teacher in Loretto Convent school, but soon her motherly feelings ......(cry) for the sufferings of the poor and the downtrodden. On the 10th September 1946, while ......... (go) to Darjeeling, she ......... (decide) to ...... (leave) the convent in order to .........(serve) the poor. She went on her heels to the slums of the city. Her 'Nirmal Hriday' at Kalighat ......... (become) the shelter of the sufferers. Her activities have now been ......... (spread) all over the world. In 1979 she was ......... (award) the Nobel Prize for Peace. She ......... (obtain) 'Bharat Ratna Award' in 1980. On her visit to African countries she was ......... (receive) as 'Angel of Peace'. Her selfless service for mankind irrespective of caste and creed ......... unforgettable. She ......... (breath) her last ......... 5th September ......... the year 1997. We ......... (mourn) her death as a loss for humanity.

### [6] SATYAJIT RAY—THE FAMOUS FILM DIRECTOR

Write a Paragraph on Satyajit Ray with the help of the following points :

**Name** : Satyajit Ray

**Date of birth** : May 2, 1921

Parentage : Father Sukumar Ray, Mother Suprabha Devi
Name of the newborn baby : Prasad
Nickname : Manik
Father's death : In 1923, at the age of about 36; Manik was only 2 then.
Education : Admitted to Class VI in Ballygunge Govt. High School, passed Matriculation Exam. in 1936, Graduation from Presidency College in 1940, Art education at Santiniketan.
Film world : 'Pather Panchali' was released in 1955 and awarded President's Gold Medal and 12 international awards. 'Aparajita' in 1956, 'Apur Sansar' in 1959, 'Mahanagar' in 1963, 'Charulata' in 1964, 'Gupi Gain Bagha Bain' in 1969, 'Ashani Sanket' in 1972 and 'Sonar Kella' in 1974. Last film 'Agantuk' in 1991.
Awards : 'Padma Bhushan' in 1965, 'Magsaysay' in 1967, 'Padma Bibhushan' in 1976, highest award of France 'Lajiyan De Nar' (Legion of Honour) awarded by Mitterand, the President of France. 'Oscar' by the Academy of Motion Pictures, U.S.A. in 1992. 'Bharat Ratna' in the same year.

Satyajit Ray, the world famous film director ...... born on May 2, 1921. His father Sukumar Ray......... a famous poet in juvenile literature and his mother Suprabha Devi ......... a strong-willed lady. The name of the newborn baby was ......... but afterwards he was ......... (name) Satyajit. His nickname was ......... and really he was a jewel among so many Indian pebbles. His father ...... (die) a premature death at the age of about 36 in 1923. Manik was ......... then. He was ......... (admit) to Class VI in Ballygunge Govt. High School in 1932 and ......... (pass) Matriculation Exmination in 1936. He ......... (pass) B.A. Exam. from Presidency College in 1940. Satyajit Ray ......... a man of versatile genius. He ...........(get) Art education at Santiniketan in 1940. A good many memorable films ........... (release) under his direction. Among them 'Pather Panchali' ......... in 1955 and he ......... (get) the honour of President's Gold Medal and 12 international awards. The other two of the trilogy 'Aparajita' and 'Apur Sansar' ......... released in 1956 and 1959, respectively. His 'Mahanagar' ......(release) in 1963 and 'Charulata' in 1964. His 'Gupi Gain Bagha Bain'...... (come) in 1969, 'Ashani Sanket' in 1972 and 'Sonar Kella' in 1974. His last film 'Agantuk' ......... in 1991. He ......... (honour) with so many awards in our country and abroad. He was ......... (award) ......... in 1965 and ......... in 1967. He was awarded ......... in 1976. The highest award of the film world 'Oscar' was ......... (award) by the Academy of Motion Pictures, U.S.A., in 1992. He ......... (obtain) 'Bharat Ratna' in the same year. He ......... (breath) his last on the 23rd April in 1992. We pay our heartiest homage to this world-famous master-artist.

## [7] DIGNITY OF LABOUR

Write a Paragraph on 'Dignity of Labour' with the help of the following hints :

Usefulness of manual labour—wrong idea of our educated people about it—position of manual labour in the society—dignity of labour should be recogniszed.

Labour is of two types—manual and mental. Each ......... of labour should ...... dignity of its own. But unfortunately, most of our ......... persons have a ......... idea about ......... We should know that ......... labour is at the root of our livelihood. The food, drink, clothes and houses without which we cannot ........., are all the gifts of .........

labour. Manual workers are thus the ......... of a nation. But many people ......... that ......... labour is not dignified. This ......... notion should be changed. The dignity of ......... is specially important in the context of the economic realities in any country. It may be a ......... means of combating the problem of unemployment. In fact, no government can ........... employment to all the ......... youths. Hence self-reliance and dignity of labour may be the only reasonable way to ......... the problem of unemployment. We should always keep in ......... "Work is worship". And in this way the dignity of ......... should be ......... in its due importance.

### [8] THE HANDICAPPED AND THEIR PROBLEMS

Write a paragraph on 'The Handicapped and their Problems' with the help of the follwing hints :

> Different kinds of the handicapped—must not be looked down upon—should be given enough opportunity to be employed in society—philanthropic organizations—role of the government—sympathetic outlook.

In our ......... there are many handicapped or disabled persons. Some of them are physically born-handicapped and some others are ......... retarded. There are others who have ......... limbs or sense organs on account of an attack of some deseases, accidents, etc. In this or ......... way, they are deprived ......... the pleasure of enjoying a normal life. So we must not look ......... upon these persons as social burdens. They must be ......... to face life boldly and to feel that life still holds charm for them. They can be ......... employed in various craft and vocations befitting ......... them. They can ......... great success if they are given ......... opportunity. We can take the example of Helen Keller who was blind, deaf and dumb but ......... a new horizon for the blind. It is our sacred duty to ......... suitable works for them and give them special training to rehabilitate with dignity in our society.

### [9] FREEDOM OF THE PRESS

Write a paragraph on 'Freedom of the Press' with the help of the follwing outlines :

> The press is a public forum—freedom of press is essential in democracy—abuses of freedom cause great harm.

"Newspaper is the people's parliament". The newspaper or the press is a ......... forum, and it plays a ......... role in democracy. The press safeguards the democratic ......... of the people and, therefore, it should be bold enough to say what is wrong and what is ......... It should bring to the public view the acts of injustice, oppression and maladministration. It should ......... the grievances of the people and criticise the authorities for their failure. And in this way, it becomes the vital organ to form the public ......... . Like the judiciary it should have an impertial outlook in ......... the news. Partial views and sensational ......... can do great harm to the nation. The press should, therefore, refrain ......... biased and distorted reportage in any way. However, the government should not impose censorship or curb the ......... of the press. At the same time, it should also be borne in mind that ......... is not the equivalent word of licence.

### [10] THE SCHOOL MAGAZINE

Write a Paragraph on 'The School Magazine' with the help of the following information-table :

> Role of the school magazine in school life—Different from a popular literary journal—Usually annual or bi-annual—The editor and the assistant editors—A training ground in literary composition—The first stepping stone for future writers—A link between the past and present students of the school.

The school magazine ........... (play) an important role in school life. It ........... different from a popular literary journal as it ........... (contain) mainly the articles of the school students. It ......... usually annual or bi-annual. The editor of the school magazine ......... a teacher and the assistant editors are always ......... (choose) from among the students. The magazine ......... (help) the students to express their feelings and thoughts. It ......... (stimulate) their imagination and ......... (develop) their creative powers. Thus it ......... (become) a training ground in literary composition and talents ........... (discover) even in most unexpected quarters. A student ........... (feel) proud and happy when he ......... (find) his writing in print. In fact, the school magazine ......... the first stepping stone for ......... Moreover, it ......... a link between the ......... students of the school. The ex-students can rightly ......... (remember) the school with all the happy memories of their childhood days when a copy of the school magazine ......... (reach) their hands.

## [11] LOAD-SHEDDING

**Write a Paragraph on 'Load-shedding' with the help of the following information :**

> Almost a daily occurrence—Condition of cinema, shops, factories, hospitals—Students before examination—Condition of the country—Necessity of measures for improvement.

Nowadays load-shedding ......... almost a daily occurrence in cities and suburbs. There ......... hardly any area which is not ......... (affect) by it. Cinema houses, shops, factories, hospitals are all ......... (affect) by it. The industrial units ......... (paralyse) for the time being. Operation ......... (stop) in hospitals for loadshedding. The students......... their books and ......... idly in darkness. They curse the authorities especially if electricity ......... (fail) before their exmination. In fact, load-shedding ........... a geat problem of our country. It should not be ......... (allow) to continue in the present manner. The whole country is bound to ......... (collapse) if the present condition of load-shedding is not ......... (improve). So the government should ......... over the matter deeply and ......... necessary steps to check it as early as possible.

## [12] YOUR AIM IN LIFE

**Write a Paragraph on 'Your Aim in Life' with the help of the folloiwng outlines :**

> What is the use of aim in life? What is your aim in life?—Reasons for choosing the aim—Motto in life.

Many people ......... no definite aim in life. They ......... like ships without rudders and without goals. So a man who......... (wish) to succeed in life must ......... (have) a definite aim in his life. My aim in life is to be a ......... It is a noble profession. But I have ......... (choose) it as my aim in life for more than one reason. More than eighty percent of people of our country ......... in villages. They ......... from various diseases for ignorance, poverty, malnutrition and want of proper sanitation. But the hospitals and the doctors........ very few in rural areas. Most of the doctors hanker after money and honour and they ........ (prefer) cities and towns to villages as their fields of practice. As a result many people in the rural area ...... like cats and dogs without proper treatment and medicine. For all these reasons I ......... to be a ......in my future life to serve the suffering humanity. My motto in life would be Vivekananda's immortal saying 'Service to man is service to God'

## EXERCISE

Write short Paragraphs on each of the following topics with the help of the following tables :

**1. A Visit to an Exhibition :**

Site of the exhibition—kinds of exhibits—qualities of exhibits—price—crowd—experience gathered by you.

**2. A Social Function in Your School :**

Date and time—decoration of the school building—enthusiasm among the students—participation of the students—audience—enjoyment—ending.

**3. Pavement-dwellers :**

City life—wealth and poverty side by side—pavement-dwellers at day-time—pavement-dwellers at night—remedy.

**4. Srinivasa Ramanujam :**

Date and place of birth—Dec. 22, 1887, at Erode in Tamil Nadu; parentage—Krippuswami Ayenger & Komalata Ammal— Matriculation from Kumbhakonam Town High School in 1903—F.A. appeared but did not come out successfully in 1907—Marriage with Janaki Ammal in 1909—To England for research work in Mathematics in 1914—Fellow of London Royal Society in 1918—Return from England with great name and fame—Death in April 26, 1920.

**5. Buddhism in Sri Lanka :**

The first confrontation of the Sinhalese king named Devanampiyatissa and Arhat Mahinda, the celebrated missionary of Buddhism in 306 B.C.—paved way for the establishment of Buddhism in Sri Lanka—the Arhat Mahinda, son of Emperor Asoka of India was then sent for this mission—brought with him the Theravada canon or orthodox Buddhism, regarded as the most ancient sect of Buddhism using the Pali language—preached the Buddha's teaching not only to rulers but also directly to common people—constant patronage of the succeeding king allowed Buddhism to flourish throughout the island —among those monasteries, the most outstanding one is the Mahavihara monastery, the historic centre of Theravada Buddhism in Sri Lanka.

**6. A religious festival : The Durga Puja :**

The greatest Hindu festival—preparation—the Puja days—decoration of the pandals and the gods and goddesses—people dressed in new garments—Vijaya Dashami—immersion.

**7. A Religious festival : The 'Muharram'/The 'Id' :**

A great Muslim festival—preparation—observance—communal harmony—significance of the day.

**8. The Most Memorable Day in Your Life :**

Date and time—description of the day—How were you involved? Why is it memorable?

**9. A Rainy Day :**

Beginning of the day—description of the heavy rainfall—condition of the roads—difficulties of the people—the school remains closed.

**10. The Game You Like Most :**

Name of the game—causes of preference—advantages and disadvantages—Is the game included in Asiad or Olympic?

**11. The Annual Sports :**

Date and place—duration—number of events—flat race, relay race, hurdle race, sum race, spoon race, high jump, long jump, discus throw, javeline throw etc.—the most interesting event—prizes—ending.

**12. The Cinema :**

What is it?—amusement—educative value—harmful sides—influence upon the young—influence upon the society—conclusion.

**13. A Football Match :**

Date and time—playground—participants—description of the game—results of the game.

**14. A Street Accident :**

Spot of the accident, date and time of the accident—casualties—eye-witness—reaction.

**15. Physical Education :**

What is it?—Utility of physical education—place of physical education in the syllabus—any suggestion for improvement.

**16. Work Education :**

What is it?—Utility of work educaiton—place of work education in the syllabus—any suggestion for improvement.

**17. Science in Daily Life :**

Comparison between the modern life and the life of our forefathers—gifts of science—electricity, newspaper, telephone, radio, T.V., trains, buses, trams—medicines—more and more mechanised civilization.

**18. Your Favourite Book :**

Name of the book—author of the book—qualities of the book—conclusion.

**19. Rocket Pad, Thumba :**

India's spacecraft—Collaboration with foreign countries—Necessity of a Rocket Pad—Where is Thumba?—activities—Success.

**20. Atomic Reactor, Trombay :**

Atomic Research of India—Where is Trombay?—Atomic power for war—Atomic power for peace—India's policy.

# 4 PRESENTING PROBLEMS AND SUGGESTING SOLUTIONS

## HOW TO PRESENT PROBLEMS AND SUGGEST SOLUTIONS?

Problems on a topic should be identified first. Next, Suggestions for the remedy should be categorized.

### [1] POLLUTION AND THE WAYS TO FIGHT IT

Here is a detailed information structure. With the help of it write a paragraph on 'Pollution and the ways to fight it' :

| | | | |
|---|---|---|---|
| Where ? | AIR | LAND | WATER |
| How ? | Factory smoke | Garbage | Untreated sewage |
| How to control ? | Controlling the haphazard growth of factories | Preserving wildlife and forest | Treating sewage |

In the beginning of the 21st century, one of our greatest problems is pollution. In our cities, the air is constantly being polluted by smoke from factories, and from carbon monoxide gases emitted by motor vehicles. Even the ground we walk on—in both urban and rural areas—is polluted by uncollected garbage. Water is also polluted, particularly as a result of untreated sewage. Also, oil tankers often clean out their tanks at sea. And power stations release hot water into rivers, which kills fish and plants. But we cannot remain idle in the face of such an alarming problem.

Steps must be taken to control the haphazard growth of industries. As the exhaust of automobiles is one of the major reasons of environmental pollution, we must take effective steps to control it. The best way to curb pollution is to plant trees and to take care of them. To maintain ecological balance, the wildlife must be preserved and the random felling of trees must be prevented. To fight against the pollution of water, sewage treatment plants must be built. We must see that industrial effluents are not released direct into the rivers. Above all, we must make peace with Nature. We must remember "Pollute and perish; preserve and flourish".

## [2] SOUND POLLUTION

| | |
|---|---|
| Problem : | Sound Pollution—a serious problem of our times—chasing us almost everywhere—schools, colleges etc. |
| How? | Indiscriminate use of microphones—bullying horns—film songs—crackers during religious & social festivals—slogans. |
| Response : | Effective control of loudspeakers—to make the people aware of the dangers of sound pollution—strict laws. |

Sound is a symptom of life. The existence of life is felt and perceived through the presence of sound. But loud and shrill sound creates a cacophony instead of a symphony. Of late, sound pollution has reached an alarming stage in human life. It is chasing us in almost every step of life. In schools, colleges, offices, and even in hospitals we often hear an explosion of deafening sound. The quietness of our life has totally vanished. Even within our homes sound has been chasing us. Many are the causes of this problem of sound pollution. Microphones blare out day in and day out. Film songs are played on cassette recorders at top volume even from the wayside betel shops! There are the aggressive bullying horns of automobiles. During social and religious festivals, crackers are burst indiscriminately and, as a result, the lives of the children and the aged persons as well as the examinees become miserable. Shouting of slogans also contributes not a little to sound pollution. One can even hear slogan-shouting in hospitals! The extent of sound pollution has already crossed the normal limits of human endurance. We have to pass strict laws to take effective steps against the misuse of microphones. Poeple must be made aware of the dangers of sound pollution. It is dangerous for patients suffering from heart diseases. In many cases it is responsible for deafness and psychological inbalance. Of late, judicial bodies are taking steps to control the sound pollution. However, everyone must cultivate the virtues of quietness in domestic as well as in public life.

## [3] DRUG ADDICTION

| | |
|---|---|
| Problem : | Drug addiction—a major problem of our society today. Many youngsters are falling victims to addiction. |
| How? | The rackets of unscruplous traders work underground— smuggling of narcotics continues unabated. Young men take to these drugs just to find a temporary pleasure. |
| Response : | The atrophy must be stopped—alarming nature of the problem must be focused on—the Government has set up anti-narcotic cells but there must be a large scale awakening of the people, especially the young generation. |

Drug addiction has now become one of the major problems of our society, particularly in the urban areas. Sometimes frustration and sometimes temptation are the cause of this addiction. Many youngsters are falling victims of this deadly curse. As a result, possibilities of these young men and women are being nipped in the bud. The dishonest traders operate underground and the deadly narcotics and drugs are smuggled into the country. It is really surprising to note that these traders manage to thrive at the cost of precious lives and rosy possibilities of our young generation. Many of these drug-addict crazy young men are tempted to continue these drugs. Once they take it, they are caught in a death trap. Slowly but surely they are led to death. But we have a duty to fight against this dangerous enemy of our social life. The alarming nature of the problem must be highlighted and people must be made aware of this evil with the help of the mass media. Seminars should be organised in schools and colleges. In West Bengal an anti-narcotic cell has been established in Lalbazar, Kolkata. Drug business is punishable and the highest punishment is death sentence in Bangladesh. But no Government action can be fruitful unless it is backed by a strong public opinion, especially of the young generation.

### [4] NATIONAL INTEGRATION

| | |
|---|---|
| Problem : | The country is in peril. The forces of disintegration have come to the surface. |
| How? | The foreign rulers had sown the seeds of disintegration in the country. External factors, regional imbalance. |
| Response : | Mass awakening, sharing of responsibilities by all sections of people, proper education. |

Vincent Smith described India as a picture of 'unity in diversity'. But at present the unity of the country is in peril. The forces of disintegration have come to the surface of our national life. The prolonged violence in Kashmir, communal riots in different parts of the country, lingual riots, agitation in West Bengal for Gorkhaland, terrorist movements in Assam, Tripura, Manipur, etc. are cruel blows to national integration. The 'Ramjanmabhumi-Babri Masjid' debate was a burning question a few years back. Illiteracy, narrow religious thinking, and regional imbalance are serious causes of this deep-rooted problem. The foreign rulers followed the policy of 'Divide and Rule' and had sown the seeds of discord. The separatist tendencies are at present very active in the country. But we must devote ourselves to preserve the unity of the country. No sacrifice is too great for the integration of the country. We must strive hard for the unity and integrity of the country. There must be a mass awakening and all sections of people must be aware to share their responsibility in this regard.

### [5] ILLITERACY—WAYS TO REMOVE

| | |
|---|---|
| Problem : | 35% people of the country illiterate. |
| Solution : | Govt. efforts necessary. Educated people and students should come forward to join literacy campaign. Holding night schools. TV, Radio, Computer, etc. as a mass media. |

Illiteracy is a social curse and it is the root of ignorance, superstition and backwardness. It prevents the people from marching ahead to set up an ideal social fabric. But unfortunately India is a country where over one-third (35%) of the population is deprived of minimum education. When such a vast section of our population remains ignorant, democracy becomes meaningless. Education makes a man conscious of his rights and duties in the society. It is the spirit that helps him to get rid of the foolish customs and superstititions.

It is the duty of every government to remove illiteracy from the grassroot level. But at the same time one must admit that the government alone will not be able to cope with the situation. It is the duty of every educated citizen to help in this matter. We, the students, should come forward with voluntary service and enable the illiterates to read and write. Students can do it easily by joining the literacy camps in their spare time. They can hold night schools for the illiterate adults and give them lessons on three R's. The emphasis should be given to the literacy of the womenfolk as well.

Thus the students have a dominant role in removing the deep-rooted problem of illiteracy in our country. TV, Radio, Computer, etc. may also play a vital role as a mass media in this concern.

## [6] CHILD LABOUR

| Problem : | (i) Child labour in mines, factories, shops, tea-stalls, etc.<br>(ii) household servants<br>(iii) want of proper food and clothing and education<br>(iv) extreme poverty of the parents |
|---|---|
| Solution : | Economic reform and spread of literacy. |

In recent times many campaigns have been organised against employing children in mines, factories, motor garages, shops, hotels, restaurants, tea-stalls, etc. But somehow lots of poor children working as household servants in middle class and upper class families have been overlooked. These children have to work like slaves round the clock. There are few households that allow their child-servant adequate food and clothing. They do not get any free time. They are deprived of even primary education! Their wages are paid to their parents and the money is rarely spent on them. No doubt, it is the extreme poverty of the parents that leads the children to adopt such humiliating means of wage-earning at a minor age.

For the solution of this problem we need not only strict laws, but also a thorough economic reform to reduce the poverty line. At the same time the spread of literacy is essential to wipe out this shameful practice still prevalent in our country.

## DO IT YOURSELF

1. **Here is a detailed information-chart. With the help of the information write on 'THE POLLUTION OF THE GANGA—Ways to Fight It' :**

| Situation : | The Ganga—the longest river of India (2,525 km)—the main stream of Indian civilization. |
|---|---|
| Problem : | The Ganga is being polluted—less than 4 milligrams of dissolved oxygen per litre of water in the Ganga (normal requirement 6 mg per litre). Contamination of drinking water—Fall in the growth of fish. The worst affected stretch from Bansberia to Birlapur in West Bengal. |

| | |
|---|---|
| **How?** | Untreated sewage of 48 Class I towns and 66 Class II towns on both sides of the Ganga—Industrial effluents (In Kanpur alone there are 70 industrial units). Throwing of junks and garbage. (In Benaras 6 crore litres of garbage thrown into the Ganga everyday). |
| **Response :** | Ganga Action Plan has been formed. It sanctioned Rs. 37 crores recently for West Bengal. People must be made aware. |

### THE POLLUTION OF THE GANGA—WAYS TO FIGHT IT

The Ganga is the longest river of India ...... (cover) 2,525 km. But it is more than a river. It is the main stream of this riverine Indian civilization. For centuries the Ganga ......... (promote) trade, commerce, transport and ......... (help) the economic, social and cultural progress of the country. But unfortunately at present this major river of India ......... (pollute). In some areas the measure of dissolved oxygen is ......... than four milligrams per litre, whereas the minimum ......... is six milligrams per litre. The stretch of the river from ......... to ......... in West Bengal is worst ......... (pollute). As a result, there is a fall in the growth of fish. There ......... 48 Class I towns and 66 Class II towns on both sides of the Ganga. The untreated sewage of all these towns ......... (release) into the Ganga. Moreover, the industrial effluents ......... also ......... for the ......... of the Ganga. In Kanpur alone, there ...... seventy industrial units. The effluents of all these mills and factories ......... (release) into the Ganga everyday. Last but not the least is the throwing of junks. In Benaras 6 crore litres of garbage ......... (throw) everyday in the Ganga. All these factors ...... responsible ......... the pollution. So we have to work out a systematic programme for ......... (control) the pollution of the Ganga. It is fortunate that the Ganga Action Plan ......... (formulate) by the Central Ganga Authority. About 37 crore rupees recently for ......... (control) the pollution of the Ganga in West Bengal. It ......... (propose) that sewage plants would be ......... (set up) where the sewage would be ......... (treat) and converted into fertilisers. This would control the pollution considerably. But everyone must be aware ......... his responsibility.

2. **From the information chart given below write a paragraph on "HOUSING PROBLEM—Ways to Solve It" :**

| | |
|---|---|
| **Problem :** | Actute shortage of houses—one of the major problems of our national life. |
| **How ?** | The cost of construction is very high. Shortage of raw materials. In rural areas houses with mud walls and thatched roof are often damaged by heavy rains and fire. |
| **Response :** | Reducing the cost and saving in the consumption of materials —successful techniques—experimental housing schemes of the National Building Organisation—cost reduction of large scale housing projects as well as houses in rural areas. |

### HOUSING PROBLEM—WAYS TO SOLVE IT

Housing is one of the major......... of our country today. Thousands of people in big cities......... (dwell) on the footpath. In rural areas also there ......... an acute shortage of houses. The problem of housing ......... (aggravate) by the rising price of the raw materials. The cost of construction ......... (go) up everyday and at present it is very difficult for the common people to .........(afford) the cost of construction. In rural areas most of the houses......... (build) with mud walls and thatched roofs. These are often ......... (damage) by heavy rains and fire. Every year thousands of people .........(remain) homeless in rural areas because mud houses collapse on account of heavy rain and consequent flood. The National Building Organisation ......... (evolve) experimental housing schemes to reduce the cost of ......... and to save the consumption of materials. These are also ........... (design) to reduce the cost of large scale housing projects as well as to adopt new techniques for construction of houses in rural areas. Techniques are in progress for water ......... (proof) of mud walls. Methods are also being ......... (work out) for making the roofs of the house fireproof. Maximum stress should be ......... (lay) on proper utilization of indigenous raw materials.

## EXERCISE

**Q. From the given information charts write paragraphs on the concerned problems and suggest a title to each :**

**1. Problem :** **AFFORESTATION**—Fast disappearance of the green in urban and rural areas.

**How ?** Large scale deforestation—rapid urban development—lack of awareness—excessive greed—active gangs engaged in cutting trees.

**Response :** Fast growing trees—such plants now being distributed by different agencies including Central and State Governments—awareness among people—responsibilities.

**2. Problem :** **DOWRY**—series of deaths—of homicide, suicide, etc.—in different parts of the country.

**How ?** Age-old beliefs—male chauvinism—passive roles of ladies—lack of stiff opposition by socio-political leaders.

**Response :** Mass protest—specially by educated men and women—Laws alone are not sufficient—creating a social atmosphere.

**3. Problem :** **TRAFFIC PROBLEM IN KOLKATA**

**How ?** Infrequent service of buses—breakdowns—number of buses less than adequate—late running of trains—other modes of transport also not satisfactory.

**Response :** To increase the number of buses—to improve the condition of roads in order to improve the maintenance of buses—special measures to tackle the over-crowding during peak hours—the Metro and the Circular Railways to help the rush of passengers—improvement of railway services to help the daily commuters.

4. Problem : **SHORT SUPPLY OF KEROSENE**—long queue for a litre of kerosene.

How ? Irregular supply of kerosene—hoarders hold the article for raising prices—available in open market on payment of higher rates.

Response : Distribution system should be effectively improved—Fair price shops should be opened—consumers' cooperative societies may be engaged—in villages kerosene should be supplied at a subsidised rate for the students.

5. Problem : **HAWKERS**—encroaching the pavements—give rise to serious inconvenience to the pedestrians.

How ? Actue scarcity of employment opportunities—number of hawkers increasing everyday—no regard for civic laws—expanding markets near railway stations to meet the needs of the daily commuters.

Response : The hawkers should be provided with alternative accommodation—the pedestrians cannot be exposed to injuries—in many areas hawkers enjoy political protection—this must be stopped —we must think of the greatest good of the greatest number.

6. Problem : **HANDICAPPED** or **DISABLED PERSONS** in our society.

How ? Some are born with handicaps—sometimes these are caused by accidents—injury to workers in factories.

Response : Person's/child's role—role of the parents and other members of the society—self-sufficiency and mental courage of the handicapped—social outlook—sympathy or indifference—role of the Government.

7. Problem : **PRICE RISE**

Causes : Artificial shortage of foodgrains—black-marketeers and hoarders—fall in food supply—population growth.

Effect : Sufferings of the common people—daily wage-earners the worst affected—daily necessaries getting costly—cost of living rises—antisocial activities on the increase.

Solution : Drive agaisnt dishonest businessmen—strict laws—buyers' resistance—'Grow More Food' campaign.

8. Problem : **BASIC HUMAN NEED**

Causes : Poverty to provide food, clothing and shelter—want of proper sanitation and treatment in illness.

Solution : Planning for economic reform and to actualise it—scope of earning wages and self-help employment—special stress on the projects in villages and slum areas in cities.

**9.** Problem : **HORN-HAPPY DRIVERS DRIVE CITY DEAF**

Causes : Unnecessary use of powerful vehicular air horns the main source of noise pollution—horns from a close range causes accidents.

Solution : Hydraulic horns should be banned—Private vehicles with two powerful horns should not be allowed—No noise and no horn in 'silent zones'.

**10.** Problem : **USE OF PLASTIC BAGS AND CUPS**

Causes : Plastic materials are non-biodegradable—lead to the blocking of sewage system—lead to poisoning of food—risk of children being choked to death while playing with plastic bags.

Solution : Say 'No' to the plastic cups and plastic bags.

# 5  RETELLING STORIES

## HOW TO WRITE A STORY?

Give a title to the story preferably Capitalised. Make out full sentences from the hints or outlines and add some sentences to the outlines. Use the Past Tense of the verbs. You may use a short dialogue within the story to make it natural and interesting. Add a moral, if any, at the end of the story.

**Stories are of different categories :**

**(i)** **Stories of eminent persons** : Interesting incidents of the celebrities.

**(ii)** **Folk tales** : Folk tales are popular stories handed down from generation to generation. They often have a moral.

**(iii)** **Fables** : Fables are short tales—usually with animal characters—and they aways have a moral.

**(iv)** **Stories describing real life and experience : Modern short stories deal with such real life experience :**

In this lesson there are stories of different categories. Read the stories and find out for yourself which categories they belong to. You may have morals in the stories.

### [1] NEWTON AND HIS DOG

Newton, a great scientist—Diamond, a little pet dog—heaps of paper on the table—a lighted candle on the table—Diamond jumped on the table—papers caught fire—Newton patted the dog.

Sir Isaac Newton was a great scientist. He had a little dog named Diamond. One day he went out of his room leaving his little dog asleep before the fire. For twenty years he was hard at work, studying a most difficult subject. On the table lay a heap of papers on which he had put down the findings of his research of twenty years. When his master left the room, little Diamond woke up, jumped on the table and overturned the lighted candle. The papers at once caught fire. Just when the papers had been completely burnt, Newton opened the door of the room. He saw that the fruits of his twenty years' labours had been turned into a heap of ashes. There stood Diamond, the cause of all this mischief. Almost any other man would have killed the dog on the spur of the moment. But Newton patted the dog on the head with kindness, although his heart was full of grief. He said, "O Diamond! Diamond! thou little knowest what mischief you have done." Then he patiently set to work again.

**Moral : Patience is the strength of character.**

## [2] KING CANUTE AND HIS COURTIERS

King Canute's courtiers often flattered him—one day they said that the sea would obey him—the king took them to the sea-shore—commanded the sea to stop but to no effect—reaction.

There was a great king named Canute. His courtiers often flattered him. One day his courtiers said, "Your Majesty, you have endless power. Even Nature obeys you. If you command the sea to stop, it will stop.' King Canute disliked such flattery and wanted to teach them a good lesson. He went to the sea-shore with his courtiers and took his seat on a chair there. The sea was rough and the waves were rolling on. The king commanded, "O sea, stop there and do not move forward." But the waves rolled on as before and drenched their clothes. Then the king turned towards his courtiers and said, "Don't flatter like this. Remember that God alone is all-powerful who can stop the sea. But no man can do this." The courtiers felt ashamed of this and gave up their flattery.

**Moral : Flattery is meanness.**

## [3] THE ENGLISH SAILOR AND THE CAGED BIRDS

An English sailor became a prisoner in France—returned home after the war—bought cages full of birds—set them free—the birdseller was surprised.

In a war with France an English sailor became a prisoner. He was confined in prison for several years. When the war came to an end, he was set free. He came to his homeland and felt very happy. One day when he visited a bird-shop in the market, he bought all the cages full of birds. He opened all the cages one after another and set all the birds free. The bird-seller was surprised to see the strange act of the man. He asked him, "Why have you spent so much money for nothing?" The man replied, "When I was a prisoner of war, I always longed to be free and see my near and dear ones. So I can feel the miserable condition of the birds. I have, therefore, spent a little money to set them free."

**Moral : Freedom is more valuable than anything else.**

## [4] A CLEVER JUDGE

A man lost his purse—complained to a judge—judge gave each servant of the man a stick—asked them to appear before him next day with their sticks—he said that the thief's stick would be longer by an inch—the thief was detected and sent to jail.

One day a rich man lost his purse. He thought that the purse had been stolen by one of his servants, but he could not detect the actual thief. Then he made a complaint before a judge. The judge summoned all the servants but all of them denied the charge. The judge then hit upon a plan to detect the thief. He gave all of them sticks of equal length and asked them to submit the sticks on the following day. He also told that the stick of the thief will increase an inch by the magic touch of his judgment-stick at that time. All the servants went home and kept their sticks as it was. But the servant who stole the purse reduced the length of his stick by an inch. Next day when all the servants submitted their sticks to the judge, one stick was found shorter by an inch and the thief was easily detected and sent to jail.

**Moral : One cannot hide one's misdeed by tricks.**

### [5] THE KING AND THE SPIDER

A king was defeated by his enemies six times—hid himself in a cave—A spider failed six times to climb up the roof of the cave—it succeeded at the seventh attempt—the king was inspired—fought against the enemies for the seventh time—became successful.

There was a king who lost his kingdom being defeated by his enemies. He wished to regain his kingdom at any cost. He collected troops and made as many as six attempts to drive away the enemies. But by irony of fate he was defeated each and every time. He then hid himself in a cave. One day when he was lying in the cave in a pensive mood, he saw a spider tyring to climb up to the ceiling of the cave. But it failed six times and succeeded the seventh time. The king was inspired by this and he fought against the enemies for the seventh time. This time he became successful and regained his lost kingdom.

**Moral : Endeavour with Patience is the mother of success.**

### [6] A TAILOR AND A MAGICIAN

A tailor regretted that he knew only one trade—A magician boasted of his hundred tricks—A famine came—The magician suffered—the tailor still lived by his honest means.

Once a tailor and a magician met together and talked on various topics. The tailor talked of his poverty and said, "I know only one trade. If this trade fails, I am undone."

"I pity you, my friend," said the magician, "but things are not so bad with me. If one trick fails, I have a hundred tricks more to help me."

"You are very lucky," said the tailor.

"Don't envy," replied the magician, "If a bad time should ever come to you, just tell me and I'll help you."

Days in and days out and a bad year of famine did really come and people suffered horribly. The tailor still lived by his honest means as people could not go without clothing. But the magician with his hundred tricks could find no customer as people had no penny for that. He moved about promising to eat fire or to vomit pins but still none cared for him.

At last in extreme misery the magician came one day to the poor tailor and said, "Friend, my pride has been humbled. Give me something to eat if you can. I am starving."

**Moral : Honest profession is more precious than a hundred tricks.**

### [7] A DISHONEST SHOP-KEEPER

A dishonest shop-keeper gives under-weight—when asked, he says, "You have to carry less load." A clever customer pays less and says, "You have to count less."

In a market there was a dishonest shop-keeper. He used to give underweight to every customer. One day a clever customer was determined to pay him back in his own tricks. He went to the shop and wanted one kilo of rice. The shop-keeper gave him under-weight as usual. The customer asked him why he had given such under-weight. The shop-keeper replied "Brother, why are you so angry? I have given you under-weight so that you'll have to carry less load." The clever customer remained silent for a while and paid him less than his dues. The shop-keeper asked, "Why have you paid me less?" The customer replied, "I have paid you less so that you may have to count less." Thus the dishonest shop-keeper was paid back in his own coin.

**Moral : Dishonesty is paid by its own coin.**

### [8] HIDDEN TREASURE

> A farmer had two lazy sons—he hit upon a plan—a hidden treasure in the field—the field was dug up and planted—golden corn came out.

A farmer had two sons. They were very lazy. They would never do any work. The farmer did not know how to make them busy. He thought and thought and on his death-bed hit upon a plan. He called his sons to his bedside and said, 'My sons, go to the yonder field. I have laid a hidden treasure there. Dig the field and you'll find it."

The boys ran to the field at once. They worked very hard and dug up all the field. But they found no treasure anywhere. They said to themselves, "Why should we leave the field all dug up? We may plant some corn here."

So they planted the field with corn. In due course golden corn came out and the sons became very happy. They now understood the meaning of the hidden treasure as told by their father.

**Moral : Honest labour is really the hidden treasure.**

### [9] WHO IS TO BELL THE CAT?

> Mice cause mischief in a house—the master of the house brings a cat—the mice are in difficulty—they hold a meeting—one of them proposes to tie a bell round the cat's neck—"Who is to bell the cat?" asks an old mouse.

In a big house there lived a large number of mice. They were doing a lot of mischief there. The master of the house was very much annoyed and made a plan to get rid of them. He brought a cat to kill the mice. The mice were in great difficulty. They could not move freely as before. They held a meeting to discuss the matter and find a way to come out of this danger. Several proposals were made, but none of the proposals was practical. At last a young mouse rose to speak. He said, "I have a good plan for your consideration. Let us tie a bell round the cat's neck. Then we shall always hear him coming and hide ourselves in time." All the mice thanked the young mouse for his plan. But an old mouse stood up and said, "No doubt, the idea is good. But pray, who is to bell the cat?" At this all remained silent as there was none to bell the cat!

**Moral : It is easy to say but hard to do.**

### [10] TWO CATS AND A MONKEY

> Two cats steal a cake—they quarrel over their share—they ask a monkey for two equal divisions of the cake—cats are deceived.

Two cats lived in a house. Once they stole a piece of cake. They could not decide how to divide the cake between themselves. So they began to quarrel over the share. At last they came to a monkey and asked him to make two equal divisions of the cake. The clever monkey took the opportunity to deprive them of the thing. So he began to weigh the cake after breaking it into two parts. Each time he put the unequal portions on the scale and bit a part of it to make them equal. Thus he ate up the entire cake. In this way the two cats were befooled by the monkey and went away.

**Moral : Quarrels create the advantage for a third person.**

## [11] THE GOLDEN GOOSE

A man had a goose—it laid a golden egg every morning—the man's wife wanted all the eggs at a time—she cut the goose's belly—lost the goose as well as the eggs.

A man had a goose. It was not a usual one as it laid one golden egg evey morning. Each egg brought the man quite a fair amount of money and he soon became rich. But his wife was not satisfied with this. She was very much greedy. She thought, "The goose has quite a number of golden eggs in its womb. Why should we not receive all the eggs at a time?" So she asked the man to do so. But the man did not agree with her. One day when the man was out of his house, his greedy wife brought a sharp knife, took hold of the goose and cut open its belly. The goose died at once. Thus the foolish woman lost the goose as well as the prospect of golden eggs.

**Moral : Grasp all, lose all.**

## [12] A FOX AND A GOAT

A fox fell into a well—a goat came—the fox invited him to drink sweet water—the goat jumped down—the fox leaped on its horns and got out of the well.

Once a thirsty fox happened to fall into a well. He tried his best to get out of it but in vain. After a while a goat came there for a drink. As the goat peeped in, he saw the fox inside the well.

"What are you doing there at the bottom of the well?" asked the goat. The cunning fox was glad to see the goat and at once made a plan. He invited the goat and said, "My friend, this well is famous for its sweet water. I have jumped in and I'm drinking to my heart's content. If you want a taste of it yourself, please jump into it."

Without a second thought the foolish goat jumped into the well. The fox at once leaped on the goat's back, then on to his long horns and got out of the well. Before leaving the place he looked back into the well and said, "Foolish goat, look before you leap."

**Moral : Look before you leap.**

## [13] TWO FRIENDS AND A BEAR

Two friends travelling together met a bear—one jumped up a tree—another lay down like a dead man—the bear smelt his nose and ears and took him to be a dead man—then left the place.

Once two friends were passing through a forest. The forest was full of ferocious animals and the two friends were very much frightened. But they promised to stand by each other in danger. Suddenly they saw a bear coming towards them. One of them knew how to climb up a tree. He at once climbed a tree and hid himself. The other man, finding no other alternative, fell flat on the ground and held his breath, pretending to be dead. The bear came up to him and smelt his nose and ears and face, took him to be a dead man, and left the place.

When the bear was gone, the man on the tree came down and said, "Thank God that you are saved. But friend, I saw the bear put its mouth very close to your ear. Did it say anything to you?"

The friend replied, "Yes, the bear told me not to trust a friend who left me in my danger to seek his own safety."

**Moral : A friend in need is a friend indeed.**

## [14] A TIGER AND A LAMB

A lamb was drinking water in a stream—a wolf came there to drink—the wolf wanted to eat the lamb—he said that the lamb was muddying the water though the lamb was drinking downstream—the wolf said that the lamb abused him one year back—the lamb said that he was not born then—the wolf said that it was his father—he killed the lamb.

One day a wolf came to a stream for a drink and found a sweet little lamb drinking in the same stream. The wolf thought of killing the lamb and eating its flesh. So he began to pick a quarrel with the lamb. He shouted, "You rogue, how dare you make the water dirty for me?" The lamb began to tremble in fear. He said, "Excuse me, sir, how can I make the water dirty for you? You are drinking upstream and I am drinking down." The wolf could say nothing to that but shouted, "Oh, I remember, you called me bad names last year about this time."

"How can that be, sir?" said the lamb meekly, "I was not even born then." But the wolf paid no heed to his reply. He growled angrily, "Then it must have been your father. And it makes no difference whether it was you or your father." So saying he sprang upon the poor lamb and ate him up.

**Moral : A tyrant never wants a plea.**

## [15] A GRASSHOPPER AND AN ANT

A hungry grasshopper in winter—hopped to an ant—begged grains of corn—"Why did you not store in summer?" asked the ant—"I sang", replied the grasshopper—"Now dance", said the ant.

It was winter. A grasshopper was hungry. He had no food. One day he saw an ant passing by. He hopped to the ant who had stored some grains for the winter. "I'm dying from hunger", said the grasshopper with folded wings and prayed, "Will you please give me a few grains of corn?" The ant frowned and asked, "Why did you not store for winter? What did you do in summer?"

"In summer I sang all day long", said the grasshopper.

"Now dance", said the angry ant.

The grasshopper now realized his mistake.

**Moral : Save something for bad days.**

## STORIES DESCRIBING REAL-LIFE EXPERIENCE

**[1] Suppose you told your friend that you had once saved a drowning boy. Tell the story in about 150 words by answering the following questions. Add a suitable title.**

Where did it happen? When? What did you see? What was the condition of the man? What did you do? How did you feel? What did your father feel for you?

### A MEMORABLE RESCUE

10th August is a memorable day in my life. On that day I went to the river for taking my bath at 9 a.m. as usual. The bathing ghat was not crowded then. Only two boys were bathing in the river at that time. Suddenly one of them fell in deep water and cried out for help. The other boy was quite puzzled and stood helplessly. Instantly I made up my mind and dived into water. I had learnt the technique of rescuing a drowning man in our social service class. So I took the drowning boy by his hair and brought him safely to the shore. In the meantime, some people came there and when they noticed how I rescued the boy, they praised me very much. I thanked my teacher for teaching me how to rescue a drowning man. When my father heard this, he felt very proud of me.

**[2] Suppose you told your uncle that you had witnessed a cottage on fire. Tell the story in about 100 words by answering the following questions. Add a suitble title.**

> Where did it happen? When? What did you see? What was the condition of the members of the family? What did you do? How did you feel?

### A COTTAGE ON FIRE

Last Sunday I went to bed at 9 p.m. and slept a sound sleep. Suddenly I woke up at about 1 a.m. when I heard a hue and cry at a little distance. I got up from bed and rushed to the spot. I saw that a cottage was burning. People were rushing towards it. The old woman and the poor little girl who lived in it could not come out. They were crying for help inside the cottage. Everybody was throwing water on the burning cottage but nobody dared to enter the room. At last I requested a brave young man to rescue the old woman and the poor little girl. My eyes were full of tears then. He looked at my face once again and suddenly rushed into the cottage. He came out with the little girl by his arm and the old lady on his back. I thanked God and felt very happy for the noble deed the youngman did. It will be treasured in my memory for a long time.

## DO IT YOURSELF

**Fill in the blanks with correct verb forms and complete the following stories :**

### [1] A DOCTOR AND HIS PATIENT

> A rich lady suffering from bad eyesight—engaged a doctor to cure her—promised a good reward—the doctor stole her costly things—asked for the reward—lady's reply.

A rich lady ........... (suffer) from bad eyesight. She ..............(engaged) a doctor to cure her and ........... (promise) to give a handsome reward to the doctor if he ........... (can) cure her. The doctor ........... (come) everyday to the house of his patient to treat her very carefully. But the doctor ......... (be) a dishonest man. He ......... (tempt) by the costly things in the room of his patient. He ......... (steal) them from her room day to day. After six months the lady ........... fully cured of her disease and she ......... (regain) her normal eyesight. Then the doctor ........... (demand) his reward. But the lady, who had been really ........... (cure), saw that her valuable articles had been ......... (steal). She understood that it ......... the act of the dishonest doctor. So she said, "Doctor, before I ......... blind, I could see that my room was ........... (furnish) with many valuable articeles, but now I can see none of them. This proves that I ......... still almost blind. So I cannot pay you the promised reward."

**Moral : Dishonesty is paid by its own coin.**

### [2] TWO RIVAL BEGGARS

> Two rival beggars—one put round his neck a plate with the word 'DUMB'—the other beggar said that he was not dumb—the first beggar shouted, "No, no, I have been dumb all my life."

Two rival beggars ......... (live) in a big city. They would ......... (compare) their earnings each day and ......... (abuse) each other. One day a beggar ......... (hit upon) a new trick. He ......... (put) round his neck a plate with the word 'DUMB' .........

(write) on it. He thus ......... (attract) greater attention of people and ......... (earn) more money than the second beggar. The other beggar ......... (shout) at the top of his voice all the day but ......... (earn) a little. He ........... (feel) jealous of this and ........... (want) to teach the first beggar a good lesson. Next day when the 'dumb' beggar ......... (sit) for begging, his rival beggar ......... (warn) all the passersby, "Beware of the cheat. He is not dumb at all." People greatly ......... (enjoy) the fun and nobody ......... (give) anything to either of them. At the close of the day, the first beggar ........... (can) bear this no longer. He ......... (shout), "Gentlemen, do not believe that liar. I have been dumb all my life."

**Moral : False tricks cannot stand for long.**

### [3] A FARMER AND HIS SONS

A farmer had three quarrelsome sons—he thought of a plan—asked his sons to break a bundle of sticks—each failed—the bundle was untied—the sticks were easily broken.

A farmer ......... (have) three sons. They always ......... (quarrel). This ......... (make) the farmer unhappy. He ........... (try) to bring them to their senses but failed. At last he ........... (think) of a plan. He ........... (call) all his sons and ........... (ask) them to bring a bundle of sticks. When the bundle ......... (bring), he asked the eldest son to break it. He ......... (try) hard but failed. Similarly he ......... (ask) his two other sons one after another, but no one ......... (succeed). He then .........(ask) them to untie the bundle and break the sticks one by one. This they ......... (do) very easily. Then the farmer ......... (say) to them, "You see, my sons, each of you ......... (break) one stick easily. But none of you could ......... (break) the bundle of sticks. Why couldn't you do it?" The eldest son ......... (reply), "In the bundle, the sticks were together and so we couldn't break it."

"That's right," said the father, "you see the strength of unity just now. You must live together and nobody can harm you." After this they ......... (live) in peace and the farmer ......... happy.

**Moral : Unity is strength.**

### [4] THE FOX AND THE GRAPES

A hungry fox stole into a vineyard—found ripe grapes hanging from vines—too high for him to reach—jumped and tried to catch the nearest bunch—missed—grapes are sour.

A fox ......... (be) hungry and thirsty too. He ......... (steal) into a vineyard. There he ......... (find) ripe grapes (hang) from vines. But they ......... (be) too high for him to reach. He ......... (take) a run and ......... (jump) to catch the nearest bunch of grapes but ......... (miss). Again and again he jumped, only to ......... (miss) the juicy grapes. At last, tired and worn out, he ........... (stop) and said, "Well, I never really ......... (want) to have the grapes. I know grapes are sour."

**Moral : A rogue always finds an excuse.**

### [5] A GREEDY DOG

A dog with a piece of meat in his mouth—saw his own reflected image in the water of a stream—thought it was another dog with another piece of meat—jumped upon the reflection—lost his own piece of meat.

One day a dog ......... (steal) a piece of meat from a butcher's shop in the market and ......... (run) away with it. On the way he ......... (have) to cross a bridge across a small stream. As he was ......... (run) along the bridge, suddenly ......... he (look down) at his own reflected image in the water of the stream. He ........... (think) it was another dog with another piece of meat in its mouth. He ......... (be) easily tempted to see that piece of meat and ........... (think) of having that piece too. So he .............. (jump) upon his own reflection with a loud bark. As soon as he ........... (open) his mouth, the piece of meat ......... (drop) from his mouth and ........... (take) away by the current of the steam. Thus the greedy dog ......... (lose) his own piece of meat as well as the one he ........... (want) to snatch.

**Moral : Grasp all, lose all.**

## EXERCISE I

**1. Retell the stories with the help of the following tables. Give a heading and a suitable moral, if any :**

(a) A king had a favourite jester—often cut practical jokes on the courtiers—grew so bold as to offend the king himself—was ordered to be put to death, but allowed to choose how he would like to die—the man chose to die of old age.

(b) The town of Hamelin badly infested with rats—Mayor promised a high reward to get rid of them—A piper played his pipe and led and drowned the rats into the river—Mayor refused him to pay the promised reward—The piper played his pipe in another tune—All the children followed him and drowned.

(c) A farmer's daughter going to market with a can of milk on her head—lost in day-dreaming—dream of being very rich—many suitors—rejects them all—nods her head in pride—the result.

(d) A grand feast in honour of Columbus, discoverer of America—a lord remarks "It was a simple thing"—Columbus asks all to make an egg stand on an end—all fail--Columbus taps one end of the egg and puts it on the table—the egg stands—credit lies in showing the way.

(e) A fisherman brings some fish to a lord—demands a hundred lashes as the price—all surprised—the fisherman sticks to the demand—lashes are given—the fisherman urges to stop it after fifty are given—says that he has a partner—the gatekeeper has demanded half of the price—the lord understands—whips and dismisses the gatekeeper—rewards the fisherman.

(f) A woodcutter cutting wood near a stream—axe fell into water—began to weep—the water-god appeared with a golden axe—woodcutter refused—the god returned with a silver axe—woodcutter refused it—the god came back with his own axe—the woodcutter received it gladly—the god gave him all the three—another greedy man tried his luck but in vain.

(g) A carter was driving a cart along a muddy road—the wheels of the cart sank into mud—the carter whipped the bullocks in vain—prayed to Hercules—Hercules came and asked the carter to put his shoulders to the wheel—the cart moved.

(h) A man hires a donkey on a summer day—halts after going some distance—both the rider and the owner want to take rest in the shadow of the donkey—quarrel—'You hired the ass and not its shadow'—come to blows—donkey runs away.

(i) Androcles, a Roman slave, severely tortured—fled to the forest—faced a lion with limping paws—removed thorn—later arrested and thrown before a lion—the lion licked his feet—spectators were amazed—the slave was set free.

(j) A wolf gets a bone stuck in his throat—howls in pain—asks all to help him—declares a reward—a crane pulls the bone out—wants the reward—the wolf says that it is already given—he has allowed the crane to put its beak into a wolf's mouth and escape safely.

(k) Sir Philip Sidney wounded in a battle—felt very thirsty—a bottle of water was brought to him—going to drink—noticed a wounded soldier wistfully looking at the bottle—Sidney gave him the bottle saying "Thy need is greater than mine."

(l) A night-watchman had a dream that he had caught a thief—in the morning he told the story—the master listened to his story—rewarded him and then dismissed him—why?

(m) A villager gazes at a sweetmeat shop in a town—the shopkeeper demands price for smelling his sweets—the poor villager at a loss—another man comes to his rescue—says, "Jingle your coins in your purse and the sound will pay for the smell."

(n) A miser hid all his money in a secret place—a thief stole it—the miser began to cry—a wise man advised him to put a piece of stone in its place—it was as good as the useless money.

(o) An ass and a buffalo fought for their right of pasture—the ass was defeated—the ass took a man on his back to help him—the buffalo was driven away—the man kept the ass as his servant.

(p) Father is worried to see his son in evil company—tries to reform him—buys a few good ripe mangoes for him—puts a rotten mango in their midst—the boy finds all mangoes rotten next day—the boy learns the lesson of the harmful effects of evil company.

(q) King Midas was crazy for gold—the god of wealth granted his prayer that everything he touched might turn into gold—Next day the king's touch turned many things, even his food and daughter, into gold—The king repented—prayed his 'golden touch' to be taken away.

(r) A good man ties a bell to a sunken rock to warn mariners—all praise the man—a pirate cuts off the bell in jealousy—some time after, the pirate's ship strikes against the rock—all on the boat are drowned.

(s) An ass with a load of salt—falls into a stream by chance—load becomes lighter—next time falls into the stream on purpose—master puts a load of cotton next time—result.

(t) A thirsty crow finds a pitcher of water—the water at the bottom of the pitcher—the crow drops some pebbles into the pitcher—water level rises and the crow drinks at ease.

(u) The limbs of the body quarrel with the belly—they work but the belly only receives—they all cease work—the belly starves—all the limbs become weak and lose strength—they learn the lesson of cooperation.

(v) Two women quarrel over a child—come to court—judge's order to cut the child into two—one gives up her claim and says, 'Do not cut the child'—the other remains silent—judge decided.

(w) An old man divides his property among three sons—sets apart a jewel for him who would do the noblest work—one makes pilgrimages—one saves a drowning child—the third saves his enemy's life—who wins?

(x) King loses a finger—minister says "God is good and kind to all"—king puts his minister in prison—goes out for hunting—falls into robbers' hand—saved by injured limb from being killed before goddess Kali—king realises the truth of the minister's remark—makes him his minister again.

(y) Two blind beggars—one said, "God alone can make one happy"—the other said, "The king alone can make one happy"—the king gave the second beggar a loaf of bread filled with gold coins—finding it heavy he sold it to the first beggar—the latter became rich and happy.

(z) In a sea-fight the captain of a warship posted his son Casabianca at a spot—the captain was killed—the ship caught fire—flames rolled on the deck—the boy would not move from the burning deck without his father's order—he was burnt alive.

## EXERCISE II

1. **Suppose you told your friend that you had once saved a boy from snake-bite by using first-aid. Tell the story in about 100 words by answering the following questions. Add a suitable title.**

   Where did it happen? When? What did your see? What was the condition of the boy? What did you do? How did you feel? What did your friend feel for you?

2. **Suppose your father told you a story of a tragic death of a woman by bursting of a stove in the kitchen. Tell the story to your friend in about 100 words by answering the following questions. Add a suitable title.**

   Where did it happen? When? What was the woman doing? How did she catch fire? What did she do then? What did the other members of her family do? What was the result? Did the police enquire into the matter? What truth was revealed then?

3. **Suppose you had read a newspaper report on rescuing an old man under a collapsed building. Tell the story to your friend in about 100 words by answering the following questions. Add a suitable title.**

> How did you know it? What is the location of the collapsed building? Why did it collapse? On what date did it collapse? Who led the rescue operation? How was the old man traced? How was he rescued?

4. **Suppose you had witnessed a bus accident. Tell the story to your class-teacher in about 100 words. Add a suitable title.**

> Where did the accident occur? How did you come to know it?—Description of the ill-fated bus—condition of the passengers and the driver and the conductor of the bus—Any casualties?—Rescue operation by the public—Involvement of the police.

5. **Suppose you were engaged as a volunteer in a flood-stricken area. Tell the story of your real-life experience in about 100 words. Add a suitable title.**

> Location of the flood-affected area—How were you included in the group of volunteers?—Description of the misery of the flood-stricken people—your participation in relief work—What was the role of the State Government?—Involvement of other welfare organisations.

# 6 DIALOGUE AND REPORTING IN A SUMMARY FORM

## HOW TO REPORT A DIALOGUE IN A SUMMARY FORM?

1. In **Reporting a Dialogue**, the rules of the change of Narration should be maintained.
2. **Reporting** should be usually made in Past Tense as it concerns past events.
3. It is not necessary to report each sentence literally, but should contain the main or important points in gist form or summary form.

## EXAMPLES WORKED OUT

### [1] PLANNING A PICNIC

**Two friends are planning a picnic after examination :**

Amal : So the awful examination is over and we are as free as air. How would you like to have a picnic now?

Kamal : Oh, it's a grand idea. We haven't had a picnic for a long time. Let us fix up a date and the site for the same.

Amal : What about going to Botanical Gardens next Sunday?

Kamal : Yes, that's a good place to go to. When are we going to start?

Amal : Let's start at 7 o'clock next Sunday from school.

Kamal : That's all right, I think.

Amal : What are we going to cook there?

Kamal : *Luchis* and fowl curry—that's all I suggest. Isn't it a good menu?

Amal : That's all right. But we'll cook our own food ourselves. We'll cook our food under the trees and listen to songs from a record-player.

Kamal : Simply wonderful. We'll put this proposal before our class and we hope our classmates as well as our class teacher will agree to this proposal.

**Summary**

Two friends are planning a picnic after their examination. Amal proposes to go to Botanical Gardens the next Sunday. They will start at 7 o'clock from the school. They will have a good menu of *luchis* and fowl curry. They will cook their food under a tree and listen to songs from a record-player. They will put their proposal before their class and they hope that their classmates as well as their class teacher will agree to their proposal.

## [2] BOOKING FOR A TRIP TO GOA

**Suparna, a girl of south Kolkata, has come to a tourist office at Esplanade in Kolkata. She wants to have her booking for a trip to Goa.**

Suparna : Would you give me a ticket to Goa, please?

Booking clerk : Certainly. Do you want to travel by our tourist bus and visit the place?

Suparna : Yes. Will there be any guide in your tourist bus?

Booking clerk : Yes, of course.

Suparna : How much will it cost for the trip?

Booking clerk : It will cost ₹ 3000 for three days. It includes charges for food and stay too.

Suparna : When does the bus leave?

Booking clerk : At 5.45 a.m.

Suparna : The bus will bring me back, won't it?

Booking clerk : Of course.

Suparna : Here's the money, please.

Booking clerk : Here's the ticket and the change.

Suparna : Thank you very much.

### Summary

Suparna has come to a tourist office at Esplanade in Kolkata. She wants to have her booking for a trip to Goa. She is informed that it will cost ₹ 3000/- for the trip. It includes charges for food too. The bus will start at 5.45 a.m. and it will bring her back after the tour. There will be a guide in the tourist bus.

## [3] A DOCTOR AND HIS PATIENT

**A doctor asking his patient about the condition of his health and prescribing medicine.**

Bimal : Good morning, Doctor.

Doctor : Welcome! How are you, Bimal?

Bimal : I feel ill again.

Doctor : Please lie down. I'll check you up thoroughly. (after checking) I find nothing wrong with you except that your nerves are rather weak. Have you again been working hard?

Bimal : Yes, sir. Our examination is knocking at the door. So I have to sit up late at night.

Doctor : I see. That's why you are pulled down again. But why do you forget that if you fall ill, you can never succeed in the examination?

Bimal : Really, sir, I'm anxious for my examination. Do please prescribe a good tonic.

Doctor : I'm sorry, Bimal. I don't prescribe any tonic for you. I'll give you another type of prescription instead.

Bimal : Do please, sir.

Doctor : Avoid strain. Rise early and take some physical exercise in fresh air. That will make you fit soon.

### Summary

A doctor visits his patient, Bimal. He checks him up thoroughly and finds nothing wrong except nervousness. He comes to know that it is for his (Bimal's) overwork and anxiety for the coming exmination. The doctor advises him to avoid strain, to rise early and take some physical exercise in fresh air.

## [4] WHO IS MORE USEFUL—A TEACHER OR A DOCTOR?

**Two friends are talking about the usefulness of a teacher and a doctor in a society. One talks for a teacher and the other for a doctor.**

Sisir : Hi, Prabir! Do you still stick to your opinion about the teachers? No doubt a teacher renders useful service to the society. But I hope you don't claim that he is more useful than a doctor.

Prabir : Yes, I do. It is the teachers who are real nation-builders. Our greatest men owe much to them.

Sisir : But this is only a sentimental way of judging things. For practical purposes, a doctor provides more useful service. If they do not serve us, we would be dying like cats and dogs.

Prabir : That's right. But you should not undervalue the teacher's work. If they stop their work, even your doctors would not come out as doctors.

Sisir : I see. The society depends on cooperation. So, we see teachers and doctors, as also farmers and workers, work side by side for the existence and betterment of the society.

### Summary

Two friends talk about the usefulness of a teacher and a doctor. Sisir suggests that doctors are more useful than the teachers. If they do not serve us, we would be dying helplessly. Prabir says that the teachers are real nation-builders and if they stop their work, even the doctors would not come out as doctors. Sisir realizes that the society depends on cooperation. So the teachers and doctors as also farmers and workers work side by side for the existence and betterment of the society.

## [5] A RAINY DAY AT SCHOOL

**Two friends are talking on a rainy day at school. They are enjoying the day.**

Suren : Hello, Naren, what a day! It has been raining and raining and nobody knows when it will stop. All the lanes and streets of our area are water-logged. What a fun it is to wade through it!

Naren : That's the reason why I've come out. I'm sure we shall have a rainy day at school.

Suren : That may be. My clothes are all spoilt. Oh! there are lots of boys thoroughly drenched. They are playing before the main gate of the school. They are all in a jolly mood. Let us join them.

Naren : Look, Suren, the street in front of the school is almost like a stream of filthy water. Trams and buses have stopped plying and so even the teachers are delayed.

Suren : Hush! The Headmaster is coming from his office to count the thin attendance of the teachers and the students. Stand out and wait for the final bell.

Naren : Hurrah! there goes the bell. So we've a rainy day at last.

Suren : Three cheers for the rainy day! Now we will have a lot of fun.

### Summary

Two friends, Suren and Naren have come out on the water-logged street on a rainy day. They are thoroughly drenched and they find lots of boys playing before the main gate of the school in a jolly mood. Trams and buses have stopped plying and even the teachers are delayed. The Headmaster counts the thin attendance of the teachers and students and decides to treat the day as a rainy day. Students take it with rejoice.

## [6] TWO BOYS ABOUT A FIRE

**A godown of clothes in Barabazar area has caught fire. The crowd rushes towards it.**

Swapan : Look, Tapan. There's a fierce fire! The sky is red with it. Let's run and see what's the matter.

Tapan : A crowd is rushing towards it. I see the flames and smoke like a dark cloud with sparks like lightning. We are very near the spot.

Swapan : There comes the fire brigade at top speed. How gallant these firemen look with their glittering helmets on! They look like soldiers marching to fight against an enemy. Don't they?

Tapan : Yes, they do. Look, another truck of fire brigade is coming up. It must be a big fire. You can feel the heat even from here.

Swapan : People say it's a big godown of clothes. What a fierce blaze! I've never seen anything like it in my life.

Tapan : Look here. The fire engine has started work. The long fat hosepipes are throwing water right on the fire. Some of the firemen have gone into the burning godown. I wonder if they are not afraid of death!

Swapan : They are specially trained for this kind of work. Thank God, they've now brought the fire under control. It is showing signs of dying out. Let's go back.

### Summary

[Next day, Swapan and Tapan reported the fact to their classmates in a summary form.]

A godown of clothes in Barabazar area caught fire yesterday. Two engines of the fire brigade came there to stop fire. The fire-engines started working. The long fat hose-pipes threw water right on the fire. Some of the specially trained firemen went into the burning godown. They brought the fire under control after a few hours.

## [7] VISITING A PATIENT IN A HOSPITAL

**Bimal had a serious accident and he was admitted to S. S. K. M. Hospital. His friend Mihir pays a visit to him.**

Mihir : How are you, Bimal? I can't imagine what a horrible accident it was!

Bimal : Yes, I shudder to think of it now. I've come back from the jaws of death. I might have died, or at least been crippled all my life.

Mihir : But now you are quite all right. You'll get back your strength and you'll be a jolly boy as before. How do they treat you here?

Bimal : Fine. I'm under the treatment of the famous surgeon Dr. N. K. Sen. He is awfully busy. Still he takes special care of me. He assures me of steady recovery.

Mihir : May God put His healing hand on you. Wish you good luck, my friend. Good-bye.

Bimal : Bye.

### Summary

Bimal had a serious accident and he was admitted to S. S. K. M. Hospital. He had a possibility of being crippled at least. But when his friend Mihir paid a visit to him, he was all right. Dr. N. K. Sen, the famous surgeon, took special care of him. He assured him of steady recovery.

## [8] A FATHER AND HIS SON ABOUT THE SON'S CAREER

**A father and his son are talking on the point of choosing a career for the son after getting general education.**

Father : My son, it's high time to choose a career for you.

Son : Why don't you choose one for me, father? You've seen life from many aspects and I know little of it.

Father : That may be so. But every man has his own bent of mind. And one should follow his own line. Otherwise, he may cut a sorry figure in life.

Son : If you allow me to say so, I should like to be a doctor.

Father : Is it? Are you tempted by the lot of money a doctor earns, my boy?

Son : Quite opposite, father. I don't think money is the sole aim of life. I want to live for an ideal. If I be a doctor, I shall have opportunities to serve many miserable people in their sufferings.

Father : That's what people say before they get into their profession. But when they are in it, they run after money.

Son : That may be so in most cases. But I can only speak for myself. My heart bleeds when I see the poor people dying for want of proper treatment. If I ever get a chance, I shall involve myself in the service of suffering humanity.

Father : May God grant you the chance you look for.

### Summary

A father and his son are talking on the point of choosing the son's career. The son wishes to be a doctor—not for money but for an ideal. Father warns him that people say so before they get into their profession. But when they are in it, they run after money! The boy expresses his sincere desire for service to suffering humanity.

## [9] PUJA PURCHASE

**Two friends go out shopping together during the Pujas.**

Malay : How busy are the businessmen, here and there and everywhere!

Milan : Of course, it's the best time for the businessmen, specially the cloth merchants.

Malay : Even the hawkers' stalls on the footpaths are full of customers!

Milan : But we must go to a reputed shop that can supply the choicest articles. Let's go to 'Haralalka'.

Malay : Sure, they have an age-old goodwill.

Milan : Oh, God! what a crowd in the shop! How can we get in?

Malay : We must push our way through the crowd. (Getting into the shop Malay asks a shop-assistant) Hello, gentleman, please show me a shirt of silk.

The shop-assistant : (Placing a bundle) Here it is. You may choose.

Malay : I choose this one. How much is it?

The shop-assistant : Rs. 300/- please.

Malay : Thank you. Here it is.

**Summary**

Two friends, Malay and Milan go out shopping together during the Pujas. They prefer 'Haralalka' and get into the shop. Malay chooses a silk-shirt and purchases it for Rs. 300/-.

## [10] TWO FRIENDS ON CINEMA SHOWS

**Two friends are talking on cinema shows—One is pleading for its bright sides and the other is trying to make a balance.**

Aparna : I'm afraid, Ruchira, you've been a film-fan.

Ruchira : But you should not blame me for that. The film-shows can teach us a lot and can remove the monotony of life at the same time.

Aparna : That may be. But too much of anything is bad. There are indecent pictures which may spoil our life. We should keep away from them.

Ruchira : You simply repeat what our elders say. But life is life and we must see both sides—good and evil. These pictures can show you that.

Aparna : But at our tender age we should see life on its good side alone. Once we have formed our character, there's no harm in seeing the evil things of the world.

Ruchira : Don't be so mechanical, my friend. One cannot always be fed with good things alone. Be a bit bad rather and see things as they are. It will help you in the struggle of life.

Aparna : No Ruchira, that's a mistake that many people make nowadays. A drunkard or a gambler too may provide you such reasons! But remember, my friend, good is always good—now and always.

**Summary**

Aparna makes her friend aware of the evil effects of bad films. But Ruchira pleads for enjoying both good and bad films. She opines that it will help one in the struggle of life. Aparna cannot approve such idea and she comes to the conclusion that good is always good.

## DO IT YOURSELF

**A young man and a gentleman on starting a business :**

**Imagine you are Samir and you are talking to a gentleman on starting a business. Fill in the gaps to complete the conversation.**

Gentleman : Samir, you've passed the Madhyamik Examination. Would you like to go in for further studies now?

Samir : No, Sir. My father has retired from service and .........

Gentleman : What would you like to do then?

Samir : I've to look for a job. I'm.........

Gentleman : Have you any chance of getting it soon?

Samir : No, sir. There are thousands of youngmen .........

Gentleman : When such is the position, why don't you start a small business of your own?

Samir : I've neither money nor experience. How can I .........?

Gentlemen : You may take help of the self-employment projects of the Government. They will give you the seed-money and necessary guidelines.

Samir : But how can I repay......?

Gentleman : Don't be worried, my boy. You can repay the same in some easy instalments.

Samir : Thank ...........

Gentlemen : Thank you my boy. Always remember—self-help is the best help.

### Summary

A youngman......... (pass) the Madhyamik Examination. He ........... (look for) a job as his father ......... (retire) from service. But as thousands of youngmen ......... unemployed, a gentleman ......... (advise) him to start a small business. He also ......... (advise) him to ......... (take) help of the self-employment project of the Government for necessary seed-money and guidelines. The loan can be ......... (repay) in some easy instalments.

## EXERCISE

**Write out conversations on the following topics and report the same in a summary form :**

(a) A teacher and his student as to how to learn English well.
(b) Two friends about the coming examination.
(c) Two friends coming out of the examination hall.
(d) Two friends about a circus show in the town.
(e) Two friends meeting unexpectedly at a railway station.
(f) Two friends about starting a rural library.
(g) Two friends about starting a night school.
(h) Two friends about what they are going to do after their final examination.
(i) Two friends about a farewell function at school.
(j) A teacher and a student on social service as a part of education.
(k) A teacher and his pupils on common civic duties.
(l) A father and his son who wishes to join the army.
(m) A Railway ticket-checker and a traveller without ticket.
(n) Two boys on the advantages and disadvantages of hostel life.
(o) Two boys on their respective hobbies.
(p) Two friends after a visit to the museum.
(q) Two friends after a visit to the zoo.
(r) A mother and her son who is going abroad.
(s) A book-seller and a customer on buying some books.
(t) Two gentlemen about the rising prices of essential commodities.
(u) Two boys after an exciting football match/cricket match.
(v) Two friends planning a holiday trip.
(w) Two friends on the usefulness of games and sports.
(x) Two friends discussing how they can use their leisure.
(y) Two boys on the development of their village.
(z) Some students and the teacher hearing complaint in an open class.

# 7 SUMMARY/PRÉCIS WRITING

## HOW TO WRITE A SUMMARY/PRÉCIS

1. **The technique of Summary/Précis writing :**

   A summary writing has its systematic technique.

   Read the passage carefully and underline the important words and phrases and essential points.

   After collecting the important points you will have to rewrite the whole thing in your own style and in your own words. The summary / précis should be written in the third person and indirect speech.

2. **The length of the summary :**

   Though there is no hard and fast rule, the summary will have to be considerably shorter than the original discourse. Normally, a summary should not be more than half of its original. And a précis should be within one-third of its original.

3. **Heading :**

   There is no compulsion about it. You may give a Heading to your summary/ précis or you may not.

## SHORTENING A SENTENCE / SENTENCES

In summary / précis writing it is very important to reduce a sentence without altering the meaning of the original sentence. Here are some specimens of long sentences to show how they can be reduced to short forms.

**Example 1**

Long sentence : He was sentenced to death because he murdered a child.
Short form : He was sentenced to death for infanticide. [one-word substitute]

**Example 2**

Long sentence : He gave me a book which I ought to read.
Short form : He game me a readable book. [one-word substitute]

**Example 3**

Long sentence : He is a man in whom no reliance can be placed.

Short form : He is an unreliable man. [one-word substitute]

**Example 4**

Long sentence : He spoke without any preparation and everybody applauded him.

Short form : Everybody applauded him for his extempore speech. [one-word substitute]

**Example 5**

Long sentence : The question is so difficult for us that we can't answer it.

Short form : The question is too difficult for us to answer. [Using too...to]

**Example 6**

Long sentence : There is nothing which needs to be explained.

Short form : There is nothing to explain. [Using 'to' Infinitive]

**Example 7**

Long sentence : Because the sea was turbulent, we did not go far a sail.

Short form : The sea being turbulent, we did not go for a sail. [Using '-ing' Participle]

**Example 8**

Long sentence : It was unfortunate that he got plucked in the examination.

Short form : Unfortunately, he got plucked in the examination. [Using Adverb]

**Example 9**

Long sentence : That he could be so foolish was a disappointment to me.

Short form : His foolishness disappointed me. [Reducing a Clause]

**Example 10**

Long sentence : I went to Kolkata. I saw the museum. I came back home.

Short form : Seeing the museum in Kolkata I returned home. [Joining of sentences]

## PASSAGES FULLY WORKED OUT

### Passage 1

The world of today has achieved much, but for all its declared love for humanity, it has based itself far more on hearted and violence than on virtues that make man human. War is the negation of truth and humanity. War may be unavoidable sometimes but its progeny are terrible to contemplate. Not mere killing, for man must die, the deliberate and persistent propagation of hatred and falsehood gradually becomes the normal habit of the people. It is dangerous and harmful to be guided in our life's course by hatreds and aversions, for they are wasteful of energy and limit and twist the mind and prevent it from perceiving the truth. Unhappily, there is hatred today in India, and strong aversions, for the past pursues us and the present does not differ from it. It is not easy to forget repeated affronts to the dignity of a proud race. Yet, fortunately Indians do no nourish hatred for long; they recover easily a more benevolent mood.

Jawaharlal Nehru

**Essential Points :**

(i) Hatred and violence prevail in the world today; (ii) War may be sometimes unavoidable; (iii) Its consequences are terrible; (iv) Hatred wastes our energy; (v) Indians do not nurse hatred.

### Précis

**Heading : Hatred and violence in the world and in India today**

Hatred and violence prevail in the world today. War may be sometimes unavoidable, but its consequences are terrible. It is dangerous to be guided in our life's course by hatreds and aversions. Hatred wastes our energy and crooks our mind. India is affected by the hatred that wars have generated. India is pursued by the repeated insults to the dignity of a proud race. But Indians do not nurse hatred. They recover love and humanity, a more benevolent mood of living.

### Passage 2

As daylight can be seen through very small holes, so little things will illustrate a person's character. Indeed character consists in little acts, well and honourably performed in our daily life. One of the most marked tests of character is the manner in which we conduct ourselves towards others. A graceful behaviour towards superiors, inferiors and equals is a constant source of pleasure. It pleases others because it indicates respect for their personality; but it gives tenfold pleasures to ourselves. Every man may, to a great extent, be a self-educator in good behaviour, as in everything else. He can be civil and kind, if he wills, though he may not have a penny in his purse. Even a kind look will give pleasure and confer happiness. Gentleness in society is like a silent influence of light which gives colour to all nature. It is more powerful than loudness of force, and far more fruitful.

**Essential Points :**

(i) Little acts of man indicate his character; (ii) One of the basic traits of character is good manners; (iii) It costs nothing to be a well-behaved person.

### Summary

**Heading : The Value of Good Manners**

Little acts of man indicate his character. Indeed one of the most marked tests of one's character is the manner in which one behaves with others. His polite behaviour to different persons gives pleasure to everybody, including himself. Good behaviour costs nothing. But its noble influence cannot be denied. Besides, a well-behaved person himself becomes more pleased than the others towards whom he behaves politely. Thus these little acts of kindness bear a powerful impact on society. In fact it is more powerful and more fruitful than the impact of force.

### Passage 3

Socrates had disciples. The greatest of them was Plato. Plato wrote many books which have come down to us, and it is from these books that we know a great deal of his master, Socrates. Evidently, Governments do not like people who are always trying to find out things by making inquries. They do not like the search for truth. The Athenian Government—this was just after the time of Priceless—did not like the methods of Socrates, and they held a trial and condemned him to death. They told him that, if he promised to give up his discussions with people and changed his ways, they would let him off. But he refused to do so and preferred the cup of hemlock which brought him death, to forsaking what he considered his duty. On the point of death he addressed his accusers and judges, the Athenians, and said, "If you propose to acquit me on condition that I abandon my search for truth, I'll say : "I thank you, O Athenians. But I will have God, who, as I believe, set me this task rather than you and so long as I have breath and strength I will continue the practice of accosting whomever I meet, and saying to him, 'Are you not ashamed of setting your heart on wealth and honours, while you have no care for wisdom and truth and making your soul better?' I know not what death is—it may be a good thing and I am not afraid of it. But I do know that it is a bad thing to desert one's post and I preferred what may be good to what I know to be bad."

**Essential Points :**

(i) Men can know about Socrates by reading the works of Plato; (ii) Governments usually discourage the search for truth. Naturally the Athenian Government disliked Socrates' methods of making inquiries and finding out truth; (iii) Socrates was condemned to death, but the Government wanted to release him if he did not try to make inquiries and seek people's company for discussions; (iv) Socrates did not agree and again addressed people and told them to lead their life for wisdom and truth.

**Précis**

**Heading : Life and Death of Socrates for a Principle**

We can know much of Socrates by reading the works of Plato, one of his disciples. As all governments usually discourage the spirit of inquiry, the Athenian Government disliked Socrates' methods of finding truth through inquiry. So the Government condemned him to death, offering to set him free if he changed his life style. But Socrates refused to change his life style and again addressed the Athenians before his death. He argued that God has given him the task of searching our truth. Addressing people and persuading them to live nobly, he further asserted that he did not fear death which might be something good but giving up duties was surely bad.

**Passage 4**

The peril involved in nuclear was is one which affects all mankind and one, therefore, in which the interests of all mankind are at one. Those who wish to prevent the catastrophe which results from a large scale H-bomb war are not concerned to advocate the interests of this or that nation, or this or that class, or this or that continent. Their arguments have nothing whatever to do with the merits or demerits for communism or democracy. The arguments that should be employed in a campaign against nuclear weapons are such as should appeal, as equal force, to eastern and western blocks and also the uncommitted nations, since they are concerned solely with the welfare of human species as a whole and not any special advantages to this or that group.

**Essential Points :**

(i) The danger from the nuclear war will affect everybody; (ii) The prevention of nuclear disaster should be made in the interests of the whole world; (iii) The objective is human welfare, as a whole.

**Summary**

**Heading : Nuclear Disaster and Its Prevention**

The danger from the nuclear was can engulf the whole world. Such dangers are to be stopped in the interests of the whole mankind. Those who plead against such wars are not concerned with the interests of any particular group of man of this or that continent. Any such campaign against nuclear disaster can be fruitful if people do not run after their narrow nationalism of the eastern and western blocks. And so people should be concerned with the welfare of the human race as a whole.

### Passage 5

But the first thing that men learned, as soon as they began to study nature carefully, was that some events take place in a regular order and that same causes always give rise to same effects. The sun always rises on one side and sets on the other side of the sky; the changes of the moon follow one another in the same order and with similar intervals, some stars never sink below the horizon of the place in which we live; the seasons are more or less regular, water always flows downhill, fire always burns, plants grow up from seeds, from which like plants grow up again; animals are born, grow, reach maturity, and die, age after age in the same way. Thus the notion of an order of nature and of a fixity in the relation of cause and effect between such things gradually entered the minds of man.

**Essential Points :**

(i) Man observed that the same causes of things produce the same effects; (ii) There is a regularity in nature; (iii) By observing the objects of nature men came to understand the principle of order and fixity in the relation of cause and effects.

### Summary

**Heading : Natural Order between Cause and Effect**

By observing different phenomena of nature for a long time men have perceived that nature has a regular order and there is a relation between the cause and effect of things. They have observed the sunrise and sunset at fixed directions, the changes of the moon in regular order, the nature of fire and water, the harmonious growth of plants and other things like birth, age and death to confirm their ideas about natural order.

### Passage 6

We are citizens of no mean country and we are proud of the land of our birth, of our people, our culture and traditions. That should not be for a romanticised past to which we have to cling; nor should it encourage exclusiveness or a want of appreciation of others' ways than ourselves. It must never allow us to forget our many weaknesses and failings or blunt our longing to be rid of them. We have a long way to go and much leeway to make up before we can take our proper station with others in the van of human civilisation and progress. And we have to hurry, for the time at our disposal is limited and the pace of the world grows ever swifter. It was India's ways in the past to welcome and absorb other cultures. That is much more necessary today, for we march to the One World of tomorrow where national cultures will be intermingled with the international culture of the human race. We shall, therefore, seek wisdom and knowledge and friendship and comradeship wherever we can find them, and cooperate with other in any tasks, but we are not suppliants for others' favours and patronage. Thus we shall remain true Indians and Asiatics, and become at the same time good internationalists and world citizens.

**Essential Points :**

(i) The past glory of India should not confine one to the past or prevent one from receiving the weakness of Indian people; (ii) It is necessary to make rapid progress and assassinate the cultures of other nations; (iii) Our aim is to retain Indian identity and to cultivate good internationalism.

### Précis

**Heading : To Retain Indian Identity and Achieve International Ideals**

India has glorious past. This idea should not be romanticised too much. It is time for every Indian to recognise the weakness too. India can make progress and keep pace with the other nations of the world if people of India show their ability to absorb good sides of other peoples' cultures. We should not ask favours of others by giving up our dignity. Our aim should be the retention of Indian identity along with the cultivation of internationalism.

**Passage 7**

The most important thing is that we should have freedom of thought. This is not as easy as it sounds, for everyone likes to have this freedom for himself, but is not ready to give it to others, when they express different opinions. This is particularly the case when the difference of opinion arises on such important matters as religion or politics. But if we refuse to let other people hold their opinions on these matters and specially, if we try to force them to accept our own, progress is impossible. If everyone went on thinking the same things as his ancestors thought, progress would come to an end. If we think exactly what our forefathers thought, we shall remain in the condition in which they were. Our thought depends a good deal upon what we read and what we talk about. Therefore, if we are to think new thoughts we must try to study all sides of the topic that comes before us and not be content with only what we read in newspapers or what others say.

**Summary**

**Heading : Freedom of thought**

Freedom of thought is wanted by all, but given by few. We lack tolerance for difference of opinions particularly on such important matters as religion or politics. But if any particular opinion is forced on all others, progress is not possible. If we do not think any new thoughts we shall be confined in the condition of our forefathers. For true progress everything has to be seen and judged with an open mind from all perspectives. Patience and a spirit of enquiry are essential for our advancement.

**Passage 8**

The mystery of Napoleon's career was this, that under all difficulties and discouragements, he pressed on. It solves the problems of all heroes; it is the rule by which to weigh rightly all wonderful success and triumphal marches to fortune and genius. It should be the motto of all, old and young, high and low, fortunate and unfortunate.

Never despair, never be discouraged, however stormy the heavens, however dark the way, however great the difficulties, and repeated the failure. "Press on!" If fortune has played false with you today, it will play true to yourself tomorrow. If your riches have taken wings and left you, do not weep your life away; but be up and doing, and retrieve the loss by new energy and new action. If an unfortunate bargain has deranged your business, do not fold your arms, and give up all for lost; but stir yourself, and work all the more vigorously.

**Summary**

**Heading : The Secret of Napoleon's Success**

The secret of Napoleon's success in life was that he was never disheartened by difficulties or depressed by failures, but steadily persevered through them like all real heroes, and thus he attained his goal. In fact, this should be the attitude of all who want to do anything great in their lives. One should never allow himself to be overcome by adverse situations, but must stand firm and try to recover what has been lost by vigorous attempts.

### Passage 9

It is language, more obviously than anything else, that distinguishes man from the rest of the animal world. At one time it was common to define man as a thinking animal, but we can hardly imagine thought without words—not thought that is at all precise, anyway. More recently man has often been described as a toolmaking animal; but language itself is the most remarkable tool that man has invented; and is the one that makes all the others possible. The most primitive tools admittedly, may have come earlier than language : the higher apes sometimes use sticks for digging, and have even been observed to break sticks for this purpose. But tools of any greater sophistication demand the kind of human cooperation and division of labour which is hardly possible without language. Language, in fact, is the great machine tool which makes human culture possible.

### Summary

Heading : The Tool of Language

In the animal world man alone is endowed with language. For his language he is distinguished from other lower animals. Another mark of distinction is the human capacity or ability to make tools. Language can also be treated as one of man's tools. It helps him make sophisticated tools based on cooperation and division of labour. In fact, language is the great machine tool for developing human culture.

### Passage 10

In the atomic bomb, man is making use of the fundamental energy process of the universe. He has used it for destructive purposes, but that is largely an accident of the time and place. All around we have abundant evidence that without this energy, life itself could not exist. The universe would become a dead thing.

Without the sun and its heat and light there could be no life. It is the sun's rays which give us our food and enable us to keep alive and healthy. Without the sun there could be no warmth. The terrific heat of the sun, of which only a small proportion reaches the earth, is due in the first place to a process exactly the same as that which makes the atomic bomb. Matter is broken down into energy—or rather transformed into energy. Untold millions and millions of atoms in the sun release their energy and give forth light and heat, which the rays bring us. Through atomic energy, therefore, nature has given the world life. This is a significant thought.

### Précis

Heading : The Life-giving Aspect of Atomic Energy

In the making of the atom-bomb man has used the fundamental energy process though it has sometimes been for destructive purposes. This energy is actually life-giving. It comes from the solar heat and light. The solar heat which comes to the Earth is generated in the manner which is used for the production of atom-bombs. In fact, matter changed into energy produces light and heat. Thus nature has given life to this planet through atomic energy.

### Passage 11

A gentleman advertised for an office-boy and quickly chose one from the fifty who applied. 'I should like to know', said a friend, 'on what ground you chose the boy. He has not a single recommendation with him'. 'You are mistaken', answered the gentleman, 'he had great many. He wiped his feet before he came in and closed the door after him showing that he was orderly and tidy. He gave his seat instantly to that lame old man showing that he was courteous. He lifted up the book which was lying on the floor, and placed it on the table while all the others stepped over it or shoved it aside. When I talked with him I noticed that his clothes were carefully brushed, his hair was in nice order and his teeth were as white as milk. When he wrote his name, I noticed that his finger nails were clean. And he waited patiently for his turn instead of pushing others aside. Don't you call these letters of recommendation?"

**Summary**

Heading : Selecting an Office-boy

A gentleman once advertised for an office-boy and among the fifty candidates he recruited one who had not a single recommendation with him in the literal sense. When his friend asked about the reason, the gentleman said that he noted the applicant's manners, cleanliness, patience and courteous habits. The applicant showed those qualities in every small thing he did since entering the room for interview. It was the real recommendation than any formal certificate for his recruitment.

**Passage 12**

The number of mouths to feed is constantly increasing, but the resources from which they may be fed are correspondingly diminishing. If present tendencies continue, if, that is to say, science continues to be mainly used for man's harm instead of for his welfare, the world may well be faced in one or to hundred years' time with famine-stricken nations competing for larger shares of a dwindling food supply.

The best way of preventing such a disaster would be to fix each nation's population with reference to the food resources likely to be available. This could be done by the wise use of birth control. But at the present time each nation tries to become as large and as numerous as possible in order that it may be strong in war, and only a world government would have the power to compel the nations to take the necessary steps to limit their populations. Thus, from many points of view it seems that man's increasing powers point unmistakably to the need of world government, if they are to be used not for man's detriment and possible destruction, but for his welfare.

**Précis**

Heading : The Rapid Growth of World Population and its Solution

With the rapid growth of population and the food supply rapidly coming down for the destructive role of science, the world is faced with a crisis of famine and starvation within nearly two hundred years. This problem can be solved only through birth control by fixing each nation's population maintaining a balance with its food resources. But the war situation in the world has made birth control ineffective. So the formation of the world government is needed for the welfare of man.

**Passage 13**

National progress is the sum of individual industry, energy, and uprightness, as national decay is of individual idleness, selfishness, and vice. What we are accustomed to decry as great social evils, will, for the most part, be found to be only the outgrowth of our own perverted life, and though we may endeavour to cut them down and extirpate them by means of Law, they will only spring up again with fresh luxuriance in some other form, unless the conditions of human life and character are radically improved. If this view be correct, then it follows that the highest patriotism and philanthropy consist, not so much in altering laws and modifying institutions, as in helping and stimulating men to elevate and improve themselves by their own free and independent action.

The Government of a nation itself is usually found to be but the reflex of the individuals composing it. The Government that is ahead of the people will be inevitably dragged down to their level, as the Government that is behind them will in the long run be dragged up. In the order of nature, the collective character of a nation will as surely find its befitting results in its law and Government, as water finds its own level. The noble people will be nobly ruled, and the ignorant and corrupt ignobly. Indeed, liberty is quite as much a moral as a political growth—the result of free individual action, energy, and independence.

**Précis**

**Heading : The Government and the National Progress**

The progress of a nation is possible when its individual members are industrious and energetic, and it becomes backward when its members are idle, selfish and vicious. Most of the social evils result from people's perversities. Any government cannot remove them by framing laws only. So the practical solution is the development of character and improvement of the condition of life. The Government of a country highlights the characters of its citizens. The ideal government requires the citizens to lead free and noble lives.

**Passage 14**

Persistent efforts are being made by nations to bring about a new social system in which all men will be provided at least with the bare necessities of life, so that in a century or so there should be no poor man in the world. Old prejudices and customs, no doubt, take time to disappear, but it is recognised by every civilized government today that every citizen has a right to be comfortable. It is estimated that in the eighteenth century eight per cent of the people of England were poor; that is to say, they had no certain means of livelihood, could not afford two meals a day, or clothe themselves properly. Today the number of such people is very small, and even that number is looked after by the state. Even in India poverty is on the decrease; and its worst form which resulted from famine, has been rooted out. There are canals to guard against uncertain rainfall. The means of transport have been developed to carry foodstuffs from one area to another when the crops fail.

**Summary**

**Heading : The Government and the New Social Order**

Every nation of the world has been continuously trying to bring about a new social system by eradicating poverty from its soil. Every civilized government has now understood the value of the citizen's right to live a comfortable life in society, though old prejudices and customs will take time to disappear. In England the problem of poverty has almost been solved. Even in India, poverty does not pose a great threat as it was in the previous years because of the improvement of the irrigation system and the transport facilities.

**Passage 15**

Self-reliance is the pilgrim's best stuff, the worker's best tool. It is the master-key that unlocks all the difficulties of life. 'Help yourself and heaven will help you' is a maxim which receives daily confirmation. He who begins with crutches will generally end with crutches. Help from within always strengthens, but help from without invariably enfeebles the recipient. It is not in the sheltered garden, but on the rugged Alpine cliff, where the storms beat most violently, that the toughest plants are reared. It is not by the use of corks, bladders and lifeboats that you can best learn to swim but by plunging courageously into the waves and buffeting them.

To wait until some charitable man passes by—to stand with arms folded, sighing for 'helping hand', is not the part of any manly mind. The habit of depending upon others should be vigorously resisted, since it tends to weaken the intellectual faculties and paralyse the judgement. The struggle against adverse circumstances has, on the contrary, a bracing and strengthening effect, like that of the pure mountain air on an enfeebled frame.

**Précis**

**Heading : The Value of Self-help**

Self-help is the best way to fight against all difficulties. It is the key to all success in life. One should not depend on other's help, because it is invariably bad—it makes a person weak while self-reliance strengthens him. Heaven helps those who help themselves. A man can learn swimming more effectively by his own effort than by the use of bladders or corks or lifeboats. The toughest plants grow and get vigour not in the seltered garden, but on the rough rocks. The struggle against adverse situation makes a man strong.

**Passage 16**

Years ago Roman Rolland declared that he regarded Gandhi as a "Christ who only lacked the Cross". We have now given him the Cross also, Gandhi's death was a classical ending to his life. He died with the name of God on his lips and love in his heart. Even as he received the bullet wounds he greeted his murderer and wished him well. He lived up to what he preached.

Possessed and inspired by the highest ideals of which human nature is capable, preaching and practising fearlessly the truth revealed to him, leading almost alone what seemed to be a forlorn hope against the impregnable strongholds of greed and folly, yet facing tremendous odds with a calm resolution which yielded nothing to ridicule or danger, Gandhi presented to this unbelieving world all that is noblest in the spirit of man. He illumined human dignity by faith in the eternal significance of man's effort. He belongs to the type that redeems the human race.

If Gandhi was able to rid himself of all rancour and hatred, to develop that flame of love which burnt up all impurities, if he feared no evil even though he walked in the valley of the shadow of death, if he represented to us the eternal voice of hope, it is because he believed in the heritage of India, the power of the inward life of spirit.

S. Radhakrishnan

**Précis**

**Heading : Gandhi as a Man**

Referring to Romain Rolland's description of Gandhiji as the Christ with no Cross, the author remarks that his death gave him the Cross. The last word on his lips was 'God'. His heart was full of love and when he fell down dead, he wished well of his murderer. He preached and practised fearlessly the truth revealed to him throughout his life. Indeed, there was no difference between his life and his teaching. He was fearless in his preaching of truth. He filled the minds of men with high hopes as he believed in the heritage of India.

### Passage 17

The aim of culture and religion is the same. Men are all members of one great whole, and the sympathy which is in human nature will not allow one member to be indifferent to the rest or to have a perfect welfare independent of the rest. The expansion of our humanity to suit the idea of perfection which forms culture, must be a general expansion. Perfection, as culture conceives it, is not possible while the individual remains isolated. He must carry others along with him in his march towards perfection. Culture lays on us the same obligation as religion which says, "To promote the kingdom of God is to increase and hasten one's own happiness."

Culture is a harmonious expansion of all the powers which make the beauty and wonder of human nature. Culture is not consistent with the overdevelopment of any one power at the expenses of the rest. Here it goes beyond religion, as religion is generally conceived by us.

**Summary**

**Heading : The meaning of Culture**

Both culture and religion aim at promoting the general welfare of man. Both of them want man's perfection and happiness. There is, however, a difference between the two. Culture is the general expansion of our humanity. It is not possible while the individual remains isolated. Moreover, culture means the development of all powers of man. Religion aims at the development of moral or religious power of an individual.

### Passage 18

Why do we want to know History? Why does History form a recognised part of education? Simply because all of us, and everyone of us ought to know how we have come to be what we are today, so that each generation need no start again from the same point and hold over the same ground, but profiting by the experience of those who came before us. History may advance towards higher points and nobler aims. As a growing child might ask his father or grandfather who had built the house they lived in, or who had cleared the fields that yield them their food, we ask the historians whence we came and how we came into the possessions of what we call our own : History may tell us afterwards many useful and amusing things such as a child might like to hear from mother to grandfather. But what History has to teach us before all and everything, is our own antecedent, our own ancestors, our own descendant.

**Summary**

**Heading : Teaching of History**

Why should we read history? It is because history forms an important part of our education. We are profited by experience through history in order to advance towards higher points and nobler aims. The study of history tells us about our heritage and of our ancestors. It also helps us to start from where our ancestors ended. It enables us to reach a highter stage too. In this way history enlightens about our past, our forefathers and our descendants.

### Passage 19

We often hear of unrest in the student world. Strikes and definance of teacher's authority are now common. But it will be sheer injustice and error of judgement if we lay all the blame on the shoulders of students alone. Boys are only too eager to show respect to those teachers who can capture their imagination by their sympathy and broad mindedness. It will be a tragedy if they cannot find such teachers because in that case their inner urge will remain unsatisfied. On the other hand if they find such teachers, they will surely place implicit faith in them. In institutions where teachers enjoy the confidence of their students, and students the sympathy and loving care of their teachers, the problem of discipline comes much easier.

**Summary**

**Heading : How to overcome students' unrest**

Students' unrest is a common event nowadays. But students are not solely responsible for this. They are generally eager to respect and trust the sympathetic teachers. The sincere teachers too enjoy the confidence of their students. But such teachers are not always available. The institutions where the teacher-student relation is cordial, care-free and kind, the problem of unrest can be easily solved and discipline can be readily restored.

**Passage 20**

You find a little hole in your coat, so small that you do not think it matters. Later, you find it has become a big tear, and it takes you more than nine stitches with needle and thread and time and trouble, to repair it. If you had mended it at once, you could have done it a minute or so and with one or two stitches. So you just take things in time and you will save yourself a lot of trouble. A small hole in a canal embankment can be stopped with very little trouble; but if it is neglected, it will widen into a great breach which will call for much labour and expense to make it right again. As the old saying teaches, a kingdom may be lost by neglecting to replace a nail in time in a horse's shoe : 'For want of a nail, the shoe was lost; for want of a shoe, the horse was lost; for want of a horse, the rider was lost; for want of a rider, the battle was lost; for want of a battle, the kingdom was lost.'

**Précis**

**Heading : Do it now**

We should mend our troubles in time. Otherwise the defect and difficulties may grow too great to be dealt with in future. This fact can be illustrated in many fields of our life. A stitch in time saves nine. If a leak in an embankment is left unattended, it can make a wide breach. If a nail is not fitted in a horse's shoe in time, it can cause defeat in war and loss of a whole kingdom.

**Passage 21**

The natural curiosity of man has produced the material civilization which we know and has added immeasurably to the storehouse of our knowledge. In modern times this desire for knowledge is expressed most forcibly in our pursuit of science. The exploration of the geographical world is now almost complete, but the spirit of Drake and Cook lives on in those who explore the inside of atoms of the complicated molecules from which living things are made.

At first sight, modern science seems to be an immensely complicated mixture of fact and fancy. Carefully observed and corroborated facts, the results of experiments made with great precision and the pictures of the way in which nature works with this mass of data are found side by side with almost as large a volume of speculation. This boiling up of hypothesis from the cold facts is the very spirit of science, for a guess suggests ways to prove it, and so the truth is slowly sorted out. Speculations which stretch out beyond existing knowledge are exciting and exhilarating. It is a duty of science to make these guesses, and it is equally a duty to test them by experiment and observation.

### Summary

[Without a Heading]

The natural curiosity of man has produced the material civilization by adding much to the storehouse of our knowledge. In modern times this curiosity is the main force in our pursuit of science. Inquisitive spirit of man has led to discoveries of geographical world and inventions of scientific truths. Researches of science combine facts and fanciful guesses to reveal mysteries of life and nature. Without speculative courage followed up by experiments science could not have advanced so far. So the duty of science is not to refuse guesses, but to test them through observation.

### Passage 22

Good English teaching in a school is essential. This does not mean efficient teaching only, it means teaching aimed at the right things; mainly at developing the pupils' skill in handling language in all types of expression and in comprehending all types of meaning with precision and alertness. So it is evident that language has a central position in the school education of children, though we must also admit that learning about language is often forced into more prominence in the school work of the younger children than is necessary for their natural and balanced development. Leaving this for discussion elsewhere, we turn to the role of language in the child's life. Language in our society at present is of such importance to the child that the development of his ability to use language effectively is closely related to the development of his mind and character. To speak it clearly, it is important to every manifestation of his mind and character in almost every moment of his private and social life.

### Summary

[Without a Heading]

Good English teaching at school level requires not only efficient teaching, but also teaching of right things. It should be done in such a way that the students are able to comprehend things and handle their language in all types of expression. It is necessary for their natural and balanced development. So language learning holds a central position in school education. The role of a language in the child's life is closely related to the developent of his mind and character in his private life as well as social life.

### Passage 23

The study of biography is a pleasant occupation. Particularly, if it happens to be the life of a great man, a hero, it is even more delightful than reading a novel. For we read fiction knowing all the time that it is a work of imagination. But to read the life of a great man is to read things that have actually happened. We have a sensation that truth can be stranger than fiction. And then there is the thought—if these have actually happened—why may not they happen again and why not in my life? This indeed is a splendid thought, an ennobling idea. Biography acts as an inspiration to achievement. We read how from petty provincial lawyer Abraham Lincoln rose to be the memorable President of the USA by dint of his integrity, ideallism, and earnestness. And today his name is a household word in America and well-known all the world over. We read how the great Vidyasagar raised himself from poverty to eminence by his iron will and high character. Such examples fill us with inspiration. They tell us that we also can make ourselves great and famous if we have character, idealism, preseverance and courage.

**Précis**

[Without a Heading]

The reading of biography of a great man or a hero is more interesting and profitable and pleasant than reading a novel. A novel is a work of imagination. But such things happened in reality in the life of great men having such a thrilling sensation that truth can be stranger than fiction. And this might happen to the reader as well. Thus the careers of Lincoln, Vidyasagar and such celebrated great men inspire us to cultivate human virtues like idealism, sincerity, perseverence and courage which constitute an ideal character.

**Passage 24**

To get great ideas we require great teachers. These teachers may be living persons whith whom we come in daily contact or they may be dead and yet reach us through great books which they have given to the world. In whichever way it comes, the teaching required is that which guides to a large outlook. Yet, after all, it is only to a limited extent that the teacher, be he living or one who though dead yet speaks, can mould his student. There is no royal road to learning. The higher it is, the harder is the toil of spirit that is required for its attainment. But this toil brings with it happiness. As we advance along the path, we see more and more new territory to traverse, new heights to scale, heights which are scaled only by patient labour, but the scaling of which promises us a new sense of possession. In all this there is much of the sweet in sad and the sad in sweet. Yet the mere endeavour, even apart from the result, brings its reward.

**Summary**

[Without a Heading]

We get great ideas from great teachers. They may be living persons in our day-to-day life, or, if dead, they may reach us through books. In any case, the good teaching requires a liberal outlook. And in this way a teacher can mould his student. There is no easy road to learning. However, to learn more and understand deeply, a student should go through harder path and take harder initiative. It involves strain and pain, which is repaid by a sense of achievement, or at least the satisfaction of an honest effort.

**Passage 25**

The highest education is that which does not merely give us information but makes our life in harmony with all existence. But we find that this education of sympathy is not only systematically ignored in schools, but it is severely repressed. From our very childhood our habits are formed and knowledge is imparted in such a manner that our life is weaned away from nature and our mind and the world are set in opposition from the beginning of our days. Thus the greatest of educations for which we came prepared, is neglected, and we are made to lose our world to find a bagful of information instead. We rob the child of his earth to teach him geography, of language to teach him grammar. His hunger is for the Epic, but he is supplied with chronicles of facts and dates. He was born in the human world, but is banished into the world of living gramophones, to expiate for the original sin of being born in ignorance. Child nature protests against such calamity with all its power of suffering, subdued at last into silence by punishment.

### Summary

[Without a Heading]

The ideal system of education does not merely give us information, but makes our life harmonious with life and nature. But, unfortunately, this education of sympathy is ignored in schools, rather repressed. From our childhood knowledge is poured in such a manner that it keeps away our life from nature and thus the true education is neglected to get a bagful of information. Thus the systematized education robs the child's pleasure and teaches dry information through grammar, geography, history of facts and dates only. A child is forced to push into it, and sometimes punished even if he rebels against it. It is regretable to neglect the essential elwment of sympathy in such system of education.

### Passage 26

My idea of society is that though we are born equal, we may not have a right to equal opportunity in every sphere as all of us have not the same capacity. To be equal in every respect is impossible in the nature of things. For instance, all cannot have the same height or colour or degree of intelligence. Therefore, in the nature of things, some will have ability to earn more, and others less. People with talents will have more and they will utilise their talents for this purpose. If they utilise their talents kindly, they will be performing the work of the state in a better way. Such people should exist in the society as trustees. I would allow a man of intellect to earn more according to his capacity. I would not cramp his talent to be equal with the inferiors. But the bulk of his greater earnings must be used for the good of the state, just as the income of all earning sons of the father goes to the common family fund. They would have their earnings only as trustees for equal distribution of the basic amenities among the common people.

### Précis

[Without a Heading]

We are born equal but we are not equally talented. All of us have not the same capacity and so it is absurd to claim a right to equal opportunity. Nature also does not permit us for that. Like physical appearance we are different in the degree of intelligence from each other. So talented perosns, by dint of their superior skill, earn more than others. But they should, like trustees, utilise the money for the welfare of the entire state.

### Passage 27

A future society can certainly be envisaged in which the length of the working day progressively decreased as a rising level of technique makes the production of the material requirements of society possible with less and less human labour. But in an unplanned society, a technological advance may be enabling one man to do work formerly requiring twenty men, throw many of the other nineteen out of work, if no steps be taken to make use of their labour-power. To make the full use of the potentialities of science for the benefit of all men, a degree of national and international planning is needed, which will enable the required goods and services to be produced, while offering to each man and woman opportunities for work. A democratic citizenship, alive to the potentialities of science, is also needed. In the modern world, the man in the street should become a citizen of scientific mind. He has to understand his role in the modern industry. He should be able to exercise his democratic rights on the basis of knowledge instead of prejudice. There is also a general cultural value of such understanding to him as an individual.

**Summary**

[Without a Heading]

Technological developments minimise human labour. But in an unplanned society technological progress threatens unemployment for a large number of people. So to make the full use of the potentialities of science for the benefit of all men a national and international planning is needed. We should admit that opportunity for work is a democratic right. So common people should be conscious of their role in the modern world. And for that their democratic rights should be bsed on knowledge instead of prejudice. It should include a general cultural value of such understanding as an individual too.

**Passage 28**

There is no doubt whatsoever about the vitality of the modern demand for equality. It has appeared in the form of the demand for equality between individuals, between classes and between nations. It has been at the root of every recent revolution and most recent wars. Nor is it a demand which would be satisfied by the formal political equality of the nineteenth century. It is specifically a demand for economic equality—for equality of economic resources or equality of economic opportunity. This problem requires, in the first instance, a positive programme. Our deliberate purposes should be to build up equality rather than to break down inequality. The process of equalisation can be achieved by gradual rather than by violent methods. Our first step should be to secure the distribution to all of what may, on a generous interpretation, be called the necessaries of life. Since in the area with which we are most likely to be concerned, this should not be difficult of attainment, the distribution of the necessaries of life may be supplemented by the distribution of many of the amenities and luxuries. Such a programme will create needs vast enough to make a full call on our resources.

**Summary**

[Without a Heading]

Demand for equality is found in all spheres of life—between individuals, between classes, between nations. Dissatisfaction on this issue has caused wars and revolutions. It is not only for the formal political equality, but for economic equality. A positive programme to build up equality rather than to break down inequality is needed to solve this problem. And it has to be gradually built up first by determining a process of distribution of necessary things and then the items of comfort, after taking a proper measure of total resources.

**Passage 29**

Our final aim can only be a classless society with equal economic justice and opportunity for all, a society organised on a planned basis for the raising of mankind to higher material and cultural levels. It should lead to cultivation of spiritual values of cooperation, unselfishness, the spirit of service, the desire to do right, goodwill and love—ultimaely a world order. Everything that comes in the way will have to be removed, gently if possible, and forcibly, if necessary. And there seems to be little doubt that coercion will often be necessary. But if force is used, it should not be in the spirit of hatred or cruelty, but with the dispassionate desire to remove an obstruction. That will be difficult. It is not an easy task; there is no easy way, and the pitfalls are numerous. The difficulties and pitfalls do not disappear by our ignoring them, but by realising their true nature and facing them boldly. All this sounds fanciful and utopian, and it is highly unlikely that many people will be moved by these noble motives. But we can keep them in view and stress them, and it may be that gradually they will lessen the hatred and passion that fill most of us.

**Summary**

[Without a Heading]

Classless society with equal economic justice and opportunity for all is our final aim. But it should be on a planned basis by improvement of all human values of cooperation, sympathy, the spirit of service, the desire to do right, goodwill and love. Obstacles to it must be removed, gently if possible, forcibly if necessary. But force, when used shoulld be devoid of hatred or cruelty. We cannot hope that difficulties will disappear by ignoring them. It can be done by realizing their true nature and facing them with courage. We cannot do it in a day, but we should always remember the noble goal.

**Passage 30**

It is almost a definition of a gentleman that he will not inflict pain on others in any way. He is mainly occupied in merely removing the obstacles which hinder the free and unembarassed action of those about him. His benefits may be considered as parallel to what are called comforts or conveniences in arrangements of a personal nature, like an easy chair or a good fire, which do their part in dispelling cold and fatigue. The true gentleman, in like manner, carefully avoids whatever may cause a jar or a jolt to the mind of those with whom he is surrounded : all clashing of opinions or collision of feeling; his great concern being to make everyone at his ease and at home. He has his eyes on all his company, he is tender towards the bashful, gentle towards the distant, and merciful towards the absurd. He makes light of favours that he does towards them and seems to be receiving when he is conferring. He never speaks of himself by a mere retort, he has no ears for slander or gossip.

**Summary**

[Without a Heading]

A true gentleman never inflicts pain on others. He only tries to remove the obstacles in his way of progress. His benefits are parallel to comforts of a personal nature. He puts much importance on the lookout for respecting others' feelings and making them feel at home in his company. He tries to avoid all clashing of opinions or collision of feeling. He tries to understand all sorts of people and adjust his own behaviour to theirs. He is gentle, free from arrogance and sympathetic towards all. He never indulges in scandals or gossip.

**Passage 31**

If you look at the men and women whom you can call happy, you will see that they all have certain things in common. The most important of these things is an acivity which at most times is enjoyable on its own account, and which, in addition gradually builds up something that you are glad to see coming into existence. Women who take an instinctive pleasure in their children...can get this kind of satisfaction out of bringing up a family. Artists and authors and men of science get happiness in this way if their own work seems good to them. But there are many humbler forms of the same kind of pleasure. Many men who spend their working life in the city devote their week-ends to voluntary and unremunerated toil in their gardens, and when the spring comes, they experience all the joys of having created beauty.

It is impossible to be happy without activity, but it is also impossible to be happy if the activity is excessive or of a repulsive kind. Activity is agreeable when it is directed very obviously to a desired end and is not in itself contrary to impulse.

**Summary**

[Without a Heading]

All the happy men and women have certain common things. One of them is activity which is mostly enjoyable on its own account. Moreover it builds up something pleasant that comes into existence. Women find an instinctive pleasure in their children. They get such kind of satisfaction when they bring up a family. Artists, authors, scientists too get happiness in their creative work. There are some humbler forms of pleasure too. Those who live in a city can find pleasure in outing in the week-ends or in gardening, etc. In all these things some kind of activity is the source of happiness. But excessive work or a repulsive work may act in opposite direction.

## EXERCISE

### Passage 1

What is a machine? It is a big tool to help man to do his work. Man has been called a tool-making animal, and from his earliest days he has made tools and tried to better them. His supremacy over the other animals, many of them more powerful than he, was established because of his tools. The tool was an extension of his hand or you may call it a third hand. The machine was the extension of the tool. The tool and the machine raisd man above the brute creation. They freed human society from the bondage of nature. With the help of the tool and the machine, man found it easier to produce things. He produced more and yet had more leisure. And this resulted in the progress of the arts, of civilisation and of thought and science. But the big machine and all its allies have not been unmixed blessings. If the machine has encouraged the growth of civilization, it has also encouraged the growth of barbarism by producing terrible weapons of warfare and destruction. If it has produced abundance, this abundance has not been mainly for the masses, but chiefly for the limited few. It has made the differene between the luxury of the very rich and the poverty of the poor even greater than it was in the past. Instead of being the tool a servant of man, it has presumed to become his master.

**Hints for Summary :** The man-made tools and machines have placed man above all other animals. The tools and machines have advantages and disadvantages. The increase of production by the use of machine results in making a few people rich and increasing poverty of the masses. Instead of being the servant of man, the tools have now become the master of man.

### Passage 2

Science affects the average man and woman in two ways. He or she benefits by its applications driving in a motor car or an omni-bus instead of a horse-drawn vehicle; being treated for a disease by a doctor or surgeon rather than a witch, and being killed with an automatic pistol or a shell in place of a dagger or a battle-axe. It also affects his or her opinions. Almost everyone believes that the earth is round, and the heaven is nearly empty, instead of solid. And we are beginning to belive in our animal ancestry and the possibility of vast improvements in human nature by biological method.

But science can do something far bigger for human mind than the substitution of one set of beliefs for another, or the inculcation of scepticism regarding accepted opinions. It can gradually spread among humanity as a whole the point of view that prevails among research workers, and has enabled a few thousand men and a few dozen women to create the science on which modern civilisation rests.

**Hints for Summary :** The passage is about the influence of science of man. It further says that modern civilisationnn owes a debt to the scientific attitude of man.

### Passage 3

Some people seem to imagine that the human mind is like a bottle, and that when you have filled it with anything, you pour it out again and it becomes empty as it was before. That is not the nature of the human mind. It is never completely empty or completely full. The boy who has been crammed has learned a good deal, and that learning has accomplished two objects. In the first place, the boy has exercised the faculties of his mind in being crammed, and in the next place, there remains in his mind a great portion of the knowledge so acquired. Depending upon it that boy who is crammed successfully, not only may succeed in the examination for which he is preparing, but is from that time forward, more intellectually better informed and more didposed to push forward the knowledge by which that cramming he has acquired.

**Hints for Summary :** The passage is a discussion of the function of human mind. The relationships between cramming and knowledge, the cramming and the preparation for future have also been dealt with.

### Passage 4

Vivekananda's writings on nationalism have made a more powerful impact than those of other writers, because they have a broader base and also because they come from a philosophy that might be called perennial. Although he was a Hindu monk, preaching a certain form of Vedanta, it is so catholic that men of all faiths, including atheists and agnostics, may draw inspiration from his writings, which preach spirituality but do not recognise any heaven beyond the earth, and he never loses sight of the temporal forces—racial, economic and political—which sustain our quest for the beyond. An important feature of this comprehensiveness is his discovery of the similarity between his philosophy or religion and other faiths, Buddhism, Judaism, Christianity and Islam and his frank criticism of them all. Thus his philosophy or religion has an appeal for all people because he has his feet firmly planted on solid earth. Although no one has shown greater contempt for pleasures that are merely sensual, his eyes were rightly fixed o the material well-being of men, and although he preachd doctrines that are acceptable to all, he had little faith in mysticism and occultism.

**Hints for Summary :** Vivekananda's broad basis of philosophy has been discussed in this passage. Swami Vivekananda cherishd a very liberal outlook about life and religion and considered the material welfare of people though he was a monk.

### Passage 5

The activity represented in human education is a worldwide one; it is a great movement of universal cooperation interlinked by different ages and countries. And India, though defeated in her political destiny, has her responsibility to hold up the causes of truth, even to cry in the wilderness, and offer her lessons to the world as the best gifts she could produce. The messengers of truth have ever joined their hands across centuriies, across the seas, across historical barriers and they help to form the great continent of human brotherhood. Education in all its different forms and channels has its ultimate purpose in the evolving of a luminous sphere of human mind from the nebula that has been rushing around ages to find in itself an external centre of unity. We, individuals, however small may be our power and whatever corner of the world we may belong to, have the claim upon us to add to the light of the consciousness that comprehends all humanity.

**Hints for Summary :** Man's educational activities have been linked up with different ages and countries. The Indians have a role in spreading education and humanity by joining other in the world.

### Passage 6

Courage is a mental state—an affair of the spirit—and so it gets strength from spiritual and intellectual sources. The way in which these spiritual and intellectual elements are blended, I think, produces roughly the two types of courage. The first, an emotional state which urges a man to risk injury or death—physical courage. The second, a more reasoning attitude which enables him coolly to stake career, happiness, his whole future, on his judgement of what he thinks either right or worthwhile—moral courage. Now these two types of courage, physical and moral, are very distinct. I have known many men who had marked physical courage but lacked moral courage. Some of them were in high places but they failed to be great in themselves because they lacked it. Moral courage is a higher and a rarer virtue than physical courage.

**Hints for Summary :** Courage has been defined as a mental state. There are two types of courage—physical and moral.

### Passage 7

We can separate a man from a beast by his quality of virtue. It is something which distinguishes him from all other creatures. It is his nature. It is his mark. It is his character. Wonderful it is to think that man is distinguished from all other creatures by this higher and grander standard of conduct we call virtue—the things worthy of a man. He goes to the rescue of someone he has never seen—a woman in a burning house, a child in a dark sea; why? Because he is a man. He goes to the stake or to the scaffold for an idea which he can never prove in this world to be true; why? Because he is a man. What do we say when we read of some cruel creature who has beaten a child or struck a woman? We say, 'He is no man.' What do we say of the traitor who sells his country to the foe? We say, 'He is no man'. Something tells us at once that a man who could do such things as these is 'no man'. He has played the traitor to himself. He has denied the man in his soul.

**Hints for Summary :** The passage is about some qualities which distinguish man from all other animals. Several deviations from the right human nature have also been pointed out in the passage.

### Passage 8

The world is like a looking glass; if you smile, it smiles, if you frown, it frowns back. If you look at it through a red glass, all seems red and rosy; if through a blue, all blue; if through a smoked one, all dull and dingy. Always try then to look at the bright side of things. There are some persons whose smile, whose voice, whose very presence seem like ray of sunshine and brighten the whole room. Greet everybody with a bright smile, kind words and a pleasant welcome. It is not enough to love those who are near and dear to us. We must show that we do that. While enjoying the blessings of life, we cannot expect to have no sorrow or anxieties. Life is indeed a tragedy at times, and comedy very often, but as a rule it is what we choose to make it.

**Hints for Summary :** Optimism has been said to have a good impact on everybody. The world will be a good place to live in if graces of life are valued.

### Passage 9

No generation leaves the world as it finds it. We shall change our cities and villages, just the men have done in the past. The great and wonderful city of Babylon consits now of ruins buried in the ground, and its glory is forgotten. Cities, like people, grow and die; increase or decrease in importance. All such changes are the result of the restless energies of man. The generation now growing up will have the same energies and will not be satisfied with what it finds in the world. Some of us will invent new machines or instruments; some will suggest new scientific theories; some will explore new places or new regions of thought. Every fresh mind is different from every other mind of the present or the past and it may have a contribution to make to the progress of mankind. And, so, the changes continue for better or for worse.

**Hints for Summary :** Changes in different ages cause human progress or its reverse. People of each generation use their energy to bring about suitable changes.

### Passage 10

A great may worries can be diminished by realising the unimportance of the matter which causing the anxiety. I have done in my time a considerable amount of public speaking; at first every audience terrified me, and nervousness made me speak very badly; I dreaded ordeal so much that I always feared I might break my leg before I had to make a speech, and when it was over I was exhausted from the nervous strain. Gradually I taught myself to feel that it did not matter whether I spoke well or ill, the universe would remain much the same in either case. I found that the less I cared whether I spoke well or badly, the less badly I spoke, and gradually the nervous strain diminshed almost to a vanishing point. A great deal of nervous fatigue can be dealt with in this way. Our doings are not so important as we naturally suppose; our successes and failures do not after all matter very much. Even great sorrows can be survived; troubles which seem as if they must put an end to happiness in a life fade with the lapse of time until it becomes almost impossible to remember their poignancy.

**Hints for Summary :** We can reduce our worries by realising the futility of the matter which is causing the anxiety.

### Passage 11

Sri Lanka's national cricket team transformed the country from underdog status to a major international team during the 1990s. The team went on to win the 1996 Cricket World Cup, beating Australia in the finals, and becoming World Champions. Since then, the team has continued to be a major force in international cricket. The Sri Lankan cricket team reached the finals of the 2007 Cricket World Cup but lost to Australia in a rain-affected final match. And in 2011 Cricket World Cup they lost to India despite a great batting performance by Sri Lankan player Mahela Jayawardene. The batting of Sanath Jayasuriya (retired) and Aravinda de Silva (retired), backed up by the bowling of Muttiah Muralitharan (retired) and Chaminda Vaas (retired), among many other talented cricketers, has underpinned the successes of Sri Lankan cricket during the last 15 years.

**Hints for Summary :** Sri Lanka emerged as an international cricket team during the 1990s and has bagged the successes during the last 15 years.

# 8 DESCRIBING A PROCESS

## WHAT IS DESCRIBING A PROCESS AND HOW CAN IT BE DONE?

**Describing a Process means description of a continued set of actions to reach some result.**

**This Process may be described in two ways :**

**(i) It may be described in Impersonal Form and in the Passive Voice.**

**(ii) It may be described by a set of Imperative Sentences.**

**(iii) It may be described by a set of Assertive Sentences.**

In both the ways the **Sentence Linkers** which are generally used are :

At first/First, now, then, next, after that, later, thereafter, finally, at last, etc.

You should have an introductory sentence like this : The preparation of ...... goes through a number of steps. (or, ...... is prepared through various steps).

**[A] USING PASSIVE VOICE**

**[1]** The flow-chart below is about the preparation of a mixture useful for rehydration or removing shortage of water in the body. It is also useful for curing diarrhoea. Use the flow-chart and describe the Process in about 80 words :

clean hands, clean pots, teaspoon → one litre boiled but cold water in a pot → sugar or honey—2 tablespoonfuls

↓

ordinary salt : $\frac{1}{4}$ teaspoonful → orange juice $\frac{1}{2}$ cup or lemon juice—a few drops → sodibicarb—commonly called edible soda—$\frac{1}{4}$ teaspoonful

↓

stirring well → ready for use

## REHYDRATION MIXTURE

Rehydration mixture is prepared through various steps. First, hands, pots, a teaspoon, a tablespoon and a cup are to be cleanly washed. A liter (litre) of boiled water, after cooling, is to be poured in a pot. Then two tablespoonfuls of sugar or honey, $\frac{1}{4}$ tea-spoonful of common salt, $\frac{1}{2}$ cup of orange juice or a few drops of lemon juice and $\frac{1}{4}$ teaspoonful of sodibicarb (commonly called edible soda) are to be added to the water in the pot. The mixture is to be stirred well. Now the Rehydration Mixture is ready. It is used for removing shortage of water in the body. It is also useful for curing diarrhoea.

**Note** British spelling : litre; American spelling : liter

**[2] Study the following flow-chart. It tells you how newspapers are produced. Write a Paragraph in about 110 words describing the Process. Use an introductory sentence.**

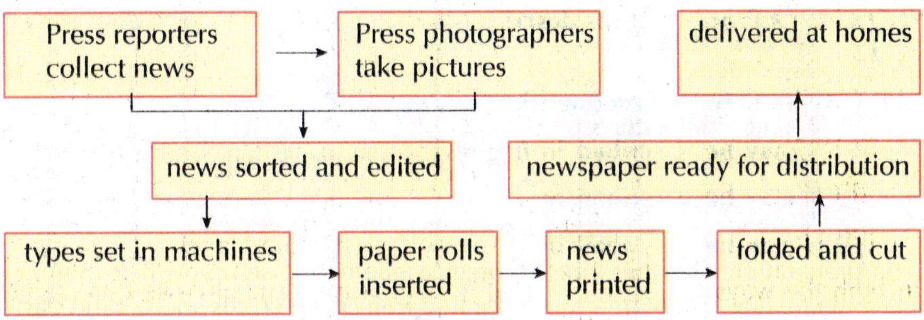


## NEWSPAPER PROCESSING

We read newspapers but very few of us know how newspapers are produced. There is a chain of activities beginning from the collection of news to the delivery of the printed newspapers at homes. First, press-reporters collect news that deserve to be published and the press-photographers take picturers illustrating the news to be published. The collected news and photos are then sorted and edited. Next comes the printing of the sorted news. Types are set in machines and paper rolls are inserted. Thus the news is printed on the newsprint. The papers are then folded and cut according to size. Newspapers are now ready for distribution to marketing agents. Finally, the newspapers are delivered at homes by hawkers.

**[3] Describe in about 70 words how clothes are washed and made ready for wear. Use the following chart :**

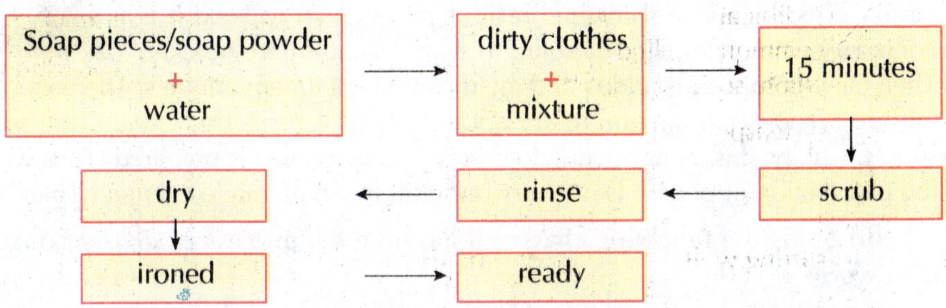


['rinse' means to remove dirt and soap lather or foam, with clean water.]

## WASHING CLOTHES

Dirty clothes are washed through a number of stages. At first, soap-pieces or soap powder is mixed with clean water. Then the dirty clothes are dipped in the mixture. It is left for 15 minutes. Next they are scrubbed and rinsed. After that they are dried in the sun. Then they are pressed or ironed. Now they are ready for wear. Thus we see, washing clothes is not very difficult and we can do it ourselves.

**[4] Describe in about 70 words how butter is made. Use the following chart :**

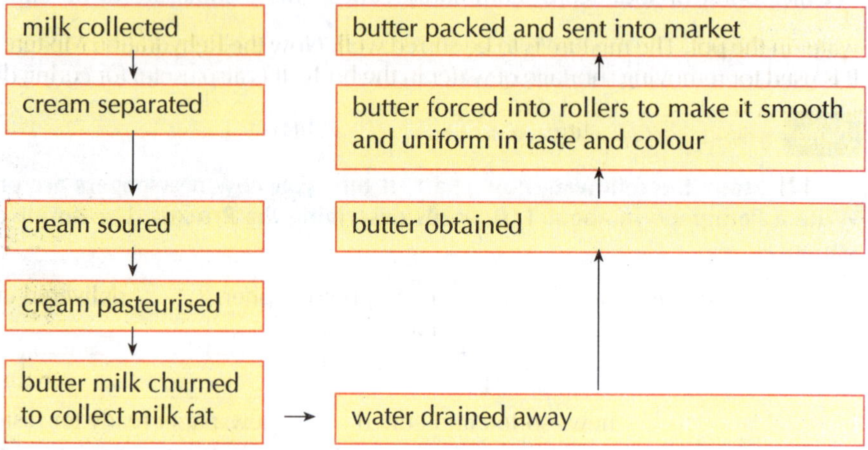


## PREPARATION OF BUTTER

The preparation of butter goes through a number of steps. At first milk is collected from the market. Then cream is separated from it. Next it is soured and pasteurised—i.e. heating to 72°C/161°F for 15 seconds followed by rapid cooling to 10 °C/50 °F. After that butter milk is churned to collect milk fat. Then water is drained away from it. Thus butter is obtained. Then the butter is forced into rollers to make it smooth and uniform in taste and colour. Finally, the butter is packed and sent off to market.

**[5] Describe the preparation of Phenyl at home with the help of the following outlines :**

Boiling castor oil—mixing crushed resin—cooling—mixing caustic soda—solution—stirring solution quickly—adding creosote oil—keeping the mixture for ten minutes—adding carbolic and potassium permanganate—pouring water—stirring the solution—keeping it for 24 hours.

## PREPARATION OF PHENYL

The preparation of phenyl goes through a number of steps. At first, castor oil is boiled. The crushed resin is mixed with it. Next it is cooled. After that caustic soda solution is mixed and stirred quickly. Then the creosote oil is added and the mixture kept for ten minutes. Thereafter, carbolic and potassium permanganate are added. Then water is poured and the solution is stirred. Finally, it is left for twentyfour hours. Now phenyl is prepared. Thus we see that the preparation of phenyl is not very difficult. It can be made even at home.

**[6] Study the following chart and describe the process of soap-making in about 100 words :**

Coconut oil, caustic soda and water—heated for thirty minutes—allowed to cool—common salt added—kept for 12 hours—cut to cakes—ready for use.

## SOAP-MAKING

Soap is very useful in our daily life. It is prepared through a number of steps. First, coconut oil and caustic soda are mixed with water. The solution is heated for thirty minutes. Then the heated solution is allowed to cool. After that, common salt is added to the solution. It is left in that condition for twelve hours. As a result the mixture becomes solid. Thereafter, it is cut to cake-like pieces. Now the soap cakes are ready for use. So we see that soap making is not very difficult. We can make it ourselves at home or in school.

**[7] Study the following chart and describe how mango-pickle is prepared :**

Mangoes—buying—sorting—removing rotten ones, if any,—cleaning—cutting into pieces—drying—spices and salt—mixing mustard oil and chilli—keeping in a big flat pot in the sun—pouring into jars.

## MANGO PICKLE

Mango pickle is a delicious food. We can easily prepare it at our homes. It is prepared through a number of steps. At first some green mangoes are bought from market. Then they are sorted and the rotten ones, if any, are rejected. After that, the good ones are cleansed and cut to pieces. Thereafter, these pieces are dried for some time in the sun. Meanwhile measured spices, salt, mustard oil and chilli are mixed up with the pieces of mangoes. Then these mixed up pieces of mangoes are kept in a big flat pot in the sun for some days. Now mango pickle is ready and poured into jars for storage.

**[8] Describe the preparation of Vegetable Polao with the help of the following flow-chart :**

| | | | | | | |
|---|---|---|---|---|---|---|
| cleaning and washing of rice, peas, carrots and beans | → | cutting carrots and beans $\frac{1}{2}$ to 1 inch ($1\text{-}2\frac{1}{2}$ cm) size | → | placing the cooker without lid on optimum heat—adding ghee and masala—frying | → | cleaning and washing of rice, peas, carrots and beans |
| | | | | | | ↓ |
| removing lid to find that the polao is ready | ← | removing the cooker from oven, allowing it to cool for 2 minutes | ← | hearing a hissing sound within ten minutes | ← | adding water and salt—stirring—placing lid |

## VEGETABLE POLAO

The preparation of vegetable polao goes through a number of steps. At first rice, peas, carrots and beans are cleaned and washed. Then the carrots and beans are cut into $\frac{1}{2}$ to 1 inch ($1\text{-}2\frac{1}{2}$ cm) size. After that, the cooker without lid is placed on simmer—optimum heat. Then the masala is fried with ghee. Thereafter, the vegetables are added and fried for two or three minutes. Then rice is added and fried till it is slightly brown. Next water is poured and stirred with required salt. The lid is placed. A hissing sound is heard within ten minutes. After that, the cooker is removed from the oven and allowed to cool for two minutes. Finally, the lid is removed and the polao is ready to serve.

**[9] The Indian Air Force sometimes recruits airmen. Below is an outline of a selection procedure. Study it and describe the process of selecting the candidates :**

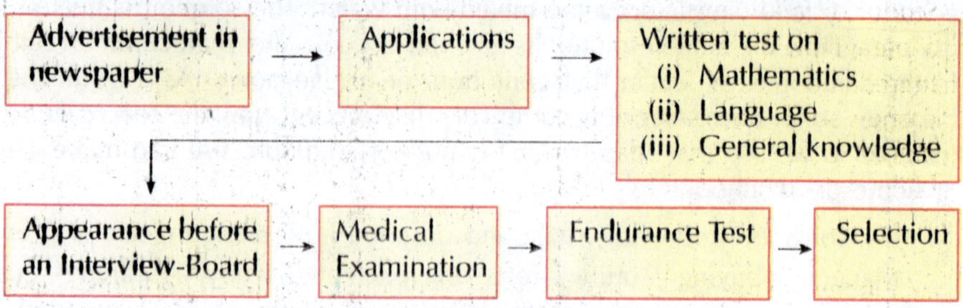


## PROCESS OF RECRUITMENT

Recruitment of the Indian Air Force is made by advertisement in newspaper. Applications are invitied from suitable candidates. Written tests on Mathematics, Language and General Knowledge are held. The eligible candidates are asked to appear before an Interview-Board by letters. After being duly interviewed the candidates have to go in for Medical Examination. They have to appear at the Endurance Test too. If they duly pass these tests, they are selected.

## [B] USING IMPERATIVE SENTENCES

So long we have described the Processes in Impersonal Form and Passive Voices. Now we can describe the Process in another way, i.e., by a set of instructions in Imperative Sentences. See the following :

**[10] Read the following flow-chart and describe the Process of making a phone-call from a public booth.**

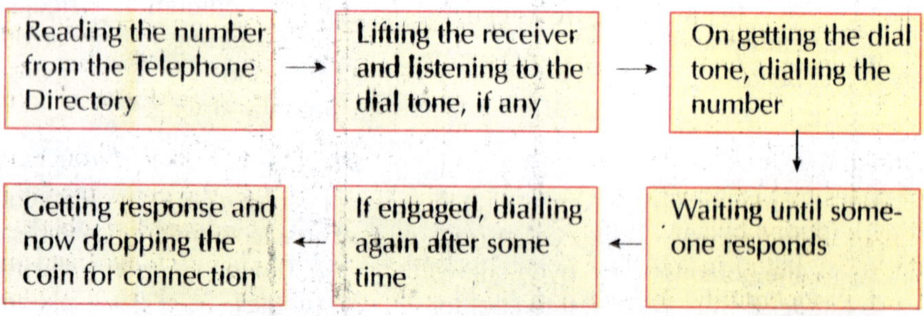


## MAKING A PHONE CALL

In making a phone call, first find out from the Telephone Directory the phone number of the person whom you like to ring (if the number is not known to you). Then lift the receiver and listen if there is a dial tone. If you get the dial tone, dial the number, one digit after another. When you get the ringing tone, wait until someone says, "Hello" from the other end. If you do not get the ringing tone or the line is engaged, dial the number once again after some time. However, when someone responds to you with 'Hello', drop a one rupee coin in the slit provided. Now the connection is established and you can talk to the person and listen to him as well on the phone.

## [C] USING ASSERTIVE SENTENCES

There is another form of describing a process by using Assertive sentences.

Study the following information table about Preparing a Cake at Home and write a paragraph on it.
Ingredients : eggs, butter, white flour, baking soda, sugar, essence of vanilla, cashew and raisin—special oven—mixing eggs into white flour—mixing other ingredients—whipping them in a blender—heating the oven—putting the cake batter into oven—cake done.

### PREPARING A CAKE AT HOME

Last Sunday we prepare a cake at home. We bought all the ingredients—eggs, butter, white flour, baking soda, essence of vanilla, cashew and raisins. Of course, we had sugar at home. But we were missing an important instrument—the baking oven. So we bought one. Now, we were ready to prepare our first cake. My mother mixed the eggs into the white flour. Then, she mixed the other ingredients and whipped them in a blender. All along I watched the process hopefully and attentively. Now, the oven was heated and she put the batter to bake on the oven for a few hours. The cake baked slowly. I kept a close eye on the rising batter. The aroma of the cake filled the whole house. Finally, the cake was done. We took it out of the oven and ate while it was still hot.

### DO IT YOURSELF

**Describe the Process how drinking water from Palta Water Works is supplied to Kolkata. (Use the Passive Voice)**

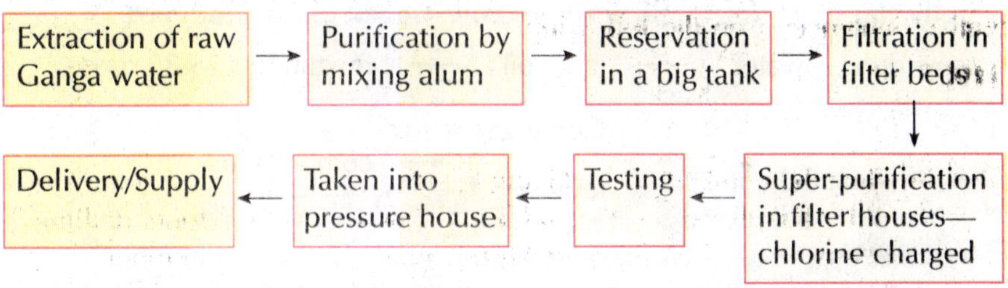


Drinking water from Palta Water Works ......... (supply), to Kolkata through a number of stages. At first, raw Ganga water ......... (extract) through the pump machines. Then it ...... (purify) by ......... (mix) alum. After that, it ......... (reserve) in a big tank. Next it ......... (filter) in the filter beds. Thereafter, chlorine ...... (charge) and the water ......... (superpurify) in filter houses. Then it ......... (test). Next it ......... (take) into pressure house. Finally drinking water ......... (supply) to the people of Kolkata.

### EXERCISE

1. **Study the flow-chart for preparing a cup of tea. Then write the process in about 80 words :**

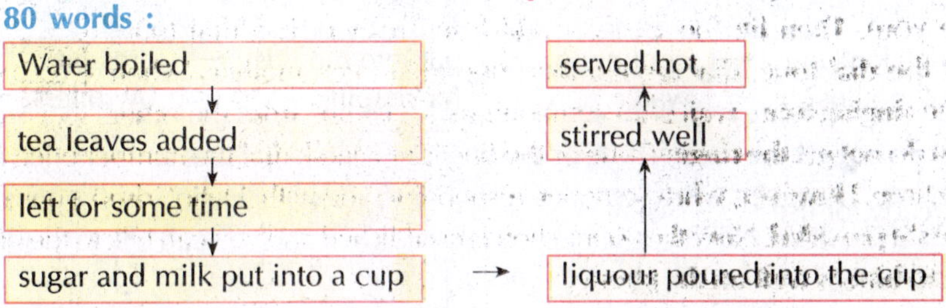

**2. Study the following flow-chart and describe how milk is processed :**

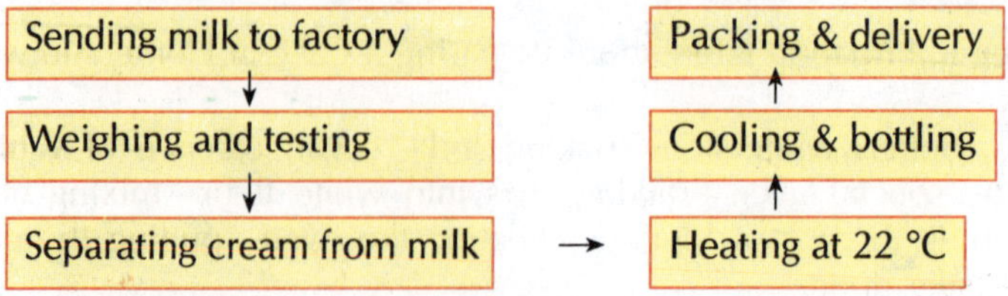


**3. Describe the process of making edible oil from mustard seed :**

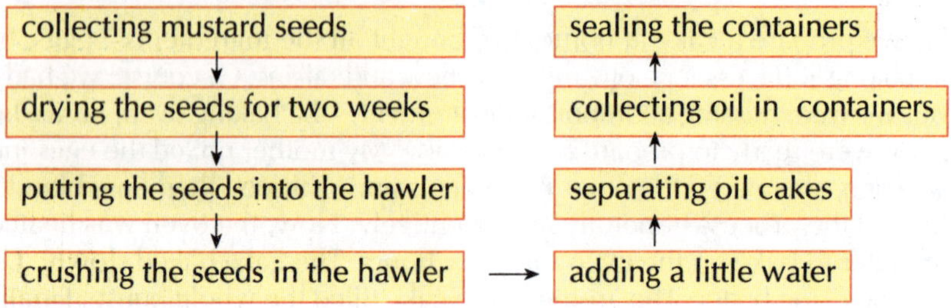


**4. Describe the Process of making paper with the help of the following flow-chart :**

Paper scrap/rags/torn clothes/straw and other raw materials→cut into small pieces→ cleaning and adding of lime → tearing to pieces and mixing of water → making soft, white pulp → mixing of colour if necessary → rolling flat to make smooth → cutting into different sizes as required → marketing and exporting.

**5. Study the flow chart and describe how Gobar gas is produced :**

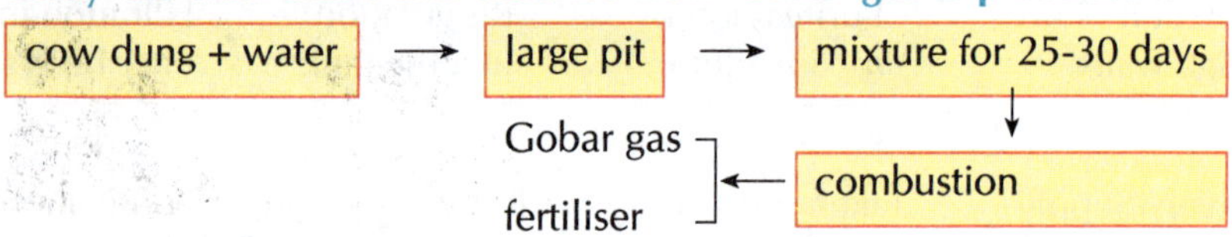


**6. Describe the process of formation and fall of rain from the following flow-chart :**

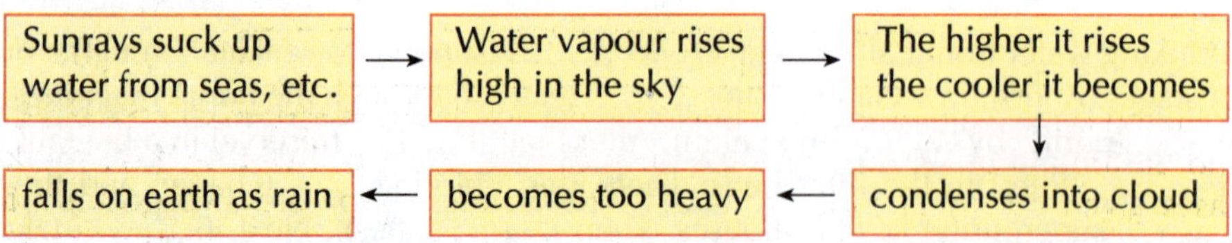


**7. Describe the process how polywood is made :**

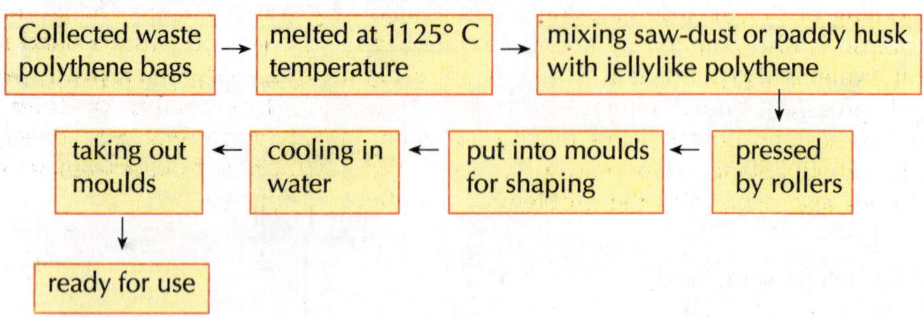

# 9 PICTURE DESCRIPTION

[ **Picture Description** is a very interesting task. It has been included in the New Syllabus in English for Madhyamik Level framed by NCRT in India and by NCTB in Bangladesh. ]

## WORKED OUT EXAMPLES

**[1] Look at the cartoons given below and write a descriptive account suggested by the cartoons. You may note that environmental pollution is the subject that needs most urgent attention of all concerned. You may add some more relevant points.**

**Fig. 1 :** Now, we'll do our environmental impact study

### ANS. [1] POLLUTION PROBLEM

Pollution is the main problem of the industrial age. Environment means the land, water and air around us. In our cities the air is always being polluted by dust, smoke and gases given out by factories and cars. The air and sound are also polluted by the bullying horns of cars, bursting of crackers and blaring of loud-speakers. Microphones are used indiscriminately during social and religious festivals and political gatherings. Shouting of slogans also contributes not a little to sound pollution. The ground we walk on is also polluted by uncollected garbage and chemical waste soaked in the soil. Water is also polluted as a result of untreated sewage, waste water, plastic packets and carcasses of dead animals released into rivers. Oil tankers clean out their tanks in the seas and power plants release hot water into rivers causing great damage to fish and aquaplants. They poison the water. Deforestation and indiscriminate felling of trees also aggravates the problem of pollution.

**[2] Study the picture given herewith. Write a description or an account of what the picture suggests to you. Your composition may be about the subject of the picture or you may take suggestions from it, but there must be a clear connection between the picture and the composition.**

## ANS. [2] THREE ESSENTIALS OF LIVING

The picture shows us the three essential elements of living—food, clothing and housing, and the economic disparity among the people in our social system. Population explosion has aggravated the situation to an alarming proportion. Now how to provide food and accommodation to this increasing mass of people is a serious problem. Instead of becoming a national asset, it has become a national liability. More children do not solely mean more workers of the future, but more people without work, more mouths to feed. Moreover, the problem is gaining more serious dimension as our national asset is not equally distributed among the people. Here the poor are becoming poorer and the rich are becoming richer—day-by-day.

**Fig. 2** Haves and Have-nots

## EXERCISE

**1. Look at the cartoon given and write a descriptive account of what happened. Your composition may be directly about the subject of the picture or you may take suggestions from it.**

**2. Study the cartoon given below and write an account of what it suggests relevantly.**

**3.** Look at the picture given. Write an account of what it suggests. The composition may be on the subject of the picture or you may take suggestions from it; but there must be a distinct relation between the picture and your composition.

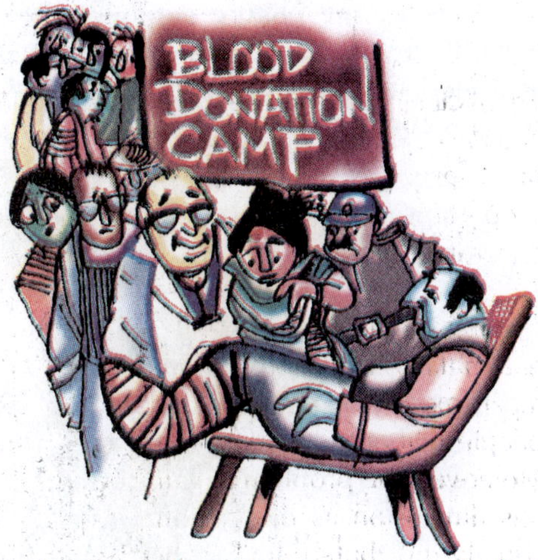


**4.** Look at the cartoon picture below and write a descriptive account of what happens.

**5.** Look at the cartoon below and write a descriptive account of what's happening. It will tell you something about the dowry system in our society.

**6.** Study the picture carefully and write a story or a description of what it suggests to you. Your composition may be directly about the subject of the picture or what it suggests to you but there must be a clear connection between the picture and the composition.

**7.** Study the picture given below. Write a story or a description or an account of what the picture suggests to you. Your composition may be directly about the subject of the picture or you may take suggestions from it, but there must be a clear connection between the picture and the composition.

**8.** Look at the cartoon given below and write a story or a descriptive account of what happened. Your composition may be directly about the subject of the picture or what it suggests to you.

**9.** Study the picture carefully and write a story or a description of what it suggests to you. Your composition may be directly about the subject of the picture or what it suggests to you, but there must be a clear connection between the picture and the composition.

**10.** Look at the cartoon picture below and write a descriptive account of what is happening. Your composition may be directly about the subject of the picture or what it suggests to you.

**11.** Study the picture carefully and write a story or a description of what it suggests to you. Your composition may be directly about the subject of the picture or what it suggests to you, but there must be a clear connection between the picture and the composition.

**12.** Study the picture carefully and write a story or a description of what it suggests to you. Your composition may be directly about the subject of the picture or what it suggests to you but there must be a clear connection between the picture and the composition.

**13.** Look at the cartoon below and write a descriptive account of what happened. Your composition may be directly about the subject of the picture or what it suggests to you.

**14.** Study the picture carefully and write a story or a description of what it suggests to you. Your composition may be directly about the subject of the picture or what it suggests to you but there must be a clear connection between the picture and the composition.

**15.** Study the picture carefully and write a story or a description of what it suggests to you. Your composition may be directly about the subject of the picture or what it suggests to you but there must be a clear connection between the picture and the composition.

**16.** Study the picture carefully and write a story or description of what it suggests to you. Your composition may be directly about the subject of the picture or what it suggests to you but there must be a clear connection between the picture and the composition.

**17.** Look at the picture given below and write a story or a descriptive account of what it suggests.

**18.** Study the picture carefully and write a story or a description of what it suggests to you. Your composition may be directly about the subject of the picture or what it suggests to you but there must be a clear connection between the picture and the composition.

**19.** Study the picture carefully and write a story or a description of what it suggests to you. Your composition may be directly about the subject of the picture or what it suggests to you but there must be a clear connection between the picture and the composi

**20.** Look at the picture below and write what the picture suggests to you. There must be a cleare connection between the picture and your composition.

# PART III

# READING COMPREHENSION

# READING COMPREHENSION

**Reading Comprehension** is meant for testing the power of understanding of the students. When a student studies something, he should try to grasp the meaning of it. Such comprehension tests do not require the students to write much but require them to have an idea of the reading material and answer the questions in a word, a few words or a sentence or by putting ticks, crosses, numbers or drawing arrows etc.

## GUIDELINES

**[1] Read the passage carefully.**

**[2] Read the questions carefully too.**

**[3] Then put ticks/crosses or write a word/number etc. as required.**

**[4] You may not know the meaning of all the words. But you may guess it in some cases.**

## COMPREHENSIONS FROM FAMILIAR EXTRACTS

**[1] Read the following text carefully and answer the questions below :**

And Jesus answering said; a certain man went down from Jerusalem to Jericho, and fell among thieves, which stripped him of his raiments, and wounded him, and deprated, leaving him half dead.

And by chance there came down a certain priest that way; and when he saw him, he passed by the other side.

And likewise a Levite, when he was at the place, came and looked on him, and passed by on the other side.

But a certain Samaritan, as he journeyed, came where he was. And when he saw him, he had compassion on him.

And went to him, and bound up his wounds, pouring in oil and wine, and set him on his own beast, and brought him to an inn, and took care of him.

And on the morrow when he departed, he took out two pence, and gave them to the host, and said unto him, "Take care of him, and whatsoever thou spendest more, when I come again, I will repay thee."

"Which now of these three, thinkest thou, was neighbour unto him that fell among the thieves?"

And he said, 'He that shewed mercy on him.' Then said Jesus unto him, 'Go and do thou likewise.'

[ **'The Parable of the Good Samaritan'** ]

**A. Answer the following questions :**

(i) What is a parable?

........................................................................................................

........................................................................................................

........................................................................................................

........................................................................................................

........................................................................................................

(ii) Who is Jesus talking to?

........................................................................................................

........................................................................................................

(iii) What question does Jesus give an answer to?

........................................................................................................

........................................................................................................

(iv) What answer does Jesus bring out to that question?

........................................................................................................

........................................................................................................

(v) What does the phrase 'a good Samaritan' mean nowadays?

........................................................................................................

........................................................................................................

........................................................................................................

........................................................................................................

........................................................................................................

**B. Put a sentence from the text against each function in the following table :**

| | |
|---|---|
| (i) Reporting | (i) |
| (ii) Requesting | (ii) |
| (iii) Enquiring | (iii) |
| (iv) Answering | (iv) |
| (v) Giving advice | (v) |

**C. The following sentences are jumbled up. Put them in order of sequence. Put 1, 2, 3 etc. in the brackets given :**

( ) The wounded man was brought to an inn.

( ) A Samaritan came and nursed the wounded man.

( ) A certain man was wounded by the thieves on the way from Jerusalem to Jericho.

( ) A Levite looked on the wounded man and passed by.

( ) A priest saw the wounded man but did not take care of him.

**ANS.**

**A.** (i) A parable is a short story having human characters with a moral. It is used in the Bible.

(ii) Jesus was talking to one of his disciples.

(iii) Jesus was giving an answer to the question "Who is your neighbour?"

(iv) Jesus brought out the answer that he who shows mercy on a person is his real neighbour.

(v) Nowadays the phrase 'a good Samaritan' means a kind-hearted man.

**B.** (i) **Reporting :** A certain man went down from Jerusalem to Jericho and fell among the thieves.

(ii) **Requesting :** Take care of him.

(iii) **Enquiring :** Which now of these three, thinkest thou, was neighbour unto him that fell among the thieves?

(iv) **Answering :** He that shewed mercy on him.

(v) **Giving advice :** Go and do thou likewise.

**C.** (5) The wounded man ........ to an inn.

(4) A Samaritan ........ man.

(1) A certain man ........ Jericho.

(3) A Levite ........ passed by.

(2) A priest ........ care of him.

**[2] Read the following and answer the questions given below :**

A wolf and a fox conspired to kill a lot of other animals and store up the meat for future meals. In the name of King Lion they called all the animals together and declared, "It is said that there is known throughout the forest a prescription for eternal youth and immortality which was handed down from the past, and it is being kept from us two and King Lion. On behalf of King Lion we order you to tell it. Anyone who refuses will be sentenced to death."

As self-appointed representatives of the king, the fox acted as the inquistitor, the wolf as executioner. The deer was the first to be called up, and of course, it knew of no such prescription. So the fox declared, "This deer is sentenced to death", and the wolf pounced on it.

The deer was followed by a goat and a pheasant and they were killed in the same way.

Who would be next? Terror loomed large in the silent forest.

Then a small white rabbit hopped in front of the fox and the wolf and said calmly, "I know the prescription."

Of course, the wolf and the fox knew there was no such thing.

"What did you say?"

"Don't you want the secret prescription? I know it."

"Out with it then."

"The prescription is that King Lion must eat the heart of the fox and lungs of the wolf freshly cut from their bodies." Then the rabbit turned to the other animals and shouted, "Brothers, it's time to act! Cut out their hearts and lungs and offer them to the King."

The other animals, united by their common hatred of the fox and wolf, pounced on them and killed them in no time.

[ **'The Rabbit's Prescription'** ]

**A. Answer the following questions :**

(a) Give a suitable title for the paragraphs above.

(b) Was the King Lion responsible for the conspiracy in the forest? Answer in one word.

(c) What was the distinguishing feature in the rabbit?

(d) Did all the animals in the text belong to the same category? If not, mention the exception.

(e) What was the feeling of the fox and wolf when they said, "What did you say?"—Use one word.

(f) Fill in the blank : All the animals of the forest ........ the fox and the wolf.

(g) What is the function of the sentence, "Brothers, it's time to act!"?

(h) Do you find any moral in the text? If so, what is it?

(i) Make sentences of your own with :
'loomed large', 'in the long run', 'on behalf of'.

(j) Give synonyms for

(i) inquisitor ...........

(ii) executioner ...........

**B. Choose the correct alternatives with tick mark (√) in the following :**

'Out with it' means

(i) Go out with it. [ ] (ii) Bring it out. [ ] (iii) Disclose it. [ ]

**C. State T/F for true and false accordingly in the boxes below :**

(i) The wolf and the fox represented another big animal. [ ]

(ii) Hunger goaded them to kill other animals. [ ]

(iii) The deer had no presence of mind. [ ]

**ANS.**

**A.** (a) The conspiracy of a wolf and a fox.

(b) No.

(c) Ready wit and courage

(d) Pheasant

(e) Wonder

(f) killed

(g) Advice

(h) Unity is strength.

(i) Silence loomed large in the class when the Headmaster asked, "Who is guilty?" In the long run the guilty was detected. The monitor on behalf of the class asked for apology.

(j) enquirer, killer.

**B.** Disclose it. [√]

**C.** (i) F (ii) F (iii) T

**[3] Read the paragraphs and answer the questions below :**

Something about the peace and quiet of the morning stirred Davy into reminiscing. Faraday's problem reminded him of his own early struggle.

In an almost inaudible voice Sir Humphry began to tell his personal history as a scientist. He was apprenticed to an apothecary at the age of fifteen. Some friends helped him get a place in the Pneumatic Institute at Bristol. Then came the famous experiments with nitrous oxide or laughing gas. He had to breathe the gas to prove that it was not poisonous. More experiments followed. These researches caught the attention of the public. Finally came the meeting and his appointment as Director of the Chemical Laboratory of the Royal Institution.

"It was mainly chance or good fortune, young man," Davy said modestly. "It may never happen to another person in a thousand years." He paused for a moment as he looked at the young book-binder. 'Stay at your trade, Mr. Faraday, I am sure you are a man of excellent abilities; but one must be practical in this world.'

Faraday's face fell with disappointment and he remained silent. That last remark depressed him. [ **'An Interview'** ]

**A. Write the events of Davy's life in the order suggested in the text. One has been done for you :**

**Example :** (iii) Experiments with laughing gas.

(i) .............. (ii) .............. (iii) .............. (iv) .............. (v) ..............

**B. Fill in the following chart :** 1 × 5

| Cause | Effect |
|---|---|
| (i) Davy advised Faraday to stay at his trade. | |
| (ii) Davy listened to Faraday's problem. | |
| | (iii) Davy wanted Faraday to be practical. |
| (iv) Nitrous oxide was suspected to be harmful. | |
| | (v) Davy joined the Pneumatic Institute. |

**C. Find out the sentences from the above paragraphs to prove that the following statements are false :**

(i) Nitrous Oxide is a harmful gas.

(ii) Davy's career was very smooth.

(iii) Davy was in doubt of Faraday's qualities.

(iv) Davy's comment made Faraday happy.

(v) People did not give importance to Davy's works.

**D. "It was mainly chance or good fortune, young man." Who said this and to whom? What does the word 'It' refer to here?**

**ANS.** **A.** (i) Apprentice to an apothecary (ii) A place in the Pneumatic Institute at Bristol (iii) Experiments with laughing gas (iv) More experiments followed (v) Director of the Chemical Laboratory of the Royal Institution.

**B.** (i) Faraday was disappointed. (ii) Davy recalled his own early struggle. (iii) Davy had bitter experience. (iv) He had to breathe the gas to prove that it was not poisonous. (v) Some friends helped Davy.

**C.** (i) He had to breathe ........ not poisonous. (ii) Faraday's problem reminded him of his own early struggle. (iii) I am sure you are a man of excellent abilities. (iv) That last remark depressed him. (v) These researches caught the attention of the public.

**D.** Davy said this to Faraday. Here 'It' refers to the position of Davy in the field of science.

**[4] Read the following text carefully and answer the questions below :**

Jute is almost entirely an Indian crop but it is cultivated on a large scale in Bangladesh, Pakistan, Brazil, Mexico, Japan, China, Argentina, Indonesia, Iran, etc. So great is its economic value that about four million farming families are engaged in the cultivation of jute in India. As an industrial crop it is quite cheap and in importance it is only next to cotton. The things made from jute are also eco-friendly.

Jute is used mainly for rough weaving. Various types of bags, ropes, sacks and covers are made of jute. The superior, long and glossy fibres are used for making carpets, twine, curtains, cloth etc. Jute butts, i.e., short fibres and pieces from the lower ends of the stalks, are used in paper-making. The white stalks are used widely in rural areas as fuel and material for walling or fencing. [ **'The Importance of Jute'** ]

**A. Answer the following questions :**

(i) Name four countries where jute is cultivated on a large scale.

..........................................................................................................

(ii) What is its economic value and why?

..........................................................................................................

(iii) What is its industrial importance and why?

..........................................................................................................

(iv) What do you mean by 'eco-friendly'? Are the jute-goods 'eco-friendly'?

..........................................................................................................

**B. Fill in the following chart :**

| What? | How used? |
|---|---|
| (a) ordinary jute fibre | (a) |
| (b) superior jute fibre | (b) |
| (c) jute stalks | (c) |
| (d) jute butts | (d) |

**ANS :**

**A.** (i) Jute is cultivated on a large scale in India, Bangaldesh, Pakistan, China, etc.

(ii) Its economic value is great as about four million farming families are engaged in the cultivation of jute in India.

(iii) Its industrial importance is next to cotton as it is a quite cheap crop.

(iv) 'Eco-friendly' means something that helps to maintain the balance of eco-system of nature.

**B.**

| What? | How used? |
|---|---|
| (a) ordinary jute fibre | (a) rought weaving of bags, ropes, sacks and covers |
| (b) superior jute fibre | (b) making carpets, twine, curtains, cloth, etc. |
| (c) jute stalks | (c) fuel and material for walling or fencing |
| (d) jute butts | (d) paper making |

**[5] Read the following text carefully and answer the questions below :**

It was a large lovely garden, with soft green grass. Here and there over the grass stood beautiful flowers like stars, and there were twelve peach trees that in the spring-time broke out into delicate blossoms of pink and pearl, and in the autumn bore rich fruit. The birds sat on the trees and sang so sweetly that the children used to stop their games in order to listen to them. 'How happy we are here!' they cried to each other.

One day the Giant came back. He had been to visit his friend the Cornish Ogre, and had stayed with him for seven years. After the seven years were over he had said all that he had to say, for his conversation was limited, and he determined to return to his own castle. When he arrived, he saw the children playing in the garden.

'What are you doing?' he cried in a very gruff voice, and the children ran away.

'My own garden is my own garden', said the Giant; 'anyone can understand that, and I will allow nobody to play in it but myself'. So he built a high wall all round it, and put up a notice board : [ *'The Selfish Giant'* ]

**TRESPASSERS WILL BE PROSECUTED**

**A. Answer the following questions :**

(i) What is the name of the Giant's friend?

..........................................................................................

(ii) How long was the Giant absent from his castle?

..........................................................................................

(iii) Why did he stay outside his castle?

..........................................................................................

(iv) What did the Giant see on his return?

..........................................................................................

(v) Which words of the Giant bring out his selfishness?

..........................................................................................

**B. State which of the following statements are true and which are false. Write T for true and F for false statements in the boxes :**

(i) The Giant had a sweet voice. ☐

(ii) The Giant was very talkative. ☐

(iii) There were twenty apple trees in the garden. ☐

(iv) The children liked to listen to the songs of the birds. ☐

**C. Pick out an expression where the speaker is expressing an intention :**

..........................................................................................................

**D. What did the Giant do to prevent the children from entering his garden?**

..........................................................................................................

**E. Pick out the nominal compound from the text and expand its meaning :**

(i) Nominal Compound : ..........................................................................

(ii) Expansion of its meaning : ...............................................................

**ANS.**

**A.** (i) The name of the Giant's friend was Cornish Ogre.

(ii) The Giant was absent from his castle for seven years.

(iii) He stayed outside his castle as he had been to visit his friend, the Cornish Ogre.

(iv) On his return, he saw the children playing in his garden.

(v) The words "My own garden is my own garden" and "I will allow nobody to play in it but myself" bring out his selfishness.

**B.** (i) F (ii) T (iii) F (iv) T

**C.** "I will allow nobody to play in it but myself."

**D.** He built a high wall all round the garden and put up a notice-board : TRESPASSERS WILL BE PROSECUTED.

**E.** (i) Nominal compound : Notice-board.

(ii) Expansion of its meaning : A board for writing notice.

**[6] Read the following text carefully and answer the questions below :**

It was spring time. From the shadow of narow lanes and alleys emerged a gaily clad crowd. The men, women and children were all going to the fair. Some walked, some rode on horses, others went in bullock-carts. One little boy ran between his parents' legs. He was very happy and filled with life and laughter.

'Come, child, come', called his parents, as he lagged behind, attracted by the toys in the shops that lined the way.

He hurried towards his parents, his feet obedient to their call, his eyes still lingering on the receding toys. As he came to where they had stopped to wait for him, he could not suppress the desire of his heart, even though he well knew the old cold stare of refusal in their eyes.

'I want that toy', he pleaded.

His father looked at him angrily. His mother, melted by the free spirit of the day, was tender and giving him her finger to hold, said : 'Look, child, what is in front of you'. The pleasure of what was in front of him filled his eager eyes. They had left the dusty road on which they had walked so far and entered a footpath in a field.

It was a flowering mustard field, pale like melting gold, as it swept across miles and miles of even land. The child looked up to his father and mother, and filled with the joy and wonder of this vast glory, left the footpath and plunged into the field, prancing like a colt. [ **'The Lost Child'** ]

**A.** **Write 'T' for true and 'F' for false statements in the boxes :**

(i) The child went to the fair with his friends. ☐

(ii) He was very obedient to his parents. ☐

(iii) The child wanted a toy. ☐

(iv) His father gladly purchased a toy for him. ☐

(v) The way to the fair ran at some place through the mustard field. ☐

**B.** **Make a list how the people were going to the fair :**

1................., 2................., 3. ....................

**C.** **Complete the table with information from the text :**

| Speech | Spoken by | Why? |
|---|---|---|
| (i) 'Come, child, come'.<br>(ii) 'I want that toy'.<br>(iii) 'Look, child, what is in front of you.' | | |

**D.** **Fill in the chart with information from the text :**

| Cause | Effect |
|---|---|
| (i)<br>(ii)<br>(iii) | (i) gaily clad crowd.<br>(ii) prancing like a colt.<br>(iii) cold stare of refusal in their eyes. |

**ANS.** **A.** (i) F (ii) T (iii) T (iv) F (v) T

**B.** 1. Some walked. 2. Some rode on horses. 3. Others went in bullock-carts.

**C.**

| Speech | Spoken by | Why? |
|---|---|---|
| (i) 'Come, child, come' | The child's parents | He lagged behind. |
| (ii) 'I want that toy' | A little boy | He was attracted by the nice toy. |
| (iii) 'Look, child, what is in front of you'. | His mother | She wanted to distract his mind from the toys. |

**D.**

| Cause | Effect |
|---|---|
| (i) They were going to the fair. | (i) gaily clad crowd |
| (ii) Filled with joy and wonder of the vast glory and beauty of the mustard field. | (ii) prancing like a colt |
| (iii) The parents did not agree to buy toys for the little boy. | (iii) cold stare of refusal in their eyes |

**[7]** **Read the following text carefully and answer the questions below :**

Dr. Vine : Sit down and don't talk. (He pulls Lester down on the chair). Now don't move. That's better.

Lester : But ......

Dr. Vine : And don't talk. How can I listen to your heart when you're talking? (Listens) Hm! Hm! I don't like this at all. Does your heart always go as fast as this? You must take a long rest, my dear Lester. No more work for you and no more parties for six months.

Lester : (putting his coat on) I'm sorry to hear that. I came here to ask you to come to a party at my house next week. And when I reached your house, I found that it was on fire. I just wanted to tell you that. [ **'Conversation'** ]

**A.** **Supply information from the text to complete the following tables :**

**(i)**

| Doctor | Patient | Findings on checking | Advice given |
|---|---|---|---|
| | | | |

**(ii)**

| What? | Who? | Purpose |
|---|---|---|
| called at Dr. Vine's chamber | | |

**B.** **Write 'T' for true and 'F' for false statements in the brackets given :**

(i) Lester had a heart disease. [ ]

(ii) Dr. Vine was annoyed because he was disturbed. [ ]

(iii) Lester's heart was going fast because he was excited. [ ]

(iv) Dr. Vine was eccentric to some extent. [ ]

(v) Lester could not tell Dr. Vine the bad news. [ ]

**C.** **Answer the following questions :**

(i) What did Lester want to tell Dr. Vine?

(ii) How does Lester come to know of Dr. Vine's house being on fire?

(iii) "I'm sorry to heart that." Who was sorry? Why was he sorry?

**D.** **Tick off (√) the correct alternatives :**

(i) Lester left his house with the object of

(a) consulting a doctor, (b) inviting Dr. Vine to a party, (c) giving Dr. Vine a bad news.

(ii) Lester's heart was going fast because of

(a) his illness, (b) weak heart, (c) some excitement.

(iii) Lester was advised a long rest because his heart-beat was

(a) normal, (b) very fast, (c) very slow.

**ANS. A. (i)**

| Doctor | Patient | Findings on checking | Advice given |
|---|---|---|---|
| Dr. Vine | Lester | Heart-beat very fast | A long rest. No more work and no more parties for six months |

**(ii)**

| What? | Who? | Purpose |
|---|---|---|
| Called at Dr. Vine's chamber | Lester | To ask Dr. Vine to come to a party at his house next week.<br>But when he reached his house, he found that it was on fire.<br>So he wanted to warn him about it. |

**B.** (i) F (ii) T (iii) T (iv) T (v) F

**C.** (i) Lester wanted to tell Dr. Vine that his house was on fire.

(ii) When he reached Dr. Vine's house, he found that it was on fire.

(iii) Lester was sorry. He was sorry to hear that his heart was going fast.

**D.** (i) (b) √ (ii) (c) √ (iii) (b) √

**[8] Read the following text carefully and answer the questions below :**

From my Uncle Podger's house to the railway station was eight minutes' walk. My uncle always said :

'Give yourself a quarter of an hour, walk gently.'

What he always did was to start five minutes before the time and run.

Many fat gentlemen lived at Ealing and caught this train to Town. They all started late; they all carried a black bag and a newspaper in one hand, and an umbrella in the other; and for the last quarter of a mile to the station, whether the weather was wet or fine, they all ran.

People with nothing else to do used to gather in the street on fine mornings to watch them pass, and shout encouragement to them. They did not run well, they did not even run fast; but they tried their hardest.

My uncle always got up early enough, but troubles seemed to come to him at the last moment. The first thing he did after breakfast was to lose his newspaper. Whenever he lost anything, my Uncle Podger did not say to himself, 'I am a careless old man. I lose everything. I never know where I have put anything. I can never find it again for myself. I must be a great trouble to everybody round me'. No, whenever he lost anything, he always blamed everybody except himself. [ **'A Daily Drama'** ]

**A. Complete the following chart with information from the text :**

| | |
|---|---|
| (i) Distance of the railway station from Uncle Podger's house | (i) |
| (ii) Uncle Podger's advice to others | (ii) |
| (iii) Uncle Podger's practice | (iii) |
| (iv) Who encouraged the commuters of Ealing? | (iv) |
| (v) The first thing Uncle Podger did after breakfast | (v) |

**B. Answer the following questions. Write not more than two sentences for each answer :**

(i) What things were common to the gentlemen of Ealing who caught the train to Town?

..................................................................................................

..................................................................................................

(ii) Who gathered in the street on fine mornings and why?

..................................................................................................

..................................................................................................

(iii) What did Uncle Podger do when he lost anything?

..................................................................................................

..................................................................................................

(iv) Why did he blame everybody except himself?

..............................................................................................

..............................................................................................

(v) Uncle Podger himself did not follow the advice he gave to others. Which sentence proves this?

..............................................................................................

..............................................................................................

**C. Write whether the following statements are true or false. Pick out the words/sentences from the text in support of your answer :**

(i) All the young people of Ealing encouraged the office-goers. [ ]

..............................................................................................

(ii) Though fat they ran fast. [ ]

..............................................................................................

(iii) Uncle Podger was a late-riser. [ ]

..............................................................................................

(iv) Uncle Podger was ashamed of his carelessness. [ ]

..............................................................................................

(v) Uncle Podger used to find the lost thing again for himself. [ ]

..............................................................................................

**ANS. A.**

| | |
|---|---|
| (i) Distance of the railway station from Uncle Podger's house | (i) eight minutes' walk |
| (ii) Uncle Podger's advice to others | (ii) to start before a quarter of an hour before the appointed hour and walk gently |
| (iii) Uncle Podger's practice | (iii) to start five minutes before the time and run |
| (iv) Who encouraged the commuters of Ealing? | (iv) People with nothing else to do encouraged them |
| (v) The first thing Uncle Podger did after breakfast | (v) to lose his newspaper |

**B.** (i) The gentlemen of Ealing carried a black bag and a newspaper in one hand and an umbrella in the other, and for the last quarter of a mile to the station, whether the weather was wet or fine, they all ran.

(ii) People with nothing else to do used to gather in the street on fine mornings.

(iii) Uncle Podger blamed everybody except himself when he lost anything.

(iv) He could not assess himself.

(v) "What he always did was to start five minutes before the time and run."

**C.** (i) False. "People with nothing else to do."

(ii) False. "They did not run well, they did not run fast; but they tried their hardest."

(iii) False. "My Uncle Podger always got up early."

(iv) False. "He always blamed everybody except himself."

(v) False. "I can never find it again for myself."

**[9] Read the following text carefully and answer the questions given below :**

Orlando and Adam also set out for the Forest of Arden. Before they had travelled very far they were both weary and hungry. While Adam rested in the shade of some trees, Orlando wandered into that part of the forest where the old duke and his band were living and came upon the band of outlaws at their meal. Desperate from hunger, Orlando rushed upon the duke and his mates with a drawn sword and demanded food. The duke immediately offered to share the hospitality of his table, and Orlando blushed with shame over his rude manner. But he would not touch a morsel until Adam had been fed. When the old duke found that Oralando was the son of his friend, Sir Rowland de Boys, he took Orlando and Adam under his protection and made them members of his band of foresters.

The forest of Arden ultimately became a place where separated friends and lovers were happily reunited. [ **'From the Court to the Woods'** ]

**Arrange the following incidents in the order in which they occur in the story :**

(a) Orlando demanded food.

(b) The Duke offered Orlando food.

(c) Adam rested in the shade of some trees.

(d) Orlando and Adam were tired and hungry.

(e) The outlaws in the forest were at their meal.

(f) Orlando would not partake a bit of food till Adam was fed.

(g) The fugitive Duke took Orlando and Adam under his protection.

ANS. (d) 1, (c) 2, (e) 3, (a) 4, (b) 5, (f) 6, (g) 7.

## [ FROM NEWSPAPERS, JOURNALS, ETC. ]

**[10] Read the passage and answer the questions below :**

In the wider sense letter-writing is now no doubt a lost art. It was killed by the penny-post and modern hurry. When Cowper, Horace Walpole, Byron and Carlyle wrote their immortal letters, the world was a leisurely place where there was time to indulge in the luxury of writing to your friend. And the cost of posting a letter made that letter a serious affair. If you could send a letter once in a month or six months, and then at heavy expense, it became a matter of great importance. The poor, of course, couldn't enjoy the luxury of letter-writing at all.

**[An extract from 'On letter-writing' by A. G. Gardiner]**

**Answer the following questions :**

**A.** Suggest a suitable title for the passage.

**B.** Find out four important names of writers from the passage.

**C.** What is the paragraph about? Put (√) against the right one :

(a) Novel-writing (b) Poetry-writing (c) Letter-writing

**D.** Say whether the statements are true or false. Put 'T' or 'F' against the statements :

| | |
|---|---|
| (a) Letter-writing is not a lost art. | |
| (b) Letter-writing was an event in earlier times. | |
| (c) Penny-post and modern hurry killed letter-writing. | |
| (d) The poor enjoyed the luxury of letter-writing. | |

**E.** A problem has been posed in the passage. Complete the Table stating the problem and its reason :

| Problems | Reasons |
|---|---|
| (a) Letter-writing is a lost art. | (a) ............................................ |
| (b) Poor men could not enjoy the luxury of letter-writing. | (b) ............................................ |
| (c) Modern people do not often write letters to their friends. | (c) ............................................ |

**F.** Fill in the blanks with suitable words :

To write a letter is not an ......1...... job. It needs some ......2....... If you want to write a good letter, you should be .........3......... and .........4......... Important letter-writers were very ......5...... about it and wrote letters which were ......6...... and still every reader reads .........7...... letters with .........8.......

**ANS.** **A.** Letter-writing, a lost art.

**B.** 1. Cowper 2. Horace Walpole 3. Byron 4. Carlyle

**C.** (b) (√)

**D.** (a) F; (b) T; (c) T; (d) F

**E.** (a) because of modern hurry and penny-post. (b) because of heavy price of post. (c) because of shortage of time.

**F.** 1. easy, 2. care, 3. cautious, 4. attentive, 5. serious, 6. excellent, 7. those, 8. attention.

**[11] Read the following text carefully and answer the questions given below :**

The Titanic was a huge ship with six different parts separated by steel doors. It was also fitted with wireless, a wonder of the time.

The night of the 14th April, 1912 was very cold. There was no moon and hardly any wind. The Titanic was in the part of the Atlantic in which icebergs cause trouble. Icebergs come from the North when the ice breaks up and they move on the water towards the South. Ice is hard enough to cut holes in steel and cannot easily be seen at night. The wireless officer of the Titanic had received several signals telling him that ice was not away and he knew very well that icebergs can send big ships to bottom of the sea. Most of these signals were passed on to the officers, but one was not. It was a signal from another ship, the Mesaba, reporting icebergs in front of the Titanic. He was so busy that he did not report it immediately. The signal lay on his table, half forgotten. The two men who were watching for icebergs suddenly saw something dark just in front of the ship. They immediately rang the ship's bell and Lee telephoned to the officer on watch to report the iceberg. The necessary orders were given at once though it was impossible to stop a great ship immediately, especially when it was moving at about twenty five miles an hour. But the officer did his best. The ship was turned away from its straight course. But it was all too late. Too late! The ship struck the iceberg with its side while it was still moving forward. In a few mintes six great holes were made in the steel. Water rushed in, not in one place but in separate places covering three hundred feet. The Titanic began to sink. The impossible happened.

**A. Complete the table using the information given in the passage. Leave a box empty or put a (x) mark if the information is not given in the passage :**

| WHAT HAPPENED? | WHEN? | WHY? | WHERE? |
|---|---|---|---|
| [i] | [ii] Icebergs came from the North | [iii] | [iv] in the sea |
| [v] There was no moon and the sea was without wind | [vi] | [vii] | [viii] |
| [ix] Two men rang the ship's bell | [x] | [xi] | [xii] |
| [xiii] Water rushed in | [xiv] | [xv] | [xvi] |

**B. Complete the following flow-chart using the information from the text.**

[i] On the 14th April 1912 the Titanic was in the Atlantic → [ii] → [iii] → [iv]
↓
[viii] The Titanic sank ← [vii] ← [vi] ← [v]

**C. Put a tick [√] in the right box.**

The extract is a (a) fable ☐ . (b) biography ☐ . (c) report ☐ .

**ANS. A.** [i] The Titanic began to sink. [ii] It dashed against icebergs. [iii] The Titanic could not be stopped immediately. [vi] on the 14th April, 1912. [vii] x. [viii] in the part of the Atlantic. [x] They suddenly saw something dark in front of the ship. [xi] to avoid the iceberg. [xii] in the ship. [xiv] at the night. [xv] six great holes were made in the steal of the ship. [xvi] in the Titanic.

**B.** [ii] A signal from the ship Mesaba reported that the icebergs were in front of the Titanic. [iii] The wireless officer received it. [iv] The signal lay on the table, half-forgotten. [v] Two men on watch suddenly saw something dark in front of the ship. [vi] They rang the ship's bell. [vii] The Titanic dashed against the icebergs, and it made six great holes in the ship.

**C.** (c) √

**[12] Read the following text and answer the questions below :**

Mother Teresa gets a number of voluntary helpers from all over the world, young men and women who spend a school or college vacation doing something for the destitute instead of just lazing about. But last week's visitor was someone who has himself become a crusader in his own right. Trevor Farrell is only 13, but for two years now he has spent most of his spare time from school, providing food, clothing, blankets and comfort to the poor and the homeless of his home-town, Philadelphia.

Moved by the spontaneous, selfless compassion of a child, adults rallied round with help in the form of cash, kind and service, leading to the foundation of a charitable organization called Trevor's Campaign. They have collected enough funds to buy a 33-room house which will be converted into a shelter.

Trevor had visited Mother Teresa earlier as well, and he helped her give injections and medicines, and food to the poor. The experience left the youngster immensely moved. It probably also gave him the inner strength to continue his mission with the hollow, emaciated face of poverty.

The nun gave him sensible advice. "You can't save everyone, but think about it in terms of one person at a time."

**Answer the following questions :**

**A.** Fill in the chart to show the effect of Trevor's natural feeling and experience on himself and others :

| Cause | Effect |
|---|---|
| 1. Trevor's feeling for the sufferings of the poor... | |
| 2. Adults were moved by his work. | |
| 3. Trevor's voluntary work under Mother Teresa moved him immensely. | |

**B.** Say whether the statements are true or false. Put a tick (√) mark against the true and put a cross (×) mark against the false :

(a) The USA is not much associated with great poverty. ☐

(b) There is no poverty in the USA. ☐

(c) USA is a poor country like India. ☐

(d) Teresa advised Trevor, "You can't save everyone, but can save one person at least." ☐

**ANS.** **A.** 1. (a) prompted him to work for the poor. (b) made him work under Mother Teresa. (c) gave him sufficient strength to continue his mission for help to the poor.

2. (a) They gathered round him with help in the form of cash, kind and service. (b) They helped him for the foundation of Trevor's campaign.

3. gave him enough strength to continue his mission for serving the poor people of his own country.

**B.** (a) √ ; (b) × ; (c) × ; (d) √

**[13] Read the passage carefully and answer the questions :**

The use of artificial scents and odours will soon play a much bigger part in our everyday lives than ever before. Already it is developing rapidly in many fields of commerce.

Unusual extracts from animals (like musk) or from plants (like rose, cloves and dozens more) are nowadays supplemented happily with chemical perfumes that have no origins outside the laboratory. Upwards of 150 different scents, ranging from "old leather" to sandalwood, are nowadays on top in everyday domestic and commercial substances.

Quite apart from the wide range of cosmetics and toiletries, perfume experts are preparing fragrances that go into floor polish, toothpaste, notepaper, shoe polish, many food and drink items, even into modern plastics for use in the home. This last kind of thing is nothing new : the Arabs of old so loved the odour of musk that they mixed it into the mortar with which they built their mosques—choosing, incidentally, the longest-lasting scent known.

[**An extract from 'Oh, what a lovely smell' by David Gunston in 'The Statesman'**]

**Answer the following :**

**A.** Suggest a title for the passage.

**B.** Answer the following questions :
Interest in scent is growing. Quote at least one sentence from the passage that suggests this.

**C.** Fill in the classification table of the two kinds of scents that you have just read about.

**D.** Indicate the correct statements with (√) and the false ones with (×) :
The writer is saying that there are

(a) more than 150 types of artificial perfumes ☐

(b) about 150 types of artificial scents ☐

(c) nearly 150 types of artificial scents ☐

(d) more than 150 types of natural scents ☐

**E.** Make a list of some things in which scent is used.

**ANS. A.** Artificial perfume and modern life.

**B.** "Upwards of 150 different scents, ranging from "old leather" to sandalwood, are nowadays on top in everyday domestic and commercial substances".

**C.**

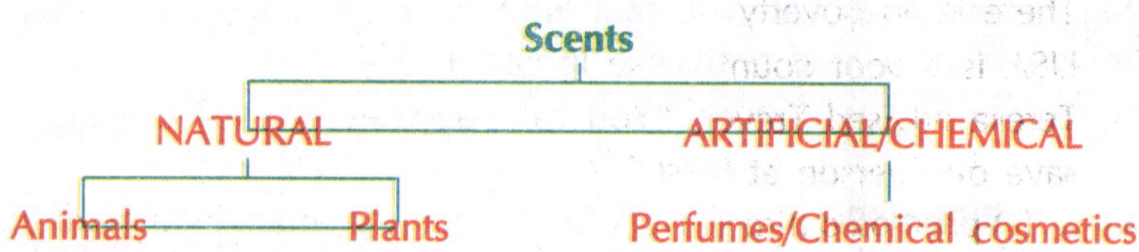


**D.** (a) ×; (b) ×; (c) ×; (d) √

**E.** (a) Toilet materials, (b) Cosmetics, (c) Toothpaste

**[14] Read the following text. Use the information in it to work out your tasks that follow :**

I was beginning to tire a little now. I had been cutting steps continuously for two hours, and Tenzing, too, was moving very slowly. As I was wondering just how long we could keep it up, I realised that the ridge ahead, instead of still monotonously rising, now dropped sharply away, and far below I could see the North Col and the Rongbuk glacier—I looked upwards to see a narrow snow ridge running up a snowy summit. A few more whacks of the ice-axe in the firm snow and we stood on the top.

My initial feelings were of relief—relief that there were no more steps to cut and no more ridges to traverse. I looked at Tenzing and in spite of goggles and oxygen mask, there was no disguising in his infectious laugh of pure delight as he looked all around him. We shook hands and then Tenzing threw his arm around my shoulders and we thumped each other on the back until we were almost breathless.

[**An extract from Recapitulation of Edmund Hillary**]

**Answer the following questions :**

**A.** What is the text about? Tick off the statement you think correct :

(a) Travelling in rural area. ☐

(b) Travelling in some seaside area. ☐

(c) Riding on hills. ☐

**B.** Complete the chart taking information from the text :

| (a) **What** | (b) **Who?** | (c) **How and For how much time** | (d) **Where** | (e) **Feelings** |
|---|---|---|---|---|
| A hill-top conquest (i.e. the conquest of Mt. Everest) | | | | |

**C.** The second paragraph contains a number of ideas :
Indicate the order in which they occur by inserting numbers 1, 2, 3, 4, etc.

| **Points** | **In order** |
|---|---|
| (a) The author looked at Tenzing. | |
| (b) They thumped each other. | |
| (c) They shook hands. | |
| (d) The feeling of the riders were of relief. | |

**D.** From the text find sentences that indicate the following functions. Write the numbers of paras and sentences in spaces provided :

| **Functions** | **Para No.** | **Sentence No.** |
|---|---|---|
| (a) cutting steps | | |
| (b) snow ridge running up | | |
| (c) getting relief | | |
| (d) laughing | | |

**E.** Study the paragraph and fill in the blanks with words or phrases from the above text :

The author became a bit __1__ as he was __2__ cutting steps to rise on the top of the hill. He was rising still __3__. The ridge was __4__ and he looked __5__ to see a __6__ snow ridge running up a snowy summit.

**ANS.** **A.** (c) √

**B.** (b) **Who? :** The writer and Tenzing

(c) **How and For how much time? :** They were moving slowly but continuously for two hours.

(d) **Where? :** On the top of the hill

(e) **Feelings :** They were happy and cheerful. There were no more steps to cut and no more ridges to traverse. Thus they had total feeling of relief.

**C.** (a) 2; (b) 4; (c) 3; (d) 1

**D.** (a) Para 1, Sent. 2; (b) Para 1, Sent. 3; (c) Para 2, Sent. 1; (d) Para 2, Sent. 2

**E.** 1. tired, 2. continuously, 3. monotonously, 4. ahead, 5. upwards, 6. narrow

## EXERCISE

### Reading Comprehension

**1. Read the following text carefully and answer the questions below :**

Being a rainy-season crop, jute thrives well in moist-heat. It can be grown in any part of the tropics and sub-tropics, provided that the soil is deep enough, rainfall is well-distributed and temperature is favourable.

Jute seeds are very small; for this, jute requires a clean and cold-free seedbed. Therefore, the land is ploughed several times (five or six times at least). All weeds are removed, preferably by raking. Additional manuring is not required in soils receiving fresh silt every year or in soils well-manured for crop preceding jute. In other soils, manure is generally used before sowing during the preparation of the land.

['The Importance of Jute']

**A. Answer the following questions :**

(i) What is the size of jute seeds?

(ii) What type of seedbed does jute require?

(iii) What do you mean by dry-heat and moist-heat? Where does jute thrive well?

**B. Put a circle for the wrong words among the following statements and correct them. You may have to use one or two words to make them correct :**

(i) Jute is an all-season crop.

(ii) Jute grows well in the tropical climate.

(iii) Manuring is essential for jute cultivation.

(iv) A roughly cultivated land is required for jute cultivation.

**C. Put down three conditions for the good production of jute :**

(i) ..........................................................................................................

(ii) ..........................................................................................................

(iii) ..........................................................................................................

**2. Read the following text carefully a1nd answer the questions below :**

One morning the Giant was lying awake in bed when he heard some lovely music. It sounded so sweet to his ear that he thought it must be the King's musicians passing by. It was really a linnet singing outside his window, but it was so long since he had heard a bird sing in his garden that it seemed to him to be the most beautiful music in the world. Then the Hail stopped dancing over his head, and the North Wind ceased roaring, and a delicious perfume came to him through the open casement. 'I believe the Spring has come at last', said the Giant, and he jumped out of bed and looked out. What did he see?

He saw the most wonderful sight. Through a little hole in the wall the children had crept in, and they were sitting in the branches of the trees. In every tree that he could see there was a little child. And the trees were so glad to have the children back again that they had covered themselves with blossoms, and were waving their arms gently above the children's heads. The birds were flying about and twittering with delight, and the flowers were looking up through the green grass and laughing. It was a lovely scene, only in one corner it was still winter. It was the farthest corner of the garden, and in it was standing a little boy. He was so small that he could not reach up to the branches of the tree, and he was wandering all around it, crying bitterly. The poor tree was still covered with frost and snow, and North Wind was blowing and roaring about it. 'Climb up! little boy," said the tree, and it bent its branches down as low as it could, but the boy was too tiny. **['The Selfish Giant']**

**A. Answer the following questions :**

(i) Pick out a sentence from the text to show that the Giant was eager for the Spring to come.

..............................................................................................

..............................................................................................

(ii) Was Nature happy to find the children again in the garden? How do you know?

..............................................................................................

..............................................................................................

(iii) Do you think the beautiful sight would soften the Giant's heart? Give your reason.

..............................................................................................

..............................................................................................

**B. Write true or false in the brackets against the statements :**

(i) The Spring came everywhere in the Giant's garden. [ ]

(ii) The Giant was sleeping when he heard a linnet sing. [ ]

(iii) The King's musicians were actually passing by. [ ]

(iv) The boy was crying standing under the tree. [ ]

(v) The song of the bird and the perfume of flowers suggested to the Giant that the Spring had come. [ ]

**C. Complete the following chart with information from the text :**

| Who / Which | Did What? | Why? |
|---|---|---|
| | jumped out of bed | |
| The tree | | to help the little boy to climb up.<br>to have the children back again. |
| | cried bitterly | |
| | could not climb the tree | |

**3. Read the following text carefully and answer the questions below :**

Suddenly he rubbed his eyes in wonder and looked and looked. It certainly was a marvellous sight. In the farthest corner of the garden was a tree quite covered with lovely white blossoms. Its branches were golden, and silver fruit hung down from them, and underneath it stood the little boy he had loved.

Downstairs ran the Giant in great joy, and out into the garden. He hastened across the grass, and came near to the child. And when he came quite close, his face grew red with anger, and he said, "Who hath dared to wound thee?" For on the palms of the child's hands were the prints of two nails, and the prints of two nails were on the little feet.

"Who hath dared to wound thee?" cried the Giant, "tell me, that I may take my big sword and slay him."

"Nay!" answered the child : "but these are the wounds of Love."

"Who art thou?" said the Giant, and a strange awe fell on him, and he knelt before the little child.

And the child smiled on the Giant, and said to him, "You let me play once in your garden, today you shall come with me to my garden, which is Paradise". And when the children ran in that afternoon, they found the Giant lying dead under the tree, all covered with white blossoms. **[ 'The Selfish Giant' ]**

**A. Complete the following chart with information from the text :**

| Cause | Effect |
|---|---|
| (i) | (i) The Giant rubbed his eyes and looked. |
| (ii) The Giant allowed the little child to play in his garden. | (ii) |
| (iii) The Giant found prints of nails on the palms and feet of the little child. | (iii) |
| (iv) | (iv) The Giant wanted to take his big sword. |
| (v) | (v) A strange awe fell on him. |

**B. Make a list of the words that describe the marvellous tree :**

..............................................................................................................

..............................................................................................................

..............................................................................................................

..............................................................................................................

**C. Pick out words, phrases or sentences that show that the little boy is not an ordinary child :**

..............................................................................................................

..............................................................................................................

..............................................................................................................

..............................................................................................................

**D. What is meant by 'the wounds of Love'?**

..............................................................................................................

..............................................................................................................

..............................................................................................................

**4. Read the following text carefully and answer the questions below :**

A man in the moving crowd heard his cry, and stooping with very great difficulty, lifted him up in his arms. 'How did you get here, child? Whose baby are you?' the man asked as he moved away from the crowd. The child wept more bitterly than ever now and only cried, 'I want my mother, I want my father.' The man tried to soothe him by taking him up to the roundabout. 'Will you have a ride on the horses?' he gently asked as he approached the ring. The child's throat tore into a thousand shrill sobs and he only shouted, 'I want my mother, I want my father.'

The man headed towards the place where the juggler still played on the flute to the dancing cobra. 'Listen to that music, child' he pleaded. But the child shut his ears with his fingers and shouted even more loudly, 'I want my mother, I want my father'.

The man took him near the balloons, thinking the bright colours of the balloons would distract the child's attention. 'Would you like a rainbow-coloured balloon?' he asked persuasively. But the child turned his eyes from the balloons and just sobbed, 'I want my mother, I want my father'.

Then, to make the child happy, the man took him to the sweetmeat shop. 'What sweets would you like, child'? he asked. The child turned his face away from the sweetmeat shop and only sobbed, 'I want my mother, I want my father'.

[ 'The Lost Child' ]

**A. Answer the following questions :**

(i) Who rescued the child? How did he rescue him?

.................................................................................................

.................................................................................................

(ii) Why was the boy not consoled? Give your reasons.

.................................................................................................

.................................................................................................

**B. Make a list of the ways the gentleman tried to console the boy :**

(i) .................................................................................................

.................................................................................................

(ii) .................................................................................................

.................................................................................................

(iii) .................................................................................................

.................................................................................................

(iv) .................................................................................................

.................................................................................................

**C. Match the following functions with the utterances :**

| Utterances | Functions |
|---|---|
| (i) "Whose baby are you?"<br>(ii) "Will you have a ride on the horses?"<br>(iii) "Listen to that music."<br>(iv) "What sweets would you like, child?"<br>(v) "I want my mother, I want my father." | |

**D. Quote sentences from the text in support of the following statements :**

| Statements | Supporting sentences |
|---|---|
| (i) The boy lost all attractions for balloons.<br>(ii) The boy would not listen to the juggler's music.<br>(iii) The boy did not like sweets. | |

**5. Read the following text and answer the questions that follow :**

The porter asked Michael Faraday to wait at the wooden bench by the window. As he sat there, he became acutely conscious of the stillness of the room. It made him feel thousands of miles away from the noisy streets and shops and general clatter of London. He became conscious of the sound of his own breathing. Sitting here was like sitting in the comforting stillness of a beautiful cathedral.

Suddenly he was roused from his dreamlike state. A man was approaching. Michael looked up and for a brief moment he did not recognize Sir Humphry Davy. He had seen him before but only from a distance. At that time he was a dignified figure on the lecture platform, dressed in a professor's black coat. Now he saw a slim round-shouldered man of medium height, with brilliant dark eyes. The face was oval and the determined chin seemed out of keeping with the soft mouth about which hovered a friendly, almost shy smile. **[ 'An Interview' from 'Michael Faraday' ]**

**Answer the following questions :**

**A.** (a) Suggest a suitable title for the text.

(b) Find out a group of words in para 2 which means 'in contrast to' .............

(c) Find out a describing word (adjective) in para 2 that helps it to maintain a sense of continuity with para 1 ..........................................................................

(d) Pick out an adverb particle from the second paragraph that connects it with the first paragraph ..........................................................................

(e) Find out the topic sentence in paragraph 2 ..............................................

**B.** Find out words in the above text which mean the following. Write down the words in brackets given against each item :

| | | |
|---|---|---|
| (i) | woke up | (        ) |
| (ii) | a very brief period of time | (        ) |
| (iii) | aware | (        ) |
| (iv) | very bright | (        ) |
| (v) | a confused noise | (        ) |
| (vi) | strongly/deeply | (        ) |

**6. Read the following text carefully and answer the questions given below :**

One day Duke Frederick commanded the two girls to attend a wrestling match between Charles, the royal wrestler, and a young man named Orlando. Orlando was the son of Sir Rowland de Boys, who in his lifetime had been one of the banished duke's most loyal supporters. When Sir Rowland died, he wanted that his eldest son, Oliver, should look after his younger brother's education. But Oliver had neglected this task. The moment Rosalind saw Orlando she fell in love with him, and he with her. She tried to dissuade him from an unequal contest with Charles, so powerful a wrestler. But the more she pleaded, the more determined Orlando became, and ultimately defeated his antagonist, and was rewarded for his prowess with a chain from Rosalind's own neck. **[ 'From the Court to the Woods' ]**

**Answer the following questions :**

(a) Who was Duke Frederick?

..........................................................................................................

(b) Who was Orlando and who was Charles?

..........................................................................................

(c) When did Rosalind fall in love and with whom?

..........................................................................................

(d) Why did Rosalind make an attempt to dissuade Orlando from the Wrestling Competition?

..........................................................................................

(e) What was the result of the Wrestling Competition?

..........................................................................................

**7. Read the following text and answer the questions that follow :**

It would be truly a shocking thing if you thought that a whale was a fish. True it lives and swims in water, and feeds on marine creatures, but there its fish-like characteristics end.

A whale is hot-blooded as you are, it came into the world in the same way as you did, and it is dependent on a sufficient supply of oxygen without which it would die, as you. If for any reason a whale is prevented from coming to the surface to breathe, it drowns. Clearly it is not a fish, for who ever heard of a drowned fish?

Whales are mammals, and they began their history ages ago as land animals. As you know, all life originally came out of water, the first animal forms being marine reptiles which gradually developed other means of locomotion, such as wings and feet. We must think of the forerunners of all the sea mammals, the whales, seals, sea-lions, sea-cows, sea-elephants, walruses, and all their kindred, as great, sprawling antediluvian animals roaming about on their four disproportionately short legs, readily taking to water, but having their proper abode on land. One day, then, a tribe of these ungainly creatures went to sea, and for some reason never came back.

**Answer the following questions :**

(i) According to the author, there are certain similarities between human beings and whales. There are also some similarities between fish and whales. Fill in the following chart with information from the text :

**A.** Similarities between human beings and whales :

(a) ..........................................................................

(b) ..........................................................................

(c) ..........................................................................

(d) ..........................................................................

**B.** Similarities between fish and whales :

(a) ..........................................................................

(b) ..........................................................................

(ii) The author has made out five stages in the process of the evolution of whales from the beginning of life. Develop the following hints and state what they are. One has been done for you :

Stage 1. Life originally appeared in the sea.

Stage 2. First animal forms ..................................................

Stage 3. They gradually developed..........................................

Stage 4. The forerunners of sea mammals were ..........................

Stage 5. One day, a group of..................................................

(iii) Some of the statements below are True and some are False. Wite 'T' or 'F' accordingly in the boxes on the right :

(a) The forerunners of whales were land animals. [ ]

(b) The whale can never drown. [ ]

(c) The whale is a kind of marine reptile. [ ]

(d) Like man the whale is a mammal. [ ]

(e) The whale can also live on land. [ ]

(iv) Answer the following questions as briefly as you can. Do not write complete sentences :

(a) Suggest an appropriate heading for the text.

(b) Where do you think the text has been taken from?

(c) Why will it be a shocking thing to think that a whale is a fish?

(d) Why can't a fish drown?

**C.** Given below are the meanings of four words which you will find in the above passage. Pick up the words and put them into the appropriate gaps on the right :

(i) living in the sea = ..........

(ii) any of the class of animals which feed their young with milk from the breast = ..........

(iii) movement = ..........

(iv) cold-blooded egg-laying animal that creeps or crawls = ..........

**8. Read carefully the following text and work out the exercises at the end of it :**

It is a matter of common knowledge that in underdeveloped countries like India with a growing population, there is an unusual pressure on land cultivation. Here, more people are engaged in agriculture partly or wholly than are necessary.

What is the result? When more people are engaged in agriculture than are really needed for the purpose, they are really surplus. If they are withdrawn from the rural areas and put in other occupations and professions it will not mean any decrease in agricultural output. On the other hand, it might increase, as it is said "Too many cooks spoil the broth". In absolute terms the total volume of rural unemployment is much larger than that of any other country. No wonder, it poses the most challenging problem for the planners to tackle.

**Answer the following questions :**

**A.** Suggest a suitable title for the text.

**B.** In which literary category would you classify the text?

Put a tick (√) mark agaisnt your choice :

[ ] a report [ ] an advertisement [ ] a story [ ] an essay

**C.** Complete the following sentences with words or phrases that best suit the context. Choose from the alternatives suggested :

(i) In India many more people are engaged in land cultivation than are—

(a) demanded (b) needed (c) expected.

(ii) "They are really surplus" means—

(a) there are too many of them

(b) they are really useless

(c) they are really needed.

(iii) India has the largest number of—
(a) unemployed persons in the urban areas
(b) unemployed persons in the village areas
(c) unemployed persons in the planning department.

**9. Read the following passage and answer the questions given below :**

The UN works through an executive council of fifteen known as the Security Council. The sponsoring nations are the permanent members. Ten others are elected. The General Assembly of the UN usually meets once a year at New York which is the permanent seat of the UN. The primary aim of the UN is to maintain international peace and no member can act unless all other members agree. This is known as the principle of 'veto'. This principle has saved the UN from breaking up in time of stress. The UN does not limit itself to its political aim of international peace. It has plans for the promotion of the general welfare of the people. With this end in view it has set up various bodies under it known as UNESCO (United Nations Educational Scientific and Cultural Organisaiton), the WHO (World Health Organisation), the IMF (International Monetary Fund) and ILO (International Labour Organisation).

These organisations have not yet made any significant headway, but their aims are so noble that they seem to give us a foretaste of a world based on complete co-operation.

**Answer the following questions :**

**A.** Select the correct alternative. While answering questions just mention the item number. You need not write the full sentences :

(i) The UN works through an executive council known as—
(a) the General Assembly.
(b) the Security Council.
(c) the Trusteeship Council.

(ii) The General Assembly of the UN usually meets—
(a) once a year. (b) twice a year. (c) frequently.

(iii) The permanent seat of the UN is in—
(a) New York. (b) Paris. (c) Geneva.

(iv) The primary aim of the UN is to—
(a) arrange for the development of the developing countries.
(b) maintain international peace.
(c) arrange for space travel.

(v) To 'veto' a proposal means—
(a) to reject a proposal with authority.
(b) to give assent to a proposal.
(c) to send a proposal for reconsideration.

**B.** Study the words in columns A and B. Match each of the words in B with a suitable one in A :

| A | B |
|---|---|
| (i) Complete | ( ) nations |
| (ii) International | ( ) members |
| (iii) Significant | ( ) peace |
| (iv) Sponsoring | ( ) aim |
| (v) Various | ( ) bodies |
| (vi) Permanent | ( ) headway |
| (vii) Primary | ( ) cooperation |

**C.** What do the following abbreviations/acronyms stand for?

(i) UNESCO (ii) WHO (iii) IMF (iv) ILO

**10. Read the passage carefully and then answer the questions set below :**

From a small town in Albania came the short slender woman whom the whole world today knows as Mother Teresa. She was born on August 27, 1910. In 1928 she joined a convent and was sent to Dublin's Loreto Abbey. Through the Bengal Mission she was sent to India, first to Darjeeling and then to Kolkata, to teach there at the Loreto Covent. One day, while she was returning from an errand, she saw the slums of Kolkata. Her heart went out to the people living there. In December 1948, she started her first school in the slums. In 1950 the Missionaries of Charity was founded. The nuns began to work for the people who were dying in the streets of Kolkata, people who were uncared for, unloved and unwanted.

Mother Teresa asked for a building where she and her workers could care for those people. In 1952 the Corporation gave her a Dharmashala in the neighbourhood of the Kali Temple which is one of Kolkata's oldest landmarks. This became : 'Nirmal Hriday, the Home for Dying Destitutes'. There is an interesting incident connected with the acquisition of this building. The priests of the nearby Kali Temple were against the setting up of the home at first. Long after the home had been established a priest entered and lay flat at Mother Teresa's feet. 'For thirty years I have served Goddess Kali in her temple,' he said. 'Now the Goddess stands before me'. He is just one of the many who have come to realise the value of Mother Teresa's work.

**A. Answer the following questions in one or two sentences :**

[a] What is the background of Mother Teresa's coming to teach at the Loreto Convent in Kolkata?

[b] What made Mother Teresa begin her work among the slum-dwellers?

**B. Fill in the table given below :**

| PERSON | DATE/PALACE OF BIRTH | PLACE OF WORK | WORK |
|---|---|---|---|
| | | (a) | (a) |
| Mother Teresa | | (b) | (b) |
| | | (c) | (c) |

**C. Answer each of the questions in one word. It will be 'Yes' or 'No' :**

[a] Is there any remark in the text that serves as a tribute to Mother Teresa?

[b] Did Mother Teresa spend some years in Loreto Convent, Kolkata?

**D. What type of text is it?**

**11. Read the following passage and answer the questions given below :**

Osama bin Laden, the world's most hunted man, was killed in an early morning fire-fight with US forces today at a fortified mansion in the Pakistan resort and army hub of Abottabad, just 4 km from the gates of the Pakistan Military Academy.

President Barack Obama made a dramatic, late-night (US time) announcement of the defining and symbolic moment in the fight against terror : the death of the September 11, 2001, mastermind who had eluded American forces for a decade.

The al Qaida chief, long thought to be hiding in some remote Afganistan mountain cave, was eventually revealed to have been sheltering just an hour's drive from Islamabad, whose government did not explain the mystery.

For India too, the hideout was too close for comfort : it borders Pakistan-administered Kashmir and is about 700 km from New Delhi. US officials said Osama resisted and was shot in the head during a special forces raid that took less than 40 minutes. Islamabad was not told in advance about the operation but Obama later called President Asif Zardari to inform him about the outcome.

The terror kingpin was later buried at sea in accordance with Islamic rites to avert creating a shrine for his followers and also because no country would want the body, US officials said. They added that the assault team identified Osama using facial recognition techniques, and that the US government was conducting a DNA test whose results would be available within a few days.

Eliminating Osama, whom George W. Bush had failed to catch, would boost Obama's chances of a second term as President.

As Obama declared "Justice has been done", crowds gathered outside the White House, some climbing nearby trees and lamp posts, and at New York's Times Square and Ground zero. They waved US flags, cheering, shouting, laughing and chanting : "USA, USA!"

But Washington avoided gloating. Amid fears of retaliatory terror strikes, the US government ordered its embassies and military installations across the world to remain alert and issued travel advisories for Americans abroad.

"The death of Bin Ladan marks the most significant achievement to date in our nation's effort to defeat al Qaida. But his death does not mark the end of our effort. There's no doubt that al Qaida will continue to pursueee attacks against us. We must and we will remain vigilant at home and abroad," Obama said.

[**The Telegraph**—3 May, 2011]

**A. Answer the following questions :**

[a] Who is Osama bin Laden?

[b] Where was he killed?

**B. Complete the following statements by selecting the correct alternatives :**

[a] Abottabad is situated in—(i) Afganistan, (ii) Pakistan, (iii) India.

[b] Osama bin Laden was so long hiding in—(i) Islamabad, (ii) Afganistan mountain cave, (iii) Pakistan-administered Kashmir.

[c] Osama bin Laden was shot in the head by—(i) the Pakistan forces, (ii) the Afganistan forces, (iii) the special forces of the US.

[d] 'Gloating' means—(i) boasting, (ii) blaming, (iii) hating.

**C. Write T for true and F for false statements in the boxes :**

[a] Osama bin Laden was arrested by the US forces. ☐

[b] Pakistan gave an explanation of Laden's hiding mystery. ☐

[c] Laden's body was buried at sea as it could not create a strine for his followers. ☐

[d] Some people climbed nearby trees and lampposts to hear Obama's announcement of Laden's death. ☐

**12. Read the following passage and answer the questions given below :**

**Explosion at nuclear plant in Japan :** Four operating nuclear reactors at the Fukushima Daiichi power station automatically shut down at 2.48 pm (Japan time) on Friday in response to the earthquake following the Tsunami. Even after the shutdown, heat from the hot reactor core needs to be removed through the coolant water. Although there is no more nuclear fission after the shutdown, the heat produced by the continued decay of fission products in the core is enough to raise further temperature. Emergency diesel generators began driving the coolant flow but stopped abruptly and inexplicably after an hour—and all emergency power was lost. This was a potential emergency situation because the residual radioactive decay in the core can continue to heat the core which, unchecked, may lead to melting and destruction of the core.

A Chernobyl-like situation where the core melts, the containment is breached, and the naked reactor spews radioactive plumes into the air may be the worst-case scenerio owing to a blast at a nuclear plant. But atomic energy regulators say this is a highly unlikely scenario in Japan. The core itself is packed within a reactor vessel and the containment (wall) is built out of reinforced concrete, typically one-metre thick, designed not to be breached.

However, if the engineers are unable to remove the residual heat from the core by circulating the water, the continued build-up of heat may lead to meltdown. A meltdown will destory the core and the reactor will become unusable. In the past, two commecial nuclear reactors have had core meltdowns. Nearly half the core melted in the Three Mile Island reactor in Pennsylvania, US, in 1979, but did not spew any radioactivity into the air because the walls remained intact. But in the 1986 meltdown in Chernobyl, Ukraine, the roof of the reactor exploded. Nuclear engineers say the worst that may happen at the Fukushima Daiichi power station is a core meltdown without radioactivity release in the atmosphere.

The plant engineers failed to cool the core, and the pressure of the radioactive steam inside rose. Operators decided to reduce pressure through partial discharge of air containing radioactive particles. This controlled dischrge occurs through a stack of filter banks—activated charcoal which absorbs most of the radioactive iodine expected in the discharge. Operators detected eight times the normal radiation levels outside the facility and 1,000 times the normal inside Unit 1 control room. At one point, the plant received each hour the amount of radiation a person normally absorbs in a year.

[**The Telegraph**—13 March, 2011]

**A. Answer the following questions :**

[a] What happened at the Fukushima Daiichi Nuclear Power Station in Japan?

[b] What may be the worst-case scenerio in this power station?

[c] Why is the nuclear reactor releasing radioactive steam?

**B. Complete the following statements by selecting the correct alternatives :**

[a] An explosion at a nuclear power station at Fukushima—(i) destroyed a hospital, (ii) destroyed the exterior walls of the reactor building, (iii) collapsed the whole plant, but not the exterior walls.

[b] Here a 'meltdown' means—(i) melting down of a steel plant, (ii) melting down of a power plant, (iii) a collapse of a powerplant system to manage temperature.

[c] The Fukushima Daiichi Plant was releasing each hour—(i) the amount of carbon-di-oxide which is fatal to a person, (ii) the amount of radiation which a person absorbs each year, (iii) the poisonous gas spreading two kilometres.

**C. Write T for true and F for false statements in the boxes :**

[a] The blast at the Fukushima Daiichi Plant was caused by the mechanical failure. ☐

[b] Four nuclear reactors at Fukushima disappeared by the earthquake. ☐

[c] The radiation leak at the nuclear power plant abruptly stopped. ☐

[d] The hot reactors were continually getting the coolant. ☐

**13. Read the passage below and answer the questions that follow :**

Man's insight into the universe began over 300 years ago, when the first optical system was turned to the heavens by the Italian astronomer Galileo.

But it was the Dutch optician Hans Lippershy who actually put one lens in front of the other and was pleasantly surprised by the magnification the system produced. The earliest use of the telescope has also been attributed to Roger Bacon of England in the 13th century.

The effects of the telescope were instantaneous. Galileo noted the rugged lunar terrain, four new planets (which we know as the Galilean moons of Jupiter), sun spots, and the countless stars that fill the night sky. Observational astronomy was born. The instrument used by Galileo consisted of lenses. In the year 1668 Isac Newton invented a new telescope using a curved mirror. These two types of telescopes in their improved formats are in use even today.

Telescopes fall broadly under the category of 'refractors' and 'reflectors'. The telescope used by Galileo was a refractor and that by Newton a reflector. A refractor uses lenses to form the image. A simple refracting system is dependent on the wave-length of light. This factor becomes a stumbling block when the object emitting light contains a number of wavelengths. The net result is the formation of an image which is blurred and tinged with different colours. The inherent defect is known as "chromatic aberration".

Chromatic aberration can be considerably reduced by using an achromatic double. This consists of cementing together a double convex lens of crown glass with a plane concave lens of flint glass. This brings lights to different colours to the same focus. The largest refractor telescope in the world is at the Yerkes Observatory and has a diameter of 40 inches. This is about the largest size possible for optical glass lenses.

[**The Telegraph**]

**A. Answer each of the following questions each in a complete sentence :**

[i] What does the word 'telescope' mean?

[ii] When did man's insight into the universe begin?

[iii] Who turned the first optical system to the heavens?

[iv] Who produced the magnification system at first?

[v] Who is credited for the earliest use of the telescope?

[vi] How was observational astronomy born?

[vii] What is chromatic aberration?

**[Or] Choose the correct alternatives or write T for True and F for False statements in the boxes :**

[i] The first optical system was turned to the heaven by the Italian astronomer (a) Newton, (b) Einstein, (c) Galileo.

[ii] The earliest use of the telescope was in the (a) 13th, (b) 16th, (c) 20th century.

[iii] Isac Newton invented a new telescope using a mirror which was (a) straight, (b) open, (c) curved.

[iv] The telescope used by Galileo was a (a) reflector, (b) refractor, (c) refrigerator.

[v] A refractor uses lenses from the (a) picture, (b) image, (c) film.

[vi] Galileo invented a new telescope using a curved mirror. ☐

[vii] The largest refractor telescope has a diameter of 40 inches. ☐

**B. Answer each of the following questions in about 20 words :**

[i] What did Galileo note through his telescope?

[ii] What is the difference between the telescopes used by Galileo and Newton?

[iii] How can chromatic aberration be considerably reduced?

[iv] Where is the largest refractor telescope in the world? How much is its diameter?

**C. Rearrange the following sentences in their proper order :**

(i) Newton invented a new telescope.

(ii) Galileo found the land in the moon through his telescope.

(iii) Observational astronomy was born.

(iv) Roger Bacon attributed much to the use of telescope.

(v) Hans Lippersy found out the use of lens.

**14. Read the passage below and answer the questions that follow :**

The view is widely held that the world would be taking a long step towards goodwill among nations if it were to adopt a universal language, and advocates of this view can offer many arguments in its favour. How pleasant for the tourists, on arrival in a foreign land, to be greeted by familiar phrases! How simple for the English businessman to cable a word that would be intelligible to Italian, Turkish, German and Chinese firms! Above all, what harmony would come to our world, if statesmen could discuss directly and accurately the problems that divide nations! We must not, however, approve an attractive idea without first examining the difficulties involved in it. The initial difficulty in adopting a common language would be to decide what that language should be. It is unlikely that all nations would agree on the adoption of one of their existing languages; and probably the very attempt would sow discord among them and, thus, defeat the ultimate purpose. The nations might prefer to create a new language, but such a language would certainly seem foreign to the first generation that employed it.

When, if ever, the nations decided what language should be universal, they would have to consider how it should be made so. Should children acquire it in infancy from their mothers? If so, they would probably never experience the full enjoyment to be gained from their national literature.

Would it be better that the universal language should be introduced as second language in the way that many of us are now taught French or German? If so, it would continue to seem a foreign language for ever and ever.

If all these difficulties were surmounted and the universal language was, in fact, universally employed, both in speech and writing, we might expect that some misunderstanding would indeed disappear. But should we dare to think that harmony among nations is assured? People of one tongue are not always of one mind.

**A. Answer the following questions each in a complete sentence :**

[i] What is the view wildly held?

[ii] Would all the nations readily agree to adopt a common language?

[iii] What would be the disadvantage of creating a new language?

[iv] What is the national language of China?

[v] Do the Italians usually understand Turkish?

[vi] Can any existing language serve as a universal language?

[vii] What does the writer expect finally?

**[Or] Choose the correct alternatives or write T for True and F for False statements in the boxes :**

[i] But such a language would certainly seem (a) native, (b) slightly known, (c) foreign.

[ii] Should children a language in infancy from their (a) fathers? (b) mothers? (c) teachers?

[iii] The universal language should be introduced as a (a) first language, (b) second language, (c) third language.

[iv] People of one tongue are not always of (a) one mind, (b) two minds, (c) different minds.

[v] Advocates of this view can offer (a) no argument, (b) a few arguments, (c) many arguments.

[vi] The world statesmen could then discuss their problems directly. ☐

[vii] There is no difficulty in adopting a universal language. ☐

**B. Answer the following questions each in about 20 words :**

[i] What is the attractive idea for taking a long step towards goodwill among nations of the world?

[ii] Why is such an idea considered attractive?

[iii] What is the initial difficulty in adopting such an idea?

[iv] What is the probable demerit of such idea?

**C. Rearrange the following sentences in their proper order :**

[i] The nations might prefer to create a new language.

[ii] All the nations would not agree to adopt one of the existing languages.

[iii] The world statesmen could then discuss their problems directly.

[iv] Adoption of a universal language would bring about complete harmony.

[v] Businessmen of different countries would be very happy.

**15. Read the passage below and answer the questions that follow :**

Ernest Rutherford was the son of a Scot emigrant to New Zealand. His father established the first flax mill in South Island. His mother was the first woman school teacher in New Zealand. They had 12 children, of whom Ernest was the fourth. He was brought up in a real frontier atmosphere and it entered into the nature of the man. Life was hard, but it was adventurous. His education was in a State Primary School from which children at the age of 13 could get grants or scholarships to secondary schools and to the infant universities. Rutherford had no intention of following an academic career. He was no bookworm. He was good in any rough-and-tumble and a keen football player, but he was good at Latin and he had a passion for music and a mechanical mind. At Nelson College, a state boarding school, he was an outstanding pupil, and because his masters expected it of him he sat for a scholarship to Canterbury College and won it.

The college in those days was a very humble academic institution with seven Professors and 150 students. Its science laboratory for both Physics and Chemistry—was a tin-shack. But he was lucky with his teachers there. The Physics Professor was an eccentric (by the academic standards of the day) who appreciated originality more than precision. But he was counterbalanced by the Mathematics professor, who was a strict pedant. The one gave Rutherford adventurous versatility of thought, the other gave him his discipline.

Rutherford, as a student, became fascinated by Hertz's work on radio-waves and in the cloakroom of the college, where the students hung their gowns, he found a corner for his own private experiments. He could detect signals at a distance of two miles. He was then 23. He won a scholarship which took him to Britain and the Cavendish Laboratory at Cambridge.

**A. Answer the following questions each in a complete sentence :**

[i] Who was Rutherford?

[ii] Where was he brought up and how was he influenced by his surroundings?

[iii] What was the homeland of Rutherford's father?

[iv] Where did he emigrate?

[v] What was the mother of Rutherford?

[vi] Where did Rutherford get his primary education?

[vii] Who was Hertz?

**[Or] Choose the correct alternatives or write T for True and F for False statements in the boxes :**

[i] Rutherford was his parents' (a) eldest child, (b) second child, (c) third child, (d) fourth child.

[ii] As a school-child Rutherford was most interested in (a) an academic career, (b) tough games and sports, (c) scholarships, (d) books.

[iii] Nelson College was a (a) boarding school, (b) big college, (c) small college, (d) new university.

[iv] The science laboratory of Canterbury College looked like (a) an ordinary laboratory, (b) an old laboratory, (c) a modern laboratory, (d) no laboratory at all.

[v] The cloak room is the place where people (a) dance, (b) make radio-waves, (c) hang their clothes, (d) make experiments.

[vi] Rutherford's mechanical mind let him have no artistic sensibility. ☐

[vii] Rutherford took no interest in Hertz's work on radio-waves. ☐

**B. Answer the following questions each in about 20 words :**

[i] Give an account of the parentage of Ernest Rutherford.

[ii] Where did he go on his higher studies? What type of institution was it?

[iii] Describe the laboratory in the college.

[iv] Who were the balancing factors for guiding Rutherford and how did they balance his character?

**C. Rearrange the following sentences in their proper order :**

[i] Rutherford won a scholarship to Canterbury College.
[ii] Rutherford won a scholarship to secondary schools.
[iii] Rutherford's father came to New Zealand.
[iv] Rutherford worked at the Cavendish Laboratory.
[v] Rutherford's hard life in his childhood helped him on his research work.

**16. Read the passage below and answer the questions that follow :**

Most of us would agree that it is admirable to be loyal—we approve of loyalty to our family, loyalty to our friends, and loyalty to our country, in fact to all those individuals and groups to whom we have reason to be grateful. And when we speak of 'loyalty', here we mean a readiness to help them when they are in difficulty or danger, and a constant interest in their well-being at all times. It is often very clear when a person is being disloyal—when he lets his parents suffer without showing any concern, for example, or when he fights in an army against his own country, killing his fellow countrymen indiscriminately. For such people most of us would feel disapproval. However, there often arise situations in which it is harder to decide if a person is being disloyal or not. A clever child may resist his parents' appeals to stop studying and begin to work in order to help them financially. He may believe that he will be able to repay his parents more fully in future if he continues his studies for a few years longer, whereas, if he stops studying now, his talents will be wasted and never serve anybody. Unimaginative people may sometimes condemn a boy or girl for making a decision like this : but often such a child, if he is conscientious and sensitive, may deserve help and encouragement rather than criticism. On the other hand, in certain circumstances—if for instance a boy's parents are in great poverty—it might be disloyal for him to refuse to help them by going out to work; and even if later in life he is successful, he may always regret his disloyalty as a boy.

**A. Answer the following questions each in a complete sentence :**

[i] Define 'loyalty'?
[ii] What should be admitted as a general rule?
[iii] To whom should we be loyal generally?
[iv] Is it right to kill one's fellow countrymen indiscriminately?
[v] What is the first duty of a boy if his parents are in great poverty?
[vi] What does the word 'talent' mean?
[vii] What does the word 'conscientious' mean?

**[Or] Choose the correct alternatives or write T for True and F for False statements in the boxes :**

[i] We must be loyal to those whom we are (a) related, (b) connected, (c) grateful.
[ii] Loyalty is the quality to help others that may be called (a) attitude, (b) willingness, (c) readiness.
[iii] In order to help parents who are in great poverty a boy should (a) stop, (b) continue, (c) begin, his studies.
[iv] A clever child who wants to continue his studies for greater interest deserves (a) criticism, (b) sympathy, (c) help.
[v] We should always remain (a) loyal, (b) grateful, (c) careless, to our family.
[vi] Loyalty means taking help from others. ☐
[vii] It is not always easy to decide who is loyal. ☐

**B. Answer the following questions each in about 20 words :**

[i] Who deserve loyalty from whom as a general rule?

[ii] Give an example where it is harder to decide if a person is loyal or not.

[iii] On which decision unimaginative people may condemn a boy or a girl?

[iv] Why may one regret for disloyalty as a boy?

**C. Rearrange the following sentences in their proper order :**

[i] A boy may help his poor parents with child labour.

[ii] A boy may not help them for his future career.

[iii] The parents of a boy are in great poverty.

[iv] People may condemn a boy for refusing to help his poor parents.

[v] The general rule of loyalty is not correct in all circumstances.

**17. Read the following passage and answer the questions given below :**

The history of human development is marked by periods when one idea has simultaneously stirred people around the world. The advancement of women is one of them. There is hardly any part of the globe which has been left untouched by this idea in recent years, even though progress in different countries may be uneven.

If there was one thing evident at Nairobi, where a United Nations Women's Conference was recently held to assess the accomplishments of the Women's Decade and to formulate strategies up to 2000 A.D., it was this worldwide ferment on the women's issue.

There are times when humankind takes a leap forward which would normally have been unthinkable. The Women's Decade provided this impetus as well as what the Secretary General of the UN Decade for Women Conference, Leticia Sahani, described as the "time frame" and the "mechanism" for this leap to take place. It was not so much an actual improvement in the lives of women; it was the consciousness of the need for women's advance. It represents "one of the most profound, quiet revolutions of our time."

The Decade has heightened consciousness about women's subordination and documented the extent of women's inequality. Today 90 per cent of governments have enacted legislations granting women equal rights, and set up national mechanisms to look after women's welfare. Half these countries were spurred to take these steps because of and during the Women's Decade; 45 of them, 75 per cent being developing nations, have established free legal aid to help women attain these rights. The number of countries which brought equal pay legislation on their statute books rose from 28 in 1978 to 90 in 1983.

**A. Answer the following questions each in a complete sentence :**

[i] Which idea stirred people all over the world?

[ii] Is the progress in the development of that idea equal in all the countries?

[iii] Where was the United Nations Women's Conference held?

[iv] What is the percentage of governments enacting legislation for granting women equal rights?

[v] How many countries have established free legal aid to help women?

[vi] Who is Leticia Sahani?

[vii] What did she describe in the conference?

**[Or] Choose the correct alternatives or write T for True and F for False statements in the boxes :**

[i] The advancement of women is an idea that has—(a) irritated people all over the world. (b) excited the imagination of the European people. (c) stirred people around the world more or less at the same time.

[ii] Progress of this idea in various countries—(a) has been equal. (b) has varied in degree. (c) has been spectacular.

[iii] At Nairobi was recently held—(a) UNESCO Conference. (b) UN Women's Conference. (c) meeting of women diplomats.

[iv] The Nairobi Conference was held to assess the—(a) importance of the women. (b) achievements of the women. (c) strength of the women.

[v] Humankind—(a) always, (b) seldom, (c) occasionally takes a leap forward.

[vi] During the Women's Decade humankind took a great leap forward. ☐

[vii] The Decade represented a shallow but noisy change. ☐

**B. Answer the following questions each in about 20 words :**

[i] What was the purpose of the United Nations Women's conference?

[ii] What was the main objective of women's decade?

[iii] What is one of the most profound and quiet revolutions of our time?

[iv] Which steps have been taken by most of the Governments for the upliftment of women?

**C. Rearrange the following sentences in their proper order :**

[i] Leticia Sahani described the time frame and mechanism of the women's Decade.

[ii] The number of countries bringing equal pay legislation on their statute books rose from 28 in 1978 to 90 in 1983.

[iii] 45 Countries have established free legal aid to help women.

[iv] 90% of governments have enacted legislations granting women equal rights.

[v] The United Nations Women's Conference was held at Nairobi in 2000 AD.

**18. Read the passage below and answer the questions that follow :**

Man alone of all creatures thinks of things as tools and uses them as such. Through his inventive genius a stick became a club with which he defended himself from the wild beast and killed the poisonous serpent. Soon he saw that if it was sharp he could thrust with it, and he had a spear. Then he threw its point first and had a javelin. Simple as this seems to us now, each step in advance was a tremendous one for a primitive man; and when, perhaps ages later, some men found that he could bend another stick with a cord stretched from end to end and shoot the javelin from that, thus having a bow and arrow, how great a further advancement it was!

It is interesting to see how man took the things which he found at hand and turned them to his own uses. Primitive man could cross shallow rivers by wading, but some streams were too deep, too swift or too wide for wading or swimming. Across a swift narrow one he might find a fallen tree and, thus, get the idea of a bridge. Across the wide, placid ones he could float a fallen log and find his first boat supplied by nature. All bridges and all ships have grown from these simple beginnings. In the same way, the stone, which was his first hammer, was his first axe when it had a sharp edge. When it was both sharp and slim, it became his first knife. From these two have come all the numberless kinds of cutting tools.

**A. Answer the following questions each in a complete sentence :**

[i] What does the word 'tools' mean?

[ii] Who can make and use tools?

[iii] What idea did the early man get from a fallen tree across a narrow stream?

[iv] What idea did he get from the floating logs?

[v] What was the first improvement on a simple stick?

[vi] What idea did he get from a sharp stick?

[vii] How did the early man use the stone with a sharp edge?

**[Or] Choose the correct alternatives or write T for True and F for False statements in the boxes :**

[i] Primitive man got the idea of a bridge with the help of—(a) a fallen tree. (b) sun-burnt bricks. (c) cement and rod.

[ii] Primitive man got his first boat by—(a) floating a fallen log. (b) swimming in the river. (c) wading through the river.

[iii] Other creatures than men have thought of things as tools. ☐

[iv] A primitive man could use a sharp stick as a spear. ☐

[v] Across a swift stream one found a fallen tree and used it to cross the river. ☐

[vi] The stone was man's first axe. ☐

[vii] The sharp and slim stone became his first knife. ☐

**B. Answer the following questions each in about 20 words :**

[i] How could the primitive man protect himself from the wild beast?

[ii] How could he invent a spear or a javelin?

[iii] How could he have a bow and arrow?

[iv] How could he have his first bridge?

**C. Rearrange the following sentences in their proper order :**

[i] The primitive man invented the bow and arrow.

[ii] The primitive man invented a javelin.

[iii] The primitive man invented a spear.

[iv] The primitive man invented a boat.

[v] The primitive man invented a bridge.

**19. Read the following passage and answer the questions given below :**

Today, around 250 million children under 14 have to work for a living in jobs ranging from shining shoes and cutting cane to making sports goods, weaving carpets or assembling fireworks.

In India and Pakistan , many children are sold by their parents to factory owners to pay off their debts, a form of slavery called bonded labour. Others are forced to work in stone quarries which can stunt their growth and cause permanent injury both physical and mental.

In India, around 30,000 children are involved in producing footballs, boxing gloves and other sports goods for British shops. Earlier this year Christian Aid discovered that little children stitch footballs which sell in Britain for 14.99 shillings while they are paid just 14 p for two hour's work—less than one cent of each ball's UK price.

More than 40 million children live on the streets of the world's cities. Many children in Brazil have been orphaned or abandoned and keep alive by begging, washing cars and scavenging for food in rubbish dumps.

In the Romanian capital of Bucharest, hundreds of orphaned, homeless children live in the city's sewers underground.

In India, the pavements of cities and railway station platforms are full of sleeping bodies at night, many of them are children who have nowhere to go.

Over the past decade two million children have killed in wars and six million seriously injured or disabled. In many African countries, children are recruited or kidnapped for the army. In Sudan, it is said, there are around 3000 boy soldiers aged between 7 and 11. The boys are made to act as porters and guards and are forced to retrieve weapons from dangerous minefields.

**A. Answer the following questions each in a complete sentence :**

[i] How many children are involved in producing sports goods in India?

[ii] How much is paid to little children for making footballs?

[iii] How are the orphaned and abandoned children kept alive in Brazil?

[iv] How many children were killed over the past decade?

[v] How many children were seriously injured or disabled in wars over the past decade?

[vi] Why are children recruited or kidnapped for the army in Sudan?

[vii] Why are the boys recruited for the army in many African countries?

**[Or] Choose the correct alternatives or write T for True and F for False statements in the boxes :**

[i] The children who live on the streets of the cities are—(a) around 250 million. (b) less than 40 million. (c) more than 40 million.

[ii] The boy soldiers in Sudan are aged between—(a) 6 and 9. (b) 7 and 11. (c) 8 and 12.

[iii] Nowadays a few number of children under 14 have to work in tedious jobs. ☐

[iv] In India and Pakistan many children are bound to be bonded labour. ☐

[v] Hundreds of orphaned children live in the underground sewers in Bucharest. ☐

[vi] In India the pavements of cities and railway platforms are used as sleeping places for many homeless children. ☐

[vii] Over the past ten years two million children have been killed in wars. ☐

**B. Answer the following questions each in about 20 words :**

[i] How many children and under what age group are forced to work to earn their livelihood ?

[ii] Why are many children sold by their parents in India and Pakistan?

[iii] How are the children affected working in stone quarries?

[iv] What did Christian Aid discover ?

**C. Rearrange the following sentences in their proper order :**

[i] The boys between 7 and 11 are recruited for the army in Sudan.

[ii] About 3000 boy soldiers are engaged in the army in Sudan.

[iii] Two million children have been killed in wars.

[iv] Footballs are sold in Britain for 14.99 shillings each.

[v] The boy labourers are paid only 14p for two hours' work.

**20. Read the following passage and answer the questions given below :**

United nations, Oct. 15 : Dr. Amartya Sen is still haunted by boyhood memories of a famine that gripped India. Neither he nor his family starved—a fact that later formed the basis of his economic theories that earned him a Nobel Prize on Wednesday.

Emaciated rural labourers died by the hundreds of thousands in 1943 while most people were untouched by wartime inflation that pushed food prices beyond reach of the poorest members of the then British India.

Dr. Amartya Sen was nine when he witnessed the effects of India's wartime famine. "I knew of no one who was affected by the famine—no relation, no friend, no one I ever associated with. That, to me, was a great lesson later, I thought, though I didn't see it at that time. I just thought we were very lucky", Dr. Sen said on Wednesday.

The experience stirred his interest in the cause of famines—an interest that led ultimately to his pioneering work in Development Economics.

Despite rumours that food supplies were plentiful, rumours he later substantiated, people still starved.

"There is hardly a famine that affects more than 10 per cent of a population, in any way," he said. "To see famine mainly as a divisive factor, whereby some people fall behind and the devil takes the hindmost is something that links, I think, my childhood memories and impressions of 1943 with the work I did in the decade following 1973."

Dr. Sen, 64, was awarded the prestigious prize for his contributions to welfare economics, which help explain the economic mechanisms underlying famines and poverty, the Royal Swedish Academy of Sciences said.

Last years's prize winners, Americans Robert Merton and Myron Scholes, were honoured for their work on valuing risky "derivatives" investments like stock options—work that generally benefited the rich. "The fact that economics is also concerned with the poor, the downtrodden, the underdogs of society is something that is close to my heart," said Dr. Sen.

**A. Answer the following questions each in a complete sentence :**

[i] What is it that still haunts Amartya Sen?

[ii] When did Dr. Amartya Sen witness the effects of India's wartime famine ?

[iii] What was the unforgettable experience of Dr. Amartya Sen's boyhood?

[iv] What did his boyhood experience supply him ?

[v] What was the effect of the famine of 1943 on food prices ?

[vi] What is mainly a famine to Dr. Sen ?

[vii] Why was Dr. Sen awarded the Nobel Prize?

**[Or] Choose the correct alternatives or write T for True and F for False statements in the boxes :**

[i] In 1943 in India deaths of the rural labourers were—(a) more than hundreds. (b) more than thousands. (c) more than millions.

[ii] During famine people starved—(a) for disease. (b) for want of food. (c) despite food supplies were plentiful.

[iii] Dr. Amartya Sen received the Nobel Prize. ☐

[iv] At the time of the famine of 1943 Amartya Sen was a boy of 9 only. ☐

[v] Many of Amartya Sen's close relatives died in the famine. ☐

[vi] Dr. Sen's theory of economics explains causes of famine and poverty. ☐

[vii] Last year's Nobel Prize in Economics was shared by African scholars. ☐

**B. Answer the following questions each in about 20 words :**

[i] What was the condition of two classes of people during wartime inflation in India?

[ii] What was a great lesson to Dr. Sen in his later life?

[iii] How did the experience of famine stir his interest ?

[iv] What is the average percentage of death during a famine?

**C. Rearrange the following sentences in their proper order :**

[i] Dr. Amartya Sen was awarded the Nobel prize.

[ii] He contributed much to welfare economics.

[iii] Dr. Sen witnessed India's wartime famine.

[iv] Neither he nor his family starved during famine.

[v] Millions of Poor people died.

**21. Read the following passage and answer the questions given below :**

A recent report on the effect of nuclear war prepared by the World Health Organisation calculated that even the use of half the existing nuclear weapons would result in more than 1,000 million deaths and another 1,000 million seriously injured. No medical services anywhere in the world would be able to deal with casualties of such gigantic proportions and the resulting epidemics of even greater dimensions, the report cautioned.

Another competent study made by the Royal Swedish Academy of Sciences presented the fearful picture of post-nuclear-war as that of a "republic of grass and insects". Besides millions of immediate casualties, a global nuclear war would cause horrible radioactive contamination in food production and food shortages throughout the world. High radiation exposure would cause widespread devastation of natural plants and animal communities. Forests would be converted into a residual vegetation of herbs and shrubs.

In a vivid description of the transformation of the global ecosystem the study says that enormous amounts of light-absorbing and light-reflecting debris will cloak the atmosphere in a dark veil which will hinder sunlight for weeks and perhaps months. Nuclear devastations will cause vast fires. These will sweep over expanses of forest land and agricultural fields and these fires along with those in oil and gas fields ignited by the thousands of nuclear explosions, would load the lower atmosphere with tiny particles of tar, soot and ash. A state of chaos will ensue, which, among other things, will make agriculture operations extremely difficult.

Moreover, there will be a large reduction of the stratospheric ozone layer, which protects life on earth from the sun's harmful rays. It would last for several years and to an increased intensity of solar ultra-violet radiation with serious consequences for humans, animals and plants. The utterly changed surroundings would be vulnerable to attack by pests and population of cockroaches and rats and carrion birds and organisms of decay would fearfully increase. Pests and those others are relatively resistant to radiation.

**A. Answer the following questions each in a complete sentence :**

[i] What is WHO?

[ii] What is the report of the study made by the Royal Swedish Academy of Science ?

[iii] How many people may die if half the nuclear stock is used?

[iv] What type of medical service would be available for seriously injured persons?

[v] What will be left for the survivors to eat in the event of a world-wide nuclear war?

[vi] How will the nuclear war affect the plant kingdom?

[vii] Why will pests and other small organisms increase after nuclear war?

**[Or] Choose the correct alternatives or write T for True and F for False statements in the boxes :**

[i] The full use of the existing nuclear weapons would cause—(a) 1,000 million deaths. (b) 2,000 million deaths. (c) 3,000 million deaths.

[ii] The solar ultra-violet radiation is—(a) harmful to life on earth. (b) helpful to life on earth. (c) useless to life on earth.

[iii] The nuclear war is surely beyond imagination. ☐

[iv] A nuclear war will render agricultural operations almost impossible. ☐

[v] As a result of nuclear war a new kind of republic will be born. ☐

[vi] The nuclear war will have no effect on the region beyond earth. ☐

[vii] A nuclear war cannot cause widespread havoc. ☐

**B. Answer the following questions each in about 20 words :**

[i] What did the WHO calculate about the effect of the nuclear war?

[ii] What will be the global ecosystem after the nuclear war?

[iii] What will be the lower atmosphere after the nuclear war?

[iv] How does the stratosphere ozone layer help life on earth?

**C. Rearrange the following sentences in their proper order :**

[i] Cockroaches and rats will increase after nuclear war.

[ii] The radiation of Solar ultra-violet rays will be increased.

[iii] The stratospheric ozone layer will be reduced.

[iv] Agricultural operations will be difficult.

[v] Nuclear war may occur.

**22. Read the following passage and answer the questions given below :**

New Delhi, Sept. 6, 2004 : A new drug developed in India has emerged as the "most promising" drug against tuberculosis in 40 years and might reduce treatment duration from eight to two months, industry and government officials claimed today.

The drug, development under a reasearch-industry partnership programme, has cleared animals trials and is now awaiting approval for clinical trials on humans, science and technology ministry Kapil Sibal said.

The drug was discovered by industry partner Lupin while several laboratories of the Council of Scientific and Industrial Research (CSIR) helped establish that it is effective in animals and does not have adverse effects. "This will change the way the world looks at India," Sibal said, "It establishes India's leadership in drug development."

TB is now treated with a combination of four drugs : the last one Rifampicin—was discovered in the early 1960s. But though the existing drugs can easily cure a patient, the treatment takes about six to eight months and scientists have long looked forward to a drug that can cure in much shorter time.

Lupin officials said their studies on animals have shown that the new drug, called Sudoterb, can completely clear tubercular infection within two months.

Lupin has sought permission from the Drugs Controller General of India to conduct clinic trials in humans. The first set of trials will be to find out whether the drug is safe for humans, while subsequent trials will examine whether it is effective.

The human trials are expected to cost Rs. 50 crore and will take about four years to complete.

The Rs. 25 crore development effort has so far been funded by the New Millennium Indian Technology Leadership Initiative programme managed by the CSIR that seeks to synthesise ideas from industry and research centres and get them to work together.

Lupin has filed patents on the new drug in India and in the US. CSIR director general R. Mashelkar said Lupin was an ideal partner because the company was the world's leading producer of standard TB drugs and had invested in research aimed at finding new drugs. [Adapted from **'The Telegraph'**]

**A. Answer the following questions each in a complete sentence :**

[i] Who is R. Mashelkar?

[ii] What is CSIR?

[iii] What is the aim of CSIR?

[iv] On whom have the trials of the new drug been successful?

[v] What was the last traditional drug against tuberculosis?

[vi] When was the last traditional drug invented?

[vii] What is the name of the new drug?

**[Or] Choose the correct alternatives or write T for True and F for False statements in the boxes :**

[i] The "most promising drug" has been invented to cure—(a) asthma. (b) cancer. (c) tuberculosis.

[ii] The said drug has been developed in—(a) India. (b) China. (c) the USA.

[iii] The new drug has been allowed for clinical trials on humans. ☐

[iv] The existing drug for curing TB is a combination of three drugs. ☐

[v] The existing drug takes time about six to eight months to cure a TB patient. ☐

[vi] The new drug can cure the patient in one month only. ☐

[vii] The name of the new drug is Sudoterb. ☐

**B. Answer the following questions each in about 20 words :**

[i] How did the new drug-experiment develop?

[ii] Why were the scientists eager to invent a new drug?

[iii] How has the new drug shortened the duration for treatment?

[iv] Why is Lupin a good partner ?

**C. Rearrange the following sentences in thier proper order :**

[i] Lupin had invested a fat amount in research for finding new drugs.

[ii] The CSIR has granted Rs. 25 crore.

[iii] The human trials are expected to cost Rs. 50 crore.

[iv] The new drug has emerged after four decades.

[v] The new drug is awaiting human trials.